INSTRUCTOR'S HANDBOOK

TO ACCOMPANY

An Introduction to Literature

FIFTEENTH EDITION

SYLVAN BARNET
Tufts University

WILLIAM BURTO
University of Massachusetts at Lowell

WILLIAM E. CAIN
Wellesley College

PEARSON
Longman

New York   Boston   San Francisco
London   Toronto   Sydney   Tokyo   Singapore   Madrid
Mexico City   Munich   Paris   Cape Town   Hong Kong   Montreal

Vice President and Editor-in-Chief: Joseph Terry
Senior Supplements Editor: Donna Campion
Electronic Page Makeup: Grapevine Publishing Services, Inc.

Instructor's Handbook to Accompany *An Introduction to Literature*, Fifteenth Edition, by Sylvan Barnet, William Burto, and William E. Cain.

Copyright © 2008 Pearson Education, Inc.

ISBN: 0-205-62038-8

1 2 3 4 5 6 7 8 9 10—OPM—10 09 08 07

Suggested video viewings are made throughout this manual.
A select quantity of videos is available free to qualified adopters.
Contact your local Longman representative for ordering assistance.
www.ablongman.com/replocator

Contents

Part II Fiction

Part III Poetry

Chapter 11: Approaching Poetry: Responding in Writing   159

Chapter 12: Narrative Poetry   161

Chapter 13: Lyric Poetry   171

Chapter 14: The Speaking Tone of Voice   193

Part IV Drama

Preface

What follows is something close to a slightly organized card file. In the course of teaching many of the materials in this book, we have amassed jottings of various sorts, and these may be of some use to others as well as to ourselves. Perhaps most useful will be the references to critical articles and books from which we have profited. We have plowed through a fair amount of material and tried to call attention to some of the best. We have also offered suggestions for theme assignments, but many of the questions printed at the ends of selections in the text are suitable topics for writing. The point of these questions is to stimulate critical thinking.

We have offered, too, relatively detailed comment on some of the stories, poems, and plays. These may serve to give an instructor a jumping-off place for these selections and others to which they are connected.

Acknowledgments. We are deeply indebted to countless published sources, and to countless discussions with colleagues and students; we hope we can be forgiven for not seeking to make a long list that would inevitably be incomplete. We do, however, wish to thank Donna Campion, Dianne Hall, and Meegan Thompson for their superb editorial work on the handbook.

Guide to
MyLiteratureLab

http://www.myliteraturelab.com

You may check the Instructor Resources section of MyLiteratureLab for a more extensive Faculty Teaching Guide.

Introduction

Welcome, instructors, to *MyLiteratureLab*. This brief guide highlights the main benefits and features of the *MyLiteratureLab* website. In this guide you will find an overview of the three main sections of the website.

1. The Literary Elements: Testing Your Knowledge
2. Where Literature Comes to Life: The Longman Lectures
3. Writing and Research

For more extensive information on the these portions of the website, including detailed descriptions of each of the Longman Lectures and teaching tips for using *MyLiteratureLab* in your classroom, please see the Instructor Resources section of the website.

The Literary Elements: Testing your Knowledge

This section of the site features *Diagnostics* (linked to the Glossary of Literary and Critical Terms) and *Interactive Readings*.

Diagnostics

The *Diagnostics*, including multiple-choice and fill-in-the-blank questions, enable students to assess their understanding of literary theory and criticism by quizzing them on terms such as imagery, archetype, point of view, and soliloquy. Upon completing each diagnostic, students are forwarded to the *Glossary of Literary and Critical Terms* to fill any gaps in their knowledge.

Interactive Readings

The *Interactive Readings* section is designed to help students understand how to use literary elements to interpret works of literature. Each reading focuses on a particular literary element, such as word choice, tone and style, and character analysis. As students read a particular selection, key passages are highlighted. When students click on the highlighted text, a box appears that contains explanations, analysis, and/or questions highlighting how the passage can be interpreted using the literary elements. These readings can be assigned as homework, and students may be required to submit their written responses to the questions.

Where Literature Comes to Life: The Longman Lectures

This section of the website features a menu of nine-minute lectures. All of the *Longman Lectures* are given by Longman's authors—critically-acclaimed writers, award-winning teachers, and performance poets. Longman's "guest lecturers" discuss some of the most commonly taught literary works and authors in depth. In the process, they encourage students to analyze stories, poems, and plays, and develop thoughtful essay ideas.

The lectures are richly illustrated with words and images to contextualize and enrich the content of each lecture. As stated earlier, each lecture is divided into three parts—Reading, Interpreting, and Writing. Each part of each lecture is accompanied by a diverse selection of Critical Thinking and Writing Questions. Some questions provide feedback and suggestions for online research and essay development. Students' answers to the questions can be e-mailed to you or used to spark class discussion.

As a whole, the lectures are designed to complement in-class discussion of particular works and augment related assignments in your syllabus. Available to students around the clock, the three-part structure of the lectures encourages students to read and interpret works more thoughtfully and spark ideas for research and writing. The lectures may also be assigned as extra-credit work or be used as an emergency substitute instructor.

Below we discuss the primary purpose of each part of the lectures and provide examples.

Part 1: Reading

Students often are reluctant readers. The first part of each lecture, "Reading," sparks student interest through the lecturer's interpretative reading. The reading of a key passage places the work within a context that appeals to students. Some readings are dramatic and performative; others provide analysis about how a work is structured. The lecturers' varying approaches to their subject matter helps reach students with different learning styles. At the same time, related visuals help students *see* the work while reading it. Here are a few examples of opening statements in Part 1 of the lectures.

- From Shakespeare's sonnets lecture: *In Shakespeare's Sonnets (published in 1609 but probably written in the middle 1590s), love—whether for the fair youth or the dark lady—is only one of several themes. Some of these themes—for instance, beauty and the tragic effect of time on beauty—are easily connected with love. Let's glimpse a few of the themes by looking at the opening lines of some of the sonnets.*

- From the Flannery O'Connor "A Good Man Is Hard to Find" lecture: *What if I told you about a writer who included in her works a youth who, in baptizing his mentally defective nephew, manages to drown him, or a woman with a wooden leg and a Ph.D. in philosophy who . . . is robbed of her wooden leg and stripped of her self-confident belief in nothing . . . ? If I then told you that this author is a devout Catholic, would you be astonished? If so, you are not yet familiar with the works of Flannery O'Connor.*

- From the James Baldwin "Sonny's Blues" lecture: *From the opening scene . . . until the final scene in a darkened nightclub when Sonny, bathed in blue light, performs the magic of improvisational jazz on his piano, these two brothers move in and out of each others' lives, attempting to communicate but most often failing.*

Part 2: Interpreting

Many students lack confidence in their ability to analyze and interpret works of literature. Some students are impatient to find the "right" answer. Part 2 of each lecture provides provocative "keys" for understanding. The lecturers' comments humanize both the work and its author. For example:

- From the Seamus Heaney "Digging" lecture: *Not only is he {Heaney} honoring the work of his father and grandfather, he is using his own kind of digging—that is, writing poetry—to show us the worth of the work they did. And in this respect, he honors and carries on their tradition—but with a different tool. As such, it's a poem about writing poetry—with digging as its metaphor.*

- From the James Joyce "Araby" lecture: *Notice how the bright images of his love, Mangan's sister, always appear out of the dreary background that surrounds them. Compare the words and phrases that are used to describe Mangan's sister and the boy's feelings about her with the language that describes his neighborhood or his everyday activities. Let the words open your senses—visualize and feel the bright, warm image of Mangan's sister as her dress swings and the soft rope of her hair tosses from side to side and contrast it with the dark, cold image of the short days of winter and the acrid smell of ashpits and horse stables in the surrounding neighborhood.*

- From the Billy Collins "The Names" lecture: *A typical Collins poem begins in the morning. The poet walks around his empty house, thinks about last night's supper or tonight's bottle of wine, puts on some jazz, goes out and runs a few errands or takes a train into the city, comes home, looks out the window, and makes a poem. To say that Collins writes a low-pressure kind of poetry is like observing that a flat tire could stand a little air. It's the poetic equivalent of an episode of Seinfeld, "the show about nothing." But . . . I sympathize. Indeed, I'm a little envious. Collins's saving grace is the wit that laces his observations of everyday* matters. Poets, he says, "have enough to do / complaining about the price of tobac-co, // passing the dripping ladle, / and singing songs to a bird in a cage. // We are busy doing nothing. . . ."

- From the Hawthorne "Young Goodman Brown" lecture: *Let's consider two specific ways to better understand and enjoy this famous story. First, can you sum up its theme—what's its central message? In some stories, the theme is easy to find. You can just underline its general statements, those that appear to sum up some large truth. In a fable, the theme is often stated in a moral at the end, such as: "Be careful in choosing your friends." In Stephen Crane's story of a shipwreck, "The Open Boat," Crane tells us, among other things, that "it occurs to a man that Nature does not regard him as important." But Hawthorne's story is trickier. If you underline its general statements and expect one of them to be its theme, you'll miss the whole point of the story. See paragraph 65: "Evil is the nature of mankind." Does Hawthorne believe that? Do you? Those are the words of the Devil, always a bad guy to believe. No, after you finish reading the story, especially pondering its closing paragraph, you can sum its theme much better in your own words.*

Part 3: Writing

In Part 3, Writing, the lectures further the discussions in Part 2 and help students form their own interpretations. The historical and cultural backdrop of the times, the writer's life experiences, and a close reading of the text all help students make connections. The lectures are peppered with ideas that students might pursue to write a critical essay or even a research paper. Here are a few examples:

- From the Seamus Heaney "Digging" lecture: *While both use natural imagery, Yeats writes of nature in idealized terms that seem to transcend everyday life. Images like "Dropping the veils of morning to where the cricket sings" and "midnight's all a glimmer, and noon a purple glow" remove us from the gritty world of toil. For Heaney, nature is anything but an escape. It is the here and now substance of everyday living—the harsh "rasping" of the spade—the "straining rump"—and the "heaving of sods." No pun intended on the title "Digging," but Heaney's poetry is much earthier and grounded than that of Yeats. And much of this attitude toward nature can be attributed to his own background.*

- From the Baldwin "Sonny's Blues" lecture: *Though the setting in Harlem in the mid-twentieth century is in many ways crucial to an understanding of the problems faced by these two African-American brothers, their story is universal. Therefore, an essay on the theme or themes in "Sonny's Blues" can be especially informative. Ask yourself what major ideas Baldwin is suggesting in the story. One theme, the theme of learning wisdom through suffering, is as old as literature, and Baldwin shows us through the searching and suffering of the two brothers that literature can share with us the wisdom of the ages, that we can learn about the agony and the beauty and the creativity within ourselves by vicariously sharing theirs.*

- From the Kate Chopin "The Story of an Hour" lecture: *Kate Chopin published several of her stories in the magazines of her time. However,* Vogue *and* The Century *initially refused to publish "The Story of an Hour." The Century regarded the story as "immoral" and* Vogue *only published it after Chopin's* Bayou Folk *became a success. Discuss "The Story of an Hour" in terms of the artistic, moral, and intellectual sensibilities of Chopin's time. Consider why Chopin's story was branded as "immoral" and why literary perceptions have changed over the years.*

- From the Sophocles *Oedipus the King* lecture: *Over time, this play has drawn many conflicting interpretations. Here are a few long-debated questions for you to think about. Is Oedipus a helpless, passive tool of the gods? Who is responsible for his terrible downfall? Does he himself bring about his own misfortune? Is he an innocent victim? If the downfall of a person of high estate (as Aristotle thought tragedies generally show) is due to a tragic flaw or weakness in the person's character, does Oedipus have any tragic flaw? If he does, how would you define it? Consider his speeches, his acts, his treatment of others. Does Oedipus seem justified in afflicting himself with blindness? Does his punishment fit, or fail to fit, his supposed crime?*

Critical Thinking and Writing by Lecture

Each part of the three-part lectures is accompanied by Questions for Thinking and Writing. These questions help reinforce the content given in the lecture and provide helpful suggestions for research and writing. Students can respond to the questions directly on screen and have their responses e-mailed to you.

Writing and Research: Tools and Techniques

From formulating an original idea to citing sources, this section of *MyLiteratureLab* offers students step-by-step guidance for writing powerful critical essays and research papers. This section of the site can reinforce and augment the writing coverage in your text. Below is a brief description of what each section covers.

Overview

Writing and Research contains eight main sections. Six are discussed here, while we cover **Exchange, Research Navigator,** and **Avoiding Plagiarism** in more detail below.

Writing About Literature facilitates effective writing by providing useful information on both the writing process and writing about literature, including such key topics as invention, planning, and strategies for organizing, drafting, and revising. **Writing the Research Paper** offers comprehensive instruction for writing research papers, including finding a topic, evaluating sources, taking notes, tips for summarizing, developing a thesis, suggestions for organizing the paper, choosing a pattern of development, guidance for writing introductions and conclusions, and comprehensive MLA documentation. A dozen **Student Papers** are integrated throughout, providing helpful models of a variety of critical essays and the research paper. Comprehensive coverage of **MLA Documentation** provides numerous models of all types for citing a range of sources, from interviews to periodicals to electronic sources.

Access to our **Tutor Center** is provided free of charge with your subscription to *MyLiteratureLab*. The Tutor Center gives your students help with reviewing papers for organization, flow, argument, and consistent grammar errors. Students can contact tutors toll-free via phone, e-mail, Web access, or fax, often at times when your campus writing center is not available.

Using *Exchange*

Exchange, Pearson's powerful interactive tool, allows students to comment on each others' drafts and instructors to review and grade papers—all online. More information about *Exchange* can be found in the Instructor Resources section of the *MyLiteratureLab* website. Please visit the Instructor Resources area to learn about creating and administering *Exchange* as part of your teaching apparatus. Highlights of *Exchange* include the ability to:

- Quickly and easily add comments at the word, sentence, paragraph, or paper level.
- Save and re-use your favorite comments.
- Help students identify and overcome common grammar errors through links to practice exercises and an online handbook.
- Decide how many students are in each group.
- Assign students by name, or create random groups.
- Let all students see comments, or only the author and instructor.
- Allow students to post comments anonymously.
- And more!

Exploring *Research Navigator*

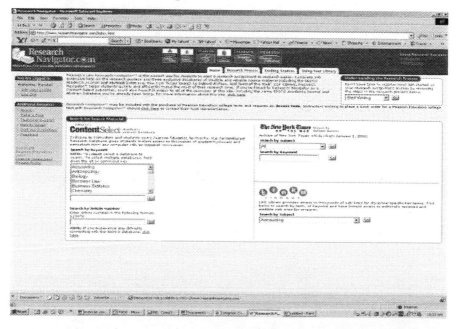

Pearson's *Research Navigator* is designed to help students develop their rhetorical knowledge, critical skills, understanding of processes, and knowledge of conventions for research writing.

Research Navigator is the easiest way for students to start a research assignment or research paper. Complete with extensive help on the research process and four exclusive databases of credible and reliable source material (EBSCO Academic Journal and Abstract Database, New York Times Search by Subject™ Archive, "Best of the Web" Link Library, and the *Financial Times* archives), *Research Navigator* helps students quickly and efficiently make the most of their research time.

Here is a brief overview of the databases available to students who use *Research Navigator*:

- **The EBSCO Academic Journal and Abstract Database**, organized by subject, contains over 100 of the leading academic journals per discipline, including literature. Instructors and students can search the online journals by keyword, topic, or multiple topics. Articles include abstract and citation information and can be cut, pasted, e-mailed, or saved for later use. The EBSCO database includes the MLA International Bibliography, MagillOnLiterature Plus, and Academic Search Premier.

- **The New York Times Search by Subject™ Archive** is organized by academic subject and searchable by keyword or multiple keywords. Instructors and students can view full-text articles from the world's leading journalists from *The New York Times*. *The New York Times Search by Subject™ Archive* is available exclusively to instructors and students through *Research Navigator*.

- **Link Library**, organized by subject, offers editorially selected "best of the Web" sites. Link Libraries are continually scanned and kept up to date, providing the most relevant and accurate links for research assignments. Subjects in the Link Library include American Literature, British Literature, Children's Literature, and World Literature.

- **FT.com** provides access to a wealth of business-related information from the *Financial Times*.

In addition to the databases, *Research Navigator* provides students with help in understanding the research process itself. The areas explored include:

- **The Research Process**: This area leads students step-by-step through the process of selecting a topic, gathering information, and developing a research paper.

- **Finding Sources**: This area provides access to the site's four databases on one page.

- **Using Your Library**: This area explores the resources available through libraries and provides library guides to 31 core disciplines. Each library guide includes an overview of major databases and online journals, key associations and newsgroups, and suggestions for further research.

- **Start Writing:** This area guides students through the writing process itself, from draft to finished paper.

- **End Notes and Bibliography:** This area provides clear and authoritative guidance about documenting sources and formatting notes and bibliographies according to a variety of styles.

You may want to provide class time for exploring this rich resource, if you have access to a computer lab, or you may want to encourage your students to explore on their own by assigning a Web-based activity.

The Research Process

From *Research Navigator*'s homepage, students have easy access to all of the site's main features, including a quick route to the databases of source content. If your students are new to the research process, however, you may want to have them start by browsing *The Research Process,* located in the upper right-hand section of the homepage. Here students will find extensive help on all aspects of the research process, including:

- Overview of the research process
- Planning your research assignment
- Finding a topic
- Creating effective notes
- Research paper paradigms
- Finding source material
- Avoiding plagiarism
- Summary of the research process

Selecting a topic is the first and often most difficult step for students completing a research assignment or research paper. In the tutorial for this topic, *Research Navigator* assists students with the process of finding an appropriate topic to research.

Once students have selected and narrowed down their research topic, they are ready to take on the serious task of gathering data. With academic research projects, student researchers quickly find out that some leads turn out to be dead ends, while other leads provide only trivial information. Some research yields repetitive results, but a recursive pattern does develop; that is, students will go back and forth from reading, to searching indexes, the Internet, the library, and back again to reading. One idea modifies another, until students begin discovering connections and refining their topics even further.

Research Navigator simplifies students' research efforts by giving them a convenient launching pad for gathering data. The site has aggregated three distinct types of source material commonly used in research assignments: academic journals (EBSCO ContentSelect), newspaper articles (*New York Times* and *Financial Times*), and websites (Link Library).

Finding Sources

Scholarly Journals

The EBSCO Academic Journal and Abstract Databases contains scholarly, peer-reviewed journals in a wide variety of disciplines, including the MLA International Bibliography, MagillOnLiterature Plus, and Academic Search Premier. If your students have not been exposed to scholarly journals, you may want to take the time to provide them with a sense of what a scholarly journal looks like and what kind of information it typically contains.

You will probably also want to clarify the differences between scholarly journals and magazines, especially as they should or should not be used in academic research writing. What sets scholarly journals apart from popular magazines like *Newsweek* or *People* is that the content of each journal is peer-reviewed. This means that each journal has, in addition to an editor and editorial staff, a pool of reviewers on whom the editorial staff relies in selecting appropriate articles for publication. Academic journal articles also adhere to strict guidelines for methodology and theoretical grounding. The information in journal articles is often more rigorously tested than that found in popular magazines or newspaper articles, or on Web pages (which have, for the most part, no scholarly or professional "filter" at all).

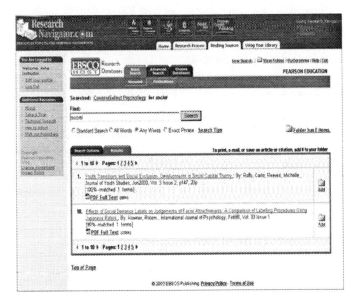

Teaching Tip: Many students shy away from scholarly journals because they are intimidated by the scientific or theoretical language, nature, and content. Instructors often require students to use such sources in their research projects in part to familiarize students with the skills needed to read this kind of information critically. Assignments based on using *Research Navigator* may give your students the confidence they need to navigate journals on their own for later assignments.

Searching for articles in EBSCO's ContentSelect is easy. Here are some tips to help students find articles for their research projects. (EBSCO Search Tips are also available at <http://www.researchnavigator.com/>.)

Sample Tips

Tip 1:	*Select a discipline.* When first entering the database, users see a list of disciplines. To search within a single discipline, click the name of the discipline. To search in more than one discipline, click the box next to each discipline and click the ENTER button.
Tip 2:	*Basic Search.* After selecting discipline(s), go to the Basic Search window, which lets users search for articles using a variety of methods: Standard Search, Match All Words, Match Any Words, or Match Exact Phrase. For more information on these options, click the Search Tips link at any time!
Tip 3:	Using *AND, OR,* and *NOT* to help the search. In Standard Search, use AND, OR, and NOT to create a very broad or very narrow search: AND searches for articles containing all of the words. For example, typing education AND technology will search for articles that contain both education AND technology. OR searches for articles that contains at least one of the terms. For example, searching for education OR technology will find articles that contain either education OR technology. NOT excludes words so that the articles will not include the word that follows "NOT": For example, searching for education NOT technology will find articles that contain the term education but NOT the term technology.
Tip 4:	Using *Match All Words.* When selecting the "Match All Words" option, you will automatically search for articles that only contain all of the words. The word "and" is not necessary. The order of the search words does not matter. For example, typing education technology will search for articles that contain both education AND technology.
Tip 5:	Using *Match Any Words.* After selecting the "Match Any Words" option, type words, a phrase, or a sentence in the window. The database searches for articles that contain any of the terms typed (but will not search for words such as "in" and "the"). For example, type the following words: rising medical costs in the United States. The database searches for articles that contain rising, medical, costs, United, or States. To limit the search to find articles that contain exact terms, use quotation marks—for example, typing "United States" will only search for articles containing "United States" together as words.
Tip 6:	Using *Match Exact Phrase.* Select this option to find articles containing an exact phrase. The database searches for articles that include all the words entered, exactly as they were typed. For example, type *Flannery*

	O'Connor's use of religion to find articles that contain the exact phrase "Flannery O'Connor's use of religion."
Tip 7:	To switch to a *Guided Search*, click the Guided Search tab on the navigation bar, just under the EBSCO Host logo. The Guided Search Window helps you focus your search using multiple text boxes, Boolean operators (AND, OR, and NOT), and various search options. • To create a search: • Type the words to search for in the "Find" field. • Select a field from the drop-down list. For example: AU-Author will search for an author. For more information on fields, click Search Tips. • Enter additional search terms in the text boxes (optional), and select *and, or, not* to connect multiple search terms (see Tip 3 for information on and, or, and not). • Click Search.
Tip 8:	To switch to an *Expert Search*, click the Expert Search tab on the navigation bar, just under the EBSCO Host logo. The Expert Search Window uses keywords and search histories for articles. NOTE: Searches run from the Basic or Guided Search Windows are not saved to the History File used by the Expert Search Window—only Expert Searches are saved in the history.
Tip 9:	Expert Searches use Limiters and Field Codes to help you search for articles. For more information on Limiters and Field Codes, click Search Tips.

Newspapers

The *New York Times* and *FT.com* (the *Financial Times*). Newspapers provide contemporary information. Information in periodicals—journals, magazines, and newspapers—may be useful, or even critical, when students are ready to focus in on specific aspects of a topic or to find the most current information. There are some significant differences between newspaper articles and journal articles and students should consider the level of scholarship that is most appropriate for their research project. Popular or controversial topics may not be well covered in journals, while coverage in newspapers and magazines like *Newsweek* and *Time* may be extensive.

Research Navigator gives students access to a one-year, "search by subject" archive of articles from one of the world's leading newspapers—the *New York Times*. (To learn more about the *New York Times*, visit them on the Web at <http://www.nytimes.com>.) The *New York Times* search-by-subject archive is a very easy-to-use search tool. Students need only to type a word, or multiple words *separated by commas*, into the search box and click Go. This search generates a list of articles that have appeared in the *New York Times* over the last year, sorted chronologically with the most recent article first. The search can be refined as needed by using more specific search terms.

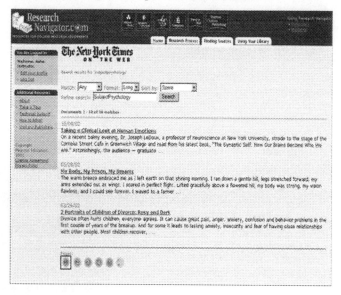

Websites

"Best Of The Web" Link Library. The collection of Web links organized by academic subject and key terms can be easily searched. Students select their subject (American, English, and World Literature or Children's Literature) from the dropdown list and find the key term for their search topic. Examples of key terms include allegory, Joyce Carol Oates, and neo-realism. Clicking on the key term reveals a list of 5–7 editorially reviewed websites that offer educationally relevant and credible content. When students use the key term "Jane Austen," for example, they find links to the OnLine Austen Journal, the Jane Austen Society of North America Home Page, and an audio reading of *Pride and Prejudice,* as well as many other Austen-specific resources. The Web links in this database are monitored and updated each week.

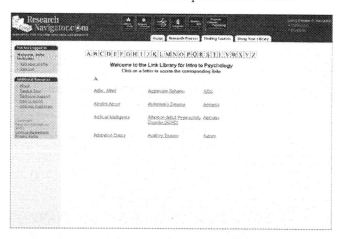

Using Your Library

After students have selected and narrowed their topic, they may want to seek source material not only from the Internet but also from their school library. *Research Navigator* should not—and does not try—to replace the library. In fact, it provides an additional resource—a guide to doing library research effectively and efficiently.

Libraries may seem foreign and overwhelming to a generation of students brought up on the easy access to information provided by the Internet. *Research Navigator* provides a bridge to the library by taking students through a simple step-by-step overview of how to make the most of library time. Written by a library scientist, the "Using Your Library" area of *Research Navigator* explores:

- Types of libraries
- Choosing the tool to use (covering electronic databases)
- Gathering data in the library

In addition, when students are ready to use the library to complete a research assignment or research paper, *Research Navigator* includes 31 discipline specific "library guides" (English is one discipline) for students to use as roadmaps. Each guide includes an overview of the discipline's major subject databases, online journals, and key associations and newsgroups. The library guide tailored to English introduces students to *Comparative Literature Studies* online, the MLA, and the online catalog JSTOR, among many other journals and associations. Encourage students to print the guide and take it to the library.

Start Writing

This writing tutorial leads students step-by-step through the process of writing an academic paper. Sections in this area include:

- Drafting a paper in an academic style
- Incorporating reference material into your writing
- Writing the introduction, body, and conclusion
- Revising, proofreading, and formatting the rough draft

Also included is a bank of sample research papers for students to peruse.

End Notes and Bibliography

The final step in the research process is the creation of endnotes and a bibliography. This area authoritatively outlines the rules for using and documenting sources in a variety of styles. These include:

- How to cite sources from *Research Navigator*
- Using MLA style

Tips for Instructors and Suggestions for Use

Student writers can benefit from the resources in *Research Navigator* throughout the different stages of the research writing process. *Research Navigator* is especially beneficial for students who feel overwhelmed with the process of handling a research project and researching online. Especially in the early stages of research writing, students tend to be over-reliant on the popular search engines with which they are already familiar, and they may be overwhelmed with too much information and unable to evaluate it critically. Students who use *Research Navigator* are assured of the credibility and reliability of the sources they find, and the information returned to them in a search is manageable and targeted.

Here are two possible Web-based activities that can help your students become familiar with *Research Navigator*:

Activity #1

- Have students explore *Research Navigator*, either individually or in small groups of two or three students. Give each student or group a particular area of the site to explore. If you are in a computer classroom and doing this activity together, provide ample time to complete the activity; fifteen to twenty minutes is usually enough.
- Ask students to share their findings with the class. In less technologically-adept classes, have students report orally on what they have found. In more skilled groups, have them report electronically, either through a class-wide e-mail, a distribution list that you have established, or as postings on a class discussion board.

Activity #2

- Ask students to pick partners and then assign each team a research topic. (You may want to brainstorm with the class to find a list of topics that the students find engaging or compelling. The topics should be broad enough that student groups have no trouble finding sources in *Research Navigator*.)
- Look at the EBSCO Search Tips with the class. Talk a little about how related terms or subtopics can affect an online search.
- If you are in a computer classroom and doing this activity together, give students fifteen to twenty minutes to complete an initial search.
- Have each team compile a bibliography of the ten most useful sources they have found. Encourage them to use the *MyLiteratureLab* resources to create accurate MLA citations.

Note: Research Navigator website does not allow students to word process or save their searches; therefore, students must have a second window open on their computers to allow them to type and save information as they find it; or they must print out their searches to have a record of their work in *Research Navigator*.

Avoiding Plagiarism

Avoiding Plagiarism allows students to work through interactive tutorials to learn how to cite and document sources responsibly in MLA format. This section guides students through a step-by-step tutorial, complete with self-tests and items for extended analysis. The steps include:

- What is Plagiarism?
- When to Document
- Using Print & Electronic Sources
- Avoiding Plagiarism
    - ✧ Attribution
    - ✧ Quotation Marks
    - ✧ Citation
    - ✧ Paraphrase
    - ✧ Loyalty to Source
    - ✧ Works Cited
    - ✧ Citation for Images
- Extended Analysis
- Wrap-Up

Each step in the MLA tutorial guides students to read and click to navigate to the next step. Students do not need to complete the tutorial on one visit to the site; they can jump ahead to continue their work or return to previous steps to review an earlier discussion.

    The *Avoiding Plagiarism* tutorial contains many practice sets for students.

Extended Analysis

The extended analysis section allows students to apply what they have learned from the "Avoiding Plagiarism" tutorials. Here students can test how well they recognize plagiarism as they read a student research paper. Students must pay careful attention to the sources that are being quoted, paraphrased, or summarized in consideration of the seven rules of avoiding plagiarism discussed during the tutorial.

Tips for Instructors and Suggestions for Use

Student writers can benefit from their work in *Avoiding Plagiarism* throughout a composition course and at different stages in the research writing process. *Avoiding Plagiarism* helps students to correctly paraphrase, summarize, and quote source material, as well as cite and document sources in both MLA and APA style.

    Students can use the *Avoiding Plagiarism* tutorials on their own, working through the tutorials at their own pace and returning to them as needed throughout their research projects. Most pages or "steps" in each tutorial can also be printed for quick student reference.

    We encourage you to explore the tutorial yourself so that you understand the tutorial's content and can make connections to your own course, your students and their research projects, and to other areas of *MyLiteratureLab*. We encourage you to identify teaching opportunities, learn the website's navigation method, and view the website's additional resources and links.

Students should also be encouraged to review *Avoiding Plagiarism* before they submit both drafts and final versions of their research projects for review. With peer review of drafts, for example, students who have reviewed the appropriate tutorial will be better prepared to give informed feedback about documentation of sources in other student papers. And students who review the tutorial before submitting papers to instructors are more likely to correct their in-text and end-of-text citations during the final editing stage.

A Note on
Reference Books

There are many good reference books, but we'll mention here the core group that we could not survive without. Most are updated every few years. When new, they are expensive, but often you can fill out your reference shelf by checking what's available in used book stores.

At the bare minimum, we urge students to read with an excellent dictionary, such as *The American Heritage Dictionary*, 3rd edition, nearby. We also recommend that they do some of their reading, especially when preparing for paper assignments, in the reference room of the library.

Annals of American Literature, ed. Richard M. Ludwig and Clifford A. Nault, Jr.

Benét's Reader's Encyclopedia, ed. Katharine Baker Siepmann

Benét's Reader's Encyclopedia of American Literature, ed. George Perkins, Barbara Perkins, and Philip Leininger

The Bible, King James Version, and a concordance, such as Strong's

Brewer's Dictionary of Phrase and Fable

The Cambridge Biographical Encyclopedia, ed. David Crystal

The Cambridge Dictionary of American Biography, ed. John S. Bowman

The Cambridge Encyclopedia of the English Language, ed. David Crystal

The Cambridge Guide to Literature in English, ed. Ian Ousby

The Columbia Encyclopedia

The Concise Dictionary of American Biography

The Encyclopedia of World Facts and Dates, ed. Gordon Carruth

The Feminist Companion to Literature in English: Women Writers from the Middle Ages to the Present, ed. Virginia Blain, Isobel Grundy, and Patricia Clements

Merriam-Webster's Encyclopedia of Literature

The New Princeton Encyclopedia of Poetry and Poetics, ed. Alex Preminger and T. V. F. Brogan

The Oxford Classical Dictionary, ed. N. G. L. Hammond and H. H. Scullard

The Oxford Companion to American Literature, 6th edition, ed. James D. Hart and Phillip W. Leininger

The Oxford Companion to Art, ed. Harold Osborne

The Oxford Companion to Classical Literature, ed. M. C. Howatson

The Oxford Companion to English Literature, ed. Margaret Drabble

The Oxford Companion to Philosophy, ed. Ted Honderich

The Oxford Companion to the English Language, ed. Tom Macarthur

The Oxford Companion to Women's Writing in the United States, ed. Cathy N. Davidson and Linda Wagner-Martin

The Oxford English Dictionary

The Oxford Guide to Classical Mythology in the Arts, 1300–1990, 2 vols., ed. Jane Davidson Reid

You'll want to supplement this list with favorites of your own, along with anthologies of American, English, and World literatures, which are handy both for their selections and headnotes.

The First Meeting

When you meet your students on the first day of classes, in addition to the usual business of taking attendance and reviewing the syllabus, you may want to spend a few minutes describing *An Introduction to Literature*. Explain how this book will enable the students to fulfill the goals of the course. Your students have purchased the book, and they will be spending lots of time working with it; they will benefit from hearing from you why you have chosen it and about the features in it that will help them to improve their writing.

On the first day, we also give the students some advice about other resources that they should draw upon. These are obvious enough: a good dictionary and a thesaurus. But we recommend that you be more specific. Bring to class the dictionary and the thesaurus that you keep on your own desk. One of us in fact carries to each and every class a dictionary he especially admires: *The American Heritage Dictionary of the English Language*, third edition (1996); he places the dictionary, open and ready for reference, on his desk in the classroom, alongside his copy of *An Introduction to Literature*.

This, we know, may seem heavy-handed. But we think the teacher needs to provide a model for the students; if you urge the students to use the dictionary to check on the meanings of words and to expand their vocabularies, show them that you do this yourself—that it is a natural part of studying literature and becoming a skillful writer.

It is tempting on this first day or during the first week to identify for students many other books and Internet resources that they can turn to. But be careful not to give students more than they can handle or absorb, especially if you are teaching first-year students in the first semester of college, who tend to feel overwhelmed anyway. We also increasingly find that many of our students are non-native speakers; indeed, it is not unusual for us to encounter students for whom English is their third language. We try to keep this point in mind, even as we set a high standard for these students and all of the others.

If you are using the text in a composition course and you assign a research paper, there will be plenty of opportunities, as the semester unfolds, to outline the elements of a research paper and the relevant print and electronic sources for them. At the outset, keep the focus on the resources that *An Introduction to Literature* itself contains from one chapter to the next, and on the value derived from regular use of the dictionary and the thesaurus.

The only exception we make to this rule is when we are teaching a course, or a section of a course, designed for English majors, say, in the second semester of the first year or the first semester of the second. In these cases, we highlight two basic tools of the trade:

> *The Oxford Companion to American Literature*, 6th edition, ed. James D. Hart and Phillip W. Leininger (1995)

> *The Oxford Companion to English Literature*, revised edition, ed. Margaret Drabble (1998)

Students who know that they will be majoring in English enjoy hearing about the reference books that matter in particular for them. We suggest that you bring your own copies of these books to class. You might even make copies of an entry or two so that the students can see for themselves how the information in such books can prove useful to them in interpreting literature and writing about it.

The night before the first class, every teacher knows the truth of Byron's observation: "Nothing so difficult as a beginning." What to do in the first meeting is always worrisome. Students will not, of course, have prepared anything, and you can't say, "Let's open the book to page such-and-such," because half of them won't have the book. How, then, can one use the time profitably? A friend of ours (Marcia Stubbs of Wellesley College) offers a suggestion. We have tried it and we know it works, so we suggest that you consider it, too, if you are looking for an interesting beginning.

Begin reading the Japanese anecdote "Muddy Road" (text, p. 100) aloud, stopping after "A heavy rain was still falling." Then ask, "What do you think will happen now?" Someone is bound to volunteer, "They'll meet someone." Whom will they meet? (It may be necessary to say at this point that Tanzan and Ekido are both men.) You will certainly be informed that if two men meet someone, it will be a woman. Continue reading, "Coming around the bend they met a lovely girl." After "unable to cross the intersection," ask again what will happen, and entertain answers until you get an appropriate response. Read again, and pause after "temple." Who are Tanzan and Ekido? The temple may suggest to someone that they are monks; if not, provide the information. Continue reading, up through "Why did you do that?" Now inform the class that the story ends with one more line of print, and ask them to supply the brief ending. The students will then see the perfect rightness of it.

The point of the exercise: First a story sets up expectations, partly by excluding possibilities. (A relevant remark by Robert Frost can be effectively introduced at the first meeting. A work of literature—Frost is talking about a poem, but we can generalize—"assumes direction with the first line laid down.") After the first line or so, the possibilities are finite. The story must go on to fulfill the expectations set up. At the same time, a story, to be entertaining, must surprise us by taking us beyond what we have imagined and expect. But the fulfillment and the surprise must be coherent or the storyteller will appear arbitrary and the story, no matter how entertaining, trivial. (Notice E. M. Forster's pertinent comment, "Shock, followed by the feeling, 'Oh, that's all right,' is a sign that all is well with the plot.")

By satisfying expectations, literature confirms the truth of our own experience, teaching us that we are not alone, not singular; our perceptions, including moral perceptions (e.g., cause leads to effect, guilt leads to punishment or retribution) are shared by other human beings, people who may not even be of our own century or culture. Something along these lines can be suggested at the first meeting; subsequent meetings can be devoted to showing that literature, by exceeding and yet not violating our expectations, can also expand our powers of observation, imagination, and judgment.

The first chapter ("Reading and Responding to Literature") is fairly short; it can be given as the first reading assignment, and since it includes four very short poems and five very short prose narratives, the discussion in class can hardly flag.

If, however, you prefer to skip the first chapter and you plan to spend the first few weeks on fiction, you may want to begin with Chapter 2, which includes four short stories and three poems, and which introduces issues of *writing* about literature. Or you may want to begin with Chapter 3, which includes Chopin's "The Story of an Hour," or Chapter 4, which includes Hemingway's "Cat in the Rain," along with comments about annotating and keeping a journal. If none of this pedagogical material appeals to you, you may want to give as the first assignment—that is, the reading for the next meeting—Poe's "The Cask of Amontillado" (Chapter 10). The story is short and arresting, and it is familiar to many students. There will almost certainly be ample discussion in class, yet even students who come to class thinking they know the story well will probably leave class having learned new things about it. And in any case, an instructor who wishes to follow up on the lessons of "Muddy Road" (p. 100)—not the theme of the story but the lessons about plot and characterization—can examine Poe's story with an eye toward the way one episode follows another, arousing curiosity and then satisfying it.

In closing, we'd like to mention one other tip for the first meeting that we have been using often in recent years, as we have tried to emphasize writing as a part of the Introduction to Literature course. Make a copy of a short poem—by Blake, Dickinson, or Frost, for example—that the students can examine. Read it aloud. And then ask two or three questions, to which students respond by writing in their notebooks. The questions can be fairly general, such as "What do you find especially interesting in this poem?" Or they can be specific, keyed to the meaning of a stanza or an image.

The value of this approach is that it connects the course, right away, to *writing.* In addition, after the students are done writing, the questions and responses can be made the basis for some discussion. Yes, it is only the first meeting, but it is good to get the students talking from the beginning, and frequently students will be more ready to speak if they have written something: they feel more committed to the response because they have set it down on paper. There is always the risk, too, that if the instructor does all of the talking on the first day, he or she might create the impression that it's the instructor's voice that really counts and that the students in the course will play secondary, rather than primary and active, roles in it.

If you are teaching a composition course, please notice that some of the suggested topics in the book use the work of literature as a point of departure for expository or persuasive essays. For instance, for an essay that takes off from Grace Paley's "Samuel," we ask:

> If you had been on the train, would you have pulled the emergency cord? Why, or why not?

We have just said that such topics use the literary work as a point of departure; we do not mean that the work gets left behind. A good essay will be based on a close reading of the text, but it will also allow the student to develop an argument on an issue larger than the work. Moreover, many of these topics can easily be made into small-scale research papers if the instructor wishes to teach research methods. In the text, three appendices on research papers provide information about documentation and about electronic sources.

In this handbook we discuss, in varying degrees of detail, every literary selection that we reprint, except for a handful that are discussed extensively within the text itself. We also offer in this handbook Additional Topics for Critical Thinking and Writing on many of the works. Unfortunately, however, assignments that work well for one instructor may not work well for another, and even an assignment that works well at nine o'clock may not work well at ten. Still, over the years we have had good luck with the selections we include and with the writing assignments given in the text and in this handbook. We will be most grateful to any instructors who write to us to suggest additional topics. In the next edition of the book, we will try to introduce new topics, and we will of course acknowledge our sources.

Note: We provide bibliographies for the authors included in this handbook, but we do not repeat this information in the case of authors for whom we have more than one selection. You will find the bibliography the first time that the author is discussed.

I

Reading, Thinking, and Writing Critically about Literature

1

Reading and Responding to Literature

This chapter begins with very short poems. If you want to begin by teaching fiction, you may want to skip this chapter and start with Chapter 3 or 4 (Chopin's "The Story of an Hour" and Hemingway's "Cat in the Rain," respectively). On the other hand, we think these poems make a good introduction to literature, and in any case, since they are closely followed by short works of prose, you can use the chapter even if you devote the first third of the course to fiction.

ROBERT FROST

Immigrants (p. 6)

PAT MORA

Immigrants (p. 8)

These two poems are discussed at some length in the text. Those words may sound ominous, even deadly, but we are sure you will find that much remains to be done in class. Enough questions are raised in the text to stimulate lots of discussion.

The text makes the point that Frost's poem was written for an anniversary celebration of the arrival of the *Mayflower*, and that is really all that students need to know about the background, but instructors may be interested in a bit more. The lines originally were the fourth stanza of a long poem that Frost wrote in 1920, "The Return of the Pilgrims," for *The Pilgrim Spirit—A Pageant in Celebration of the Landing of the Pilgrims at Plymouth, Massachusetts, December 21, 1620,* organized by George Pierce Baker. The literary aspects of the pageant were published (under the title just given) in 1921, but Frost never again reprinted the entire poem. Instead, he extracted only this one stanza from his poem, called it "Immigrants," and printed it in *West-Running Brook* (1928) and in many of his later volumes.

In the text, in our discussion of Frost, we ignore one large matter—the speaking voice. We omitted this issue because we felt we had talked enough (maybe more than enough) about the poem, and because the matter of voice is fairly subtle, but instructors may want to ask several students to read the poem aloud, and then to discuss the voice. Briefly, it seems to us that in this poem we get an authoritative voice—a voice which is by no means offensive but which is highly confident and which by its confidence (and its mastery of form) inspires confidence or faith in its assertion.

Pat Mora's voice in her "Immigrants" is marvelously different—for one thing, we get (as our comment in the text tries to suggest) *several* voices in her poem. Where Frost gives us the voice of the poet as an assured elder statesman (though he was only 46 at the time), Mora gives us the voices of the uneasy immigrants as well as the voice of the ironic commentator.

At least three voices are heard in Mora's poem: the voice of the immigrant who hopes that his or her child will resemble Americans (WASPS, that is); the voice of the immigrant who fears that the child will not be liked because the child will not seem sufficiently American; and the ironic voice of the poet, expressing skepticism about the hopes for assimilation to an Anglo-American model.

The almost comic glimpse of imperfect pronunciation given in line 7 ("hallo, babee, hallo")—the speaker of the poem here seems to have a somewhat superior attitude—disappears in the last three lines which, though written in English, sympathetically represent the fear that is thought "in Spanish or Polish." If you discuss these lines, you may want to invite students to express their opinions about why "american" is not capitalized in the last two lines, even though it is capitalized in the first ("the American flag"), and "Spanish" and "Polish" are capitalized. It's our guess that by not capitalizing "american" in the last two lines the poet implies that it's not all that wonderful to become an "american"; indeed there may be a loss in changing from "Spanish" or "Polish" to "american."

Put it this way: the poem shifts from the eager activity of immigrant parents (presented almost comically in lines 1–7) to a more sympathetic presentation of deep fears in lines 8–13, but the whole is complicated by the author's implied criticism (chiefly through "american") of the immigrants' understandable but mistaken activity.

In short, we think that if you ask several students to read both of the poems aloud, students will enjoy what Frost in a letter called "the sound of sense," and they will also see that works of literature have an almost palpable sensuous appeal. They will see, too, that Mora's poem is able to hold its own in the company of Frost's. We confess that we are unable to think of a more effective way than this if one wants to introduce students to the idea of "multiculturalism."

One last word about this part of the chapter, specifically about Frost's poem. A reader of our manuscript objected that Frost offered an offensive mythic view of America (the land of freedom and opportunity) and that in our commentary we had bought this myth. He suggested that many immigrants—especially the Asian laborers in the nineteenth century—had been imported as cheap labor and existed virtually as chattel. And before the Asians came, thousands of English, for instance, had come as indentured servants, obliged to work for years before they could be free. Still, it seems evident to us that even for these people life in America promised opportunities that were unavailable in the Old Country. Similarly, for those Asians who came here, life in this country (or Hawaii)—however grinding—must have seemed preferable to life in China or Japan or the Philippines. For instance, the Japanese who worked in the sugar plantations of Hawaii (beginning in 1868) endured terrible conditions, but the prospects were better for them than was life in Japan, and at the end of their contractual period most of them elected *not* to return to Japan. In time, of course, many of these people migrated to the mainland. Our own instinct is *not* to go into this issue in discussing Frost's poem, partly because we do not find his view offensive, but chiefly because we want to talk about literature, not about history.

Note: Our text includes a fair number of other poems by Robert Frost, and three other poems (also on conflicting identities) by Pat Mora.

The best book on Robert Frost is Richard Poirier, *Robert Frost: The Work of Knowing* (1977). Also helpful are Reuben A. Brower, *The Poetry of Robert Frost: Constellations of Intention* (1963); William H. Pritchard, *Frost, A Literary Life Reconsidered* (1984); and Mark Richardson, *The Ordeal of Robert Frost: The Poet and His Poetics* (1997). For a good collection of Frost's prose pieces and letters on literary criticism and poetry, see *Robert Frost on Writing*, ed. Elaine Barry (1973). Serious students will consult *Robert Frost: Collected Poems, Prose, and Plays*, published in the Library of America series (1995).

We tend ourselves not to refer much, if at all, to secondary sources during the early weeks of the course. The main goal then, for us, is to focus the attention of students on the text at hand and equip them to state their responses to it. But from experience we know that a student is likely to ask early on, usually at the time of the first paper assignment, "Do you want us to use criticism?" Here, each instructor will fall back on his or her own preferences. Some will agree with us and judge that students, in getting underway, benefit most from their own engagement with the works; these instructors see criticism as coming into play later, once students are more confident about their own interpretations. Other instructors, however, find it valuable to use criticism right from the start, as a means of encouraging students to connect their experiences in the classroom and in papers to the larger "conversation" about this or that particular author.

Perhaps the main point is that instructors should give some thought to the question that, no doubt, a number of students will be wondering about: "Am I allowed to use criticism?" Take the question seriously, and have your answer ready for it. If no student asks the question, raise it yourself: rest assured that members of the class will be glad that you did.

Whether you are willing to let your students use criticism or not, we suggest that you stress to them that *they* have the capacity themselves to analyze literary texts well. In our view, one of the important aims of the first weeks is to boost the students' confidence, making them see and believe that they *can* respond cogently and coherently to literature, and, furthermore, that their pleasure in literary works will grow as they become more articulate about describing the nature and shape of their responses.

LYDIA DAVIS

City People (p. 10)

In our second question in the text we ask if it is reasonable to offer a conjecture as to *why* these people have moved from the city to the country. We are aware that the characters in "City People" are fictional, that they have no "real" lives—they are only what Lydia Davis tells us they are, and we cannot speculate about their earlier experiences any more than we can speculate on Hamlet's days at the university. That is, we cannot speculate on (for instance) whether Davis's characters moved to the country from New York or from San Francisco, whether they lived in more than one city, whether they now are middle-aged or younger or older, and so forth. Still, our answer to our question is, Yes, we can guess why they have moved from the city to the country. It is because they are unhappy, isolated, alienated—perhaps that is the human condition—and they have moved thinking they will find some sort of tranquility. But, in this Beckett-like world a change in locale is meaningless. Someone—maybe Horace?—said something to the effect that travelers change only the skies, not themselves.

We think it is worth discussing, in class, the physical form of the story, its shape on the page even though, unfortunately, in our text we cannot print it with the abundance of white space that surrounds the story in Davis's book. In the first paragraph Davis gives us a solid block of third-person omniscient narration, chiefly short simple sentences. The effect of the sentences is almost childlike, especially near the end of the paragraph:

> He hates the mice. The pump breaks. They replace the pump. They poison the mice. Their neighbor's dog barks. It barks and barks. She could poison the dog.

Even as one silently reads the first paragraph, the reader's eye sees the next (and only other) paragraph, a very short paragraph. This second paragraph, a single sentence, gives us some dialogue. We at last *hear* these people (or at least one of them) rather than get the narrator's report of their action. And what do we hear? The stupid yet pitiful "'We're city people,' he says, 'and there aren't any nice cities to live in.'" In terms of thoughtfulness, the line bears comparison with an inane line in Flannery O'Connor's "A Good Man Is Hard to Find," where the grandmother says, "People are certainly not nice like they use to be." But our point here is not to comment on the shallowness of the man's speech; rather, our point is to comment on the shape of the story: In its original format the text is centered on the page, with generous margins at the top, bottom, and sides so we get a block of print, varied only by a slight indentation (the beginning of the second paragraph) near the bottom of the block, followed by the inane line of dialogue. And then we are left on our own, with ample space at the bottom of the page, i.e., we are in this isolated world of these city people, surrounded by blankness.

LUKE

The Parable of the Prodigal Son (p. 11)

A bibliographic note about parables may be useful. In the *Encyclopedia Britannica,* in a relatively long article entitled "Fable, Parable, Allegory," fable and parable are defined as "short, simple forms of naive allegory," and yet a few paragraphs later the article says that "The rhetorical appeal of a parable is directed primarily toward an elite, in that a final core of its truth is known only to an inner circle, however simple its narrative may appear on the surface. . . ." Perhaps, then, a parable is not a "naive allegory." Two other passages from the article are especially interesting: "The Aesopian fables emphasize the social interaction of human beings," whereas "parables do not analyze social systems so much as they remind the listener of his beliefs." That may not always be true, but it is worth thinking about.

The traditional title of this story is unfortunate, since it makes the second half of the story (the father's dealings with the older brother) superfluous. Joachim Jeremias, in *The Parables of Jesus* (1972), suggests that the work should be called "The Parable of the Father's Love."

Here is a way to provoke thoughtful discussion of the parable. Roger Seamon, in "The Story of the Moral: The Function of Thematizing in Literary Criticism," *Journal of Aesthetics and Art Criticism* 47 (1989): 229–36, offers an unusual way of thinking about this parable. He summarizes his approach as follows:

> I want to reverse the traditional and common sense view that stories convey, illustrate, prove or emotionally support themes. Morals and themes, I argue, convey to audiences what story is to be made out of sentences. The story flows, so to speak, from theme, rather than the theme following from the story. (230)

He goes on to suggest an experiment. "Imagine," he says, that instead of reading a story that traditionally is called "The Prodigal Son,"

> we were to find the same set of sentences in another book under the title "The Prodigal Father," and at the end we found the following moral: "waste not your heart on the unworthy, lest you lose the love of the righteous." We now go back and re-read the sentences, and we find that *we are now reading a different story.* In the new story the father's giving the son money is wrong.

Seamon goes on to say that in *this* story the son's confession is "a way of evading responsibility for his error," and that the father is as prodigal with his love as he was with his property. In this version (remember: the sentences are identical, but the title is different), Seamon claims, "The story concludes with the father happily returning to his error. The absence of poetic justice at the end is meant to arouse our indignation" (232).

It's interesting to hear students respond to this view. Of course Seamon's title, "The Prodigal Father," is merely his own invention, but the conventional title ("The Prodigal Son") has no compelling authority. The question is this:

Once we apply Seamon's title, do we read the story the way he suggests—that is, do we see the father as blameworthy and the stay-at-home son as justified? If not, why not? Again, Seamon's point is that although the common-sense view holds that the story yields a moral, in fact the reverse is true: the moral (i.e., the theme we have in mind) yields the story. For Seamon, "A thematic statement conveys information about how the critic constructs the *nature and motivations of the characters,* [and] *the value of their actions* . . ." (233). True, but can't we add that the skilled critic, i.e., reader, is in large measure guided by the author who knows (again, at least in large measure) how to control the reader's response? Seamon apparently takes a different view, for he holds that "the sentences used to project the events are not, in themselves, sufficient to tell us how we are to characterize or evaluate what is going on." Our response to Seamon is of no importance; what is important is to get students to think about why they do or do not accept the view that the story might be entitled "The Prodigal Father."

We spend some time in class teaching this parable because we find the artistry admirable—and also because the story is profound. One small but telling artistic detail may be noted here, a detail mentioned by Joachim Jeremias, who points out that the elder son, speaking to his father, "omits the address"; we had never noticed this, but now it seems obvious, and surely it is revealing that when the younger son addresses his father he says, "Father," and that when the father addresses the older son he says, "Son." The older son's lack of address, then, speaks volumes. He refuses to see himself as bound by family ties of love—a position evident also when, talking to his father, he identifies the prodigal not as "my brother" but as "this thy son." The story is (among many other things) an admirable example of work in which a storyteller guides an audience into having certain responses.

It's also worthwhile in class to spend some time cautioning against a too-vigorous attempt to find meaning in every detail. Professionals as well as students sometimes don't know when to leave well enough alone. For instance, a writer in *Studies in Short Fiction* 23 (1986), talking about Updike's "A & P," says that Queenie's *pink* bathing suit "suggests the emerging desires competing with chastity." But come to think of it, this statement isn't surprising, considering what has been said about the pink ribbon in "Young Goodman Brown." One writer, for instance, says it symbolizes feminine passion, and another says it symbolizes a state between the scarlet of total depravity and the white of innocence.

To illustrate the danger of pressing too hard, you might mention medieval allegorizations of the story. The gist of these is this: the older brother represents the Pharisees and teachers who resented the conversion of the Gentiles. Thus the fact that the older brother was in the fields when the prodigal returned was taken as standing for the remoteness of the Pharisees and the teachers from the grace of God. The younger brother, according to medieval interpretations, represents the Gentiles, who wandered in illusions and who served the devil (the owner of the swine) by tending the devil's demons (the swine). The pods that the prodigal ate represent either the vices (which cannot satisfy) or pagan literature (again, unsatisfying). The father represents God the Father; his going forth to meet the prodigal stands for the Incarnation; his falling on the neck of the prodigal stands for the mild yoke that Christ places on the neck of his followers (Matthew 11.29–30). The music which the older brother hears represents the praise of God, and the feast of the fatted calf represents the Eucharist. A great deal more of this sort of thing can be found in Stephen L. Wailes, *Medieval Allegories of Jesus' Parables* (1987, 236–45). The point should already be clear. On the other hand, it's also worth mentioning that the medieval interpreters of the parable at least paid it the compliment of taking it seriously. Odd as the interpretations now seem, they were the result of an admirable love of the word, and surely such an excess is preferable to indifference.

Is the parable an allegory? No, and yes. Certainly it does not have the detailed system of correspondences that one associates with allegory. Moreover, since the prodigal says, "Father, I have sinned against heaven and . . . thee," the father cannot be said to represent heaven, i.e., God. And yet, as Jeremias says (131):

> The parable describes with touching simplicity what God is like, his goodness, his grace, his boundless mercy, his abounding love.

Need a reader believe in God or in the divinity of Jesus in order to value this story? The point is surely worth discussing in class. Many students will say that religious belief is not necessary to appreciate the artistry of the parable and to benefit from the moral lesson that it teaches. But for other students, this parable will be understood within the context of their own religious views and values. The discussion in class of the parable, we have found, can often take on a curious shape, with some students sounding like literary critics and others a bit like priests and ministers.

Usually all that's needed is some acknowledgment from the instructor that the story of the prodigal son is profound on at least two levels, meaningful (and moving) for believers and nonbelievers alike. But we have sometimes used the occasion to describe briefly for students the connections between reading the sacred books of religious traditions and interpreting literature, as the students are learning to do in their course. "Close reading" can come to strike some students as more accessible, as more *possible* for them, when they realize that versions of it can be found outside the college and university classroom. It's curious that students frequently begin their literary work by saying that they find "close reading" to be strange, foreign, forced, even though they are in fact accustomed to careful analysis of texts in their religious practices and observances. You might help them move more readily into their literary work by pointing out the connections between what they have done, if they are religiously observant and are students of sacred scriptures, and what they are now learning to do.

GRACE PALEY

Samuel (p. 13)

"All those ballsy American stories," Grace Paley has said of much of the American canon, "had nothing to say to me." Is she, then, a feminist writer? She denies it, insisting that she is something rather different, "a feminist and a writer." Some instructors may wish to have a class consider in what ways, if any, "Samuel" is the work of a feminist.

There is a particularly female insight in the last two paragraphs of "Samuel" which (though the second of these mentions Samuel's father) focus on Samuel's mother. The first of these paragraphs emphasizes the mother's agony when she learns of her son's death; the final paragraph, describing a later time, emphasizes a grief that is less visible or audible but that is perhaps even more painful, for this grief is stimulated by the sight of her newborn baby: "never again will a boy exactly like Samuel be known."

Interestingly, the narrator (can we say the female author?) conveys a good deal of enthusiasm for what some people might regard as offensive macho displays of jiggling on the subway, riding the tail of a speeding truck, and hopping on the tops of trucks. Paley makes these actions sympathetic partly by implying that they take real skill, partly by implying that the show-off performing kids usually turn out to be very decent guys (one daredevil has graduated from high school, is married, holds a responsible job, and is going to night school), and partly by mildly discrediting those who oppose them. Thus one lady who disapproves of the jigglers thinks, "Their mothers never know where they are," but the narrator immediately assures us that the mothers of these boys did know where they were, and, moreover, the boys had been engaged in the thoroughly respectable activity of visiting a "missile exhibit on Fourteenth Street."

Like this woman, the man who pulls the alarm cord is somewhat discredited: He is "one of the men whose boyhood had been more watchful than brave." Although it's no disgrace for a boy to be "watchful," the sentence probably guides most readers to feel some scorn for the man who (so to speak) was never a boy. Many readers will feel that although the man "walked in a citizenly way" to pull the cord, he is motivated less by an impulse of good citizenship than (though probably he doesn't know it) by resentment, by irritation that these children are experiencing a joy that he never experienced in his childhood. On the other hand, Paley does not present him as a villain, and the story is not chiefly concerned with his guilt. By the end of the story, readers are probably so taken up with the mother's grief that they scarcely remember the man.

Although "Samuel" resembles a fable in that it is fairly brief, is narrated in an apparently simple manner, and concludes with a message, it differs significantly from a fable. Most obviously, it does not use the beasts, gods, and inanimate objects that fables commonly use. In fact, these are not essential in fables. More significantly, the characters in "Samuel" are more complicated, since the noisy boys are treated sympathetically and the apparently respectable adults are treated ironically. Finally, where the fable traditionally utters or implies a hard-headed, worldly wise (and often faintly cynical) message, the message uttered at the end of "Samuel" arouses the reader's deepest sympathy.

On Paley, see N. Isaacs, *Grace Paley, A Study of the Short Fiction* (1990); J. Taylor, *Grace Paley, Illuminating the Dark Lives* (1990); and Judith Arcana, *Grace Paley's Life Stories: A Literary Biography* (1993). Students might also be directed to Paley's *Collected Stories* (1994).

ADDITIONAL TOPICS FOR CRITICAL THINKING AND WRITING

1. If you had been on the train, would you have pulled the emergency cord? Why, or why not?
2. Write a journalist's account (250–300 words) of the accidental death of a boy named Samuel. Use whatever details Paley provides, but feel free to invent what you need for an authentic news story.

JAMAICA KINCAID

Girl (p. 17)

Jamaica Kincaid, like her fictional heroine Annie John, lived in Antigua, a much doted-on only child, until she was seventeen, when she came to the United States to continue her education. In an interview in the *New York Times Book Review* (April 7, 1985, 6), she said, "I did sort of go to college but it was such a dismal failure. I just educated myself, if that's possible." She has published three collections of short stories based on her life in the West Indies.

In this story we meet a girl in her early adolescence, under the constant tutelage of her mother for her coming role as a woman. In today's terminology, we see the social construction of gender. The mother is a powerful presence, shrewd and spirited as well as overprotective and anxious about her daughter's burgeoning sexuality. The girl is attentive to her mother, and mostly submissive; we sense that it is through her reverie that we hear her mother's monologue, which the daughter twice interrupts briefly. But the repetition of instruction and correction in the monologue, especially of the incessant "this is how to," suggests the tension between the two that we know, from our own experience, will lead to a confrontation that will permanently alter the relationship. Despite the references to the island culture, which provide the story's rich, exotic texture, the central drama of coming of age could be happening anywhere.

A good way to teach the story is to have two students read it aloud in class. It's short, humorous, and in passages pleasantly rhythmical. The students will hear the shift in voices, and will want to discuss the characters and the conflict.

We especially admire Kincaid's novel, *Annie John* (1985), which consists of eight interrelated chapters (which were first published separately in *The New Yorker*) that explore a mother-daughter relationship.

See also: Selwyn R. Cudjoe, "Jamaica Kincaid and the Modernist Project: An Interview," *Callaloo* 12 (Spring 1989), 396–411; and Donna Perry, "An Interview with Jamaica Kincaid," in *Reading Black, Reading Feminist*, ed. Henry Louis Gates, Jr. (1990), 492–509.

ADDITIONAL TOPICS FOR CRITICAL THINKING AND WRITING
1. What is the conflict in this story?
2. Is the girl naive? Explain.
3. Taking "Girl" as a model, write a piece about someone—perhaps a relative, teacher, or friend—who has given you more advice than you wanted.

TOBIAS WOLFF

Powder (p. 18)

The first paragraph provides the necessary background. The parents are separated, the mother is sensible, and the father is irresponsible—but even at this stage one may wonder if perhaps there isn't something especially engaging about a father who sneaks his young son into a nightclub in order to see Thelonious Monk.

The father's irresponsibility is underlined in the second paragraph. He promised to get the boy home to the mother for Christmas Eve dinner, but "he observed some quality [in the snow] that made it necessary for us to get in one last run. We got in several last runs." The father tries to be reassuring at the diner, but the boy, a worrier, is distressed. He's a strange kid, as he himself knows, someone who bothers "teachers for homework assignments far ahead of their due dates" so he can make up schedules. But with a father like his, and a mother who clearly is not sympathetic to the father's adventurous (or childish?) enthusiasms, who can blame the boy? And though the boy in his orderliness is his mother's son, the last paragraph of the story validates the father. Although the father is "bankrupt of honor," the ride (or the boy's experience of the ride) is something so special that it is "Impossible to describe. Except maybe to say this: If you haven't driven fresh powder, you haven't driven."

One detail may escape some readers. When the father makes a phone call from the diner, the boy quite reasonably thinks the father must be calling the mother, but this man-child in fact is calling the police, with some sort of bull that causes the officer to drive away and thus gives the father a chance to put aside the barrier and drive home. The evidence? After making the call, the father stares through the window, down the road, and says, "Come on, come on." (He is impatiently waiting for the result of his call.) As soon as the trooper's car passes the window, the father hurries the boy out of the diner. When the boy asks the father where the policeman may have gone, the father ignores the question.

"Bankrupt of honor," yes, and one can easily imagine the impossibility of being married to such a man. But the father desperately wants to keep the family intact, and he wants to get the boy home for dinner with the mother in an effort to buy "a little more time," though we are not surprised to learn that the mother decides "to make the split final."

Wolff's stories have been published in two excellent collections: *Back in the World* (1985) and *The Night in Question* (1996). He has also written a somber, disturbing book about his childhood in the 1950s, *This Boy's Life: A Memoir* (1989), and an excellent book about his experiences in Vietnam, *In Pharaoh's Army: Memories of the Lost War* (1994).

JAMES MERRILL

Christmas Tree (p. 21)

Your students doubtless have encountered some poems other than the two that we give earlier in this chapter, but they may not have encountered "shaped poetry" or "pattern poetry," or, if they have, perhaps nothing beyond George Herbert's "Easter Wings" and Lewis Carroll's poem in the shape of a mouse. (We give two additional examples of shaped poetry in Chapter 20.) But Merrill's poem differs from Herbert's and Carroll's in that the speaker is the shape. That is, whereas "Easter Wings" is not spoken by Easter, or by Jesus, and Carroll's poem is not spoken by a mouse, Merrill's poem is spoken by a Christmas tree, the shape made by the lines.

You may want to begin the discussion by talking about the speaker of this poem or of any poem—a topic addressed later, in Chapter 16 ("The Speaking Tone of Voice"). Many inexperienced readers assume that a poem is spoken by the poet and that it expresses the poet's feelings. Of course, poems do express their authors, but only if one understands that a mask may allow the writer to express ideas and emotions otherwise inexpressible.

Before we talk about Merrill's poem, we want to mention that the beginning of the course is a good time to alert students to the fact that the shape of any poem—its look on the page—may be part of its meaning. The very fact that a line ends well short of the right-hand margin tells us something about how we are to read the line. After all, poems could be printed (and in some medieval manuscripts were indeed written) continuously, filling the entire page. A new line, and especially a new line that follows an extra line of empty space, prepares us for some change, even perhaps for a change of speaker. In Whitman's "A Noiseless Patient Spider" (Chapter 15) the varying lengths of the lines are significant, a part of the meaning. A related point: One would not want to begin a poem by reading two lines at the bottom of a right-hand page, and then, upon turning the page, find a single line followed by an extra space and then several more tercets. If a poem is in tercets, we should see the form at the outset. (Are we being too sensitive? We don't think so, and while we are on this topic we might mention that we object to those texts that number all poems in units of five. A sonnet ought to be numbered 4, 8, 12, and quatrains ought to be numbered in 4s, not in 5s, though copy editors are distressed by the apparent inconsistency.)

Students don't have to be told that shaped poetry, or pattern poetry, is an ancient form (there are a few Greek poems in simple shapes—an egg, wings, an altar, a panpipe) but they should understand (to repeat) that Merrill's poem is not only shaped like a tree but is spoken by a tree, and this fact may lead into a discussion of the speakers of poems. In classical rhetoric, the word *prosopopoeia* (from Greek *prosopon* mask, person + *poein*, to make) was used to denote a speech invented for an imagined person or an absent person, and schoolboys were required to invent speeches for famous persons, e.g., for Antony's first encounter with Cleopatra, or Brutus's dying words. These speeches, like Merrill's invented speech for his Christmas tree, were of course in the first person, and the term *prosopopoeia* is often used for a speech uttered by an inanimate object.

It is the job of poets (in Ezra Pound's words) "to make it new," and Merrill makes us look freshly at Christmas trees and Christmas. Probably most of us at one time or another have sensed a sad undercurrent in Christmas festivities, but Merrill makes it evident. In this celebration of the birth of Jesus, which takes place at the end (death?) of the year, Merrill imagines the Christmas tree as aware that it has been "Brought down at last"; now in its glory, "it would be only a matter of weeks" before it meets its end. The tree perceives the irony of the enthusiastic welcome ("Warmly they took me in, made much of me") that precedes its demise. Throughout the poem run words suggesting illness and finally death: "Brought down," "it would be only a matter of weeks," "there was nothing more to do," "It did help" (note the visual pun in "wound" in this line: "It did help to be wound in jewels"), "I ended before long," "a primitive IV" (i.e., intravenous device, in this case the electric wire that keeps the lights going), "what lay ahead / Was clear," "back into the Earth," "To have grown so thin. / Needles and bone," "Holding up wonderfully," "the last time."

But the poem is not, we think, primarily about sickness and death. It ends with "praise." From the slightly self-pitying lines of the opening we move through a witty, bitter-sweet Christmas of gifts, children, and music—all presented in the context of the dying tree—to an unsentimental resolution: everything that occurred in the "room aglow" is recalled and celebrated.

Some of your students might enjoy Merrill's *A Different Person: A Memoir* (1993). The best book on Merrill is Stephen Yenser, *The Consuming Myth: The Work of James Merrill* (1987). For illuminating discussion of Merrill, as well as of Elizabeth Bishop, John Ashbery, and other poets, we recommend Vernon Shetley, *After the Death of Poetry: Poet and Audience in Contemporary America* (1993).

2

The Pleasures of Reading— and of Writing Arguments about Literature

TOBIAS WOLFF

Say Yes (p. 30)

In line with Question 1 below, students might be invited to give their responses to the man, based only on the first paragraph. (You may want to make this assignment before the students read the story, and ask them to jot down their responses immediately after reading—or reading twice—the first paragraph.) Is he a decent guy? Is his "I try" nicely modest, or is it a bit too self-congratulatory? In the last sentence of the first paragraph ("Helping out with the dishes was a way he had of showing how considerate he was") do we hear the voice of an objective narrator— or do we get inside of the husband's mind, and hear him congratulating himself on how considerate he is? (Of course this issue gets into matters of point of view—a topic discussed elsewhere in the text—but there is no harm in raising the issue.)

How do students respond to the husband and wife during the quarrel? (It will be interesting to see if the class divides along the lines of sex.) Perhaps the husband is at his nastiest when, saying "These are dirty," he dumps the silver back into the sink. His aggressive (and defensive?) action is understandable— we probably have all done something like this—but it is also revealing. And, even more important, this perfectly normal (if nasty) action leads to something significant; his wife, reaching into the sink, cuts her hand. We didn't expect that, but now it has happened and it seems perfectly natural. Her action, in turn, leads to further actions: his solicitude (genuine, no doubt, but, since "he hoped that she appreciated how quickly he had come to her aid," a very self-conscious and therefore somewhat tainted display of his goodness), her continuation of the argument (though by now the issue has somewhat turned from the general topic of interracial marriage to whether he would marry *her* if she were black), his rejection ("No"), his pretense of indifference (in order to equal her pretended indifference), the glimpse of the outside world (a few stars, light traffic, two dogs that scrap but then amicably trot off).

The effect of the husband's (and our) breif contact with the outdoors, and especially with the scrapping dogs who apparently really get along well together, is to bring him to his senses. One might almost say that nature helps to heal him. He apologizes to Anne. Because a reader feels the sincerity of the apology ("Anne, I'm really sorry. . . . I'll make it up to you, I promise"), when Anne (apparently rather coldly) says, "How?" and "We'll see," a reader may at first be taken aback but then will see the appropriateness of her response.

In short, everything naturally follows from what has come before, and yet perhaps nothing could easily have been predicted. It's pretty much in accord with E. M. Forster's famous statement:

> Shock, followed by the feeling, "O, that's all right," is a sign that all is well with plot: characters, to be real, ought to run smoothly, but a plot ought to cause surprise.

The final paragraph is complex, maybe even ambiguous. On one level, their wedding night is repeated. He has said that he will marry her, and now the bride, insisting that he turn out the lights (she is modest?) approaches, and his heart pounds "the way it had on their first night together." At the same time, the paragraph introduces the menacing idea of a stranger in the house, an intruder who awakens one and who causes anxiety. Have the husband and wife, by means of the quarrel, become strangers to each other? Adam and Eve after the Fall? *Is* the final effect that of a menacing estrangement between the husband and wife? Or is it rather of the excitement of newlyweds, going to bed for the first time— strangers (sexually) to each other, but united by love? Perhaps the ultimate effect of the final paragraph is to convey the trepidation and excitement of a first sexual experience, an experience during which the stranger becomes the beloved spouse. Some such experience is now relived by this couple, who had been briefly estranged, and now are in the process of becoming reunited.

DIANE ACKERMAN

Pumping Iron (p. 36)

Women's bodybuilding and weight lifting for strength, conditioning, and appearance have become very popular, and there are many books now available on the subject that provide all sorts of "how-to" advice. From a quick visit to the local bookstore, we noted in the "Health and Fitness" section such titles as *Bone-Building/Body-Shaping Workout: Strength, Health, Beauty, in Just 16 Minutes a Day* and *Supervixen: Secrets for Building a Lean and Sexy Body.* But there are other books on the subject to be found in the Cultural Studies and Women's Studies sections, which perhaps some of your students might find intriguing.

Combining scholarly analysis and personal experience and reflection, the poet, art historian, bodybuilder, and performance artist Joanna Frueh, in her 400-page *Monster/Beauty: Building the Body of Love* (2000), examines female bodybuilders but also "traditional models of beauty" (e.g., Aphrodite) and a host of other topics. Also interesting: Maria R. Lowe, *Women of Steel: Female*

Bodybuilders and the Struggle for Self-Definition (1998); and Leslie Heywood, *Bodymakers: A Cultural Anatomy of Women's Body Building* (1998).

Perhaps the most absorbing of all is *Picturing the Modern Amazon* (New Museum Books, 2000), ed. Joanna Frueh, Laurie Fierstein, and Judith Stein, published to accompany an exhibition at the New Museum of Contemporary Art in New York City. Through photographs, art reproductions, and essays, this book explores the history of strong and "hypermuscular" women, from the era of classical sculpture to the present (e.g., the circus, the cartoons, and bodybuilding), but focusing on the eighteenth, nineteenth, and, especially, twentieth centuries. Among the artists whose works are considered: Matthew Barney, Louise Bourgeois, Annie Leibovitz, Cindy Sherman, and Nancy Spero.

The "she" of Ackerman's poem is worth thinking about. Some of our students have said that the "she" is a woman whom Ackerman is describing, perhaps with a satiric tone in her voice, while others have claimed that the "she" is really a stand-in for Ackerman herself, as though she were looking at herself "from the outside"—which would make sense in a poem about a speaker who wants to present her body in a striking, attention-seizing form.

On a related note, the point of view of the poem is likely something that your students will want to discuss and debate. On one level, we may tend to assume that a woman poet writing about this subject—this phenomenon—will be critical of it. But the question then becomes, does the language of the poem support this interpretation, or, instead, is the language actually making a different kind of point? Maybe the poem is meant to be funny: look at the intensity of this woman's quest for a strong, impressive physique—one suited to a woman, not to a man (the "male lifters").

That's what one student claimed in a recent class we taught. But she in turn was countered by other students who argued that Ackerman is showing here the ways in which women feel obliged to sculpt the perfect body, making themselves into versions of the "strong woman" that women's health and fitness magazines promote. At this juncture, we jumped in: but what about the men? Are they (we used some dramatic terms) brainwashed, victimized, etc., into straining and wrenching *their* bodies into the perfect mold that *their* magazines feature?

Ackerman's poem is short in its number of lines and in its use of line lengths. But it engages a compelling topic—body size and body image—that is connected to gender roles, sexual identity, and self-definition. "Pumping Iron" works very well in class because it highlights how a poem, with its *literary* organization of language, can probe and inquire into the ideas, images, and practices of the culture.

In an interview in the August 1999 issue of *January* magazine, Ackerman observes: "Poetry has so much to teach us about who we are, where we come from, what we wish to become." You might consider using this quote in a writing assignment, which students could be asked to relate to "Pumping Iron."

ANONYMOUS

Tweed to Till (p. 37)

We have never seen this little poem in a textbook, but we find it intriguing and moving, and we wonder what sort of response it will get from instructors and students.

First, the language. An occasional instructor has told us that he or she does not teach any of the popular ballads that we include ("The Twa Corbies," "The Three Ravens," "Edward," "Sir Patrick Spence") because the archaic or Scots words turn students off. Our own experience in the classroom has been different: We are under the impression that our students enjoy the strange language, and we connect this pleasure with the pleasure that we see and hear when children recite chants, songs, counting-rhymes, etc., with strange words, such as "Yankee Doodle," or "Eeny, meeny, miny, mo." Further, only one or, at most, two of the words in "Tweed to Till" are in fact obscure ("gars" and possibly "ae"); no one is put off by such words as "rins," "slaw," "droun," and "twa." We do hope that you will give the poem a chance.

Rivers don't speak, but beneath the poem, in the final words of Tweed we hear the voice of a remorseless nature, a nature that indeed seems proud of its destructiveness ("For ae man that ye droun / I droun twa"). And surely this is the way nature does seem to us, at least on some occasions. Perhaps the most famous statement of this view is a passage in Tennyson's *In Memoriam*, in which Nature rejects the view that, if she destroys individuals, she at least cares for the species ("the type"):

> "So careful of the type?" but no,
>   From scarped cliff and quarried stone
>   She cries, "A thousand types are gone;
> I care for nothing, all shall go."

Or one might call to mind the beginning of Robert Frost's "Once by the Pacific":

> The shattered water made a misty din.
> Great waves looked over others coming in,
> And thought of doing something to the shore
> That water never did to land before.

Very close to "Tweed to Till" in theme and also in form are the first four lines of Frost's "Lodged":

> The rain to the wind said,
> "You push and I'll pelt."
> They so smote the garden bed
> That the flowers actually knelt . . . .

In *Introduction* we express our hope that students enjoyed reading "Tweed to Till" and we ask them—if they did enjoy it—to try to explain their response. Our own explanation would include remarks along these lines: (1) the short rhyming lines have an incantatory effect; (2) the idea of rivers engaging in dialogue is, well, engaging; (3) the strange language is catchy; (4) the story, if we may put it that way, is absorbing: One river, a sort smarty-pants, taunts another river because it runs quietly, slowly. What will come of this confrontation? The slow river responds first by agreeing ("I rin slaw") but then it delivers a knock-out punch: "For ae man that ye droun / I droun twa." In the world of rivers, it seems, it's not so much a matter of running slow or fast, but of deadliness.

WILLIAM BLAKE

The Clod and the Pebble (p. 37)

ADDITIONAL TOPICS FOR CRITICAL THINKING AND WRITING

1. What does it mean to say (lines 1–4) that self-sacrificing love "builds a Heaven in Hell's despite"? And (lines 9–12) that selfish love "builds a Hell in Heaven's despite"?
2. What would be the effect of beginning with lines 9–12, and ending with 1–4—and, of course, revising the middle stanza?

KATHERINE MANSFIELD

Miss Brill (p. 38)

Few students have any trouble perceiving that Miss Brill is a friendless older woman living in France, seeking out a living by such genteel activities as teaching English and reading the newspaper to an "old invalid gentleman" (who sleeps while she reads). She is "Miss Brill" to us because that is what she is, presumably, to her pupils, to the invalid gentleman, and to anyone else who has any dealings with her. In short, she has no intimate acquaintances. Probably by the end of the first paragraph most readers have a pretty good idea of her emotionally starved life—though to put it this way is perhaps misleading, since Miss Brill herself seems quite content, delighting in the weather and in her shabby fox, as later she will delight in much of what she sees in the park. In the first paragraph most readers probably identify her with the fox—an identification that is insisted on in the final paragraph, when Miss Brill has returned to "the little dark room—her room like a cupboard"—and the fox is returned to its box.

Between the beginning and the end, of course, the unfeeling (or at least careless) boy and girl sitting on the bench jolt Miss Brill out of her comfortable role as delighted spectator at a play, and (in her view of things) as a performer, too. The third question following the story, asking if Miss Brill is "justly punished for her pride," is the result of several uncomfortable experiences teaching the story. The first time that a student offered this view, we were surprised. It seems evident to us that during most of the story Miss Brill is a sympathetic figure; pitiful, yes, but admirable too, chiefly because she is not given to *self-pity*. She is a bit snobbish about the other regulars who attend the concert ("They were odd, silent, nearly all old, and from the way they stared they looked as though they'd just come from dark little rooms or even—even cupboards!"), but she does no harm to anyone, and she is a person of good will.

Her pride in setting the scene around her is, if anything, pathetic rather than morally offensive. After her rude awakening, we pity her even more. However, students in several classes have argued that Miss Brill seeks to play God, to assign roles, to judge others (as when she says, "The Brute! The Brute!"), and at last she herself is judged by the boy and girl. A slightly less harsh version, also offered in class, goes like this: Miss Brill thinks she plays a significant part in the activities in the park, as a listener, as an appreciator of what is going on, and even as a performer. Stimulated by such thoughts, she seeks to arrange all that goes on, but when the "hero and heroine" (that's the way she sees them) arrive, and Miss Brill is "prepared to listen," reality breaks in, forcing Miss Brill to recognize what she is.

Again, it seems to us to be inappropriate to judge Miss Brill severely, but those students who do judge her severely have not been impressed by arguments to the contrary.

Students are not the only severe judges. In *College English* 23 (1962): 661–63, a university teacher judges her mercilessly. He begins by discussing the action:

> What happens in the story is that with each main event Miss Brill's mind moves higher and higher up the hierarchy of unrealities, until she has reached a point from which she can only fall with a thump back to the hard ground of the real world of her humdrum life. (661)

According to this writer, the first "unreality" is her view of the fox as a "rogue." We realize, he says, "that here is a character who is not averse to wandering in the realms of fancy." He then goes on to assert that "her imaginative coloring of what she sees next is a little more preposterous," for she sees the musicians as (he says) "not a group of hired musicians, but rather a single, responsive and very sensitive creature." This does not seem to us a preposterous way to regard a band of musicians, but the author— very stern with Miss Brill—goes on to assert that she is "ignorant of music." The evidence: she doesn't know whether the "flutey bit" will be repeated, and "the bit to her is 'a little chain of bright drops,' not music." (Teachers who believe that metaphor is not a bad thing, and is indeed a way of conveying fresh perceptions, may be surprised at this condemnation of metaphor.)

The critic continues:

> The episode of the "ermine toque and the gentleman in grey," as it is inter-preted by Miss Brill, is considerably more preposterous than her coloring of her fur and the orchestra. The woman in the ermine hat is obviously a prostitute who is propositioning the gentleman; but to the heroine she is merely a nice lady whose attempt to be friendly is rebuffed by a not-nice man. (661)

There is a great deal more of this sort of thing. Instructors who take up the story in detail in class may want to invite students to express their opinions about the identity of the "ermine toque." (Is she not more plausibly taken as a woman who formerly had a relationship with the gentleman?) More important, of course, is our attitude toward Miss Brill, and our sense of the author's attitude. Although we should always trust the tale, not the teller, following D. H. Lawrence's admirable advice, perhaps it is not utterly illegitimate to keep in mind some words Mansfield wrote in a letter to her husband. She had sent him this story, and in a letter he told her that he shared her enthusiasm for it. In response to his letter she wrote [quoted in Marvin Magalaner, *The Fiction of Katherine Mansfield* (1971), p. 17],

> One writes (*one* reason why is) because one does care so passionately that one *must show* it—one must declare one's love.

Finally, a word about the protagonist's name. We have already mentioned that she is "Miss" because that presumably is the way all of her acquaintances know her, but why "Brill"? James W. Gargano pointed out [*Explicator* 19:2 (November 1960), Item 10] that the brill is a European flatfish, edible though not especially esteemed for its taste. The name certainly does not convey dignity, but whether it conveys ridicule or absurdity is another matter. (The American equivalent would be something like Miss Perch.) In fact, "Brill" is not an exceptionally uncommon name, as a glance at a large telephone directory will reveal. (There are a few dozen in the Boston area.) In any case, students might be invited to discuss the name. Does it fit the person? (Perhaps the important thing is that the name of a character *not* mislead the reader by *in*appropriate connotations, unless these are used for purposes of irony.)

TONI CADE BAMBARA

The Lesson (p. 42)

It would be hard to find a less strident or more delightful story preaching revolution. At its heart, "The Lesson" calls attention to the enormous inequity in the distribution of wealth in America, and it suggests that black people ought to start thinking about "what kind of society it is in which some people can spend on a toy what it would cost to feed a family of six or seven" for a year. That the young narrator does not quite get the point of Miss Moore's lesson—and indeed steals Miss Moore's money—is no sure sign that the lesson has failed. (Presumably, Miss Moore doesn't much care about the loss of her money; the money is well lost if it helps the narrator, who plans to spend it, to see the power of money.) In any case, the narrator has been made sufficiently uneasy ("I sure want to punch somebody in the mouth") so that we sense she will later get the point: "I'm going . . . to think this day through." The last line of the story seems to refer to her race to a bakery, but it has larger implications: "ain't nobody gonna beat me at nuthin."

The difference between Sylvia's response and Sugar's response to Miss Moore's lesson is worth discussing in class. As Malcolm Clark, of Solano Community College, puts it, "The obvious question of the story is, 'What is the lesson?' . . . It's clear that Miss Moore is trying to teach these children a lesson in economic inequity. . . . Sugar learns this lesson, as her comments to Miss Moore indicate. However, Sylvia has also learned this lesson, though she does not reveal her understanding to Miss Moore." As Clark goes on to point out, Miss Moore's lesson is not simply that some people are rich and others are not. She wants to bring the children to a state where they will demand their share of the pie. And it is in learning this part of the lesson that Sylvia and Sugar part company. Despite Sugar's obvious understanding of the lesson and her momentary flash of anger—strong enough to make her push Sylvia away—her condition is only temporary.

"At the end of the story she is unchanged from the little girl she was at the beginning. It is she who wants to go to Hascomb's bakery and spend the money on food, essentially the same thing they intended to do with the money before the lesson began. . . . Sylvia, however, is greatly changed. She does not intend to spend the money with Sugar; instead, she plans to go over to the river and reflect upon the lesson further."

For students who would like to read more of Bambara's work, the best place to begin is with her two collections of stories: *Gorilla, My Love* (1972), and *The Sea Birds Are Still Alive* (1977). A posthumous book, *Deep Sightings and Rescue Missions: Fiction, Essays, and Conversations* (1996), is also well worth reading. For secondary sources, see Keith Byerman, *Fingering the Jagged Grain: Tradition and Form in Recent Black Fiction* (1986), and Elliott Butler-Evans, *Race, Gender, and Desire: Narrative Strategies in the Fiction of Toni Cade Bambara, Toni Morrison, and Alice Walker* (1989). See also the entry in the *Dictionary of Literary Biography*, vol. 38 (1985), 12–22. There is a section on Bambara in *Black Women Writers (1950–1980): A Critical Evaluation*, ed. Mari Evans (1984), 41–71.

ADDITIONAL TOPICS FOR CRITICAL THINKING AND WRITING

1. Let's suppose Bambara had decided to tell the story through the eyes of Miss Moore. Write the first 250 words of such a story.
2. Miss Moore says, "Imagine for a minute what kind of society it is in which some people can spend on a toy what it would cost to feed a family of six or seven. What do you think?" In an essay of 500 words, tell a reader what you think about this issue.
3. Describe the relationship between Sugar and Sylvia. What is Sugar's function in the story?
4. What does the last line of the story suggest?
5. In a paragraph or two, characterize the narrator. Do not summarize the story—assume that your reader is familiar with it—but support your characterization by some references to episodes in the story and perhaps by a few brief quotations.

3

More about Writing about Literature: From Idea to Essay

KATE CHOPIN

The Story of an Hour (p. 50)

The first sentence of the story proves to be essential to the end, though during the middle of the story the initial care to protect Mrs. Mallard from the "sad message" seems almost comic. Students may assume, too easily, that Mrs. Mallard's "storm of grief" is hypocritical. They may not notice that the renewal after the first shock is stimulated by the renewal of life around her ("the tops of trees . . . were all aquiver with the new spring life") and that before she achieves a new life, Mrs. Mallard first goes through a sort of death and then tries to resist renewal: Her expression "indicated a suspension of intelligent thought," she felt something "creeping out of the sky," and she tried to "beat it back with her will," but she soon finds herself "drinking in a very elixir of life through that open window," and her thoughts turn to "spring days, and summer days." Implicit in the story is the idea that her life as a wife—which she had thought was happy—was in fact a life of repression or subjugation, and the awareness comes to her only at this late stage. The story has two surprises: The change from grief to joy proves not to be the whole story, for we get the second surprise, the husband's return and Mrs. Mallard's death. The last line ("the doctors . . . said she had died . . . of joy that kills") is doubly ironic: The doctors wrongly assume that she was overjoyed to find that her husband was alive, but they were not wholly wrong in guessing that her last day of life brought her great joy.

In a sense, moreover, the doctors are right (though not in the sense they mean) in saying that she "died of heart disease." That is, if we take the "heart" in a metaphorical sense to refer to love and marriage, we can say that the loss of her new freedom from her marriage is unbearable. This is not to say (though many students do say it) that her marriage was miserable. The text explicitly says "she had loved him—sometimes." The previous paragraph in the story nicely calls attention to a certain aspect of love—a satisfying giving of the self—and yet also to a most unpleasant yielding to force: "There would be no one to live for her during those coming years; she would live for herself. There would be no powerful will bending her in that blind persistence with which men and women believe they have a right to impose a private will upon a fellow creature."

A biographical observation: Chopin's husband died in 1882, and her mother died in 1885. In 1894 in an entry in her diary she connected the two losses with her growth: "If it were possible for my husband and my mother to come back to earth, I feel that I would unhesitatingly give up every thing that has come into my life since they left it and join my existence again with theirs. To do that, I would have to forget the past ten years of my growth—my real growth."

Note: The chapter includes another work by Chopin, "Ripe Figs," and Chapter 4 includes "Désirée's Baby."

Good secondary sources include Per Seyersted, *Kate Chopin* (1969), and a more recent biography, Emily Toth, *Kate Chopin* (1990).

TOPIC FOR CRITICAL THINKING AND WRITING

Chopin does not tell us if Mrs. Mallard's death is due to joy at seeing her husband alive, guilt for feeling "free," shock at the awareness that her freedom is lost, or something else. Should the author have made the matter clear? Why, or why not?

KATE CHOPIN

Ripe Figs (p. 72)

This story teaches marvelously. Some stories supposedly teach well because the instructor can have the pleasure of showing students all sorts of things that they missed, but unfortunately stories of that kind may, by convincing students that literature has deep meanings that they don't see, turn students away from literature. "Ripe Figs" teaches well because it is a first-rate piece that is easily accessible.

Elaine Gardiner discusses it fully in an essay in *Modern Fiction Studies* 28:3 (1982), reprinted in Harold Bloom's collection of essays, *Kate Chopin* (1987, 83–87). Gardiner's essay is admirable, but instructors will be interested to find that their students will make pretty much the same points that Gardiner makes. Gardiner emphasizes three of Chopin's techniques: her use of *contrasts*, *natural imagery*, and *cyclical plotting*.

The chief contrast is between Maman-Nainaine and Babette, that is, age versus youth, patience versus impatience, experience versus innocence, staidness versus exuberance. Thus, Chopin tells us that "Maman-Nainaine sat down in her stately way," whereas Babette is "restless as a humming-bird" and dances. Other contrasts are spring and summer, summer and fall, figs and chrysanthemums.

Speaking of natural imagery, Gardiner says, "Not only are journeys planned according to when figs ripen and chrysanthemums bloom, but places are defined by what they produce; thus, Bayou-Lafourche, for Maman-Nainaine, is the place 'where the sugar cane grows.'" Gardiner calls attention to the references to the leaves, the rain, and the branches of the fig tree, but of course she emphasizes the ripening of the figs (from "little hard, green marbles" to "purple figs, fringed around with their rich, green leaves") and the flowering of the chrysanthemums. The contrasts in natural imagery, Gardiner says, "ultimately convey and emphasize continuity and stability."

Turning to cyclical plotting—common in Chopin—Gardiner says, "With the ripening of the figs in the summertime begins the next period of waiting, the continuance of the cycle, both of nature and of the characters' lives. . . . The reader finishes the sketch anticipating the movements to follow—movements directed by the seasons, by natural happenings, by the cyclical patterns of these people's lives."

WILLIAM STAFFORD

Traveling Through the Dark (p. 73)

The speaker is matter-of-fact, but by the end of the poem we realize that he is not only thoughtful in the sense of consideration of others (unlike the motorist who killed the deer, he pushes the deer off the road so that others won't have an accident) but also thoughtful in the sense of meditative. Although he realizes that he cannot possibly save the unborn fawn, he cannot dispose of the doe casually, knowing that he will also be killing its fawn.

We take it, then, that when he says "I thought hard for us all" (line 17) he means not only "our group" (line 16), but everything, including the fawn. He briefly hesitates—his "only swerving"—but he does what he has to do, lest a motorist "swerve [and] . . . make more dead" (line 4).

In teaching this poem we usually try to reserve comment on the title until late in the discussion. If the poem has been talked about for a while, students can usually see that the title implies something about the human condition. All of us are "traveling through the dark," moving through a difficult, demanding world, sometimes swerving a bit, but by and large guided by principles. The resonance of Stafford's title will become especially clear if you ask students how it compares with some invented title, such as "The Dead Deer," or "On the Edge of the Wilson River."

A postscript. Is it absurd to compare the poem to Frost's "Stopping by Woods on a Snowy Evening"? We have in mind especially Frost's contrast between the speaker and the little horse that, being only a horse, can't share the speaker's values. In Stafford's poem, the automobile serves somewhat as the horse; its parking lights are on, and its engine purrs steadily. No swerving here, no decisions to make. But unlike machines, human beings have to make hard decisions in a world of danger (the tail-light turns the exhaust red).

ADDITIONAL TOPICS FOR CRITICAL THINKING AND WRITING

1. What do we know (or believe we know) about the speaker of these lines?

2. Rereading the second stanza, note the pauses in line 6. What do they seem to tell you about the speaker's frame of mind?
3. Line 11 also has three pauses. In reading the line, what do you sense about the speaker's feelings?
4. Line 12 tells us that the speaker hesitated—and then the poem hesitates. Instead of moving forward to the conclusion of the story, the fourth stanza offers some description. What is described and how is it described? Try to imagine the poem without stanza 4. Do you find the stanza necessary? If so, why?
5. In the final stanza who does "us all" refer to? Does it include the same members as "our group" (in line 16) or not? Why does the speaker characterize his thinking (in line 17) as "swerving"?
6. What choices does the speaker of "Traveling" have? Do you think he makes the right choice? Explain.

LORNA DEE CERVANTES

Refugee Ship (p. 74)

Most students will quickly grasp the significance of the title. Like a refugee on a ship, the speaker is isolated from her origins and she is uncertain—indeed desperate—about her future. In the original version (see question 3 in the text) the repetition in the last two lines ("a ship that will never dock / a ship that will never dock") perhaps indicates a condition of numbed hopelessness, a sense that she is doomed to drift forever and will never be able to achieve a stable identity. (We are *not* saying that repetition always has this effect. The repetition in the last two lines of Frost's "Stopping by Woods" probably has quite a different effect.) But in the revision, printed in our text, the line is in Spanish rather than in English, which suggests to some readers of our acquaintance that she is no longer "orphaned" from her Spanish name and that Spanish is no longer "foreign" (line 7) to her.

The change, thus interpreted, is somewhat puzzling, since the recovery of Spanish (i.e., the regaining of her Spanish heritage) would seem to contradict the idea of the boat never landing. A related point: The original poem (1974) did *not* end with a period (it had no final punctuation), so it seemed inconclusive, unfinished, unending, and thus appropriate to the idea of a speaker who can't find her identity. The period at the end of the revision (1981) of course adds a note of finality—but is the idea that the ship will never dock or (since the final line is in Spanish) that the Spanish heritage has been regained?

Still another conspicuous difference between the original and the revision is in a figure of speech in line 9 of the revision, where the speaker refers to her "bronzed skin." In the original (see below, line 9) she spoke of her "brown skin." Students might be asked to comment on the change. Our own view is that "bronzed" is somewhat more elevated, perhaps even suggesting heroic monuments in bronze. Other changes are in the lineation, and from "I am an orphan to my spanish name," by virtue of the lowercase initial letter, somewhat diminished. Here is the 1974 version:

Refugee Ship

like wet cornstarch I slide past *mi abuelita's* eyes
bible placed by her side
she removes her glasses
the pudding thickens

mamá raised me with no language   5
I am an orphan to my spanish name
the words are foreign, stumbling on my tongue
I stare at my reflection in the mirror
brown skin, black hair

I feel I am a captive   10
aboard the refugee ship
a ship that will never dock
a ship that will never dock

By the way, in class a Chicano student brought up a point that provoked considerable discussion. He mentioned that many people with Spanish names are by no means rightly characterized as "Hispanic," since they are descended largely or entirely from Native Americans, and they were deprived of their own languages by the Spaniards. Some of these people may think of themselves as "Spanish," but in Cervantes's words they really are "orphaned," persons who have lost their original (i.e., indigenous) culture. The student was somewhat surprised to find himself saying that just as these people who have lost their original identity have come to regard themselves as Spanish or "Hispanic," so the Chicanos of today may in time forget their "Spanish" identity (really something imposed on many of them) and they may become as assimilated to the Anglo world as they now are to the "Spanish" world. That is, although the student fully sympathized with the speaker's anguish, he found it ironic that she presumably regards the grandmother as at ease in a Spanish culture that probably struck the grandmother's ancestors as foreign and undesirable.

Most students probably will feel that the second and third stanzas present few if any difficulties, but they may be puzzled by the first stanza, especially by the images of "wet cornstarch" and "pudding." We confess our own uncertainty. Perhaps part of the idea is that "wet cornstarch" has no permanent shape, no identity, just as the speaker feels she has no identity. Or, on the contrary, is the point that "wet cornstarch" is sticky, thereby suggesting that the speaker can't move easily, can't get anywhere (like a ship that can't dock)? (But the speaker does not in fact say that she feels "like wet cornstarch"; rather, she is saying something about the way in which the grandmother perceives, or doesn't perceive, her.) A more evident point is that cornstarch is white, which perhaps is the way the grandmother sees the speaker. That is, although the speaker has "bronzed skin, black hair," since she speaks English rather than Spanish (her mother's words are "foreign") she is an Anglo to the grandmother.

And what about "the pudding" in the last line of the first stanza? Again, it's our understanding that the first stanza gives the speaker's interpretation of the way in which the grandmother perceives her. "The pudding thickens," then, is a description of the way in which the grandmother, who has removed her glasses, perceives the speaker. Someone who is not wearing the glasses that she needs might well feel that the scene is "thickening." But why "pudding"? Probably there is a connection with "cornstarch," but exactly what is the connection? Is a pudding thought to be (like the wet cornstarch of the first line) shapeless? But in fact a pudding that thickens (with the aid of cornstarch) is not shapeless; it has considerable consistency or identity.

For a very different attitude toward being a Latina in the United States, see Aurora Levins Morales's poem "Child of the Americas" in Chapter 24.

JOSÉ ARMAS

El Tonto del Barrio (p. 75)

If you have any Spanish-speaking students in your class, or even students whose acquaintance with Spanish does not go beyond a few years of high school study, you might ask them how they would translate the title. We thought of glossing "El Tonto" as "The Fool" or "The Idiot," but "Fool" is a bit old-fashioned and "Idiot"—as Armas suggested to us—is too strong. Armas's own suggestion, "Dummy," strikes us as exactly right.

While one is reading the story, say through the first one-third, it may seem to be chiefly a character sketch of Romero and a sketch of the community in which he lives, but then come two sentences that mark a turning point:

> Romero kept the sidewalks clean and the barrio looked after him. It was a contract that worked well for a long time.

"Worked well *for a long time*" implies that something happened that broke the contract, and we are promptly introduced to this disruptive element.

> Then, when Seferino, Barelas' oldest son, graduated from high school he went to work in the barber shop for the summer. Seferino was a conscientious and sensitive young man and it wasn't long before he took notice of Romero and came to feel sorry for him.

In the light of what happens next, some readers may think that the narrator (or the author?) is being ironic, even sarcastic, when he characterizes Seferino as "conscientious and sensitive," but Seferino really *is* conscientious and sensitive. He just isn't mature, wise in the ways of the barrio, and (an important point) isn't able to understand that not everyone feels as he does. Thus, when he argues with his father he says, "How would you like to do what he does and be treated the same way?" That's a reasonable position (we all know that we should do unto others as we would have others do unto us)—but Barelas's answer is wiser than Seferino's question: "I'm not Romero." Further, and this may seem to be a paradox, Barelas is not only wise enough to know that he is not Romero, but he is also wise enough to know (as Seferino does not) *why* Romero sweeps the sidewalks: "He sweeps the sidewalks because he wants something to do, not because he wants money."

Although the conflict between Seferino and Romero is the obvious conflict, the conflict (though that is almost too strong a word) between Seferino
and Barelas is worth discussing in class. (The question in the text about
Barelas's character is one way of approaching it.) This conflict is amusingly
resolved when the well-meaning Seferino disappears into Harvard, thus spar-
ing us a potentially embarrassing or painful scene in which the boy acknowledges his error. Indeed, instead of emphasizing the conflict between Barelas
and his son, we get a scene in which Barelas—whose son has caused Romero
to misbehave—is pitted against the rest of the community, which now seeks
to confine Romero. And although Barelas again is on the right side, in one tiny
detail he reveals that he too has been rattled, we might even say corrupted, by
his son's well-intentioned plan. When one of the men of the barrio says, "What
if [Romero] hurts . . . ," Barelas interrupts: "He's not going to hurt anyone."
Tino replies: "No, Barelas. I was going to say, what if he hurts himself." It's a
lovely touch, showing that Barelas (who is right about so much) can be mistaken, and, more important, showing that even though the community wants
to lock Romero up, it is concerned chiefly for Romero's well being.

These comments are obvious, and perhaps a bit too solemn, since the story
has a good deal of delightful humor in it. (One can ask the class what it finds
amusing in the story.) Our own favorite passage is the bit recounting how
Romero, after breaking with Seferino, at first simply skipped the barber shop
in his sweeping, but then refined his action and pushed all of the trash from
elsewhere in front of the barber shop.

Fiction

4

Approaching Fiction: Responding in Writing

ERNEST HEMINGWAY

Cat in the Rain (p. 83)

To the best of our knowledge, "Cat in the Rain" has not been anthologized in college textbooks of this sort, but we think that it ought to be better known, and we find that it provokes lively discussion when used as an introduction to fiction.

The best published discussion is David Lodge's "Analysis and Interpretation of the Realist Text," *Poetics Today* 1 (1980): 5–19; it is conveniently reprinted in Lodge's *Working with Structuralism* (1981). Lodge begins by summarizing Carlos Baker's discussion, in which Baker (in *Ernest Hemingway: The Writer as Artist* [1952]) assumed that the cat at the end is the cat at the beginning. As Lodge puts it, in this reading

> [T]he appearance of the maid with a cat is the main reversal in Aristotelian terms in the narrative. If it is indeed the cat she went to look for, then the reversal is a happy one for her, and confirms her sense that the hotel keeper appreciated her as a woman more than her husband.

On the other hand, Lodge points out, if the cat is not the same cat,

> We might infer that the padrone, trying to humour a client, sends up the first cat he can lay hands on, which is in fact quite inappropriate to the wife's needs. This would make the reversal an ironic one at the wife's expense, emphasizing the social and cultural abyss that separates her from the padrone, and revealing her quasi-erotic response to his professional attentiveness as a delusion.

Lodge goes on to discuss a very different interpretation by John Hagopian, published in *College English* 24 (Dec 1962): 220–22, in which Hagopian argued that the story is about "a crisis in the marriage . . . involving the lack of fertility, which is symbolically foreshadowed by the public garden (fertility) dominated by the war monument (death)." For Hagopian, the rubber cape worn by the man in the rain "is a protection from rain, and rain is a fundamental necessity for fertility and fertility is precisely what is lacking in the American wife's marriage." Put bluntly, Hagopian sees the rubber cape as a condom. Lodge correctly points out that although rain often stands for fertility, in this story the rainy weather is contrasted with "good weather." What the rubber cape does is emphasize the bad weather, and thus emphasizes the padrone's thoughtfulness (and the husband's indifference).

Lodge's careful and profound article can't be adequately summarized, but we'll give a few more of his points. Near the end of the story, when we read that "George shifted his position in the bed," a reader may feel that George will put down the book and make love to his wife, but this possibility disappears when George says, "Oh, shut up and get something to read."

Taking Seymour Chatman's distinction between stories of *resolution* (we get the answer to "What happened next?") and stories of *revelation* (events are not resolved, but a state of affairs is revealed), Lodge suggests that this story seems to share characteristics of both: it is, one might say, a plot of revelation (the relationship between husband and wife) disguised as a plot of resolution (the quest for the cat). The ambiguity of the ending is therefore crucial. By refusing to resolve the issue of whether the wife gets the cat she wants, the implied author indicates that this is not the point of the story.

On point of view, Lodge demonstrates that Hemingway's story is written from the point of view of the American couple, and from the wife's point of view rather than the husband's. (Of course he doesn't mean that the entire story is seen from her point of view. He means only that we get into her mind to a greater degree—e.g., "The cat would be around to the right. Perhaps she could go along under the eaves"—than into the minds of any of the other characters.) Lodge's argument is this: At the end, when the maid appears, "the narration adopts the husband's perspective at this crucial point," and so that's why we are told that the maid held *a* cat rather than *the* cat. After all, the man had not seen the cat in the rain, so he can't know if the maid's cat is the same cat.

Finally, another discussion of interest is Warren Bennett, "The Poor Kitty . . . in 'Cat in the Rain,'" *Hemingway Review* 8 (Fall 1988): 26–36. Bennett reviews Lodge's discussion of Baker and Hagopian and insists that the wife is not pregnant (Lodge had suggested, in arguing against Hagopian, that the wife *may* be pregnant). Bennett says that

> [T]he girl's feelings as she thinks of the padrone pass through three stages, tight inside, important, and of momentary supreme importance, and these stages reflect a correspondence to the sensations of desire, intercourse, and orgasm.

Not all readers will agree, though probably we can all agree with Bennett when he says that "The wife's recognition of the padrone's extraordinary character suggests that her husband, George, lacks the qualities which the wife finds so attractive in the padrone. George has neither dignity, nor will, nor commitment."

In any case, Bennett suggests that when the wife returns to the room "her sexual feelings are transferred to George. She goes over to George and tries to express her desire for closeness by sitting down 'on the bed.'"

Bennett's article makes too many points to be summarized here, but one other point should be mentioned. He says that female tortoise-shell cats do not reproduce tortoise-shells, and that males are sterile. Since he identifies the woman with the cat, he says that the woman's "destiny is that of a barren wandering soul with no place and no purpose in the futility of the wasteland *In Our Time.*"

Bennett's article is reprinted in the excellent collection, *New Critical Approaches to the Short Stories of Ernest Hemingway*, ed. Jackson J. Benson (1990). There have been a number of noteworthy biographies of Hemingway published recently, including Kenneth S. Lynn, *Hemingway* (1987), and James R. Mellow, *Hemingway: A Life Without Consequences* (1992).

5

Stories and Meanings: Plot, Character, Theme

W. SOMERSET MAUGHAM

The Appointment in Samarra (p. 95)

In the text we use this short short story in connection with Aesop's fable as an example of a fiction that, like a parable, obviously makes no pretense at being history. These stories are clearly didactic; they seek to shape the behavior of the auditors by setting forth some sort of truth. In the text we go on to mention the anecdote (our example is Parson Weems's fable of George Washington and the cherry tree), and we make the point that although one can easily moralize most anecdotes, the emphasis nevertheless is not on a truth to be contemplated but rather on an engaging story (how X led surprisingly but on reflection decisively and satisfyingly to Y). If the impulse behind the parable or fable is chiefly didactic (to improve people by telling them something true about the world), the impulse behind the anecdote is chiefly aesthetic (to entertain people by telling them a shapely story).

And if one can contrast *parables* (and fables) with *anecdotes*—that is, *moral tales* with *entertaining happenings*—one can also contrast (as we do later in the book, in Chapter 10, "A Collection of Short Fiction") *stories of resolution* (e.g., anecdotes of the sort associated with Maugham and his teacher Maupassant) with *stories of revelation* (Chekhov, Joyce). At this point we confess that we uneasily recall Robert Benchley's wry observation that the world can be divided into two groups: those who divide the world into two groups, and those who do not. And so we will retract a bit, and now will say that Maugham's story is a fable in that it seeks to tell us something true about the world, and it is an anecdote in that it seeks to entertain, for instance, by its exotic setting and also by the symmetry asserted in the plot—the servant, fleeing Baghdad, unwittingly fulfills his allotted destiny. Samarra (now called

Kuibyshev or Kuybyshev, in Russia, on the Volga) and Baghdad—especially Baghdad, city of the *Arabian Nights*—immediately take us out of the realm of our experience and into an exotic world, an aesthetic world, we might say. But the events in this exotic world, in which a servant sees Death in the market-place and in which the servant's master can engage in a conversation with Death, are easily interpreted with reference to our own world. The underlying idea, evidently, is not only that we cannot avoid death but also that the place and date of our death is determined.

This idea that destiny prevails has had a powerful hold on humanity. One thinks of *karma*, of the proverb *che sarà sarà*, of "Man proposes, God disposes," of Laius's unsuccessful attempt to avoid death at the hand of his son Oedipus, of the gravedigger in *Hamlet* who began to dig graves on the very day that Hamlet was born, of Hamlet's reflection that "There is special providence in the fall of a sparrow," of "We also, as soon as we were born, ceased to be" (*Wisdom of Solomon*), of George Herbert's "Death is still working like a mole, / And digs my grave at each remove," of the youthful Alan Seeger's poem, "I have a rendezvous with Death" (and indeed soon after writing the poem Seeger did die, in the Battle of the Somme), of the common idea that "When my time comes, it will come" (with the soldiers' variant, "The bullet will have my name on it"), of Mary Stuart's "In my end is my beginning" (quoted by Eliot in "East Coker," which uses not only Mary's line but also an inversion, "In my begin-ning is my end")—the idea is everywhere.

Why is Maugham's story so powerful? Partly because the idea is all but universal. The gist of "The Appointment in Samarra" conforms to our sense of reality, our sense that in the final analysis we do not have control of our lives—witness the fact that we all die, whether we will or no. If the story confirms our intuition, it also confirms a famous remark of Hemingway's, in *Death in the Afternoon*: "Madam, all stories, if continued far enough, end in death, and he is not a true-story teller who would keep that from you." But of course Maugham's story is especially potent because it is so short. In *The Tales of a Wayside Inn* (through the mouth of the Spanish Jew) Longfellow tells substantially the same story, at somewhat greater length and to much less effect. (We had thought of including Longfellow's version but, short though it is—36 lines—it is no match for Maugham's; Maugham wins, hands down.)

The story is, so to speak, all plot. One can, of course, talk a bit about char-acter—the servant quite naturally trembles at the sight of Death, the master is sufficiently kind-hearted to let the servant take a horse and ride off for some two thousand miles, the servant "dug his spurs in its flanks and as fast as the horse could gallop he went," the merchant somewhat huffily speaks to Death, and Death (perhaps this is the biggest surprise) courteously offers an explana-tion. But it would be perverse to say that characterization is important in this story; the interest is in the plot, in the ironic turn of events. Maugham briefly discusses his sort of fiction in an engaging book, *The Summing Up* (1938; Mentor, 1946), where he unattractively condescends to Chekhov ("Chekhov was a very good short story writer, but . . . he had no gift for devising a com-pact, dramatic story, such a story as you could tell with effect over the dinner-table," 130) and then he comments on his own kind of writing:

As a writer of fiction I go back, through innumerable generations, to the teller of tales round the fire in the cavern that sheltered neolithic men. . . .

It has been my misfortune that for some time now a story has been despised by the intelligent. I have read a good many books on the art of fiction and all ascribe very small value to the plot. . . . From these books you would judge that it is only a hindrance to the intelligent author and a concession that he makes to the stupid demands of the public. Indeed, sometimes you might think that the best novelist is the essayist, and that the only perfect short stories have been written by Charles Lamb and Hazlitt. . . .

. . . There are a number of clever writers who, with all sorts of good things in their heads to say and a gift for creating living people, do not know what on earth to do with them when they have created them. They cannot invent a plausible story. Like all writers (and in all writers there is a certain amount of humbug) they make a merit of their limitations and either tell the reader that he can imagine for himself what happens or else berate him for wanting to know. They claim that in life stories are not finished, situations are not rounded off and loose ends are left hanging. This is not always true, for at least death finishes all our stories; but even if it were true it would not be a good argument. (137)

A final ironic story, said to be true: When Lord Palmerston (1784–1865), twice elected Prime Minister, was told by his doctor that he was fatally ill, he scoffingly replied, "Die, my dear doctor! That's the last thing I shall do!" Of course, dying is indeed the last thing that each of us does, but these were Palmerston's last words.

Maugham's *Of Human Bondage* (1915) was once a popular choice for Advanced Placement English courses in high school, but this novel seems to have faded from view and is rarely taught these days. For the enterprising, we recommend Maugham's *Complete Short Stories*, 3 vols. (1957). For biography, see Ted Morgan, *Maugham* (1980), and Jeffrey Meyers, *Somerset Maugham* (2004).

ANTON CHEKHOV

Misery (p. 97)

Like all good stories, this one can be taught in many ways. Since we teach it at the beginning of the course, we tend to emphasize two things—the artistry of the story and the reader's response, especially the reader's response to the ending. But first we want to mention that plot is given little emphasis. The cabman encounters several passengers, but these encounters do not generate happenings—actions—in the obvious or usual sense, though of course they are in fact carefully arranged and lead to the final action when Iona speaks to the mare. Second, we want to mention that we believe that writers usually express their values in the whole of the story, not in a detachable quotation or in a statement that a reader may formulate as a theme. Chekhov himself made a relevant comment to an editor: "You rebuke me for objectivity, calling it indifference to good and evil, absence of ideals and ideas, etc. You would have me say, in depicting horse thieves, that stealing horses is evil. But then, that has been known for a long while, even without me. Let jurors judge them, for my business is only to show them as they are."

By "the artistry," we mean chiefly the restrained presentation of what could be a highly sentimental action. Chekhov does not turn Iona into a saint, and he does not turn the other characters into villains. The passengers are unsympathetic, true, but chiefly they are busy with their own affairs, or they are drunk. (One of the drunks is a hunchback, and although we feel that he behaves badly toward Iona, we feel also that nature has behaved badly toward him.) Second, Chekhov does not simply tell us that the world is indifferent to Iona; rather, he takes care to *show* the indifference before we get the explicit statement that Iona searched in vain for a sympathetic hearer. Third, it seems to us that the episodes are carefully arranged. First we get the officer, who, despite his initial brusqueness, makes a little joke, and it is this joke that apparently encourages Iona to speak. The officer displays polite interest—he asks of what the boy died—and Iona turns to respond, but the passenger immediately (and not totally unreasonably) prefers the driver to keep his eyes on the road. Next we get the drunks, who can hardly be expected to comprehend Iona's suffering. All of this precedes the first explicit statement that Iona searches the crowd for a single listener. Next, in an extremely brief episode (we don't need much of a scene, since we are already convinced that Iona cannot find an audience) the house-porter dismisses him, and finally, again in a very brief scene, even a fellow cabman—presumably exhausted from work—falls asleep while Iona is talking. But again Chekhov refrains from comment and simply shows us Iona going to tend his horse. At this point Iona does not intend to speak to the animal, but the sight of the horse provokes a bit of friendly talk ("Are you munching?"), and this naturally leads to a further bit of talk, now about the son, couched in terms suited to that horse—and this, in turn, opens the floodgates.

So far as responses go, all readers will have their own, but for what it's worth, we want to report that we find the ending not so much painful as comforting. The tension is relieved; Iona finds an audience after all, and if the thought of a man telling his grief to his horse has pathos, it also has its warmth. It seems to us to be especially satisfying, but we will have to explain our position somewhat indirectly. First, we will talk about attempts to state the theme of the story.

In the text we give the attempts of three students to state the theme. Of the three, we find the third ("Deep suffering is incommunicable, but the sufferer must try to find an outlet") the closest to our response. That is, we are inclined to think that the reason Iona cannot tell his story to the officer or to any other person is that grief of this sort cannot be communicated. It isolates the grief-stricken person. One notices in the story how much physical effort goes into Iona's early efforts to communicate with people. As a cabman, of course, he is in front of his passengers, and he has to turn to address his audience. At first his lips move but words do not come out, and when he does speak, it is "with an effort." Near the end of "Misery," just before he goes to the stable, Iona thinks about how the story of his son's death must be told:

> He wants to talk of it properly, with deliberation. . . . He wants to tell how his son was taken ill, how he suffered, what he said before he died, how he died. . . . He wants to describe the funeral, and how he went to the hospital to get his son's clothes. He still has his daughter Anisya in the country. . . . And he wants to talk about her too. . . . Yes, he has plenty to talk about now.

Now, we are all decent people—not at all like the brusque officer or the drunken passengers or the indifferent house-porter or the sleepy young cabman—but which of us could endure to hear Iona's story? Which of us really could provide the audience that he needs? Which of us could refrain from interrupting him with well-intended but inadequate mutterings of sympathy, reassurances, and facile pity? Iona's grief is so deeply felt that it isolates him from other human beings, just as the indifference of other beings isolates them from him. Overpowering grief of this sort sets one apart from others. We hope we are not showing our insensitivity when we say that the mare is the only audience that can let Iona tell his story, in all its detail, exactly as he needs to tell it. And that is why we think that, in a way, this deeply moving story has a happy ending.

Chekhov once said that the aim of serious literature is "truth, unconditional and honest." He stated, too, that, in his estimation, "the artist should be, not the judge of his characters and their conversations, but only an unbiased witness." Both of these observations can prove useful in opening up the story for discussion. Ask students to point to moments in the text where Chekhov's intentions for his art are realized.

Much of the best scholarship focuses on Chekhov's plays, but for the stories (and for sensitive treatments of his central themes) we can recommend the discussions in D. Rayfield, *Chekhov: The Evolution of His Art* (1975); Beverly Hahn, *Chekhov: A Study of the Major Stories and Plays* (1977); and *Chekhov: New Perspectives*, ed. René Wellek and N. D. Wellek (1984). A cogent recent study of both the stories and the plays is Donald Rayfield's *Understanding Chekhov: A Critical Study of Chekhov's Prose and Drama* (1999).

For biography, see Ernest J. Simmons, *Chekhov: A Biography* (1962); Philip Callow, *Chekhov, The Hidden Ground: A Biography* (1998); and Donald Rayfield, *Anton Chekhov: A Life* (1998).

Students can be encouraged to seek out an excellent selection of stories, supplemented by critical essays: *Anton Chekhov's Short Stories: Texts of the Stories, Backgrounds, Criticism*, ed. Ralph E. Matlaw (1975).

KATE CHOPIN

Désirée's Baby (p. 104)

Students tend to differ in their responses to this story, and in particular to the ending. In the final lines, Armand learns that his own mother "belongs to the race that is cursed with the brand of slavery." The point is that he carries within himself the traces of the "black" race that he found intolerable in his wife, whom he has exiled from his presence and who, apparently, commits suicide along with their child.

But what exactly is it that Armand learns? Is he learning with a shock something he never suspected, or, instead, something he sensed was true (or might have been true) all along? Some students contend that the letter from his mother that Armand reads stuns him with its sudden, shocking disclosure, whereas others maintain that he really knew the truth all along, or that he may not have known the truth for sure but likely suspected it.

We tend to start the class, then, by asking the students for their responses to the ending of the story. And we have always found some version of this sharp difference in interpretation to emerge from the opening discussion. There is of course a risk in keying the structure of the class to a debate; sometimes the positions can become too polarized, too rigidly upheld. The way to avoid this is to keep pressing the students to connect their positions to details in the language, moments in the story's unfolding narrative. As the students talk about the ending, ask them to explain where, earlier in the story, they find evidence that supports their interpretation.

On the one hand, this reminder spurs the students to seek evidence for their statements about the text: they must return to the text and its organizations of language. On the other hand, this close attention to passages usually complicates the polarized terms of the debate, making the story more complex and harder to simplify.

Notice, for example, the detail about Armand that Chopin gives halfway through: "And the very spirit of Satan seemed suddenly to take hold of him in his dealings with the slaves." This is the kind of detail that is worth lingering over. Does Armand begin to act cruelly because of his rising anger at his wife and child? Or, somewhat differently, because he knows on some level that he cannot deny the truth about who he is—the truth that his mother's letter will later confirm?

In her biography of Chopin (1990), Emily Toth states that "Désirée's husband, Armand, has a relationship with the slave La Blanche." We are not sure that the text sustains this intriguing idea, but it's a useful comment to mention in class, for it returns the students once more to the text, leading them to focus on a key passage in order to test whether they agree with Toth or not. Students are frequently unsure about how to make use of secondary sources in their own analytical essays, and an example like this one, which a student could cite for agreement or disagreement and *work with*, can be instructive to them.

We might mention a couple of assignments that have gone over well for Chopin's story. On occasion we have asked students to "complete the story" by writing a new final paragraph that presents Armand's reaction to his mother's letter. Sometimes we have also assigned a student to present an oral report on the term *miscegenation*, which derives from the title of a faked anonymous pamphlet written during the Civil War. The authors, David Goodman Croly and George Wakeman, were Democratic newspapermen, and their pamphlet (which they pretended had been written by a member of the Republican Party) was designed to discredit Abraham Lincoln and his fellow Republicans by revealing that they favored interracial marriages—which was untrue. The student might be directed to dictionaries and encyclopedias and, for more detail, to George M. Fredrickson, *The Black Image in the White Mind: The Debate on the Afro-American Character and Destiny, 1817–1914* (1971), which includes an insightful account of how the term *miscegenation* arose and gained prominence.

ALICE WALKER

Everyday Use (p. 109)

The title of this story, like most other titles, is significant, though the significance appears only gradually. Its importance, of course, is not limited to the fact that Dee believes that Maggie will use the quilts for "everyday use"; on reflection we see the love, in daily use, between the narrator and Maggie, and we contrast it with Dee's visit—a special occurrence—as well as with Dee's idea that the quilts should not be put to everyday use. The real black achievement, then, is not the creation of works of art that are kept apart from daily life; rather, it is the everyday craftsmanship and the everyday love shared by people who cherish and sustain each other. That Dee stands apart from this achievement is clear (at least on rereading) from the first paragraph, and her pretensions are suggested as early as the fourth paragraph, where we are told that she thinks "orchids are tacky flowers." (Notice that in the fifth paragraph, when the narrator is imagining herself as Dee would like her to be on a television show, she has glistening hair—presumably because the hair has been straightened—and she appears thinner and lighter-skinned than in fact she is.) Her lack of any real connection with her heritage is made explicit (even before the nonsense about using the churn top as a centerpiece) as early as the paragraph in which she asks if Uncle Buddy whittled the dasher, and Maggie quietly says that Henry whittled it. Still, Dee is confident that she can "think of something artistic to do with the dasher." Soon we learn that she sees the quilts not as useful objects but only as decorative works; Maggie, on the other hand, will use the quilts, and she even knows how to make them. Dee talks about black "heritage," but Maggie and the narrator embody this heritage and experience a degree of contentment that eludes Dee.

Many white students today are scarcely aware of the Black Muslim movement, which was especially important in the 1960s, and they therefore pass over the Muslim names taken by Dee and her companion, the reference to pork (not to be eaten by Muslims), and so on. That is, they miss the fact that Walker is suggesting that the valuable heritage of American blacks is not to be dropped in favor of an attempt to adopt an essentially remote heritage. It is worth asking students to do a little work in the library and to report on the Black Muslim movement.

Houston A. Baker, Jr., and Charlotte Pierce-Baker discuss the story in *Southern Review* (new series 21 [Summer 1985]), in an issue that was later published as a book with the title *Afro-American Writing Today*, ed. James Olney (1989). Their essay is worth reading, but it is rather overheated. Sample:

> Maggie is the arisen goddess of Walker's story; she is the sacred figure who bears the scarifications of experience and knows how to convert patches into robustly patterned and beautifully quilted wholes. As an earth-rooted and quotidian goddess, she stands in dramatic contrast to the stylishly fiery and other-oriented Wangero. (131)

The essay is especially valuable, however, because it reproduces several photographs (in black and white only, unfortunately) of quilts and their makers. Lots of books on American folk art have better reproductions of quilts, but few show the works with the artists who made them. It's worth bringing to class some pictures of quilts, whether from the essay by the Bakers or from another source. Even better, of course, is (if possible) to bring some quilts to class.

Many students have read Walker's novel *The Color Purple* (1982)—it is one of the most widely taught novels in U.S. colleges and universities—and seen the film adaptation directed by Steven Spielberg (1985). In our judgment this is Walker's best book, though we also value an earlier novel, *Meridian* (1976), and two collections from the 1980s: *In Search of Our Mothers' Gardens: Womanist*

Prose (1983) and *Living by the Word: Selected Writings, 1973–1987* (1988). For a selection of critical essays on the story we have chosen, see *Everyday Use*, ed. Barbara T. Christian (1994). Also helpful: *Alice Walker: Critical Perspectives Past and Present*, ed. Henry Louis Gates, Jr., and K. A. Appiah (1993).

ADDITIONAL TOPICS FOR CRITICAL THINKING AND WRITING

1. "Everyday Use" is by a black woman. Would your response to the story be the same if you knew it were written by a white woman? Or by a man? Explain.

2. How does the narrator's dream about her appearance on the television program foreshadow the later conflict?

3. Compare "Everyday Use" with Bambara's "The Lesson." Consider the following suggestions: Characterize the narrator of each story and compare them. Compare the settings and how they function in each story. What is Miss Moore trying to teach the children in "The Lesson"? Why does Sylvia resist learning it? In "Everyday Use," what does Dee try to teach her mother and sister? Why do they resist her lesson? How are objects (such as quilts, toys) used in each story? How in each story does the first-person narration enlist and direct our sympathies?

MARGARET ATWOOD

Happy Endings (p. 116)

This story is an example of metafiction, i.e., a work of fiction that itself is an examination of the nature of fiction, a work that by drawing attention to its artificiality forces the reader to think about the nature of fiction in a way that the realistic short story or novel presumably does not. (Consult Robert Scholes, *Fabulation and Metafiction* [1979].) Unlike such a story as Joyce's "Araby" or Updike's "A & P," Atwood's story does not take us into a world that makes us say, as we read it, "Yes, how convincing these characters are, how close to life this report is." Rather, from the very start—even by labeling the units "A," "B," and so on—we see that the author will not be trying to take us into a consistently presented world that at least for a few minutes seems real. Further, even by the end of A it is clear that the title is ironic; B gives us a suicide, and C a triple murder.

We have only to read the second sentence, with its preposterous clichés ("They both have worthwhile and remunerative jobs which they find stimulating and challenging") to realize that the writer is not aiming at realism. "Stimulating and challenging" would be bad enough once in a straight story, but we get it three times in the first paragraph (and it reappears in section C), so we realize that the writer *must* be saying something about writing rather than something about life.

In B we get a somewhat different sort of play with language; the second sentence gives us the clichés of pop psychology ("selfish pleasure and ego gratification"), and the third and fourth sentences run to about 100 words apiece—sentences that we would never find in a straight story. After these two monstrous sentences, what do we get? "Mary gets run-down." And how does Part B end? "John marries Madge and everything continues as in A."

Part C introduces a new character, if we can say that the words "someone called James" introduce a character, and it repeats a cliché that we heard three times in A, "stimulating and challenging." In A we had read, "Eventually they die," but now in C death is given further emphasis—in a story that is called "Happy Endings"—though death is not the end of even this part of the story, since we are told that "everything continues as in A, but under different names."

Part D employs additional clichés ("working out any little difficulties," "charming house") and again returns to the beginning, with "continue as in A." Part E continues to use clichés ("how kind and understanding they both are," "devotes herself to charity"), and calls attention to the business of story-writing by inviting the reader to write part of the story.

With F we get to the final part: The author addresses the reader more aggressively ("see how far that gets you," "You'll have to face it") and forces the reader to think about the kinds of things that authors think about, for instance, "The endings are the same however you slice it." Probably there is a good deal of truth in the three sentences near the end of the story:

> So much for endings. Beginnings are always more fun. True connoisseurs, however, are known to favor the stretch in between, since it's the hardest to do anything with.

If we value this story, surely it is not because of the story about John and Mary, or James, or Fred; it is because "Happy Endings" makes us think about the nature of fiction, perhaps beginning with the very idea of happy endings. Come to think of it, the middle of the story probably *is* the hardest part to write, and that's something that had never occurred to us until we read Atwood's "Happy Endings."

Speaking of happy endings, two proverbial thoughts pop into our head: "The end crowns all" and "All's well that ends well." We have never been convinced of the truth of either of these, but our views are of no importance. Here is one additional comment about the ends of stories, this one from Hemingway's *Death in the Afternoon:*

> Madame, all stories if continued far enough, end in death, and he is no true story-teller who would keep that from you.

WILLIAM CARLOS WILLIAMS

The Use of Force (p. 119)

One student took the story as an account of a rape. Our own view is different: the story certainly is an account of a doctor's forcible assault on a patient, but we take it that the assault is exactly what the doctor says it is, an attempt to examine the child's throat. Still, we grant that there are sexual implications. As we see it, the chief evidence consists of the following passages:

> The child was fairly eating me up with her cold, steady eyes. . . . [She was] an unusually attractive little thing, and as strong as a heifer in appearance. . . . She had magnificent blond hair, in profusion. (paragraph 3)

> After all, I had already fallen in love with the savage brat. . . . (21)

and of course the passage that we cite in topic 4:

> Will you open it now by yourself or shall we have to open it for you? (18)

But this last passage actually seems to us the least substantial, almost an accident, in the way that many sentences—in daily life, not just in this story—with "it" can be given an unintended and irrelevant sexual significance.

As we see it, the doctor is indeed taken with girls' beauty ("magnificent blond hair, in profusion") and especially with her defiant spirit ("The child was fairly eating me up with her cold, steady eyes") but evidence of this sort does not mean that he rapes her, even in fantasy. In our view, the doctor is charmed by the girl, especially in contrast to her well-meaning but thoroughly conventional parents. Thus, when the mother says to the girl, "Such a nice man. . . . Look how kind he is" (14), the doctor is disgusted by the banal (though of course well-intentioned) remark: "At that I ground my teeth in disgust" (15). Similarly, when the mother says to the girl after the girl has knocked the doctor's glasses from his face, "You bad girl" (17), the doctor says, "Don't call me a nice man to her. I'm here to look at her throat on the chance that she might have diphtheria and possibly die" (18).

And this last quotation gets us to our main point: when it comes down to it, the doctor is indeed doing his job, serving not only the girl but the society around her, and if she has diphtheria, it is his job to cure her, to save her and those around him, even if it means *not* being "a nice man." So in our view the assault on the girl is more or less medically necessary (he is telling the truth when he says, "I had to have a throat culture for her own protection" [19]), *but*—and this is a big but—the doctor several times admits that he lost control over himself:

> But now I also had grown furious—at a child. (28)

> Perhaps I should have desisted and come back in an hour or more. (30)

> But the worst of it was that I too had got beyond reason. (30)

We take these admissions to be essential to the story. As we see it, it is not a story about a literal rape, or even (despite some sexual imagery) about a fantasy rape. It is what it is, a story about a doctor's forcible examination of a physically and psychologically attractive child. The doctor begins the attempted examination (11) with a professional manner ("Well, I said, suppose we take a look at the throat first. I smiled in my best professional manner"), and he continues for a moment ("Aw, come on, I coaxed" [13]), but he soon loses his professional cool. Still, it can be said that (a) he does have professional reasons for doing what he does, and (b) he realizes that his behavior was tainted ("It was a pleasure to attack her" . . . "blind fury"), so we can hardly call him a monster. What the story "shows" is that doctors are human. (We fear that some students may say the story "proves "or "teaches" this or that. Although we keep telling our students that the essays they write are arguments, we regularly remind them that, once we get beyond such forms as proverbs and fables, most works of literature do not seek to argue or prove or teach: rather, they invent situations that we find memorable and meaningful.)

As we see it, the story is about a doctor who is aware that—being human—in professional situations he sometimes behaves unprofessionally, and who is contemptuous of laymen who think doctors are inherently nice, dispassionate guys. By the end of paragraph 30, or 31 at the most, the reader knows all this, but the story continues through paragraph 33. In paragraph 32 we at last learn that the girl's throat is indeed diseased, but this point is almost irrelevant to the story as we see it. Why, then, does it continue to paragraph 33? In 30 and 31 the doctor repeats his social justification ("I have seen at least two children lying dead in bed of neglect in such cases," "Others must be protected against her. It is a social necessity") and he also repeats that he was acting not rationally ("I too had got beyond reason," "blind fury"). In the next-to-last paragraph he speaks of his "unreasoning assault" but we know all this; the only new information is that indeed the girl was ill. Nor does the final paragraph tell us anything that is very new—but it is important, in our view, because it is a sort of tribute to the girl. The story ends thus:

> Now truly she was furious. She had been on the defensive before but now she attacked. Tried to get off her father's lap and fly at me while tears of defeat blinded her eyes.

We take this concluding paragraph to be the doctor's reaffirmation of the doctor's praise of the girl's vitality.

In short, although some of the language evokes rape, we disagree with the student who argued that the story is a veiled report of a girl who is sexually violated. But she certainly is in a significant sense violated. The somewhat extenuating circumstances are (a) the medical necessity, and (b) the doctor's awareness that, like the child, he too had "got beyond reason" (30).

6

Narrative Point of View

A good deal of critical discussion about point of view is in Wayne Booth, *The Rhetoric of Fiction* (1961); for a thorough history and analysis of the concept, consult Norman Friedman, "Point of View in Fiction," *PMLA* 70 (December 1955): 1160–84. Also of interest is Patrick Cruttwell, "Makers and Persons," *Hudson Review* 12 (Winter 1959–60): 487–507.

Among relatively easy stories in other chapters that go well with discussions of point of view are Poe's "The Cask of Amontillado," Alice Walker's "Everyday Use," Toni Cade Bambara's "The Lesson," and Amy Tan's "Two Kinds"—all first-person stories. (More difficult first-person stories are Gilman's "The Yellow Wallpaper" and Joyce's "Araby.")

JOHN UPDIKE

A & P (p. 126)

It may be useful for students to characterize the narrator and see if occasionally Updike slips. Is "crescent," in the fourth sentence, too apt a word for a speaker who a moment later says, "She gives me a little snort," and "If she'd been born at the right time they would have burned her over in Salem"? If this is a slip, it is more than compensated for by the numerous expressions that are just right.

"A & P" is, in its way, about growing up. Invite students to characterize the narrator as precisely as possible. Many will notice his hope that the girls will observe his heroic pose, and some will notice, too, his admission that he doesn't want to hurt his parents. His belief (echoing Lengel's) that he will "feel this for the rest of [his] life" is also adolescent. But his assertion of the girls' innocence is attractive and brave.

Some readers have wondered why Sammy quits. Nothing in the story suggests that he is a political rebel, or that he is a troubled adolescent who uses the episode in the A & P as a cover for some sort of adolescent emotional problem. An extremely odd article in *Studies in Short Fiction*, 23 (1986): 321–23, which seeks to connect Updike's story with Hawthorne's "Young Goodman Brown," says that "Sammy's sudden quitting is not only a way of attracting the girls' attention but also a way of punishing himself for lustful thoughts." Surely this is nonsense, even further off the mark than the same author's assertion that Queenie's pink bathing suit "suggests the emerging desires competing with chastity" (322). Sammy quits because he wants to make a gesture on behalf of these pretty girls, who in appearance and in spirit (when challenged, they assert themselves) are superior to the "sheep" and to the tedious Lengel. Of course Sammy hopes his gesture will be noticed, but in any case the gesture is sincere.

What sort of fellow is Sammy? Is he a male chauvinist pig? An idealist? A self-satisfied deluded adolescent? Someone who thinks he is knowledgeable but who is too quick to judge some people as sheep? Maybe all of the above, in varying degrees. Certainly his remark that the mind of a girl is "a little buzz like a bee in a glass jar," is outrageous—but later he empathizes with the girls, seeing them not as mindless and not as mere sex objects but as human beings who are being bullied. If we smile a bit at his self-dramatization ("I felt how hard this world was going to be to me hereafter"), we nevertheless find him endowed with a sensitivity that is noticeably absent in Lengel.

Helpful studies of Updike include George W. Hunt, *John Updike and the Three Great Secret Things: Sex, Religion, and Art* (1980); *Critical Essays on John Updike*, ed. William R. McNaughton (1982); Donald J. Greiner, *John Updike's Novels* (1984); and Julie Newman, *John Updike* (1988).

Students will likely be familiar with Updike's name; some will have seen the film version of his novel, *The Witches of Eastwick* (1984). But because he has written so much, students may be unsure what by Updike they should read. For starters, we recommend the early novel, *Rabbit, Run* (1960), and the short story collections, *Pigeon Feathers* (1962) and *Problems* (1979). Updike is also an extraordinarily versatile and accomplished literary critic. His essays and reviews have been collected in *Hugging the Shore: Essays and Criticism* (1983); *Odd Jobs: Essays and Criticism* (1991); and *More Matter: Essays and Criticism* (1999).

ADDITIONAL TOPICS FOR CRITICAL THINKING AND WRITING

1. Sammy: comic yet heroic?
2. What kind of person do you think he is?
3. Question 5 in the text quotes Updike, thus:

> I want stories to startle and engage me within the first few sentences, and in their middle to widen or deepen or sharpen my knowledge of human activity, and to end by giving me a sensation of completed statement.

What do *you* want stories to do?

GRACE PALEY

A Man Told Me the Story of His Life (p. 131)

The structure of this story is simple enough. Vicente, opposed by "the school," is dissuaded from becoming a doctor. Authority triumphs. Later, when he consults a doctor on behalf of his wife, the doctor brushes him off. Again authority triumphs. But Vicente correctly diagnoses his wife's ailment and the doctor admits it, though he remains puzzled by Vicente's ability. The conflict is resolved, then, and Vicente saves a life—but the reader understands that the ending is scarcely a happy one. For one thing, although Vicente has saved his wife's life, part of his own life has been lost. That's put too strongly, of course, since Vicente is alive and he doesn't seem to be deeply embittered, but Vicente has been prevented from living the rewarding, successful life that he had wanted. We can even assume that if the authorities had not prevented him from becoming a doctor he would have saved additional lives.

The first question in the text asks why Paley begins by saying, "Vicente said"; she could have begun with Vicente's own words, and called the piece "The Story of My Life." One can put the question a bit differently, shifting attention from the author's intention to the reader's response: How would your responses be different if . . . ? If Vicente narrated the story, we might feel that he is tugging too directly on our heartstrings. We might even feel that he has a chip on his shoulder, since he is telling anyone and everyone how he was prevented from becoming a doctor. In Paley's version, on the other hand, Vicente tells *one* person that he wanted to be a doctor, and this one person passes the story on to us. In its present form, the story slightly distances him from us, and his story is, one might say, vouched for by the narrator.

It's noteworthy that Paley doesn't describe "the school" as being composed of villains. "The school" doesn't mean to oppress Vicente; it just can't conceive that he can be anything other than "an excellent engineer."

Why the information about Vicente's service as an army cook? Presumably his ability to see connections and proportions served him as a cook ("I prepared food for two thousand men"), and the passage hints both at his competence and his justifiable pride in being of use to humanity. And, again, the reader is guided to believe that Vicente could have been of *more* use if "the school" had been more open-minded.

Is Vicente characterized (Question 2), or is he simply "a man"? Although he is a bit puzzled and a bit aggrieved, his mind has not been poisoned by the shabby treatment he received. Students might be invited to comment on the last two paragraphs especially. In the penultimate paragraph, Vicente tells the doctor that he has looked in a book, diagnosed the pain, etc. In the last paragraph, the doctor tests the girl, confirms Vicente's diagnosis, and (apparently unable to comprehend the fact that Vicente looked at a book and understood what he read) asks Vicente how he knew. By ending this way, with the doctor's stupidity, and without any concluding bitter remark by Vicente, Paley makes sure that the reader will hold Vicente in esteem.

Perhaps a bit more can be said about a reader's perception of Vicente. Because he has been deprived of substantial higher education, he sounds a bit childish, as in the choppy beginning of the last paragraph: "The doctor made a test. He said. . . ." (This point can't be pressed too hard, since the voice of the narrator, which we hear in the title and in the first two words of the story, is equally simple.) His pride is engaging, not offensive ("Did you know I saved her life?"), and his affection for his wife is especially evident when he mentions her *name*. Other people are, for him, simply "the teacher," "the principal," "the army," and "the doctor," but his wife is not simply "my wife," she is Consuela.

The brevity, the apparently simple narrative style, and the presence of a strongly felt message (even though it is not explicitly stated) give this story a fable-like quality. For a brief comment on fables, see the discussion of Paley's "Samuel" in this manual.

JEAN RHYS

I Used to Live Here Once (p. 132)

The first question in the text draws on an interpretation offered by a student who had lived in the Caribbean. It provides a good opportunity to discuss in class the relative merits of looking only at the text (or at least trying to look only at it) versus drawing on one's personal responses. For what it's worth, our own feeling about this story is that it is a ghost story and that it is not by any reasonable (or useful) interpretation a story about the return of an emigrant.

The story is so short that one might think of it as a parable or fable, but surely it is not. There is no reason to squeeze a moral out of it, and indeed one can use this story along with a parable or fable to illustrate something of the range of storytelling: At one extreme, meaning or significance is primary, and at the other (as here), there is sheer happening with no "relevance" to us.

"I Used to Live Here Once" can be used to talk about foreshadowing, and since it is so short the entire story can be read aloud in class as a prelude to any discussion. Once we know how it ends (the woman discovers that she is dead), on rereading we see how cunningly contrived it is. The first thing that we encounter, the title, turns out not to be the mere casual statement that any of us might make when we visit a former residence; "I used to live here once" turns out to mean "I once was alive, I once inhabited the earth." And the first paragraph, describing a journey across a river, turns out to be a journey across Styx, that is, across the boundary between the world of the living and the world of the dead.

Once we know how the story ends, the second paragraph conveys a suggestion of the messiness of life as it must appear to those in the next world. The third paragraph, calling attention to the unfamiliar "glassy" look of the sky, also suggests that something is not quite right, and then at the end of the paragraph we get another reference to the "unfinished" or messy state of our daily world. The next paragraph plays the sense of familiarity against the sense of loss and strangeness.

The next three paragraphs, narrating her attempts to communicate with the children, end with her "longing to touch them," a natural action, yet one that is chilling because, although "her arms went out," we are not told that she did touch them. Indeed, the atmosphere becomes literally chilling, for the boy, in the presence of this revenant, remarks, "Hasn't it gone cold all of a sudden," and we're told "her arms fell to her sides" ("lifelessly," we almost add), whereas the living children are seen "running across the grass." In the final paragraph the protagonist and the reader alike come to see what really has been going on.

If you read the story aloud in class (or have a student read it aloud), there is plenty to discuss, as indicated in the preceding paragraphs. But if you teach it on the first day of class, you may also want the discussion to get into larger issues. For instance, you may want to develop with the class the idea that there are two extreme views of fiction:

1. Things exist independently, objectively, and a good work of fiction represents them accurately. Good fiction helps us to see what reality is. (Among the implications are: (1) reality is knowable; (2) art pleases because it corresponds to reality.)
2. Everything we think and see is a fiction. For instance, democracy is an invented idea, a fiction, and then we try to create a reality (our country) that resembles it. (Or, another version: there may be a reality, but we can't know it. We perceive it only through our own personalities, and these are conditioned by our circumstances. What we announce as reality is only our projection.)

But of course other views are possible, and it may be well to discuss the story first, and then (if there is some remaining time) to ask the students whether they enjoyed the story, why or why not, and, finally, if they would call it "literature"—and the reasons for their answer.

ANONYMOUS

The Judgment of Solomon (p. 134)

The story is told chiefly to emphasize Solomon's wisdom, or, more specifically, to indicate that "the wisdom of God was in him, to do judgment" (1 Kings 3.28), but we include the story here because it seems to us to be a moving tale of a mother's love and (a lesser reason, but a respectable one) because it relates to Raymond Carver's "Mine," included in Chapter 8.

The biblical story is, in a way, a sort of early detective story. There is a death, a conflict in the testimony of the two witnesses, and a solution by a shrewd outsider. We say "shrewd" because although any of us could have reached the correct judgment after the two women had responded to Solomon's proposal to divide the child, few of us would have been shrewd enough to have devised the situation that led each woman to declare what she really was.

Consider Solomon's predicament. There seems to be nothing that distinguishes the two claimants. There came before him "two women, that were harlots." Until late in the story—that is, up to the time that Solomon suggests dividing the child—they are described only as "the one woman," "the other woman," "the one," "the other." The reader, like Solomon, has nothing to go on, since neither of the witnesses is known to be morally superior, and since there are no other witnesses. Solomon's inspired wisdom, then, is to set up a situation in which each claimant will reveal her true nature—the mother will reveal her love, and the culprit will reveal her hard heart.

Instructors interested in discussing the literary structure of the story may want to call attention to the nice way in which the author takes the cry of the true mother (in which she gives up her suit), "Give her the living child, and in no wise slay it," and then puts these identical words, without change, into Solomon's mouth as his final judgment, though of course the meaning of "her" shifts from (in the first case) the liar to (in Solomon's sentence) the true mother. This exact repetition of a sentence is, of course, especially appropriate in a story about two seemingly indistinguishable women and about a proposal to divide an infant into two.

We have already mentioned that it is important for the two women to be, in effect, indistinguishable, but why did the author make them harlots? We can offer a few guesses: (a) the story demands that there be no witnesses, and by making the women harlots the author thus disposed of husbands, parents, and siblings who might otherwise be expected to live with the women; (b) the author wishes to show that Solomon's justice extended to all, not only to respectable folk; and (c) the author wished to dispel or at least to complicate the stereotype of the harlot as thoroughly disreputable by calling to mind another—overriding—stereotype of the mother as motivated by overwhelming maternal love.

One other point: The basic motif of two women fighting over an infant, and the true mother revealing her identity by rejecting a proposal that will kill the infant, is found in many cultures. For instance, in an Indian Jataka story (a story of the lives of the Buddha before he reached his final incarnation as the Historical Buddha, Siddhartha), a mother brought her child to a river bank, where a she-demon claimed it as her own. The two brought the case to the Buddha-to-be, who ordered the women to engage in a tug-of-war with the child in the center, but the mother yielded her claim rather than destroy the child. See E. B. Cowell and W. H. D. Rouse, *Jataka Stories* 6 (1912): 163.

For a strong feminist reading—a reading very much against the grain of the traditional interpretation that Solomon's deep wisdom solved a difficult problem—see Anne C. Dailey, "The Judgment of Women," in *Out of the Garden,* ed. Christina Buchmann and Celina Spiegel (1994). We quote a few extracts; you may want to try them out with your students.

> Shouldn't we question Solomon's responsibility for raising the sword in the first place? Had he not called for the sword, the other woman might never have expressed her seemingly violent impulse. . . . (147)

> But does the second woman really *choose* to have the child killed? Maybe she would have picked up the sword and slain the child with her own hands, but we certainly do not know that. All we know is that she says, "Cut him up." Her response may have represented many things besides a heartless desire to see the child killed: futility, hopelessness, anger, or perhaps a disbelief that Solomon would follow through on his murderous threat. . . . (147)

> The institutional violence that the two women confront in the sword of Solomon mirrors the violence that women face in their everyday lives. Women are expected to back down, negotiate, settle, and accept arbitrary assaults of men at home, on the street, and in the workplace. They are

expected to respond with the self-sacrifice of the first prostitute. And when they do not, when they defiantly transgress the laws of men, women must endure, Eve-like, the punishment meted out to them. . . . (148)

Blind faith in the correctness of Solomon's judgment can be maintained only because we hear so little from the women. When the sword is raised and the command given to divide the child, the women know that they have but moments to plead their case. Their speech is uttered in a fearful rush, a female cry in the face of seemingly arbitrary male violence. Had Solomon recognized that the women's initial responses were incomplete, had he desired to *know* these women rather than to judge them immediately according to a preconceived ideal, then, had he been truly wise, he would have listened with a patient ear to all they had to say. . . . (148)

Solomon succeeds in resolving the dispute over the child in a swift and expedient manner, but he fails to comprehend the cost in human terms of doing so. By judging the women on the basis of a few frantic words, he erases the fullness and complexity of their lives. (148–49)

AMBROSE BIERCE

An Occurrence at Owl Creek Bridge (p. 135)

Some students will have read this story in high school. One can ask them if it retains its interest on a second reading even when they know the ending. Experience has shown that students like it as much (or more) on rereading. Their reasons for liking it can provide a valuable introduction to the topic of what makes a work of art enduring. Our own feeling, as will become apparent below, is that the story is chiefly a clever trick, but we either keep this opinion to ourselves, or raise it but don't press it. We've never found it worthwhile to suggest strongly that students ought not to enjoy any work of literature. To let students express their enjoyment, and then to suggest that their tastes are low, is to seriously inhibit any further expression of opinion.

The opening paragraphs seem highly objective, reportorial ("A man stood upon a railroad bridge," and so on), but in fact they contain another voice, a voice marked by mild cynicism or irony. We hear it, for example, near the end of the first paragraph ("It did not appear to be the duty of these two men to know what was occurring at the center of the bridge"), and again in the last two sentences of the second paragraph, in the somewhat portentous remarks about death, and yet again in such an expression as "The man who was engaged in being hanged" (opening of paragraph 3). (One can reasonably speak of being engaged in hanging someone, but to speak of being engaged in being hanged is to imply, wryly, that the victim is an active participant.

The seeming objectivity yields (in the latter part of paragraph 4) to an inner view of the victim, but even here, where "the arrangement commended itself to his judgment as simple and effective," sometimes the tone and the perception are so cool as to seem ironic. The remainder of the first part, except for the last sentence, gets more openly into the victim's mind, and we hear of his desperate hopes, but still it is fair to say that most of the section (until we get to Farquhar's thoughts) is narrated from the point of view of a detached observ-er. Notice, too, how literal the language is. True, we get a few metaphors (in paragraph 2 the soldiers stare "stonily"; they "might have been statues"), but these figures are scarcely imaginative. Similarly, the figurative language in Farquhar's own thoughts in this part of the story (for instance, the ringing sound that is "as slow as the tolling of a death bell") is, again, chiefly a matter of clichés. It is only in the third part, describing Farquhar's hallucination, that we get fresh perceptions, such as the description of "the strokes of the water-spiders' legs, like oars which had lifted their boat."

Part Two, a flashback giving the antecedent action, is again chiefly objec-tive, though its last, flat sentence ("He was a Federal scout") sends a chill through the reader. The rest of the story (except, of course, the final paragraph, which again is objective and chilling), is in a different vein, for it seems to record in detail, from Farquhar's point of view, Farquhar's sensations and expe-riences. Some of this is in the Gothic vein of Poe's "The Tell-Tale Heart" (notice, for instance, that Farquhar thinks that he hears a blacksmith's hammer when he in fact hears the ticking of his own watch), but chiefly we get his des-perate struggle to live, and (in the next-to-last paragraph) to rejoin his wife. By the way, many hints appear, at least when one rereads the story, suggesting that all is not what it seems to be. Even as early as the first part we get the pas-sage about the ticking watch. Examples from Part Three include the following: "He looked at the forest on the bank of the stream, saw the individual trees, the leaves, and the veining of each leaf—saw the very insects upon them"; "A strange, roseate light shone through the spaces"; "He had not known he had lived in so wild a region"; "Whispers in an unknown tongue." In contrast to Part One, the emphasis in this part is on the freshness of the sensations. On rereading, too, we notice that the story is rich in deception. Thus, the Confederate soldier who approaches Farquhar and his wife is not what he seems to be; he is a Federal scout. Like Farquhar, the reader is tricked.

The second part of this story, the summary of how Farquhar, prompted by the scout, came to try to destroy the bridge, most obviously gives us the pic-ture of an individual seeking to fulfill his duty to society, an action that brings about his death. We are told that "Circumstances . . . had prevented him from taking service with the gallant army," but circumstances now seem to provide him with an opportunity to perform a heroic action, and he does not hesitate. In the event, he accomplishes nothing (though presumably he does not regret his effort), and despite a tenacious will to live, he loses his life. We are told that Peyton "assented to at least a part of the frankly villainous dictum that all is fair in love and war." How seriously are we to take the author's judgement of the dictum? If we take it seriously, we may end up saying that Farquhar is just-ly punished for acting villainously, but surely Bierce's interest here is less in justice than in the cruelty of war and the psychology of the dying man.

Responses to Farquhar—those published and those offered in the class-room—vary remarkably. F. J. Logan, in an essay in *Critical Essays on Ambrose Bierce*, edited by Cathy N. Davidson (1982), finds him foolhardy, callous, and stupid, all-in-all a "satiric object" (page 198). On the other hand, Stuart C. Woodruff, in his book entitled *The Short Stories of Ambrose Bierce* (1974), finds Farquhar "an attractive figure: brave, sensitive, highly intelligent" (page 156). Assertions of this sort are easily made. The real question is, what evidence sup-ports them? When evidence is adduced, the classroom discussions (and essays) are interesting.

It may be useful to compare this story with Chopin's "The Story of an Hour"; both deal with prisoners (speaking metaphorically of Mrs. Mallard) who for a moment feel released from their bonds but who both die before they can live their newly imagined lives. Bierce's story is certainly as clearly contrived as Chopin's, but one can question whether it adds up to more than a good read (though that's not a bad achievement in itself). One can admire the artistry, or, better, the artifice, but one can doubt the psychological plausibility (especially when compared also with Porter's "The Jilting of Granny Weatherall," which also deals with the thoughts of a dying person), and perhaps one may argue that even if a hanged person can experience such thoughts in an instant (we can never know), the story remains remote from life; to put it another way, it does not convince us, on reflection, that despite its ingenuity and elaborate detail, it is genuinely insightful.

Students can also be invited to make comparisons between this story and Frank O'Connor's "Guests of the Nation."

Note: Robert Enrico's effective film of this story (which won an Academy Award in 1963) was remarkably successful in finding cinematic ways of indicating states of mind. When Farquhar sees his wife, for instance, she moves toward him in slow motion, thus stimulating a viewer to question the reality of the episode.

KATHERINE ANNE PORTER

The Jilting of Granny Weatherall (p. 142)

Students do not always understand that there are two narratives here: one of a woman's dying hour and another of the past that floods her mind. The old lady, a tough Southerner or Southwesterner with an intense love of life, has "weathered all," even a jilting; she had expected a groom, George, and was publicly disappointed when he failed to show up. Now, at her death, again a priest is in the house, and again she is disappointed or "jilted": The bridegroom (Christ) fails to appear. (It surely is worthwhile to call attention to the parable of the wise and foolish virgins, in Matthew 25.1–13, where the bridegroom does appear, but the foolish virgins miss him.) The first jilting could in some measure be overcome, but the second is unendurable.

Porter gives us the stream of Granny's consciousness, and if we are not always perfectly clear about details (did Hapsy die in childbirth?), we are nevertheless grateful for the revelation of an unfamiliar state of consciousness.

Exactly who is Hapsy? We assume that Hapsy was her last child, "the one she really wanted," and that is why Hapsy plays such an important role in Granny's consciousness. Presumably she had at last come to love her husband. (On this point, it is relevant to mention, too, that one of her sons is named George—presumably for the man who jilted her—and the other son is not named John, for his father, but Jimmy.) But other readers interpret Hapsy differently. Among the interpretations that we find far-fetched are (1) Hapsy was a black friend and midwife who secretly delivered Ellen of an illegitimate child, but George learned of this and therefore jilted Ellen, and (2) Hapsy was Ellen's illegitimate child, fathered by George, and George then jilted her.

Also, who is the "he" who, at the first jilting, "cursed like a sailor's parrot and said, 'I'll kill him for you'"? Among the answers usually given are: her father, a brother, the man she later married. Probably the question can't be answered authoritatively. And who is the driver of the cart, whom she recognizes "by his hands"?

These details probably do not affect the overall interpretation of the story. To return to a larger matter, what interpretation of the story makes the most sense? What happens if we consider the story chiefly in the light of the Parable of the Ten Virgins? "The Jilting of Granny Weatherall" has engendered considerable comment in books on Porter, in journals, and especially in the instructors' manuals that accompany textbooks, but it is probably fair to say that the story is usually interpreted as setting forth the picture of an admirable—even heroic—woman who finds, at the end of her life, that there is no God, or, more specifically, that Christ the Bridegroom does not come to her. That is, putting aside the matter of the author's own beliefs (and putting the whole matter rather crudely), the story shows us an energetic woman who at the end of her life learns that she lives in a godless world.

This is the way we have long seen the story, and we still have a strong attachment to that view, but a rereading of the parable (Matthew 25.1–13), may raise some doubt:

1. Then shall the kingdom of heaven be likened unto ten virgins, which took their lamps, and went forth to meet the bridegroom.
2. And five of them were wise, and five were foolish.
3. They that were foolish took their lamps, and took no oil with them.
4. But the wise took oil in their vessels with their lamps.
5. While the bridegroom tarried, they all slumbered and slept.
6. And at midnight there was a cry made, Behold, the bridegroom cometh; go ye out to meet him.
7. Then all those virgins arose, and trimmed their lamps.
8. And the foolish said unto the wise, Give us of your oil; for our lamps are gone out.
9. But the wise answered, saying, Not so; lest there be not enough for us and you: but go ye rather to them that sell, and buy for yourselves.
10. And while they went to buy, the bridegroom came; and they that were ready went in with him to the marriage: and the door was shut.
11. Afterward came also the other virgins, saying, Lord, Lord, open to us.
12. But he answered and said, Verily I say unto you, I know you not.
13. Watch therefore, for ye know neither the day nor the hour wherein the son of man cometh.

Before we learned (chiefly from Wimsatt and Beardsley) of "the Intentional Fallacy," we might have studied Porter's letters, prefaces, and other stories in an effort to ascertain her view of the parable—we still might try to do so, but if we do we will be frustrated since Porter apparently did not comment on the parable, except in this story. Nor does the fact that she had a Catholic education tell us much about what she made of the parable. It appears that to understand the story we can do nothing more than read the story, and perhaps read the parable.

Matthew's final line, "Watch [i.e., remain awake] therefore, for ye know neither the day nor the hour wherein the son of man cometh," somewhat confuses the point of the parable, since the wise virgins as well as the foolish virgins slept, but the point nevertheless is very clear: the foolish virgins—foolish because they were shortsighted—overlooked the possibility of the bridegroom's delay. The bridegroom may come unexpectedly.

Can one (or should one) interpret the story in the light of the evident meaning of the parable? If one interprets it thus, the point or theme might be roughly stated along these lines: Granny, despite all of her apparently commendable worldly activity—ministering to the sick, keeping the farm in good repair, etc.—is (in a spiritual sense) improvident. The second bridegroom does not appear at the moment that she expects him, and she therefore despairs and abandons her belief:

> For the second time there was no sign. Again no bridegroom and the priest in the house. She could not remember any other sorrow because this grief wiped them all away. Oh, no, there's nothing more cruel than this—I'll never forgive it. She stretched her self with a deep breath and blew out the light.

One might almost say Granny Weatherall is guilty of the sort of hubris shown by some of Flannery O'Connor's characters, who think (for example) that because they wear clean clothing (the grandmother in "A Good Man Is Hard to Find") or hose down their pigs (Mrs. Turpin in "Revelation") they will be saved. Some support for this reading can be found in this passage:

> Granny felt easy about her soul. . . . She had her secret comfortable understanding with a few favorite saints. . . .

However, another way of looking at the story is to emphasize the point that, although at the end she is deeply disappointed, she remains active; she blows out the light. Against this, David C. Estes argues [*Studies in Short Fiction* 22 (1953)], "Her final act . . . reveals the ironic futility of all that has kept her so busy."

The interpretation that she is hubristic is offered very tentatively, and certainly not as one that gives *the* meaning of the story. But a reading of the parable is bound to call into question the usual view that "The Jilting of Granny Weatherall" is a story about a strong woman's perception that her faith is delusive.

ADDITIONAL TOPICS FOR CRITICAL THINKING AND WRITING

1. The meaning of the title, "The Jilting of Granny Weatherall."
2. The reader's developing response to Ellen Weatherall.
3. Religious imagery in "The Jilting of Granny Weatherall."
4. The meaning of "duty" in "The Jilting of Granny Weatherall."
5. The two narratives of "The Jilting of Granny Weatherall."
6. The imagery of darkness and light in "The Jilting of Granny Weatherall."

7

Allegory and Symbolism

Allegory and *symbolism* have accumulated a good many meanings. The best ref erences to consult are several oldish books, Edwin Honig, *The Dark Conceit* (1959); C. S. Lewis, *The Allegory of Love* (1936); and Dorothy Sayers, *The Poetry of Search* (1963).

"Araby" is a good story to focus on if one wants to get into a discussion of how far to press details for symbolic meanings.

In our discussion of "The Parable of the Prodigal Son" (in this handbook, Chapter 1), we talked about pressing a work very hard in an effort to make it an allegory, and we have also mentioned that some readers put an awful lot of weight on details. How much emphasis should one put on the fact that a girl's bathing suit is pink (in Updike's "A & P") or on a rusty bicycle pump (in "Araby")? Different readers will have different answers. (Our own answer is that much depends on the amount of weight that the author gives to the details.)

NATHANIEL HAWTHORNE

Young Goodman Brown (p. 152)

Lea B. V. Newman's *A Reader's Guide to the Short Stories of Nathaniel Hawthorne* (1979) provides a valuable survey of the immense body of criticism that "Young Goodman Brown" has engendered. (By 1979 it had been discussed in print at least five hundred times.) We can begin by quoting Newman's remark that the three chief questions are these: "Why does Brown go into the forest? What happens to him there? Why does he emerge a permanently embittered man?"

Newman grants that there is a good deal of "ambivalence" in the story, but she finds most convincing the view that Brown is a victim, a man who "is deluded into accepting spectral evidence as conclusive proof of his neighbors' depravity." Newman also finds convincing another version of the "victim" theory, this one offered by psychologists who hold that "Brown is a sick man with a diseased mind who cannot help what he sees in the forest or his reaction to it." But her survey of course also includes references to critics who see Brown "as an evil man who is solely responsible for all that happens to him" (342–44).

Various critics—it almost goes without saying—press various details very hard. For instance, one critic says that Faith's pink ribbons symbolize Brown's "insubstantial, pastel-like faith." (Instructors expect to encounter this sort of reductive reading in essays by first-year students, but it is disappointing to find it in print.) How detailed, one might ask, is the allegory? Probably most readers will agree on some aspects: the village—a world of daylight and community—stands (or seems to stand) for good, whereas the forest—a dark, threatening place—stands (or seems to stand) for evil. The old man—"he of the serpent"—is the devil. But, again, as Newman's survey of criticism shows, even these interpretations have been debated.

The journey into the forest at night (away from the town and away from the daylight) suggests, of course, a journey into the dark regions of the self. The many ambiguities have engendered much comment in learned journals, some of which has been reprinted in a casebook of the story, *Nathaniel Hawthorne: Young Goodman Brown*, ed. Thomas E. Connolly. Is the story—as David Levin argues in *American Literature* 34 (1962): 344–52—one about a man who is tricked by the devil, who conjures up specters who look like Brown's neighbors in order to win him a damnable melancholy? Does Faith resist the tempter? Does Goodman (i.e., Mister) Brown make a journey or does he only dream that he makes a journey? Is the story about awareness of evil, or is it about the crushing weight of needlessly assumed guilt? That is, is the story about a loss of faith (Austin Warren, in *Nathaniel Hawthorne*, says it is about "the devastating effect of moral skepticism"), or is it about a religious faith that kills one's joy in life? And, of course, the story may be about loss of faith not in Christ but in human beings; young Goodman Brown perceives his own corruption and loses faith in mankind.

With a little warning the student can be helped to see that the characters and experiences cannot be neatly pigeonholed. For example, it is not certain whether or not Faith yields to "the wicked one"; indeed, it is not certain that Brown actually journeyed into the woods. Richard H. Fogle points out in *Hawthorne's Fiction* (1952) that "ambiguity is the very essence of Hawthorne's tale." Among other interesting critical pieces on the story are Marius Bewley, *The Complex Fate* (1952); Thomas Connolly, "Hawthorne's 'Young Goodman Brown': An Attack on Puritanic Calvinism," *American Literature* 28 (November 1956): 370–75; and Frederick C. Crews, *The Sins of the Fathers: Hawthorne's Psychological Themes* (1989). Connolly argues that Brown does not lose his faith, but rather that his faith is purified by his loss of belief that he is of the elect. Before the journey into the woods, he believes that man is depraved but that he himself is of the elect and will be saved. In the forest he sees "a black mass of cloud" hide "the brightening stars," and (according to Connolly) his faith is purified, for he comes to see that he is not different from the rest of the congregation.

On the other hand, one can point out (as J. L. Capps does, in *Explicator*, Spring 1982), that only once in the story does Hawthorne use the word "hope" ("'But, where is Faith?' thought Goodman Brown; and, as hope came into his heart, he trembled"), and the word "charity" never appears, indicating that Brown lacks the quality that would have enabled him to survive despair.

Speaking a bit broadly, we can say that critics fall into two camps: those who believe that Goodman Brown falls into delusion (i.e., misled by the devil, he destroys himself morally by falling into misanthropy), and those who believe that he is initiated into reality. Thus, for readers who hold the first view, Brown's guide into the forest is the devil, who calls up "figures" or "forms" of Brown's acquaintances, and it is Brown (not the narrator) who mistakenly takes the figures for real people. Even what Brown takes to be Faith's pink ribbon is for the narrator merely "*something* [that] fluttered lightly down through the air and caught on the branch of a tree." In this view, (1) the fact that Faith later wears the ribbon is proof that Brown has yielded to a delusion, and (2) we are to judge Brown by recalling the narrator's objective perceptions. For instance, Brown's guide says that "evil is the nature of mankind," and Brown believes him, but the narrator (who is to be trusted) speaks of "the good old minister" and of "that excellent Christian," Goody Cloyse. There is much to be said for this view (indeed much has been said in journals), but against it one can recall some words by Frederick Crews: "The richness of Hawthorne's irony is such that, when Brown turns to a Gulliver-like misanthropy and spends the rest of his days shrinking from wife and neighbors, we cannot quite dismiss his attitude as unfounded" (*The Sins of the Fathers* [1989], 106).

We'd urge instructors to pay special attention to the words spoken by the "sable form" among the fiend worshipers, about three-quarters into the story: "There are all whom ye have reverenced from youth." This is one of Hawthorne's most powerful visions of evil, and it is notable how he involves and implicates the mind of the reader in his dark imaginings. Hawthorne does not state explicitly, for example, that the widow referred to in this paragraph has *poisoned* her husband. Nor does he say outright that the fair damsels are burying children conceived out of wedlock, children whom, apparently, the fearful, ashamed mothers have murdered. The point of the words used in the speech—we find them terrifying—is that they evoke sins and crimes that Hawthorne makes the reader imagine and identify in himself or herself. You might ask the class why Hawthorne does this, and what it is about the nature of the heart and mind he is seeking to explore through this technique.

Note: In Chapter 8 we reprint a student's essay on the pink ribbons in this story.

ADDITIONAL TOPICS FOR CRITICAL THINKING AND WRITING

1. Discuss ambiguity in "Young Goodman Brown."
2. What are the strengths and weaknesses of the view that Brown is tricked by the devil, who stages a show of specters impersonating Brown's neighbors, in order to destroy Brown's religious faith?
3. Brown's guide says, "Evil is the nature of mankind," but does the story say it?

4. Is the story sexist, showing Brown more horrified by his wife's sexuality than his own?
5. Retell the story using a modern setting. Make whatever changes you wish, but retain the motif of the temptation of a man and a woman by evil.
6. What do you think Hawthorne gains (or loses) by the last sentence?

JOHN STEINBECK

The Chrysanthemums (p. 162)

Because most students find this story accessible, it can be effectively taught early in the semester. To say that most students find it accessible, however, is not to say that they see all its workings. Some class discussion can be devoted to the opening paragraph on the setting: "A closed pot" suggests that there may be an explosion, and the flaming leaves similarly prepare one for violence. The first description of Elisa, too, can be studied, with an eye toward the implications of the fact that she wears a man's hat and almost completely covers her "figured print dress." Like the winter fog that has "closed off the Salinas Valley from the sky and from all the rest of the world," Elisa's clothing seems to suppress her femininity.

One can go on to talk about her energy, which turns out to be devoted not to any children but to the "neat white farm house" and to her flowers. The flowers are an expression of her vitality, or of her otherwise unexpressed drive to procreate. The shrewd traveling repairman brings out her femininity ("She tore off the battered hat and shook out her dark pretty hair") and her generosity or creativity. The story becomes strongly sexual in Elisa's comment about the pointed stars driven into her body, and in the narrator's report that "her hand went out toward his legs," but as soon as the man receives the saucepans his manner changes; he becomes "professional." Elisa, however, remains in a state of excitement (the hot bath, the vigorous scrubbing, the look at her body in the mirror, the ritual of putting on feminine clothing and makeup); her womanliness revived, she confronts a husband who is somewhat puzzled by her new, attractive vitality. Then comes her disillusionment when she perceives that the tinker wanted only some work and the pot, not her gift of flowers, a disillusionment that at first finds an outlet in her thoughts of drinking wine, and of seeing men pummeled (i.e., of vicariously pummeling a male), and finally in tears.

There is, however, another angle from which the story may be viewed, for one can also see "The Chrysanthemums" as a story of two ways of life, that of the solid, rooted citizen (here the farmer) versus the amoral wanderer who scratches out a living. The wanderer's treatment of Elisa is despicable, but it is part of a way of life that Steinbeck implies is not without its strengths. Like his mismatched team, he gets along; and like his dog—who wisely refrains from taking on two shepherds—he knows how to survive as an outsider. The story is not the tinker's—it is chiefly Elisa's—but he is worth attention. During the course of class discussion, students may come to feel that he is not the villain they may at first have taken him to be.

One other point: Judging from the published criticism of the 1960s and early 1970s, many readers saw in Elisa's gardening a sublimation of her maternal instincts. Today perhaps readers are more likely to see Elisa's gardening as a woman's effort to establish a creative role in a man-dominated society.

EUDORA WELTY

A Worn Path (p. 170)

In an essay in the *Georgia Review* (Winter 1979), Eudora Welty (speaking mainly of her first story, "The Death of a Traveling Salesman") says that her characters "rise most often from the present," but her plots are indebted to "the myths and fairy tales I steeped myself in as a young reader. . . . By the time I was writing stories I drew on them as casually as I drew on the daily newspaper or the remarks of my neighbors."

Clearly "A Worn Path" draws on the myth of the phoenix, the golden bird that periodically consumes itself in flames so that it, rising from the ashes, may be renewed. Phoenix Jackson renews her ancient body on each visit to the doctor's remote office. The chief clues: the woman's name ("Phoenix"), the story's early description of her (her stick makes a sound "like the chirping of a solitary little bird"; "a golden color ran underneath, and the two knobs of her cheeks were illuminated by a yellow burning under the dark"), a reference to cyclic time ("I bound to go to town, mister. The time come around"—and the time is Christmas, i.e., a time of renewal), her "ceremonial stiffness" in the doctor's office, and finally, the words "Phoenix rose carefully."

The myth is wonderfully supported by details, details that are strictly irrelevant (e.g., Phoenix's deception of the hunter, which nets her a nickel, and her cadging of a nickel's worth of pennies from the nurse) but that make the character unsentimental and thoroughly convincing.

A writer in *Studies in Short Fiction* 14 (1977): 288–90 argues: "The journey to Natchez . . . becomes a psychological necessity for Phoenix, her only way of coping with her loss and her isolation. . . . Having at first made the journey to save the life of her grandson, she now follows the worn path each Christmas season to save herself" (289). On the other hand, not all of the criticism of the story is on this level. For a good discussion, see Alfred Appel, *A Season of Dreams: The Fiction of Eudora Welty* (1965).

Students will enjoy browsing in Welty's *Collected Stories* (1980). Also worthy of mention are her novels *Delta Wedding* (1946) and *The Optimist's Daughter* (1972); her prose collection, *The Eye of the Story: Selected Essays and Reviews* (1978); and her eloquent account of her youth and writing career, *One Writer's Beginnings* (1984).

For secondary sources, see Michael Kreyling, *Eudora Welty's Achievement of Order* (1980); Ruth M. Vande Kieft, *Eudora Welty* (rev. ed., 1987); and Peter Schmidt, *The Heart of the Story: Eudora Welty's Short Fiction* (1991). For biography, see Ann Waldron, *Eudora: A Writer's Life* (1998).

ADDITIONAL TOPICS FOR CRITICAL THINKING AND WRITING

1. Is the story sentimental? (We'd say no, for several reasons: Phoenix, though old and—at moments—mentally failing, is dignified and never self-pitying; the writer, letting Phoenix tell her own story, never asks us to pity Phoenix; Phoenix exhibits both a sense of humor and a sense of self-

reliance, and on those occasions when she needs help she exhibits no embarrassment. Her theft of the nickel and her shrewdness in getting the nurse to give her another nickel instead of "a few pennies" also, as mentioned a moment ago, help to keep her from being the sentimental old lady of Norman Rockwell pictures.)

2. Write a character sketch (250–300 words) of some old person whom you know. If possible, reveal the personality by showing him or her engaged in some characteristic activity.

GABRIEL GARCÍA MÁRQUEZ

A Very Old Man with Enormous Wings: A Tale for Children (p. 176)

A neighbor is the first to call the winged man an angel, and then other characters call him an angel—maybe he is, but maybe he is just a winged old man. That is, despite the references to an angel, and even to the somewhat biblical sounding start with its "third day," its torrent of rain (in the Old Testament such a torrent is symbolic of God's power), and its "newborn child," we need not assume that the story is about the human response to the divine.

Most of our students, like most of our colleagues, argue that the story satirizes the inability of people to perceive the spiritual. Thus the angel attracts attention only briefly and is, when not abused, finally neglected. All of this, in the common view, constitutes a satire on humanity, an attack that suggests we are like those contemporaries of Jesus who saw in him only a troublemaker.

But this is to assume that García Márquez, like Flannery O'Connor, subscribes to a Christian view of reality. Such an assumption is highly doubtful. Moreover, the assumption that in this story García Márquez is talking about our inability to perceive and revere the miraculous neglects the fact that he deals in fantasy or, perhaps more precisely, that he employs fantasy in order to write about the individual's isolation in an unintelligible world. Such worlds as he gives us in his stories and novels are, he would say, projections of his mind rather than pictures of objective reality.

In short, we doubt that the story is about the ways in which human beings ignore, domesticate, or in other ways maltreat the divine. Of course, there is some satire of churchgoers and of the church: the old lady who thinks angels live on meatballs, the inappropriate miracles, and especially the correspondence with the authorities in Rome and the business about the priest who suspects that the winged man is an imposter because he doesn't speak Latin. But satire in this story is directed less at religious faith than at exploitative capitalism—selfishness, gullibility, etc.

To say that the story is satiric is to say also that it is comic. One ought not to be so concerned with creating a religious allegory that one fails to see the humor, for instance, in the comments on the priest, the mail from Rome, and the "lesson" taught by the spider-woman. (In this last we hear a jibe at the conventional morality of fairy tales and of bourgeois standards.) As in other satire, the vision of human stupidity and cruelty is as unnerving as it is amusing. And what perhaps is especially unnerving is the fact that Pelayo and Elisenda are, at least when they discover the man, not particularly villainous. "[T]hey did not have the heart to club him to death," and so they at first (kindly, by their standards) plan to set him adrift on a raft for three days and "leave him to his fate on the high seas." Such is the depth, or rather the shallowness, of decency.

For a good discussion of the story, see John Gerlach, "The Loss of Wings," in *Bridges to Fantasy*, ed. George E. Slusser et al. (1982), reprinted in *Gabriel García Márquez*, ed. Harold Bloom (1989). Rejecting the fairly common view that the story of a feeble old flyer is meant to explode our taste for antiquated myths, Gerlach points out that many passages are puzzling. For instance, a line such as "he answered in an incomprehensible dialect with a strong sailor's voice" makes the careful reader wonder what a "sailor's voice" is. Or take, for instance, the last sentence of the story, which says that the old man "was no longer an annoyance in [Elisenda's] life but an imaginary dot on the horizon of the sea." First, there is the odd contrast between an "annoyance" (an abstraction) and a "dot" (something barely visible); Gerlach calls the sentence grammatically uncomfortable. Second, Gerlach points out that an "imaginary dot" is strange; Elisenda is simultaneously seeing and imagining. Briefly, Gerlach's gist is that although the world of myth seems to be demeaned by this story about a winged old man who looked "like a huge decrepit hen," the story gives us a world of mystery, partly in the almost miraculous patience of the old man and partly in its puzzling statements. One mystery is that the mysterious, winged old man seems more real (in his behavior) than the others in the story. Drawing heavily on Tzvetan Todorov's *The Fantastic* (1973), Gerlach's overall point is that this story, like other works of fantasy, evokes "hesitation" (we'd say uncertainty). In Todorov's view, fantasy is not simply a matter of improbable happenings. The happenings in an allegory are usually improbable, but allegories are not fantasies, Todorov says, because the supernatural events can be interpreted on a naturalistic level. But in "A Very Old Man," there remains a strong sense of uncertainty, an uncertainty that survives such an allegorical interpretation as "There is a winged aspect of man that can fly despite the lack of appreciation of others."

García Márquez's best novels are *One Hundred Years of Solitude* (1967; trans. 1970) and *The Autumn of the Patriarch* (1975; trans. 1975). There have been a number of scholarly studies, including Kathleen McNerney's *Understanding Gabriel García Márquez* (1989); but for the stories, we suggest Raymond L. Williams, *Gabriel García Márquez* (1984).

For the study of García Márquez's work, an excellent online resource is "Gabriel García Márquez: Macondo–Author Homepage": http://www. themodernword.com/gabo/.

D. H. LAWRENCE

The Horse Dealer's Daughter (p. 181)

Despite the title, the story is about Dr. Fergusson as well as about Mabel. The deadness that characterizes her at the outset is later seen to be relevant to him as well, though he has managed to retain some vitality by keeping in touch with "the rough strongly-feeling people."

Mabel's lifelessness, consequent upon the breakup of the family, brings her to her dead mother's tomb (she feels secure in the churchyard); the "gray," "deadening" landscape contributes to the bleakness. Her devotion to her mother suggests not only a spiritual death but also a deep capacity for love, and it is therefore fitting that her attempt to commit suicide by drowning herself in the mucky winter pond turns out to lead to rebirth; the doctor, though he cannot swim, enters the pond to rescue her, goes over his head, and yet saves her. Both rise out of the foul water changed persons, having undergone a sort of baptism or rebirth from a womb. In short, character *evolves* and is not simply revealed.

The change is also suggested by the change of clothing and in the references to fire and light. Their new love is passionate and frightening, but that is (presumably) a sign of its vitality. (Lawrence originally called the story "The Miracle.") Kate Chopin's "The Story of an Hour" deals somewhat similarly with a sort of rebirth and can be compared usefully.

Donald Junkins, in *Studies in Short Fiction* [6 (1968–1969), 210–212], points out that:

> [r]itual overtones pervade the action: the silence, the solemn purification rite at her mother's grave, the personal ritual washing, the dedicatory vows, the commitment to water and death. The resuscitation of Mabel's flesh prefigures the resurrection of her spirit.

Junkins also calls attention to fairy tale or "mythological motifs: there are three brothers; the real mother has died and the father married again . . . the girl experiences a death-like unconsciousness; the hero braves death to rescue the maiden; there is a kiss of recognition remembered." (Again, it should be remembered that Fergusson too evolves and comes to life.)

Other useful discussions of the story can be found in T. H. McCabe, *PMLA* [87 (1972): 64–68], and Steven R. Phillips, *Studies in Short Fiction* [10 (1973): 94–97].

We don't hesitate to say to our students that we think that *The Rainbow* (1915) and *Women in Love* (1920) stand among the very best novels of the twentieth century. We also believe that Lawrence is one of the masters of the short story; see his *Collected Stories* (1994). For a biography, see *The Priest of Love* by Harry T. Moore (1974). Older important critical books that are still useful include Mark Spilka, *The Love Ethic of D. H. Lawrence* (1955); F. R. Leavis, *D. H. Lawrence, Novelist* (1955); George Ford, *Double Measure: A Study of the Novels and Stories of D. H. Lawrence* (1965); and David Cavitch, *D. H. Lawrence and the New World* (1969). See also Janice Hubbard Harris, *The Short Fiction of D. H. Lawrence* (1985).

SHIRLEY JACKSON

The Lottery (p. 193)

This story is based on fertility rituals of the sort described in Sir James Frazer's *The Golden Bough*: a community is purged of its evil, and fertility is ensured, by the sacrifice of an individual, that is, by killing a scapegoat. "Lottery in June, corn be heavy soon," Old Man Warner says. In "The

Lottery," the method of execution is stoning, which Frazer reports was a method used in ancient Athens.

Until the last six paragraphs we think we are reading a realistic story about decent small-town life. Probably on rereading we notice that, despite all the realism, the time and the place are never specified; we may feel we are reading about a twentieth-century New England town, but we cannot document this feeling. On rereading, too, we pay more attention to the early references to stones, and to the general nervousness, and of course we see the importance of Tessie Hutchinson's outburst. (Consult Helen E. Nebeker, "'The Lottery': Symbolic Tour de Force," *American Literature* 46 [1974]: 100–107.) With the last six paragraphs the horror comes, and it is described in the same matter-of-fact, objective tone used in the earlier part of the story.

Inevitably a discussion turns to the question, "Does the story have any meaning for a modern society?" Students in the 2000s may have to be reminded that a lottery was used as recently as the Vietnam War to pick the people who would be subject to slaughter.

In *Come Along With Me*, Shirley Jackson discusses the furor "The Lottery" evoked after its original publication in *The New Yorker* in 1948. Lenemaja Friedman, in *Shirley Jackson* (1975), reports that Jackson said of the theme: "Explaining just what I hoped the story to say is very difficult. I suppose I hoped, by setting a particularly brutal ancient rite in the present and in my own village, to shock the story's readers with a graphic demonstration of the pointless violence and general inhumanity in their own lives." On the other hand, Jack O'Shaughnessy in *The New York Times Book Review* (August 18, 1988, p. 34), said that after reading the story in *The New Yorker* he wrote to Jackson, asking, "What does it mean?" He says that Jackson replied, on a postcard, "I wish I knew. Shirley Jackson."

Perhaps this story should not be pressed for its meaning or theme. Formulations such as "Society engages in ritualized slaughter," or "Society disguises its cruelty, even from itself," or "Even decent people seek scapegoats" do not quite seem to fit. Isn't it possible that the story is an effective shocker, signifying nothing? As many people have pointed out, much of the effect of the story depends on the contrast between the objective narration and the horrifying subject. The story is clever, a carefully wrought thriller, but whether it is an allegory—something about the cruelty of humanity, a cruelty which is invisible to us because it is justified by tradition—is a matter that may be reasonably debated.

The date of the story is significant, June 27, close to the summer solstice, and the season for planting. Some of the names, too, are obviously significant: the ritual is presided over by Mr. Summers, the first man to draw a lot is Mr. Adams, and conservative warnings are uttered by Mr. Warner. Note, too, that the leaders of the attack on Mrs. Hutchinson are Adams (the first sinner) and Graves (the result of sin was death).

One last point about the ritual: Clyde Dunbar, at home with a broken leg, does not participate. Why? Because a sacrificial victim must be unblemished.

For biography: Judy Oppenheimer, *Private Demons: The Life of Shirley Jackson* (1988).

Note: In Chapter 8 we reprint two essays by students on "The Lottery."

8

Writing about Stories

Nothing in this chapter requires our comment, but we do want to mention that the chapter is somewhat unusual in providing students with help if they are going to write about a story that has been adapted into a film.

Students who want further help with this sort of assignment might consult some of the following sources. The first is a general reference work. The second is a website. The third is a new scholarly study. The next three are monographs devoted to the works of specific authors.

We include—the last five items below—monographs on authors whose fiction is not represented in our *Introduction to Literature*. We include these titles because some instructors supplement our book with a novel, and if they use a novel by Jane Austen, Henry James, Joseph Conrad, or Thomas Hardy they may well want to students to look at a filmed version and to write about the book in comparison with the film.

Literature and Film: A Guide to the Theory and Practice of Film Adaptation, ed. Robert Stam Alessandra Raengo (2005)
Fiction into Film Database: http://fifdb.com/
Thomas Leitch, *Film Adaptation and Its Discontents: From Gone with the Wind to The Passion of the Christ* (2007)
Jane Austen on Screen, ed. Gina Macdonald and Andrew Macdonald (2003)
Henry James Goes to the Movies, edited by Susan M. Griffin (2002)
Conrad on Film, ed. Gene M. Moore (1997)
Laurence Raw, *Adapting Henry James to the Screen: Gender, Fiction, and Film* (2006)
Thomas Hardy on Screen, ed. T. R. Wright (2005)

We will comment here about only one of the essays by students, the essay on "Revenge, Noble and Ignoble."

Ann Geraghty's "Revenge, Noble and Ignoble" seems to us to be an excellent essay—clearly written and effectively argued—but we think that if it had been revised yet once more it would have been even better. As we see it, the writer offers not one thesis but two: (1) Montresor is insane, and (2) the story is appealing because Montresor's insanity is of a special sort, rooted in his concept of honor, a concept that leads him to think of the killing as a solemn sacrifice (an "immolation").

We would have been happier if the student had somehow combined these two points more clearly and had perhaps indicated the thesis (the combined points) earlier in the essay, perhaps even in the title. For instance, the essay might have been called "Insane but Noble Revenge." Having said what we have just said, we want to reiterate our view that we think the essay is strong. We should add that, in a conference after the essay was returned, the student said, quite reasonably, that her thesis was that Montresor is mad and that the material about the family honor was offered not as a second point but as an explanation of exactly what sort of madness was displayed.

The basic thesis, stated at the end of the second paragraph, is that Montresor is insane. Again, we would have liked a title that glanced at the point made in the second half of the essay, but we find Geraghty's title sufficiently interesting and sufficiently relevant, and we find the first two paragraphs (and the third paragraph, which supports the thesis) effective.

The fourth paragraph is something of a transition between what the writer has already established (Montresor is insane) and the extremely interesting idea that Montresor's insanity is understandable and interesting because it is based on his concept of family honor, a concept that allows him to think that killing Fortunato is a solemn sacrifice, an "immolation." A colleague thinks that Geraghty makes too much of the word "immolation," but one might say the same of almost any interpretation of any work; that is, in focusing on one point one almost inevitably overemphasizes it.

9

A Fiction Writer in Depth: Flannery O'Connor

FLANNERY O'CONNOR

A Good Man Is Hard to Find (p. 249)

In the early part of this story the grandmother is quite as hateful as the rest of the family—though students do not always see at first that her vapid comments, her moral clichés, and her desire to be thought "a lady" are offensive in their own way. Her comment, "People are certainly not nice like they used to be," can be used to convince students of her mindlessness and lack of charity.

The Misfit, like Jesus, was "buried alive"; he believes that "Jesus thrown everything off balance," and he finds no satisfaction in life (i.e., his life without grace). Life is either a meaningless thing in which all pleasure is lawful (and, ironically, all pleasure turns to ashes), or it derives its only meaning from following Jesus. The Misfit, though he does not follow Jesus, at least sees that the materialistic view of life is deficient. Confronted by the suffering of The Misfit, the nagging and shallow grandmother suddenly achieves a breakthrough and is moved by love. She had earlier recognized The Misfit ("'You're The Misfit!' she said. 'I recognized you at once!'"), and now she has a further recognition of him as "one of [her] own children," that is, a suffering fellow human. Faced with death, she suddenly becomes aware of her responsibility: her head clears for an instant and she says, "You're one of my own children!" This statement is not merely an attempt to dissuade The Misfit from killing her; contrast it with her earlier attempts, when, for example, she says, "I know you come from nice people! Pray! Jesus, you ought not to shoot a lady. I'll give you all the money I've got!" Rather, at last her head is "cleared." This moment of grace transfigures her and causes her death. The Misfit is right when he says, "She would of been a good woman if it had been somebody there to shoot her every minute of her life."

On the "moment of grace" in O'Connor's fiction, see *College English* 27 (December 1965): 235–39, and R. M. Vande Kiefte in *Sewanee Review* 70 (1968): 337–56. Vande Kiefte notes that the description of the dead grandmother ("her legs crossed under her like a child's and her face smiling up at the cloudless sky") suggests that death has jolted the grandmother out of her mere secular decency into the truth of eternal reality. See also Martha Stephens, *The Question of Flannery O'Connor* (1973).

For Flannery O'Connor's comments on this story, see our text. In her collected letters, entitled *The Habit of Being* (1979), O'Connor says (letter to John Gawkes, Dec. 26, 1959) that she is interested in "the moment when you know that Grace has been offered and accepted—such as the moment when the Grandmother realizes The Misfit is one of her own children" (367).

O'Connor's letters, fiction, and essays are included in the volume of her work in the Library of America series (1988). See also *Conversations with Flannery O'Connor*, ed. Rosemary M. Magee (1987). Good points of departure for further study include *Critical Essays on Flannery O'Connor*, ed. Melvin J. Friedman and Beverly Lyon Clark (1985); Suzanne Morrow Paulson, *Flannery O'Connor: A Study of the Short Fiction* (1988); and Miles Orvell, *Flannery O'Connor: An Introduction* (1972; rpt. 1991).

FLANNERY O'CONNOR

Good Country People (p. 261)

We agree with Blanche H. Gelfant and Lawrence Graver, in *The Columbia Companion to the Twentieth-Century American Short Story* (2000):

> Few storytellers are as initially appealing and ultimately inaccessible as Flannery O'Connor. Her clear, energetic style, humorously delineated cartoonlike characters, and wild mixture of narrative ingredients make an irresistible combination. (413)

"Good Country People" sometimes has been described as a story about innocence and experience. However, before we begin with our students to explore the story's themes, we ask them to summarize the plot: Who are the main characters, and what happens during the course of the story? This helps to make explicit the oddities of the characters, and the strange turns and twists of their behaviors.

As we proceed, we also start to raise questions that are more specific in order to move from a summary of the story to a consideration of the choices that O'Connor has made in it. Why, for example, does O'Connor give Joy/Hulga an academic background and a doctorate in philosophy?

Note: Anthony Di Renzo, in *American Gargoyles: Flannery O'Connor and the Medieval Grotesque* (1995), remarks: "Hulga Hopewell, the story's protagonist, is a deluded egghead who prides herself on her brains but is oblivious to her body" (pp. 73–74). Hilton Als, in "This Lonesome Place," *The New Yorker*, January, 29, 2001, adds, more generally: "In many of [O'Connor's] stories, intellectuals are depicted as grumpy poseurs, mean and homely failures who can't get on with life and are often driven into the ground by its brutality.

O'Connor was like her chicken, walking backward, staring at others as she removed herself from them."

What might be O'Connor's reasons for giving Hulga (as we will call her in this discussion) an artificial leg? How does this disability function in thematic terms in the story?

We also find ourselves drawn fairly soon to ask about the title: Why *this* title? Who are the "good country people"?—people like Mrs. Hopewell? Or like Mrs. Hopewell and her daughter? Or like neither one, but, instead, Manley Pointer? Consider, by the way, the significance of O'Connor's choices of names (Mrs. Freeman too!), which highlights the biting irony and satire that this author takes such pleasure—often it is a grotesque pleasure—in.

In this vein, Marshall Bruce Gentry, in *Flannery O'Connor's Religion of the Grotesque* (1986), who emphasizes the "harsh laughter" that the story induces in the reader, observes that "Manley Pointer" is "certainly one of the most phallic names in fiction" (116).

In a helpful overview, Preston M. Browning, Jr. contends:

> Joy and her mother, Mrs. Hopewell, make up the prime configuration: the disaffected young rebel, more often than not cynical but most certainly imbued with pretensions to intellectualism, and typically alienated from the smug, uncritical parent; the parent, self-satisfied, optimistic, endowed with what seems an inexhaustible repertoire of platitudes of a moral or religious cast but actually dedicated to philistine values and the profit motive. Mrs. Hopewell, as her name implies, is a regular subscriber to the "life can be beautiful" philosophy. In contrast to her daughter Joy, whose distinguishing features are a nasty disposition and an artificial leg, Mrs. Hopewell staunchly maintains that "people who looked on the bright side of things would be beautiful even if they were not." Joy is brilliant but cynical, and derives a perverse pleasure from affronting her mother's flaccid optimism with a look expressing her characteristic emotion of outrage. Joy's perversity prompts her to adopt the name Hulga, the most unpleasant sound she can think of; and she complements the ugliness of her new name with a sullen rudeness of behavior to her mother and the latter's "companion," Mrs. Freeman. A self-styled atheist, with a Ph.D. in philosophy, Hulga is rendered almost physically ill by the intensity of her contempt for what she considers the utterly fatuous and banal world of her mother, who appears incapable of thought more profound than the sentiment that "good country people"—of whom, in her opinion, Mrs. Freeman is a notable example—are "the salt of the earth."
> —*Flannery O'Connor* (1974), p. 42

At one point, Hulga says: "I don't have illusions. I'm one of those people who see through to nothing." O'Connor, through the action of the story, shows the self-regard, the self-delusion, of such a claim. Hulga is smugly confident about the rightness of her nihilistic attitude, but its emptiness is exposed when she falls prey to Manley's evil manipulations. Hulga is humiliated and realizes, painfully, how little she knows about herself and others.

"Good Country People" intrigues students, but it also makes many of them uncomfortable because they are not quite sure they grasp its point—the lesson that O'Connor is seeking to teach. We recall one student saying, "I don't like what O'Connor does to Hulga—it's cruel."

Yes: It *is* cruel—that is O'Connor's aim, administering to Hulga a deserved intellectual, emotional, and spiritual chastisement. Hulga is not the grown-up person she thinks she is; she is little more than a child, as Anthony Di Renzo suggests:

> The theft of [Hulga's] leg brings her in touch with own infantilism, her own physical limitations. Indeed, throughout the story, Hulga has been depicted as a bratty toddler. She is sulky, moody, and incompetent, completely dependent on her mother. She even dresses the part: "She went about all day in a six-year-old skirt with a faded cowboy on a horse embossed on it. She thought this was funny; Mrs. Hopewell thought it was idiotic and showed simply that she was still a child."

Other students in our courses have wondered about the relationship between O'Connor's devout Catholicism and the meaning of this story. From one point of view, O'Connor seems to be satirizing and mocking atheism, yet from another point of view (so our students have maintained) she appears to be mocking religion—as is evident perhaps in the hollowed-out Bible that Manley Pointer uses for seduction and sex. Note the shocked Hulga's statement to Manley, late in the story, that he is a "perfect Christian."

O'Connor herself, in a lecture at Rollins College in 1962, stressed that she based her stories on "the central Christian mysteries," sin, redemption, grace, salvation: "there are perhaps other ways than my own in which [the stories] could be read, but none other by which [they] could have been written."

About "Good Country People," Preston M. Browning, Jr. concludes:

> O'Connor's intention in the dramatic encounter of Hulga and Pointer appears to be the exposure of a facile, superficial, and finally sentimental nihilism as it meets head-on a nihilism which, while entirely nonintellectual, is nonetheless real and implacable. Seen from this vantage point, Hulga's mean-spirited perversity proves merely a façade; and when she is compelled to acknowledge the existence of perversity profounder than her own–more a part of the true scheme of things, because partaking more fully of evil as a metaphysical reality–she responds with incredulity, shock, and impotent outrage. Thus is portrayed Hulga the positivist, experiencing the shock of evil which initiates her into what Hawthorne called "the sinful brotherhood of mankind." In this respect Hulga is like many another O'Connor character who experiences a sense of utter helplessness as he is made to confront a dimension of reality whose very existence his positivism or his positive thinking has prompted him to deny or ignore. (p. 51)

You might consider grouping O'Connor with Hawthorne, Kafka, and Faulkner, who are included in this textbook. What are the similarities and differences among them, in style and theme? Along these lines, Frederick S. Frank, Douglass H. Thomson, Jack G. Volle, in *Gothic Writers: A Critical and Bibliographical Guide* (2002), state: "O'Connor's pervasive use of the grotesque does not so much suggest a dispiriting worldview of the kind one finds in many of her modernist contemporaries; instead, it is primarily strategic, a means to a higher end." (316)

FLANNERY O'CONNOR

Revelation (p. 274)

This story, like "A Good Man Is Hard to Find," is concerned with a moment of grace, which most obviously begins when Mary Grace hurls a hook at Mrs. Turpin—an action somewhat parallel to The Misfit's assault on the grandmother. The doctor's office contains a collection of wretched human beings whose physical illnesses mirror their spiritual condition. There is abundant comedy ("The nurse ran in, then out, then in again"), but these people are treated sympathetically too. Mrs. Turpin's pitiful snobbery—especially her desperate effort to rank people in the eyes of God—is comic and horrible, but it at least reveals an uneasiness beneath her complacency, an uneasiness that finally compares well with the monumental hatred that characterizes Mary Grace. Yet Mary Grace, a pimply girl, is a messenger of grace. And so when the blow comes (from a book nicely called *Human Development*), it is not in vain. The girl's accusation ("Go back to hell where you came from, you old wart hog") strikes home, and later, among the pigs that Mrs. Turpin so solicitously cleans, the message produces a revelation, a revelation that forces upon her an awareness of the inadequacy of "virtue" (her horrible concept of respectability) as she has known it. Virtue is of as little value to fallen humanity as a hosing-down is to a pig; in her vision she sees that even virtue or respectability is burned away in the movement toward heaven.

On the one hand, some students have difficulty seeing that Mrs. Turpin is not simply a stuffy hypocrite; on the other, some students have difficulty seeing that her respectability is woefully inadequate and must be replaced by a deeper sympathy. But perhaps students have the greatest difficulty in reconciling the comic aspects of the story with its spiritual depth, and here the instructor can probably not do much more than read some passages and hope for the best.

In O'Connor's writings the sun is a common symbol for God. Here, the light of the sun transforms the hogs, so that they appear to "pant with a secret life," a parallel to the infusion of grace into Mrs. Turpin, which causes her to see the worthlessness of her earlier "respectable" values.

The story is deeply indebted to the Book of Revelation, traditionally attributed to St. John the Evangelist and probably written at the end of the first century A.D. (A revelation is, etymologically, an "unveiling," just as an apocalypse is, in Greek, an unveiling. What is unveiled in the Book of Revelation is the future.) Numerous details in O'Connor's story pick up details in the biblical account: O'Connor's "red glow" in the sky echoes the fiery heaven of Revelation; the "watery snake" that briefly appears in the air echoes the water-spewing "serpent" of Revelation (12.15), and even the "seven long-snouted bristly shoats" echo the numerous references to seven (angels, churches, seals, stars) in Revelation. But the details should not be pressed too hard; what matters most is the apocalyptic vision of the oppressed rejoicing and shouting hallelujah at the throne of God.

The story is not difficult, and no published discussions of it are essential reading, though it is of course discussed in books on O'Connor and in general comments on her work, such as A. R. Coulthard, "From Sermon to

Parable: Four Conversion Stories by Flannery O'Connor," *American Literature* 55 (1983): 55–71. Two essays devoted entirely to "Revelation" are "'Revelation' and the Book of Job" by Diane Rolmedo, *Renascence* 30 (1978): 78–90, and Larve Love Slone's "The Rhetoric of the Seer: Eye Imagery in Flannery O'Connor's 'Revelation,'" *Studies in Short Fiction* 25 (1988): 135–45.

10

A Collection
of Short Fiction

CHRIS ADRIAN

Every Night for a Thousand Years (p. 298)

Chris Adrian begins this story with a reference to the Civil War battle of Fredericksburg, in northern Virginia, which took place in November–December 1862. The Union forces were led by General Ambrose Burnside (1824–1881), and the Confederate forces by Robert E. Lee (1807–1872). The Union suffered a disastrous defeat, with horrific casualties, many of which were the result of foolhardy frontal attacks that Burnside ordered. Newspaper stories that described the Union's losses caused widespread dismay in the North about the course of the war.

In *Walt Whitman* (2005), David S. Reynolds cogently describes Whitman's involvement in the war, which began for the poet when he read a report that indicated his brother had been wounded in action:

> [Whitman] had direct knowledge of the war through his brother George, who joined a New York regiment in September 1861 and spent four years fighting in many important battles. In February 1862, Walt was working as a journalist in New York when he read on a casualty list the report that "George W. Whitmore" had been wounded in the battle of Fredericksburg. Alarmed, Walt went to Washington and tracked down his brother in a nearby military camp in Alexandria, Virginia. It turned out that George had suffered a minor cheek wound and would soon return to army service.

> Walt stayed on in Washington, where he got a job as a clerk in the Bureau of Indian Affairs, a division of the Department of the Interior. He spent

much of his time in Washington's crowded war hospitals, where he served as a volunteer nurse. During the six years that he was in Washington, he saw over 100,000 wounded soldiers in the war hospitals. Although he would sometimes help doctors and regular nurses in their medical work, his main contribution was providing companionship and supplies to wounded soldiers. He distributed candy, fruit, oysters, stationery, and small sums of money to the soldiers. He gained a deep appreciation of the courage and devotion to a cause on the part of both Union and Confederate soldiers. (18–19)

Here, we might also cite the stirring words of James M. Cox, in an essay about Whitman's and Twain's activities during the Civil War:

Whitman's role in the Civil War stands as one of the triumphs of our culture. That this figure should have emerged from an almost illiterate background to become a national poet, that he should have at the age of forty-two gone down into the wilderness of Virginia to walk across the bloody battlefields ministering to the sick and wounded, that he should have paced through the hospitals and kept a vigil over the mutilated victims on both sides, that he should have created the war in prose and poetry of an extraordinarily high order—that he should have done these deeds shows how truly he had cast himself in the heroic mould.
—"Walt Whitman, Mark Twain, and the Civil War," *The Sewanee Review* 69 (1961): 185–204

In many of his prose writings and letters, as well as in his poetry, Whitman spoke of the impact of the Civil War on his life and work. In, for example, "A Backward Glance O'er Travel'd Roads," the preface to *November Boughs* (1888), he said:

I went down to the war fields in Virginia (end of 1862), lived thenceforward in camp—saw great battles and the days and nights afterward—partook of all the fluctuations, gloom, despair, hopes again arous'd, courage evoked—death readily risk'd—*the cause*, too—along and filling those agonistic and lurid following years, 1863–'64–'65—the real parturition years (more than 1776–'83) of this henceforth homogeneous Union. Without those three or four years and the experiences they gave, *Leaves of Grass* would not now be existing.

When we have taught Chris Adrian's story, we begin with this background and context, and then we ask the class: What might have led Adrian to choose this episode from Whitman's life as the subject for a modern-day short story? Why might he have wanted to turn into fictional form a set of events and experiences that Whitman, in so much of his own poetry and prose, already described so vividly, so evocatively?

From this general question, we turn to specific comparisons and contracts. Consider, for instance, this passage from Adrian's story:

In the summer he saw the President almost every day, because he lived on the route the President took to and from his summer residence north of the city. Walking down the street, soon after leaving his rooms in the morning, he'd hear the approach of the party. Always he stopped and waited for them to pass. Mr. Lincoln, dressed in plain black, rode a gray horse, surrounded by twenty-five or thirty cavalry with their sabres drawn and held up over their shoulders. They got so they could exchange bows, he and the President, he tipping his broad, floppy felt hat, Lincoln tipping his high stiff black one and bending a little in the saddle. And every time they did this the same thought bloomed large in Walt's mind: A sad man.

Now, here are two passages from Whitman's prose writings:

"Memories of President Lincoln," August 12, 1863: I see very plainly Abraham Lincoln's dark brown face, with the deep-cut lines, the eyes always, to me, with a deep latent sadness in the expression. We have got so that we exchange bows, and very cordial ones.

"The Inauguration," March 4, 1864: The President very quietly rode down to the Capitol in his own carriage, by himself, on a sharp trot, about noon, either because he wished to be on hand to sign bills, or to get rid of marching in line with the absurd procession—the muslin temple of liberty and pasteboard monitor. I saw him on his return, at three o'clock, after the performance was over. He was in his plain two-horse barouche, and looked very much worn and tired; the lines, indeed, of vast responsibilities, intricate questions, and demands of life and death cut deeper than ever upon his dark brown face; yet all the old goodness, tenderness, sadness, and canny shrewdness underneath the furrows. (I never see that man without feeling that he is one to become personally attached to for his combination of purest, heartiest tenderness, and native Western form of manliness.)

A second example for comparison and contrast: Note the passage below from Adrian's story:

Hank's fevers waxed and waned, too. Once Walt came in from a blustery snowstorm, his beard full of snow. Hank insisted on pressing his face into it, saying it made him feel so much better than any medicine had, except maybe paregoric, which he found delicious, and said made him feel like he was flying in his bed.

Walt read to him from the New Testament, the bit about there being no room at the inn.

"Are you a religious man?" Hank asked him.

"Probably not, my dear, in the way that you mean." Though he did make a point of dropping by the Union Square chapel whenever he was there. It was a little building, with a quaint onion-shaped steeple. He would sit in the back and listen to the services for boys whom he'd been visiting almost every day. He wrote their names down in a small leatherbound notebook that he kept in one of his pockets. By Christmas he had pages and pages of them. Sometimes at night he would sit in his room and read the names softly aloud by the light of a single candle.

Here is "A New York Soldier," from Whitman's prose:

> THIS afternoon, July 22d, I have spent a long time with Oscar F. Wilber, company G, 154th New York, low with chronic diarrhea, and a bad wound also. He asked me to read him a chapter in the New Testament. I complied, and ask'd him what I should read. He said, "Make your own choice." I open'd at the close of one of the first books of the evangelists, and read the chapters describing the latter hours of Christ, and the scenes at the crucifixion. The poor, wasted young man ask'd me to read the following chapter also, how Christ rose again. I read very slowly, for Oscar was feeble. It pleased him very much, yet the tears were in his eyes. He ask'd me if I enjoy'd religion. I said, "Perhaps not, my dear, in the way you mean, and yet, may-be, it is the same thing." He said, "It is my chief reliance." He talk'd of death, and said he did not fear it. I said, "Why, Oscar, don't you think you will get well?" He said, "I may, but it is not probable." He spoke calmly of his condition. The wound was very bad, it discharg'd much. Then the diarrhea had prostrated him, and I felt that he was even then the same as dying. He behaved very manly and affectionate. The kiss I gave him as I was about leaving he return'd fourfold. He gave me his mother's address, Mrs. Sally D. Wilber, Alleghany post-office, Cattaraugus county, N. Y. I had several such interviews with him. He died a few days after the one just described.

Adrian concludes his story with an account of Whitman's visits to a soldier named "Henry Smith." Here again, Adrian adapts and supplements Whitman's accounts of his experiences with wounded and dying soldiers. Adrian writes at one point:

> Dear Friends,
>
> I thought it would be soothing to you to have a few lines about the last days of your son, Henry Smith—I write in haste, but I have no doubt anything about Hank will be welcome.
>
> From the time he came—there was hardly a day but I was with him a portion of the time—if not in the day then at night—(I am merely a friend visiting the wounded and sick soldiers). From almost the first I felt somehow that Hank was in danger, or at least was much worse than they supposed in the hospital. As he made no complaint they thought him nothing so bad. I told the doctor on the ward over and over again he was a very sick boy, but he took it lightly and said he would certainly recover; he said, "I know more about these fever cases than you do—he looks very sick to you, but I shall bring him out all right—" Probably the doctor did his best—at any rate about a week before Hank died he got really alarmed, and after that he and all the other doctors tried to help him but it was too late. Very possibly it would not have made any difference...

Now, we have Whitman, presenting a letter he wrote to the parents of a soldier:

Washington, August 10, 1863. Mr. and Mrs. Haskell.

Dear Friends: I thought it would be soothing to you to have a few lines about the last days of your son Erastus Haskell, of Company K 141st New York Volunteers—I write in haste, but I have no doubt anything about Erastus will be welcome.

From the time he came into Armory-Square, until he died, there was hardly a day but I was with him a portion of the time—if not in the day, then at night (I am merely a friend visiting the wounded and sick soldiers). From almost the first I felt somehow that Erastus was in danger, or at least was much worse than they supposed in the hospital. As he made no complaint, they thought him nothing so bad. I told the doctor of the ward over and over again he was a very sick boy, but he took it lightly, and said he would certainly recover; he said: "I know more about these fever cases than you do—he looks very sick to you, but I shall bring him out all right...."

Note: See also the entry in this Manual for Whitman's poem, "A Sight in Camp" (p. 413).

On Whitman and the Civil War, and for further quotations from his poems, letters, and prose writings, see: *Walt Whitman and the Civil War: A Collection of Original Articles and Manuscripts*, ed. Charles I. Glicksberg (1933); Walter Lowenfels, *Walt Whitman's Civil War* (1960); Justin Kaplan, *Walt Whitman: A Life* (1980); *The Sacrificial Years: A Chronicle of Walt Whitman's Experiences in the Civil War*, ed. John Harmon McElroy; and Roy Morris, Jr., *The Better Angel: Walt Whitman in the Civil War* (2000).

MARGARET ATWOOD

Gertrude Talks Back (p. 307)

We have not taught this very short short story, but we think students will enjoy it. We imagine that they will like the idea of treating a classic irreverently, of thinking of Hamlet not so much as the melancholy prince but as a royal pain in the neck. Indeed some respectable scholars have suggested that Hamlet makes much too much of a fuss—he makes a big deal out of everything, not just the death of his father but, for instance the nature of acting— and that Claudius probably was a pretty effective king. If we had to spend an evening either with Claudius or with Hamlet, this argument runs, we probably would much prefer the company of Claudius.

Students will enjoy catching references in Atwood's story to passages in *Hamlet*, chiefly in 3.4 (the so-called "closet scene"). Thus, Hamlet's "Leave wringing of your hands" (3.4.35) is echoed in Atwood's Gertrude's "I am *not* wringing my hands. I'm drying my nails" (paragraph 3). Other passages: Hamlet's "You go not till I set you up a glass" (3.4.20) connects with Atwood's Gertrude's "Stop fidgeting with my mirror" (paragraph 4); Hamlet's "Look here upon this picture, and on this" (3.4.54) and Atwood's Gertrude's "Yes, I've seen those pictures" (paragraph 5); Atwood's Gertrude's remark that her husband liked a drink "now and then" (paragraph 5), and Hamlet's condemnation of

Claudius's drinking (1.4.8–20); "the bloat king" (*Hamlet* 3.4.189, and Atwood, paragraph 7); Hamlet's "rank sweat of an enseamed bed" (3.4.94) and Atwood's Gertrude's "the rank sweat of *what?*" (paragraph 8); Hamlet's "nasty sty" (3.4.96) and Atwood's paragraphs 8 and 10. Atwood's Gertrude says, of Ophelia, that "Any little shock could push her right over the edge" (9) and she uses the word "mad" in paragraph 11. Atwood's Gertrude also suggests (paragraph 11) that Hamlet Senior was not keen on sex (the business about "flesh" in paragraph 11, a trait that she relates to Hamlet's disdainful comments about sex).

Again, we think students will enjoy seeing the connections and seeing a classic treated spoofingly. We are not worried that Atwood has diminished the play. *Hamlet* remains unscathed. Come to think of it, the tone is somewhat like Anthony Hecht's tone in his "The Dover Bitch," a joke that is amusing but that doesn't dent Arnold's poem. (For Hecht's poem, see the text, page 909).

JORGE LUIS BORGES

The Gospel According to Mark (p. 309)

The two questions we give at the end of this discussion ask the students to connect Borges's story with biblical episodes, so it will be convenient here to list the chief points.

1. The protagonist's first name, Baltasar, evokes the traditional name (it's not specified in the Bible) of one of the Three Magi, i.e., one of the three wise men who paid homage to the infant Jesus; more important, the student's family name, Espinosa ("thorny"), evokes the crown of thorns placed on Jesus's head. His age is thirty-three, the age at which according to tradition Jesus was crucified. Perhaps the woman who weeps suggests Mary Magdalene.
2. Like Jesus, Baltasar is a skilled orator.
3. The pet lamb that Baltasar heals recalls not only the miraculous healings worked by Jesus but also recalls Jesus as the sacrificial lamb and, from the Gutres's point of view, Baltasar as a sacrifice that will redeem the Gutres.
4. The goldfinch, too, was a traditional symbol of the Passion; according to legend, it acquired its red spot when it withdrew a thorn from Christ's brow and was splashed with a drop of blood.
5. Baltasar's dream of the Flood and of the construction of the Ark foreshadows his fate at the hands of the Gutres. (In the Middle Ages the Flood was taken as a prefiguration of baptism. Noah—who saved humankind and the animal world in his wooden ark—was interpreted as an anticipation or prefiguration of Christ, who saved the world by his sacrifice on the wooden cross. The sacrifice of Baltasar redeems the Gutres.)
6. The Gutres "steal the crumbs [Baltasar] had dropped on the table" because they identify him with Jesus, and Jesus identified himself with bread, as in Mark 14.22: "And as they did eat, Jesus took bread, and blessed, and brake it, and gave it to them, and said, Take, eat: this is my body."

The narrator mentions that for generations people

have always told and retold two stories—that of a lost ship which searches the Mediterranean seas for a dearly loved island, and that of a god who is crucified on Golgotha.

These two archetypal stories of human experience make a symbolic contrast. The first, *The Odyssey*, is relevant to the Gutres, who have sailed from civilized Europe (Scotland) and who in a remote barbaric land have lived a life without beliefs. The second, a story of redemption, is relevant to the Gutres's discovery, in Baltasar's reading, of the story of the god who is crucified and who redeems their otherwise meaningless lives. This second story they reenact.

A few more words about the persistence of certain stories. Without making any reference to Borges, J. Hillis Miller, in "Narrative" [*Critical Terms for Literary Study*, ed. Frank Lentricchia and Thomas McLaughlin (1990)], raises the question, "Why do we need the 'same' story over and over?" Earlier in his essay Miller has argued, "Fictions may be said to have a tremendous importance not as the accurate reflectors of a culture but as the makers of that culture and as the unostentatious, but therefore all the more effective, policemen of that culture. Fictions keep us in line and tend to make us more like our neighbors" (69). Then, after asking why we need the "same" story over and over, he says:

> If we need narratives in order to give sense to our world, the shape of that sense is a fundamental carrier to the sense.   If we need stories to make sense of our experience, we need the same stories over and over to reinforce that sense making. Such repetition perhaps reassures by the reencounter with the form that the narrative gives to life. Or perhaps the repetition of a rhythmic pattern [i.e., the basic or archetypal plot] is intrinsically pleasurable, whatever that pattern is. The repetitions within the pattern are pleasurable in themselves, and they give pleasure when they are repeated. . . .
>
> Narrative may therefore have as its function . . . the affirmation and reinforcement, even the creation, of the most basic assumptions of a culture about human existence, about time, destiny, selfhood, where we come from, what we ought to do while we are here, where we go—the whole course of human life. (70–71)

Now to return to this particular story. As George R. McMurray points out in a brief but thoughtful comment in *Jorge Luis Borges* (1980), the essential irony is this: The non-believer—Espinosa, the free-thinking medical student—emerges as an ironic Christ. Or, to put it a little differently, the good man Espinosa unwittingly provides the older truth that the Gutres crave.

Borges's *Collected Fictions*, *Selected Non-Fictions*, and *Selected Poems* were published in 1999.

TOPICS FOR CRITICAL THINKING AND WRITING

1. Why does Borges include the bit about the pet lamb? About Noah's Flood and the building of the Ark? About the Gutres "secretly stealing the crumbs he had dropped on the table"?

2. What would be lost (or gained) if Espinosa were a believing Christian rather than a free-thinking (i.e., atheistic) medical student? By the way, why do you suppose Borges called his medical student "Espinosa" ("thorny")?

RAYMOND CARVER

Cathedral (p. 313)

You might begin by asking students to indicate what sort of impression the narrator makes on them in the first paragraphs. (You may want to assign a short writing requirement of this sort along with the story. If students come to class with a paragraph or two on the topic, the discussion is usually good.)

Probably no single word adequately describes the narrator at this stage, but among the words that students have suggested in their paragraphs are "mean," "cynical," "bitter," "sullen" (this seems especially apt), "unfeeling," "cold," and "cruel"; all of these words are relevant. He is also (though fewer students see this at first) jealous, jealous both of the blind man and of the officer who was his wife's first husband. His jealousy of the officer emerges in his wry reference to "this man who'd first enjoyed her favors." (Later in the story his hostility to the officer is more open, for instance, in this passage: "Her officer—why should he have a name? he was the childhood sweetheart, and what more does he want?—came home from somewhere, found her, and called the ambulance.")

With the blind man, too, the narrator's characteristic form of aggression is the ironic or mocking comment, as when he tells his wife that he will take the blind man bowling. His jealousy of the affectionate relationship between his wife and Robert is understandable if unattractive, and equally unattractive is the way in which he at last reveals that he does not fear this intruder into his house, when he flips open her robe, thus "exposing a juicy thigh." Still, this action is a step toward his accepting Robert and ultimately responding to Robert's influence. One other characteristically aggressive response also should be mentioned: only rarely does he call Robert by his name. In speaking about him, as early as the first sentence of the story but pretty much throughout the story, he usually calls him "the blind man," a way of keeping him at a distance. (Not surprisingly, we soon learn that the narrator has no friends.) Late in the story, when Robert asks the narrator if he is "in any way religious," the narrator replies, "I guess I don't believe in it. In anything." This reply is not surprising; all of his behavior has shown that he doesn't believe "in anything."

The narrator seems to us, until near the end, to be a thoroughly unattractive figure. His irony is scarcely witty enough to make us deeply interested in him, so why do we continue reading the story after we have read the first few paragraphs? Mark A. R. Facknitz interestingly suggests in *Studies in Short Fiction* (Summer 1986) that "perhaps what pushes one into the story is a fear of the harm [the narrator] may do to his wife and her blind friend" (293).

Despite the narrator's evident aggressiveness, fairly early in the story he does profess some sympathy for Robert and especially for Robert's late wife, who died without her husband

> having ever seen what the goddamned woman looked like. It was beyond my understanding. Hearing this, I felt sorry for the blind man for a little bit. And then I found myself thinking what a pitiful life this woman must have led. . . . A woman whose husband could never read the expression on her face, be it misery or something better. Someone

who could wear makeup or not—what difference to him? . . . And then to slip off into death, the blind man's hand on her hand, his blind eyes streaming tears—I'm imagining now—her last thought maybe this: that he never even knew what she looked like, and she on an express to the grave. Robert was left with a small insurance policy and half of a twenty-peso Mexican coin. The other half of the coin went into the box with her. Pathetic.

But to say that the narrator displays "sympathy" here is, obviously, to use the word too loosely. What is displayed, again, is his bitterness, cynicism, and (despite his "imagining") his utter inability to understand the feelings of others. (Later, when the blind man's hand rests on the narrator's as the narrator draws a box—like his house—that turns into a cathedral, he will presumably come close to the experience that here he so ineptly imagines.)

Almost by chance the blind man enters into the narrator's life and thaws the ice frozen around his heart, or better, the blind man enables the narrator to see. As Facknitz puts it,

> Carver redeems the narrator by releasing him from the figurative blindness that results in a lack of insight into his own condition and which leads him to trivialize human feelings and needs. Indeed, so complete is his misperception that the blind man gives him a faculty of sight that he is not even aware that he lacks. (293)

The narrator so dominates the story that there is a danger in class that no other matters will get considered, but it's worth asking students to characterize the wife and also Robert. Carver has taken care not to make Robert too saintly a fellow, full of wisdom and goodness and all that. True, Robert does have an uncanny sense of the difference between a black-and-white television set and a color set, but Carver nicely does not dwell on this; he just sort of lets it drop. Further, Robert's use of "bub" is maddening, and his confidence that he has "a lot of friends" in "Guam, in the Philippines, in Alaska, and even in Tahiti" suggests that he takes quite a bit for granted. It is easy, in fact, to imagine that one wouldn't much like Robert. The man who brings the narrator to a new consciousness is not sentimentalized or etherealized.

The story also invites comparison with Flannery O'Connor's "Revelation," which is about unearned grace, although the word "grace" should be used metaphorically when talking about Carver, whereas O'Connor was literally concerned with the working of the Holy Spirit. Talking of several of Carver's stories (including "Cathedral"), Facknitz puts the matter thus:

> Grace, Carver says, is bestowed upon us by other mortals, and it comes suddenly, arising in circumstances as mundane as a visit to the barber shop, and in the midst of feelings as ignoble or quotidian as jealousy, anger, loneliness, and grief. It can be represented in incidental physical contact, and the deliverer is not necessarily aware of his role. Not Grace in the Christian sense at all, it is what grace becomes in a godless world—a deep and creative connection between humans that reveals to Carver's alienated and diminished creatures that there can be contact in a world they supposed was empty of sense or love. Calm is given in a touch, a

small, good thing is the food we get from others, and in the cathedrals we draw together, we create large spaces for the spirit. (295–96)

One last point: Obviously a cathedral is a more appropriate and richer symbol for what Carver is getting at than is, say, a gas station or shopping mall. Notice, too, that in the television program about cathedrals there is an episode in which devils attack monks; that is, an assault is made on the soul. Presumably the narrator is unaware of morality plays, but some readers will understand that this scene introduces the possibility of a sort of spiritual change. A little later the inner change is further prepared for by the narrator's comments about a change in physical sensation. When he goes upstairs to get a pen so that he can draw a cathedral, he says, "My legs felt like they didn't have any strength in them. They felt like they did after I'd done some running."

For a stimulating study of the themes of isolation, retreat, and self-enclosure in Carver's work, focusing on the collection titled *Cathedral* (1983), we recommend Kirk Nesset, "Insularity and Self-Enlargement in Raymond Carver's *Cathedral*," *Essays in Literature* 21 (Spring 1994): 116–28. Also relevant: William L. Stull, "Beyond Hopelessville: Another Side of Raymond Carver," *Philological Quarterly* 64 (Winter 1985): 1–15; and Nelson Hathcock, "'The Possibility of Resurrection': Re-vision in Carver's *Feathers* and *Cathedral*," *Studies in Short Fiction* 28 (Winter 1991): 31–39. For an approach to Carver's literary career, consult Randolph Paul Runyon, *Reading Raymond Carver* (1992).

OSCAR CASARES

Yolanda (p. 323)

The story is told in the first-person, a common enough device, especially in stories about the transition from innocence to experience (cf. Updike's "A & P"), but in this instance the narrator's voice is an engaging combination of the mature man that he now is and the boy that he was at the time of the episode. In the first paragraph, he is all adult:

> When I can't sleep at night I think of Yolanda Castro. She was a woman who lived next door to us one summer when I was growing up. I've never told Maggie about her because it's not something she'd appreciate knowing. Trust me. Tonight, like most nights, she fell asleep before I was even done brushing my teeth. And now all I can hear are little snores. Sometimes she even talks to herself, shouts out other people's names, and then in the morning says she can't remember any of it. Either way, I let her go on sleeping. She's over on her side of the bed. It's right where she ought to be. This thing with Yolanda doesn't really concern her.

There is plenty to discuss here—not merely the narrator's sense that Maggie would not "appreciate" knowing about the attractive Yolanda who spent some time in bed with him but also his report that (a) Maggie falls asleep even before he gets into bed at night, and (b) Maggie has her own life in dreams, when she calls out names that she later (when awake) claims she can't remember. Presumably Maggie, like the narrator, has her own secrets, and the narrator has enough sense not to pry. Live and let live: "She's over on her side of the bed. It's right where she ought to be. This thing with Yolanda doesn't really concern her."

Although the story concerns infidelity and violence, the treatment is somewhat comic, occasionally almost farcical, with such details as a drunken driver who runs over "the Baby Jesus that was still lying in the manger," Frank with forearms "like Popeye's," a Jehovah Witness who tries to give Frank a pamphlet, Frank knocked off balance when "his head hit the clothesline," and of course Yolanda pressing her breasts against the boy's back—and how he "never turned around and always regretted it."

What might have been a tender initiation into sexuality is, at least as we see it, here presented as a comic story of a missed opportunity and a golden memory. Notice, however, that Casares does not sentimentalize Yolanda: In the next-to-last paragraph the reader learns that she has been having an affair with an assistant manager, that she is pregnant, and that "she'd been taking money out of the register and was about to be caught." (Presumably the bonuses that in paragraph 19 she claimed had been given to her are in fact dollars she has taken out of the till. The brutal Frank was right to wonder where her money came from.) But, as the narrator says in the last sentence of the next-to-last paragraph, "that's not the part of the story I like to remember." What he likes to remember is set forth in the final paragraph, which more or less summarizes the gist of what the innocent-eye narrator told us, the experience of being with Yolanda, safe, though now romanticized into a vision wherein they are "riding off to some faraway place on an Appaloosa." No need to tell his wife Maggie about this private world, and she, we recall from the first paragraph, has her own private world too.

DIANA CHANG

The Oriental Contingent (p. 329)

The title comes from a remark in paragraph 15, when a voice—presumably belonging to Lisa's Caucasian husband—refers to the two Asian-American women as "[t]he Oriental contingent." Is the remark offensive? The man sees two Asian-Americans together, and he (quite naturally?) sees them as a unit. The Asian-Americans, too, regard themselves (quite naturally?) as having something in common, although it turns out that Lisa, born in Buffalo, was not even brought up by Chinese parents.

It's hard to think of Lisa as Chinese in any significant way, other than that her biological parents were Chinese. And yet, of course, to Caucasians she will always be "Oriental," and when two people like Lisa are chatting they will (in Caucasian eyes) be "the Oriental contingent." And in their own eyes, too, they are not a hundred percent American; at one point Lisa thinks of her "American friends," and then remembers that she too is American. But if an American with Asian features, or, for that matter, with Indian features or black African features is in some degree an outsider to a Caucasian, such an individual is also in some degree—indeed, probably to a much greater degree—an outsider to persons with those features who were born in Asia, India, or Africa. Connie feels inferior to Lisa, who she mistakenly thinks is a more "authentic" Chinese than Connie, but it turns out that Lisa is so fearful of being insufficiently Chinese that she avoids visiting Asia.

One way to talk about the story is to talk about the degree to which any American—even someone from an Anglo background—feels an identity with some ethnic subgroup and therefore sees others as the Other. Of course the old idea was that all who came to the United States were turned into Americans, which more or less meant Anglos, or, let's say, Northern Europeans. America was a "melting pot," a term invented or at least popularized by Israel Zangwill in a play, *The Melting Pot* (1914): "America is God's crucible, the great Melting-Pot where all the races of Europe are melting and reforming." The idea was dominant in the late nineteenth century and survived almost unchallenged into the middle of the twentieth century, but today the image of the melting pot has been replaced by other images, including "the salad bowl" and "the mosaic." These newer images emphasize the idea that each part retains its identity and also contributes to the whole. (You might ask students if they are familiar with other metaphors. In recent years we have noticed the occasional use of America as a kaleidoscope.)

Here are two relevant quotations:

Fortunately, the time has long passed when people liked to regard the United States as some kind of melting pot, taking men and women from every part of the world and converting them into standardized, homogenized Americans. . . . Just as we welcome a world of diversity, so we glory in an America of diversity—an America all the richer for the many different and distinctive strands of which it is woven. (Hubert H. Humphrey, 1967)

And:

The crucial thing about the melting pot was that it did not happen: American politics and American social life are still dominated by the existence of sharply-defined ethnic groups. (Charles E. Silberman, 1964)

It would be easy to find many quotations in which African-Americans call attention to their sense of having two identities as Americans or to the inadequacy of the image of the melting pot. Here is an example of each:

One ever feels his twoness—an American, a Negro, two souls, two thoughts, two unreconciled strivings; two warring ideals in one dark body, whose dogged strength alone keeps it from being torn asunder. (W.E.B. Du Bois, 1903)

And:

I hear that melting-pot stuff a lot, and all I can say is that we haven't melted. (Jesse Jackson, 1969)

Perhaps in class you may want to examine the following hasty generalizations. How much truth is in any of them?

1. It is probably true that, until some thirty years ago, most people who immigrated to this country wanted to enter the melting pot, i.e., wanted to put "the old country" behind them and to become "Americans."
2. Most African-Americans, too, probably wanted to get into the pot, but they were excluded by whites.
3. Even immigrants who were or are eager to become 100 percent American probably retain a good deal of ethnic identity, perhaps unto the third and fourth generations (an idea implicit in Silberman's quotation).
4. Many recent immigrants emphasize their desire to retain their ethnic identity, but they too—or, rather, their children and grandchildren—will retain very little of the older generation's identity; they will, in fact, be like the Chinese Americans in Chang's story.

"The Oriental Contingent" provides an excellent opportunity for students to write—in journals, and then in essays and in their own fiction—about their ethnic backgrounds or about what they have seen in the behavior of second- and third-generation people of other backgrounds. (You may also want to refer students to Pat Mora's poem, "Immigrants," in Chapter 1, and to Martín Espada's poem, "Bully," in Chapter 24.)

Note: In Chapter 24, "American Voices: Poems for a Diverse Nation," we include several poems about the thoughts of non-Anglos in the United States.

KATE CHOPIN

The Storm (p. 333)

Chopin wrote this story in 1898 but never tried to publish it, presumably because she knew it would be unacceptable to the taste of the age. "The Storm" uses the same characters as an earlier story, "The 'Cadian Ball," in which Alcée is about to run away with Calixta when Clarisse captures him as a husband.

Here are our tentative responses to the topics for discussion and writing in the text.

1,2. (On the characters of Calixta and Bobinôt). In Part I, Bobinôt buys a can of shrimp because Calixta is fond of shrimp. Our own impression is that this detail is provided chiefly to show Bobinôt's interest in pleasing his wife, but Per Seyersted, in Kate Chopin, finds a darker meaning. Seyersted suggests (p. 223) that shrimp "may represent a conscious allusion to the potency often denoted by sea foods." (To the best of our knowledge, this potency is attributed only to oysters, but perhaps we lead sheltered lives.) At the beginning of Part II Calixta is "sewing furiously on a sewing machine," and so readers gather that she is a highly industrious woman, presumably a more-than-usually diligent housekeeper. The excuses Bobinôt frames on the way home (Part III) suggest that he is somewhat intimidated by his "overscrupulous housewife." Calixta is genuinely concerned about the welfare of her somewhat simple husband and of her child. The affair with Alcée by no means indicates that she is promiscuous or, for that matter, unhappy with her family. We don't think her expressions of solicitude for the somewhat childlike Bobinôt are insincere. We are even inclined to think that perhaps her encounter with Alcée has heightened her concern for her husband. (At least, to use the language of reader-response criticism, this is the way we "naturalize"—make sense out of—the gap or blank in the narrative.)

3. Alcée's letter to his wife suggests that he thinks his affair with Calixta may go on for a while, but we take it that the affair is, like the storm (which gives its title to the story), a passing affair. It comes about unexpectedly and "naturally": Alcée at first takes refuge on the gallery, with no thought of entering the house, but because the gallery does not afford shelter, Calixta invites him in, and then a lightning bolt drives her (backward) into his arms. The experience is thoroughly satisfying, and it engenders no regrets, but presumably it will be treasured rather than repeated, despite Alcée's thoughts when he writes his letter.

4. Clarisse's response. By telling us, in Part V, that Clarisse is delighted at the thought of staying a month longer in Biloxi, Chopin diminishes any blame that a reader might attach to Alcée. That is, although Alcée is unfaithful to his wife, we see that his wife doesn't regret his absence: "Their intimate conjugal life was something which she was more than willing to forego for a while."

5. Is the story cynical? We don't think so, since cynicism involves a mocking or sneering attitude, whereas in this story Chopin regards her characters affectionately. Blame is diminished not only by Clarisse's letter but by other means. We learn that at an earlier time, when Calixta was a virgin, Alcée's "honor forbade him to prevail." And, again, by associating the affair with the storm, Chopin implies that this moment of passion is in accord with nature. Notice also that the language becomes metaphoric during the scene of passion. For instance, Calixta's "lips were as red and as moist as pomegranate seed," and her "passion . . . was like a white flame," suggesting that the characters are transported to a strange (though natural) world. There is, of course, the implication that people are less virtuous than they seem to be, but again, Chopin scarcely seems to gloat over this fact. Rather, she suggests that the world is a fairly pleasant place in which there is enough happiness to go all around. "So the storm passed and everyone was happy." There is no need to imagine further episodes in which, for instance, Calixta and Alcée deceive Bobinôt; nor is there any need to imagine further episodes in which Calixta and Alcée regret their moment of passion.

Two additional points can be made. First, there seems to be a suggestion of class distinction between Calixta and Alcée, though both are Creoles. Calixta uses some French terms, and her speech includes such expressions as "An' Bibi? he ain't wet? Ain't hurt?" Similarly Bobinôt's language, though it does not include any French terms, departs from standard English. On the other hand, Alcée speaks only standard English. Possibly, however, the distinctions in language are also based, at least partly based, on gender as well as class; Calixta speaks the language of an uneducated woman largely confined to her home, whereas Alcée—a man who presumably deals with men in a larger society—speaks the language of the Anglo world. But if gender is relevant, how can one account for the fact that Bobinôt's language resembles Calixta's, and Clarisse's resembles Alcée's? A tentative answer: Bobinôt, like Calixta, lives in a very limited world, whereas Clarisse is a woman of the world. We see Clarisse only at the end of the story, and there we hear her only through the voice of the narrator, but an expression such as "The society was agreeable" suggests that her language (as might be expected from a woman rich enough to take a long vacation) resembles her husband's, not Calixta's.

ALICE ELLIOTT DARK

In the Gloaming (p. 337)

We begin with a comment by the author, printed in *Best American Short Stories 1994*, ed. Tobias Wolff:

> After "In the Gloaming" was published, I got a lot of letters asking if it was really fiction; apparently it seemed autobiographical. I suppose it is, in the sense that I see it as a story about a woman trying to be a decent mother, a subject that was very much on my mind at the time I wrote it. I had recently become a mother, and was having bouts of vertigo whenever I thought of the scope of this new relationship. There were so many contradictory feelings to cope with; I wanted to encourage my son to have his own life, yet I hoped he would like me; I wanted to help him feel brave going out into the world, yet when I imagined it, I instantly feared harm that could come to him.
>
> The story was not conceived as being about any disease in particular. AIDS came in when Laird made a remark about his immune system, and I left it at that. I never thought of it as an AIDS story; from what I've seen of AIDS, the end of the disease is not as gentle as this, nor do most victims have situations as idyllic as Laird's. (333)

We agree that it is not "an AIDS story." The central issue, as we see it, is the mother's relationship with her son—and the adjacent issue is her relationship with her husband, hence we include the story in this chapter. To say this, however, is not to say that AIDS is peripheral to the story; the story as we have it is about such constructions as manliness and motherliness.

We begin with a few remarks about stereotypes, which may reveal that we are Politically Incorrect, or since these things have a way of changing almost overnight, Politically Correct. One hears that stereotypes are a Bad Thing, but one also hears about pride in ethnic identity, which assumes that individuals within groups have certain identities. Proud advocates of ethnic or racial or religious identity claim to have certain characteristics, let's say a sense of humor or some sort of special courage or love of nature, or whatever; almost all groups seem to claim to be special by virtue of having loving families, and by virtue of having strong mothers. To this degree they stereotype themselves, and they are proud of their stereotypes. On the other hand, they strongly object to outsiders imposing what seems to be negative stereotypes. About the only exception we can think of is the occasional Asian objection to the favorable stereotype of the Asian as the ideal immigrant. Some Asians argue that this favorable stereotype is damaging because it makes others expect too much of Asians.

But to get back to Dark's story: It is not a story about AIDS and it is not a gay story, but we do have some of the signs that are said (or used to be said) to mark gay relationships. A father who is "ambitious, competitive, self-absorbed" (paragraph 74) and away too much; a mother who loves her son to the exclusion of the father; a boy who perhaps is too eager to please his mother (125) and who perhaps is a bit more attracted to sensuous pleasures (the cashmere lap blankets of paragraph 141) than a Real Man should be. We are not complaining that Dark's story is a tissue of stereotypes. Rather, we are saying that the characters are thoroughly believable—wonderfully believable—and yet if one stands back, one sees that they more or less fit a traditional pattern of a family with a homosexual son. Even in the first paragraph we get (appropriately) gender stereotyping when the narrator comments on Laird's openness: "No one [Janet] knew talked that way—no man, at least." The implication surely is this: Men talk one way, women another—and a gay man, dying of AIDS, may talk like a woman. By the way, students may have a good deal to say on the alleged differences between the ways women and men speak—especially if the students have used a freshman reader that includes essays by such popular writers as Robin Lakoff and Deborah Tannen.

Although in this story the mother is infinitely more interesting than the father, students might begin tracking the comments about the father. He makes himself scarce now (paragraphs 4, 62), as he always did (64, 66, 68–69, 73); he has often let his son know that he is disappointed in the boy (72); he knows that his son is homosexual but apparently can't bring himself to admit it or discuss it with the boy (121). Of course—and it is important that this point comes up in class—we know the father chiefly through the mother. We never enter the father's mind; if he were to tell the story, we would get a somewhat different story. But we do see him weep (183), and he does suggest that bagpipes should provide the funeral music, a choice that we must believe the mother is fully in accord with. And, most moving of all, the story ends with his plaintive words, "Please tell me—what else did my boy like?" In short, the father of this gay boy held certain ideas of manliness that prevented him from being close to the boy during his life. Now that the boy is dead he admits that he failed as a father, and he desperately wants to know what his son was really like.

About the title: The words and the music to "In the Gloaming" were written in 1877 by Annie Fortescue, who married Lord Alfred Hill, comptroller of Queen Victoria's household. Here is the text:

In the gloaming, oh my darling!
When the lights are dim and low,
And the quiet shadows falling
Softly come and softly go,
When the winds are sobbing faintly
With a gentle, unknown woe,
Will you think of me and love me
As you did once long ago?
In the gloaming, oh my darling!
Think not bitterly of me!
Though I passed away in silence,
Left you lonely, set you free,
For my heart was crushed with longing
What had been could never be.

It was best to leave you thus, dear,
Best for you and best for me.

Students might enjoy the film *In the Gloaming* (1997), directed by Christopher Reeve and starring Glenn Close as Janet.

RALPH ELLISON

Battle Royal (p. 350)

The term "battle royal" has two chief meanings: (1) a fight involving several or many contestants, and (2) a bitterly fought battle. Both meanings are relevant to this story, most obviously in the contest between the boys in the ring, and almost as obviously in the battle between blacks and whites.

The battle between blacks and whites in many ways is evident enough to all of the participants, but in two important ways it is not evident to some of them. First, the whites presumably did not perceive that the narrator's grandfather was a traitor and a spy; presumably they mistakenly accepted his feigned acquiescence as genuine submission, not realizing that in fact he was an enemy, maintaining his ideals in the only way available to him. Second, the narrator, who in his youth accepted the traditional answers, did not understand that a war was going on, or ought to be going on. In his immaturity he sought to please the whites, subjecting himself to all sorts of indignities—not only by fighting against blacks for the amusement of whites and grabbing for counterfeit coins on an electrified rug, but also by giving a speech that he thinks is impressive but reduces him to a puppet mouthing ideas that lend support to his enemy. He is so unaware of his plight that even during the fisticuffs he wonders if his speech will impress his audience. (Ellison emphasizes the point a little later in various ways, for instance, when the M.C. introduces the boy as someone who "knows more big words than a pocket-sized dictionary," and when the narrator tells us that he was swallowing his own blood while giving his speech to the amused audience.) As the narrator says at the beginning of the story, it took him a long time to realize that he must be himself—not the creature that white society wants him to be—and that as far as white society goes, a black is an invisible man, i.e., a person of no identity.

As long as he accepts the role the whites give him, he serves the purpose of whites. In fact, because he is verbally talented, he is extremely useful to whites; he will persuade other blacks to perceive themselves as the whites perceive them. As the school superintendent puts it, the boy will "lead his people in the proper paths." Thus the scholarship is used by the whites to strengthen their army by recruiting a man who betrays the blacks. If the narrator had not ultimately come to understand this, he would have become a traitor of a sort very different from his grandfather. Fortunately, however, the nightmarish experience of the battle and the subsequent speech are balanced by another sort of nightmare, a dream (presided over by his grandfather) in which the briefcase contains not a scholarship but a note: "Keep This Nigger-Boy Running." (The message is rooted in a horrible practical joke, in which a white plantation owner would send an illiterate African American to another plantation owner, with a letter supposedly recommending the bearer but which actually said, "Keep This Nigger-Boy Running." The second owner would say he could not offer a job, but would recommend that the bearer go to a third plantation, and so on.) The narrator's dream is as real as the battle, and more real than the scholarship, since the scholarship (though of course literally real) was not at all what the young man had thought it was.

"Battle Royal" became part of Ellison's novel, *Invisible Man* (1952). On this important book, see *New Essays on Invisible Man*, ed. Robert G. O'Meally (1988), and *Approaches to Teaching Ellison's Invisible Man*, ed. Susan Parr and Pancho Savery (1989). All students of modern and contemporary American and African American literatures should explore *The Collected Essays of Ralph Ellison*, ed. John F. Callahan (1995). Another essential resource is *Conversations with Ralph Ellison*, ed. Amritjit Singh and Maryemma Graham (1995). Callahan, Ellison's literary executor, has also edited *Flying Home and Other Stories* (1998) and *Juneteenth* (1999), a version of the novel-in-progress (some 2,000 pages in manuscript) that Ellison left unfinished at the time of his death.

LOUISE ERDRICH

The Red Convertible (p. 360)

"The Red Convertible" is one of those literary works that teaches itself. Our students always find the story powerful and moving, as they respond keenly to the account of brotherly love and loss that Louise Erdrich presents in it.

The narrator Lyman loves his brother Henry and tries to help him recover from the shock of his experiences in Vietnam. Lyman wrecks the car, in the hope that Henry will become absorbed in the work of repairing it—which he does, though the narrator learns later that his brother knew that he was being tricked. Erdrich brings out well the intensity of the connection between the brothers, especially toward the close: ". . . I felt something squeezing inside me and tightening and trying to let go all at the same time. I knew I was not just feeling it myself: I knew I was feeling what Henry was going through at that moment. . . ." We notice throughout the sharp-eyed, vivid quality of Lyman's descriptions, as when he tells of Henry's TV-watching:

> He sat in front of it, watching it, and that was the only time he was completely still. But it was the kind of stillness that you see in a rabbit when it freezes and before it will bolt. He was not easy. He sat in his chair gripping the armrests with all his might, as if the chair itself was moving at a high speed and if he let go at all he would rocket forward and maybe crash right through the set.

The phrase "watching it" makes the reader zero in on Henry's numb absorption in the television programs. This was the "only" time he was still, and not just "still," but "completely" still. The "you" engages us even more directly in the scene, and the image of the rabbit brings out Lyman's perception of his brother's panic and fright, and vulnerability and helplessness, even as the same image dramatizes the fact that for Henry there will be no escape from his fearful, disordering memories. Henry "was not easy": He is not easy to be with, because he is not at ease with himself. This short sentence is followed by a longer one that fixes for us Henry's frozen position in the chair, "gripping the armrests" (he is the opposite of being at "rest"), and, through the image of the "rocket," evokes the out-of-control energies that swirl inside Henry and the violent feelings he is barely able to contain—and that eventually will hurl him to his death.

These are small and simple word choices, but we nonetheless point them out to students when we read this passage aloud and comment on it. We want the students to understand how Erdrich is using specific words and images and to perceive how her pacing of sentences increases the tension as she builds toward the fight between the brothers and Henry's death.

As an experiment, we once asked students to imagine that the story ended without its final paragraph. What kind of story would "The Red Convertible" be if it ended, "And I go in"? On one level, the answer to this question is obvious enough: Erdrich wanted to tell her story in the first person, and that would only be possible if Lyman were a survivor. But this choice is itself worth pondering. Why does Erdrich write this story in the first person? Why does she want Lyman to live?—after all, she could have told the story in the third person and ended it with the death of both of the brothers. But Erdrich wanted the first-person form; she wanted *this* voice; and it mattered to her that Lyman not die—which is perhaps in keeping with his uncanny luck in making money that he notes in the first lines of the story.

You might recommend to students three of Erdich's books: *The Beet Queen* (1989); *Tales of Burning Love* (1996); and *Love Medicine*, new and expanded version (1998). For critical commentary, see Peter G. Beidler, *A Reader's Guide to the Novels of Louise Erdrich* (1999).

TOPICS FOR CRITICAL THINKING AND WRITING

1. Did the ending of the story surprise or perhaps even shock you? When you reread the story, what details do you notice that foreshadow the ending?

2. Why does Lyman let the red convertible roll into the river? Why with the lights on?

3. Is the fact that Lyman and Henry are Indians important to the story? Explain.

4. In the first paragraph Lyman speaks of himself in the third person. What is the effect of this device? Taking the story as a whole, how would you characterize the tone of this first-person narrator? Focus on specific phrases and sentences that enable us to know and to understand the narrator and, in particular, the nature of his relationship with his brother.

5. Many authors have written stories or novels about the impact of the Vietnam War on the soldiers who fought in it. What makes Erdrich's story distinctive? What does she accomplish in this story that might lead us to say, "I have read stories about this subject before, but here is something new, something different"?

WILLIAM FAULKNER

A Rose for Emily (p. 367)

The chronology of the story—not very clear on first reading—has been worked out by several writers. Five chronologies are given in M. Thomas Inge, *William Faulkner: "A Rose for Emily"* (1970); a sixth is given in Cleanth Brooks, *William Faulkner: Toward Yoknapatawpha and Beyond* (1978, 382–84). Brooks conjectures that Miss Emily is born in 1852, her father dies around 1884, Homer Barron appears in 1884 or 1885, dies in 1885 or 1886, the delegation calls on Miss Emily about the smell in 1885/86. In 1901 or 1904 or 1905, Miss Emily gives up the lessons in china-painting. Colonel Sartoris dies in 1906 or 1907, the delegation calls on her about the taxes in 1916, and Miss Emily dies in 1926.

The plot, of course, is gothic fiction: a decaying mansion, a mysteriously silent servant, a corpse, necrophilia. And one doesn't want to discard the plot in a search for what it symbolizes, but it is also clear that the story is not only "about" Emily Grierson but also about the South's pride in its past (including its Emily-like effort to hold on to what is dead) and the guilt as well as the grandeur of the past. Inevitably much classroom discussion centers on Miss Emily's character, but a proper discussion of her character entails a discussion of the narrator.

(This next paragraph summarizes an essay on this topic by John Daremo, originally printed in S. Barnet, *A Short Guide to Writing about Literature* [1975].) The unnamed narrator is never precisely identified. Sometimes he seems to be an innocent eye, a recorder of a story whose implications escape him. Sometimes he seems to be coarse. He mentions "old lady Wyatt, the crazy woman," he talks easily of "niggers," and he confesses that because he and other townspeople felt that Miss Emily's family "held themselves a little too high for what they really were," the townspeople "were not pleased exactly, but vindicated" when at thirty she was still unmarried. But if his feelings are those of common humanity (e.g., racist and smug), he at least knows what these feelings are and thus helps us to know ourselves. We therefore pay him respectful attention, and we notice that on the whole he is compassionate (note especially his sympathetic understanding of Miss Emily's insistence for three days that her father is not dead). True, Miss Emily earns our respect by her aloofness and her strength of purpose (e.g., when she publicly appears in the buggy with Homer Barron, and when she cows the druggist and the alderman), but if we speak of her aloofness and her strength of purpose rather than of her arrogance and madness, it is because the narrator's imaginative sympathy guides us. And the narrator is the key to the apparently curious title. Presumably the telling of this tale is itself the rose, the community's tribute (for the narrator insistently speaks of himself as "we") to the intelligible humanity in a woman whose unhappy life might seem monstrous to less sympathetic observers. Another meaning, however, may be offered (very tentatively) for the title. In the story Faulkner emphasizes Miss Emily's attempts to hold on to the past: her insistence, for example, that her father is not dead, and that she has no taxes to pay. Is it possible that Homer Barron's corpse serves as a sort of pressed or preserved will, a reminder of a past experience of love? If so, the title refers to him.

For a feminist reading, see Judith Fetterley, in *The Resisting Reader: A Feminist Approach to American Fiction* (1978), reprinted in *Literary Theories in Praxis*, ed. Shirley F. Staton (1987). Fetterley sees the story as revealing the "sexual conflict" within patriarchy (whether of the South or the North, the old

order or the new). Emily's confinement by her father represents the confinement of women by patriarchy, and the remission of her taxes reveals the depen-
dence of women on men. Emily has been turned into a "Miss," a lady, by a
chivalric attitude that is "simply a subtler and more dishonest version of her
father's horsewhip." The narrator represents a subtle form of this patriarchy.
According to Fetterley, the narrator sees her as "'dear, inescapable, impervious,
tranquil, and perverse'; indeed, anything and everything but human."

Fetterley—the "resisting reader" of her title, i.e., the reader who refuses to
accept that text—argues that the story exposes "the violence done to a woman
by making her a lady; it also explains the particular form of power the victim
gains from this position and can use on those who enact their violence. . . . Like
Ellison's invisible man, nobody sees *Emily*. And because nobody sees *her*, she
can literally get away with murder."

We have enjoyed and learned from the biographies of Faulkner by David
Minter (1980), Joseph Blotner (the one-volume abridgement, 1984, of his
three-volume work), Joel Williamson (1993), and Richard J. Gray (1994).
We have also roamed around in the meticulously detailed biography written
by Frederick R. Karl, but we confess that, at 1,200 pages, it feels long to us.
There are far too many critical studies to mention here. But we will say that
two older books still strike us as good introductions for undergraduate readers: Michael Millgate, *The Achievement of William Faulkner* (1966), and Irving
Howe, *William Faulkner: A Critical Study*, 3rd ed., rev. and expanded (1975).

TOPICS FOR CRITICAL THINKING AND WRITING

1. How valid is the view that the story is an indictment of the decadent
   values of the aristocratic Old South? Or a defense of these values
   (embodied in Emily) against the callousness (embodied in Homer
   Barron) of the North?
2. Suppose Faulkner had decided to tell the story from Miss Emily's point of
   view. Write the first 200 or 300 words of such a version.
3. Characterize the narrator.

WILLIAM FAULKNER

Barn Burning (p. 377)

Against his vision of the ideals of the Confederacy, embodied in Major de
Spain and Colonel Sartoris in much of Faulkner's writing, Faulkner sets his
vision of a more widely held ideal—cunning and self-centeredness—embodied
in the Snopes family. (Flem Snopes, the older brother in "Barn Burning," is a
major character in *The Town, The Mansion,* and *The Hamlet*; Abner Snopes, the
father in "Barn Burning," is a lesser character in *The Unvanquished* and in *The
Hamlet*. But the boy, Colonel Sartoris Snopes, does not appear in the novels.)

It would be wrong, however, to see the Snopes family—and especially,
here, Abner Snopes—as merely contemptible. Abner's single-mindedness,
however unlovely and destructive, gives him a hero's aspect, for example,
when he walks resolutely on toward the great house and refuses to deviate by
even a single step that would enable him to avoid stepping in the horse-
dung. Abner Snopes has, we might say, something of the air of the tragic
hero who, like Job confronted with what seems to be an assault on his

integrity, will maintain his own ways even before God. He has, in Faulkner's words, a "ferocious conviction in the rightness of his own actions." Or, to quote again, a deep sense of the importance of "the preservation of integrity, else breath were not worth the breathing." This second passage, by the way, comes in the discussion of "the niggard blaze" that is part of Snopes's way of life. Coupled with the burning barns, it suggests that Snopes is a Promethean figure—not the Prometheus of the ancients, who gave fire to man out of pity, but a romantic Promethean figure who sets his blaze in defiance of authority.

As we read "Barn Burning" we are reminded of Alfred North Whitehead's comment that tragedy shows us "the remorseless working of things," an action that cannot be stopped, partly because the hero, insisting on asserting himself, is determined that it shall not be stopped. We can scarcely *like* Snopes, but we can scarcely fail to admire (especially in the older sense of "wonder at," "be awed by") him. Indeed, if we compare Major de Spain's justifiable but somewhat fussy anger over the rug ("You must realize you have ruined that rug") with Snopes's smoldering rage at any limitations imposed on him, we may feel that Snopes is by far the more vital figure. One notes, too, and cannot dismiss, Snopes's charge that Major de Spain's big white house has been built out of "sweat. Nigger sweat. Maybe it ain't white enough yet to suit him. Maybe he wants to mix some white sweat with it." We may feel that in large measure Snopes's ruthlessness proceeds from a sense of social inferiority, but we can scarcely deny that he offers a telling criticism of his social superiors.

Finally, a few words about Sarty, the boy. He too is a sort of hero, moved by the most painful kind of conflict—not good with evil but good with good, for he must choose between his sense of decency and his sense of loyalty to the family.

TOPICS FOR CRITICAL THINKING AND WRITING

1. Point of view in "Barn Burning." (Sarty is not the narrator, but we hear the story as the boy perceives it. We enter his mind only; when the language used to present his thoughts is clearly not his own language, it is usually given in italics.)
2. Is Faulkner on Major de Spain's side, or Abner Snopes's, or both, or neither?
3. Is Sarty's action at the end adequately motivated?
4. Imagine a situation in which your loyalty to your family would be severely tested by loyalty to your own values or to society's values. Then set forth what you *hope* you would do, and what you *probably* would do.
5. Many people claim that Faulkner is one of the greatest American writers. Do you think that this story supports such a view? Is this a great story, or a good story?

JACK FORBES

Only Approved Indians Can Play: Made in USA (p. 389)

One way to begin a discussion of this story is to ask students what kind of story they anticipated from the title. What did they expect, and why?

(Consider especially "Approved Indians," and "Made in USA.") Sooner or later, of course, the discussion will shift to the narrator's tone. Recited in a matter-of-fact colloquial voice ("Excitement was pretty high," "A lot of people were betting"—both in the first paragraph), the story for the most part is a goodhearted, farcical, wry narrative, but with the last line (the white BIA official tearfully says, "God Bless America. I think we've won") it becomes evident that the irony is scathing.

By the way, the Bureau of Indian Affairs really does concern itself with "official" Indians. For instance, the Indian Arts and Crafts Law of 1990 defines an Indian as a person of at least one-quarter Indian blood. Only such persons (in the BIA view) can sell their work as a Native American product. Many Native Americans, however, refuse to acknowledge the authority of the BIA and therefore don't seek enrollment in its records.

CHARLOTTE PERKINS GILMAN

The Yellow Wallpaper (p. 391)

In this story the wife apparently is suffering from postpartum depression, and her physician-husband prescribes as a cure the things that apparently have caused her depression: isolation and inactivity. Victorian medical theory held that women—more emotional, more nervous, more fanciful than men—needed special protection if they were to combat lunacy. As Gilman tells us in her autobiography, *The Living of Charlotte Perkins Gilman* (1935), the story (published in 1892) is rooted in the author's experience. After the birth of her child, Gilman became depressed and consulted Dr. S. Weir Mitchell (physician and novelist, named in the story), who prescribed a rest cure: "Live as domestic a life as possible. Have your child with you all the time. Lie down an hour after each meal. Have but two hours intellectual life a day. And never touch pen, brush or pencil as long as you live." Gilman in fact tried this routine for a month, then took a trip to California, where she began writing and recovered nicely. Thinking about Mitchell's plan later, Gilman concluded that such a way of life would have driven her crazy.

Although the prescribed treatment in the story is not exactly Mitchell's, it does seem clear enough that the smug husband's well-intended treatment is responsible for the wife's hallucinations of a woman struggling behind the wallpaper. The narrator is mad (to this degree the story resembles some of Poe's), but she is remarkably sane compared to her well-meaning husband and the others who care for her. Elaine R. Hedges, in the afterword to the edition of *The Yellow Wallpaper* published by the Feminist Press (1973), comments on the narrator:

> At the end of the story the narrator both does and does not identify with the creeping women who surround her in her hallucinations. The women creep through the arbors and lanes along the roads outside the house. Women must creep. The narrator knows this. She has fought as best she could against creeping. In her perceptivity and in her resistance lie her heroism (or heroineism). But at the end of the story, on her last day in the house, as she peels off yards and yards of wallpaper and creeps around the

floor, she has been defeated. She is totally mad. But in her mad sane way she has seen the situation of women for what it is. (53)

Judith Fetterley offers a thoughtful interpretation of Gilman's story in "Reading about Reading" in *Gender and Reading: Essays on Readers, Texts, and Contexts*, ed. Elizabeth A. Flynn and Patrocinio P. Schwieckart (1986). Here (in direct quotation) are some of Fetterley's points, but the entire essay (147–64) should be consulted.

> Forced to read men's texts [i.e., to interpret experience in the way men do], women are forced to become characters in those texts. And since the stories men tell assert as fact what women know to be fiction, not only do women lose the power that comes from authoring: more significantly, they are forced to deny their own reality and to commit in effect a kind of psychic suicide. (159)

> The nameless narrator of Gilman's story has two choices. She can accept her husband's definition of reality [that his version is sane and that her version is mad] . . . or she can refuse to read his text, refuse to become a character in it, and insist on writing her own, behavior for which John will define and treat her as mad. (160)

> Despite the narrator's final claim that she has, like the women in the paper, "got out," she does not in fact escape the patriarchal text. Her choice of literal madness may be as good as or better than the "sanity" prescribed for her by John, but in going mad she fulfills his script and becomes a character in his text. Still, going mad gives the narrator temporary sanity. It enables her to articulate her perception of reality and, in particular, to cut through the fiction of John's love. (163)

> The narrator's solution finally validates John's fiction. In his text, female madness results from work that engages the mind and will; from the recognition and expression of feelings, and particularly of anger; in a word, from the existence of a subjectivity capable of generating a different version of reality from his own. (164–65)

> More insidious still, through her madness the narrator does not simply become the character John already imagines her to be as part of his definition of feminine nature; she becomes a version of John himself. Mad, the narrator is manipulative, secretive, dishonest; she learns to lie, obscure, and distort. (164)

> This desire to duplicate John's text but with the roles reversed determines the narrator's choice of an ending. Wishing to drive John mad, she selects a denouement that will reduce him to a woman seized by a hysterical fainting fit. Temporary success, however, exacts an enormous price, for when John recovers from his faint he will put her in a prison from which there will be no escape. (164)

Of the many feminist readings of the story, perhaps the most widely known is that of Sandra M. Gilbert and Susan Gubar, *The Madwoman in the Attic* (1979). For Gilbert and Gubar, the wallpaper represents "the oppressive structures of the society in which [the narrator] finds herself" (90). The figure behind the wallpaper is the narrator's double, trying to break through.

But Jeanette King and Pam Morris, in "On Not Reading Between the Lines: Models of Reading in 'The Yellow Wallpaper'," *Studies in Short Fiction* 26 (1989): 23–32, raise questions about this interpretation. Their essay, influenced by Lacan, is not easy reading (one finds such terms as "decentered subject," "signified and signifier," "a polysemic potential"), but they present some impressive evidence against the widespread view that the woman behind the paper is "the essential inner psyche which has been trapped by repressive social structures" (25). First, they argue that if the woman indeed is the essential inner psyche, "the breaking free, even if only in the hallucination of madness, ought surely to indicate a more positive movement than the chilling conclusion of the tale suggests" (25). They point out that the wallpaper is not described in terms of "a controlling order"; rather, the narrator says it has "sprawling flamboyant patterns," and it resembles "great slanting waves" that "plunge off at outrageous angles . . . in unheard-of contradictions." For King and Morris, the wallpaper's "energy and fertility are anarchic and lawless, at times aggressive. It displays, that is, an assertive creativity and originality that have no place in the wifely ideal constructed by patriarchal ideology" (29). They therefore interpret it not as a metaphor of a repressive society but as a metaphor of the "forbidden self" (29), "the repressed other" (30). The narrator, seeking to comply with the male ideals, is thus threatened by the wallpaper, and her "attempts to tear down this obdurate wallpaper are not intended . . . to free her from male repression . . . but to eliminate the rebellious self which is preventing her from achieving ego ideal" (30). That is, she wishes to remove the paper (the image of her secret self, which she strives to repress) in order to gain John's approval. "When the woman behind the paper 'gets out,' therefore, this is an image not of liberation but of the victory of the social idea." We get a "grotesque, shameful caricature of female helplessness and submissiveness—a creeping woman." Nevertheless, King and Morris argue, the narrator does indeed have "a desperate triumph . . . : she crawls over her husband" (31).

King and Morris assume that "Jane" (mentioned only near the end of the story) is the narrator, but, like most earlier critics, they do not greatly concern themselves with arguing this point. William Veeder, in "Who Is Jane?," *Arizona Quarterly* 44 (1988): 41–79, does argue the point at length. He writes "By defining a context beyond Poesque horror and clinical case-study, Kolodny, Hedges, and others have convincingly described the heroine's confrontation with patriarchy. What remains to be examined is another source of the heroine's victimization. Herself" (41). Veeder discusses Gilman's difficult childhood (an absent father and a "strict and anxious mother"), and, drawing on Freud and Melanie Klein, argues that the history is not only about a repressive marriage but also about "the traumas wrought by inadequate nurturing in childhood" (71). To escape bondage to men, "Jane moves not forward to the egalitarian utopia of *Herland* but back into the repressive serenity of the maternal womb" (67).

We've had good luck recently with a paper assignment keyed to the final paragraphs of Gilman's story. It takes as its point of departure an observation by Edith Wharton, a contemporary of Gilman's and the author of *The House of Mirth* (1905) and *The Age of Innocence* (1920), who said that in structuring her novels she sought to "make my last page latent in my first."

Wharton wanted her readers, after they had completed the final page, to be able to return to the first chapter and see the sources for the conclusion there: The novel would have a logic that would be developed throughout the story, which would give the whole work its effectiveness and coherence. Ask the class to apply Wharton's statement to the conclusion of "The Yellow Wallpaper" where the narrator "creeps" over her husband. Is Gilman's last page "latent in her first"?

For sources, contexts, and critical commentaries, we recommend *The Yellow Wallpaper: A Bedford Cultural Edition*, ed. Dale M. Bauer (1998), and *Charlotte Perkins Gilman's "The Yellow Wallpaper" and the History of Its Publication and Reception: A Critical Edition and Documentary Casebook*, ed. Julie Bates Dock (1998).

TOPICS FOR CRITICAL THINKING AND WRITING

1. In the next-to-last paragraph the narrator says, "I've got out at last." What does she mean, and in what way (if any) does it make sense?
2. Is the narrator insane at the start of the story, or does she become insane at some point during the narrative? Or can't we be sure? Support your view with evidence from the story.
3. How reliable do you think the narrator's characterization of her husband is? Support your answer with reasons.
4. The narrator says that she cannot get better because her husband is a physician. What do you take this to mean? Do you think the story is about a husband who deliberately drives his wife insane?

PATRICIA GRACE

Flies (p. 402)

This story is about children's play, which means that it is about enthusiasm, about a rule-governed activity, and especially about cruelty.

The enthusiasm is evident, and so is the concern for doing things the right way: "You had to be careful tying the flies"; "They put themselves into teams and had partners;" "You were allowed a new fly if your fly died, but you weren't allowed to stamp on your fly just so that you could get a better one." This last comment makes evident the cruelty too, though it is apparent everywhere in the story. Of course, tormenting flies is scarcely a new activity. Gloster in *King Lear* says, "As flies to wanton boys arer we to the gods: / They kill us for their sport."

It would be inappropriate for us to talk about the origins of the cruelty of children's play, but we want to call attention to the paragraph in which Grace writes,

> But the main thing was *you* were in charge. You could lengthen the cottons to see whose fly could go highest, or you could shorten the cottons to make the flies wild and crazy, pulling and buzzing for their lives. . . . But the flies couldn't go anywhere you didn't want them to go. You were the boss of the flies.

Yet not all of the story so clearly reveals the desire for power by the unempowered. (That the children are empowered is clear enough from their comments about their teacher. But of course all children are especially powerless.) Much of the play seems to result not from cruelty but from sheer exuberance, and from a desire to see what will happen. Consider: "After a while Denny Boy said that they could have a war and that the flies could be soldiers. Good idea." And the children gave medals and words of congratulations to the surviving flies.

The last three paragraphs especially blend exploratory play with cruelty, when the flies are linked into a convoy. "It wasn't easy, and some of the flies died, but at last the convoy was ready." (We are far from the episode of the grove of death in *Heart of Darkness*, where the narrator sees six black men, each fitted with an iron collar, "and all were connected with a chain," but how far?) Grace's narrator says that the children launched the convoy "and off went the flies, crazily, pulling this way and that. It made you laugh your head off. It made you die." Laughing and dying. Bion has a relevant comment: "The boys throw stones at the frogs in sport, but the frogs die not in sport but in earnest." And yet if the ending of Grace's story forces us to see the persistence of the children's cruelty, it also lets us see the children's utter unawareness of their cruelty, and the joy of their playfulness: "Go flies. . . . Up. Goodbye. Go to Jesus. Go to Jesus, flies. Goodbye. . . . Goodbye. . . . Goodbye."

GISH JEN

Who's Irish? (p. 405)

Rather than say much about our own "reading" of this story, we'd like to take this opportunity to talk about the approach that we take to it—an approach that bears on the sorts of lessons about literature and literary study that we highlight and hope to convey to our students. We take this approach most of the time, but especially at the introductory level.

When we teach Gish Jen's story, we focus on the "voice" of its first-person narrator. In all of our classes, we urge students to "ask lots of questions" about what they read, questions large and small that will help them to become active rather than passive readers. "Who's Irish?" is an excellent case study for this question-asking approach, because the voice in it that the author develops is so engaging and interesting to hear and think about.

Start with the title. Encourage the students to linger over it and to consider the kinds of questions it prompts (and it is a question itself, after all) and the expectations that it raises. We may wonder, for example, why Gish Jen, a daughter of Chinese immigrants (so the headnote mentions) would be writing a story that deals with the Irish in some way. And what is the answer to the title's question? That's something we assume we will learn more about as we continue to read.

Ask these and other questions about the title, and remind the students that the title is not only something that opens the story but, further, it is something to which the reader returns after his or her reading of the story is done. How do we respond to the title *then*, when we come back to it?

Once we have made this first foray into question-asking, we read aloud the first paragraph. After we are done, we ask a student to read it aloud. And then another student to do the same.

Sometimes, of course, when teaching a story or poem, we ask a student to do the first reading aloud. But that is both necessary and, on occasion, a little awkward, if it turns out that the student stumbles over an unfamiliar word or two (or three) or a twist of syntax. If you do the first reading, you can give the right pronunciation to words and enable everyone to hear how this or that phrase or sentence is meant to sound. Then, give a couple of the students a chance; it is valuable for them to have the experience of hearing well-written prose as well as silently reading it, and they'll now feel more at ease.

We then work on the first paragraph carefully, asking lots of questions together about the speaker, her tones of voice, her clear and articulate but also somewhat rough relationship to the English language. We zero in on specifics (e.g., "I am work hard my whole life") and on more general matters (e.g., Why might Gish Jen have chosen a first-person narrator? Why not present this character from a third-person point of view?).

Again, the goal is to help students realize that they need never feel at a loss for material for an in-class writing assignment or an essay they have been assigned. We seek to get them to understand that none of us can simply wait for something to pop out at us from the page; we have to do the creative and critical question-asking that generates the ideas, issues, puzzles, etc., that provide us with the material we need to sift through, develop, and organize.

In a way, this is what happens when a student comes to see us in conference about his or her paper on a poem or story or play. We ask lots of questions of them: So are you claiming that . . . ? Have you thought about how the scene when . . . fits into your argument? What's your take on the bitter tone of the middle section of the story? All of us do this with and for our students—it's why conferences are so important for them. But ultimately the trick is to equip the student to carry on that conversation with himself or herself.

Once we have finished up with Gish Jen's first paragraph, we then move to the final paragraph. We want the students to be asking, How does the speaker sound *here*, and how is her voice the same and yet different from the voice when we encountered it in the first paragraph? More broadly: What has transpired between here and there? What occupies the large middle of the story, *this* story with *this* beginning and *this* ending?

Then we back away a bit from the analytical labors that we have performed. A final question we ask of the students: Did you enjoy this story?

Perhaps we are not obliged to raise this question, but it is good, we think, to do so after an intense period of analysis and explication. Students often acknowledge that analytical work on a piece of literature will indeed make it more interesting, more stimulating, more enjoyable. But there will be some students in the room who feel, or believe that they should feel, that interpreting a story (and going on and on about it) spoils it, drains the pleasure from the experience. Keep in mind this possible objection (or, as it is with some of our students, this silently held but strong view), and see what you can do to circumvent (that is, to disprove) it.

You want the students to hear you saying, or sense that you are implying, all the time: "Yes, we are here in a literature classroom, studying this story or that poem in an academic setting. That means we will be treating it differently from a poem or story we might read on our own. But we still are looking for pleasure, for enjoyment, from literature, and in fact expect that the better interpreters (the better question-askers) we become, the richer our pleasure in literature will be."

Students interested in Gish Jen might visit Voices from the Gaps: Women Writers of Color: Gish Jen (http://voices.cla.umn.edu/vg/Bios/entries/jen_gish. html). This site includes biography, criticism, selected bibliography, and related links.

JAMES JOYCE

Araby (p. 412)

Probably the best discussion of "Araby" remains one of the earliest, that of Cleanth Brooks and Robert Penn Warren in various editions of *Understanding Fiction*. Among more recent discussions, L. J. Morrissey, "Joyce's Narrative Strategies in 'Araby,'" *Modern Fiction Studies* 28 (1982): 45–52, is especially good.

Students have difficulty with the story largely because they do not read it carefully enough. They scan it for what happens (who goes where) and do not pay enough attention to passages in which (they think) "nothing is happening." But when students read passages aloud in class, for instance, the first three paragraphs, they *do* see what is going on (that is, they come to understand the boy's mind) and enjoy the story very much. To help them hear the romantic boy who lives in what is (from an adult point of view) an unromantic society, it is especially useful to have students read aloud passages written in different styles. Compare, for instance, "At night in my bedroom and by day in the classroom her image came between me and the page I strove to read" with "I asked for leave to go to the bazaar on Saturday night. My aunt was surprised and hoped it was not some Freemason affair."

That the narrator is no longer a boy is indicated by such passages as the following:

. . . her name was like a summons to all my foolish blood.

Her name sprang to my lips at moments in strange prayers and praise which I myself did not understand. My eyes were often full of tears (I could not tell why).

What innumerable follies laid waste my waking and sleeping thoughts. . . .

Morrissey points out that in addition to distancing himself from his past actions by such words as "foolish" and "follies" (and, at the end of the story, "vanity"), the narrator distances himself from the boy he was by the words "imagined" and "seemed," words indicating that his present view differs from his earlier view.

The narrator recounts a story of disillusionment. The first two paragraphs clearly establish the complacent middle-class world into which he is born—the houses "conscious of decent lives within them" gaze with "imperturbable faces." This idea of decency is made concrete by the comment in the second paragraph that the priest's charity is evident in his will: He left all of his money to institutions and his furniture to his sister. (Probably even the sister was so decent that she too thought this was the right thing to do.) Morrissey, interpreting the passage about the priest's will differently, takes the line to be the boy's innocent report of "what must have been an ironic comment by adults."

As a boy he lived in a sterile atmosphere, a sort of fallen world:

- The house is in a "blind," or dead-end, street.
- The rooms are musty.
- The priest had died (religion is no longer vital?).
- A bicycle pump, once a useful device, now lies rusty and unused under a bush in the garden.
- An apple tree stands in the center of the garden in this fallen world.
- Nearby are the odors of stable and garbage dumps.

Nevertheless the boy is quickened by various things, for instance, by the yellow pages of an old book, but especially by Mangan's sister (who remains unnamed, perhaps to suggest that the boy's love is spiritual). He promises to visit "Araby" (a bazaar) and to return with a gift for her.

The boy for a while moves through a romantic, religious world:

- He sees her "image."
- He imagines that he carries a "chalice."
- He hears the "litanies" and "chanting" of vendors.
- He utters "strange prayers."

Delayed by his uncle, whose inebriation is indicated by the uncle's "talking to himself" and by "the hall-stand rocking" (his parents seem not to be living; notice the emphasis on the boy's isolation throughout the story, e.g., his ride alone in the car of the train), he hears the clerks counting the day's receipts—moneychangers in the temple.

"The light was out. The upper part of the hall was now completely dark." The darkness and the preceding trivial conversations of a girl and two young men reveal—Joyce might have said epiphanize—the emptiness of the world. The boy has journeyed to a rich, exotic (religious?) world created by his imagination and has found it cold and trivial, as dead as the neighborhood he lives in.

The boy's entry through the shilling entrance rather than through the sixpenny (children's) entrance presumably signals his coming of age.

This brief discussion of "Araby" of course seems reasonable to its writer, even the remarks that the rusty bicycle pump suggests a diminished world, and that the entry through the shilling entrance rather than the sixpenny entrance suggests, implies, or even—though one hesitates to use the word—symbolizes (along with many other details) his initiation into an adult view. But how far can (or should) one press the details? An article in *James Joyce Quarterly* 4 (1967): 85–86 suggests that the pump under the bushes stands for the serpent in the garden. Is there a difference between saying that the rusty pump—in the context of the story—puts a reader in mind of a diminished (deflated) world, and saying that it stands for the serpent? Is one interpretation relevant, and the other not? Students might be invited to offer their own views on how far to look for "meaning" or "symbols" in this story, or in any other story. They might also be advised to read—but not necessarily to swallow—the brief discussions of symbolism in the text and in the glossary.

When teaching Joyce's stories, we turn often to the textual glosses in *Dubliners: Text, Criticism, and Notes*, ed. Robert Scholes and A. Walton Litz (1969); Don Gifford, *Joyce Annotated: Notes for Dubliners and A Portrait of the Artist as a Young Man* (2nd ed., 1982); and, especially, John Wyse Jackson and Bernard McGinley, *James Joyce's Dubliners: An Illustrated Edition* (1993), which includes many helpful drawings, maps, and photographs.

TOPICS FOR CRITICAL THINKING AND WRITING

1. Joyce wrote a novel called *A Portrait of the Artist as a Young Man*. Write an essay of about 500 words on "Araby" as a portrait of the artist as a boy.
2. In an essay of about 500 words, consider the role of images of darkness and blindness and what they reveal to us about "Araby" as a story of the fall from innocence into painful awareness.
3. How old, approximately, is the narrator of "Araby" at the time of the experience he describes? How old is he at the time he tells his story? On what evidence do you base your estimates?
4. The boy, apparently an only child, lives with an uncle and aunt, rather than with parents. Why do you suppose Joyce put him in this family setting rather than some other?
5. The story is rich in images of religion. This in itself is not surprising, for the story is set in Roman Catholic Ireland, but the religious images are not simply references to religious persons or objects. In an essay of 500 to 750 words, discuss how these images reveal the narrator's state of mind

FRANZ KAFKA

A Hunger Artist (p. 417)

The events of this story are recorded so reasonably and the characters are (in a way) so recognizable that much of the story seems to report the commonplace. And yet, of course, the story necessarily strikes a reader as incredible, and one searches this fantastic tale for some sort of allegorical meaning.

The title suggests that it may be about art or the role of the artist, and most interpretations begin with the idea that it is about the alienated artist of the twentieth century, the difficulty of the artist in a coarse world. But one can hardly publish an essay that says only this, and so, if one is writing about "A Hunger Artist," one begins to work out a more specific interpretation, a detailed allegorical reading of Kafka's highly concrete world. All right, the hunger artist and the public may be clear enough, but what does the cage stand for? The impresario? The position of the hunger artist's cage near the managerie? The "raw lumps of flesh" that are fed to the beasts? The panther? And almost as soon as a critic—whether an undergraduate or a professional— offers answers to these self-imposed questions, readers find the essay forced and dreadfully reductive. (This manual, in briefly talking about "The Parable of the Prodigal Son," mentioned that medieval interpretations press the parable too hard, assuming that every detail has an equivalent. Interpretations of Kafka tend to share this approach.)

If the most common interpretation is that the story is about the plight of the artist—perhaps especially the artist in the twentieth century—isolated in (and rejected by) a philistine world, there are at least two others, and there is no reason why the story can't include all three. A second interpretation is that "A Hunger Artist" is about the alienation of the spiritual man, perhaps a distinctive alienation that began in the Renaissance; and a third interpretation holds that the story is about the defeat of humanity's idealistic nature (the hunger artist) by the physical (the panther).

Before commenting briefly on the second and third views, let's spend another moment on the first. One might begin by asking, In what way is the hunger artist an artist? An artist is someone who is imaginative, skilled, and creative, but what does the hunger artist create? As soon as one asks this question, however, one is tempted to withdraw it, since it is exactly the sort of question a philistine would ask any artist. The hunger artist apparently regards himself as a creator, for he hopes to engage in a fast "beyond human imagination." Further, like most (all?) artists, he is self-compelled to do what he does: "I have to fast, I can't help it." In the next-to-last paragraph he says, to our amazement, that he would have eaten if he had found any food he had liked. Perhaps here we get the (romantic) idea that the artist's gift is a curse, isolating him from the normal pleasures of the world. He is like the poet in Coleridge's "Kubla Khan," nourished by the milk of Paradise. Finally, one notices that although the hunger artist scorns the world, he nevertheless desperately wants to be appreciated, appreciated for the right reasons: "I always wanted you to admire my fasting." (But this is complicated when, only two sentences later, he says, "But you shouldn't admire it.") He can compel people to look at him, but he cannot compel them to understand what he offers, or to give him the nourishment of valuing it. In summary, we might say that the hunger artist, like other artists, feels he has a vision to offer to society, and if he feels superior to that society, he nevertheless also hungers for its approval.

The religious interpretation is most vigorously set forth by Harry Steinhauer, in an article in *Criticism* [4 (Winter 1962): 28–43]. Steinhauer categorically (and unnecessarily) rejects the idea that the story is in any way about the role of the artist. Rather, he says, it is "a clear allegory . . . of the fate that has overtaken religion since about the Renaissance." The hunger artist, in this view, is the ascetic saint who is displaced by the materialism of organized religion. Steinhauer probably was the first person to emphasize certain details that cannot be ignored, for instance, that the hunger artist's longest fast, forty days, was the length of the fasts of Moses and Jesus. Still, Steinhauer seems to go needlessly far in insisting that the story is only about the decline of religion.

The third view mentioned above (and ineptly summarized as "the defeat of humanity's idealistic nature by the physical") is usually developed without the insistence on detailed allegory that accompanies the first view. At its broadest, the idea is that in the hunger artist we see a person—not necessarily an artist—in a certain psychological state, a person consumed with a lofty vision, but (psychologically) living in an alien society. Richard Sheppard offers this interpretation in *German Quarterly* [46 (March 1973): 219–233]. Society for a while bestows its attention on the visionary, but then loses interest and turns its attention to a symbol of life, the panther who loves food, who is full of athletic energy, and who, though caged, seems free. "Seems," of course, is an important word here; Kafka does not let us give full approval to the life of the panther.

It is unusual to point out that Kafka had good reason to feel alienated: He was a Jew in a Gentile world, a German speaker in Prague, a son neurotically estranged from his authoritative father, a victim of tuberculosis, a literary man in a bourgeois society, and a writer who urged his literary executor to destroy his unpublished writing.

TOPICS FOR CRITICAL THINKING AND WRITING

1. Why the hunger *artist*, rather than, say, the hunger *man*, or even the *hungerer*? In what ways is the hunger artist an artist, or like an artist?
2. How sympathetic a figure is the hunger artist?
3. What do you make of the statement that "he was working honestly, but the world was cheating him of his reward"?
4. What do you make of the hunger artist's statement, in the next-to-last paragraph, that he would have eaten if he could have found food that he liked?

   I couldn't find the food I liked. If I had found it, believe me, I should have made no fuss and stuffed myself like you or anyone else.

   Has he become deranged from too long a fast? Or what?
5. Why does the public lose interest in the hunger artist and shift its interest to the panther?
6. What effect is gained by withholding all dialogue until the last two paragraphs?

JACK LONDON

To Build a Fire (p. 423)

London wrote an earlier story with this same title for a boys' magazine called *The Youth's Companion* (1902). Earle Labor and King Hendricks reprint it as an appendix to an article on the two stories [*Studies in Short Fiction* 4 (1966–67): 334–47]. The first version, in which the man succeeds in building a fire but carries lifelong scars of frostbite, has two strong morals: "Never travel alone" and "Pay attention to the advice of your elders." Labor and Hendricks characterize this version as an *exemplum*, a story that subordinates atmosphere and characterization to didactic explicitness.

   The revision of 1907 (published in 1908), more than twice the length of the earlier version, is really a new story. It not only changes the ending but drops the explicit moralizing, or at least alters the emphasis, turning from the simple point that one needs a companion to the more subtle point that one needs "imagination." We are told that the man "was quick and alert in the things of life, but only in the things, and not in the significances." Thus the extreme cold "did not lead him to meditate upon his frailty as a creature of temperature, and upon man's frailty in general."

   The story, using only one character and one setting, is something of a tour de force; the dog serves as a sort of second character, for the dog (which instinctively knows that there is not the time to travel) lets us see how a creature should behave when confronted with this aspect of nature. (Nature, by the way, is not hostile here, only unyielding. The man dies not because nature toys with him, or because existence is absurd, but because he does not take the proper precautions.) Then, too, at the end when the dog trots off to find some other provider of food and fire, we get a glimpse of life going on, indifferent to any one person.

Labor and Hendricks, saying that the use of the dog as a "reflector" (Henry James's term) is "the masterpiece of London's revised version," make the obvious point that the dog serves as a foil to the man. The dog's "natural wisdom of conduct is juxtaposed against the foolish rationality of his master's behavior." More controversial is their claim that the man's dealings with the dog show that the man has no sense of "true comradeship." Labor and Hendricks go so far as to say that the man's "inner coldness correlates with the enveloping outer cold. And there is a grim but poetic justice in his fate."

Earle Labor discusses the story again in his book, *Jack London* (1974), where he treats it as an Aristotelian tragedy:

> It is a representation of an action that is serious, whole, complete, and of a certain magnitude. . . . The protagonist, neither an especially good man nor an especially bad man, falls into misfortune because of a tragic flaw, notably hubris: an overweening confidence in the efficacy of his own rational faculties. . . . The narrator [when commenting on the man's failure to think about the meaning of fifty degrees below zero] functions as the chorus, who mediates between the action and the reader and who provides moral commentary upon the action.

Labor goes on to argue that "also in keeping with the tragic mode is the sense of inevitability in the catastrophe," and that there is irony in the man's premature self-congratulation when he thinks, "Those old-timers were rather womanish, some of them. . . . All a man had to do was to keep his head, and he was all right." And when the fire in effect extinguishes itself by precipitating an avalanche from the snow-laden tree, there is a reversal (Aristotle's *peripeteia*) and a discovery (*anagnorisis*). London writes,

> The man was shocked. It was as though he had just heard his own sentence of death. For a moment he sat and stared at the spot where the fire had been. Then he grew very calm. Perhaps the old-timer on Sulphur Creek was right. If he had only had a trail mate he would have been in no danger now. The trail mate could have built the fire.

Labor concludes his discussion of the Aristotelian qualities in the story by saying that "the man achieves true heroic stature; and his tragic action inspires both pity and fear in leading his audience toward the cathartic relief prescribed by Aristotle."

London of course drew in part on his firsthand knowledge of the klondike, but he also drew on a book, Jeremiah Lynch's *Three Years in the Klondike* (1904). Lynch's account of a man who dies because he cannot build a fire is reprinted in Franklin Walker, *Jack London and the Klondike* (1966).

BOBBIE ANN MASON

Shiloh (p. 434)

Writers in all periods have occasionally used the historical present in telling stories (Katherine Anne Porter, for example, used it for "Flowering Judas"), but in America in our century—until the early 1970s—few storytellers used it, except for melodramatic historians eager to convey a sense of immediacy: "The German armies march into Paris. . . ." At first glance it seems that Updike uses the present in "A & P," a story whose opening line is this: "In walks these three girls in nothing but bathing suits." But Updike uses a first-person narrator, who occasionally talks in a sort of "So he says to me . . . and I says to him" manner.

Exactly why so many writers in the 1970s and 1980s used the present tense (Mason wrote her story in 1982) is not clear, but some explanations attribute its widespread use to television, film, the new journalism, and drugs. But what sort of useful generalization can one make about the effect of this device? Usually it is said that the present adds realism and immediacy, but such an assertion is dubious.

Still, it seems true that contemporary writers who narrate in the present usually write in what can be called a plain style; i.e., they use (for instance) little subordination, few words with strong connotations, and few figures of speech. (In fact, in "Shiloh" Mason uses more figures than are commonly found in fiction of its type.) Such writing often seems "flat," lacking in energy, free from value judgments, uninvolved. Sample:

> When Leroy gets home from the shopping center, Norma Jean's mother, Mabel Beasley, is there. Until this year, Leroy has not realized how much time she spends with Norma Jean. When she visits, she inspects the closets and then the plants, informing Norma Jean when a plant is droopy or yellow. Mabel calls the plants "flowers," although there are never any blooms. She always notices if Norma Jean's laundry is piling up.

The narrator is just reporting on what passes before his or her eyes, not responding or evaluating. In "Shiloh," after the first surprising sentence ("Norma Jean is working on her pectorals"), almost no sentence seems to have been written to give the reader a special little thrill. But this is only to say that Mason writes the story in an appropriate style, since the story is about confused, almost numbed people, people whose lives (like their child) seem to have died, people who can't make out who they are, what they are, or even where they are:

> Now that Leroy has come home to stay, he notices how much the town has changed. Subdivisions are spreading across western Kentucky like an oil slick. The sign at the edge of town says "Pop: 11,500"—only seven hundred more than it said twenty years before. Leroy can't figure out who is living in all the new houses. The farmers who used to gather around the courthouse square on Saturday afternoons to play checkers and spit tobacco juice have gone. It has been years since Leroy has thought about the farmers, and they have disappeared without his noticing.

Perhaps when storytellers customarily used the past tense they were (to some degree) implying that something had happened, was over and done with, and they were reporting on it because they thought they had made something out of it; further, they thought that what had happened and what they had made out of it were worth reporting. Perhaps when writers use the present tense they are (to some degree) implying that "such-and-such is passing in front of my eyes, I'm telling you about it, but I am not able to interpret it any more than the participants themselves are able to." In any case, "Shiloh" is obviously a story about a man and wife who don't know what to make of each other or of themselves. Leroy has his kits and his hope of building a real log cabin, and Norma Jean has her weights, her music, her cooking, and her English composition course, but none of these things provides a center. There was once a marriage, and there was once a baby, but the baby died and the marriage has fallen apart. This is not at all the world that existed when Leroy and Norma Jean got married; it's a new world, a world in which women engage in weight lifting, men engage in needlepoint, and a doctor's son pushes dope. It's all very confusing, especially to Leroy.

Mabel, Norma Jean's mother, thinks things can be as they were in the past (Norma Jean should be a dutiful daughter and not smoke, Leroy and Norma Jean should go on a second honeymoon—to Shiloh, where Mabel went on her honeymoon), but of course there is no going back to the way things were. The trip to Shiloh proves to be a disaster. Norma Jean walks away from Leroy, leaving him to realize that he doesn't understand his wife, himself, or their marriage. He remembers some events, but

he knows he is leaving out a lot. He is leaving out the insides of history. History was always just names and dates to him. It occurs to him that building a house out of logs is similarly empty—too simple.

Early in the story, when we first hear about Leroy's interest in kits, we are told that "Leroy has grown to appreciate how things are put together" (that's the way he sees it, of course), but at the end of the story we see that he has no idea of how the pieces of his life can be put together.

A few words about the names "Leroy" and "Norma Jean." Some readers suggest that Leroy (French for "the king") puts us in mind of Elvis Presley. Further, they say, the name evokes an image of a romantic knight errant, now reduced to a maimed man who does needlepoint of a scene from *Star Trek* while his truck rusts. Norma Jean of course evokes Marilyn Monroe.

For Mabel, Shiloh has the pleasant associations of a honeymoon, and she thinks that the happiness she experienced at Shiloh can now be transferred to Leroy and Norma Jean. But Shiloh, though now a site for picnics, was a scene of vast destruction, and it is at Shiloh that Leroy sees that his marriage has come apart.

(The Battle of Shiloh took its name from Shiloh Church, a meeting house at the site. The church was named for the ancient Hebrew sanctuary about ten miles north of Bethel. It is thought that the word means "tranquility," so the name adds irony to the story.)

We admire Mason's novels, *In Country* (1985) and *Spence and Lila* (1988), but value her short stories, in *Shiloh and Other Stories* (1982) and *Love Life: Stories* (1989), even more. For studies of "Shiloh," see Leslie White, "The Function of Popular Culture in Bobbie Ann Mason's *Shiloh and Other Stories* and *In Country*," *Southern Quarterly* 26 (Summer 1988): 69–79, and Barbara Henning, "Minimalism and the American Dream: 'Shiloh' by Bobbie Ann Mason and 'Preservation' by Raymond Carver," *Modern Fiction Studies* 35 (Winter 1989): 689–98. Andrew Levy devotes a chapter to "Shiloh"—really to Mason's kind of writing—in *The Culture and Commerce of the American Short Story* (1993).

TOPICS FOR CRITICAL THINKING AND WRITING

1. Whose feelings—Leroy's or Norma Jean's—are more fully presented in the story? Do we know exactly what Norma Jean wants? Do you think that she herself knows?

2. The story is written in the present tense, for instance, "Leroy Moffitt's wife, Norma Jean, is working on her pectorals," rather than (as would be more common in fiction) ". . . was working on her pectorals." What is gained by using the present in this story?

3. Why is Leroy preoccupied with kits, and why is Norma Jean so eagerly attempting to improve her body and her mind?

4. When we first meet Mabel, Norma Jean's mother, we learn that she has made "an off-white dust ruffle for the bed." Leroy jokes about it, and Mason refers to it in the last line of the story, a place of great emphasis. Why this business about a dust ruffle for a bed?

5. Why does Norma Jean leave Leroy?

6. Do you think "Shiloh" is a good title? Why?

GUY DE MAUPASSANT

Mademoiselle (p. 444)

Anthologists who want to include a story by Maupassant surely have a duty to find something other than the grotesquely over-anthologized "Necklace." We browsed through his stories and came upon "Mademoiselle," a story that we find both moving and puzzling. To the best of our knowledge this story about gender-identity has not been anthologized in any book comparable to ours.

What do we make of the story? We are inclined to think that the chief point is this: Society (beginning with the boy's mother) has made him into what at first sight might seem to be a cross-dresser. That is, the family has dressed this delicate, weak boy in girl's clothing, and the rest of society follows, giving him approval in this guise. The boy accepts the role, perhaps partly because he is simple, but chiefly, we imagine, because the role provides him with the warmth (approval and affection) that he needs. He accepts this role, and so does society (the family, and the whole village). Why does society accept it? The boy is mentally and perhaps physically unusual for a male, and society therefore finds it convenient to treat him as something other than a male. Those around him give him a feminine identity, and, to repeat, he responds by acting out a feminine gender role. Notice, however, that in the middle of the story we are told that "he thought more of his nickname than he did of his dress." The story clearly is not about someone who is sexually excited by wearing clothes of the opposite sex, but rather is (up to this point) about a young man who finds apparent satisfaction in a role society creates for him.

By accepting the role that society has given to him, he gets the warmth that a human being requires. When, however, he dresses like a boy, society rejects him. His use of male clothing

> created quite a disturbance in the neighborhood, for the people who had been in the habit of smiling at him kindly when he was dressed as a woman, looked at him in astonishment and almost in fear, while the indulgent could not help laughing, and visibly making fun of him.

The distress of the community when it sees male clothing on a female-like person is paralleled by the distress of the boy: "Suppose that, after all, I am a girl?"

The boy knew before that he was not a girl, and that he was "in disguise," but he did not fully understand what the disguise consisted of. He thought it was a matter only of clothing, yet when he wears male clothing the disguise does not end: "He had totally lost all masculine looks and ways."

Later in the story he makes a second attempt to assert his maleness, this time when he tries to have sex with Josephine. She screams (understandably), and he is seized (again understandably). Society for a second time will not let him assert or express his masculinity. And in fact, this attempt to confirm his sex is no more successful than was the exchange of female clothes for male clothes. Each of his attempts to declare his biological nature encounters difficulty: Society is angry when he prances in male garb, and society is angry when he attacks Josephine. Both events imply a tragic side to the old collusion between the boy and the world around him, to call him "Mademoiselle." That is, it robbed him of the ability to bring his behavior in line with his biological nature.

In our view, the story is largely about the way in which society establishes gender (masculine or feminine behavior). Gender usually corresponds with external genitals, but in this case society has (for its own reasons) preferred to see the boy as feminine, and the boy for a while has acquiesced. After he finds (by observing couples, and in the encounter with Josephine) his erotic orientation, he learns that he is locked into the wrong gender.

We offer this reading with some hesitancy (and only after we have modified it in line with discussions with Professor Donald Stone, a specialist in French literature), since we don't quite know what to make of certain passages in the story. For instance, although the boy says that he dresses like a girl "only . . . for a joke," he also says, "But if I dress like a lad, I shall no longer be a girl; and then, *I am a girl*" (our italics). Still, although we find a contradiction between these passages, we think that the statement (already quoted) that he values his nickname more than his dress clearly indicates that the dress itself is of only minor importance to him; it does not in itself give him pleasure, but it is the means whereby he gets approval from the community.

The story ends with the boy asserting his maleness. It does not tell us what happened thereafter, that is, whether (for example) from that time onward he refused to wear female clothing, or (again, for example) whether society continued to treat him as a girl. Donald Stone finds the dark irony thoroughly in Maupassant's vein. He points out that there is even a similarity with Maupassant's "Necklace," in which a woman, eager to shine (see also the boy's quest for affection), borrows a diamond necklace, loses it, spends much of the rest of her life in efforts to pay for it, and at last finds out that the necklace was of no value.

Students might be invited to write a paragraph to be added to the ending, or to write an essay explaining why the present ending is preferable.

Developing an insight of Henry James's, the novelist Wallace Stegner has noted: "Maupassant saw with great clarity the small characteristic, the tiny episode, the telling relationship, the perverted motive, and he focused on it— wrung it, as James said, 'either until it grimaces or until it bleeds.'"

Much of the best critical work on Maupassant's stories and novels is in French—for example, A. Vial, *Guy de Maupassant et l'art du roman* (1954); but Edward D. Sullivan, *Maupassant the Novelist* (1972) is helpful. For biography: Francis Steegmuller, *Maupassant: A Lion in the Path* (1949). Henry James's keen study of Maupassant is included in *Partial Portraits* (1888), and has been reprinted, along with a second shorter piece, in the Library of America's two-volume collection of James's critical writings (1984).

GUY DE MAUPASSANT

The Necklace (p. 447)

This story apparently remains a favorite among instructors and students, though perhaps because (at least for many readers) it is a story they love to hate. When we typed "Maupassant necklace" into a search engine, a couple of student essays came up, including one by someone—presumably an undergraduate—named Gregory Weston. His essay ends thus:

> I earlier compared "The Necklace" with "Cinderella," but the story reminds me more of the myth of Icaris [sic]. Mathilde wanted more then [sic] what was given to her and used her natural talents to get what she aspired to. She did, and her only crime was trying to fly too [sic] high. Maupassant delights in melting her wings, and then cheapens her fall with his "ironic twist" at the end. Why someone would write such a vicious and cynical story is beyond me.

Why someone would post such an essay is beyond us, but, come to think of it, instructors might well start a class discussion by distributing copies of this paragraph and inviting comment. Does Mathilde "use her natural talents" to get what she aspires to? Does Maupassant "delight" in reducing her? Is the story "vicious and cynical"?

A second essay that we found on the Internet is an anonymous piece entitled "Diamonds and Paste: A Marxist Reading of Guy de Maupassant's 'The Necklace.'" There is absolutely nothing Marxist about it, other than that it talks about "class distinction," "the social ladder," and "different economic classes." That is, it reveals no understanding of Marxist views of the role of the artist in bourgeois society or of class relationships. Here is the final paragraph:

> This story illustrates the different perspectives on value that are created by different economic classes. Value is viewed differently by different classes because of their different perspectives. The couple in the story would not have had to go into so much debt if they had simply realised that the necklace might not have much monetary value. Their social class made them believe that only expensive things are valuable and this brought them down.

Are we to understand that only lower-middle-class people "believe that only expensive things are valuable" and that, for instance, Mme. Loisel's rich friend holds a different view?

We confess that "The Necklace" is not our favorite Maupassant story, but we do think it is far richer than these two essayists indicate. Yes, the heart of the story is the ironic twist, the idea that the couple engaged in ten years of needless drudgery, that a moment or two of humiliating confession would have spared them a decade of slavery. But Maupassant is convincing in his swift characterization, for instance, in the husband's "triumphant air" (paragraph 7) when he presents the invitation to his wife, in the wife's unexpected (but to us natural) expression of "disdain" (11), in the husband's embarrassment that he had not thought about what she might wear to the affair (15–18), in the wife's "intoxication" at the ball (54) and then her shame as she leaves, dressed in the "modest wraps of common life" rather than in the furs of the other women (55). We might notice, too, Maupassant's unsentimental (is it cynical—or merely realistic?) statement that her years of drudgery coarsened her ("she went to the fruiterer, the grocer, the butcher, her basket on her arm, bargaining, insulted, defending her miserable money sou by sou").

All these skillful touches of characterization raise the story to a level far above a merely ironic anecdote. Notice, too, how Maupassant darkens the tale when the couple leave the ball, first by the wife's thoughts about her wraps, then by the difficulty they have in finding a cab. From here on, things go downhill swiftly. In class one might talk about the ways in which Maupassant from the very beginning prepares for the outcome. For instance, the very first paragraph speaks of "destiny," more specifically of "a mistake of destiny." Admittedly a reader does not put much weight on this phrase at first but on rereading, it takes on significance. There is something odd, something almost unnatural or freakish, Maupassant suggests, in the fact that this pretty, charming girl was born into the class she finds herself. Further in this paragraph we are told that "she let herself be married to a little clerk," that is, she seems to have no will of her own; her fate is settled for her. And surely we all realize that although we feel we are acting freely, chance plays an enormous part in our lives: Had we gone to a different college, we might well now have a different spouse, and we might be engaged in a different career. And (unless we smoke cigarettes) we do not choose to fall ill or to die the way we will die. And—nagging thought—had our parents not met (an act that was not of our doing), we would not be here, thinking these thoughts. For the most part we feel as though our actions are free—we may think we are the captain of our fate, the master of our soul—but most of us probably recognize that in many ways we are puppets. A good deal of proverbial wisdom holds this view: Man proposes, God disposes; *che sarà sarà* (what will be will be); *ça ira* (it will go its own way—supposedly said by Benjamin Franklin about the American Revolution, when he was in Paris in 1776–77).

Our point is, in brief, that Maupassant's characterization is convincing (the people behave plausibly) and that the overarching idea is scarcely shocking: Our mistakes, sometimes rooted in a combination of our character and bad luck, can be catastrophic. If Mme. Loisel out of pride borrows jewelry, loses it, and later makes the mistake of not admitting that she has lost it, all three actions are entirely intelligible to us—we might do exactly what she has done. As for disastrous mistakes, well, if we haven't made them ourselves, we know of other people who have. Further, even as we say, "Why *of course* X *should* have done such-and-such," we realize that X (for whatever reasons) couldn't have done it, or perhaps didn't do it because there seemed to be no need to do it at the time.

Still, it might be worth asking students whether they do indeed find the story "cruel." One could ask them, even more generally, what it means for an author to treat his or her characters cruelly.

What's behind this question is a common fact of the students' experience as readers—that characters in novels and stories can take on for them and, for that matter, for us a life of their own, a life that we feel keenly interested in and that—so compelling does the illusion seem—we believe the writer himself or herself should not interfere with. The character is, on the one hand, the writer's creation, yet, on the other hand, the character enters into the reader's imagination as more than that, as an independent person rather than as something that the writer controls. There is a magic and mystery in the creation of a literary character that teachers are sometimes hesitant to admit to, but that they, and certainly their students, respond to when caught up in the story of, for example, Emma Woodhouse, Jane Eyre, or Anna Karenina.

Thus, when a writer seems to us to be imposing an unfair fate on a character we care about, a fate that the character does not deserve or that is not in keeping with his or her nature, or that makes the character no more than a victim, we may be led to protest that the author or story is a cruel one. Again, this touches on a dimension of the students' experiences as readers, and perhaps the analysis of "The Necklace" can invite some discussion of it.

Here are some questions we have raised in class, with our responses to the questions.

1. *What do we learn about Mme. Loisel from the first six paragraphs of the story? What is your response to the narrator's generalizations about women in paragraph 2?*

All generalizations are suspect (including even William Blake's assertion that "To generalize is to be an idiot"), but we find something attractive in the narrator's comment that "Natural fineness, instinct for what is elegant, suppleness of wit, are the sole hierarchy," and in his comment that lowborn women may thus be the equals of great ladies. In this period, with very few exceptions women had no way of rising, other perhaps than by selling their bodies, and so we take Maupassant to be asserting that even though a woman may be of low status, she make indeed be the mental equivalent of "the very greatest ladies."

2. *Is Maupassant's point that Mme. Loisel is justly punished for her vanity and pride? What about her husband and the impact of the apparent loss of the necklace on his life?*

We don't think so. Yes, she shows traces of vanity and pride, but what kind of justice requires that vanity be sentenced to ten years at hard labor?

3. *In paragraph 98, as Mme. Loisel decides she must pay the debt, Maupassant writes: "She took her part, moreover, all of a sudden, with heroism." Why the word "heroism"? Isn't this a strange way to characterize Mme. Loisel's behavior?*

We are glad that Maupassant used this word. Up to now, Mme. Loisel has exhibited petulance, vanity, and some other less-than-attractive qualities, though she has certainly not been villainous. Now, confronted with adversity, we are heartened to see her accept responsibility: "She took her part, moreover, all of a sudden, with heroism. That dreadful debt must be paid. She would pay it." And so she begins a decade of hard work, in which she comes to know "the horrible existence of the needy." Notice that Maupassant does not sentimentalize her behavior. Her heroic willingness to pay for the necklace does not mean that she became noble-minded. Rather, the reverse is true, as we indicated when we quoted the passage that tells us she harangued the fruiterers, the grocer, the butcher. Suffering doesn't ennoble, it harshens (or at least it usually does). But surely readers are able to see something heroic—however mistaken, however ironic—in her struggle.

4. *Maupassant, in a discussion of fiction, said that a serious writer's "goal is not to tell a story to entertain us or to appeal to our feelings, but to make us think and to make us understand the hidden meaning of events. By dint of having observed and having meditated, the writer sees the world, facts, people, and things in a distinctive way, a way that is the result of all of his thoughtful observation. It is this personal view of the world that a writer strives to communicate to us. . . . To make the spectacle of life as moving to us as it has been to him, he must bring life before our eyes with scrupulous accuracy. He must construct his work with great skill—his art must seem artless—so that we cannot detect his contrivance or see his intentions."*

Among the big ideas in these few sentences are these: (a) The purpose of fiction is "to make us understand the hidden meaning of events"; (b) writers give us a "personal view"; (c) readers should be moved by the story but should not be aware that the artist has foisted a personal view on them. Do you agree with some or with all of these assertions? And do you think that "The Necklace" effectively illustrates Maupassant's points? What might be "the hidden meaning of events"? What would you guess is Maupassant's "personal view"? Would you agree that the story is so skillfully constructed that we are unaware of the author's methods and of his intentions?

We isolate three issues: the purpose of fiction ("to make us understand the hidden meaning of events"); the assertion that fiction gives the reader a "personal view"; and the assertion that readers should be moved but should not be aware that the writer has foisted a personal view on them, i.e., the writer's purpose and artistry should be inconspicuous. We have already indicated that we think Maupassant's highly anecdotal story does imply a view of life, a revelation of "the hidden meaning of events," and it does indeed seem that Maupassant's "personal view" was that we have little control over our destiny. Finally, we think that the work has been constructed so skillfully that— despite the outrageous irony—the reader cannot say, "Oh, no; people do not behave this way. Maupassant, like the writer of a soap opera, is inventing crazy improbabilities and crazy inconsistencies in the characters merely to create a gripping story." In our view, the characters are sketched convincingly, and the plot is plausible enough. People *are* sometimes motivated by vanity, and they *do* lose things, and they *do* conceal embarrassing truths. For us, the behavior of Mme. Loisel and her husband is entirely believable.

In our view, the great improbability is that the Loisels could somehow find a real diamond necklace that was so similar to the paste necklace that the owner, Mme. Forestier, would not notice the difference. Curiously, we don't recall a student ever bringing up this point—further proof, of course, that Maupassant has done his work very well.

One other point: The valuable necklace presumably belongs to the Loisels. They have thus—unknowingly—prepared for a life of comfortable retirement. Should they be delighted?

KATHERINE MIN

Courting a Monk (p. 453)

Readers of this story need to know nothing, or almost nothing, about Buddhism, and we decided to limit our annotations to a single note, on *dukkha* in paragraph 66, a Pali word literally meaning "unpleasantness," "disease," but usually translated as "suffering"—not merely physical suffering but also the suffering that results from desire. "Desire" (or "craving" or "thirst for life" or "attachment to the world") in Buddhist thought is not merely the desire of the flesh—the sort of desire that St. Augustine saw all around him in Carthage, and, for that matter, that he himself felt when he prayed, "Give me chastity and continence, but not just now." Nor is it merely desire for worldly goods; rather, it is any sort of attachment, even to things and ideas that the West considers noble. We will speak further (very briefly) about Buddhism, but first we want to make a few obvious comments about the structure of the story.

Broadly speaking, Min's structure employs *chiasmus*, an X-like arrangement, "a placing crosswise." (The classical example of the ABBA structure that constitutes chiasmus is Shakespeare's "Remember March, the ides of March remember," in *Julius Caesar* 4.3.18.) What we have in mind is this: The story begins with Micah as a chaste monk and Gina (the narrator) as a woman consumed by desire. At the end, although Gina tells us that Micah sometimes appears to be removed from the world, he is a high school teacher of biology, the father of two children, and a man who "makes it sound as though he were crazy to ever consider becoming a monk." Gina, by contrast, has "taken to reading books about Buddhism," and in the penultimate paragraph she briefly recounts the story of how Siddhartha (the Historical Buddha) gained Enlightenment (Sanskrit *bodhi*, in the United States, best known by the Japanese word *satori*, which some specialists prefer to translate as "awakening"). Obviously chiasmus can be a highly effective way of concluding, as the very brief example from *Julius Caesar* indicates. When we go beyond a sentence or two and get into a plot, this structure can provide not only a sense of finality but also a rich sense of irony. In "Courting a Monk" the irony is evident but the finality is diminished; although Micah has put aside his early ambitions and views, he is still (at least according to Gina) given to moments of meditation, and although Gina is studying Buddhism, she has by no means achieved enlightenment ("awakening"). Gina is still attached to the world, but she is pondering a *koan* of her own invention, "What is the sound of a life not lived?" (We will talk about *koans* later.)

Within the story there is another sort of X that deserves a bit of comment. The narrator's father opposes his daughter's marriage to a Caucasian, yet during the dinner, despite his insistence on his daughter's Korean blood, he says to her, "This boy more Korean than you." Interestingly, what apparently appeals to the father is Micah's fondness for Korean food (cabbage kimchi), which Gina does not care for. Micah's interest in Buddhism does engage the father's attention, but chiefly as something to react against; the father is no longer a Buddhist, and Buddhism does not provide a bond. Food is another thing; we do find kinship with the people who share our tastes in food. One can almost say that shared tastes for food are in the blood (we have in mind the father's insistence that blood makes for identity), something deeper than shared intellectual interests. It is our impression that for many Americans, their deepest connection with their European or Latin American or Asian or African backgrounds is not in their religion but in the foods they ate as children and (despite assimilation in other matters) continue to cherish.

We said at the outset that readers need no knowledge of Buddhism, but we nevertheless want to offer a few comments about it since the subject may come up in class, especially if you have some Asian or Asian-American students or indeed native-born Caucasian students who have converted to Buddhism. (*Caution*: Do not assume that your Asian students are Buddhists. Most of the Korean and Korean-American students whom we have met in our classes have been Christians.)

The subject of desire (Sanskrit: *trishna*), or attachment, is emphasized in the story. In paragraph 34 Micah tells Gina that "Buddhism is all about the renunciation of desire," and the topic is discussed in the ensuing paragraphs. In paragraph 43 Gina offers an extremely interesting definition: "I understood what desire was then, the disturbance of a perfect moment in anticipation of another." The discussion of desire reappears in paragraph 69, when Gina says that Buddhists "believe in physical desire. . . . They have sex," but Micah parries with "Buddha believes in physical desire. . . . It's impermanent, that's all. Something to get beyond." All of this talk may lead to some classroom discussion of Buddhism, so we will offer a brief comment.

Buddhism of course is immensely complicated. It has a long history, it has developed many schools, and there is much argument about terms such as "self" (see paragraphs 94–95), but we can probably say that the heart of Buddhism is the belief that suffering (*dukkha*) is omnipresent. The Four Noble Truths (paragraph 66) are these:

1. All existence is characterized by suffering; the human condition (though it includes temporary pleasures) is one of dis-ease.
2. Suffering is caused by desire (or "craving," or "attachment"), by a thirst for selfish pleasure, by orientation to the transient.
3. Suffering can be eliminated, but only by ceasing to crave.
4. One can cease to crave only by leading a disciplined, moral life, and this is set forth in the Eightfold Path, which takes one from the realm of suffering to Nirvana.

Before we go on to list the constituents of the Eightfold Path we want to say, in all seriousness, that the image of the father trying to hard-boil an egg by running hot water over it strikes us as a wonderful metaphor for the life of craving. Doubtless the father had been frustrated in earlier endeavors, and later he would be frustrated by others, most notably by his desire to have a daughter whose behavior shows filial piety. Indeed, in the final paragraph of the story Gina specifically connects the father's futile effort to cook the egg with his futile effort to shape his daughter. But, again, we think this image of the father trying to boil an egg by putting it in a sock and holding it under hot water wittily (and in a very Zen-like way) conveys the Buddhist idea of the suffering inherent in desire, or, to put it only a bit less grandly, the image embodies the frustration that the unenlightened mind experiences.

With some hesitation—this is getting complicated—we give one version of the Eightfold Path, which the Buddha taught in his first sermon. These are not eight successive stages, but are eight practices that are engaged in simultaneously. We are aware that each of the following points needs considerable amplification, and it may be that you will want some students to give reports on some aspects of Buddhism.

1. Right understanding, or right views (understanding reality, which means understanding the Four Noble Truths)

2. Right thinking (resolution to renounce desire, ill will, and cruelty)
3. Right speech (avoidance of lying, angry words, gossip)
4. Right action (avoidance of stealing, rape, pederasty, etc.)
5. Right livelihood (avoidance of harmful ways of making a living, e.g., hunting, fishing, palmistry, astrology)
6. Right effort (cultivation of what is wholesome)
7. Right mindfulness (good thoughts, contemplation, including—as a corrective to vanity—contemplation of corpses)
8. Right concentration (a stage in meditation in which mental activity ceases and the mind is united with the object of meditation)

By these practices, it is said, one extinguishes the passions (which produce ignorant actions) and arrives at enlightenment. Attempts to eliminate passion, to detach oneself from the things of this world, are not, of course, limited to Buddhism. One can easily find Christian texts that urge renunciation.

> But I say unto you, That whosoever looketh on a woman to lust after her hath committed adultery with her already in his heart. / And if thy right eye offend thee, pluck it out, and cast it from thee: for it is profitable for thee that one of thy members should perish, and not that the whole body should be cast into hell.
>
> Matthew 5.28–29

> He that loveth father or mother more than me is not worthy of me: and he that loveth son or daughter more than me is not worthy of me.
>
> Matthew 10.37

> And everyone that hath forsaken houses, or brethren, or sisters, or father, or mother, or wife, or children, or lands, for my name's sake, shall receive an hundredfold, and shall inherit everlasting life.
>
> Matthew 19.29

We are not saying that in the matter of renunciation Christianity and Buddhism are the same. We daily try (especially when we ask students to write a comparison) to keep in mind a profound remark by Bishop Joseph Butler: "Everything is what it is, and not another thing." Still, if some students find the Buddhist ideal of renunciation odd, we think it is worth citing some Christian texts.

One other aspect of Buddhism that is given some emphasis in the story is the *koan*, which Micah introduces in paragraph 47. In 51 he explains that "It's a question that has no answer, sort of like a riddle. You know, like 'What is the sound of one hand clapping?' Or 'What was your face before you were born?'" (By the way, although "What is the sound of one hand clapping?" is probably the best-known *koan* in the United States, in fact the correct translation of this *koan* invented by the Japanese monk Hakuin is "What is the sound of one hand?" For a painting by Hakuin, showing him with one hand raised, and inscribed at the top, "Young people, no matter what you say, everything is nonsense unless you hear the sound of one hand," see Sylvan Barnet and William Burto, *Zen Ink Paintings* [1982], 54, or Penelope Mason, *History of Japanese Art* [1993], 285.) Buddhist teachers (especially Zen Buddhists of the Rinzai sect) use *koans*, which are often paradoxical and which in any case cannot be solved by logic, as a device to force the student to make an intuitive leap into a world beyond logical contradiction. Here are two of the responses that are said to have satisfied some Zen masters: (1) the pupil said, "Whether it's from the front or the back, you can hear it as you please"; (2) the pupil thrust one hand forward. (These are given in *The Sound of One Hand*, trans. Yoel Hoffman [1975], 47–49.)

Gina in one of her least likeable moments trivializes the whole procedure by asking (paragraph 56) "What's the sound of one cheek farting?" Even as late as paragraph 129 she is clowning around when, in the ice cream parlor, she asks "What is the sound of Swiss chocolate almond melting?" By the way, the *koan* about the sound of a hand is so well known that journalists take it for granted. On the very day that we wrote this page (August 6, 1999) *The New York Times* had an article (C5) about Abercrombie and Fitch's advertising campaign that featured "lubricious images of toothsome campus types." The article ended, "It's not unlike the riddle asking about the sound of one hand clapping. What does a college student tugging off his boxers sound like?"

The coarseness of the newspaper account is more or less of a piece with Gina's coarseness during most of the story, but, again, at the end she is a different person. Not enlightened, but seriously meditating: "What is the sound of a life not lived?"

Suggested reference: The literature, even in English, on Buddhism is enormous, but in our view the best introduction is a collection of Buddhist texts with admirable short introductions: W. M. Theodore De Bary, ed., *The Buddhist Tradition in India, China, and Japan* (1969).

LORRIE MOORE

How to Become a Writer (p. 463)

This story will work wonderfully for some students, less so for others. The students who enjoy it will find it funny, while the students who don't enjoy it will complain that Moore is aiming for comedy but not achieving it. Some will be impressed by Moore's virtuosity; others will judge her voice to be too insistent, repetitive, irritating.

Who is speaking in this story? When we first read it, we were inclined for a time to identify the voice as Moore's: This is the author speaking, parodying in a How-To form the steps that a writer must follow in order to become successful at her craft. But the references to "Francie" in the story soon make clear that the voice is not Moore's; rather the voice is that of a character whom she has imagined. The point of view is complicated further by the fact that the tips and suggestions are delivered to "you," to the second-person pronoun, from beginning to end. Is Moore poking clever, fast-paced ironic fun at herself? Is she satirizing earnest but simpleminded aspiring writers like Francie? Or is she scoring comic points at the reader's expense, especially readers (this means *you*) who might dream of becoming a novelist or short story writer and are eager for guidance: So, how is it done? Where do I start, what should I do, how should I gain experience?

For the story's comedy to succeed, the advice presented has to seem off-center, skewed, crazy, and yet based on a measure of sense. Disillusionment, pain, suffering—these are described ironically in the first paragraph, even as they do strike us as part of the writer's necessary knowledge. A writer cannot be naive, innocent, limited in his or her emotional range; the writer must feel and know a great deal to understand his or her own life and the lives of others and then to project this understanding in characters he or she creates. To say this is to utter a cliché and also a truth. It's something that a genuine writer takes to heart, learns through labor, and weaves into the activity of writing. It's also something that a poor or superficial, or sincere but unskilled, writer believes and attempts to put into practice but cannot: The magic is not there.

There are many sharp turns and absurd twists in Moore's story. Some of the jokes are very good, as when Francie wonders whether fate, rather than computer error, has led her to the creative writing class. "Perhaps," she observes in a report of parental wisdom, "this is what your dad meant when he said, 'It's the age of computers, Francie, it's the age of computers.'" Other jokes are bad but are intended to be bad—clumsy and clunky, as in the paragraph about "Fishmeal" and "Mopey Dick."

After we discuss the point of view and tone of "How to Become a Writer," and its elements of irony and comedy, we ask the class, "Is this a good story?" The answers that we have received are intriguing. The students admire Moore's stylistic gifts, but, in our experience, most of them are not convinced that "How to Become a Writer" is a good story. Nothing happens in it, they frequently say—which is an interesting complaint, given the criticisms of Francie's writing that she reports in the story itself. Francie is told that she shows a fine feeling for imagery and for rhythm, but, it is said, she has little or no conception of plot. Moore is very canny; she anticipates our criticism and embeds it into the story. This will not keep students from noting the absence of plot, but it makes them seem to be expressing a charge that Moore herself is aware of: How can she be criticized for lacking a plot when she knows that already?

But press the students, "So, I'll ask again, is this a good story or not?" "How to Become a Writer" offers a good opportunity for the members of the class to say what they want to find in a story, what Moore does and does not offer in comparison with other writers studied in the course, and, furthermore, what makes a story like this one "contemporary." If it turns out that too many students are unresponsive to or critical of Moore, tell them how acclaimed (and successful) she is: "Well, what do you make of that?" This story comes from Moore's highly regarded first collection, *Self-Help*, in which several stories are presented in a How-To structure and feature the second-person pronoun "you" ("How to Be an Other Woman," "The Kid's Guide to Divorce," "How," "How to Talk to Your Mother (Notes)"). She is responding to the cascade of self-help manuals and instruction books on the market and to the staggering popularity in the media for advice about everything from losing weight to getting into the best college to being your own best friend. Many readers of *Self-Help* have praised Moore as a shrewd explorer of contemporary life. And her recent collection *Birds of America* (1998) has been even more successful, reaching the fiction best-seller list for a month and receiving one glowing review after another.

For differing perspectives on *Self-Help*, consult the reviews by Michiko Kakutani, *The New York Times*, March 6, 1985; and Jay McInerney, *The New York Times Book Review*, March 24, 1985. Kakutani admires Moore's gifts but finds the stories too limited and the collection as a whole not coherent as a work of art, whereas McInerney comes to a different conclusion, commending

Moore's flexible, well-modulated voice. See also Carol Iannone, "Post-Counterculture Tristesse," which examines both Moore and David Leavitt, *Commentary* 83 (February 1987): 57–61.

The March 24, 1985 issue of the *Book Review* also includes this brief profile, written by Caryn James:

> At the age of 28, Lorrie Moore often strikes others as precocious. "I'm not one of those people who always wanted to be a writer; everyone assumes I am," she said in a telephone interview, pointing out that, like the heroine of her story "How to Become a Writer," her career began haphazardly. She signed up for a high school linguistics course, was shunted off to creative writing instead and stayed. But success came early, while she was a student at St. Lawrence University in Canton, N.Y. The first story she ever sent out won first prize in *Seventeen* magazine's fiction contest. "When I won, I thought, this is easy, but I also felt a little sheepish—I was competing against 13- and 14-year-olds, and I was 19."
>
> After graduation she worked as a paralegal for two years—"I was still writing. I had a lot of energy; I even took tap-dance lessons"—then got an M.F.A. at Cornell University. Last September she began teaching writing workshops at the University of Wisconsin at Madison. Asked about influences on *Self-Help*, she said, "When I was 18 or 19, my favorite writer was Margaret Atwood. For the first time I read fiction about women who were not goddesses or winners. In some ways they were victims, but they weren't wimps. They were stylish about their victimization." She sets herself apart from other savvy short-story writers with whom she might be linked. Ann Beattie's "male characters seem to get all the good lines. I give the women in my stories more than equal time." A major influence is a timeless one, with a twist. "I suppose it's arrogant, but every writer is influenced by Shakespeare. I'm always trying to write *Romeo and Juliet* and it comes out as something else, like in *Alice in Wonderland*, when she tries to recite poetry and it comes out as that awful poem about crocodiles."

For a longer and more recent profile, direct your students to Don Lee, "About Lorrie Moore," *Ploughshares* 24:2–3 (Fall 1998): 224–29.

For an excellent essay on the contemporary short story, which includes discussion of Moore, see Vince Passaro, "Unlikely Stories: The Quiet Renaissance of American Short Fiction," *Harper's* (August 1999): 80–89.

ALICE MUNRO

Boys and Girls (p. 468)

A good way to begin the discussion of this story is to have a student read the first paragraph aloud, and then ask if the sentences about the calendar have any relevance to the rest of the story. Of course this passage would be justified if it did no more than give a glimpse of the sort of decorations that might be found on a Canadian fox farm, and one doesn't want to press too hard for a deep meaning, but surely the picture of "plumed adventurers" (male, naturally) who use "savages" as pack animals introduces, however faintly, a political note that can be connected with the treatment of distinctions between the sexes.

This is not to say that the story suggests that women are comparable to the Indians who bend their backs in service to the whites. The wife works hard, but so does the husband. And the early part of the story indicates that the female narrator, when a child, eagerly engaged in what the mother must have thought was "man's work." Certainly the girl, feeling quite superior to her little brother, had no sense that she was oppressed. She came to learn, however, that she must "become" a girl. If we hear a note of protest in this statement that society expects us to assume certain roles, the story nevertheless seems also to suggest that females are, by nature rather than by nurture, mentally or emotionally different from males. Despite the narrator's early enthusiasm for her father's work, and despite her sense of superiority to her brother (she can handle the wheelbarrow used for watering the foxes, whereas Laird, carrying a "little cream and green gardening can," can only play at watering), she is more shaken by the killing of Mack than she will admit. "My legs were a little shaky," she says, and later she adds that she "felt a little ashamed," but for the most part she deals with her response by talking about another episode, the time when she endangered Laird's life, and afterwards felt "the sadness of unexorcised guilt." Of course we may think that anyone—male or female—might feel shaky and guilty upon first witnessing the death of a harmless animal, but in fact Laird does not seem even mildly disturbed. Rather, after witnessing the shooting of Mack, Laird is "remote, concentrating."

The guilt engendered by watching Mack die prompts the narrator to let Flora escape. (A question: If the first horse killed had been a female, would the narrator have let the second horse, a male, escape? One answer: The story is right as it is. Don't monkey with it. If the horses were reversed, the story would be less coherent.) The narrator is irretrievably female. (Notice too the passage recounted after the episode with Flora, about the narrator's attempt to prettify her part of the bedroom and, in the same paragraph, the discussion of her new fantasies, in which she no longer performs heroic rescues but is now the person rescued and is wondering about her hairstyle and her dress.) Having let Flora escape, she of course has no desire to join in the chase, but Laird does, and when he returns, daubed in blood (this passage, however realistic, seems almost a parody of Hemingway and Faulkner on rituals of initiation), he is quite casual about what happened: "'We shot old Flora,' he said, 'and cut her up in fifty pieces.'" Laird, no longer his sister's partner but now firmly aligned with the men, soon betrays the narrator, reducing her to tears. Her father means well in absolving her ("She's only a girl"), but, as the narrator says, the words not only absolve but also "dismiss" her. On the other hand, the narrator recognizes that the father's words may be "true."

In teaching this story, one might get around to making the point that a work of literature doesn't "prove" anything. *Hamlet* doesn't prove that ghosts exist, or that one should not delay, or that revenge is morally acceptable. Similarly, Munro's story doesn't prove that girls are by nature more sensitive to the killing of a horse than boys are. We won't attempt here (or anywhere) to say what a work of fiction does do, but the point is worth discussing—probably early in the course and again near the end, after students have read a fair amount of literature.

Among Munro's books, we remain partial to her first two collections of stories: *Dance of the Happy Shades* (1968) and *Lives of Girls and Women* (1971).

But the best point of departure for students is her volume *Selected Stories* (1996). For a concise survey, see E. D. Blodgett, *Alice Munro* (1988).

GLORIA NAYLOR

The Two (p. 478)

Although instructors will be interested in matters of technique—especially the metaphors of the quilt and of the smell, and the shift in point of view from (at the start) the outside view of the two women to (midway) the inside view of Lorraine and Theresa—discussion in class is likely to center on the characterization of "the two" (we don't learn even their names until we have read about one-third of the story), their relationship to each other, and society's relationship to them.

The differences between the two women are clear enough—Lorraine is shy, soft, and in need of the approval of the community; Theresa is tougher (but "the strain of fighting alone was beginning to show")—but both are at first lumped together as "nice girls," and this point is worth discussing in class. Why, at first, does the community find them acceptable? Because they don't play loud music, they don't have drunken friends, and—the next most important point—they do not encourage other women's husbands to hang around, that is, they are not a threat to the married women. But it is precisely this "friendly indifference to the men on the street" that (when its source is detected) becomes "an insult to the [neighborhood] women."

By the way, we have fairly often encountered in the popular press articles with such titles as "Why Are Gay Men Feared?" (the usual answer is that men insecure about their own heterosexuality feel threatened by gay men, who, the theory goes, in effect tell the supposed straight men that maybe they aren't really so straight), but we don't recall ever encountering an article on the response of heterosexual women to lesbians. Perhaps some students will want to confirm or dispute Naylor's view of why the straight community resents "the two." As we understand the story, Naylor is suggesting that heterosexual women welcome other women who are not threats to their relationships with men, but then reject lesbians (who fit this category) because lesbians, by virtue of their indifference to or independence from males, seem to be a criticism of heterosexuality. (Can we go so far as to say that lesbians, in this view, upset straight women because lesbians make other women aware of their need for men?)

There are two stories in this story, the story of the relationship between the community and "the two," and the story of the relationship between Lorraine and Theresa. This second story, we take it, is about two women who (like the members of most straight couples) differ considerably in personality and who have their problems, but who are tied to each other by deep affection. The last we hear in the story is a bit of good-natured bickering that reveals Lorraine is doing her best to please Theresa. Lorraine, who had tried to talk Theresa into avoiding fattening foods, is preparing a (fattening) gravy for the chicken, and Theresa is pretending to disapprove.

"The Two" is included in Naylor's first and, we think, her best book, *The Women of Brewster Place* (1982). But students might be directed to her later novels: *Linden Hills* (1985); *Mama Day* (1988), which blends African-

American folklore with stories derived from Shakespeare's *The Tempest*; and *Bailey's Cafe* (1992).

For background and context, see Gloria Naylor and Toni Morrison, "A Conversation," *Southern Review* 21 (July 1985): 567–93; Gloria Naylor, "Love and Sex in the Afro-American Novel," *Yale Review* 78 (Autumn 1988): 19–31; and Barbara Christian, "Gloria Naylor's Geography: Community, Class, and Patriarchy in *The Women of Brewster Place* and *Linden Hills*," in *Reading Black, Reading Feminist*, ed. Henry Louis Gates, Jr. (1990), 348–73.

JOYCE CAROL OATES

Where Are You Going, Where Have You Been? (p. 483)

The title seems to be derived from Judges 19.17 ("So the old man said, 'Where are you going, and where do you come from?'"), a point made in a rather strained discussion of the story in *Explicator* (Summer 1982).

Tom Quirk, in *Studies in Short Fiction* 18 (1981): 413–19, pointed out that the story derives from newspaper and magazine accounts (especially one in *Life*, March 4, 1966) of the activities of a psychopath known as "The Pied Piper of Tucson," who drove a gold-colored car and seduced and sometimes murdered teenage girls in the Tucson area. Because he was short, he stuffed his boots with rags and flattened tin cans, which caused him to walk unsteadily. Oates herself has confirmed, on various occasions, her use of this material (e.g., *New York Times*, March 23, 1986).

According to Oates, in an early draft of her story "Death and the Maiden" (she is fond of a type of fiction that she calls "realistic allegory"), "the story was minutely detailed yet clearly an allegory of the fatal attractions of death (or the devil). An innocent young girl is seduced by way of her own vanity: She mistakes death for erotic romance of a particularly American/trashy sort." The story went through several drafts. Oates has said she was especially influenced by Bob Dylan's song, "It's All Over Now, Baby Blue." One line of Dylan's song ("The vagabond who's standing at your door") is clearly related to the story, and note that in the story itself Connie wishes "it were all over."

In speaking of the revisions, Oates writes that "the charismatic mass murderer drops into the background and his innocent victim, a 15-year-old, moves into the foreground. She becomes the true protagonist of the tale. . . . There is no suggestion in the published story that Arnold Friend has seduced and murdered other girls, or even that he necessarily intends to murder Connie." Oates goes on to explain that her interest is chiefly in Connie, who "is shallow, vain, silly, hopeful, doomed—perhaps as I saw, and still see, myself?—but capable nonetheless of an unexpected gesture of heroism at the story's end. . . . We don't know the nature of her sacrifice [to protect her family from Arnold], only that she is generous enough to make it." Instructors who are interested in discussing the intentional fallacy (and is it a fallacy?) will find, if they use this passage, that students have strong feelings on the topic.

The story has abundant affinities with the anonymous ballad called "The Demon Lover." The demon lover has "music on every hand," and Connie "was hearing music in her head"; later, Arnold and Ellie listen to the same radio station in the car that Connie listens to in the house; the demon lover's ship has "masts o' the beaten gold," and Arnold's car is "painted gold."

The second sentence tells us that Connie "had a quick nervous giggling habit of craning her neck to glance into mirrors." Her mother attributes it to vanity, and indeed Connie does think she is pretty, but a more important cause is insecurity. Connie's fear that she has no identity sometimes issues in her a wish that "she herself were dead and it were all over with." "Everything about her had two sides," which again suggests an incoherent personality.

Arnold Friend has a hawklike nose, thick black lashes, an ability to see what is going on in remote places, a curious (lame) foot, a taste for strange bargains, incantatory speech, an enchanted subordinate, and a charismatic personality; all in all he is a sort of diabolical figure who can possess Connie, partly because he shows her an enormous concern that no one else has shown her. (The possession—"I'll come inside you, where it's all secret"—is possession of her mind as well as of her body.) Notice, too, that like a traditional evil spirit, Arnold Friend cannot cross the threshold uninvited.

The dedication to Dylan has provoked considerable comment. Marie Urbanski, in *Studies in Short Fiction* 15 (1978): 200–03, thinks it is pejorative, arguing that Dylan made music "almost religious in dimension among youth." Tom Quirk, on the other hand, says it is "honorific because the history and effect of Bob Dylan's music had been to draw youth away from the romantic promises and frantic strains of a brand of music sung by Buddy Holly, Chuck Berry, Elvis Presley, and others." A. H. Petry, in *Studies in Short Fiction* 25 (1988): 155–57, follows Quirk and goes on to argue that Ellie is meant to suggest Elvis Presley (lock of hair on forehead, sideburns, etc.). According to Petry, Oates is seeking "to warn against the dangerous illusions and vacuousness" generated by Elvis's music, in contrast to Bob Dylan's.

Perhaps the most astounding comment is by Mike Tierce and John Michael Crafton (*Studies in Short Fiction* 22 [1985]: 219–24). Tierce and Crafton argue that Arnold Friend, the mysterious visitor, is not satanic but rather a savior, and that he is (as his hair, hawklike nose, unshaved face, and short stature suggest) an image of Bob Dylan. Arnold's visit, in their view, is a fantasy of Connie's "overheated imagination," and it enables her to free herself "from the sense of confinement she feels in her father's house. . . . She broadens her horizons to include the 'vast sunlit reaches of the land' all around her."

Many readers find resemblances between the fiction of Oates and Flannery O'Connor, but in an interview in *Commonweal* (Dec. 5, 1969), Oates said that although she at first thought her fiction was indebted to Flannery O'Connor, she came to see that in O'Connor there is always a religious dimension whereas in her own fiction "there is only the natural world."

The story has been made into a film called *Smooth Talk* (Spectra Films, 1986).

For further study of this story, we recommend the casebook *"Where Are You Going, Where Have You Been?"*, ed. Elaine Showalter (1994). For biography, see Greg Johnson, *Invisible Writer: A Biography of Joyce Carol Oates* (1998). A good critical overview is Johnson's *Understanding Joyce Carol Oates* (1987). Other helpful resources include *Critical Essays on Joyce Carol Oates*, ed. Linda W. Wagner (1979), and Francine Lercangee, *Joyce Carol Oates: An Annotated Bibliography* (1986). Oates is best known for her fiction, but her criticism is worth reading as well. See, for example, *Contraries: Essays* (1981) and *The Profane Art: Essays and Reviews* (1983).

TOPICS FOR CRITICAL THINKING AND WRITING

1. Characterize Connie. Do you think the early characterization of Connie prepares us for her later behavior?
2. Is Arnold Friend clairvoyant—definitely, definitely not, maybe? Explain.
3. Evaluate the view that Arnold Friend is both Satan and the incarnation of Connie's erotic desires.
4. What do you make of the fact that Oates dedicated the story to Bob Dylan? Is she perhaps contrasting Dylan's music with the escapist (or in some other way unwholesome) music of other popular singers?
5. If you have read Flannery O'Connor's "A Good Man Is Hard to Find" (text), compare and contrast Arnold Friend and the Misfit.

TIM O'BRIEN

The Things They Carried (p. 495)

A few words should be said about the movement away from the highly anecdotal story of, say, the Middle Ages and even of the late nineteenth century (e.g., Maupassant)—a movement toward what has been called the lyric style of, say, Chekhov and Joyce.

Most stories, even those of the twentieth century, retain something of the anecdotal plot, a fairly strong element of conflict and reversal. Howard Nemerov offers a satirical summary in *Poetry and Fiction* (1963):

> Short stories amount for the most part to parlor tricks, party favors with built-in snappers, gadgets for inducing recognitions and reversals; a small pump serves to build up the pressure, a tiny trigger releases it, there follows a puff and a flash as freedom and necessity combine; finally a celluloid doll drops from the muzzle and descends by parachute to the floor. These things happen, but they happen to no one in particular.

Some writers, however, have all but eliminated plot, and it's not unusual for twentieth-century writers of stories to disparage narrative (especially the novel) and to claim some affinity with poets. Frank O'Connor, in an interview in *Paris Review* (reprinted in *Writers at Work* [1958], edited by Malcolm Cowley), said that the short story was his favorite form

> because it's the nearest thing I know to lyric poetry—I wrote lyric poetry for a long time, then discovered that God had not intended me to be a lyric poet, and the nearest thing to that is the short story. A novel actually requires far more logic and far more knowledge of circumstances, whereas a short story can have the sort of detachment from circumstances that lyric poetry has.

In his book on the short story, *The Lonely Voice* (1963), O'Connor amplifies this point.

Faulkner makes pretty much the same point in another *Paris Review* interview that is reprinted in the same collection. Faulkner says:

> I'm a failed poet. Maybe every novelist wants to write poetry first, finds he can't, and then tries the short story, which is the most demanding form after poetry. And failing at that, only then does he take up novel writing.

Doubtless, Faulkner is being at least somewhat facetious, but we can't quite dismiss his implication that the short story is allied to the poem—by which he must mean the lyric.

If the course is being taught chronologically, students probably have already encountered Chekhov, Joyce, and Hemingway; if, for instance, they have read "Araby" they have read a story in which (many of them think) "nothing happens." In the "lyric story" (if there is such a species) the emphasis is not on telling about a change of fortune, marked by a decisive ending, but rather is on conveying (and perhaps inducing in the reader) an emotion—perhaps the emotion of the narrator. There is very little emphasis on plot, that is, on "What happened next?" (Chekhov said, "I think that when one has finished writing a short story one should delete the beginning and the end"), though of course there is a good deal of interest in the subtle changes or modulations of the emotion.

Certainly in "The Things They Carried"—a story set in a combat zone—there is none of the suspense and catastrophic action that one would expect in a war story of the nineteenth century, say a story by Ambrose Bierce or Stephen Crane. In "The Things They Carried" we learn fairly early that Ted Lavender got killed; because no one else gets killed, an inexperienced reader may conclude that nothing much happens in the story.

Of course, as far as plot is concerned, what "happens" is that Lieutenant Cross, feeling that his thoughts of Martha have led him to relax discipline with the result that one of his men has been killed, determines to pay attention to his job as a military leader, and he therefore burns Martha's letters and photographs. But this narrative could scarcely sustain a story of this length; or, to put it another way, if that's what the story is about, much of the story seems irrelevant.

Even inexperienced readers usually see that "The Things They Carried" is not to be judged on its plot, any more than is (say) "Born in the U.S.A." If some passages are read aloud in class, even the least-experienced readers—who may miss almost all of the subtleties when they read the story by themselves—will see and hear that O'Brien interestingly varies "the things they carried," from physical objects (chewing gum and the latest gear for killing) to thoughts and emotions. In short, he uses verbal repetition (which creates rhythm) and metaphor to a degree rarely if ever found in the novel.

Not least of "the things they carried" are themselves and their minds. "For the most part they carried themselves with poise, a kind of dignity." "For the most part" is important. O'Brien doesn't sentimentalize the soldiers; they can be afraid and they can be wantonly destructive. He tells us, fairly late in the story, that "They shot chickens and dogs, they trashed the village well." He tells us, too, that "They carried the soldier's greatest fear, which was a fear of blushing." "They carried all the emotional baggage of men who might die." "They carried shameful memories." This insistent repetition, rather like the incremental repetition in the old popular ballads (e.g., "Edward," "Lord

Randall," "Barbara Allen"), serves less to record a sequence of events than to deepen our understanding of a state of mind.

Still, there is, as has already been said, something of the traditional narrative here: Lieutenant Cross at last does something overt (burns Martha's letters and photographs). He thus "carries" less, literally, since the first line of the story is "First Lieutenant Jimmy Cross carried letters from a girl named Martha." Whether by burning the letters and photos he will in fact lighten his load—his guilt—is something about which readers may have different opinions. He may indeed impose stricter discipline, but it's hard to imagine that he will think less of Ted Lavender. Cross himself seems skeptical. "Lavender was dead. You couldn't burn the blame." One may lighten one's load by shooting off fingers and toes, and thus gain release from combat, and one can dream of flying away ("the weights fell off; there was nothing to bear"), but a reader may doubt that when Cross lightens his physical load he will find that the weights will fall off, and that he will have nothing, or only a little, to bear. He will still be a participant in a war where "men killed and died, because they were embarrassed not to." One may wonder, too, if Cross will be able to forget about Martha, or, so to speak, to keep her in her place. He thinks he will be able to do so, but the matter is left unresolved:

> Henceforth, when he thought about Martha, it would be only to think that she belonged elsewhere. He would shut down the daydreams. This was not Mount Sebastian, it was another world, where there were no pretty poems or midterm exams, a place where men died because of carelessness and gross stupidity. Kiowa was right. Boom-down, and you were dead, never partly dead.

This quotation, however, raises yet another question, and perhaps a central question if one takes the story to be about Cross rather than about the soldiers as a group. Cross here seems to assume that death comes only to those who are careless or stupid. He thinks, presumably, that it is his job as an officer to prevent the carelessness and the stupidity of his men from getting them killed. But of course we know that in war even the careful and the bright may get killed. Further, nothing in the story tells us that Lavender was careless or stupid. He was killed while urinating, but even the careful and the bright must urinate. We are told that he was shot in the head, and perhaps we are to understand that, contrary to standard operating procedure, he was not wearing his helmet, but the point is not emphasized. When we first hear of Lavender's death we are told that Cross "felt the pain" and that "he blamed himself," although the reader does not know exactly why the lieutenant is blameworthy. Later perhaps a reader concludes (though again, this is not made explicit) that it was Cross's job to insist that the men wear their helmets. In any case, the reader is probably much easier on Cross than Cross is on himself.

To the extent that the story is about Cross's isolation—and, as Kiowa knows, Cross is isolated—it fits Frank O'Connor's remark (in *The Lonely Voice*) that a short story is "by its very nature remote from the community—romantic, individualistic, and intransigent." But, to repeat, it's probably fair to say that O'Brien is as much concerned with celebrating the state of mind of all the "legs or grunts" as he is with recording the sequence of actions that constitutes Lieutenant Cross's attempts to deal with his sense of guilt.

This story has been reprinted in a book called *The Things They Carried,* where it is one of twenty-two related but discontinuous pieces ranging from two to twenty pages. The book is dedicated to "the men of Alpha Company," and the names in the dedication correspond to the names in the stories. Further, in the book the narrator identifies himself as Tim O'Brien. A question thus arises: Is *The Things They Carried* a collection of stories, or is it biography, history, or whatever? Perhaps one's first thought, given the dedication and the name of the narrator, is that the book reports what O'Brien experienced—and yet in an interview in *Publisher's Weekly* O'Brien said, "My own experience has virtually nothing to do with the content of the book." He claims he used his own name for that of the narrator merely because he thought it would be "neat." (In another interview, he said the use of his own name was "just one more literary device.") If we believe what he told the interviewer, the book is fiction. But perhaps O'Brien is toying with the interviewer. Or perhaps he is behaving in accordance with a point made in the book: "In war you lose your sense of the definite, hence your sense of truth itself, and therefore it's safe to say that in a true war story nothing is ever absolutely true." Has O'Brien been infected by the "fact-or-fiction?" game of much recent writing? If so, should someone tell him that what we value in his writing is his ability to bring the Vietnam War home to us, rather than his philosophizing?

TOPICS FOR CRITICAL THINKING AND WRITING

1. What is the point of the insistent repetition of the words "the things they carried"? What sorts of things does Lieutenant Cross carry?
2. We are told that "Kiowa admired Lieutenant Cross's capacity for grief." But we are also told that although Kiowa "wanted to share the other man's pain," he could think only of "Boom-down" and of "the pleasure of having his boots off and the fog curling in around him and the damp soil and the Bible smells and the plush comfort of night." What might account for the different responses of the two men?
3. Near the end of the story, Lieutenant Cross "burned the two photographs." Why does he do this?

CYNTHIA OZICK

The Shawl (p. 508)

This story may be the hardest in the book to teach, not because it is the most difficult but because it is the most painful. Other stories deal with people in anguishing circumstances, but perhaps only "The Shawl" provides no catharsis, no release for our sense of horror. Consider, by way of contrast, Ellison's "Battle Royal." The whites treat the blacks abominably, but the protagonist is the narrator of the story; his survival, his ability now to tell the tale, offers proof that he endured, that his plight (however dreadful) has been at least partly overcome. But in "The Shawl" nothing affords the reader even a glimmer of relief.

Speaking of "catharsis" (a word whose meaning is admittedly much disputed), we can say that the protagonist finds no release, and partly for this reason the reader finds none either. Or, rather, Rosa's only release is into madness, and though perhaps a reader is grateful that she is spared (at least so far as this story goes) further perception of horror, the price is enormous, almost more than a reader can bear. Not surprisingly, readers differ in their interpretations of the ending:

> She took Magda's shawl and filled her own mouth with it, stuffed it in and stuffed it in, until she was swallowing up the wolf's screech and tasting the cinnamon and almond depth of Magda's saliva; and Rosa drank Magda's shawl until it dried.

According to one commentator, the last line means that the shawl nourished Rosa until the memory of her baby's death became bearable. This is a comforting interpretation, and if right, it does provide the reader with a release from suffering; but will it do? Doesn't the end of the story strongly suggest that Rosa has become infantile and has gone mad? Madness is a way of coping with an unbearable reality, of course, but (from the reader's point of view) scarcely one that affords relief. In short, the curious statement that "Rosa drank Magda's shawl until it dried" seems to say that through madness Rosa escaped from the horror ("drank Magda's shawl"), but then even madness didn't work ("until it dried"). The shawl is an ordinary shawl, of course, but it is also (as the first sentence in the fourth paragraph says) in some ways a magic shawl: it hides the infant and keeps her quiet, thereby preserving her life, it stifles Rosa's cry; and in Rosa's madness it provides sustenance. However, in the end not even a magic shawl can overcome the horror of the Holocaust.

Observations of this sort can bring us to the question of whether any work of literature about the Holocaust can be satisfactory—satisfactory as literature, and at the same time satisfactory as a response to an unimaginable historical event. One can almost argue that if a work on this topic is satisfactory as literature, it will strike readers as unsatisfactory as a response to or a comment on history, for it seduces us into an aesthetic pleasure that is at odds with reality. In various critical writings Ozick has argued that, in the light of the Holocaust, a Jew must write either in the tradition of George Eliot, Dickens, and Tolstoy—that is, one must write about conduct and the consequences of conduct—or one must write (and this she finds unacceptable) the "new fiction," literature that is self-referential and purely aesthetic, what she has called "aesthetic paganism." Thus, in an essay entitled "What Literature Means," Ozick rejects "art for its own sake," and insists that (except for lyric poetry) "literature is the moral life," giving a "corona of moral purpose." In short, she takes the old-fashioned view that literature may refer to a world outside the text.

But is "What Literature Means" entirely compatible with "The Shawl"? The essay argues that the best literature conveys "the sense that we act for ourselves rather than are acted upon," yet the story seems to show a woman who is acted upon so monstrously that her only action can be to enter madness. Surely the story does enter, as Ozick says an artist must enter, into the deepest evil, but does the story meet Ozick's requirement that "at the last moment steeples of light spurt up from the corona, and the world with its meaning is laid open to our astonished sight"? To put the issue more simply, we might ask if "The Shawl" finally provides "meaning," and indeed if any "meaning" can be attributed to the Holocaust.

An examination of the artistry of the story is worthwhile. First, one can call attention to the surreal effect of the story, evident most obviously in the near-absence of dialogue (Question 3), and also in the rather flat, disjointed style that is varied with occasional fanciful images (Question 2). The first technique probably evokes the reality of the prison camps, where prisoners were forbidden to speak, and where silence served to protect. (Silence is what preserves Magda's life, short though it is, and what preserves Rosa's at the end of the story.) Silence—the inability to express oneself—is also part of what drives Rosa over the brink. One thinks in *Macbeth* of Malcolm's commonsense advice to Macduff when Macduff learns that his wife and children have been slain:

> Give sorrow words. The grief that does not speak
> Whispers the o'erfraught heart, and bids it break.

One thinks too of Tennyson's grieving Princess:

> All her maidens watching said,
> She must weep, or she will die.

The other point is probably more subtle and complicated. There is, first of all, a deep irony in flatly recounting monstrous doings. It is as if indignation could not come near to the truth, and so the writer chooses another way, recounting the story simply, letting the actions speak for themselves. The first paragraph illustrates this point. Even its most conspicuous metaphors are not imaginatively daring: "Her knees were tumors on sticks, her elbows chicken bones." In the second paragraph the figures are similarly rather ordinary: Rosa while marching feels like "a floating angel," and the baby's round face is like "a pocket mirror of a face." At this stage, although Rosa has been almost dehumanized she still retains her sanity and so Ozick presents Rosa's thoughts in thoroughly familiar and intelligible terms. (One sign of Rosa's sanity is her awareness, in the third paragraph, that if she attempts to give away the baby she may be shot, or the intended recipient may drop the baby, or refuse it.) But even this paragraph, with its rather ordinary language, contains a striking metaphor comparing the baby's tooth to "an elfin tombstone of white marble"; it also includes the strange observation that the shawl's flavor was like the "milk of linen." Much of the later writings is more conspicuously strange, corresponding to Rosa's madness, though for the most part the language continues to seem simple—and monstrous:

> Stella did not menstruate. Rosa did not menstruate. Rosa was ravenous, but also not; she learned from Magda how to drink the taste of a finger in one's mouth.

Still later come odder figures, such as "blue tigers," "butterflies in summer" (nothing odd in the words here, but the image is grossly inappropriate), "grainy sad voices" in the electrified fence, and, perhaps oddest of all, "The light tapped the helmet and sparkled into a goblet." All of these passages, and others, indicate that the world around the protagonist—the world of the concentration camps—is now beyond the possibility of human comprehension, and that Rosa at the end of the story has been driven into a world as infantile as that of Magda.

Note: "The Shawl" first appeared in *The New Yorker* in 1981. In 1984 Ozick published a sequel called "Rosa" in the same magazine, though she wrote both stories in 1977. In 1989 the two stories were published in a book called *The Shawl*. "Rosa," set thirty years later than "The Shawl," tells how Rosa gave up her New York furniture store and now, grudgingly supported by Stella, lives a squalid life in Miami, where she rarely ventures from her room. She has fantasies (conjured up by the magic shawl) of Magda as a doctor, or as a professor. Stella accuses Rosa of idolatry, of being "like those people in the Middle Ages who worshipped a piece of the True Cross, a splinter from some old outhouse as far as anybody knew." Far from causing readers to distance themselves from Rosa, however, Ozick's presentation of Rosa's idolatry frees readers to encounter her experience. Ozick has said [*New York Times Book Review*, 10 (September 1989): 39] that although she worries that the Holocaust "is corrupted by fiction and that fiction in general corrupts history," her aim in writing fiction is "to make everybody a witness."

TOPICS FOR CRITICAL THINKING AND WRITING

1. The fourth paragraph begins, "It was a magic shawl." Why does the narrator say this? Now notice the last clause in the story: "Rosa drank Magda's shawl until it dried." Does this mean that the magic stopped working? Or that, for some reason, there was no longer a need for a magic shawl? Or what?

2. The story combines an apparently simple, matter-of-fact, realistic style with a highly figurative style. What is the effect of this combination?

3. There is very little dialogue in the story. What is the effect of the relative absence of dialogue?

EDGAR ALLAN POE

The Tell-Tale Heart (p. 511)

We will list here the key interpretive questions and issues that we highlight when we teach this story:

The narrative point of view: What kind of person is this narrator? Why does Poe use first-person point of view, rather than third-person omniscient? This might be the opportunity for you to linger with the class over the famous opening: "True—nervous—very, very dreadfully nervous I had been and am; but why will you say that I am mad?" Poe, we know, was a deliberate, painstaking craftsman, and we might help students to think about his sense of style and structure by taking note of this first sentence and then moving to the final one: "I admit the deed!—tear up the planks!—here, here!—it is the beating of his hideous heart!" How does Poe get from here (opening sentence) to there (final sentence)?

What is the narrator's purpose in telling his story? Along these lines, we might mention that one scholar has said that Poe wanted in "The Tell-Tale Hart" to present a narrator who is both "highly rational and insane." We could also quote here the following comments by James W. Gargano, who praises Poe's technique while perhaps intimating some reservations about it:

In "The Tell-Tale Heart" the cleavage between author and narrator is perfectly apparent. The sharp exclamations, nervous questions, and broken sentences almost too blatantly advertise Poe's conscious intention; the protagonist's painful insistence in "proving" himself sane only serves to intensify the idea of his madness. Once again Poe presides with precision of perception at the psychological drama he describes. He makes us understand that the voluble murderer has been tortured by the nightmarish terrors he attributes to his victim: "He was sitting up in bed listening;—just as I have done, night after night, harkening to the death watches in the wall"; further, the narrator interprets the old man's groan in terms of his own persistent anguish: "Many a night, just at midnight, when all the world slept, it has welled up from my own bosom, deepening, with its dreadful echo, the terrors that distracted me." Thus, Poe, in allowing his narrator to disburden himself of his tale, skillfully contrives to show also that he lives in a haunted and eerie world of his own demented making.
—James W. Gargano, "The Question of Poe's Narrators," *College English* 25:3 (December 1963): 177–81.

Does the narrator make clear the nature of his relationship to his victim? What is the meaning of the "evil eye"? E. Arthur Robinson argues that the key to the story is:

the murderer's psychological identification with the man he kills. Similar sensory details connect the two men. The vulture eye which the subject casts upon the narrator is duplicated in the "single dim ray" of the lantern that falls upon his own eye; like the unshuttered lantern, it is always one eye that is mentioned, never two. One man hears the creaking of the lantern hinge, the other the slipping of a finger upon the fastening. Both lie awake at midnight "hearkening to the death-watches in the wall." The loud yell of the murderer is echoed in the old man's shriek, which the narrator, as though with increasing clairvoyance, later tells the police was his own. Most of all the identity is implied in the key psychological occurrence in the story—the madman's mistaking his own heartbeat for that of his victim, both before and after the murder.
—E. Arthur Robinson, "Poe's 'The Tell-Tale Heart,'" *Nineteenth-Century Fiction* 19:4 (March 1965): 369–78.

Is there a "real" version of events that Poe wants us to perceive behind the version that his deranged narrator recounts?

Who or what is the old man? Some critics contend that in this story Poe is dramatizing human wickedness—the narrator's motiveless malignity, his killing of an innocent man. Other critics have maintained that in killing the old man, the narrator is seeking to kill himself—that is, that the narrator projects onto the old man his own self-loathing. Still other critics have proposed that, in truth, there is no old man at all—that he is a fantastical creation of the narrator's deranged mind.

In a study of Poe published in 1885, the scholar George Woodberry states that "The Tell-Tale Heart" is a "tale of conscience." What makes it *that*, yet also more than that?

Does Poe lead us to sympathize with his murderous narrator? Some students, we have found, believe that he does, while others steadfastly do not.

This question bears, too, on the tone of the story. It is likely that your students have seen countless horror movies and scary TV shows. And the aim of many of them is to be extreme and excessive—on the one hand, to horrify and shock us, but, on the other hand, to make us laugh, maybe as a release from fear, maybe as the sign of our knowing recognition that the events we are witnessing are, deliberately, overblown and exaggerated. You might ask your students: Is "The Tell-Tale Heart" at all funny? Or: If we told Poe that we found ourselves laughing at his narrator, what might be his response? Would Poe be pleased, or would he reply that we have misunderstood his intention?

We conclude with this stimulating remark by Edward H. Davidson, in *Poe: A Critical Study* (1957): "The tragedy (if it is a tragedy) of the Poe heroes is that they suffer from a war between their own faculties, body and mind, or mind and soul; and once that struggle has begun, it ends only with death. This disease of being is the enormous distension of any one perception or faculty at the expense of the others; and the Poe protagonists nearly all have in common the death-wish." (203)

EDGAR ALLAN POE

The Cask of Amontillado (p. 514)

Because many students will have read this story in high school, it can be used effectively as the first assignment. They will start with some ideas about it, and at the end of the class discussion they will probably see that they didn't know everything about the story. It may be well to begin a class discussion by asking the students to characterize the narrator. The opening paragraph itself, if read aloud in class, ought to provide enough for them to see that the speaker is probably paranoid and given to a monstrous sort of reasoning, though, of course, at the start of the story we cannot be absolutely certain that Fortunato has not indeed heaped a "thousand injuries" on him. (In this paragraph, notice too the word "impunity," which we later learn is part of the family motto.) When we meet Fortunato, we are convinced that though the narrator's enemy is something of a fool, he is not the monster that the narrator thinks he is. And so the words at the end of the story, fifty years later, must have an ironic tone, for though *in pace requiescat* can apply to Fortunato, they cannot apply to the speaker, who is still talking (on his deathbed, to a priest?) of his vengeance on the unfortunate Fortunato.

The story is full of other little ironies, conscious on the part of Montresor, unconscious on the part of Fortunato:

- The narrator is courteous but murderous.
- The time is one of festivity but a murder is being planned.
- The festival of disguise corresponds to the narrator's disguise of his feelings.
- Fortunato thinks he is festively *disguised* as a fool, but he is a fool.
- He says he will not die of a cough, and the narrator assures him that he is right.

- Fortunato is a Freemason, and when he asks the narrator for the secret sign of a brother, the narrator boldly, playfully, outrageously shows him the mason's trowel that he will soon use to wall Fortunato up.

But what to make of all this? It has been the fashion, for at least a few decades, to say that Poe's situations and themes speak to our anxieties, our fear of being buried alive, our fear of disintegration of the self, and so on. Maybe. Maybe, too, there is something to Marie Bonaparte's interpretation. She sees the journey through the tunnel to the crypt as an entry into the womb; the narrator is killing his father (Fortunato) and possessing his mother. And maybe, too, there is something to Daniel Hoffman's assertion in *Poe Poe Poe Poe Poe Poe Poe* (223) that Montresor and Fortunato are doubles: "When Montresor leads Fortunato down into the farthest vault of his family's wine-cellar, into a catacomb of human bones, is he not . . . conducting his double thither? My treasure, my fortune, down into the bowels of the earth, a charnel-house of bones." Maybe.

In addition to Hoffman's book (1972), we can recommend Kenneth Silverman's fine biography, *Edgar Allan Poe: Mournful and Never-Ending Remembrance* (1991).

A videocassette of Edgar Allan Poe's "The Cask of Amontillado" is available from Longman Publishers.

MICHELE SERROS

Senior Picture Day (p. 519)

This engaging story will cause no difficulty for students, or, rather, they can easily understand it, but it is conceivable that some students will be offended by the depiction of a young woman of Middle American Indian ancestry who is disturbed by her large nose.

Some but not all of your students may know that the Maya esteemed a large nose as a sign of high social status: Sculptures of high priests and of aristocrats always show them with large noses; in fact, the bridges of the noses extend well up into the forehead. Other cultures, too, esteemed a long nose. Some of your students may know a line from the Song of Solomon (7.4):

Thy nose is as the tower of Lebanon which looketh toward Damascus.

Our own favorite quotation about noses appears in William Hazlitt's *My First Acquaintance with Poets* where Hazlitt—who had an ample nose—describes Coleridge:

His nose, the rudder of the face, the index of the will, was small, feeble, nothing.

Alas, an adolescent with a large nose is not likely to take comfort in the fact that the Maya, the biblical world, and William Hazlitt endorsed large noses.

In the book we ask students what their response is toward the narrator. It is our guess that many, especially students who themselves are close in age to the narrator, will condemn her for her snobbism; she talks about "snooty" people in the first paragraph, but clearly she regards herself as superior to persons of Indian heritage, even though she herself is such a person. Our own view, and the view of some other older readers, is more charitable. Yes, her snobbism is deplorable, and so is her self-hatred (though that term is a bit strong), but, well, she is young. She is an adolescent, and much can be forgiven. Adolescence has its problems, and one of its characteristics is shame of one's parents—with the funny speech (especially if the parents are immigrants), their flabby flesh, and, yes, in some cases their big noses. We happen to have come across a comment about adolescence that we think we may test in class when we teach this story:

> The conflict between the need to belong to a group and the need to be seen
> as unique and individual is the dominant struggle of adolescents.
>   —Jeanne Elium and Don Elium, *Raising a Daughter* (1994), 11

The narrator very much wants to belong to the group of blond Californians, to Terri's group, though, as we learn, Terri does not have much use for this girl— this girl who, in Terri's words, has "this nose, a nose like . . . like an *Indian*"; and Terri's father is scarcely a role model.

Given the Anglo society's view of Indian physiognomy it is not surprising that the narrator is ashamed of her nose. And surely the narrator will in time find that squeezing her nose is not going to make it smaller. Meanwhile a reader can deplore her pretensions and yet smile a bit at them and can wish her well in the long run.

LESLIE MARMON SILKO

The Man to Send Rain Clouds (p. 523)

The church—especially perhaps the Roman Catholic Church—has often adapted itself to the old ways and beliefs of new converts, sometimes by retaining the old holidays and holy places but adapting them and dedicating them to the new religion. For instance, although the date of the birth of Jesus is not known, from the fourth century it was celebrated late in December, displacing pagan festivals of new birth (e.g., the Roman *Saturnalia*, which celebrated the sowing of the crops on December 15–17, and the feast of the *Natalis Solis Invicti*, celebrating the renewal of the sun a week later).

Practices of this sort have facilitated conversion, but from the church's point of view the danger may be that the new believers retain too much faith in the old beliefs. In Silko's story the priest has every reason to doubt that his parishioners have fully accepted Christianity. The unnamed priest—he's just "the priest" or "the young priest," not anyone with a personal identity, so far as the other characters in the story are concerned—is kind and well-meaning, and he is even willing to bend the rules a bit, but he knows that he does not have the confidence of the people. He is disturbed that they didn't think the Last Rites and a funeral Mass were necessary, and he is not at all certain that they have given up their pagan ways: "He looked at the red blanket, not sure

that Teofilo was so small, wondering if it wasn't some perverse Indian trick—
something they did in March to ensure a good harvest. . . ." He is wrong in
suspecting that Teofilo (the name means "beloved of God," from the Greek
theos = God, and *philos* = loving) is not in front of him, but he is right in suspecting that a "trick" is being played, since the reader knows that the holy
water is wanted not to assist Teofilo to get to the Christian heaven but to bring
rain for the crops. In Part One we hear Leon say, "Send us rain clouds,
Grandfather"; in Part Three we hear Louise express the hope that the priest
will sprinkle water so Teofilo "won't be thirsty"; and at the very end of the
story we hear that Leon "felt good because it was finished, and he was happy
about the sprinkling of the holy water, now the old man could send them big
thunderclouds for sure."

We aren't quite sure about what to make of the passage in which the
water, disappearing as soon as it is sprinkled on the grave, "reminded" the
priest of something, but the passage is given some emphasis and surely it is
important. Our sense is that the priest vaguely intuits an archetypal mystery,
something older and more inclusive than the Roman Catholic ritual he
engages in.

During most of the story the narrator neither editorializes nor enters the
minds of the characters; we are not told that the characters are reverential, and
(for the most part) we are not allowed to hear their thoughts. Rather, we see
them perform ceremonies with dignity, and, because the point of view is
chiefly objective, we draw our own conclusions. Possibly, too, by keeping outside of the minds of the characters the narrator helps to convey the traditional
paleface idea that Native Americans are inscrutable people, people of few
words. Certainly Leon hoards words when, responding to the priest's admoni-
tion not to let Teofilo stay at the sheep camp alone, he says, "No, he won't do
that any more now." But we do get into the priest's mind, notably in the passage in which he suspects trickery, and we get into Leon's mind at the end of
the story when, in what almost seems like a thunderstorm of information, we
are told his thoughts about the water.

Because the narrator, like the characters, is taciturn, some readers may
think that Leon and his companions are callous. "After all," one student
said, "don't they first round up the sheep before attending to the burial
rites? And why don't they weep?" Class discussion can usually bring out
the dignity of the proceedings here, and some students may be able to provide specific details about burial customs unfamiliar to other members of
the class.

We do not know if the different colors of paint—white, blue, yellow, and
green—have specific meanings, but perhaps blue suggests the sky and the
water, yellow suggests corn meal, and green suggests vegetation. White is a
fairly widespread sign of purity, but we have not been able to find out how
Pueblo people regard it. (If you know about these things, we'll be most appre-
ciative if you write to us, in care of the publisher.)

Silko has written two novels: *Ceremony* (1977) and *Almanac of the Dead*
(1991). Short stories and prose poems are included in *Storyteller* (1981). Per
Syersted has written a cogent introduction, *Leslie Marmon Silko* (1980), but it
needs to be updated. For additional commentary, see Alan R. Veile, *Four
Indian Masters* (1982). For students working on the stories, we recommend
Helen Jaskoski, *Leslie Marmon Silko: A Study of the Short Fiction* (1998).

AMY TAN

Two Kinds (p. 526)

It's not a bad idea to ask a student to read the first two paragraphs aloud and then to invite the class to comment. What, you might ask them, do they hear besides some information about the mother's beliefs? Probably they will hear at least two other things: (1) the voice of a narrator who does not quite share her mother's opinion, and (2) a comic tone. You may, then, want to spend some time in class examining *what the writer has done* that lets a reader draw these inferences. On the first point, it may be enough to begin by noticing that when someone says, "My mother believed," we are almost sure to feel some difference between the speaker and the reported belief. Here the belief is further distanced by the fivefold repetition of "You could." The comedy—perhaps better characterized as mild humor—is evident in the naivete or simplicity of ambitions: open a restaurant, work for the government, retire, buy a house with almost no money down, become famous. Many readers may feel superior (as the daughter herself does) to this mother, who apparently thinks that in America money and fame and even genius are readily available to all who apply themselves—but many readers may also wish that their mother was as enthusiastic.

The second paragraph adds a sort of comic topper. After all, when the mother says, in the first paragraph, "you could be anything you wanted to be in America," the ambitions that she specifies are not impossible, but when in the second paragraph she says, "you can be prodigy too," and "you can be best anything," we realize that we are listening to an obsessed parent, a woman ferociously possessive of her daughter. (In another story in Tan's *Joy Luck Club* a mother says of her daughter, "How can she be her own person? When did I give her up?") Obsessions, of course, can be the stuff of tragedy—some students will be quick to talk about Macbeth's ambition, Brutus's self-confidence, and so forth—but obsessions are also the stuff of comedy; witness the lover who writes sonnets to his mistress's eyebrow, Harpo Marx in pursuit of a blonde, the pedant, and all sorts of other monomaniacs whose monomania (at least as it is represented in the work of art) is not dangerous to others.

The third paragraph, with its references to the terrible losses in China, darkens the tone, but the fourth restores the comedy, with its vision of "a Chinese Shirley Temple." The fifth paragraph is perhaps the most obviously funny so far. When Shirley Temple cries, the narrator's mother says to her daughter: "You already know how. Don't need talent for crying!"

There's no need here to belabor the obvious, but students—accustomed to thinking that everything in a textbook is deadly serious—easily miss the humor. They will definitely grasp the absurdity of the thought that "Nairobi" might be one way of pronouncing Helsinki, but they may miss the delightful comedy of Auntie Lindo pretending that Waverly's abundant chess trophies are a nuisance ("all day I have no time to do nothing but dust off her winnings"), and even a deaf piano teacher may not strike them as comic. (Of course, in "real life" we probably would find pathos rather than comedy in a deaf piano teacher—and that's a point worth discussing in class.) So the point to make, probably, is that the story is comic (for example, in the mother's single-mindedness, and in the daughter's absurd hope that the recital may be going all right, even though she is hitting all the wrong notes) but is also serious (the conflict between the mother and the daughter, the mother's passionate love, the daughter's rebelliousness, and the daughter's later recognition that her mother loved her deeply). It is serious, too, in the way it shows us (especially in the passage about the "old Chinese silk dresses") the narrator's deepening perception of her Chinese heritage.

As a child, she at first shares her mother's desire that she be a "prodigy," but she soon becomes determined to be herself. In the mirror she sees herself as "ordinary" but also as "angry, powerful"; she is an independent creature, not an imitation of Shirley Temple. The question is, Can a young person achieve independence without shattering a fiercely possessive parent? Or, for that matter, without shattering herself? We can understand the narrator's need to defy her mother ("I now felt stronger, as if my true self had finally emerged"), but the devastating effect when she speaks of her mother's dead babies seems almost too great a price to pay. Surely the reader will be pleased to learn that the narrator and her mother became more or less reconciled, even though the mother continued to feel that the narrator just didn't try hard enough to be a genius. It's worth reading aloud the passage about the mother's offer of the piano:

> And after that, every time I saw it in my parents' living room, standing in front of the bay window, it made me feel proud, as if it were a shiny trophy that I had won back.

As a mature woman, the narrator comes to see that "Pleading Child" (which might almost be the title of her early history) is complemented by "Perfectly Contented." Of course, just as we have to interpret "Pleading Child" a bit freely—let's say as "Agitated Child"—so "Perfectly Contented" must be interpreted freely as, say, "Maturity Achieved." We get (to quote the title of the story) "two kinds" of experience and "two kinds" of daughter, in one.

See Marina Heung, "Daughter-Text/Mother-Text: Matrilineage in Amy Tan's *Joy Luck Club*," *Feminist Studies* 19 (Fall 1993): 597–616.

TOPICS FOR CRITICAL THINKING AND WRITING

1. Try to recall your responses when you had finished reading the first three paragraphs. At that point, how did the mother strike you? Now that you have read the entire story, is your view of her different? If so, in what way(s)?
2. When the narrator looks in the mirror, she discovers "the prodigy side," a face she "had never seen before." What do you think she is discovering?
3. If you enjoyed the story, point out two or three passages that you found particularly engaging, and briefly explain why they appeal to you.
4. Do you think this story is interesting only because it may give a glimpse of life in a Chinese-American family? Or do you find it interesting for additional reasons? Explain.
5. Conceivably the story could have ended with the fourth paragraph from the end. What do the last three paragraphs contribute?

JAMES THURBER
The Secret Life of Walter Mitty (p. 534)

Class discussion may begin with an examination of the point at which it is apparent that this story is comic. Anyone who knows Thurber's name will of course expect comedy, but not every student has heard of him. The first two sentences do not (on first reading) reveal themselves as comic, though in hindsight one sees that at least the first sentence is from the world of inferior adventure stories. An alert reader may become suspicious of the third sentence with its "full-dress uniform" and its "heavily braided white cap pulled down rakishly over one cold gray eye." Suspicions are confirmed with "ta-pocketa-pocketa-pocketa-*pocketa-pocketa*"; the ludicrous "eight-engined Navy hydroplane" and the cliché about the Old Man make the comedy unmistakable.

Instructors may find it useful to introduce the concept of pathos and to lead the class in a discussion of the relation of the pathetic to the tragic and the comic. Here, of course, Mitty's daydreams are comic; we may pity him because of his weakness, but we can only laugh at his daydreams, which (1) are so greatly in contrast with the actual event, and (2) are so indebted to bad movies and pulp magazines.

Brooks and Warren provide an interpretation of the story in various editions of *Understanding Fiction;* Charles S. Holmes's *The Clocks of Columbus* (1972) is a useful study of Thurber. Carl Sundell examines the structure of the story (e.g., it begins and ends with Mitty dreaming) [*English Journal* 56 (1967): 1284–1287]. James Ellis [*English Journal* 54 (1965): 310–313] points out that Mitty's fantasies are made even more fantastic by various bits of misinformation. For example, Mitty the sea captain calls for "full strength in No. 3 turret," mistakenly thinking that the turrets move the ship; the surgeon nonsensically speaks of obstreosis (primarily a disease of cattle and pigs) of the ductal tract and thinks coreopsis (a flower) is a disease; the marksman refers to a 50.80-caliber pistol (its diameter would be more than four feet); the pilot speaks of von Richtman but means von Richthofen.

One other study of the story should be mentioned, Ann Ferguson Manx's in *Studies in Short Fiction* 19 (1982): 315–357. This essay is a vigorous defense of Mrs. Mitty, who is usually thought of as a nag. Manx argues that Mitty's fantasies are not provoked by Mrs. Mitty's naggings. Rather, Mitty is a hopeless fantasist, and it's a good thing for him that he has Mrs. Mitty to see that he wears his galoshes, doesn't drive too fast, and so on. Manx writes: "If we think seriously about what life with a man like Mitty would be like, Mrs. Mitty seems responsible and concerned." Perhaps the best thing is not to "think seriously" about what living with Walter Mitty would be like.

For a well-annotated selection of Thurber's work, along with a detailed chronology of his life, see *James Thurber: Writings and Drawings* (Library of America, 1996). See also Charles Shiveley Holmes, *The Clocks of Columbus: The Literary Career of James Thurber* (1972), and Robert Emmet Long, *James Thurber* (1988).

TOPICS FOR CRITICAL THINKING AND WRITING

1. In a paragraph, characterize Mrs. Mitty.
2. In an essay of 500 words, evaluate the view that Mrs. Mitty is exactly the sort of woman Walter Mitty needs.

LEO TOLSTOY

The Death of Ivan Ilych (p. 538)

No author need apologize for writing about death, a topic of such enormous interest that it is rivaled only by sex. But if we think for a moment about "The Death of Ivan Ilych," we realize that it is largely about the life of Ivan Ilych, or, more precisely, about his deathbed realization that he has scarcely lived. Despite the recurrent references to Ivan Ilych's illness, the story reveals not a morbid interest in illness and dying but a heartening interest in living.

The first sentence of the second part of the story makes this clear: "Ivan Ilych's life had been most simple and most ordinary and therefore most terrible." In the remainder of the story Tolstoy (clearly the narrator is Tolstoy, or someone so close to him that we need scarcely speak delicately of "the narrator") goes on to demonstrate the terribleness of this ordinariness. Superficially Ivan Ilych's life would seem to be unusual and successful: He climbs fairly high up the social ladder, achieves a substantial salary, has a wife, children, and an ample home, and he has some power which he savors even if he does not abuse it.

But the point, of course, is that after he falls ill and nears death, he becomes aware—as Tolstoy has kept the reader aware—that Ivan Ilych's interests are so narrow, and even his vices so trivial, that however he may be envied, he can scarcely be said to have lived. He learns this through sickness, which forces intense awareness of oneself, as anyone realizes who has had even so trivial a sickness as a running nose. And one of the facts about us, which we are scarcely aware of until we become sick, is that some day we will die.

Tolstoy makes it clear that, in a way, Ivan Ilych knew this. In a logic text he had learned that "Caius is a man, men are mortal, therefore Caius is mortal," but, Tolstoy says, these words "had always seemed to him correct as applied to Caius, but certainly not as applied to himself." And here we can digress for a moment on one of the differences between literature and philosophy. Literature, it has long been recognized, has a concreteness or immediacy that at least in some considerable degree forces the reader to sense or experience the reality that is being presented; to some degree we believe in and understand the experiences of the characters in good literature (at least in realistic prose fiction such as this story). Why do we identify with such figures? Probably for at least two reasons: (1) We are given a fairly convincing detailed picture of their surroundings, and (2) we are given revelations of character or psychological insights whose truth we recognize from our own experiences. Each of these two points may be discussed a bit.

Most novels, long or short, carefully build up a picture of the characters' surroundings. Thus, "The Death of Ivan Ilych" begins with a reference to an apparently public event ("the Melvinski trial") and to a public building (the "Law Courts"), specifies the name of a particular person, and moves through other people's names to the name of a newspaper. We know, of course, that we are reading fiction, but it is fiction that insists on facts, rather than fiction that begins, "Once upon a time in a far-off country there lived a woodsman who had three sons." But it is not merely the specification of names of buildings, people, and newspapers that gives us a sense of a believable world. Tolstoy continually gives us a sense of the solidity of things. For example, describing the players beginning a card game, Tolstoy mentions that "they dealt, bending the new cards to soften them." We need not look here for symbolism, we need not fancy that the cards, like Ivan Ilych, are being forced into a new shape; we can be content simply with our sense of the reality of this (fictional) card game. It is through such details, which pervade the story, that the writer gains our confidence.

Illustrations need not be multiplied, but we might look briefly at one other scene before proceeding to the second point, the author's psychological astuteness. In the first section of the story there is a highly comic scene in which Peter Ivanovich sits "on a low pouffe, the springs of which yielded spasmodically under his weight." There again, most literally, is the sense of the weight of things. When Peter must get up to assist the widow in detaching a shawl that catches on the carved edge of a table (again, convincing even if apparently irrelevant detail), "the springs of the pouffe, relieved of his weight, rose also and gave him a push." It probably is not fanciful to see here, in the pouffe's mechanical behavior, satiric commentary on the mechanical (conventional, unspontaneous) behavior of Peter and the widow, but it would be wrong to neglect the fact that Tolstoy also sees the pouffe as a pouffe, a thing with a density of its own, and it is through a world of believable things that his characters move.

Now for the second point, the revelation of convincing characters. Possibly the presentation of convincing *things* is a sort of sleight of hand whereby authors win our confidence in their perceptions. After all, it does not follow that because a writer is perceptive enough to notice that card players bend new cards and that pouffes have springs, he or she is a shrewd perceiver of human nature. But in page after page Tolstoy does indeed give us shrewd perceptions of human nature. He catches the irritability and the hypersensitivity of a sick man, for example, in the scene when his partner "pushed the cards courteously and indulgently towards Ivan Ilych that he might have the pleasure of gathering them up without the trouble of stretching out his hand for them." Ivan Ilych's mental response is, "Does he think I am too weak to stretch out my arm?"

As we begin to read the story, perceiving the mutual insincerity that passes between Peter Ivanovich and the widow he is supposed to be consoling, and perceiving Ivan Ilych's shallowness, we may feel superior to the characters, but it soon becomes evident that although these people are not very amiable, we can scarcely look down on them. Too much is revealed about them that we recognize in ourselves. We have been pushed by pouffes, we have experienced "the complacent feeling that, 'it is he who is dead and not I,'" we have said to widows what we believe we are supposed to say, and—most telling—we know from experience the truth of Tolstoy's assertion that after Peter pressed the widow's hand because it was "the right thing," "both he and she were touched." That hurts, this perception that we are moved by our own calculating gestures.

Most of all, of course, we are concerned with Ivan Ilych, not with his widow or his acquaintances, and here again, we are compelled to recognize that we cannot take a superior attitude. We simply find him too recognizable, too human, too much ourself, to take refuge in thoughts of our superiority. Interestingly, he is not given much external characterization. He has a name, he is somewhat bald, he has a prominent nose and a graying beard, but he is not described in such detail as to become a "character" and therefore someone apart from us. The story, after all, is the story of Everyone: Near the end of one's life one finds that death terrifies and that one has not loved and therefore in any significant sense one has scarcely lived. Ivan Ilych very late and very painfully comes to an awareness of these things; his body racks him first into an awareness of physical existence and then into an awareness of spirit whereby he is at last able to recognize his lifetime of failure and to experience—terribly late—a compassion that banishes the fear of death.

In a very crude sense, then, the story has a happy ending—a man in his last couple of hours experiences a pity for others that is perhaps indistinguishable from love and dies without fear—but Tolstoy does not let us off that easily with a comforting message. We continue to remember the agony of Ivan Ilych's dying months and the waste of his life.

The discussion of Tolstoy's story is often one of the high points of any course in which it is taught. This is testimony to Tolstoy's art and intention, his desire to make his literary gifts serve the teaching of a compelling moral lesson. But instructors might use the students' responses here, more generally, to bring home to the class the powerful connection between literature and life. This is a truism that we frequently express but that perhaps is not always evident to students, who tend to compartmentalize their literary experiences, seeing them as separate from the lives they lead. Tolstoy shows that a literary work can directly engage us in reflecting on the choices by which we organize our lives from day to day. He addresses each reader: "Is this the way you should be living?" And what is wonderful, even breathtaking, we think, is the manner in which he asks this question through the highest form of narrative artistry. There is something essential here about the value of literature that instructors should talk about with their students.

Biographies of Tolstoy have been written by Ernest J. Simmons (1946), Henri Troyat (1967), and A. N. Wilson (1988). A good introduction to his literary career is R. F. Christian, *Tolstoy: A Critical Introduction* (1969). For commentary on "The Death of Ivan Ilych," see the relevant sections in Philip Rahv, *Image and Idea* (1949); *Tolstoy: A Collection of Critical Essays,* ed. Ralph E. Matlaw (1967); E. B. Greenwood, *Tolstoy: The Comprehensive Vision* (1975); Gary R. Jahn, *"The Death of Ivan Ilich": An Interpretation* (1993); and Gary R. Jahn, *Tolstoy's "The Death of Ivan Ilich": A Critical Companion* (1999).

TOPICS FOR CRITICAL THINKING AND WRITING

1. What do you think of the way the story opens? Why, in your opinion, does Tolstoy begin not by telling us about Ivan's early years but by having Ivan's colleagues learn of his death during a pause in some business?

2. Tolstoy tells us a good deal about Ivan's house. What does the house tell us about its owner?

3. What, if anything, did you find comic in the story? And if you did find some comic passages, what do they contribute?

4. Summarize the change (and the reasons for the change) in Praskovya, from a bright and attractive woman to the woman we meet early in the story.

5. Of Ivan's death, the narrator says near the very end of the story, "He tried to add, 'forgive me,' but said, 'forgo.'" Why did Ivan say "forgo"? Is the word relevant to the story?

JOHN UPDIKE

The Rumor (p. 577)

One might almost have thought that the emergence of the gay liberation movement had put an end to all talk about "latent" homosexuality, but it hasn't; indeed, although sexual identity is much talked about, it remains at least as mysterious as ever.

One of the interesting things about "The Rumor" is that it is about sex and yet it has very little sexual action in it. We hear that Sharon had sex with Frank when she was sixteen, that they "made love just two nights ago," that Frank had a "flurry of adulterous womanizing," and (about a third of the way through the story) that Frank, after the rumor has changed everything, engages in "pushing more brusquely than was his style at her increasing sexual unwillingness," but that's pretty much it, as far as sexual activity goes. Yet the story glances at a wide spectrum of sexual activity. We can begin with heterosexuality:

1. Frank and Sharon married partly as a way of getting out of Cincinnati. ("Their early sex had been difficult for her; she had submitted to his advances out of a larger, more social, rather idealistic attraction. She knew that together they would have the strength to get out of Cincinnati and, singly or married to others, they would stay.")
2. Frank has had adulterous heterosexual affairs—but after the rumor has reached his ears, he wonders if these were not really a manifestation of his homosexuality.

As for homosexuality, there is:

1. The unambiguous homosexuality of Walton Forney and Jojo, and of others who make up "the queer side" of the art world.
2. The part of Frank's nature that, as he now sees it, is homosexual. Here too we find a spectrum. Probably some of Frank's speculations strikes a reader as tenuous (e.g., his belief that his attraction to "stoical men" had a homosexual component). The passage about the golfing trip in Bermuda, however, is more convincing; Frank "had felt his heart make many curious motions, among them the heaving, all-but-impossible effort women's hearts make in overcoming men's heavy grayness and achieving—a rainbow born of drizzle—love." Finally, at the end of the story, it seems clear that Frank's interest in Jojo, which he characterizes as "Hellenic fellowship," is a mixture of the physical ("That silvery line of a scar . . . lean long muscles . . . white skin") and the intellectual and paternal (Jojo now seems "unexpectedly intelligent," and someone who "needed direction").

Is Frank a homosexual? Any answer would of course have to say what homosexuality is, or, more precisely, would have to say what it means to be a homosexual. It's our sense of the story that as the rumor persists, Frank finds in himself things that seem to confirm it, that is, he begins to take his identity from the identity ascribed to him. He now looks back on various episodes and sees in them a homosexual slant which cannot quite be disproved, though it cannot be proved either; for example, the idea that his adulterous affairs were an attempt to deny his essential homosexuality.

The first half of the story pretty clearly establishes Frank—or seems to establish him—as heterosexual, though even here there are some ambiguous notes. For instance, when he first denies that he has a lover, he does so "too calmly." We take the comment to reflect Sharon's perception, but it comes from the omniscient narrator and therefore can at least be conceived as an authoritative comment. Similarly, Frank's hostile comment about gays—"You know how gays are. Malicious. Mischievous"—sounds like the unambiguous comment of a straight male; yet of course it can be taken as a reflection of Frank's insecurity, a disparaging comment made by someone unsure of his own masculinity. (By the way, the comment is *Frank's*, not—as some students may think—Updike's.)

The idea that gays are "malicious" probably is fairly common among straight men; what is especially interesting in this story is that Updike goes on to use the words "malice" and "maliciousness" in connection with Frank's behavior: "Frank sensed her discomfort and took a certain malicious pleasure in it," and Sharon's belief in the rumor "justified a certain maliciousness" on Frank's part. So, again, we get Frank taking his identity from society's view; if (at least in Frank's view) gays are malicious, Frank—now rumored to be gay—will be malicious. In any case, the first half of the story is largely devoted to setting forth the rumor and to giving evidence of Frank's heterosexuality, and the second half of the story is largely devoted to Frank's perception (creation?) of himself as a homosexual. Whereas in the first half of the story, his denial increased his wife's belief in the truth of the rumor and indeed the very "outrageousness" of the rumor paradoxically served to confirm her suspicions, now, in the second half we find a new belief (Frank's) based, it may seem to most readers, on evidence almost equally insubstantial. In the first half she spied on him, looking for tiny clues (e.g., his response to a waiter) and interpreting them in one way, and in the second half he spies on himself, equally attentive to tiny clues, and equally seeing the evidence only one way.

Does Updike take a stand on the nature/nurture argument about gender identity? We don't think so (and we certainly don't think a writer of fiction need do so), but he does force the issue into a reader's mind. Frank himself sometimes seems to incline to the "nature" view, for instance, when he thinks of himself as someone likely to be a homosexual because he is a man "slight of build, with artistic interests," but at other times he senses that what he is depends on who is around him: "Depending on which man he was standing with, Frank felt large and straight and sonorous, or, as with Wes, gracile and flighty."

III

Poetry

Approaching Poetry: Responding in Writing

LANGSTON HUGHES

Harlem (p. 587)

In the eight lines enclosed within the frame (that is, between the first and next-to-last lines) we get four possibilities: the Dream may "dry up," "fester," "crust and sugar over," or "sag." Each of these is set forth with a simile, for example, "dry up / like a raisin in the sun." By the way, the third of these, "crust up and sugar over—like a syrupy sweet," probably describes a dream that has turned into smiling Uncle Tomism. Similes can be effective, and these *are* effective, but in the final line Hughes states the last possibility (*"Or does it explode?"*) directly and briefly, without an amplification. The effect is, more or less, to suggest that the fancy (or pretty) talk stops. The explosion is too serious to be treated in a literary way. But, of course, the word "explode," applied to a dream, is itself figurative. That is, the last line is as "literary" or "poetical" as the earlier lines, but it is a slightly different sort of poetry.

A word about the rhymes: Notice that although the poem does use rhyme, it does not use a couplet until the last two lines. The effect of the couplet (load / explode) is that the poem ends with a bang. Of course, when one reads the poem in a book, one sees where the poem ends—though a reader may be surprised to find the forceful rhyme—but an audience hearing the poem recited is surely taken off-guard. The explosion is unexpected (especially in the context of the two previous lines about a sagging, heavy load) and powerful.

Note: Later in the textbook we present Hughes in depth.

See *The Collected Poems of Langston Hughes,* ed. Arnold Rampersad (1995), an excellent edition. Rampersad's two-volume biography (1986, 1988) is superb. On the poetry: Onwuchekwa Jemie, *Langston Hughes: An Introduction to the Poetry* (1976). See also James A. Emmanuel, *Langston Hughes* (1967);

Langston Hughes, Black Genius: A Critical Evaluation, ed. T. B. O'Daniel (1972); Richard K. Barksdale, *Langston Hughes: The Poet and His Critics* (1977); Steven C. Tracy, *Langston Hughes and the Blues* (1988); and R. Baxter Miller, *The Art and Imagination of Langston Hughes* (1989).

A "Voices and Visions" videocassette of Langston Hughes is available from Longman Publishers.

TOPIC FOR CRITICAL THINKING AND WRITING

One might keep the first line where it is, and then rearrange the other stanzas—for instance, putting lines 2–8 after 9–11. Which version (Hughes's or the one just mentioned) do you prefer? Why?

APHRA BEHN

Song: Love Armed (p. 594)

Although the allegory may at first seem unfamiliar to relatively inexperienced readers, if you ask students whether they have ever heard of any connections between love and war, they will quickly come up with phrases such as "the battle of the sexes" and "all is fair in love and war," and someone will mention that Cupid is armed with a bow and arrows. And although we don't want to push this delightful poem too far in the direction of realism, probably many students will find Behn's characterization of love as "tyrannic" quite intelligible.

It happens, however, that what especially interests us about the poem is the issue we raise in our first question: Why do people enjoy songs about unhappy love? Because it gives us a chance to impose form onto suffering, and thus implies a kind of mastery over suffering? In any case, many students will be familiar with the motif and will be able to offer explanations accounting for the pleasure they take in the material.

Aphra Behn was not only a poet but also a playwright and novelist, and when teaching her poetry, we often take note of her powerful narrative of slavery and colonization, *Oroonoko* (1688). On this work, which has received much attention recently, see Katharine M. Rogers, "Fact and Fiction in Aphra Behn's *Oroonoko*," *Studies in the Novel* 20 (Spring 1988): 1–15. See also George Woodcock, *The Incomparable Aphra* (1948; rpt. as *Aphra Behn: The English Sappho*, 1989), and Angeline Goreau, *Reconstructing Aphra* (1980).

12

Narrative Poetry

Half a century ago virtually all students in grammar school and high school became familiar with narrative poetry by Longfellow ("The Wreck of the Hesperus," "Hiawatha," "Paul Revere's Ride"), Whittier ("Barbara Fritchie"), and Kipling ("Gunga Din," "The Ballad of East and West"). These poems (and indeed their authors) seem to have utterly vanished from the curriculum, and it may well be that the only narrative poem you can count on most of your students knowing is "The Night before Christmas," though from time to time we encounter students who have read *The Iliad* and *The Odyssey* in one version or other.

ANONYMOUS

There Was a Young Fellow of Riga (p. 598)

Almost all students will know some limericks, and these can provide an entrance into narrative poetry, though the danger is that most of the limericks they know will be obscene. We are reminded of a comment by the late Bennet Cerf, the publisher. His company, Random House, sponsored a limerick contest, and when he was asked how he chose the winning limerick he said, "When we discarded all the obscene submissions, the one that was left was awarded the prize."

The limerick with which we introduce our chapter seems to us to be an admirable narrative:

> There was a young fellow of Riga,
> Who smiled as he rode on a tiger.
>   They returned from the ride,
>   With the fellow inside,
> And the smile on the face of the tiger.

We shouldn't make too much of these lines, but first we want to mention that other versions exist, notably "young lady" instead of "young fellow," and "Niger" instead of "Riga." But to get to the narrative: The poem admirably follows Aristotle's principle that a plot should have a beginning, a middle, and an end. We begin with an interesting situation: Somebody is riding a tiger. No reader or auditor asks how this person got on the tiger, or why, or where the rider is headed. We just accept the situation as an interesting one, and we wonder what it will lead to. That is, we wonder where the writer will take us. The rider's smile is thoroughly understandable (a sort of enthusiastic "Look Ma! I'm riding, no hands!"), and the narrator then picks up this detail and uses it in an unexpected but (when we think about it) thoroughly reasonable and thoroughly satisfying way: The smile reappears on the face of the tiger. We couldn't have predicted this ending, but once we hear it we realize that it makes excellent sense. It is indeed the natural ending (cf. the Chinese proverb, "He who rides a tiger is afraid to dismount," or "What goes around comes around," or "The chickens come home to roost"), and there is nothing more to be said. In short, the story is told efficiently, effectively, memorably. It fits E. M. Forster's comment that a good plot does two things, fulfills expectations and offers a slight surprise: "Shock, followed by the feeling, 'Oh, that's all right,' is a sign that all is well with plot."

ANONYMOUS

Sir Patrick Spence (p. 600)

We have found that traditional ballads teach well, partly because they are narrative, partly because they are musical, and partly because students can be invited to talk about other ballads that they know. If you are lucky, a student in your class will sing some ballads.

Albert B. Friedman, in *The Viking Book of Folk Ballads*, reissued as *The Penguin Book of Folk Ballads* (1977), gives additional versions of "Sir Patrick Spence," a comic version of "The Three Ravens," and an American version of "Edward." An American version of "Edward" is recorded on an album, *Child Ballads Traditional in the United States*, 1, issued by the Library of Congress (AAFS L57). Some of these may be useful in class discussion.

Discussion of the questions in the text ought to fill a good part of the hour and ought to help students to see the virtues in this great ballad. One might also call attention to the fact that the poem does not begin with Sir Patrick—whose initial appearance is effectively held off and built up to—and to the fact that the first lines, with their reference to the king drinking, suggest a life of courtly ease that contrasts with Sir Patrick's life of seamanship. But notice too the dark or tragic implication in the second line: The wine is "blude-reid." And we should also call attention to the contrast between the nobles, who are "loath" to wet their shoes, and Sir Patrick, who is not eager for the trip and is much more than "loath," for he knows that the trip is virtually a death mission. The nobles are associated with ladies with fans and combs. The courtiers will be mourned by the ladies, but we are not told of any mourners for Sir Patrick. However, we see Sir Patrick as master of the lords in death by virtue of having done his duty with full awareness.

Here are some of our thoughts about the questions we give in the text.

Our own response is that the poem is much more about loyalty than about a storm at sea. There's no way of being sure about the "eldern knicht," but, as we suggested a moment ago, we think this poem is chiefly about Sir Patrick's loyalty. Whether the knight is malicious or not does not, finally, matter. Students sometimes have trouble understanding the sharp transition. Apparently at first Sir Patrick thinks the order to sail is a joke, but then he sees it is serious, and he foresees the ironic consequences. The two states are sharply juxtaposed, without a transition. We prefer the first version, since we find the second melodramatic. We much prefer the conclusion in the version given in the text, since it ends quietly and with dignity.

We think these questions can help to get a lively discussion going, but we want to mention also that we think students can have fun—can learn a lot about poetry—by doing some ballad-making of their own. Alice Munro, in a fairly recent story, "Before the Change" (first published in *The New Yorker,* August 24 and 31, 1998), has the narrator say, "One of our teachers had got us reading old ballads like 'Patrick Spence' . . . and there'd been a rash of ballad-making at school:

> I'm going down the corridor
> My good friend for to see
> I'm going to the lav-a-to-ry
> To have myself a pee."

The narrator, a doctor's daughter, then reports a stanza that she had made, based on what she saw when she spied on people coming to her father—who, she later learns, performs abortions at a time when abortions were illegal:

> A lady walks on a long long path
> She's left the town behind.
> She's left her home and her father's wrath
> Her destiny for to find.

There is a good deal to say for urging students to try their hand at writing ballad stanzas.

Students who become interested in the form might enjoy browsing in *The Oxford Book of Ballads* (1969) and *The Faber Book of Ballads* (1965).

ANONYMOUS

The Demon Lover (p. 602)

Not all ballads include supernatural elements, but a good many of them do. This is not to say, however, that these ballads are purely fanciful or escapist. Many of them, including "The Demon Lover," are deeply rooted also in the passions (which, finally, are mysterious) of this world.

"The Demon Lover" nicely illustrates several of the characteristics mentioned in the text. That is, the process of oral transmission probably has eliminated the dross (the antecedent action may once have been given at length but now it can be gleaned only from the dialogue) and has left us chiefly with memorable speech, swiftly drawn pictures, and strong passions. There is no comment on the action, no reflection on the theme. Rather, whatever "meaning" the poem has is conveyed only through the action. It begins not with the introduction of a speaker but with dialogue. In a similarly abrupt fashion, without telling us that after A spoke B replied, we get the words of the second speaker. As in most ballads (or at least in most of the ballads that are regarded as the best) the plot is vigorous but highly abbreviated, and the characters—perceived through what they say rather than through description—are sharply drawn, not in the sense that they are rounded but in the sense that they are embodiments of intense passions. (One thinks of Yeats's remark that comedy gives us "characters" but in tragedy we get not character but pure passion, intense versions of ourselves.)

Between lines 28 and 29 (between the seventh and eighth stanzas) the woman decides to go with the demon lover. In the final stanza the lover suddenly appears to become gigantic, striking the topmast (one thinks of him striking the top of the mast) and the foremast simultaneously. That is, his overwhelming power is given a physical dimension that corresponds to its force.

For a selection of ballads, see Francis Child's *English and Scottish Popular Ballads* (1904), ed. Helen Child Sargent and George Lyman Kittredge. See also *The Oxford Book of Ballads* (1910); *The Faber Book of Ballads* (1965); and *The Viking Book of Folk Ballads of the English-Speaking World* (1956), rptd. as *The Penguin Book of Folk Ballads of the English-Speaking World* (1977).

JOHN KEATS

La Belle Dame sans Merci (p. 605)

"La Belle Dame" is elaborately discussed in Earl Wasserman, *The Finer Tone* (1953), and more reasonably discussed in books on Keats by Walter Jackson Bate, Douglas Bush, and Charles Patterson, and in Harold Bloom's *The Visionary Company* (1962). Here are a few points: In the first stanza, nature ("withered") reflects the condition of the knight ("*palely* loitering"). The second stanza further establishes the time as autumn, and though nature is abundant ("The squirrel's granary is full"), the knight seems starved, and the implication is that he is approaching winter, that is, death. Line 22 ("And nothing else saw all day long") indicates his total absorption in the lady's song, which (along with "roots of relish sweet, / And honey wild, and manna dew") nourished him for a while, and brought him to a vision of people who resemble him in his present condition ("pale"). This vision is presumably a vision of mortality, and he awakes to find himself "On the cold hill's side"—in the physical world unredeemed by the imagination.

SIEGFRIED SASSOON

The General (p. 607)

As Sassoon found in his day and as we know in ours, any criticism of a nation when it is engaged in fighting a war is likely to be viewed as an act of disloyalty. In Sassoon's case, because he had been wounded and decorated for courage, the government suggested that he was suffering from "shell-shock," put him in a hospital, and thus shrewdly muted his criticism.

Some of your students may be familiar with Tennyson's "The Charge of the Light Brigade" (1854), a poem celebrating—well, exactly *what* does it celebrate? The poem concerns an episode in the Crimean War, when a brigade of British cavalry was mistakenly ordered to charge entrenched Russian artillery, with the result that some 400 of the 600 British soldiers were killed. Tennyson celebrates British courage and discipline ("Theirs not to reason why, / Theirs but to do and die. Into the valley of death / Rode the six hundred"). The poem ends:

> When can their glory fade?
> O the wild charge they made!
>   All the world wondered.
> Honor the light Brigade,
> Noble six hundred!

In its day the poem was taken as a tribute to the soldiers; today it is hard not to engage in a bit of reading against the grain, hard not to see it as an exposé of the incompetence of the officers, the blind obedience of soldiers, and all in all the horrors—especially the terrible waste of life—that war entails.

Sassoon's affable general is still with us. The writer of these pages recalls an occasional visit (during World War II) of a general to the mess hall where enlisted men ate, some patting on the back, some encouraging words, and indeed in our own time we have seen on television a President visit combat troops and speak encouragingly. This is as it should be—but one hopes that the troops are supported by wise commanders, not by affable incompetents.

Sassoon's storyteller (to answer our questions) is a soldier who has been sent to the frontline ("the line" in line 2), and who is one of the few survivors. He reports the General's courtesy and cheerfulness in the first two lines, but in the third line he lets us know that most of the soldiers now are dead. In the fourth line, "And we're cursing his staff for incompetent swine," he clearly aligns himself with the indignant survivors, but in the next line he takes us back to the point of view of the simple soldiers who were taken in by the General:

> "He's a cheery old card," grunted Harry to Jack

Jack is grunting and slogging toward Arras (and, we learn in the last line, toward his death), but he seems to be a good-natured fellow, loyal to his incompetent commander.

The space before the last line represents a pause, before the speaker delivers the devastating comment—devastating to the reader, for although we know little of Harry and nothing at all of Jack, we feel their deaths strongly precisely because the line is so flatly delivered, with its colloquial "he did for them both," i.e., he destroyed them both. (Further, the triple rhyme—unexpected because the preceding quatrain rhymes *abab*—hammers the point home.) In short, although the narrator is part of the group cursing the staff in line 4, we never hear him curse; we hear him quote a favorable testimony (Harry's), and at the end we hear him speak idiomatically and simply—but under this calm façade we also hear Jonathan Swift's *saeva indignatio*.

See also: Michael Thorpe, *Siegfried Sassoon: A Critical Study* (1967); and Jean Moorcroft Wilson, *Siegfried Sassoon: The Making of a War Poet: A Biography, 1886–1918* (1999).

COUNTEE CULLEN

Incident (p. 607)

The poem seems to be of the utmost simplicity: twelve lines without any figures of speech and without any obscure words. But it has its complexities, beginning with the title.

Our first question in the text asks students to think about the word "incident." It's our impression that an "incident" is usually a minor affair—something detached from what comes before and after, and of little consequence. For instance: "During the banquet a waiter dropped a tray full of dishes, but apart from this incident the affair was a great success." There are of course plenty of exceptions, such as the famous "Incident at Harpers Ferry," but we think that on the whole an incident is (1) minor and (2) a distinct occurrence.

Cullen's title therefore is ironic; the episode might seem to be minor, but in fact it has left an indelible mark on the speaker's mind (and on the minds of countless readers). And since it continues to have its effect, it is not something separate and done with. The apparent simplicity, then, of the title and of the entire poem, is deceptive, since this seemingly trivial and unconnected episode stands for, or embodies, an enormous force in American life.

It's a good idea to ask a student to read the poem aloud in class (true for all poems, of course), so that students can hear the rhythms. On the whole, "Incident" sounds like a happy jingle, but of course that is part of the irony. Two details that strike us as especially effective are the enjambments in lines 7 and 11.

Of the other ten lines, eight end with some mark of punctuation, and the other two ("I saw a Baltimorean" and "I saw the whole of Baltimore") could be complete in themselves. But in the seventh line we are propelled into the horrible event of the eighth line ("And so I smiled, but he poked out / His tongue, and called me 'Nigger'"); and in the eleventh line we are propelled into the final line, the line that tells us that this whole "incident" was by no means trivial ("Of all the things that happened there / That's all that I remember").

Studies of Countee Cullen include Helen J. Dinger, *A Study of Countee Cullen* (1953); Stephen H. Brontz, *Roots of Negro Racial Consciousness—The 1920s: Three Harlem Renaissance Authors* (1954); Blanche E. Ferguson, *Countee*

Cullen and the Negro Renaissance (1966); and Margaret Perry, *A Bio-Bibliography of Countee P. Cullen* (1969).

Instructors will find these secondary sources to be helpful, but none of them offers help on one issue that will be in the air when Cullen's poem is discussed. "Nigger," in line 8, is an ugly, offensive word—which is central to Cullen's point in the poem, but which is nonetheless a hard word for the teacher and for students to say aloud and to analyze.

We know some instructors who press hard on the word "Nigger" in class; they want the students to feel very vividly the crude bigotry and shock of the term. This approach, we confess, does not work for us, and so we follow a different path. Often, after we have read the poem and begun to examine it with students, we have paused to say outright that it's hard to use and talk about offensive racial and ethnic slurs and epithets. Yes, one of them is in Cullen's poem, and thus it has to be considered as essential to its meaning. But, still, we tell and teach ourselves that such words are wrong—that they should not be used, ever, because they are offensive—and thus it cuts against our principles and (we hope) our practice to hear ourselves voicing them.

This may or may not be the best approach, but at the least it acknowledges for students that *something* is awry and uncomfortable in the room when the instructor and students start using the word "nigger" or other words like it. Keep in mind what the students are or might be thinking and feeling. Be aware of and talk about it. The tone of the class will be better, we believe, if you are sensitive to this issue and seek as best you can to address it carefully. The mistake would be to assume that, in a classroom context, ugly, offensive words will be heard by students neutrally, dispassionately.

EDWIN ARLINGTON ROBINSON

Richard Cory (p. 608)

The point is not that money doesn't bring happiness; even a thoroughly civilized spirit (grace, taste, courtesy) does not bring happiness. The protagonist's name is significant. "Richard" suggests "Rich," and probably his entire name faintly suggests Richard Cœur de Lion (and *cœur* = heart and core, and also suggests *cour* = court). These suggestions, along with "crown," "favored," "imperially," "arrayed," "glittered," "king," emphasize his superiority. Other words emphasize his dignity, courtesy, and humanity: "gentleman," "clean favored," "quietly," "human," "schooled," "grace." Everything combines to depict him as a man of self-sufficiency, dignity, and restraint—yet he kills himself. Still, even his final act has some dignity: It is stated briefly, and it takes place on "one calm summer night." Students might be asked if anything is lost by substituting (what might on first thought seem more appropriate) "one dark winter night." If this rewriting is not bad enough, listen to Paul Simon's version of the poem. He sings it, with Art Garfunkel, on *Sounds of Silence*, Columbia CS 9269.

There is a *Collected Poems* (1937) but this huge volume (1,500 pages) is not the place where students should begin. Direct them instead to *Selected Poems*, ed. M. D. Zabel (1965). They will profit from these secondary sources: Emory Neff,

Edwin Arlington Robinson (1948); Ellsworth Barnard, *Edwin Arlington Robinson: A Critical Study* (1952); and Wallace Anderson, *Edwin Arlington Robinson: A Critical Introduction* (1967). See also Nancy Carol Joyner, *E. A. Robinson: A Reference Guide* (1978).

EMILY DICKINSON

Because I could not stop for Death (p. 609)

In Dickinson's "Because I could not stop for Death," the fact that a grave is suggested in lines 17–20 eludes many students; the reference to the grave contributes to toughening the poem. This stanza, by the way, is a good example of the closeness of some metaphors to riddles, a point worth discussing in class. Allen Tate, in a famous essay, praised the poem because "we are not told what to think." J. J. McGann, rightly taking issue with Tate, points out that "the message about the benevolence of Death is plain enough." McGann also takes issue with the widespread idea that in this poem death is a "gentlemanly suitor." He argues, on the contrary, that since the penultimate line speaks of "horses," Dickinson is talking not about a suitor—who would drive only one horse—but about an undertaker, who is driving a hearse. (McGann's essay originally appeared in *New Literary History*, 12 [1981], and is reprinted in *Literary Theories in Praxis* [1987], ed. Shirley F. Staton.) Selections from a number of commentaries (including, among others, Allen Tate, *Reactionary Essays*; Yvor Winters, *In Defense of Reason*; and Richard Chase, *Emily Dickinson*) are collected in *Fourteen by Emily Dickinson*, ed. Thomas M. Davis (1964). See also Clark Griffith, *The Long Shadow* (1964, 128–34), and Charles R. Anderson, *Emily Dickinson's Poetry* (1960, 241–466).

Camille Paglia, in *Break, Blow, Burn* (2005), a volume of short essays on poems ranging from Shakespeare to Joni Mitchell, offers an unconventional reading (97–100). We give a very few excerpts:

> In this ingenious allegory . . . a proper, respectable lady is courted and then kidnapped and murdered by a smooth gentleman caller. Dickinson's protagonist. . . never comprehend[s] the dark forces at work in the world. . . .
>
> The trusting speaker fails to see that her suitor's good manners ("Civility" 8) are a ruse. He is a seducer and cad, a trickster or confidence man. . . .
>
> "Ring" [10] is the competitive arena of earthly life, a gated paddock where men are schooled like horses. It's also a communal circle dance, . . . suggesting order and regularity on the one hand but conformity and entrapment on the other. . . .
>
> At the poem's exact midpoint, there is a hesitation or stutter ("Or rather—"), as the personified Sun obliviously vanishes ("He passed Us") and the lady's mental powers start to dim (13). . . .
>
> After the first stanza's carefree regularity, the rest of the poem uses unsettling, daringly modern off rhymes to hint at the speaker's loss of control as well as the gradual breakdown of meaning ("away"/"Civility"; "Ring"/"Sun"; "chill"/"Tulle"). . . .
>
> God himself is the suave kidnapper. That the carriage's apocalyptic "Horses' Heads" are steering "toward eternity," however, raises the ques-

tion of whether God is the driver or the driven, himself a victim of larger, impersonal forces (23–24).

Paglia's reading clearly is off-beat. You may want to consult the entire short essay in her book.

JOHN LENNON AND PAUL MCCARTNEY

Eleanor Rigby (p. 610)

We aren't explicitly told what Eleanor Rigby is waiting for, but presumably it is for a handsome man who will rescue her from loneliness, such being the ideal of materialistic male-dominated society. But Father McKenzie is also lonely, a spiritual figure in a materialistic world. The two are brought together at Eleanor Rigby's funeral (to which nobody comes), and this perhaps arouses thoughts of his own funeral, about which no one will care.

The Beatles' version of the song is in their album *Revolver* (Capitol ST76).

ADDITIONAL TOPIC FOR CRITICAL THINKING AND WRITING
What do you make of "Wearing the face that she keeps in a jar by the door" (7)? Is the sermon (14) only a sermon, or are there further implications?

E. E. CUMMINGS

anyone lived in a pretty how town (p. 611)

It can be useful to ask students to put into the usual order (so far as one can) the words of the first two stanzas, and then to ask students why Cummings's version is more effective. Here are a few rough glosses: line 4: "danced his did" = lived intensely (versus the "someones" who in 18 "did their dance," that is, unenthusiastically went through motions that might have been ecstatic); 7: "they sowed their isn't they reaped their same" gives us the little-minded or small-minded who, unlike "anyone," are unloving and therefore receiving nothing; 8: "sun moon stars rain" = day after day; 10: "down they forgot as up they grew" implies a mental diminution that accompanies growing up; 17: "someones," that is, adults, people who think they are somebody; 25: "anyone died," that is, the child matured, stopped loving (and became dead as the other adults). The last two stanzas imply that although children grow into "Women and men" (33), the seasons continue the same. (This reading is heavily indebted to R. C. Walsh, *Explicator* 22 no. 9 [May 1964], Item 72. For a more complicated reading, see D. R. Clark, *Lyric Resonance* [1972, 187–94].)

Norman Friedman has written two books, *E. E. Cummings: The Art of His Poetry* (1960) and *E. E. Cummings: The Growth of a Writer* (1964), and edited a third, *E. E. Cummings: A Collection of Critical Essays* (1972). Also helpful is Cary Lane, *I Am: A Study of E. E. Cummings' Poems* (1976).

13

Lyric Poetry

One can engage in more profitable activities than in fretting about whether a given poem is a narrative poem or a lyric, but the topic is worth at least a little thought. Something, of course, depends on the way in which the text is rendered. Spirituals, for instance, often have considerable narrative content, and yet one feels that their affinities are with the lyric and that the story is subordinate to the state of mind. This sense of lyrical meditation is heightened by the refrains—repetitions that do not advance the story and that help to communicate and to induce a visionary state. An instructor who wants to pursue this topic may want to discuss such work as "Go Down, Moses," which is included in the text.

There is much fascinating material about the theory of nineteenth-century lyric poetry in M. H. Abrams, *The Mirror and the Lamp* (1971). See also C. Day Lewis, *The Lyric Impulse* (1965), and W. R. Johnson, *The Idea of the Lyric: Lyric Modes in Ancient and Modern Poetry* (1982).

ANONYMOUS

Michael Row the Boat Ashore (p. 613), Careless Love (p. 613), The Colorado Trail (p. 615)

Versions of "Michael" were in print in the 1870s, and the song is still popular. Among effective recordings is one by Pete Seeger on Columbia (CS9717). "Careless Love" easily leads to a discussion of the blues. Here is a brief part of Ralph Ellison's comment on the genre in an essay on Richard Wright in Ellison's *Shadow and Act*: "Their attraction lies in this, that they at once express both the agony of life and the possibility of conquering it through sheer toughness of spirit. They fall short of tragedy only in that they provide no solution, offer no scapegoat but the self."

In Chapter 18 on rhythm, we quote a remark by Ezra Pound that an instructor may wish to use in connection with "Michael," "Careless Love," or "The Colorado Trail." Pound says (789), "Poetry withers and dries out when it leaves music, or at least imagined music, too far behind it. Poets who are not interested in music are, or become, bad poets." In "Colorado Trail," surely the repetitions of sounds help to make the poem singable and memorable. Ask students if they find "Blow winds blow" as attractive to the ear (as well as to the mind) as the poem's "Wail winds wail," or "all along the length of" as attractive as the poem's "all along, along, along." One can also try to account for the difference between, say, "Annie was a pretty girl," and "Laura was a pretty girl." Our own feeling is that the liquids in Laura (l, r) go better with the other liquids in the line ("pretty girl"), but other ears may hear something different.

ANONYMOUS

Western Wind (p. 615)

"Western Wind" has been much discussed. Probably most readers will find acceptable R. P. Warren's suggestion (*Kenyon Review*, 1943, 5) that the grieving lover seeks relief for the absence of his beloved in "the sympathetic manifestation of nature." But how do you feel about Patric M. Sweeney's view (*Explicator*, October 1955) that the speaker asserts that "he will come to life only when the dead woman returns, and her love, like rain, renews him"? In short, in this view the speaker "cries out to the one person who conquered death, who knows that the dead, returning to life, give life to those who loved them." We find this reading of the poem hard to take, but (like many readings) it is virtually impossible to *dis*prove.

One other point: Some readers have asked why other readers assume that the speaker is a male. A hard question to answer.

JULIA WARD HOWE

Battle Hymn of the Republic (p. 616)

Although in the last few decades women in considerable numbers have written poetry on political and social issues, in earlier periods their chief topics were love, children, death, and God, for the most part treated personally, intimately, rather than publicly. But religion allowed, in hymns, for personal expression on a public topic, and the Abolitionist movement especially provided a subject about which women could exhort society to action.

Lines 1–4 of "Battle Hymn of the Republic" are indebted to Revelations 19.11 ("And I saw heaven opened, and behold a white horse; and he that sat upon him was called Faithful and True, and in righteousness he doth judge and make war"), 14 ("And the armies which were in heaven followed him upon the white horses"), and 15 ("And out of his mouth goeth a sharp sword, that with it he should smite the nations: and he shall rule them with a rod of iron: and he treadeth the winepress of the fierceness and wrath of Almighty God"). Isaiah 63.3–6 ("I have trodden the winepress . . . ; I will tread down the people in mine anger"), describing God's punishment of His enemies, also exerted an influence. Line 15 is indebted to Genesis 3.15 (God tells the serpent that woman's seed shall bruise the serpent's head), and in line 18 "sifting" is related to Isaiah 30.28 (God will "sift the nations"). The "fiery gospel" of the third stanza perhaps comes from Deuteronomy 33.2 ("from his right hand went a fiery law"). The lilies of line 21 probably come from the Song of Songs and the Sermon on the Mount; the connection between holiness and freedom (23) is common in Paul, though of course in "Battle Hymn" (published in 1861) the allusion to freedom in line 23 is to freeing the black slaves.

In *Redeemer Nation*, Ernest Tuveson briefly discusses the poem in the context of American apocalyptic writing. He points out that although many who have sung the hymn have thought that the biblical images are merely "fitting metaphors for a war between right and wrong," the images in fact convey "a message about the precise place and point of the war in the pattern of salvation." (The idea was that the Civil War is the fruit of the accumulated evils of the reign of Satan; the day of the Antichrist is ending.)

The hymn has recently been the subject of some controversy. In July 1986 a committee of the United Methodist Church (a denomination formed in 1968 when the Methodist Church and the Evangelical United Brethren merged) narrowly voted to eliminate "Battle Hymn of the Republic" (along with "Onward, Christian Soldiers") from the hymnal. The committee received thousands of letters of protest and reversed its decision in July 1987. Students might well be invited to discuss the appropriateness (or inappropriateness) of the military metaphor and the reasons for the appeal of the hymn.

Two other issues: "Glory, Glory, Hallelujah" (a shout of triumph at the fall of Babylon) was not in the "Hymn" when it was first published. The final stanza, with its two lines about Christ, may seem incongruous or inept, but it introduces the Incarnation and Atonement, which made possible the last triumphs over evil on earth. Hermes Nye sings "Battle Hymn" on a record entitled *Ballads of the Civil War*, vol. 1 (Folkways FA 2187 [FP 48/7]).

WILLIAM SHAKESPEARE

Spring (p. 618) and *Winter (p. 619)*

No music of the period is known for these songs, sung by unspecified singers at the end of *Love's Labor's Lost*.

The songs obviously make a contrasting pair, but as every commentator says, each song contains conflicting elements within it. "Spring" celebrates joys of the season (meadows in flower, shepherds singing, "merry larks," turtledoves copulating ["when turtles tread"]), but in its picture of abundance and fertility it also introduces, with the cuckoo's call, the idea of adultery. (The cuckoo lays its eggs in the nests of other birds—though why the word "cuckold" is applied to the unwitting husband rather than to the adulterer is unclear.)

"Winter" similarly embodies conflicting elements. The poem begins by emphasizing the rigors of winter and the labors involved, but by the end of the first stanza we are indoors, with "greasy Joan"—not perhaps the most pleasant company, but the pot she cools is most welcome. The second stanza (beginning with line 10) returns us briefly to the outdoors ("the wind doth blow"), but in its second line we are in the church; the coughing congregation drowns out the parson's saws (wise sayings, but perhaps there is also a suggestion that these words have been repeated too many times). Marian's nose is "red and raw" but against these unpleasantnesses we have the joy of contemplating crab apples while they are roasting—and indeed, the entire poem, with its tribulations, is joyful so far as the reader is concerned.

A number of commentators have been disturbed by the characterization of the owl's "Tu-whit, tu-who" as "a merry note," but we take it as a sort of transferred epithet, i.e., the speaker (or reader) is "merry," and the word is applied to what he or she hears.

W. H. AUDEN

Stop All the Clocks, Cut Off the Telephone (p. 620)

Even students who have little familiarity with traditional literature will enjoy the poem, but readers familiar with traditional elegies (such as "Lycidas") will especially enjoy it, since it is a modern version of the classical pastoral elegy. From the days of the Greek Sicilian poet Theocritus, the pastoral elegy called upon all nature to mourn for the deceased shepherd; the poet ordered the trees to shed their leaves, the streams to stop flowing, etc., all in order to express proper grief for the great loss that the speaker had experienced in the death of his beloved.

Auden wryly introduces into this form the paraphernalia of our world—clocks, telephones, airplanes, and so on—and yet keeps the basic motifs of the original. A phrase such as "let the mourners come" (line 4) might occur in almost any classical elegy (from Theocritus to Milton or Matthew Arnold), where customarily there is a procession of mourners. Next we would expect to hear something about the depth of their expression of grief—perhaps the heavens would reverberate with their cry. In Auden's poem, however, the invocation to mourners is followed by "Let aeroplanes circle moaning overhead / Scribbling on the sky the message He Is Dead."

But we do not take the poem as merely a joke, or as lacking in feeling. Yes, it uses hyperbole and it has comic elements, but it also seems to us to effectively express the emotions of a grieving lover, someone who—though of course knowing better—nevertheless feels that the beloved is the moon and sun, someone who might reasonably say that the beloved was "my North, my South, my East and West, / My working week and my Sunday rest." Incidentally, the poem is recited in the film *Four Weddings and a Funeral*. It aroused much favorable comment—so much that the publisher promptly issued a little book with this poem and a few others by Auden and announced on the cover that the book contained the poem from the film.

Collected Poems (1976) and *The English Auden: Poems, Essays, and Dramatic Writings, 1927–1939* (1977), both edited by Edward Mendelson, are full of interesting work, but they give more than most undergraduates will be able to absorb. We tend to direct students to the selections by Auden that are included in the Norton and Oxford anthologies of English literature and in the *Norton Anthology of Modern Poetry*. *The Dyer's Hand and Other Essays* (1968) and *Forewords and Afterwords* (1973) collect many of Auden's best literary essays and reviews.

Two useful books for students: John Fuller, *A Reader's Guide to W. H. Auden* (1970), and Monroe K. Spears, *The Poetry of W. H. Auden: The Disenchanted Island* (1963). More advanced students will find value in Anthony Hecht, *The Hidden Law: The Poetry of W. H. Auden* (1993). Biographies have been written by Humphrey Carpenter (1981) and Richard Davenport-Hines (1995). For literary and social contexts, see Samuel Hynes, *The Auden Generation: Literature and Politics in England in the 1930s* (1976). See also Edward Mendelson, *Early Auden* (1981) and *Later Auden* (1999).

EMILY BRONTË

Spellbound (p. 621)

We first came across this poem in *The New Oxford Book of English Verse*, ed. Helen Gardner (1972), where it is given the title "Spellbound," though we have since seen it printed without this title as well. Here is a good place to begin: Ask the students what it means to be "spellbound," and how this word creates in us a set of associations—about enchantment, fascination—that in the poem itself Brontë seeks to capitalize upon and develop. You can return to a version of this question after you have reached the end of the poem: How much does the poem benefit from this title? Would the poem change, for better or worse, if it were printed not with this title, but (as it sometimes is) with the opening line as the title?

Another good question for the class: Where is the speaker? More precisely: Is she outside, with the night "darkening" around her and the winds blowing? Or is she—less likely, but still possible—inside, looking outward on a wintry scene from which she cannot break free? Or—another possibility—is the description of the scene not something that is happening "outside" the speaker, but, rather, the expression of something within her? This is how she feels—in the dark, cold, alone.

When we pitch the discussion in this way, we are trying to prompt the students to perceive that a description is not only *that* but is also a means through which a writer can dramatize the temperament and personality of a speaker. What counts is not just the description in its own terms but the description as it serves to reveal to us the speaker's thoughts and feelings. The point is perhaps an obvious one, but we have found that it needs to be made explicitly and demonstrated to the students through examples.

Still another question: What is it that has overtaken the speaker? It is more than a little hard to say. She gives us some indication—"a tyrant spell has bound me." "Tyrant" tells us that the spell is oppressive, harsh, and cruel; and "bound" suggests the physical force of the spell, as if it had literally tied down the speaker. But what about the spell itself? What does it consist of, and from where has it come?

Brontë does not explain or clarify the nature of the spell. It is present, and it is powerful—so powerful that the storm's intense power cannot shake the speaker free from it.

The spell seems terrible and terrifying, but not entirely. It is one thing for you or I to say, "I cannot go," which implies that a force is holding us back, and another thing to say, as does the speaker in the final line, "I will not" go, which intimates that the choice is one's own. Perhaps, one suspects, the speaker will not go because she needs to discover what this spell is about.

"Drear" is a curious word. *The American Heritage Dictionary* defines it simply as "dreary," which is unhelpful. *Webster's Third New International Dictionary* is better: cheerless and depressing; uninteresting and dull. The *Oxford English Dictionary* weighs in with dreariness, sadness, gloom. But how then does this word fit in the poem? Is the speaker saying, "No matter how cheerless and gloomy the scene is around me, I will not, cannot, go from it—the spell is too powerful"? Maybe, but one might have expected to find here a different, stronger phrase: "But no great fear can move me." As poetry, this revision may not be appealing, but it has the virtue of naming the speaker's predicament more directly.

It could be that the modern dictionaries we consulted are not the right ones for this word. When our curiosity led us to Samuel Johnson's *Dictionary of the English Language* (4th ed., 1773), we found that he includes for "drear" the meaning "dread, terror." This would give the forcefulness to the line that we might otherwise assume is oddly missing from it. And it seems likely that Brontë's own sense of the word would be close to or the same as Johnson's.

"Spellbound" is an alluring, yet mysterious, poem—it has a spellbinding power itself. The speaker tells us that something intense is happening to her, but she leaves unstated its exact source or cause. We can probe and speculate, but this speaker remains distant from us even as she tells us that paralysis has overtaken her. Unless, that is, we are drawn to say that this speaker is not addressing us at all, but, rapt as she is, is speaking solely to herself.

For students interested in reading more of Brontë's poetry, *The Poems of Emily Brontë*, ed. Derek Roper with Edward Chitham (1995), is recommended. Chitham has also written a good biography: *A Life of Emily Brontë* (1987). For the study of the Brontë family, there is a superb, richly detailed biography: Juliet Barker, *The Brontës* (1994). Barker has also edited *The Brontës: A Life in Letters* (1997), an illuminating selection of the family's correspondence.

ANONYMOUS AFRICAN AMERICAN

Go Down, Moses (p. 622) and
Swing Low, Sweet Chariot (p. 624)

One of the chief themes in spirituals is the desire for release, and this theme is often set forth with imagery from the Hebrew Bible. Some additional points should be mentioned. Most of what follows here is derived from Albert J. Raboteau, *Slave Religion* (1978).

Although the passages about release undoubtedly refer to the release from slavery, the songs should not be taken only as disguised statements about secular life. Many slaves—like at least some of their masters—believed that the Bible was the book of the acts of God, which is to say that they "believed that the supernatural continually impinged on the natural, that divine action constantly took place within the lives of men, in the past, present, and future" (Raboteau, 250).

Raboteau makes a second very important point:

Identification with the children of Israel was, of course, a significant theme for white Americans, too. From the beginnings of colonization, white Christians had identified the journey across the Atlantic to the New World as the exodus of a new Israel from the bondage of Europe into the promised land of milk and honey. For the black Christian, as Vincent Harding has observed [in *The Religious Situation*, ed. Donald R. Cutter], the imagery was reversed: the Middle Passage had brought his people to Egypt land, where they suffered bondage under Pharaoh. White Christians saw themselves as a new Israel; slaves identified themselves as the old. (250–51)

Instructors who have time for some additional reading may wish to consult— for a survey of scholarship on the topic—John White, "Veiled Testimony: Negro Spirituals and the Slave Experience," in *Journal of American Studies* 17 (1983): 251–63. White is especially concerned with adjudicating between those who see spirituals (of the type that we reprint) as highly revolutionary and, on the other hand, those who see the songs as in effect serving the cause of the masters, since the songs seem to suggest that suffering in this world is transient, and that God will later reward the sufferers. (As an example of this second view, White quotes E. Franklin Frazier, an African-American scholar who in *The Negro Church in America* [1964] rejected "the efforts of Negro intellectuals . . . encouraged by white radicals, to invest the spirituals with a revolutionary meaning.")

Other recommended works (in addition to Raboteau and White): John Lovell, *Black Song: The Forge and the Flame* (1972); James H. Cone, *The Spirituals and the Blues* (1972); and Lawrence Levine, *Black Culture and Black Consciousness* (1977).

Obviously this song (like all oral literature) really ought to be heard, not simply read. Many excellent recordings are available, but if you are lucky you may find a student who will give a live performance in class.

Dena J. Epstein, in a fascinating book called *Sinful Tunes and Spirituals* (1977), offers extremely interesting information about "Go Down, Moses." According to Epstein, the earliest written report of the song is by the Reverend Lewis C. Lockwood, who visited Fort Monroe, a Virginia fort at the entrance to the Chesapeake Bay. Lockwood arrived there on September 3, 1861, and commented on his first experience of African-American singers. In his report, published under the title of *National Anti-Slavery Standard* 22 (Oct. 12, 1861): 3, and reprinted by Epstein (244), he wrote:

Last evening . . . on the piazza of the hotel, I overheard music, and directed my footsteps thither, and in a long building, just outside the entrance of the Fortress, I found a number of colored people assembled for a prayer-meeting. The brother who led in the concluding prayer had a sing-song manner, but his sentiments and expressions were very scriptural and impressive. He prayed that He who brought Israel out of Egypt, Jonah out of the mouth of the whale, and Daniel out of the den of lions, might bring them out into full deliverance, spiritually and temporally.

I told my mission in few words, and the message was received with deep, half-uttered expressions of gladness and gratitude. They assured me that this was what they had been praying for; and now that "the good Lord" had answered their prayers, they felt assured that some great thing

was in store for them and their people. There are some peculiarities in
their prayer-meetings. Their responses are not boisterous; but in the gentle, chanted style. . . . The themes are generally devotional; but they have
a prime deliverance melody, that runs in this style

"Go down to Egypt—Tell Pharoah
Thus saith my servant, Moses
Let my people go."

Accent on the last syllable, with repetition of the chorus, that seems every
hour to ring like a warning note in the ear of despotism.

Epstein's account (246) includes another version of the song.

LANGSTON HUGHES

Evenin' Air Blues (p. 626)

Though perhaps when we first think of blues we think of songs of disappointed love, blues include songs concerned with other kinds of loneliness, and
some at least implicitly relate this loneliness to an oppressive society that is
built on segregation and that engenders wandering and alienation. Hughes's
"Evenin' Air Blues," then, is genuinely related to the blues tradition, though
not surprisingly the note of social protest is a little more evident.

The last stanza, chiefly by virtue of its first line, seems to make a natural
conclusion, but as in most blues, the stanzas can pretty much stand independently; perhaps less blueslike is the perfection of the rhyme (one almost feels
that the single near-rhyme [by the standards of standard English] *fine:mind* in
the first stanza is a conscious imitation of such blues rhymes as *ride:by* or
dime:mine). The blues often uses a three-line stanza, in which the second line
repeats the first; Hughes's six-line stanza, in which the fourth line repeats the
second, is a variation on the usual form.

A "Voices and Visions" videocassette of Langston Hughes is available from
Longman Publishers.

LI-YOUNG LEE

I Ask My Mother to Sing (p. 627)

Singing is infectious; the speaker asks his mother to sing, and his grandmother
joins her. The reference to the deceased father—who would have joined in too
if he had been there—adds a note of pathos and thus anticipates the second
stanza, where we learn that the song is about the land of the speaker's ancestors, a land he has never seen.

The song apparently is joyful (picknickers—though admittedly the picnic
is dispelled by rain), but since it is about a lost world it is also sorrowful (the
women begin to cry). Yet, even singing about sorrow provides the singer with
joy, or, we might say, the making of a work of art (here, singing a song) is plea-

surable even when the content is sorrowful. One way of mastering sorrow, of course, is to turn it into art.

We strongly suggest that you ask students if any of them wish to tell their classmates about how songs figured in their family history.

EDNA ST. VINCENT MILLAY

The Spring and the Fall (p. 627)

We begin with the rhyme scheme of the poem.

year	*a* (with internal *a*)
dear	*a*
wet	*b*
year	*a* (with internal *b*)
peach	*c*
reach	*c*
year	*a* (with internal *a*)
dear	*a*
trill	*d*
year	*a* (with internal *d*)
praise	*e*
ways	*e*
falling	*f* (with an internal *f*; but as an off-rhyme)
calling	*f*
hear	*a*
year	*a* (with internal *d*)
days	*e*
ways	*e*

Obviously there's lots of rhyme here; this is a highly lyrical lyric, close to song. In addition to the repetition of sound gained through rhyme, there are other repetitions—not only in the form of alliteration (e.g., "bough . . . blossoming," "rooks . . . raucous") and consonance (e.g., "trees . . . see") but also in the form of entire words. The first half of the first line is repeated verbatim in the second half of the line; "In the spring of the year" (1) becomes "In the fall of the year" (7), words repeat verbatim in the second half of the line, and in the third stanza the two phrases about the seasons are joined in line 16, but with a significant change: "the" year becomes "a" year.

Many highly lyrical poems employ what can be called a repetitive or perhaps an intensifying structure, each stanza going over the same ground, deepening the feeling but not advancing a narrative, even a narrative of the progress of a feeling. "The Spring and the Fall," however, is a lyric that includes a narrative, a progression, as a reader probably suspects immediately from the title. The first stanza deals with spring, the second with fall. Further, in the first stanza the lovers are physically and emotionally united (they walk together, and he obligingly—lovingly—presents her with "a bough of the blossoming peach"); in the second stanza the lovers are together only physically, not emotionally: "He laughed at all I dared to praise." Instead of giving her a gift, he laughs at (not with) her, and we hear of rooks making a "raucous" sound. The last line of the second stanza explicitly announces the break: "And broke my heart, in little ways." (The word "way," incidentally, was introduced in the first stanza—the peach-bough he gave her as a sign of his love "was out of the way and hard to reach." And in the last stanza "ways" appears again, in the last line, where we are told that when love went it "went in little ways.")

Another notable difference between the first two stanzas: Ordinarily the stanzas in a lyric poem repeat a metrical pattern, but in this poem the last two lines of the third stanza are shorter than the last two lines of the first two stanzas, thus conveying a sense of something cut short. The difference is made especially evident by the fact that the change is unanticipated; the first two lines of the second stanza closely resemble (as one expects) the first two lines of the first stanza.

The narrative, then, in effect is completed at the end of the second stanza. Or nearly so: Although at the end of the second stanza we learn that the speaker's heart was broken "in little ways," we don't learn until the last two lines of the third stanza that what especially hurts is that love went "in little ways." The third stanza, as has already been mentioned, brings the two seasons together; its first four lines seem joyous and loving, but its last two lines comment on the end of this love affair. The third stanza differs from the first two in several technical details. For example, as we have already mentioned, the first line of the first stanza, like the first line of the second stanza, repeats a phrase ("In the spring of the year, in the spring of the year," "In the fall of the year, in the fall of the year"). The third stanza, however, reflecting a different state of mind, begins with a different form of repetition: "Year be springing or year be falling." Another difference, admittedly small, is that the third stanza is the only stanza to use a feminine rhyme ("failing . . . calling").

We think that Millay is an underrated poet, and we urge students to turn to *Collected Poems: Edna St. Vincent Millay*, ed. Norma Millay (1956). The critical work on her verse is somewhat disappointing, though we can recommend Norman A. Brittin, *Edna St. Vincent Millay* (1967), and James Gray, *Edna St. Vincent Millay* (1967), as useful points of departure.

WILFRED OWEN

Anthem for Doomed Youth (p. 628)

Here are our responses to the questions we put in the text:

1. An anthem is (a) a hymn of praise or loyalty or (b) a sacred composition set to words of the Bible. In Owen's poem, "orisons," "prayers," "save," "choirs," "flowers," "holy glimmers," and even "die" and "pall" might be found in an anthem, but among the unexpected words and phrases are "die as cattle," "stuttering rifles'. . . . rattle," "mockeries," "demented," and perhaps "blinds." (One might, or might not, want to talk about the onomatopoeia in "stuttering rifles' rapid rattle.")
2. This question anticipates Chapter 16, "The Speaking Tone of Voice," but we see no reason not to anticipate it. We'd characterize the tone thus: The

first line asks a pained question, but in "monstrous anger" (2) we begin to hear indignation, and in line 3 ("stuttering rifles' rapid rattle") bitterness. In this poem the word "mockeries" is not unexpected; the speaker is not, of course, mocking the dead, but his pain and indignation seem to find an outlet in mockery. For instance, in calling his poem an "anthem" he mocks traditional praises of the glory of dying in war. (Owen's "Dulce et Decorum Est" pretty decisively sums up Owen's view not only of the First World War but of all wars. A different poet, however, might have mocked not war in general but only a specific war. That is, a satiric poet might have used the word "anthem" ironically, mocking a specific war precisely because it is ignoble in comparison with those wars for which anthems might fittingly be composed.) He finds some comfort, however, in the "holy glimmers of good-byes" which shine in the soldiers' eyes, in the "pallor of girls' brows," which are the pall, and in the "tenderness of patient minds," which serves as "flowers" (a floral tribute more worthy than wreaths accompanied by conventional funeral oratory). What sad comfort there is, then, is provided by those who die and their loved ones, not by church and state. By the last line the indignation has quieted, though the sadness remains.

It is interesting to compare the final version with the first draft of the poem, printed in Owen's *Collected Poems* (1964) and in Jon Stallworthy's *Wilfred Owen* (1983). The first version, untitled and chiefly unrhymed, goes thus:

What minute bells for these who die so fast?
    Only the monstrous anger of our guns.
Let the majestic insults of their iron mouths
    Be as the priest-words of their burials.
Of choristers and holy music, none;
    Nor any voice of mourning, save the wail
The long-drawn wail of high, far-sailing shells.
    What candles may we hold for these lost souls?
Not in the hands of boys but in their eyes
Shall many candles shine, and [?] light them.
Women's wide-spreaded arms shall be their wreathes,
Their flowers, the tenderness of all men's minds,
And every dusk, a drawing-down of blinds.

Owen showed the draft to Siegfried Sassoon, who suggested some changes and who also suggested a title, "Anthem for Dead Youth." Owen accepted the changes and the title and wrote at least three more versions, facsimiles of which can be found in Stallworthy. When Owen showed the final version to Sassoon, Sassoon suggested changing the title to "Anthem for Doomed Youth."

There are some excellent secondary sources, to which students can be referred for background and context: Bernard Bergonzi, *Heroes' Twilight: A Study of the Literature of the Great War* (1965); Paul Fussell, *The Great War and Modern Memory* (1975); and Samuel Hynes, *A War Imagined: The First World War and British Culture* (1990). See also *The Penguin Book of First World War Poetry*, ed. Jon Silkin (2nd ed., 1981).

WALT WHITMAN

A Noiseless Patient Spider (p. 629)

Whitman's "A Noiseless Patient Spider" is in free verse, a form discussed later in the text in connection with Whitman's "When I Heard the Learn'd Astronomer," but most instructors find it appropriate to say a few words about the form at this stage. In fact, of course, the poem is not terribly "free"; each stanza has five lines, helping to establish the similitude of spider and soul, and the first line of each stanza is relatively short, the other lines being longer, helping to establish the idea of "venturing, throwing." The near-rhyme at the end helps to tie up the poem, as though finally the bridge is at least tentatively "form'd," the "anchor" holding, but the fact is that the action is not yet complete, the soul is not yet anchored. A discussion of this poem will also necessarily get into Whitman's use of figurative language. Implicitly, the speaker's soul is a noiseless, patient spider, "ceaselessly musing, ceaselessly venturing," building a "bridge" in the vastness (i.e., uniting the present with eternity—or are the filaments that the soul flings poems that unite mankind?).

In addition to the biographies by Gay Wilson Allen (1967) and Justin Kaplan (1980), we admire Paul Zweig's sensitively written study, *Walt Whitman: The Making of the Poet* (1984). A brisk, informative overview of the period can be found in David S. Reynolds, *Walt Whitman's America: A Cultural Biography* (1995). Harold Bloom's chapter, "Walt Whitman as Center of the American Canon," in his book, *The Western Canon* (1994), is also stimulating, though students unfamiliar with the culture and canon wars may lack the context to perceive Bloom's polemical aims here.

ADDITIONAL TOPICS FOR CRITICAL THINKING AND WRITING

1. In about 250 words describe some animal, plant, or object that can be taken as a symbol of some aspect of your personality or experience.
2. The text gives Whitman's final version of "A Noiseless Patient Spider." Here is Whitman's draft, written some ten years earlier. Compare the two poems and evaluate them.

The Soul, Reaching, Throwing Out for Love

The soul, reaching, throwing out for love,
As the spider, from some little promontory, throwing out filament after
     filament, tirelessly out of itself, that one at least may catch and form
     a link, a bridge, a connection
O I saw one passing along, saying hardly a word—yet full of love I
     detected him, by certain signs
O eyes wishfully turning! O silent eyes!
For then I thought of you o'er the world,
O latent oceans, fathomless oceans of love!
O waiting oceans of love! yearning and fervid! and of you sweet souls
     perhaps in the future delicious and long:
But Death, unknown on the earth—ungiven, dark here, unspoken, never
     born:
You fathomless latent souls of love—you pent and unknown oceans of
     love!

A "Voices and Visions" videocassette of Walt Whitman is available from Longman Publishers.

JOSEPH ADDISON

Ode: The Spacious Firmament on High (p. 630)

In our biographical note we mention the Argument from Design. We do not mention the current topic of Intelligent Design, but some students may raise the issue.

For a good short discussion of the Argument from Design, as Addison Would have thought of it, see "Design Argument" in *Dictionary of the History of Ideas* (1973–74), ed. Philip Wiener. The following account is partly indebted to this source.

In brief, the Argument from Design is this: If one looks at the world around one, one sees evidence of intelligent planning (design), so one may reasonably conclude that the world was created by an intelligence. This idea has a long history, and in one form or another it was held by such distinguished thinkers as Plato, Aquinas, and Newton. (Aristotle seems not to have held it, despite Addison's reference to him in the comment that we quote in the text. Addison was drawing on a quotation by Cicero, attributing the idea to Aristotle.) Newton, for instance, in a comment added in 1713 to his *Principia*, wrote: "This most beautiful system of the sun, planets, and comets, could only proceed from the counsel and dominion of an intelligent and powerful Being." In fact, Newton went further, and deduced more than intelligence and power: "He is eternal and infinite, omnipotent and omniscient; that is, his duration reaches from eternity to eternity; his presence from infinity to infinity; he governs all things, and knows all things that are or can be done."

The Argument from Design reached what perhaps is its most memorable and most popular form in the writings of William Paley (1745–1805), an English theologian, especially in his *Natural Theology; or, Evidences of the Existence and Attributes of the Deity Collected from the Appearances of Nature* (1802). The gist is this: If we examine (for instance) a watch and a stone, we see a contrast. The watch has been designed, its parts all work together for some purpose, and the purpose is evident. Similarly, if we look at human anatomy, we see that every part is so cunningly constructed and so suited to a particular end (e.g. the fingers for grasping, the eye for seeing) that it must have been created by "an intelligent designing mind." (Whereas Newton looked to astronomical phenomena, Paley looked chiefly to the biological world around him, though the passage that was most widely quoted concerned the watch.) If a savage found a watch, he (today we would say he or she) would infer the existence of a watchmaker. Well, Paley argued, we find a cunningly constructed universe, and so we must infer the existence of a universe-maker, God. And from our perception of this universe we can infer the characteristics of the creator. But he was more cautious than Newton; he denied that "omnipotence" and "omniscience" can be inferred from the creation.

Paley wrote, of course, in pre-Darwinian days, and before Tennyson had told us that nature is "red in tooth and claw," but one wonders how he overlooked the violence evident in nature. Obviously he was able to conclude that the creator is benevolent not because he saw benevolence throughout the creation but because the Christianity of his day had taught him that God is benevolent.

Perhaps the strongest criticism of the Argument from Design was advanced (even before Paley wrote) by David Hume, in *Dialogues Concerning Natural Religion* (posthumously published in 1779). Hume pointed out that the argument is based on an analogy. Analogy is most reliable when the things being compared are closely related, but in this case we are comparing the universe with things created within the universe. The universe is *unique*, we have no experience of its origin, whereas we do have experience of the origin of watches.

A second reply to the Argument from Design points out that if we take the analogy seriously, we can ask, Who created the Intelligence that created the world? That is, if the analogy leads us to conclude that the world has a designer, it is legitimate for us to take the next step and to ask who designed the designer.

Hume also offers a third criticism. Why conclude from the evidence that the creator is intelligent, benevolent, etc.? Why not take notice of sickness and evil, and conclude that the creator is malicious or stupid or incompetent? (In fact, if we argue from analogy, we probably will have to argue that the creator is *im*perfect, since all creators—e.g., those of watches—are imperfect.)

Finally, a few words about Addison's poem. The third (final) stanza, which begins by referring to "Silence," is a response to the ancient but, by Addison's day, discredited idea of the music of the spheres. Pythagoras had argued that the planets move at different rates; that they must make sounds in their motion, according to their rates; and that (since in nature all things are harmonious) the combined sounds of the motions of the planets must be musical. Obviously Addison, a spokesman for "reason," could not go along with this as a matter of fact, but he could (and *did*) say, "In Reason's ear" the planets sing, i.e., they don't literally sing but nevertheless our reason tells us that their very existence says something to us—and what it says is, of course, what the Christianity of Addison's day taught.

JOHN KEATS

Ode on a Grecian Urn (p. 631)

Let's begin at the end, with the issue of the punctuation of the last two lines. Does the urn speak the two lines, or does it speak only "Beauty is truth, truth beauty"? The matter has been thoroughly discussed by Jack Stillinger, in an appendix to his book called *The Hoodwinking of Madeline* (1971). The problem is this: When the poem was first published, in *Annals of the Fine Arts* (1819), the lines were printed thus:

> Beauty is Truth,—Truth Beauty—That is all
>   Ye know on Earth, and all ye need to know.

When Keats published the ode in his book *Lamia and Other Poems* (1820), the lines were punctuated thus:

"Beauty is truth, truth beauty,"—that is all
   Ye know on earth, and all ye need to know.

The two printed versions thus set off "Beauty is truth, truth beauty" as a unit separate from the remaining words. But Keats probably did not supervise the publication in *Annals*, and because he was ill when *Lamia* was in production he may not have read the proofs, or may not have read them attentively. Many scholars therefore do not feel obliged to accept the punctuation of the two printed texts. They point to the four extant manuscript transcripts of the poem (none by Keats, but all by persons close to Keats). Because none of these transcriptions uses quotation marks or a period after "beauty," these scholars argue that the punctuation suggests that the urn speaks all of the last two lines:

Beauty is Truth,—Truth Beauty,—that is all
   Ye know on earth, and all ye need to know.

Stillinger points out that none of the six readings (the four transcripts and the two published versions) offers conclusive proof of Keats's intention. He goes on to summarize the interpretations, and we now summarize Stillinger:

1. **Poet to reader.** The urn speaks the first five words of line 49 ("Beauty is truth, truth beauty"), and the poet, addressing the reader, speaks the rest of the last two lines ("that is all / Ye know on earth, and all ye need to know"). The objection to this view is that earlier in the last stanza the poet and the reader are "us," and the poet says that later woes will belong to a generation other than "ours." Why, then, does the poet shift the address to "ye," where we would expect "we"? Second, the statement is obviously false; we need to know much more than that "Beauty is truth, truth beauty."
2. **Poet to urn.** The poet speaks the end of line 49, and all of the last line, to the urn. The poet tells the urn that *it* need know no more—but that we need to know a great deal more. The objection, Stillinger points out, is that "ye" is normally a plural pronoun—though in fact Keats did sometimes use it as a singular. A second objection: What can Keats possibly mean by saying to the urn, "that is all / Ye know *on earth*. . ."?
3. **Poet to figures on urn.** The poet speaks the end of line 49 and all of the last line to the figures on the urn. This fits with "ye" as a plural. The objection is that the figures are not "on earth," and, further, that the poet is no longer thinking of them as alive and capable of hearing. Further, *why* should the figures on the urn know this and only this?
4. **Urn to reader.** The urn speaks all of the two last lines. The objection is that the statement seems to defy common sense, and more important, it is *not* the way the *Lamia* volume punctuated the line. Some critics have suggested that the quotation marks were meant to set off these five words as a sort of motto within a two-line statement by the urn.

It is our impression that most editors today disregard the *Lamia* punctuation, put the whole of the two lines within quotation marks, and take the lines as spoken by the urn to the reader. In any case, a reader is still left to wonder whether the passage is profound wisdom or is nonsense.

Now to begin at the beginning. In the first line "still" probably has several meanings (motionless; as yet; silent); the urn is the "foster-child of silence and slow time" because its real parent is the craftsman who made it, but it has been adopted, so to speak, by silence and the centuries. Although the poet begins by saying that the urn can tell a tale "more sweetly" than a poet can, in fact by the end of the stanza it is clear that the urn cannot tell a tale; it can only (of course) show some isolated moment, and let the viewer try to guess what actions came before and will come after. It is worth mentioning, too, that this stanza praises the urn's staying-power ("slow time") but is rich in words that imply transience: "Sylvan," "flowery," "leaf-fringed," "haunts" (suggesting the insubstantial or ethereal). The stanza ends with urgent questions conveying agitation and implying that the urn cannot tell a tale satisfactorily.

The second stanza begins on a note of composure; in the space between the stanzas, so to speak, the poet has stilled his questioning spirit and has progressed to a state where he can offer something for meditation ("Heard melodies are sweet, but those unheard / Are sweeter"). As the stanza continues, a slightly painful note is introduced: The pastoral landscape will never die—but the lover will never kiss the woman. The poet urges the lover not to grieve, which means that he in fact introduces into this Arcadian world the idea of potential grief. Although the stanza ends by asserting the youth's eternal love and the woman's eternal beauty, there is something almost painful in the last words of the next-to-last line of the stanza, "though thou hast not thy bliss."

The third stanza begins with a renewed note of joy, again apparently gained in the blank space that precedes the stanza, though perhaps we may also detect a note of hysteria in the repetition of "Ah, happy, happy boughs!" This stanza too, despite its early expressions of joy, moves toward distress. We are told that the figures on the urn are "far above" human passion, but the last lines dwell on the pains of human passions: "a heart high-sorrowful and cloyed, / A burning forehead, and a parching tongue."

We cannot quite say that the fourth stanza begins with the by-now expected note of composure, because in fact it begins with a question, but it is true to say that in fact this stanza too begins in a quieter mood. The poet is contemplating with interest a new scene on the urn, a scene showing a "mysterious priest" and a "heifer lowing at the skies, / . . . her silken flanks with garlands drest." As the poet describes this highly picturesque scene, again we hear a note foreign to the beginning of the stanza. The poet begins by conveying his interest in what he sees—"the mysterious priest," the "heifer," and the "folk, this pious morn"—but then his mind turns to the "little town" that is "emptied of this folk" and whose "streets for evermore / Will silent be." The last two lines of the stanza are deeply melancholic: "not a soul to tell / Why thou art desolate can e'er return." Jack Stillinger, in an essay on the odes (reprinted from his *Twentieth Century Views*) in *The Hoodwinking of Madeline* suggests that "'Desolate' in line 40 is the counterpart of 'forlorn' in *Ode to a Nightingale*. It brings the speaker back to his sole self" (106).

The fifth stanza begins with the expected renewed joy, but it is worth noticing that the urn, which in the first stanza was a "Sylvan historian" capable of telling a "flowery tale" now is a "shape" and a "silent form" and a "Cold Pastoral." The poet by now has clearly seen that what he at first took for a world of idealized love is "cold," and its figures are "marble men and maidens." That is, if it is perfect and permanent it is also cold, bloodless, without the passion that (however painful) is what we want from life. Stillinger puts it this way:

> Like the nightingale, [the urn] has offered a tentative idea—momentarily "teas[ing]" the speaker "out of thought"—but has also led the speaker to understand the shortcomings of the ideal. (108)

Stillinger's comment on the last two lines is also worth quoting:

> The final lines present a special problem in interpretation, but it is clear that, while the urn is not entirely rejected at the end, its value lies in its character as a work of art, not in its being a possible substitute for life in the actual world. However punctuated, the urn's "message" amounts to what the speaker has come to realize in his speculations—that the only beauty accessible to mortal man exists "on earth." The urn is "a friend to man" for helping him to arrive at this conclusion through just such ponderings as we have witnessed in the course of the poem. (108–09)

For students, we advise they read Keats in (or alongside) *The Poems of John Keats*, ed. Miriam Allott (1970), which includes detailed annotations. W. J. Bate's biography (1963) is an impressive work, but the shorter studies by Douglas Bush (1966) and Robert Gittings (1968) may be better for introductory students. Among critical studies, we have benefited from Christopher Ricks, *Keats and Embarrassment* (1974), and Helen Vendler, *The Odes of John Keats* (1983). Also useful is *Twentieth Century Interpretations of Keats's Odes*, ed. Jack Stillinger (1968). For paper assignments, students can consult Jack Walter Rhodes, *Keats's Major Odes: An Annotated Bibliography of the Criticism* (1984). Ian Jack, in *Keats and the Mirror of Art* (1967), has an interesting, well-illustrated chapter on urns—and pictures of urns that Keats is likely to have seen, but, unfortunately, no one urn is the model; in fact, "that heifer lowing at the skies" probably came not from an urn but from the Elgin Marbles. Jack's concern is only with identifying motifs; he does not offer an interpretation of the poem.

PAUL LAURENCE DUNBAR

Sympathy (p. 633)

It is worth getting students to talk about the title. Most will say that it suggests a feeling of pity, but some may be familiar with another sense of the word, "fellow-feeling," or "feeling-along-with" (it comes from a Greek word whose elements are *like* + *feelings*). The speaker's "sympathy," then, is not merely that he feels sorry for the caged bird, but that he *shares the feelings* of the bird. Incidentally, after graduating from high school Dunbar worked as an elevator operator, and it has been suggested—we can't recall where we read this—that he well might have seen a literal as well as a metaphorical connection between himself, working in a cage-like elevator, and the bird.

We value Dunbar as a poet, in, for example, *Lyrics of Lowly Life* (1896), and as a writer of short stories, in such collections as *The Strength of Gideon and Other Stories* (1900). Secondary studies include *A Singer in the Dawn:*

Reinterpretations of Paul Laurence Dunbar, ed. Jay Martin (1975), and Peter Revell, *Paul Laurence Dunbar* (1979). But the best resource for texts, commentary, and bibliography is *The Collected Poetry of Paul Laurence Dunbar*, ed. Joanne M. Braxton (1993).

JACK FORBES

Something Nice (p. 634)

We have taught this poem on one occasion, and the discussion of it went well. We began by reading the poem aloud, but after that was done, there was a conspicuous silence in the room. We could sense the students saying to themselves, "What's so special about this?" Indeed, we had the suspicion that some students might be thinking, "this is so simple—what's the point of it?"

That is the question we then asked: What is the point of this poem? What we were really after, was: Is "Something Nice" a poem, and if it is, what *makes* it a poem, and if it *is* a poem, is it a good one?

There are details in Forbes's language that you might encourage your students to notice and comment on: the repetitions of "nice" and "really," for example. You might also invite them to consider the effect of the poem's structure: what is the difference between a prose statement of the two sentences that Forbes has written, and a presentation of these same sentences in verse, with the special line arrangements and endings that Forbes has devised?

As we discussed the poem with the students, we sought to lead them to reflect on the literal meaning of Forbes's work: In a literal sense, what do his lines say? From there, we moved to consider whether the lines might mean more than they say, or appear to say, on a literal level. Perhaps even more than we should, we asked leading questions: Is the speaker being sarcastic when he tells us that his wife said something "really nice"? Is she, in turn, being sarcastic when she (according to the speaker) says that she is "really glad" she married the man who is her husband?

We dramatize the point by stressing in our tone the word *really*, so that the students hear the edge of barbed irony in our voice—the tone we use when we say "I was *really* glad to see him" when our point (as the tone reveals) is that we decidedly were *not*.

We think that your students will enjoy their exploration of "Something Nice." It both is and is not straightforward, and you can delve into Forbes's choices in ways that will interest and give pleasure to the class. Encourage them to ask questions: why, for instance, does Forbes give *these* words, *this* explanation, to the wife? Why is it significant, to her, that her husband saves these creatures from being hit by cars? After all, Forbes could have given her many other "nice" things to say—why this one?

As we completed our treatment of "Something Nice," we found ourselves summing up for the students not the meaning of the poem, but, rather, the kinds of questions about poetry, and the analysis of poetry, that Forbes helps us to articulate and think about. The poem is a good one for this purpose because just about every student will feel he or she can say something about it: It is not an intimidating poem. It is also a good one because the students will perceive that there is more here than at first they might have imagined.

LINDA PASTAN

Jump Cabling (p. 634)

The physical appearance of a poem on the page is always important. As anthologists, we are unhappy that we must add line numbers, and that a poem sometimes begins near the bottom of a right-hand page so that most of the poem is invisible at the start. With Pastan's poem, the appearance is especially important. True, if "Jump Cabling" is read aloud, something of the physical appearance can be conveyed (1) by pausing, to indicate the space between the two columns—the space between the two cars or the two people—and (2) by not pausing when one reads the final line; still, this is a poem that must be seen as well as heard.

We take the poem to be about what it explicitly says it is, but obviously the journey together will include bodily contact. The words *touched, intimate workings, underneath*—and we can include *lifted the hood*—add a strong sexual element.

In the past we have recommended Pastan's *PM/AM: New and Selected Poems* (1982), but it has now been superseded by *Carnival Evening: New and Selected Poems, 1968–1998* (1998).

BILLY COLLINS

The Names (p. 635)

When we typed "Billy Collins" into Google, among the things that came up was a short piece he wrote in 2002, "Poetry and Tragedy," in which Collins, then the nation's poet laureate, offered a two-paragraph comment about poetry and the aftermath of September 11, 2001. Here is the second half of the second paragraph:

> It's not that poets should feel a responsibility to write about this calamity. All poetry stands in opposition to it. Pick a poem, any poem, from an anthology and you will see that it is speaking for life and therefore against the taking of it. A poem about mushrooms or about a walk with a dog is a more eloquent response to Sept. 11 than a poem that announces that wholesale murder is a bad thing.

That's worth discussing in class. Sooner or later one wants to talk in some detail about this particular poem, "The Names," and one way of getting into it is by asking students to think of names or naming in association with disaster or tragedy. Some of them will mention Maya Lin's *Vietnam Veterans Memorial*, where the names of the Americans who died are inscribed not in alphabetic order (Collins's principle) but in the order of the dates of their deaths. Discussion may include comment on names on tombstones, inscribed in an effort to give the deceased a continuing life in the mind of the viewer. And in a discussion of names it is conceivable that if you are blessed with exceptionally well-prepared students someone may mention Yeats's "Easter 1916," which concludes thus:

> I write it out in a verse—
> MacDonagh and MacBride

And Connolly and Pearse
Now and in time to be,
Wherever green is worn,
Are changed, changed utterly:
A terrible beauty is born.

Yeats here is working in the tradition of the epic catalog, naming the heroes.
(Epic catalogs are not limited to heroes: they include names of beautiful people, ships, places, even—in *Paradise Lost*—fallen angels.) The inventory is normally presented in order to honor its subject, to give new life to it, to remind
hearers that these people or things or traits must never be forgotten. The catalog, often presented in ritualistic or incantatory manner, summons up things
that have vanished and thus gives them new life. Some students may be familiar with genealogical passages in the Bible, for instance, the descendants of
Noah in Genesis 5.1–30, or the descendants of Adam down to the descendants
of Saul (I Chronicles 1.1–9), where, again, the act of naming affirms the
importance of persons and gives them new life in the minds of the hearers.
(The New Testament also includes genealogies, naming the ancestors of Jesus
[Matthew 1.1–17; Luke 3.23–38], but here the primary purpose is to establish Jesus as the prophesied Messiah.)
    Collins, working in the epic tradition, celebrates the individuals. The
poem begins with the sleepless poet, "unhelped by any breeze" (no quickening
breeze animates his mind, apparently there is no *inspiration* in the literal sense
of "breathing into"), yet the "soft rain" stimulates thought of the names, and
perhaps it is not fanciful to see a connection between the "soft rain" and new
life. Collins begins with five names, in alphabetic order, then comments a bit
(lines 7–14), mentioning "Twenty-six willows," at which point we can guess
that the twenty-six willows will stand for the letters of the alphabet. Why willows? Because the willow, especially the weeping willow, is an emblem of
mourning: during the Babylonian exile the Jews wept for Zion and they hung
their harps on willows (Psalms 137. 1–2); rejected by her husband,
Desdemona sings a song about a rejected woman ("The poor soul sat sighing
by a sycamore tree, / Sing all a green willow," *Othello* 4.3); a somewhat comic
version of the suicidal lover appears in *The Mikado* ("On a tree by a willow a
little tomtit / Sang 'Willow, titwillow, titwillow'"). The willow is a common
motif on nineteenth-century tombstones. But from this motif of nature,
Collins then moves to walking "barefoot / Among thousands of flowers"
(11–12), and it is easy enough to see the flowers as emblems of rebirth.
    He then moves to the next five letters of the alphabet, F, G, H, I, and J,
cleverly connecting this list with his previous reference to flowers by calling
up a victim named Fiori, Italian for "flower." After this second group of five
names, he again comments (17–23), sometimes speaking figuratively ("Names
written in the air") and sometimes literally ("A name under a photograph
taped to a mailbox"). Then come what at first might seem to be five more
names, K, L, M, N, and O, but after a very brief comment we get six additional names, beginning with P, Q, R, S, T, and U, providing some variety,
assuring us that the poem is not proceeding mechanically by fives. And then
another comment, again part metaphoric ("Names written in the pale sky")
and part literal ("Names silent in stone / Or cried out behind a door").
    The final group of five names includes X, but probably there was no vic-
tim whose name began with X, so Collins effectively solves the problem by

saying "let X stand, if it can, for the ones unfound." The poem ends by at first taking us out into green nature—a world of fields and birds—but that might seem too glib an ending so Collins takes us from nature to

> the dim warehouse of memory.
> So many names, there is barely room on the walls of the heart.

That is, Collins returns us to the victims themselves ("so many names") and to ourselves, the living, who in "the walls of the heart" give the victims whatever life they retain.

In our fourth question we invite students to think about defining "sentimentality," and to discuss Collins's poem in the context of their definition. We suggest that when you assign the poem, you might ask students to come to class prepared to discuss question 4.

You might dare to ask the students, is "The Names" truly a moving and effective poem, or does it possess power primarily because of its connection to a terrible and tragic event?

In an interview published in the *New York Times*, December 19, 1999, Collins emphasizes his keen attention, as he constructs his poems, to the responses of the reader. "As I'm writing," he says, "I'm always reader conscious   I have one reader in mind, someone who is in the room with me, and who I'm talking to, and I want to make sure I don't talk too fast, or too glibly. Usually I try to create a hospitable tone at the beginning of a poem. Stepping from the title to the first lines is like stepping into a canoe. A lot of things can go wrong." This implies one of Collins's strengths, but perhaps also one of his limitations. Sometimes he seems less to be expressing and exploring—really exploring—an issue or theme than presenting it in a form that will surprise, disconcert, or ruffle the reader a little but not a lot. Collins is clever and sincere, and that does not always lead to complex poems.

The poet-critic Jeredith Merrin, in "Art Over Easy," *The Southern Review* 38:1 (Winter 2002), 202–214, has sharply criticized Collins as superficial and unchallenging. She concludes he "is not without some rhetorical skills, charm, and wit. . . . But what he finally offers is disappointingly monotonous and slight."

14

The Speaking
Tone of Voice

GWENDOLYN BROOKS

We Real Cool (p. 641)

The unusual arrangement of the lines, putting what ordinarily would be the first syllable of the second line at the end of the first line, and so on, of course emphasizes the "we"—and therefore emphasizes the absence of "we" in the final line, which consists only of "Die soon," the "we" having been extinguished. The disappearance of the "we" is especially striking in a poem in which the "we" is so pleased with itself.

By emphasis we don't necessarily mean a heavy stress on the word. An emphasis can be gained by the slightest of pauses (even though the word is not followed by a comma or a shift in tone). In *Report from Part One* (1972), Brooks comments on this poem:

> The ending WE's in "We Real Cool" are tiny, wispy, weakly argumentative "Kilroy-is-here" announcements. The boys have no accented sense of themselves, yet they are aware of a semidefined personal importance. Say the "we" softly. (185)

"We" presumably refers to a gang of seven confident pool players, but if seven is traditionally a lucky number, it brings these people no luck. The subtitle allows one to infer that at the Golden Shovel they are digging their own graves.

Students might be directed to Brooks's autobiography, *Report from Part One* (1972). See also D. H. Melhem, *Gwendolyn Brooks: Poetry and the Heroic Voice* (1987).

GWENDOLYN BROOKS

The Mother (p. 641)

It's our guess that discussion in class will concentrate on the last three lines. For what it's worth, we find those lines convincing, partly because of their simplicity (no metaphors, no inversions, no unusual diction) and partly because of the repetition. Of course the repetition *might* suggest insincerity, the speaker's awareness that she does not sound convincing and so she piles it on (some readers may feel that the lady doth protest too much), but we do not hear any such suggestion.

LINDA PASTAN

Marks (p. 642)

The graders (husband, son, daughter) give steadily lower marks to the speaker, moving from A to B plus to "average," and then to "pass" (which everyone knows can mean just barely passing); but the speaker, in a surprise ending, then awards a sort of mark or academic label to herself, a label which might seem to suggest a still further diminution but which here suggests a course of vigorous action that will greatly affect those who so casually have been grading her: "I'm dropping out."

But how seriously, we ask our students, does a reader take the poem? To our ear, the speaker is good-natured and at least semi-playful. She mocks the treatment she receives from those who take her for granted, but the mockery (if that is not too strong a word) seems genial enough—though perhaps that is what many a compacent man thought until his wife explained that, no, she wasn't kidding and, yes, she really was walking out on him (shades of Ibsen's Nora). Perhaps it comes down to this: Does your ear hear a voice that conveys affection even while it complains and threatens—or does it hear a voice speaking in deadly earnest?

STEVIE SMITH

Not Waving but Drowning (p. 643)

All his life the dead man in Stevie Smith's "Not Waving but Drowning" sent messages that were misunderstood. His efforts to mask his loneliness and depression were more successful than he intended. His friends mistook him for a "chap" who "always loved larking," as they now mistake the cause of his death. But true friends would have seen through the clowning, the dead man seems to protest, in lines 3 and 4 (when of course it is too late to protest or to explain). The second stanza confirms his view of the spectators. They are imperceptive and condescending; their understanding of the cause of his death is as superficial as their attention to him was while he was alive. But they didn't know him "all [his] life" (11). The dead man thus acknowledges, by leaving them out of the last stanza, that, never having risked honest behavior, he is at least as responsible as others for his failure to be loved and to love.

Stevie Smith is an underrated poet, whom students enjoy when they encounter her work. Her *Collected Poems* were published in 1976. See also Jack Barbera and William McBrien, *A Biography of Stevie Smith* (1985). There are good studies of Smith's poetry in Calvin Bedient, *Eight Contemporary Poets* (1974), and Christopher Ricks, *The Force of Poetry* (1984).

WISLAWA SZYMBORSKA

The Terrorist, He Watches (p. 644)

It is a commonplace among teachers of rhetoric that one person's "terrorist" is another's "freedom fighter," and indeed it is appropriate for students to scrutinize the language that they use and that they hear. Discussions of "terrorist" versus "freedom fighter," however, often hinge not on the nature of the action but on whether or not one approves the particular cause. That is, we can perhaps agree that terrorism is the use of violence in order to coerce a government. We might agree on this but strongly disagree about a particular episode, and the argument would turn to such issues as whether the people who engage in this activity are driven to it and have no other recourse, whether their cause is just, etc.

The thing that especially interests us in Szymborska's poem is that the terrorist in question seems *not* to have any political motivation. Terrorism is so closely associated with particular political causes (until recently, with the IRA, most recently with Palestinian suicide bombers) that the poem seems surreal in its lack of politics. The speaker seems to be an apolitical voyeur, an obsessive observer:

> A woman in a yellow jacket, she goes in.
> A man in dark glasses, he comes out.

None of this has anything to do with the viewer's political beliefs, or the identity (ethnic, political) of the persons viewed. In so far as we can characterize the terrorist, beyond saying that he is an obsessive observer, we can perhaps say that he harbors feelings of superiority:

> The girl's not there any more.
> Was she dumb enough to go in, or wasn't she?

And:

> Instead a fat baldy's coming out.

At the end, we sense the terrorist's satisfaction—not because a political act has been completed but simply because the momentary game in which he is the only spectator has reached the final moment of play.

Who is the speaker? Strictly speaking, not the terrorist, who (beginning with the title) is talked about in the third person, but certainly someone who has complete access to the terrorist's mind. The speaker can tell us, for instance, the exact time when the bomb will detonate, and he can tell us not only the terrorist's responses to the passers-by ("That shorter guy's really got it made") but also the terrorist's state of mind just before the bomb goes off ("The time, how it drags"). The speaker's language is idiomatic ("a sight for sore eyes," "a fat baldy," "any moment now") but the title ("The Terrorist, He Watches") and the final line ("The bomb, it goes off") suggest that the speaker is not a native speaker. Put it this way: Some of the language, beginning with the title, suggests a degree of alienation. We have already said, however, that this terrorist seems to have no political stance; the alienation is that of a psychopath, someone whose only interest is in seeing what will come out of a game he has devised.

For further study, students might begin with either *Poems, New and Collected, 1957–1997*, translated from the Polish by Stanislaw Baranczak and Clare Cavanagh (1998), or *Miracle Fair: Selected Poems*, translated by Joanna Trzeciak (2001).

We have benefited from Stanislaw Baranczak, "Eastern Europe: The Szymborska Phenomenon," *Salmagundi* 103 (Summer 1994): 252–65; he observes that nearly all of Szymborska's poems are keyed to the expression and exploration of "questions" that are directed against dogmatic assertions or opinions. See also Jacqueline Osherow, "'So These Are the Himalayas': The Poetry of Wislawa Szymborska," *The Antioch Review* 55 (Spring 1997): 222–28. In "The Sky, a Sky, Heaven, the Heavens, a Heaven, Heavens: Reading Szymborska Whole," *The American Poetry Review* 29:4 (July/Aug. 2000): 41–47, Stephen Tapscot and Mariusz Przybytek deal well with the poet's treatments in her work of history and memory.

JOHN UPDIKE

Icarus (p. 645)

This is a troubling poem. In the aftermath of the destruction by terrorists of the World Trade Center on September 11, 2001, your students will react to "Icarus" strongly—some positively, others negatively.

First, a word or two about the title, which puzzles us somewhat. The title led us to expect that Updike would be giving his interpretation of the classical myth, which in full form includes the stories of both the craftsman and inventor Daedalus and his son Icarus:

> After killing his apprentice Talos in envy, Daedalus fled from Greece to Crete. There, he arranged the liaison between Pasiphaë and the Cretan Bull that resulted in the Minotaur. At the order of King Minos, he built the Minotaur's labyrinth. When Minos refused to let him leave Crete, Daedalus built wings of wax and feathers for himself and his son Icarus. Together they flew away, but Icarus flew too close to the sun and fell to his death when the wax melted. Daedalus escaped to Sicily. (*Columbia Encyclopedia*, 6th ed., 2001)

In *The Age of Fable*, Thomas Bullfinch (1796–1867) tells the relevant part of the Daedalus/Icarus story this way, which you may wish to share in class with your students:

"Minos may control the land and sea," said Daedalus, "but not the regions of the air. I will try that way." So he set to work to fabricate wings for himself and his young son Icarus. He wrought feathers together, beginning with the smallest and adding larger, so as to form an increasing surface. The larger ones he secured with thread and the smaller with wax, and gave the whole a gentle curvature like the wings of a bird.

Icarus, the boy, stood and looked on, sometimes running to gather up the feathers which the wind had blown away, and then handling the wax and working it over with his fingers, by his play impeding his father in his labours. When at last the work was done, the artist, waving his wings, found himself buoyed upward, and hung suspended, poising himself on the beaten air. He next equipped his son in the same manner and taught him how to fly, as a bird tempts her young ones from the lofty nest into the air. When all was prepared for flight he said, "Icarus, my son, I charge you to keep at a moderate height, for if you fly too low the damp will clog your wings, and if too high the heat will melt them. Keep near me and you will be safe."

While he gave him these instructions and fitted the wings to his shoulders, the face of the father was wet with tears, and his hands trembled. He kissed the boy, not knowing that it was for the last time. Then rising on his wings, he flew off, encouraging him to follow, and looked back from his own flight to see how his son managed his wings.

As they flew the ploughman stopped his work to gaze, and the shepherd leaned on his staff and watched them, astonished at the sight, and thinking they were gods who could thus cleave the air.

They passed Samos and Delos on the left and Lebynthos on the right, when the boy, exulting in his career, began to leave the guidance of his companion and soar upward as if to reach heaven. The nearness of the blazing sun softened the wax which held the feathers together, and they came off. He fluttered with his arms, but no feathers remained to hold the air.

While his mouth uttered cries to his father it was submerged in the blue waters of the sea which thenceforth was called by his name. His father cried, "Icarus, Icarus, where are you?" At last he saw the feathers floating on the water, and bitterly lamenting his own arts, he buried the body and called the land Icaria in memory of his child.

Or perhaps, we wondered as we began, Updike may be responding more directly to W. H. Auden's "Musée des Beaux Arts" (see p. 807 in the text), or William Carlos Williams's "Landscape with the Fall of Icarus," which are keyed to Brueghel's "Fall of Icarus" painting. There's also the well-known photograph of a construction worker by Lewis Hine, *Icarus Atop Empire State Building* (1931; the photograph is sometimes also titled *Sky Boy*).

But these lofty expectations were immediately upended by the colloquial "O.K." with which Updike starts the poem, as if picking up a casual, if maybe insistent or intense, conversation in the middle. The poem, as it turns out, explores a scene of air flight—two persons next to one another on a plane. Yet it does not (to us) feel connected to the Icarus tale and its exploration of aspiration and folly, youth and age, and so on. Updike is, however, a keen, purposeful writer, and—ask your students for their views—there is likely an intention at work here, in the choice of title, that we are not understanding clearly.

In the first line, Updike makes bold contact with his reader, the "you." And he places the "you" in an airplane seat. Fine. It's the next part when things start to get interesting—and highly provocative. Updike says that he wants you to imagine you are seated next to a man of "Middle Eastern origin." "Sweaty" and "swarthy": Updike knows that right away we may sense that this man is a terrorist, or might be. Reading the lines in dangerous times, we almost surely make this assumption, linking the man's appearance to his aim—well, at least to his possible aim. We do not know he is a terrorist, but the whole point is our fear that he could be.

But we proceed in our analysis too quickly. Updike writes "sweaty, swarthy" in the second line, and then "gentleman." "Gentleman" is a very nice strategy. Is Updike seeking to correct our stereotypical assumptions— our preconception, our prejudice? In part, yes. He is also using the language of stereotypes, as when a clerk at an airport counter says, "Do you gentlemen have any luggage?" or "I'll be with you as soon as I finish with this gentleman." He is also, we suspect, seeking here to evoke the mind's recoil at its own conclusion: "This person is sweaty and swarthy and Middle Eastern—he frightens me. But I shouldn't think that way—he looks like a gentleman." Or maybe he is all the more suspicious because he is a gentleman—that might be his sly choice of disguise.

Of course we are leaving out something important: Who, precisely, is the "you"? Is Updike creating a reader in his own image? The "you" thus would be (forgive our own stereotyping) a white, Christian, older man. Perhaps, more broadly, Updike wants the "you" to be, in effect, any person who is not one of them, who is not someone from the Middle East. This "you" connects the poem to the "us versus them" polarity ("the clash of civilizations") that figures so often in newspaper and TV discussions and commentaries about "the war on terrorism."

In our classroom, we always have "Middle Eastern" students, and if you do as well, or even if you do not, the conversation may become awkward and uncomfortable at this juncture. The "Middle East" is not a designation that our students from that part of the world feel at all comfortable with, precisely because the phrase is so loosely (and they would say, coarsely) deployed about a vast range of countries and cultures. Someone from Egypt is from the Middle East. So is someone from Iran. And so is someone from Israel. So what does it mean to say "Middle Eastern"? This is indeed a question that, as we read and reread "Icarus," Updike wants us to be raising and delving into.

Notice again how Updike keeps the reader off balance. The man carries a briefcase; it's black and bulky. . . . Maybe there's a bomb inside, and maybe the man "stashes" it—that is, hides it, stores it away—for an ominous reason. But maybe not: If he is stashing the briefcase, he is simply acting in compliance with the rules and regulations of the airline. "Stash" hence is descriptive; it need not carry the menacing implication that we initially assign to it.

Updike performs similarly in the final lines of the first stanza. He makes us hear the ticking bomb but the verb is "seems," not "is." The bomb is there; it isn't there. The reader, the "you," is caught in the grip of a stereotype—and knows it—even as he or she worries that on this occasion the stereotype might be all too accurate.

We work through "Icarus" slowly and carefully, attending to the interanimations of the words and the bearing of one phrase and line upon the next.

Updike's choice of details is, we think, terrific—the beauty and horror, for example, of the "rainbow scum of jet fuel," which Updike knows we will connect to the terrible, terrifying scenes of desolation after a plane crash at sea that we've seen all too frequently on television news reports. And the "docile hopes of a plastic-wrapped meal," which catches so exactly the wan wish on the part of any air traveler, looking for the time to go by, that maybe this time the mass-produced, prepackaged meal served on board will have some taste and appeal. The final line of the poem, "like a frozen lake at your elbow": quite brilliant, we think, perfectly describing the illusion that the wing's metal can create as we look out the small window, and so aptly evocative for this poem about illusion and reality, appearance and truth.

Updike is having some devilish fun with the reader, too, we suspect, as in the reference to the "exploding bubbles" of the glass of Sprite. And it's a "plastic" cup, which is, to be sure, the material from which the cups on planes are made, but which is also a wordplay on "plastic" explosives.

Here are several other points to pursue:

1. Why does Updike use dialogue in the middle of the poem?
2. What is the nature of the shift in tone, in point of view, in the fourth stanza?
3. What is the conclusion that the speaker reaches in the final stanza? Or, rather, what is the conclusion that he records for the reader?
4. What is the lesson that Updike is teaching? Or, if "lesson" seems heavy-handed, what is the insight about our ways of thinking and feeling that Updike is offering in "Icarus"?

John Updike has been widely admired for his fiction and literary criticism, but he is also an accomplished poet in, for example, *Midpoint, and Other Poems* (1969) and *Facing Nature: Poems* (1985). Your advanced students may enjoy *Hugging the Shore: Essays and Criticism* (1983) and *More Matter: Essays and Criticism* (1999), which are extraordinary in the array of topics that Updike examines in alert and thoughtful ways. We also recommend *The Best American Short Stories of the Century* (1999), which Updike selected.

A stimulating critical study is William H. Pritchard, *Updike: America's Man of Letters* (2000), a cogent, accessible reader's guide to Updike's career as a writer, which began in 1954 with the publication of a short story in *The New Yorker*. See also Jack De Bellis, *The John Updike Encyclopedia* (2000).

AURORA LEVINS MORALES

Child of the Americas (p. 647)

The author, born in Puerto Rico of a Puerto Rican mother and of a father whose origins went back to the ghetto in New York and beyond that to Europe, came to the United States when she was thirteen and has lived in Chicago, New Hampshire, and now in the San Francisco Bay Area. Her heritage and her experience thus are considerably different from those of most Puerto Ricans who are now in the United States.

Whereas other Latinas in this book emphasize the difficulties of their divided heritage (see Pat Mora's "Immigrants" and Lorna Dee Cervantes's "Refugee Ship," p. 52), Morales celebrates her diversity and apparently is at ease as a Latina in the United States. She is "a light-skinned mestiza of the Caribbean, / a child of many diaspora," she was born "at a crossroads," she is "a U.S. Puerto Rican Jew, / a product of the ghettos of New York," "Spanish is in [her] flesh," but in the next-to-last stanza she insists that she is "not african," "not taína," "not european." Most significantly, she insists that she is not fragmented but is, on the contrary, "whole."

In short, Morales holds to the old idea of the United States as a melting pot, an idea not heard so often today. The conception of the melting pot has largely given way to the conception of America as a "gorgeous mosaic," a "salad bowl," a kaleidoscope, i.e., a place where there is great variety but where each ingredient maintains its identity.

You can recommend to students two books by Morales. The first, coauthored with her mother Rosario Morales, *Getting Home Alive* (1986), includes short essays, stories, and poems about their lives, languages, cultures, and religions. Rosario was born in Puerto Rico, the daughter of Russian Jewish immigrants who moved to New York when she was a child; Aurora was born in New York and, when she was a child, moved with her parents to Puerto Rico. In *Medicine Stories: History, Culture and the Politics of Integrity* (1998), Morales presents essays on social identity, ecology, children's liberation, and other topics.

JOSEPH BRUCHAC III

Ellis Island (p. 648)

Ellis Island, in Upper New York Bay, southwest of Manhattan Island, from 1892 until 1943 was the chief immigration station of the United States. In its first year, it saw 450,000 immigrants arrive, and in its peak years in the first decade of the twentieth century the annual number exceeded a million; the total number of Ellis Island graduates was over seventeen million. When the island closed, immigration was at a low point, and for some years the buildings fell into ruin. They have now been renovated and form a museum of immigration. In 1965 Ellis Island became part of the Statue of Liberty National Monument (the statue—on its own island, separated from Ellis Island by a few hundred yards of water—had been declared a national monument in 1924).

In the first decade of the twentieth century about 8.7 million immigrants entered the country, most of them via Ellis Island. This means, of course, that the great-grandparents or even the grandparents or parents of an enormous number of today's Americans are alumni of the island, and it has a hold on their affections.

Bruchac begins by calling up an image of two of his grandparents who had endured the long journey and "the long days of quarantine." He implicitly contrasts their journey and their anxiety—about 10 percent of the visitors were denied admission for reasons of health—with "a Circle Line ship," a ship that makes a daily pleasure cruise of a few hours around the islands, chiefly patronized by tourists. He goes on to evoke "the tall woman, green / as dreams of forests and meadows," i.e., the green patina of the *Statue of Liberty* connects it with nature.

In the second stanza he says that like millions of others he has come to the island, but of course there is a distinction between the millions who, pursuing a dream (lines 10 and 17), came as immigrants and the millions who now come as tourists, perhaps in homage to their ancestors and to the nation that accepted them.

There is, then, a contrast between the first and second stanzas, but the two harmonize. The third stanza, however, introduces a serious complication. If the immigrants were pursuing a dream, they nevertheless also were invading the "native lands" (20–22) of others. (Bruchac himself, as we mention in the headnote, is part Native American and part Slovak.) The Native Americans are characterized as people "who followed / the changing Moon," people who have or who had "knowledge of the seasons / in their veins," so they too, like the green statue, are associated with nature. Is the reader to think that these people are gone—or, on the contrary, that their heritage lives on, for example, in the "veins" of the poet? To our mind, the fact that Bruchac *ends* the poem with a reference to a knowledge that is in the "veins" suggests that he sees the heritage as still living—and the violence wrought by later immigrants as also still living.

Bruchac is a prolific author who has written poetry, fiction, and many books for children and young adults. We especially value the work he has done as an editor; his edited collections include *Breaking Silence: An Anthology of Contemporary Asian American Poets* (1983); *Songs from This Earth on Turtle's Back: Contemporary American Indian Poetry* (1983); and *Survival This Way: Interviews with American Indian Poets* (1987).

ROBERT BROWNING

My Last Duchess (p. 649)

Robert Langbaum has a good analysis of "My Last Duchess" in *The Poetry of Experience* (1957). On this poem, see also Laurence Perrine, *PMLA* 74 (March 1959): 157–59. W. J. T. Mitchell, in "Representation," in *Critical Terms for Literary Study* (1995), ed. Frank Lentricchia and Thomas McLaughlin, discusses the poem at some length. One of his points is: "Just as the duke seems to hypnotize the envoy, Browning seems to paralyze the reader's normal judgment by his virtuosic representation of villainy. His poem holds us in its grip, condemning in advance all our attempts to control it by interpretation. . . ."

It may be mentioned here that although every poem has a "voice," not every poem needs to be a Browningesque dramatic monologue giving the reader a strong sense of place and audience. No one would criticize Marvell's "To His Coy Mistress" on the grounds that the "lady" addressed in line 2 gives place (in at least some degree) to a larger audience—let us say, a general audience—when we get to "But at my back I always hear / Time's winged chariot hurrying near."

See also James A.W. Heffernan, in *Museum of Words: The Poetics of Ekphrasis from Homer to Ashbery* (1993). For background and context, see *A Browning Handbook*, ed. W. C. DeVane (rev. ed., 1955), and Norman B. Crowell, *A Reader's Guide to Robert Browning* (1972). See also Ian Jack, *Browning's Major Poetry* (1973), and Herbert Tucker, *Browning's Beginnings* (1980). For a cross-section of critical essays, see *Robert Browning*, ed. Isobel Armstrong (1974). Biographies include Betty Miller, *Robert Browning: A Portrait* (1952).

PAULA GUNN ALLEN

Pocahontas to Her English Husband, John Rolfe (p. 651)

According to legend, Pocahontas (c. 1596–1617), whose name means "playful one," saved the English Captain John Smith from execution at the hands of Algonquin Chief Powhatan and his men in 1607. Scholars have disagreed about the exact nature of what happened. If it was a ceremonial feast whose customs Smith misunderstood, Smith's life may not really have been in danger. It appears that after this incident, Pocahontas—twelve years old at the time—mediated between the English settlers and the Indians and helped for several years to improve relations between them before hostilities broke out again.

In 1613, Captain Samuel Argall captured Pocahontas and held her hostage, as part of his effort to compel Powhatan to cease war against the English. She converted to Christianity, took "Rebecca" as her Christian name, and in 1614 married John Rolfe, who became wealthy from developing and cultivating a new species of tobacco. In 1616, the Virginia Company brought Rolfe, his wife, and their son to England, in order to promote the splendors of the "new world" and spur emigration to America and investments there. Pocahontas/"Rebecca" became widely known and was even presented at court. She died in March 1617 aboard a ship bound from England to Virginia. Rolfe was killed in an Indian attack in 1622. Their son and his descendants lived in Virginia.

We have found that a good strategy in teaching this poem is to begin with "perfidious" in line 2. The Latin root means faithless, dishonest; the word itself suggests deceit, treachery, and is sometimes particularly associated with Judas, the betrayer of Christ. We then ask students to circle words that express other dimensions of Pocahontas's critique of Smith and to note along the way how she characterizes his perceptions of her.

See Philip L. Barbour, *Pocahontas and Her World* (1970); Frances Mossiker, *Pocahontas: The Life and Legend* (1977); Robert S. Tilton, *Pocahontas: The Evolution of an American Narrative* (1994); and Klaus Lubbers, *Born for the Shade: Stereotypes of the Native American in United States Literature and the Visual Arts* (1994).

Allen has also written or edited a number of scholarly books, including *Studies in American Indian Literature: Critical Essays and Course Designs* (1983) and *The Sacred Hoop: Recovering the Feminine in American Indian Traditions* (1986). Instructors might also turn students toward Brian Swann, ed., *Coming to Light: Contemporary Translations of the Native Literatures of North America* (1955).

VICTOR NEHLIG

Pocahontas and John Smith (painting, p. 651)

Although all schoolchildren learn how Pocahontas saved John Smith in Virginia, historians are skeptical about the story. The gist of the narrative, though with different characters and a different setting—a Spaniard named Juan Ortiz, and a Ucita woman known as Ulele, in Florida—had been recorded almost eighty years before John Smith set foot in Virginia. The Ortiz/Ulele story, which is said to have occurred in 1528, was first published in English around 1605, two years before Smith sailed from London to America. Of course history may have repeated itself; the gist of the Ortiz/Ulele drama in Florida may have been reenacted with Smith and Pocahontas in Virginia, in December 1607, the date Smith gave, but the evidence is nonexistent. The episode does not appear in Smith's earliest account of his adventures, *A True Relation . . . of Virginia* (1608)—Smith first mentioned it in 1616—nor does any other colonist of the time mention it.

Some modern historians explain the absence of an earlier account as in accordance with orders given not to publish anything that might scare off potential colonists. In any case, the gist of Smith's story, whether or not it happened, is that the beautiful Pocahontas, moved by pity or love or both, intervened and persuaded her savage father to spare Smith's life. (The father is customarily called Powhatan, a name given him by the British, but in fact Powhatan was the name of the Indian nation, not of an individual.) The basic idea behind the story is that although Indians by and large are savages, some savages are capable of virtuous deeds. The further implication is that savages can be brought, perhaps by slow degrees, to recognize the superiority of white, Christian culture, and to adopt it. This idea achieved its most memorable formulation in Kipling's poem, "The White Man's Burden." Speaking of white, we want to mention that in Nehlig's picture the Indian princess's skin is notably lighter than that of the other Indians, hinting at or symbolizing her superior nature.

The male figures, in poses calculated to display their muscles, are indebted to Michelangelo. Europeans could never quite decide if Indians were ugly, deformed creatures with wicked minds or were by nature perfectly proportioned and mentally uncorrupted Adam-like creatures. If the latter, their unspoiled minds and their simple, primitive existence made them "noble savages," a topic discussed at length in Hugh Honour's fascinating book, *The New Golden Land* (1975). On this topic see also Julie Schimmel's chapter, "Inventing 'the Indian,'" in *The West as America: Reinterpreting Images of the Frontier, 1820–1920*, ed. William Truettner (1991). This book—originally the catalog for an exhibition—is extremely well illustrated but it is often naive in its relentless political correctness. The authors are shocked, truly shocked, that painters and writers in the nineteenth century did not represent Indians accurately—which is to say in the way that these late twentieth-century academicians see them.

The composition of Nehlig's painting, with one figure standing higher than all of the others and seeming to preside over the action, is obviously indebted to baroque paintings that show such scenes as Solomon judging the two harlots who quarreled over the baby, or God watching Abraham as he prepares to sacrifice Isaac. But there must also be a strong influence of baroque scenes of martyrdom, with Pocahontas substituting for an intervening angel; certainly the light behind her is a secular equivalent of an angel's aureole.

In *Pocahontas: The Evolution of an American Narrative* (1994), Robert S. Tilton studies representations of the Pocahontas story in painting, fiction, drama, and historical writing from the earliest days of the colonies through the Civil War. Students might enjoy reading Tilton's book, with its many helpful illustrations. The full history of the impact of European settlement on the native peoples of the Americas receives detailed, disturbing treatment in David E. Stannard, *American Holocaust: Columbus and the Conquest of the New World* (1992).

ROBERT HERRICK

To the Virgins, to Make Much of Time (p. 654)

On Herrick's "To the Virgins," see E. M. W. Tillyard in *The Metaphysicals and Milton* (1956); Tillyard argues effectively that in "To the Virgins," "the trend of the poem is urgency, touched with reflection."

This wonderful lyric seems ideally suited to introduce students to matters of persona and tone. We have found that when asked, "Who is speaking?" most students will answer, "A man." (Possibly some offer this opinion simply because a man wrote this poem.) A few will say that a woman is the speaker, and we have found it interesting to ask them why. (Those who say that a woman is the speaker usually suggest that she is unmarried and is speaking regretfully.) Almost all students hear the voice of an older person, though they cannot always say why. Similarly, although a few students find the speaker aggressively offering unsolicited advice, most hear a friendly voice. True, the first and last stanzas begin with imperatives ("Gather ye rosebuds," "Then be not coy"), but most students hear in "Old Time," "a-flying," and "a-getting" an engaging old-codgerliness. They may hear, too, even a touch of elderly loquacity in the explanation of a fairly obvious figure: "The glorious lamp of heaven, the sun."

One other point about Herrick's poem: The shift to "you" in the last stanza (from the earlier "ye") gives the moral great emphasis.

The *carpe diem* motif allows the poem to be related easily to Marvell's "Coy Mistress." What is especially interesting, however, is the difference in tone, even though the poems share both a motif and a structure—the logical argument.

Is the poem offensive to women? Some of our students have found it so. Our hope is that readers will be able to read the poem not so much as advice to women to submit passively to marriage, as advice (which can apply to males as well as to females) "to make much of time." Against "dying" and "setting," we can "gather," "smile," and "run."

John Press (1961) and Roger B. Rollin (1966) have written good introductions to Herrick's life and work.

TOPIC FOR CRITICAL THINKING AND WRITING

This seventeenth-century poem suggests that a woman finds fulfillment only in marriage. Can the poem, then, be of any interest to a society in which women may choose careers in preference to marriage?

EZRA POUND

The River-Merchant's Wife: A Letter (p. 655)

One of Pound's comments to William Carlos Williams may be useful (from *Letters of Ezra Pound, 1907–41*, edited by D. D. Paige, 3–4):

> To me the short so-called dramatic lyric—at any rate the sort of thing I do—is the poetic part of a drama the rest of which (to me the prose part) is left to the reader's imagination or implied or set in a short note. I catch

the character I happen to be interested in at the moment he interests me, usually a moment of song, self-analysis, or sudden understanding or revelation. And the rest of the play would bore me and presumably the reader.

Pound learned much from Browning's dramatic monologues, and this comment could, in a general way, apply to Browning's poems. But it is worth exploring with students the way in which "The River-Merchant's Wife" differs from "My Last Duchess." For one thing, Pound's speaker (like many of the speakers in his early poems) is relatively naive, and so the poem gives us an impression of a "pure" and universal sort, whereas Browning's gives us an impression of a particular case history. Moreover, Browning customarily gives us considerably more sense of a particular period than Pound does or, to put it a little differently, Browning—even in "My Last Duchess"— gives us a greater sense of a particular character interacting with particular circumstances of the age. Pound based his poem on a prose translation by Ernest Fenollosa of a poem by the Chinese poet Li Po (in Japanese, called Rihaku). A transcription of the Fenollosa manuscript is printed in Michael Reck, *Ezra Pound: A Close-up*, 168–71.

For Pound, see *Selected Poems* (1949; rev. ed. 1957) and *Literary Essays* (1954). A good introduction is M. L. Rosenthal, *A Primer of Ezra Pound* (1960); for a more advanced approach, we recommend Hugh Kenner, *The Pound Ezra* (1972).

WILFRED OWEN

Dulce et Decorum Est (p. 656)

There are plenty of comments about the horrors of war—for instance, Tacitus's "They make a desert and call it peace," and Sherman's "War is Hell"—but even Tacitus and Sherman probably believed that war is necessary and can be heroic. It's our guess that they would even have agreed with Horace: *"Dulce et decorum est / Pro patria mori."*

Owen is asserting that modern war is so dehumanizing that Horace's line—if it were ever true—is now certainly false. We say "dehumanizing" because even from the start Owen gives us images of ruined creatures: "Bent double," "old beggars," "hags." There is nothing here of Tennyson's Light Brigade charging manfully into the Valley of Death.

Death comes to a battered, knock-kneed, limping soldier who is seen as "flound'ring" rather than falling in some heroic pose. The speaker relives the sight of witnessing (through the eyepiece of his gas mask) his companion destroyed by what seemed to be a sea of poison gas, but equally horrible is the memory of the appearance of the dead body when it was carted away.

It's probably true to say that as long as war was (for the most part) something executed by professionals in remote places, politicians and poets and even the mass of citizens comfortable at home could find it easy to praise war. Speaking of war as it was in the eighteenth century, the Swiss philosopher Emerich de Vattell (1714–1767) said, "The troops alone carry on war, while the rest of the nation is at peace." But modern war—it is sometimes said that the Civil War was the first modern war—is quite another thing. First, an army can get its supplies from remote sources, which means from the civilians back home, who therefore become fair game for the enemy. Second, newspaper photography and television have brought the horrors of the battlefield into the home—and this, in effect, is what Owen does in the poem.

What of the structure of the poem? The first stanza (8 lines) consists of two quatrains (*ababcdcd*). Line 4 ends with a period, so why did Owen not begin a new stanza with line 5? Apparently he thought of the first two quatrains as an octave—possibly he even began by thinking he would write a sonnet. The next stanza is a sestet, rhyming *efefgh*. The fifth and sixth lines of this sestet will rhyme with the next two lines, so from the point of view of the rhyme scheme Owen has again written two quatrains, but he interrupted the second of these two, separating it from its last two lines by putting a space between lines 14 and 15. Surely this arrangement of lines has a meaning, and probably has an effect. Although the speaker uses "we" in line 2 and "our" in line 4, and thus identifies himself with the scene, until the last line of the sestet (i.e., until the second half of line 14) the impression is chiefly of a description of something out there, rather than a revelation of the self. But if for thirteen and a half lines the speaker seems chiefly to be an observer, the second half of the fourteenth line emphatically introduces the speaker's response: "I saw him drowning." In the next stanza, which consists of only two lines (15–16), considerable emphasis is given to the dead man, but an even greater emphasis is given to the speaker's response to the sight:

> In all my dreams, before my helpless sight,
> He plunges at me, guttering, choking, drowning.

The final stanza (twelve lines—three quatrains, the third of which grimly rhymes "glory" with "*mori*") begins by drawing the reader ("you") into the nightmare world of the narrator and the dead soldier. The speaker insistently holds onto this "you," addressing him (or her?) not only in line 17, but also in 21 and ironically (as "My friend") in line 25. The poem ends with a noble Latin sentiment, but this ending is scarcely designed to provide a quiet or upbeat ending; rather, it is designed to keep the squirming reader squirming.

THOMAS HARDY

The Man He Killed (p. 657)

The speaker's diction is that of a simple, uneducated rustic ("old ancient," "Right many a nipperkin," "list," "off-hand-like"). He tells us (line 15) that he enlisted because he was out of work and broke, but line 10 reveals that he also responded to customary wartime propaganda and appeals to patriotism. He is still too trusting to reject what he was told about his "foe," but in the third stanza the repetitions, abrupt pauses, and attempts to reassure himself in "of course he was," and "That's clear enough" all indicate his struggle to overcome incipient doubts. The heavy pauses in the fourth stanza show the difficulty a man unused to thinking about large matters has when what he has been taught by his "betters" conflicts with his own feelings. In the fifth stanza he resolves his doubts with a platitude—war is "quaint and curious"—but we feel that he'll be retelling his story at one pub or another and pondering his experience for the rest of his life.

One can have a field day talking about irony; here the ironic distance between poet and speaker and between speaker and reader, the "irony of fate" in which the soldier is trapped, the dramatic irony in the fact that the speaker had to kill a man before he could recognize him as a potential neighbor or friend, a man like himself. And, finally, this simple man is one of us. Like him, we are mere pawns trapped between forces whose meaning, though it continues to elude us, we continue to question.

ADDITIONAL TOPIC FOR CRITICIAL THINKING AND WRITING

What state of mind would you have to be in to think of war as "quaint and curious"? To think of a man you killed as a "foe"? *Is* the speaker convinced by the words he utters? Whether your answer is "Yes" or "No," why do you think so?

THOMAS HARDY

The Ruined Maid (p. 658)

Obviously there are two voices here, the voice of 'Melia (the "ruined maid" who now shows signs of "prosperi-ty") and the voice of a nameless rural woman. But there is also another voice, the voice of the author. Such a voice is especially evident in poems that employ irony. The ostensible speaker or speakers say X and Y, but the reader also hears the author saying Z, i.e., saying, in effect, "Of course the reality is quite different from what you are hearing, maybe even the opposite."

What the reader hears, most obviously, is an encounter which reveals that a "ruined" girl—a girl who has lost her virginity—in fact can do very well materially. (Incidentally, we hasten to add that Hardy did not always joke about prostitution. In another poem, "The Chapel Organist," he reports the suicide of a young woman who works for a miserable wage as a chapel organist. In order to survive she turns to prostitution; when the miserly deacons learn of her supplementary activity they fire her, and the desperate girl poisons herself.) Obviously 'Melia enjoys her condition ("'Yes: that's how we dress when we're ruined,' said she"), and surely a reader can infer that Hardy is at least mildly amused—rather, than, say outraged as a Victorian moralist might be. A line such as "Some polish is gained with one's ruin" (12) similarly may provide evidence that Hardy was not at all disturbed by what some of his contemporaries regarded as an indecent life, and in "'We never do work when we're ruined' said she" we may detect wry amusement in Hardy, and even an amused glance at the Victorian glorification of hard work. And in the next-to-last stanza, when 'Melia says she no longer has the megrims or the "melancho-ly," surely we can say that Hardy is indicating that the life of a "ruined" woman is nothing for us to get indignant about.

But what about the final stanza, and especially about 'Melia's use of the word *ain't*, in "'You ain't ruined' said she")? *Ain't* is a contraction, originally for "am not" but it came to be used also for "is not," "are not," and "have not (as in "They ain't gone yet"). The first printed use (1695), spelled "an't," is in Congreve's *Love for Love*: "I an't deaf," and the word is common in Restoration comedy, where (again, spelled "an't") it is often used by upper-class speakers, though admittedly they are often foppish. It is not until the early eighteenth century that it is criticized—along with *can't, don't, won't, shouldn't,* and other contractions that we find perfectly acceptable today. Henry Alford, in *A Plea for the Queen's English* (1866), condemns "ain't" but significantly he mentions that it is used "even by highly educated persons." 1866, by the way, is the very year in which Hardy wrote "The Ruined Maid."

All of this discussion of *ain't* is a preliminary to our response to a question that (in different words) we raise in the text: Does 'Melia's use of the word *ain't* indicate that despite her self-satisfied view of herself as a sophisticated women, she is pretty much the ignorant country girl? The usual response is that the line shows that 'Melia is indeed the ignorant girl she was when she was digging potatoes and using the local dialect (see lines 9–10). We are not so sure. Although today the use of *ain't* indicates ignorance—unless the word is playfully used—the word was most certainly not always a sign of illiteracy. In short, in Hardy's day prescriptive grammarians—often a narrow-minded bunch—were pretty much agreed that *ain't* was offensive but in fact the word was used by people of all classes.

We want to offer a further complication. The word is often used playfully—we might even say kittenishly—by persons who ordinarily would not use it. Thus, *Webster's Dictionary of English Usage* (1989) in its discussion of *ain't* cites examples from (among others) Charles Lamb, Winston Churchill, Robert Frost, and Flannery O'Connor, and it mentions the occurrence of the word in songs such as "It ain't necessarily so," "The old gray mare, she ain't what she used to be," and "Ain't she sweet." We also want to mention that some phrases, such as "Ain't it the truth?" and "You ain't seen nothing yet" require the word. In short, in our view, 'Melia's use of *ain't* in the last line may or may not indicate that despite her fashionable clothes she remains unsophisticated.

If in the last line Hardy's little joke is that 'Melia remains unsophisticated despite her fancy clothes, he is satirizing her. This interpretation may be correct, but it gives us a Thomas Hardy who is something of a snob, and we are not keen on that image. We prefer the alternate view, that 'Melia is quite appropriately playing the fashionable lady, and with tongue in cheek she is using the current lingo. Far from satirizing her, Hardy admires her realism and cheekiness.

WALTER DE LA MARE

An Epitaph (p. 659)

The form of course is an epitaph (literally, "over a tomb"), and it is also an epigram, not in the relatively late sense of a witty comment but in the old sense of something intended to be engraved or inscribed: "writing [engraved] on," "inscription." (Because inscriptions were brief they customarily were highly packed, and in time the word became applied to brief witty writings, but originally an epigram simply was "an inscription.")

The words are imagined to be carved on a tombstone, and the speaker is the tombstone itself ("when I crumble. . ."). The form was common in the ancient world and is especially known in the *Greek Anthology*, a collection edited and reedited many times, from the earliest version by the poet Meleager around 60 B.C. until versions as late as the tenth century A.D., by which time the *Greek Anthology* included some 4,500 poems, by more than 300 poets. Sometimes the tombstone itself speaks (as in de la Mare's poem), but sometimes the deceased person speaks, as in what is perhaps the most famous of all ancient epigrams, Simonides's sepulchral epigram spoken by one of those who died at Thermopylae. When the huge Persian army led by Xerxes sought to conquer Greece, the small Greek army established itself at a narrow pass at Thermopylae. The Greek position was betrayed, and the soldiers withdrew, except for some three hundred soldiers from the Greek city-state of Sparta (also called Lacedaemon), who remained and fought to the death. A monument was said to have been erected on the spot:

> Go, tell the Lacedaemonians, passer-by,
> That here obedient to their laws we lie.

Here's another version:

> Stranger, let Sparta learn that here we lie,
> Obedient to her call who bade us die.

(A literal translation might go thus: "Stranger, tell the Spartans that we lie here obeying their orders.")

De la Mare's "An Epitaph" has a slightly archaic flavor in the fourth line, where the accent in "West Country" falls on the final syllable (a common occurrence in ballads, for instance, in "Sir Patrick Spence," where the accent on "sailor" is on the second syllable).

The poem consists of relatively short lines, and it is full of heavy pauses. What is the effect? To us, given the subject matter, the pauses contribute to the speaker's sense of a painful loss. The one line that is enjambed is the next-to-last, when the stone speaks of crumbling, and we take this over-running to be imitative of the stone losing its form. Notice, too, that in the first line the stone speaks of "a most beautiful lady," thus preserving at least the memory of the lady's beauty, but in the last line—when the stone imagines its own demise—the lady's beauty is utterly gone, and we hear only of "This lady," and indeed the context ("who will remember / This lady") suggests that the lady as well as her beauty is gone.

Students might turn next to de la Mare's *Selected Poems*, ed. R. N. Green-Armytage (1954); and *A Choice of de la Mare's Verse*, ed. W. H. Auden (1963).

GERARD MANLEY HOPKINS

Spring and Fall: To a Young Child (p. 660)

In our experience, students will have considerable difficulty if they simply read the poem silently to themselves, but if they read (and reread) it aloud, it becomes clear—and more important, it becomes something they value.

We begin, then, as we usually do with poems, by having a student read the poem aloud, and then we invite comments about the title and its connection with the two people in the poem. Students usually see that the poem presents youth and age, that Margaret is associated with spring and the speaker with the fall, and this leads to discussion of the Fall in Christian thought. Many students, however, do not know that in Christian thought the disobedience of Adam and Eve brought consequences that extended to nature, and that the perennial spring of Eden therefore yielded to autumn and winter; that is, "Goldengrove" inherited death. ("Goldengrove," incidentally, might seem to suggest preciousness and eternity, but here the golden leaves are a sign of transience and death.)

In the original version of "Spring and Fall" (1880), line 8 ran, "Though forests low and leafmeal lie." When he revised the poem in 1884, Hopkins changed "Though forests low and" to "Though worlds of wanwood," thus introducing the pallor of "wanwood" and also wonderfully extending the vista from "forests" to "worlds." Margaret's sorrow for the trees stripped of their golden foliage is finally sorrow for the Fall, whose consequences are everywhere. Her mouth cannot formulate any of this, but her spirit has intuited it ("ghost guessed").

On "Spring and Fall," see Paul L. Mariani, *A Commentary on the Complete Poems of Gerard Manley Hopkins* (1970); Marylou Motto, *The Poetry of Gerard Manley Hopkins* (1984); and Peter Milward's essay in Milward and R. V. Schoder, *Landscape and Inscape* (1975). George Starbuck has a modern version ("Translations from the English") in his book of poems, *White Paper* (1966).

Recent work on Hopkins includes *Gerard Manley Hopkins (1844–1889): New Essays on His Life, Writing, and Place in English Literature*, ed. Michael E. Allsop and Michael W. Sundermeier (1989); Robert Bernard Martin, *Gerard Manley Hopkins: A Very Private Life* (1991); and Norman White, *Hopkins: A Literary Biography* (1992).

COUNTEE CULLEN

For a Lady I Know (p. 661)

Although Cullen sometimes wrote about African-American life he also wrote on other topics and in traditions other than the vernacular tradition employed by Langston Hughes.

"For a Lady I Know" is indeed about white/black relations, but it is in the tradition of the polished epigram of Martial and other Roman satirists and their successors. "Low" diction occurs in "snores," but for the most part the diction is refined, echoing the language that the "lady" might use: "lies late," "poor black cherubs," "rise at seven," "celestial chores." The satiric force of the poem comes largely from stating a repulsive idea elegantly.

An excellent resource for further study is *My Soul's High Song: The Collected Writings of Countee Cullen, Voice of the Harlem Renaissance*, ed. Gerald L. Early (1991).

LYN LIFSHIN

My Mother and the Bed (p. 661)

Students enjoy this poem, and classroom discussion may be animated, especially concerning the second question in the text, which asks if bitterness overshadows geniality.

Our first question, concerning the unexpected extra spaces in the poem, calls attention to the need to pay close attention to—to enjoy—the physical appearance of the poem. Of course readers of this book have already seen, in Pastan's "Jump Cabling" in Chapter 15, a poem whose meaning is partly conveyed by its appearance on the page, but it is useful to remind students to consider the physical appearance of every poem. Long lines convey a feeling different from short lines, and the breaks between stanzas can say a lot. True, we should read poems aloud, if possible, but we should also look at them closely—"hear with eyes," in Shakespeare's words—and take their appearance seriously.

E. E. CUMMINGS

next to of course god america i (p. 663)

"next to of course god america i" uses Cummings's characteristic unconventional typography, but here the effect is not so much to break with lifeless convention as it is to emphasize the mindless, unvarying, unstoppable jabbering of politicians.

MARGE PIERCY

Barbie Doll (p. 664)

The title alerts us to the world of childhood, so we are not surprised in the first line by "This girlchild" (like "This little pig") or by "pee-pee" in the second line. The stanza ends with the voice of a jeering child. The second stanza drops the kid-talk, adopting in its place the language of social science. (The stanza has much of the sound of Auden's "The Unknown Citizen.") We have not, then, made much progress; the "girlchild" who in the first stanza is treated like a Barbie doll is in the second treated like a healthy specimen, a statistic. The beginning of the third stanza sounds more intimate, but she is still an object, not a person, and by the end of this stanza, there is a painful explosion. The two preceding stanzas each ended with a voice different from the voice that spoke the earlier lines of the stanza (in 6, "You have a great big nose and fat legs," we hear a jeering child, and in 11, "Everyone saw a fat nose on thick legs," we hear an adolescent imagining how others see her), but the third stanza moves to something of the flatly stated violence of a fairy tale: "So she cut off her nose and her legs / and offered them up." In the final lines of this last stanza she is again (or better, still) a doll, lifeless and pretty.

In recent years, in addition to white Barbies there have been African-American, Hispanic, and Asian Barbies, but until the fall of 1990 the TV and print ads showed only the fair-skinned blue-eyed version. For additional information about Barbie, see Sydney Ladensohn Stern and Ted Schoenhaus, *Toyland: The High-Stakes Game of the Toy Industry* (1990), and M. G. Lord, *Forever Barbie* (1994). Barbie's wardrobe has changed from flight attendant to astronaut, and from garden-party outfits to workout attire. She has a dress-for-success and a briefcase—but they are pink.

Piercy has written many books of poetry and novels. We suggest that students turn to the poems in *Circles on the Water* (1982), *My Mother's Body* (1985), and *Available Light* (1988). See also *Ways of Knowing: Essays on Marge Piercy*, ed. Sue Walker and Eugene Hamner (1991).

LOUISE ERDRICH

Dear John Wayne (p. 665)

The title suggests a fan letter (and therefore a naive, adoring writer-speaker), but the poem turns out to be a witty, vigorous satire, with a good deal of Swiftian *saeva indignatio* under the wit.

The mock heroic diction of "to vanquish the hordes of mosquitoes" quickly yields to the simplicity of "Nothing works," but the mosquitoes as enemies reappear in "They break through the smoke screen for blood," where the line also evokes thoughts of cowboys and Indians in battle. Other elevated passages include "There will be no parlance" and "die beautifully," but such terms are mixed with "ICBM missiles" and "this wide screen," so they are undercut; the apparent heroism is Hollywood phoniness, as phony as John Wayne's smile, "a horizon of teeth."

Satire, of course, is a way of talking seriously, of expressing indignation under a veil of comedy. If the absurdity of what is happening on the screen causes the Indians to laugh and "fall over the hood / slipping in the hot spilled butter," these lines about Native Americans eating popcorn remind us of the cliché about people slipping in blood during battle, and the cliché reminds us of the reality of the battles in which, finally, the whites took the land from the Native Americans.

ALEXANDER POPE

Engraved on the Collar of a Dog (p. 667)

In our headnote we characterize the poem as an epigram, and we offer a brief definition, "a short, witty observation." You may want to quote Coleridge:

> What is an epigram? A dwarfish whole,
> Its body brevity, and wit its soul.

Pope's first line, "I am his Highness' dog at Kew," is civil enough; the beast is politely introducing himself. (Incidentally, in case some uppity kid asks, the device of giving speech to an animal or an inanimate thing is called prosopopoeia.) The next line, still seemingly polite with its "sir," gets down to business: The dog assumes that the reader of the verse on the collar is, well, is subservient to someone, just as the dog is. Is Pope absurdly cynical? Or is he on to something? Discuss.

15

Figurative Language: Simile, Metaphor, Personification, and Apostrophe

If the idea that metaphors are like riddles is appealing, ask the class why the camel is "the ship of the desert." They will see that the figure goes beyond saying that the camel is a means of transportation, for the figure brings out both the camel's resemblance (at a great distance) to a sailboat and the desert's resemblance to an ocean.

If one wants to get into this business of metaphors as riddles (and we recommend it), one can have great fun in class by asking students to ask their classmates riddles. *Note*: We are *not* talking about riddles that depend on puns, such as "What's black and white and red all over?" (Answer: A newspaper, because "read" is mistaken as "red.")

On figurative language, consult Monroe Beardsley, *Aesthetics* (1958); Isabel Hungerland, *Poetic Discourse* (1958); W. K. Wimsatt, Jr., and Cleanth Brooks, *Literary Criticism* (1957), 749–50; and Terence Hawkes, *Metaphor* (1972). Probably as good as any statement about figurative language is Shelley's, that the language of poets "is vitally metaphoric; that is, it marks the before unapprehended relations of things and perpetuates their apprehension."

At some point during our classroom discussion of metaphor we usually manage to give students Kenneth Burke's comment on metaphor (from his essay on Marianne Moore): Metaphor is "a device for seeing something *in terms of* something else. It brings out the thisness of a that, or the thatness of a this!"

ROBERT BURNS

A Red, Red Rose (p. 669)

Probably few instructors will feel the need to discuss this poem in class, but we include it in the book because we like it and because it offers figures that are easily perceived. What do we like about it? Well, we like the figures

213

(even though they are obvious); we like the repetition: "red, red rose" (line 1), "And I" (7, 11, 15), "Till a' the seas gang dry" (8, 9), "my dear" (9, 11), and especially "luve" (a noun in 1 and 3, referring to the beloved; a noun in 6, referring to the speaker's mental state; a verb in 7; a noun in 13 and 15). We like the fact that the poem scarcely advances, but keeps returning to the beloved. Of course, one can find a structure (e.g., the song moves from the local and familiar ["a red, red rose"] to the remote ["ten thousand mile"]), but chiefly one feels that the poet keeps coming back to his beloved and to his love for her.

David Daiches, in *Robert Burns* (1971), praises the poem for its "combination of swagger and tender protectiveness" (312). Somehow, this characterization doesn't seem exactly right to us, and you may want to ask your students if his view corresponds to theirs:

> Nowhere in literature has that combination of swagger and tender protectiveness so characteristic of the male in love been so perfectly captured, and it is all done by simple similes and simple exaggeration.

Burns is best studied in the one-volume edition in the Oxford Standard Authors series, ed. James Kinsley (1969). An older but still valuable book on Burns is John Delancey Ferguson, *Pride and Passion* (1939). See also *Critical Essays on Robert Burns*, ed. Donald A. Low (1975), and *The Art of Robert Burns*, ed. R. D. S. Jack and Andrew Noble (1982).

SYLVIA PLATH

Metaphors (p. 671)

Sylvia Plath's "Metaphors," in nine lines of nine syllables each, with nine metaphors, is a sort of joking reference to the nine months of pregnancy, which is what this riddling poem is about.

There are many biographies and critical studies of Plath, but the best place to start is with Janet Malcolm's fascinating account of Plath, her husband (and poet) Ted Hughes, and her biographers, *The Silent Woman: Sylvia Plath and Ted Hughes* (1994).

A "Voices and Visions" videocassette of Sylvia Plath is available from Longman Publishers.

RICHARD WILBUR

A Simile for Her Smile (p. 672)

The comparison is not of her smile to the approaching riverboat (the "packet," in line 9), but of the pause in the speaker's mind (a pause that follows the "hope, the thought" of her smile) to the pause in traffic when the boat approaches the drawbridge. In the second stanza some of the words describing the life around the speaker can easily be thought to refer also to the woman: "the packet's *smooth* approach," "the *silken* river." Probably the last line, with its rather grand image ("And slow cascading of the paddle wheel"), comes as a pleasant surprise.

There is no need to get into matters of versification (though no harm, either), but you may want to point out that the poem is divided into two sestets, and that the open space between them corresponds to the space made as the drawbridge starts to rise. The space also stands for the silence that comes over the horns and motors.

For more of Wilbur's poetry, see his *New and Collected Poems* (1988). Critical studies include Donald Hall, *Richard Wilbur* (1967); *Richard Wilbur's Creation*, ed. Wendy Salinger (1983); and Bruce Michelson, *Wilbur's Poetry: Music in a Scattering Time* (1991). See also the special issue of the journal *Parnassus*, Spring–Summer 1977, and *Conversations with Richard Wilbur*, ed. William Butts (1990).

JOHN KEATS

On First Looking into Chapman's Homer (p. 673)

In "On First Looking into Chapman's Homer," Keats uses figures to communicate to the reader the poet's state of mind. Figures of traveling (appropriate to a poem about the author of *The Iliad* and *The Odyssey*, and also, via "realms of gold" or El Dorado, to the Elizabethans) give way in the sestet to figures of more breathtaking exploration and discovery. (By the way, it is not quite right to say that at line 9 we pass from the octave's images of land to the sestet's images of discovery. An important shift occurs in line 7, with "Yet" no less important than line 9's "Then." "Breathe" in line 7 is probably transitional, linked to the octave's idea of foreign travel and also to the sestet's early reference to the skies.)

It is probably fair to say that the octave (or at least its first six lines as compared with the sestet) has a somewhat mechanical, academic quality. "Realms of gold," "goodly states," "bards in fealty to Apollo," "demesne," etc., all suggest something less than passionate utterance, a tone reinforced by the rather mechanical four pairs of lines, each pair ending with a substantial pause. But in the sestet the language is more concrete, the lines more fluid (it can be argued that only line 10 concludes with a pause), and the meter less regular, giving a sense of new excitement that of course corresponds to the meaning of the poem.

Almost all critics agree that Keats erred in giving Cortez for Balboa, but C. V. Wicker argues in *College English* 17 (April 1956): 383–87 that Keats meant Cortez, for the point is not the first discovery of something previously unknown, but an individual's discovery for himself of what others have earlier discovered for themselves. Still, it seems evident that Keats slipped, and instructors may want to spend some class time discussing the problem of whether such a factual error weakens the poem.

In line with much contemporary criticism that sees poetry as being reflective discourse concerned with itself, Lawrence Lipking, in *The Life of the Poet* (1981), sees this poem as being about Keats's discovery of Keats. Well, yes, in a way, but surely the poem is also about the discovery of the world's literature, a world other than the self. See also P. McNally, in *JEGP* 79 (1980): 530–40.

MICHAEL DRAYTON

Since There's No Help (p. 674)

The first quatrain (though joined to the next quatrain by a semicolon) is in effect a complete sentence. The speaker seems resolute, though perhaps in retrospect we feel that the repetition of "glad" in line 3 ("I am glad, yea, glad with all my heart") is a clue that insincerity causes him to protest too much. The second quatrain, which also can stand as a sentence, continues the matter-of-fact tone. But then, after the eighth line, comes the turn, or *volta*, so often found in sonnets. In the third quatrain and couplet—this quatrain cannot stand as a sentence, but passionately overflows into the couplet, and so the quatrain and couplet together can be taken as a sort of sestet—we hear a new breathlessness or sense of urgency that dispels the earlier apparent confidence. The personified abstractions, too, are new (Passion, Faith, etc.); they do *not* indicate insincerity or lack of feeling, but, on the contrary, take us into a world of bruised feelings, evident earlier in such an expression as "you get no more of me." Even the shift from "you" in line 2 to the more intimate "thou" in line 13 is significant in establishing the change. The poem ends with a feminine rhyme, probably to keep it from ending too emphatically or, to put the matter a bit differently, to indicate that the speakeer is not the master of the situation.

EDMUND WALLER

Song (p. 675)

If the chapters have been read in order, students will have encountered roses in "To the Virgins, to Make Much of Time" and in Burns's "A Red, Red Rose." In the next chapter they will encounter Blake's "The Sick Rose." In line 2, "wastes" is perhaps more potent than many students at first find it, for it implies not simply squandering but destroying, as in, for instance, "to lay waste a city." Thus the idea of death, explicit in lines 16–17, is present almost from the start of the poem.

The only edition of Waller's poetry is a reprint (1968) of a volume published in 1893. Jack G. Gilbert, *Edmund Waller* (1975), surveys the life and writings.

WILLIAM CARLOS WILLIAMS

The Red Wheelbarrow (p. 677)

Roy Harvey Pearce, in *The Continuity of American Poetry* (1987, 339), regards William Carlos Williams's "The Red Wheelbarrow" as sentimental (but of some value) and says that what depends is the poet: "He assures himself that he is what he is by virtue of his power to collocate such objects into sharply annotated images like these." Charles Altieri, in *PMLA* 91 (1976): 111, suggests that although the items are stripped of associations, "No poem in English is more metonymic. Three objects evoke a mode of life in the sparsest, most succinct manner possible. The poverty of detail, like that in the rural paintings of Andrew Wyeth, at once intensifies the starkness of rural life and exemplifies it." Altieri also points out that in each of the last three stanzas, the first line "depends" on the second, for the word that ends each first line is often a noun ("wheel," "rain," "white"), but in the poem turns out to be an adjective. Thus the reader's mind "is made to hover over details until its waiting is rewarded, not only within the stanza, but also as each independent stanza emerges to fill out this waiting and to move us beyond details to a complex sense of a total life contained in these objects." John Hollander (*Vision and Resonance* (1975), 111) suggests that cutting "wheelbarrow" and "rainwater" (with no hyphens to indicate that "rain" and "wheel" are parts of the compounds) helps to convey what the poem is about: seeing the constituents of things in the freshness of light after rain.

Camille Paglia, in *Break, Blow, Burn* (2005)—a volume devoted to explications of poems—offers some interesting (and challengeable) comments, of which we reprint a very few. She says, in part:

> The poem is a single sentence consisting of a series of prepositional phrases that dangle from the verb "depends" in the first line. The root meaning of "depend" is to hang down: hence the poem seems to rappel down the page on a smooth chain of words. Movement slows, then speeds up again at the surprise split of "wheelbarrow" in two: when "barrow" drops to the next line (cleverly sliding off "wheel"), we must pause and take breath (3–4). . . .
>
> Indeed, each of Williams's neat, tiny stanzas has a recessive wheelbarrow shape: the first line is the wheelbarrow's long handles, while the daringly terse, one-word second line mimics the sloping cart. . . .
>
> What "depends / upon" the wheelbarrow? For Williams, it is the act of *focus*, the effort to see clearly. Within its frame, art establishes relationships, even if the result of chance. . . . (128–30)

Two older studies remain useful: Linda Wagner, *The Poems of William Carlos Williams* (1964), and James E. Breslin, *William Carlos Williams: An American Artist* (1970). Paul Mariani's biography, *William Carlos Williams: A New World Naked* (1981), is detailed and definitive, but for students, Reed Whittemore's *William Carlos Williams: Poet from Jersey* (1975) might be a better place to start.

A "Voices and Visions" videocassette of William Carlos Williams is available from Longman Publishers.

ALFRED, LORD TENNYSON

The Eagle (p. 677)

Tennyson's concise account in "The Eagle" seems literal enough, but from the first the bird is personified, by being called "He" instead of "it" and by being given "hands" instead of talons. Note also that "his mountain walls" implies that the bird is lord of a fortress. "Wrinkled sea" and "crawls" are other obvious figures, giving us the sea from a human-bird's eye view. The simile "like a thunder bolt he falls" returns us from the eagle's point of view to the observer's. "Ringed with the azure world," we should mention, has been interpreted as expressing the bird's view of the earth spread out in a circle before him, but "azure" may indicate that the description is not of the earth but of the sky around the bird, and so the line is from an observer's point of view.

Robert Graves assaults the poem in *On Poetry: Collected Talks and Essays* (1969, 402–05). Graves suggests that if the eagle's claws are hands, when we are told that the eagle "stands" he must be standing on his wings, and Graves claims that line 3 adds nothing: "Since the eagle perches on his crag close to the sun, a background of blue sky has already been presumed." Graves goes on to complain that "lands" has been chosen for the rhyme with "hands" and "stands," not for the sense, because "the eagle can stand only in one land." And "close to the sun" is objectionable; "What," Graves asks, "are a few hundred feet, compared with 92,000,000 miles!"

In teaching "The Eagle," we have occasionally found that a student too familiar with the ways of English teachers may insist that the bird is symbolic of something or other. Christ has been suggested, on the grounds that the bird descends from heaven ("Close to the sun") to earth, and the word "falls" has been said to contain an allusion to the Fall of Man. Such a symbolic rendering can be gently but firmly rejected, though perhaps it contains a germ of truth: The bird is presented as an intent watcher of the world beneath it. To this degree perhaps one can say that the bird resembles the keen-eyed poet, though this is not to claim that the bird is a symbol for the poet. The bird is a bird, in fact an eagle.

Christopher Ricks skillfully edited Tennyson's poetry in a one-volume edition in 1969 and in a revised three-volume edition in 1988. Ricks's *Tennyson* (1972) and A. Dwight Culler's *The Poetry of Tennyson* (1977) are fine critical studies.

SEAMUS HEANEY

Digging (p. 678)

The comparison of the pen resting in the hand, "snug as a gun," may especially remind a reader that in Ireland literature has often been closely connected with politics and with war, but of course the idea of the pen as a weapon is widespread, best known in the adage that "The pen is mightier than the sword." Less well known, but in the same vein, is Napoleon's preference of newspapers to battalions.

The image of the weapon is then largely replaced by the lines about the speaker's father digging—now flowerbeds, but twenty years ago he dug nourishing potatoes—but such words as "lug," "shaft," and "cool hardness" (though said of potatoes) keep the gun in our midst, at least faintly. Similarly, the emphasis on the father's posture (careful, professional, expert) suggests the discipline of a marksman—and of a writer.

Heaney then goes further back in time, to his grandfather digging not potatoes but turf, the fuel that cooks the potatoes and that heats a home, thus a substance no less necessary to life than food. But the evocation of these pictures of father and grandfather digging serves to remind the poet that he has "no spade to follow . . . them" (line 28). What, then, is his place in the family, and his role in society? What nourishment, what fuel can he contribute? And so we come back to the pen: "The squat pen rests" (30, a repetition of the first half of line 2). "I'll dig with it" (31). The "squat pen" is the poet's spade and gun, to be used with the energy and precision with which his father and grandfather used their spades, and to be used, presumably, with the same life-sustaining effect.

For further reading, see *Selected Poems, 1966–1987* (1990). Heaney's sharp, sensitive prose writings include *Preoccupations: Selected Prose, 1968–1978* (1980); *The Government of the Tongue* (1988); and *The Place of Writing* (1989). Critical studies: Blake Morrison, *Seamus Heaney* (1982); *The Art of Seamus Heaney*, ed. T. Curtis (1982); Robert Buttel, *Seamus Heaney* (1985); and Neil Corcoran, *Seamus Heaney* (1986). The journals *Salmagundi* no. 80 (1988) and *Agenda* 27, no. 1 (1989) have devoted issues to Heaney's work.

DANA GIOIA

Money (p. 679)

It's our guess that only two terms may be unfamiliar to most of your students, "rhino" (money), a term that is chiefly British and whose origin is unknown, and "Ginnie Maes," the plural of Ginnie Mae, the nickname of the Government National Mortgage Association.

The pleasure that we take in this poem is partly the pleasure one takes in catalogs—an old device, at least as old as the catalog of ships in Homer—and partly the pleasure of reveling in variety. Who would have thought there were so many terms for money?

But of course there is a further pleasure; even in this short playful poem there is a sort of plot, or at least a mild shift in the speaking tone of voice. The poem begins merely by enunciating nouns that mean money ("Money, the long green, / cash, stash, rhino, jack / or just plain dough"). That is, the first stanza simply gives us nouns; it simply names something, though in an entertaining way (notice the rhyme in the second line). In the second stanza we get verbs and sentences ("Chock it up, fork it over"). In the third stanza the voice gets more excited ("To be made of it! To have it / to burn!"), and in the fourth and fifth stanzas the voice becomes more meditative, reflective, philosophic ("It greases the palm, feathers a nest"). The final stanza continues the philosophizing, and rather wittily brings together the idea of filthy lucre ("You don't know where it's been") with the idea that money is nevertheless something we hold dearly ("you put it where your mouth is"), and it then picks up the idea of "mouth" by ending with the grand truth about money: "it talks."

Here are two additional wise remarks about money:

"Money is like muck; not good except it be spread." (Francis Bacon, *Essays*)

"You can be young without money but you can't be old without it." (Tennessee Williams, *Cat on a Hot Tin Roof*)

LINDA PASTAN

Baseball (p. 680)

Our Topics for Critical Thinking and Writing suggest the kinds of questions that we highlight when we teach Pastan's poem. You might begin, for example, by asking students what is the meaning of the claim that baseball is a "metaphor / for life." But as you do so, note for the students that this claim is presented as part of a conversation that the speaker recalls, and that some sign of the speaker's resistance (her inability to understand, or her refusal to accept) the other person's view is implied in the phrase "when you *tried* to tell me" (our emphasis). Furthermore, remind your class that the words "for life" are given extra stress by being placed at the beginning of a new stanza (and by the placement of the colon, too).

In other words, keep alive for the students that Pastan's "Baseball" is a *poem*, and that we therefore need to be mindful of the speaker's tone, the dramatic situation, and Pastan's choices in structure, imagery, and word and emphasis (e.g., in something simple—seeming as capitalizing "Sacrifice"— why does Pastan do that?).

One of the nice features of Pastan's poem, especially for student readers and writers, is the simplicity of the final stanza—simple, but eloquent, in the way that richly completes the exchange between the speaker and the other person. Just who is this other person? What is the nature of his or her relationship to the speaker? And "Yes": Are we to interpret this word as coming from the other person ("that's it, *yes*, you're right") or from the speaker herself ("yes, when you say 'that's it', you are right on target—I am glad that you agree with me").

See "'Whatever Is at Hand': A Conversation with Linda Pastan," in *The Post-Confessionals: Conversations with American Poets of the Eighties*, ed. Earl Ingersoll, Judith Kitchen, and Stan Sanvel Rubin (1989).

CRAIG RAINE

A Martian Sends a Postcard Home (p. 681)

We like to begin most discussions by talking about the title—about what expectations are set up by the title—and we especially recommend the procedure for this poem. Most students will find the combination of "Martian" and "postcard" at least a bit incongruous (Martians have spaceguns and "thoughtgrams"); some students (even without having read the poem) will guess that the poem will be the report of a traveler impressed by the strange things he sees on earth. And, of course, an outsider's report of something strange (here, a Martian's report of things on earth) may itself seem to be strange when read by those who are familiar with the thing described (here, by us earthlings). A large part of the point of such writing is to help us to see freshly things we have taken for granted.

The Martian, in his report, of course gets a few things slightly wrong. He thinks that all books are called "Caxtons" and that all cars are called "Model T." Probably the hardest part of the poem is the opening, the first four lines, describing books ("mechanical birds with many wings") which can make one cry ("cause the eyes to melt") and can make one laugh ("cause . . . the body to shriek without pain"). The car (13), the rear-view mirror (15–16), and the watch and clock (17–18) cause little difficulty; the telephone (19–24) is fairly easily guessed, even though American phones, unlike English phones (at the time when the poem was written) do not make a snoring noise when lifted from the cradle. The bathroom (25–30) is only a little more riddling. Raine (at a poetry reading) mentioned that the Martian, who during his short visit presumably saw only children cry, assumes that when adults suffer and cry, they do so privately, in the "punishment room" (26) where there is water but no food. (Martians apparently do not excrete.) In the final two lines, the Martian, speaking of couples dreaming, thinks they are reading "with their eyelids shut." The poem thus ends, as it begins, with reading.

But what does one make of what the Martian makes of us? He (or she?) seems to be very decent, sensitive to earthly phenomena, and endowed with the gift of metaphor, the sign of the poet. (In fact, when Raine reads the poem to audiences, he usually says that the Martian is not only a Martian, but also a metaphor for the poet.) The passage on mist is a good example: "the world is dim and bookish / like engravings under tissue paper" (9–10). (In our discussion of metaphor in the text we make the point that metaphors are closely related to riddles. Many passages in Raine's poem are almost riddles.)

One other point: We have been able to explain a few puzzling details (especially the mistaken account of why adults go to the bathroom) because the poet has told us what's going on. But is the poet's intention binding? Suppose a reader says that the last two lines describe not people dreaming, but people falling asleep while watching television. Are they wrong?

WILLIAM SHAKESPEARE

Sonnet 130 (p. 682)

Later in the book, in Chapter 18, in our discussion of poetic forms we give additional Shakespeare's sonnets, but in the present chapter, where we are concerned chiefly with figures of speech, we could not resist giving Sonnet 130, an apparent rejection of figurative language.

Shakespeare is not, it should be emphasized, satirizing his mistress; rather, he is satirizing the fanciful comparisons that were the conventions of the day. Here is an Elizabethan sonnet of the sort that Shakespeare has in mind. It is from Thomas Watson's *The Hekatompathia or Passionate Centurie of Love* (1581). You may want to distribute copies to your students.

> Harke you that list to heare what sainte I serve:
> Her yellowe lockes exceede the beaten goulde;
> Her sparkeling eies in heav'n a place deserve;
> Her forehead high and faire of comely moulde;
>   Her wordes are musicke all of silver sounde;
>   Her wit so sharpe as like can scarce be found:
> Each eybrowe hanges like Iris in the skies;   / *Iris*: personification
> Her Eagles nose is straight of stately frame;   of the rainbow
> On either cheeke a Rose and Lillie lies;
> Her breath is sweete perfume, or hollie flame;
>   Her lips more red than any Corall stone;

Her necke more white, then aged Swans yt mone;   / *yt:* that
Her brest transparent is, like Christall rocke;
Her fingers long, fit for Apolloes Lute;
Her slipper such as Momus dare not mocke;   / *Momus:* god of mockery
Her vertues all so great as make me mute:
    What other partes she hath I neede not say,
    Whose face alone is cause of my decaye.

What Shakespeare is doing, of course, is praising his mistress by saying in the couplet that she needs no such comparisons—that she need not be "belied with false compare" (line 14). The fact that the couplet is introduced with an oath, "And yet, by heaven," emphasizes his simple honesty.

16

Imagery and Symbolism

For a discussion of the difference between *natural* symbols (items that are meaningful on the literal level but that mean much more too) and symbols that have no literal existence, such as a man who does not cast a shadow, see N. Friedman, "Symbol," in *The New Princeton Encyclopedia of Poetry and Poetics*, ed. Alex Preminger and T. V. F. Brogan (1993).

The references suggested for Chapter 15 are relevant here too. In addition, see Barbara Seward, *The Symbolic Rose* (1960).

Among the highly relevant poems in Chapter 28 are Donne's "Valediction," Keats's "To Autumn," Ginsberg's "A Supermarket in California," and especially Pound's "In a Station of the Metro." William Carlos Williams's "Spring and All" is an interesting example of a poem with almost no figurative language—until near the end.

WILLIAM BLAKE

The Sick Rose (p. 684)

"The Sick Rose" has been much interpreted, usually along the lines given in the text. (See Reuben Brower, *The Fields of Light* [1951] and Rosenthal and Smith, *Exploring Poetry* [1955].) But E. D. Hirsch, Jr., in *Innocence and Experience* (1975), argues that "The rose is being satirized by Blake as well as being infected by the worm. Part of the rose's sickness is her ignorance of her disease. Her ignorance is her spiritual disease because in accepting 'dark secret love' she has unknowingly repressed and perverted her instinctive life, her 'bed of crimson joy.'" Hirsch argues his point for a couple of pages.

We especially like Helen Vendler's comment on this poem in her introduction to *The Harvard Book of Contemporary American Poetry* (1985):

The world of the poem is analogous to the existential world, but not identical with it. In a famous created world of Blake's, for instance, there is a rose doomed to mortal illness by the love of a flying worm who is invisible. We do not experience such a poem by moving it piecemeal into our world deciding what the rose "symbolizes" and what the worm "stands for." On the contrary, we must move ourselves into its ambience, into a world in which a dismayed man can converse with his beloved rose and thrust upon her, in his anguished jealousy, diagnosis and fatal prognosis in one sentence. . . . After living in Blake's world for the space of eight lines, we return to our own world, haunted and accused.

Allen Ginsberg has "tuned" the poem (MGM Records FTS-3083).

The best edition of Blake for the scholar is *The Poetry and Prose of William Blake*, ed. David Erdman and Harold Bloom, rev. ed. (1982). For the student, a better place to start is *William Blake: Selected Works*, ed. David Stevens (1995). Influential books on Blake have been written by Northrop Frye (1947), David Erdman (1954, 3rd ed., 1977), Harold Bloom (1963), and Kathleen Raine (1968). But these are difficult books and are likely to overwhelm the beginning student. More useful are the selections included in *Blake's Poetry and Designs: A Norton Critical Edition*, ed. John Ernest Grant, John F. Grant, and Mary L. Johnson. Peter Ackroyd's *Blake* (1996) is a vivid, illuminating biography.

WALT WHITMAN

I Saw in Louisiana a Live-Oak Growing (p. 685)

Whitman spent two months in New Orleans, in the spring of 1848.

As Whitman sees it, the tree is like him in that it is "rude, unbending, lusty" (this is the Whitman who from the first version of *Leaves of Grass* onward celebrated himself as "one of the roughs, a kosmos, / Disorderly, fleshly and sensual . . . eating drinking and breeding"), but the tree is *un*like him in that it grows in solitude.

In line 3 "uttering" ("uttering joyous leaves") strikes us as especially interesting, since it attributes to the tree a voice, or, rather, sees its organic growth as akin to human speech. Whitman conceived himself as one who by nature writes poetry, as a tree by nature produces leaves.

On at least one occasion Whitman suggested that the poems in "Calamus" could be thought of as something like a group of sonnets, and some readers have felt that this poem has the feel of a sonnet with an octave and a sestet, even though it is not rhymed, is not in iambic pentameter, and has thirteen rather than fourteen lines.

The first four lines can be thought of as a quatrain (or, in terms of the structure of the whole, as roughly equivalent to the octave in an Italian sonnet) in which the poet presents the image—the tree—and relates it to himself. Then, at the beginning of line 5, comes a turn (the *volta* in an Italian sonnet), strongly marked by "But," and we get a sort of comment on the first unit, rather as a sestet in an Italian sonnet may comment on the octave. (Here the second unit runs to nine lines rather than to six.) The gist is this: The poet dwells on his difference from the tree—even as he talks about the souvenir twig that he has brought back with him. One can of course divide this second unit variously, for instance, one can distinguish between the first five lines (5–9)—a group about the twig—and the remaining four lines (10–13)—a group in which the poet's thought returns to the original tree that is not only like him ("joyous") but is also unlike him ("without a friend a lover near").

SAMUEL TAYLOR COLERIDGE

Kubla Khan (p. 687)

Among the interesting discussions of "Kubla Khan" are Brooks and Warren, *Understanding Poetry* (1976), 4th ed.; Humphry House, *Coleridge* (1953) (House's material on "Kubla Khan" is reprinted in *Romanticism and Consciousness* [1970], ed. Harold Bloom); Harold Bloom, *The Visionary Company* (1961); Walter Jackson Bate, *Coleridge* (1968); and Jerome J. McGann, *The Romantic Ideology* (1983).

Most critics tend to see the fountain, river, and chasm as symbols of the poet's consciousness and "the pleasure dome" as a symbol of poetry. Charles Patterson (*PMLA* 89 [October 1974]: 1033–42) believes that the river (suggestive of poetic consciousness) is called "sacred" because it is "given over to and seemingly possessed by a god presenting through the poet's furor divinus a vision of beauty." The "deep delight" of line 44 is, Patterson suggests, "a daemonic inspiration, an unrestricted and amoral joy like that of the pre-Christian daemons." Patterson's judicious article deserves close study. Given the continuing interest in drugs, the instructor also may wish to consult Elisabeth Schneider, *Coleridge, Opium, and Kubla Khan* (1975), or Alethea Hayter, *Opium and the Romantic Imagination* (1968). Apparently it is unsound to attribute the poem to opium. As someone has said, Coleridge didn't write "Kubla Khan" because he took opium; he took opium because he was the sort of person who writes poems like "Kubla Khan."

Blake's "Lamb" and "Tyger," printed later in our text, are useful when talking about symbolism, as are Keats's "La Belle Dame sans Merci" and Yeats's "Sailing to Byzantium."

We start our students with Humphry House, *Coleridge* (1953), and Walter Jackson Bate, *Coleridge* (1968). On the Wordsworth-Coleridge relationship: Paul Magnuson, *Coleridge and Wordsworth* (1988), and G. W. Ruoff, *Wordsworth and Coleridge* (1989).

ADDITIONAL TOPIC FOR CRITICAL THINKING AND WRITING

Discuss "Kubla Khan" as a celebration of the energy of life. (It can be argued that even the references to ice and to the "sunless sea" and "lifeless ocean" in this context suggest mystery rather than lifelessness; certainly the Khan, the river, the fountain, the dome, the wailing woman, and the poet—among other things—combine to give a vision of a powerful and mysterious creativity.)

EMMA LAZARUS

The New Colossus (p. 690)

The poem (which should be compared with the next poem, by Aldrich), is almost inseparable from its history. It was written in support of a campaign to raise funds for a pedestal for the *Statue of Liberty*—the manuscript was auctioned and the proceeds given to the fund. In 1886 the poem was read at the dedication of the statue, and in 1903 (the twentieth anniversary of the writing of the poem) a bronze tablet with the poem was placed on an interior wall of the pedestal. In 1945 the bronze tablet was moved from the second-story landing inside the pedestal to the main entrance of the statue. The poem is inevitably joined to a cherished national image, and probably millions of schoolchildren (among them the writer of this note) took pride in memorizing the lines.

When we came to prepare this section of our book, there was never any doubt that we would include the poem—the last four and a half lines alone demand inclusion. But in rereading the poem we did feel a tad uneasy about the highfalutin' opening lines, with their classical allusion and their overall "poetic" tone. Lazarus is writing in the genteel tradition—the tradition that derived from classically educated English poets such as Tennyson—rather than, obviously, in the tradition of Whitman. No "barbaric yawp" would come from the mouth of this New Yorker who was descended from a prosperous Sephardic family that had lived in the United States since the eighteenth century. Her lines praise America in a rather academic way, by comparing it favorably to the classical world.

It is not surprising, therefore, that the colossus is periphrastically evoked as "the brazen giant of Greek fame," or that electricity in the torch is "the imprisoned lightning," or that ancient lands are places of "storied pomp." It is all very declamatory, possibly right for a bronze plaque—but (at least to our ear today) a trifle inflated or stiff. Having said this, we want to add that we are still moved by the final words, spoken by the statue. The words spoken by this colossal symbol of a lofty ideal seem to us less inflated than the earlier lines, spoken by the poet or by the reader. (Here we are expressing the idea that when readers read lyric poems, as opposed to dramatic monologues such as "My Last Duchess," the readers themselves are the speakers, the poems are *their* utterances.)

A few additional points:

1. Lazarus calls the statue "Mother of Exiles," thereby anticipating the great final passage, in which the statue welcomes "the wretched refuse" of countries across the sea, i.e., low-status persons scorned by the powerful. In France the statue was officially called *Liberté Eclairant le Monde* ("Liberty Enlightening the World"), though in the United States it is popularly known as the *Statue of Liberty*. (The French title emphasizes the torch, symbolizing illumination, i.e., knowledge, and, by extension, freedom since knowledge is supposed to free us from the bonds of ignorance. The French did not intend to symbolize America as a haven for the oppressed, but as an example of a republican government. But the great increase in immigration in the following years, and Lazarus's poem, have given the statue a meaning it did not originally have.)

2. In line 8, "air-bridged" and "twin cities" deserve a bit more comment than we give them in our headnote in the text. New York (which was confined to the island of Manhattan) and Brooklyn were separate cities when Lazarus wrote the poem; not until 1898 did the two cities, and some other communities, combine into "Greater New York." The Brooklyn Bridge was the world's first great suspension bridge, i.e., the roadway is supported not on arches or pillars but rather is suspended from vertical cables that are attached to main cables; the main cables are hung on two towers, and their ends are anchored in bedrock. This method of construction requires far fewer intermediate supports beneath the bridge, thus giving it a sense of airiness (hence "air-bridged" in line 8).

3. The words "wretched refuse" in line 12 have disturbed some people, and we raise this point below, in our first question. Our own feeling is that there is nothing bothersome here. The poet is not saying that these people are unworthy or without value; rather, she is saying that they are distressed or afflicted ("wretched") and they are rejected ("refuse") by those in power in their own lands.

4. The poem ends with the words, "the golden door." Naive immigrants supposedly thought that the streets were paved with gold—the idea goes back at least to the conquistadors who searched for El Dorado, the legendary kingdom rich in precious metals—but surely "the golden door" is a metaphor for opportunity, for a chance not only to make money but also to live a new kind of life, a life of freedom.

Lazarus wrote the poem in 1883; obviously in discussing the poem in a course in literature it is not essential to talk about the pros and cons of today's immigration policies. Still, an instructor may well be interested in relating the poem to the life around us, so here is a brief history of our immigration policy. The Open Door policy of nineteenth- and early twentieth-century America was changed, in 1924, to a national origins quota system which favored Northern and Western Europe and severely restricted immigration from everywhere else. This system was replaced in 1965 by a law (with amendments) that said there were three reasons to award visas to immigrants:

1. An immigrant might possess certain job skills, especially skills that this country needs. (Relatively few visas were awarded on this basis.)

2. An immigrant might be a refugee from war or from political persecution, and we would offer "political asylum."

3. An immigrant might be related to an American citizen or to a legal alien (the "family reunification policy").

In 1965, when this policy was formulated, there was little immigration from Latin America, the Caribbean, and Asia. Today, 90% of all immigration to the United States comes from those areas. Upwards of 80% are people of color. Whatever our policy is, is it *not* racist? What about numbers, rather than percentages? The peak decade for immigration was 1901–1910, when about 8.7 million immigrants arrived, chiefly from Southern and Eastern Europe. Probably 1981–1990 matched this, if illegal immigrants are included, but in any case in 1901–1910 the total United States population was less than one-third of what it is today. After 1910, immigration declined sharply; in all of the 1930s, only about 500,000 immigrants came to the United States, and in all of the 1940s there were only about 1,000,000, including refugees from Hitler. The figure now is about 1.5 million annually, plus an unknown number of illegal immigrants (the usual guess is half a million annually). In 1970 Latino immigration was 4.5%; in 1990 it was 9%.

Some Words about the Statue of Liberty

Strictly speaking, Auguste Bartholdi's sculpture is entitled *Liberty Enlightening {i.e., illuminating} the World*. Paid for by public subscription, it was the gift of the French people (not the government), presented in memory of French assistance during the War of Independence. The statue was built in sections in France, shipped to the United States, and unveiled and inaugurated in October 1886.

The statue, 150 feet tall, is made of thin sheets of beaten copper affixed to an iron and steel framework designed by Gustave Eiffel, who later built the Eiffel Tower. A classically draped woman, her left foot advanced and stepping on the broken shackles of tyranny, she holds a torch in her raised right hand and a tablet in her left hand. Her face is traditionally said to be that of Bartholdi's mother, but even if this pleasant story is true, the face is highly stylized in a severe classic manner.

Liberty was an ancient Roman goddess—but she was the goddess of personal freedom (i.e., of the condition opposite to slavery), not the goddess of a political idea. From the late eighteenth century, however, the goddess was interpreted in terms of political freedom and democracy. The symbolism of Bartholdi's statue is very clear:

1. The tablet, which doubtless is meant to call to mind the tablets held by Moses, is inscribed "JULY IV MDCCLXXVI." Thus, Liberty is associated both with God and with American history; the idea is that liberty, divinely ordained, flourished in America in 1776 and will spread throughout the world.
2. The torch represents the dispelling of darkness, i.e., the dispelling of political ideals which enslave. Probably, too, there is an association here with Christ, who in John 8:12 calls himself "the light of the world."
3. The radiant or sunburst crown is a sort of halo, making the figure a secular saint. The seven rays suggest the seven planets, the seven seas, the seven continents, etc.
4. The base stands on a star fortress (Fort Wood, on what used to be called Bedloe's Island but is now Liberty Island), suggesting that liberty is indomitable.

For a readable account, see Marvin Trachtenberg, *The Statue of Liberty* (rev. ed. 1986). Also useful is June Hargrove et al., *Liberty: The French-American Statue in Art and History* (1986).

There are plenty of pictures of the *Statue of Liberty* shot, like this one, against a heavenly background, i.e., shot from below in order to emphasize the heroic, godlike quality of the figure, but this photo by Tseng Kwon Chi is unusual, not least because it contains a comparable image of him as well as of the statue. There he stands, self-assured, taking his own picture along with Liberty (notice the cable release in his hand). The fact that the picture is in black and white helps to unify the photographer with the image and its pedestal, and for that matter, with the background.

Also unusual, of course, is the fact that the man is an Asian. Until fairly recently, most Asians entered the United States through Angel Island, the largest island in San Francisco Bay, not through Ellis Island (a few hundred yards from the small island on which the statue stands), and probably few Asian tourists bothered to photograph themselves with the Statue of Liberty. Viewers are used to seeing pictures of immigrants from Europe approaching the Statue of Liberty, but they are probably surprised by a picture of an Asian with the statue. It is a vigorous reminder that the old patterns of immigration and also of tourism, in which immigrants and tourists came chiefly from Europe, have been markedly changed.

ALFRED, LORD TENNYSON

The Kraken (p. 691)

E. Cobham Brewer (1810–1897), in his *Dictionary of Phrase and Fable* (1898), provides some helpful background:

- kraken: A supposed sea-monster of vast size, said to have been seen off the coast of Norway and on the North American coasts. It was first described (1750) by Erich Pontoppidan (1698–1764), in his *Natural History of Norway* (1753; English edition, 1755). The Roman scholar and naturalist Pliny (23–79) speaks of a sea-monster in the Straits of Gibraltar, which blocked the entrance of ships.

- Pontoppidan speaks of sea serpents 600 feet long. The great sea serpent was said to have been seen off the coast of Norway in 1819, 1822, 1837. Hans Egede affirms that it was seen on the coast of Greenland in 1734. In 1815, 1817, 1819, 1833, and in 1869, it made its appearance near Boston. In 1841 it was "seen" by the crew of Her Majesty's frigate Dædalus, in the South Atlantic Ocean. In 1875 it was seen by the crew of the barque Pauline. Girth, nine feet.

The scholar Lee Krystek provides additional information:

Probably no legendary sea monster was as horrifying as the Kraken. According to stories this huge, many armed, creature could reach as high as the top of a sailing ship's main mast. A kraken would attack a ship by wrapping its arms around the hull and capsizing it. The crew would drown or be eaten by the monster.... The Kraken of legend is probably what we know today as the giant squid. While a colossal octopus might also fit the description, the squid is thought to be much more aggressive and more likely to come to the surface where it might be seen by man. Though giant squids are considerably less then a mile and a half across, some are thought to be large enough to wrestle with a whale. On at least three occasions in the 1930's they reportedly attacked a ship. While the squids got the worst of these encounters when they slid into the ship's propellers, the fact that they attacked at all shows that it is possible for these creatures to mistake a vessel for a whale.

Could a large squid, say a hundred feet long and weighing two or three tons, attack a small ship by accident and capsize it? Given that some ocean crossing vessels at the time were very small (for example, Columbus's *Pinta* was only 60 feet in length), it certainly seems a possibility.

"The Kraken" was included in Tennyson's *Poems, Chiefly Lyrical*, a volume that was published in 1830, when he, age twenty-one, was a student at Cambridge.

Scholars sometimes slight or speak disapprovingly about the poems from early in Tennyson's career, which, it is said, lack the brooding doubt and genuine struggle and profound anguish that one finds in *In Memoriam* (1850) and later writings. Valerie Pitt, for example, in *Tennyson Laureate* (1969), says about the early work:

> At this stage in his development, the state of Tennyson's perception is not especially interesting. He sees a world which is faintly morbid, faintly theatrical, an adolescent world in which the prevailing note is gloom. The technical achievement of poems like "The Kraken"…, in which this mood is enshrined, is very remarkable, but their substance belongs to a passing phase of adolescent nostalgia and nightmare which it would be a pity to confuse with the very real problems of Tennyson's later life. (39)

Earlier in her book, however, Pitt herself speaks cogently about the kind of real interest that readers can perceive in "The Kraken" and other poems from this period:

> Tennyson's sensibility appears then to have a double quality. The world of trance, the world of sleep and dream, in which the identities of things are lost, shares his vision with a world which is sharply defined, clear, and even minute in detail. His imagination is always slipping from the real to the fantastical, but his careful observation of real things imparts solidity to the very fantasy. In entering Tennyson's mind we are entering a world in which reality does not repel, as it so often does, the fantastic; on the contrary it is often the fantasy which interprets or symbolizes something discerned in the real. (33)

What, one might ask, does the figure of the kraken symbolize for Tennyson? Here, you might both examine this poem in its own right and compare it to other poems in this section of our book: Coleridge's "Kubla Khan," Lazarus's "The New Colossus," and Chiasson's "The Elephant." In such a context, we find it helpful to remind students during class discussion that a symbol possesses richness and depth—a fullness and complexity of meaning; and this holds true whether the poet is working with something familiar (e.g., the Statue of Liberty) or unfamiliar (e.g., a monstrous creature with a strange-sounding name). A symbol does not represent a meaning, but, rather, it accrues meanings as the writer presents, considers, and reflects upon it.

About "The Kraken," Robert Preyer makes a keen observation that takes us into the action of the poem's language:

> We begin with an active troubled surface motion and proceed directly into a distanced, quiet, dreamlike stasis. The abrupt transition between worlds is controlled and drawn out in a series of contrasts, slowed further by repetitions and parallel statements, and almost brought to a standstill as actions dissolve into antitheses.
> —"Tennyson as an Oracular Poet," *Modern Philology*, 55 (May 1958), 239–51, at p. 241

Christopher Ricks, in *Tennyson* (1972), adds that the focus of "The Kraken" is "Tennyson's pained fascination with the thought of a life which somehow is no life at all...—a life which is no life, and which waits for death" (44–45). He points out that Tennyson accents this theme through his double use of "deep" and "sleep," evoking a kind of death in life.

The kraken, as portrayed in this poem, is remote, horrid, extraordinary, and magnificent, but truly magnificent only for the brief moment when it soars and roars into view. As soon as it emerges from its long sleep, it expires. This, in broad terms, is the story that Tennyson tells, but this big effect is dramatized through weird, immense, captivating details, such as the "huge sponges," "giant arms," and "huge sea worms."

We recall once teaching this poem and having a student remark about the kraken, "he's disgusting," to which another student immediately replied, "I kind of like him." The student who liked the kraken said she found him somewhat comical, in all of his grotesqueness, and in his long-term slumbering. We would not want to press that point too much, but there may be something to it.

Perhaps in this same vein, we always enjoy lingering over the final line. We ask for volunteers to "roar" as the kraken does, in dying—and we get some impressive sound effects from students. Some bring out a fierceness, a ferocity, in the kraken, while others in their tone highlight desperation and despair, the grandeur and futility of the single glorious deed that the kraken performs—it almost seems, suicidally—and the sound that it makes.

As they ponder how the symbol of the kraken functions here, our students always offer some intriguing observations. It is striking to us, for instance, how frequently the class has used the phrase "buried life" or a similar phrase to describe what Tennyson might be up to. Possibly—we are just speculating—students have a sense of themselves as not really being present in public—that it is not "the real me" we are seeing. Something is blocking *that*, keeping it from appearing, making it stay submerged. Even more: it *cannot* appear, because if it did, it would have a terrible effect or consequence.

We hope this does not sound far-fetched, because we do suspect that in some way or other our students are in contact with the young Tennyson (he was the age of our students when he wrote the poem)—his state of mind and emotion. It is a complicated, perhaps elusive, yet vivid and compelling, form of symbolism that Tennyson presents in "The Kraken." You will find that this is a poem that your students will remember.

If you have time, you might invite students to look on the internet for Tennyson's "The Dying Swan" and Yeats's "The Second Coming," both of which can be profitably compared with "The Kraken."

DAN CHIASSON

The Elephant (p. 692)

We have the good fortune to know the author of this poem, and we asked him some questions about it, which he was kind enough to answer.

Do you remember where you were and what you were doing when you wrote this poem?

I was sitting in my home office at 26 Green Street, Jamaica Plain, Massachusetts. I remember its coming very fast. I had been reading all morning with the express intent of writing a poem. I had no idea what I would write but I knew that the day would go in the "failure" column if I didn't write something. Some days it matters tremendously to me to get something written.

What inspired you to write it?

I had been reading some essays by Calvino, the Italian writer; they are collected in a wonderful book called *The Uses of Literature*. Calvino has an essay on the ancient author and natural philosopher Pliny called "Man, The Sky, and The Elephant."

I love encyclopedias—I have since I was a kid. I also love the occult and other irrational or anti-rational systems. Not because I believe in them—I don't, but simply because I am moved by human attempts to reconsecrate the world for wonder. Pliny's *Natural History* is a little like an encyclopedia and a little like a book of mirabilia—wonders, astounding feats and records.

Did the poem require much revision?

None, actually. That's not typical for me. Maybe I changed a word or two long after writing it.

Was there any part of it that gave you special trouble or difficulty?

The project in general of making animals "speak" is a problem and a difficulty. I think Wittgenstein says, "If a lion could speak, we wouldn't understand him." There are so many ways to go wrong when you give words to animals (moralizing, sentimentalizing, etc.)

What kind of reader do you imagine for your poems?

I never think about it! I had an email from a veterinarian who is teaching my book to his class on animal ethics. That seems like in some ways (in many ways not) "the ideal reader."

For you, when a poem is done, is it really done once and for all, or do you ever look back at it on the printed page and wonder, "Should I have done this, or that, instead, with this line or stanza?

I do, I do look back and wish I had done this or that or avoided this or that, and I find the remorse or regret I feel actually gives me a reason to write new poems, "corrections" of the old, flawed poems. Of course new information, new language keeps coming in at all times. You want poems that live in the new streams of your thinking and speaking and feeling; in light of one's new mind the old poems often feel naive or incomplete.

CLAUDE MCKAY

The Tropics in New York (p. 693)

Students divide about evenly when we discuss this poem: Some praise McKay for his evocative account of his yearning for home, while others criticize the poem for being "sentimental" or "too subjective." We value the poem, especially for its luscious listing of the fruits that the speaker craves. But we do think that it runs the risk of sentimentality. By this, we mean to say that the poem does not really *earn* the response that McKay seems to want at the end. To put the point another way: Readers may feel too far "outside" the speaker, outside his sense of loss, because he does not reveal much about who he is or what his experiences in the tropics were.

Maybe this is part of McKay's intention. Possibly he wants to evoke not only the speaker's longing but also the isolation, the aloneness, that this speaker feels in New York City. It has reminders of his authentic home, yet it is not his real home, nor has he found in New York City other persons with whom he can share his regret.

It is interesting that the speaker recalls, in a vaguely mystical way, the *place* from which he came. He does not tell of people he knew, his family, or work. The memories are of the dawn, the blue skies, the hills. That is what he remembers— what is summoned up for him by the sight of the fruits brought from the tropics to New York City. His longing is powerful, beyond his control: "a wave of longing through my body swept." He then weeps, and there the poem concludes.

Once we asked the class to compose a new fourth stanza for this poem: Write a new final stanza that depicts what happens next, and the feelings that the speaker expresses after this moment of weeping. The results, we must confess, were not very good. But we found this assignment helpful nonetheless. The students agreed that nearly all of the new stanzas seemed *more* sentimental, more emotionally neat and tidy, than did the prior stanzas. Everyone ended up agreeing that McKay had concluded his poem in the right place, even as students continued to disagree about whether the poem was a good one or not.

See James R. Giles, *Claude McKay* (1975), and Wayne F. Cooper, *Claude McKay: Rebel Sojourner in the Harlem Renaissance* (1987). For a good collection of McKay's writings: *The Passion of Claude McKay, 1912–1948*, ed. Wayne F. Cooper (1973).

ADRIENNE RICH

Diving into the Wreck (p. 694)

Most responses identify the wreck as either (1) the speaker's life (persons familiar with Rich's biography may identify it specifically as her unhappy marriage to a man who committed suicide in 1970, about three years before the poem was published) or (2) more broadly, our male-dominated society. Another way of putting it is to say that the poem is about sexual politics. The poem is discussed by Wendy Martin and by Erica Jong in *Adrienne Rich's Poetry* (1975), ed. Barbara C. Gelpi and Albert Gelpi. Part of the following comment is indebted to their discussions.

Armed with a book of myths (an understanding of the lies society has created?) and a camera and a knife (an instrument of vision and an instrument of power?) she goes, alone, in contrast to Cousteau assisted by a team, to explore the wreck. (This sort of exploration can be done only by the individual. One might add, by the way, that it is a new sort of exploration, an exploration for which Rich had no maps. Before the second half of the twentieth century, there was virtually no poetry about what it was like to be a wife or a woman living in a male-dominated society. The earlier poetry written by women was chiefly about children, love, and God.) More exactly, she is there, exploring the wreck ("I came to explore the wreck" implies that she is speaking from the site itself). She has immersed herself in the primal, life-giving element and has now arrived in order "to see the damage that was done / and the treasures that prevail," that is, to see not only what is ruined but also what is salvageable. Her object is to find truth, not myth (lines 62–63).

Lines 72–73, in which she is both mermaid and merman, and line 77, in which "I am she; I am he," suggest that she has achieved an androgynous nature and thus has become the sort of new woman who will tell the truth. According to lines 92–94, the names of such true persons, or androgynes, persons who may rescue civilization, do not appear in the book of myths.

CHRISTINA ROSSETTI

Uphill (p. 696)

How can one be sure that the poem is metaphorical? This is part of what we are getting at in our first question, in which we ask the student to respond to a reader who assumes the speaker is making inquiries preparatory to a bit of touring.

The question is not meant to be frivolous. Instructors know that this is a poem about larger matters, but that's because instructors are used to reading poems and are therefore used to figurative language. Most students are unfamiliar with the way poems work—which is why they sometimes read too literally and why, on other occasions, they read too freely, ignoring some passages and imposing highly personal readings on others.

Our second question asks, Who is the questioner? The poem is not a Browningesque dramatic monologue, and we think it is enough to say that the questioner is the poet, or the poet as a universal spokesperson. By the way, we don't know exactly what to make of the suggestion of a student that the answerer in "Uphill" is a ghost, that is, someone who has made the journey and who therefore answers authoritatively.

As for our final question in the text, we do find the answers (with their dry understatement, as in "You cannot miss that inn," i.e., "Don't worry, you will certainly die") chilling as well as comforting, but we are unconvinced that a reader is supposed to imagine a dialogue between the poet and a revenant. Rather, we believe (guided by Jerome J. McGann's essay on Christina Rossetti in his *The Beauty of Inflections* [1985]) that the poet is speaking with what McGann calls "her divine interlocutor" (242). McGann points out that the ending of "Uphill" is easily misinterpreted. Rossetti is not saying that the pilgrimage of the Christian soul ends with an eternal sleep. Rather, she is alluding to the Anabaptist doctrine known as "Soul Sleep" (technically, psychopannychism), which holds that at death the soul is put into a condition of sleep until the millennium. On the Last Day the soul awakens and goes to its final reward. McGann fully discusses the point in his essay.

From time to time, we have taught students who have become very interested in Rossetti's verse. For specialized work, we can recommend *The Complete Poems of Christina Rossetti*, ed. R.W. Crump, 3 vols. (1979–90). But students might profit even more from reading Rossetti in the midst of other Victorian women poets; see *Victorian Women Poets: An Anthology*, ed. Angela Leighton and Margaret Reynolds (1995). See also Dolores Rosenblum, *Christina Rossetti: The Poetry of Endurance* (1986); Antony H. Harrison, *Christina Rossetti in Context* (1988); and Angela Leighton, *Victorian Women Poets* (1992), 118–63.

WALLACE STEVENS

The Emperor of Ice-Cream (p. 697)

On "The Emperor of Ice-Cream," first a comment by Stevens, in a letter (*Letters of Wallace Stevens*, ed. Holly Stevens) of May 16, 1945. He says of "concupiscent curds" that the words "express the concupiscence of life, but, by contrast with the things in relation to them in the poem, they express or accentuate life's destitution, and it is this that gives them something more than a cheap lustre" (500).

If "emperor" suggests power and splendor, "ice-cream" suggests pleasure, especially sensuous enjoyment, triviality, and transcience. Put together, and in this context of a wake, the implication is that a human for a while shapes and enjoys the tawdry world, as the dead woman embroidered fantails on her sheets, which were too short. We can take pleasure in the world (there is certainly pleasure in the shifting diction and in the alliteration in line 3, "In kitchen cups concupiscent curds"), but if Stevens insists on the pleasure (cigars, ice cream, flirting girls), he also insists on looking at ("Let the lamp affix its beam") transcience ("last month's newspapers," the dresser lacking knobs) and death (the corpse's horny feet). The two stanzas juxtapose a world of cuncupiscence and a world of death. The pleasures described, then, to return to Stevens's letter, "accentuate life's destitution."

In another letter, published in the *Southern Review* (Autumn 1979): 773–74, Stevens freely paraphrases part of the poem: "let us have a respite from the imagination (men who are not cigar makers, blondes, costumes, theology), and, in short, suppose we have ice cream. Not that I wish to exalt ice cream as an absolute good, although my little girl might. It is a symbol, obviously and ironically, of the materialism or realism proper to a refugee from the imagination." Stevens goes on, however, to insist that "ambiguity [is] essential to poetry."

A "Voices and Visions" videocassette of Wallace Stevens is available from Longman Publishers.

EDGAR ALLAN POE

To Helen (p. 698)

The best discussion that we have come across is an old one, by M. L. Rosenthal and A. J. Smith, in *Exploring Poetry* (1955), 603–604, in a chapter on symbolism. Rosenthal and Smith begin by pointing out that the speaker is telling a sort of story: "Helen's beauty, the speaker says, has borne him 'homeward' gently and pleasurably—'o'er a perfumed sea.'" If the poem had ended with the second stanza, they add, it might seem to argue that the beauty of the woman who is addressed (if he is not addressing the original Helen) "has led him to appreciate the kindred beauty of classical art." But in the third stanza "the emphasis on classical beauty is minimized." Helen has brought the speaker, who has sailed on "desperate seas," to security, but she is nevertheless still remote, strange, and statuelike in a window-niche. By calling her Psyche he endows her "with a spiritual, unreachable quality." Further, Rosenthal and Smith suggest, because the name Psyche reminds us of the legend of Cupid and Psyche, in which the beautiful Psyche inadvertently burned Cupid with a drop of oil from her lamp and thus lost him as a husband, she is a "symbol both of beauty and of frustration." The poem therefore is not chiefly about the values of classical art. Rather, it may be about "the speaker's feelings for a particular woman," or it may even be "a confession of failure in love or in poetic achievement."

Thomas O. Mabbott, in his valuable edition, *Collected Works of Edgar Allan Poe* (1969), confidently offers a simpler, no-nonsense summary of the theme:

> It is spiritual love that leads us to beauty, a resting place from sorrow and the homeland of all that is sacred in our being. Beauty is the lasting legacy of Greece and Rome, and its supreme symbol is the most beautiful of women, Helen of Troy, daughter of Zeus, who brings the wanderer home and inspires the poet. (I:164)

Who is the wanderer? Candidates include Odysseus, Dionysus, Menelaus, and Catullus. For instance, lines 2–5 may faintly recall Book XIII of *The Odyssey*, in which a Phaeacian bark carries the sleeping Odysseus to his native Ithaca. The various claims—none wholly convincing—are summarized in Mabbott's edition. Incidentally, the "desperate seas" of line 6 offer a nice example of a transferred epithet; the traveler is desperate, not the seas.

Poe revised the poem steadily, from 1831 to 1843. The most notable revisions are these:

Line 9: *from* beauty of fair *to* glory that was
Line 10: *from* And the grandeur of old *to* And the grandeur that was
Line 11: *from* that little *to* yon brilliant
Line 13: *from* folded scroll to agate book *to* agate lamp

HERMAN MELVILLE

DuPont's Round Fight (p. 700)

Melville opposed slavery and he unambiguously supported the North, but he saw the Civil War as something more (or deeper) than right versus wrong.

He seems to have regarded it as the product of tragic human error and unthwartable historic forces, and he thought that out of the bloodshed would come some sort of purification. Here we can quote from his "Supplement": "Let us pray that the terrible historic of our time may not have been enacted without instructing our whole beloved country through terror and pity. . . ."

In "DuPont's Round Fight," however, he does clearly indicate that one side is "Right" (line 5), and the other side is unambiguously characterized as "The rebel." This explicit partisanship is, as we say, somewhat unusual in Melville's poems, but even in this poem one feels that Melville is less concerned with celebrating the North than he is with celebrating order, or "time and measure" (1), geometry (7), and law (12).

For a fairly obvious reason, Melville's reference to "stars" (3) and "LAW" (12) brought to our mind George Meredith's "Lucifer in Starlight," which we quote here, on the off chance that an instructor may happen to want to quote it if the discussion in class turns to the idea that the stars are a type (i.e., prototype) of law, law that binds poems and everything else.

Lucifer in Starlight

On a starred night Prince Lucifer uprose.
Tired of his dark dominion swung the fiend
Above the rolling ball in cloud part screened,
Where sinners hugged their spectre of repose.
Poor prey to his hot fit of pride were those.
And now upon his western wing lie leaned,
Now his huge bulk o'er Afric's sands careened,
Now the black planet shadowed Arctic snows.
Soaring through wider zones that pricked his scars
With memory of the old revolt from Awe,
He reached a middle height, and at the stars,
Which are the brain of heaven, he looked, and sank.
Around the ancient track marched, rank on rank,
The army of unalterable law.

[1883]

For Melville, no less than for Meredith, the stars represent heavenly law and order, and therefore rebellion—whether that of Lucifer or of the South—is bound to fail.

NAOMI SHIHAB NYE

The Traveling Onion (p. 700)

We value this poem because of its adroit combination of the silly and the serious. It is in a way a silly thing to write a poem about an onion. On the other hand, poets like to do such things: they focus our attention on objects we might not have imagined a poem ever could be written about. They give themselves a challenge, even as they reorient our vision and understanding of the world around us.

In truth, Nye is taking up a special challenge in this poem because (this may surprise you, as it surprised us), the onion is a popular subject for poets. There is Marge Piercy's "Bite into the Onion," for example. Pablo Neruda has written "An Ode to the Onion," and then there's Wislawa Szymborska's "The Onion," which begins, "Onion, now that's something else...." When you bring this point to the attention of the class, you might ask, "Why *is* the onion a good subject for a poem?"

We can think of lots of poems about vegetables: corn, asparagus, cauliflower, bell peppers, celery, etc. Potatoes may be the most popular of all. OK, but what are the properties of the onion that make it special—that might prompt a poet to choose it?

You might ask your students to respond to Nye's choice of title, and, next, to her epigraph—how does *that* function in the poem's structure?

We proceed carefully through the text from beginning to end, taking note in particular of its shifts and subtleties of tone. We hear something comic in the first two lines: the onion makes its entry into the speaker's stew, which leads the speaker to want to "kneel" and offer praise for "all" miracles of this kind. The word "miracles," with its religious and sublime connotations, may move the tone beyond the comic, informing and influencing how we hear the details of the "crackly paper" and "pearly layers."

The comic note may resonate in the final lines of stanza one as well, but with a darker, even disquieting twist: we find ourselves unnerved by the phrase "knife enters onion." Moreover, there is a clever, but grisly, edge to the reference to "chopping block."

The second stanza begins with "And," which we seize upon as a cue to ask the class: Could the poem have ended with stanza one? Should the poem have ended there? "What happens" in the second stanza that Nye felt she needed—needed to add, develop, explore?

Note, too, other, more specific questions you can ask: Why, for instance, does the poem end on the single word "disappear"? How would the effect change if this word were placed at the end of the previous line, with *that* as its conclusion?

About Naomi Shihab Nye, the poet William Stafford has observed: "Her poems combine transcendent liveliness and sparkle along with warmth and human insight. She is a champion of the literature of encouragement and heart. Reading her work enhances life."

Nye herself has said that from her childhood on, she has always been drawn to the special nature of poetic language and organization: "I liked the portable, comfortable shape of poems. I liked the space around them and the way you could hold your words at arm's length and look at them. And especially the way they took you to a deeper, quieter place, almost immediately." In an interview, when queried about poetry as a "form of conversation," she replied: "Absolutely, conversation with the world, conversation with those words on the page allowing them to speak back to you— conversation with yourself."

A Note on Haiku (p. 701)

The haiku in our text, along with the editorial comment, is enough to give students an idea of the form and to allow them to write their own haiku. We have found that most students enjoy—because they can achieve at least a decent degree of success—writing haiku.

For collections of haiku, with substantial commentaries, see Harold G. Henderson, *An Introduction to Haiku* (1958), and Kenneth Yasuda, *The Japanese Haiku* (1957). For a shorter but still moderately detailed history of the form, see the article on haiku in *The Kodansha Encyclopedia of Japan* (1983). We summarize the last part of the Kodansha article, "On Writing Haiku in English." As you will see in a moment, the author takes us through several versions of a haiku. You may want to write the first version on the board, discuss it, and then move on to the second, and so on.

The author begins by saying what a haiku does: "When a haiku is successful, it endows our lives with freshness and new wonder and reveals the charm and profundity of all truly simple things." Almost any subject is possible, from the stars on a stormy night to a heron in the evening breeze. He gives as an example (in the traditional 5–7–5 syllable pattern) a roadside encounter:

> Meeting on the road,
> we chat leisurely awhile
> and go on our ways.

"The problem with this verse," he says, "is that it tells us something but evokes nothing. It is flat and one-dimensional." What is needed, among other things, is a sharper "cutting" (usually indicated by a colon or dash) after either the first or the second line, thus:

> A roadside meeting:
> we chat leisurely awhile
> and go on our ways.

But there still is not enough of a cutting here; there is no imaginative distance between the two elements. Another try:

> A baby's crying:
> we chat leisurely awhile
> and go on our ways.

Here, however, the distance between the two parts is too great. One would have to be deaf or cruel to chat while a baby cries. The two images don't somehow connect. The next version:

> A peaceful country:
> we chat leisurely awhile
> and go on our ways.

Not bad; the peaceful country provides a grand background for this pleasant encounter between two friendly people; or, to put it the other way around, the encounter between the two people "crystallizes the abstract notion of a peaceful country."

The two parts of the poem, then, must be remote to a degree and yet must somehow connect, and each must enhance the other. Further, in the traditional Japanese haiku there must be a seasonal theme. When does a leisurely chat occur? Probably not in winter (too cold to stand chatting); nor does spring (the author says) seem right for this sort of talk, since spring is the time for "the fresh encounters of the young." Autumn? No, "Autumn is too suggestive of reflective maturity and eventual partings." Only summer is right:

> Another hot day:
> we chat leisurely awhile
> and go on our ways.

But, the author of the article says, the word "leisurely" is wrong here; one wouldn't chat in a leisurely fashion on a hot day. A summer chat is characterized not by leisureliness but by "involuntary lethargy." The final version:

> Another hot day:
> yawning "good-bye" and "take care"
> we go on our ways.

The author's final judgment of this work: "Not a haiku masterpiece, but not discreditable for a first try."

Reminder: Ezra Pound's "In a Station of the Metro" (Chapter 24) is deeply influenced by Pound's reading of haiku. We discuss the poem at some length in this handbook.

Note: Chapter 23 is devoted to translation.

17

Irony

PERCY BYSSHE SHELLEY

Ozymandias (p. 707)

James Reeves, in *The Critical Sense* (1957), does a hatchet job on Shelley's "Ozymandias." (Ozymandias, incidentally, was the Greek version of the name User-ma-Ra, better known as Ramses II, the name the Greeks used for the thirteenth century B.C. pharaoh who, like other pharaohs, built monuments to celebrate his own greatness. One such monument was a colossus sixty feet tall, carved in stone by Memnon. Diodorus, a Sicilian Greek historian of the first century, saw the statue and wrote that it was inscribed, "I am Osymandyas, king of kings; if any would know how great I am, and where I lie, let him excel me in any of my works." At some later date, the statue tumbled, leaving only fragments.) Reeves's objections include: "vast" (line 2) means "of great extent," but the legs would be tall rather than vast; "on the sand" (3) is hardly necessary after "in the desert"; if the visage is "shattered" (4), which Reeves takes to mean "broken to pieces," it would be difficult to recognize the facial expression; the speaker says that the sculptor "well . . . read" (6) the subject's passions, but we cannot know if this is true, since we have no other information about the subject; if it is argued that the inscription is evidence of cold-hearted tyranny, the sestet should begin "For," not "And" (9); to speak of "the decay" of a "wreck" is tautological (12–13); in lines 13–14 "boundless" makes unnecessary "stretch far away," and "bare" makes "lone" unnecessary. Some of Reeves's objections are telling, some are niggling; in any case, the power of the poem is chiefly in the essential irony and the almost surrealistic scene of legs arising in the desert, the face on the ground nearby, and no trunk anywhere.

A small point: Lines 4–8 are unclear, for it is not certain if "the hand . . . and the heart" belong to the sculptor, in which case the idea is that the sculptor "mocked" ("mimicked," "imitated in stone") the passions and "fed" them by creating them in stone, or if the hand and the heart belong to Ozymandias, whose hand mocked the passions of his foes and whose heart fed his own passions.

Shelley's friend, Horace Smith, a banker with a taste for literature, wrote a sonnet on Ozymandias at the same time that Shelley did. You may want to ask students to compare the two poems:

On a Stupendous Leg of Granite, Discovered Standing by Itself in the Desert of Egypt

In Egypt's sandy silence, all alone,
Stands a gigantic Leg, which far off throws
The only shadow that the desert knows.
"I am great Ozymandias," said the stone,
"The King of kings; this mighty city shows
The wonders of my hand." The city's gone!
Naught but the leg remaining to disclose
The sight of that forgotten Babylon.

We wonder, and some hunter may express
Wonder like ours, when through the wilderness
Where London stood, holding the wolf in chase,
He meets some fragment huge, and stops to guess
What wonderful, but unrecorded, race
Once dwelt in that annihilated place.

For additional background material on Shelley's poem, see H. M. Richmond, "Ozymandias and the Travellers," *Keats-Shelley Journal* 11 (1962): 65–71. For a discussion of Shelley's poem and Smith's, see K. M. Bequette, "Shelley and Smith: Two Sonnets of Ozymandias," in *Keats-Shelley Journal* 26 (1977): 29–31.

There are excellent biographies by Richard Holmes (1974) and Kenneth Neill Cameron (2 vols., 1950, 1974), and many critical studies, including those by Carlos Baker (1948), Harold Bloom (1959), Earl Wasserman (1971), and William Keach (1984). The scholarship on Shelley, because of its engagement with the poet's dense ideas and passionate, but often obscure, social and philosophical views, can prove daunting to undergraduates. It might be preferable to recommend instead two books that combine primary texts with extensive annotations and contextual materials: *The Lyrics of Shelley*, ed. Judith Chernaik (1972), and *Shelley's Poetry and Prose*, ed. Donald H. Reiman and Sharon B. Powers (1977).

ANDREW MARVELL

To His Coy Mistress (p. 707)

Marvell's "To His Coy Mistress" is well discussed by J. V. Cunningham, *Modern Philology* 51 (August 1953): 33–41; by Francis Berry, *Poets' Grammar* (1958); by Joan Hartwig, *College English* 25 (May 1964): 572–75; by Bruce King, *Southern*

Review 5 (1969): 689–703; and by Richard Crider, *College Literature* 12 (Spring 1985): 113–21. Incidentally, "dew" in line 34 is an editor's emendation for "glew" in the first edition (1681). Grierson suggests "glew" means a shining gum found on some trees. Another editor, Margoulieth, conjectures "lew"—that is, warmth.

Marvell's poem can be the subject of a paper involving a comparison with Herrick's "To the Virgins." Although both poems take as their theme the *carpe diem* motif, their tone and imagery differ greatly. For example, the sun in Herrick's poem ("the higher he's a-getting") does not race through the sky, but in Marvell's poem the lovers will force the sun to hurry. Or, again, in Herrick's poem the speaker is concerned not with satisfying his own desires but with the young women, whereas in Marvell's poem one strongly feels that the speaker is at least as concerned with himself as with the woman.

We have usually found it best to teach Herrick's poem before Marvell's partly because Herrick's is shorter, but chiefly because most students find it simpler.

Naturally none of the early discussions of the poem consider whether it is outrageously sexist—and, if it is, whether it should be taught. Such a discussion is probably inevitable in the classroom today, and no reader of this handbook can be in need of our opinion on this topic. We will therefore comment only on some formal matters.

The poem consists of three parts, developing an argument along these lines: "If . . . But . . . Therefore." The first of these three parts is playful, the second wry or even scornful or bitter, and the third passionate. Or, to put it in slightly different terms, the poem is an argument, spoken (as the title indicates) by a male suitor to a reluctant woman. It begins with a hypothetical situation ("Had we but world enough, and time") in which the speaker playfully caricatures Petrarchan conventions (fantastic promises, incredible patience). Then (lines 21–32), with "But at my back," he offers a very different version of life, a wry, almost scornful speech describing a world in which beauty is fleeting. Finally (33–46) he offers a passionate conclusion ("Now therefore").

The conclusion, and especially the final couplet, perhaps require further comment. The "am'rous birds of prey" of line 38 replace the doves of Venus found in more traditional love poetry. The destructiveness suggested by the birds is continued in the image of a "ball," which is chiefly a cannonball hurtling "Thorough the iron gates of life" but is also the united lovers—that is, the ball is made up of their "strength" (chiefly his?) and "sweetness" (chiefly hers?). Some commentators find in "tear" a suggestion of a hymen destroyed by "rough strife." The violence and the suggestions of warfare are somewhat diminished in the final couplet, but they are not absent, for the sun, though advancing, is partly imagined as an enemy that is being routed ("yet we will make him run").

We have some small uncertainties about the metrics of lines 21–22, "But at my back I always hear / Time's winged chariot hurrying near." Are "chariot" and "hurrying" disyllabic or trisyllabic? If they are trisyllabic the line contains two extra syllables, forcing the reader to hurry through the line. But of course different readers will read almost any line differently. For instance, in the first of these lines some readers will put relatively heavy stresses on the first four syllables ("But at my back"); others may rush through the first three words and put an especially heavy stress on "back," compensating for the lack of an earlier stress. In any case, these two lines surely are spoken differently from the earlier lines. Similarly, the third section, beginning with line 33, starts by sounding different. In this case almost everyone would agree that "Now therefore" gets two consecutive stresses.

Good selections of Marvell's poetry have been edited by Frank Kermode (1967), George de F. Lord (1968), and Elizabeth Story Donno (1972). Students might enjoy John Dixon Hunt, *Andrew Marvell: His Life and Writings* (1978), which includes well-chosen illustrations.

JOHN DONNE

Holy Sonnet XIV ("Batter my heart, three-personed God") (p. 709)

"Batter my heart" has been discussed several times in *Explicator* (March 1953, Item 31; December 1953, Item 18; April 1954, Item 36; October 1956, Item 2). In *College English* 24 (January 1963): 299–302, John Parrish summarized these discussions, rejecting the idea that in the first quatrain, especially in lines 2 and 4, God is compared to a tinker mending a damaged pewter vessel, and offering his own reading. All these are conveniently reprinted in the Norton Critical Edition of *John Donne's Poetry* (1991), ed. A. L. Clements.

Our own winnowings from these essays follow. Although the first line introduces the "three-personed God," it is impossible to associate each quatrain with only one of the three persons. Still, the idea of the trinity is carried out in several ways: "knock, breathe, shine" becomes "break, blow, burn." And there are three chief conceits: God as a tinker repairing the speaker, damaged by sin; the speaker as a town usurped by satanic forces; God as a forceful lover who must ravish the sinful speaker; or (lest one get uneasy at the thought that Donne presents himself as a woman) God as a lover who must fully possess the speaker's soul (the soul is customarily regarded as female). "O'erthrow" in the first quatrain, in line 3, leads to the image of the besieged town in the second quatrain; "untrue" at the end of the second quatrain leads (because it can refer to marital infidelity) to the conceit of the lover in the third quatrain; and "ravish" in the final line can take us back to "heart" in the first line of the poem.

A useful, relatively long explication by M. T. Wanninger appeared in *Explicator* (December 1969), Item 37. M. H. Abrams, *Natural Supernaturalism* (1971, 50–51), points out that in "Batter my heart" Donne draws on Revelation 21.5 ("Behold, I make all things new"), and that "the ultimate marriage with the Bridegroom, represented as the rape of the longingly reluctant soul" draws on "commonplaces of Christian devotion."

For a lively, provocative study, we recommend John Carey, *John Donne: Life, Mind, and Art* (1981). For an example of a New Historicist approach, see Arthur Marotti, *John Donne, Coterie Poet* (1986). We should note that we often consult editions of Donne's writings that include annotations and commentaries: *The Songs and Sonnets*, ed. Theodore Redpath (rev. ed., 1983); *John Donne's Poetry*, ed. A. L. Clements (rev. ed., 1992); and *John Donne: The Complete English Poems*, ed. A. J. Smith (1971). See also Robert H. Ray, *A John Donne Companion* (1990).

ADDITIONAL TOPIC FOR CRITICAL THINKING AND WRITING
How do you feel about an observation made in *Explicator* (Spring 1980) to the effect that "no end" (line 6) is an anagram for "Donne"? What is the point? According to the author of the note, "This anagram is, I think, another of the

many ingenious samples of Donne's playing upon his name for poetic effect."
Is this reading helpful? Why? Why not?

LANGSTON HUGHES

Dream Boogie (p. 710)

The *American Heritage Dictionary* defines boogie-woogie as "a style of jazz characterized by a repressed rhythmic and melodic pattern in the bass."
"Repressed" has unconscious ironic echoes, since jazz grew in part from the
white repression of blacks.

Many whites, noticing the musical accomplishments of some blacks,
falsely assumed that these musicians were happy: If they weren't happy, why
were they singing? But as Langston Hughes says in *The Big Sea*, blacks put
their life into their music, singing "gay songs because you had to be gay or die;
sad songs, because you couldn't help being sad sometimes. But gay or sad, you
kept on living and you kept on going." In "Dream Boogie" Hughes says that
if you "Listen . . . closely," you can hear the injustice that in part gave birth to
jazz and forced blacks to express their sorrow rhythmically and in a masked
form. The enthusiasm of the opening line soon yields to a hint of a menace
("rumble," 3), and the point becomes almost explicit in the reference (4) to "a
dream deferred." (Instructors who already have assigned "Harlem" doubtless
will make connections between the two poems.) In lines 8–9 ("*You think / It's
a happy beat?*") the speaker pretty clearly says it is an unhappy beat, but by
putting the words in the form of a question, he stops short of making a flat
assertion, and of course he doesn't—and lines 22–26 are explicit, for instance,
in "*We knows everybody / ain't free!*" The next passage (27–34), including the
quotation from the Pledge of Allegiance, is hard-hitting, but the speaker then
shifts to another manner, using the jive-talk that to unthinking whites suggests the happiness of blacks, but the message is clear to the reader.

In the preface to *Montage of a Dream Deferred* (1951), Hughes wrote:

> This poem on contemporary Harlem, like be-bop, is marked by conflict-
> ing changes, sudden nuances, sharp and impudent interjections, broken
> rhythms, and passages sometimes in the manner of the jam session, some-
> times the popular song, punctuated by the riffs, runs, breaks, and dis-
> tortions of the music of a community in transition.

A "Voices and Visions" videocassette of Langston Hughes is available from
Longman Publishers.

MARTÍN ESPADA

Tony Went to the Bodega but
He Didn't Buy Anything (p. 711)

The basic irony of course is that Tony leaves the projects (i.e., his Hispanic
background) for law school and Boston and (presumably) material success,

but, finding that he is dissatisfied, he searches out the projects and a bodega. Why didn't he buy anything? Because it's enough for him to savor "la gente . . . hablando español." And now a smaller irony: Earlier (lines 14–15) we are told that as an incipient merchant he engaged in "practicing the grin on customers / he'd seen Makengo grin," but now, luxuriating in the "beautiful" atmosphere of the bodega, he "grinned / his bodega grin"— without any thought of trying to charm customers. Success, we are told at the end, is a return to one's roots.

We recommend a book that Espada has edited: *El Coro: A Chorus of Latino and Latina Poets* (1997). It includes a rich, diverse selection of poems by Julia Alvarez, Rafael Campo, Sandra Cisneros, and others.

EDNA ST. VINCENT MILLAY

Love Is Not All: It Is Not Meat nor Drink (p. 713)

Late in the poem a phrase in line 13 ("the memory of this night") identifies the speaker (a lover), the audience (the beloved), and the time (a night of love), but the poem begins drily, even rather pedantically. A somewhat professorial voice delivers a lecture on love, beginning authoritatively with four almost equally stressed monosyllables ("Love is not all"). Then, warming to the subject, the speaker becomes more expansive, with "It is not . . . nor . . . Nor . . . nor . . . And . . . and . . . and . . . and . . . can not . . . Nor . . . nor," all in the octave. Of course, in saying that love cannot do this and that we sense, paradoxically, a praise of love; if we have read a fair amount of love poetry, perhaps we expect the octave to yield to a sestet that will say what love *can* do. But this sestet too begins with apparent objectivity, as if making a concession ("It well may be"). Then, like the octave, the sestet introduces a romantic note while nominally proclaiming realism, although its images are somewhat less exotic (there is nothing like the "floating spar" of line 3, for instance) than the images of the octave. On the other hand, insofar as it introduces a more personal or a more intense note ("the memory of this night"), and reveals that the poem is addressed to the beloved, it is *more* romantic. In any case the sestet comes down to earth, and at the same times reaches a romantic height, in its last line, which consists of two sentences: "It well may be. I do not think I would." The brevity of these two sentences, and the lack of imagery, presumably convey a dry humor that the octave lacks, and at the same time they make an extremely romantic claim. (Surely "I do not think I would" is an understatement; in effect, it is a passionate declaration.) Put it this way: Although the octave asserts, for example, that love is not meat and drink and cannot heal the sick, and the first part of the sestet asserts that the speaker "might" give up the beloved's love in certain extreme circumstances, the understated passion of the conclusion serves to dismiss these assertions as unlikely—indeed, a reader feels, as untrue. Although to the rational mind "love is not all," to the lover it is "all," and a lover here is doing the talking.

SHERMAN ALEXIE

Evolution (p. 714)

Like much of Alexie's other work—fiction as well as poetry—"Evolution" is a wonderful mixture of fantasy ("The Indians / pawn their hands, saving the thumbs for last") and down-to-earth realism, not only with its "24 hours a day, 7 days a week," and its "television sets, a VCR, a full-length beaded buckskin outfit," but the cutting realism of the fact that Buffalo Bill opens his reservation pawn shop "right across the border from the liquor store."

The fantasy gives the poem something of the atmosphere of the tall tale, especially in the passage about the Indians pawning hands except thumbs, then thumbs, then skeletons, and finally the last Indian pawns his heart, but where the usual tall tale (say of the Baron Munchausen) is merely meant to be entertaining, Alexie's tale is certainly meant to stimulate thought, to be taken seriously. Notice that Alexie tells his story in a deadpan manner, and he does not explicitly put all the blame—or even any of the blame—on the whites. He tells us that "the Indians come running in," presumably sometimes from the liquor store, or perhaps en route to the liquor store. *Why* alcoholism is a problem on some reservations is not something he chooses to discuss.

The irony of Indians paying to see their own culture in "THE MUSEUM OF NATIVE AMERICAN CULTURES" (established by Buffalo Bill!) is evident enough, but what of the title, "Evolution"? We take it to play on the mistaken popular idea that "evolution" is a matter of moving upward, of progress—rather than a mere matter of change. Clearly the progress that is reported here is a sort of devolution, not anything to be aimed at.

HENRY REED

Naming of Parts (p. 714)

Most students will immediately hear—if the poem is read aloud in class—two voices. One voice is that of a riflery instructor, who maddeningly uses—four times in the first four lines—what has been called the "Kindergarten We"; and he uses it again in lines 6, 12, 20, 21, and 30. Recruits were required to know the names, and supposedly to be able to assemble the parts of a rifle in darkness. But from the middle of the fourth line of each stanza to the end of the stanza there is a countervoice, or, rather, we hear the thoughts of the recruit, whose mind turns from the numbing lecture to thoughts of "the neighboring gardens" (5) and of spring, a world of which the drill instructor apparently is unaware. The first and most obvious irony, then, is the contrast between the earnest, oblivious instructor and the recruit who is thinking of other things.

Some of the instructor's phrases (e.g., in 9–10, where he speaks about swivels, "Which in your case you have not got") are echoed but given a different context by the student ("in our case we have not got," in 12, the silence of the trees in spring).

The poem is delightfully comic, not least because of the boring talk of the instructor, because of the contrast between his talk and the recruit's thoughts, with puns on "easing the spring" (22, 24, and 25) and "point of balance" (27–28), and with mildly dirty allusions, but we don't think we are being hypersubtle when we say that these sexual puns arise from a not-at-all-comic desperation in the recruit's mind. Forced to listen to the droning instructor, who is talking about how to kill, the recruit mentally escapes to the abundant life going on around him. There is an assault in nature, too ("The early bees are assaulting and fumbling the flowers," 23), but that assault (in contrast to the instructor's lesson) is life-producing.

Or put it this way: Spring is associated with love (cf. Tennyson's "In the spring a young man's fancy lightly turns to thoughts of love"). Immediately following the pun on "spring" we get a vision of the bees assaulting the flowers, in a kind of rape, and indeed it is easy to see sexual suggestions in other passages, such as "released / With an easy flick of the thumb," "open the breech," "We can slide it / Rapidly backwards and forwards," "fumbling," "cocking-piece," and even in the word "parts" (in olden days, when this poem was written, and sex was rarely discussed publicly, genitals were spoken of as "private parts," even by sergeants).

SARAH N. CLEGHORN

The Golf Links (p. 715)

Cleghorn's poem uses no figures of speech. It is entirely literal. Offhand, it is the only poem we can think of in our book—though almost surely there must be a few others—that uses no similes, no metaphors, no apostrophes, no personifications. The only other poems in the book that we can think of, of which one might say the same, are Frost's "The Pasture" and "The Span of Life," but "The Pasture" is so clearly an invitation to visit the world of Frost's poetry—not just the world of the literal pasture—and "The Span of Life" is so clearly not just a comment about a dog that almost all readers know, consciously or not, that the poems are metaphoric as a whole.

What there *is* in Cleghorn's poem is plenty of irony: men are playing and children are laboring. There is a further irony, because the reader detects, or assumes, that although the speaker's tone is matter-of-fact, he or she must be horrified and enraged.

Cleghorn was writing in an age when ten-year-old children worked ten- or even fifteen-hour days, six days a week, in mills, glass factories, canneries, and coal mines—and of course also in agricultural tasks, where they might work seven days a week.

We include "The Golf Links" in a chapter on "evaluation," and it will be interesting to hear what students have to say about the poem's merits. Our own feeling is that it is pretty good: for us, much of the merit is in the sharp juxtaposition of "laboring children" and "men at play," and, second, the matter-of-fact tone that, given the context, must convey outrage.

In the text we ask if the poem is dated, given the fact that child labor is now outlawed in the United States. In our view, the poem is not dated, partly because child labor still exists elsewhere, and partly because the poem remains a reminder that in this very country—indeed, in the lifetime of today's nonagenarians—this horror existed. It is the job of writers to tell us, in memorable words, things that must be known. We are reminded of a famous passage in Lady Murasaki's *The Tale of Genji*, in which Genji sets forth his idea of *why* writers write:

> Again and again something in the writer's own life or in that around him will seem so important that he cannot bear to let it pass into oblivion. There must never come a time, he feels, when people do not know about it.

In our view, Cleghorn's four lines give us a tiny glimpse of an aspect of American history that we would like not to know about, but that we *must* always remember.

18

Rhythm and Versification

Paul Fussell, Jr.'s *Poetic Meter and Poetic Form*, rev. ed. (1979), is a readable discussion of metrics. Derek Attridge, *The Rhythms of English Poetry* (1982), though more massive, is also readable and will be of special interest to teachers or students who themselves write poetry. John Hollander's *Rhyme's Reason: A Guide to English Verse* (1981) illustrates forms of verse with self-descriptive poems. Also of interest are Harvey Gross, *Sound and Form in Modern Poetry* (1968), and *Mid-Century American Poets* (1950), ed. John Ciardi (which includes useful comments by Wilbur, Roethke, Jarrell, and others). More difficult, and much more specialized, are W. K. Wimsatt, Jr.'s "One Relation of Rhyme to Reason," in his *The Verbal Icon* (1954), and Charles O. Hartman, *Free Verse: An Essay on Prosody* (1980).

We think it is a mistake to spend an hour discussing nothing but meter. It seems to us better to work some discussion of metrics into the daily meetings than to devote a meeting exclusively to this topic. This chapter is meant to provide a summary and a convenient dictionary, but instructors probably will already have made use of some of the material. For example, the instructor, in teaching Keats's "On First Looking into Chapman's Homer," may have already mentioned (in commenting on the last line, "Silent upon a peak in Darien") that when a line in a predominantly iambic poem begins with a trochaic adverb or adjective, "we often get an effect of sudden quiet," as Paul Fussell notes in *Poetic Meter* (1965, 65). Incidentally, a similar metrical effect occurs in Shakespeare's Sonnet 29 (printed in Chapter 28), where the ninth line (in effect the first line of the sestet) begins with a trochee ("Yet in"), marking the start of an energetic rejection of the depressed condition set forth in the octave.

A. E. HOUSMAN

Eight O'Clock (p. 720)

A. E. Housman's "Eight O'Clock" is discussed by Rosenthal and Smith, *Exploring Poetry* (1955), and by Richard Wilbur, "Alfred Edward Housman," *Anniversary Lectures 1959* (Library of Congress, 1959, 42–43). Wilbur points out that we learn almost nothing about the condemned man—not even what his crime was—we get only the last half-minute of his life. A clock strikes eight, the conventional hour for executions in England; to the victim, and to the reader, it is a machine that strikes down not merely hours but men. Note the ticking in "clock collected," and the effect of the enjambment in the seventh line, where the clock collects its strength and (after a heavy pause) strikes the hour and ends the man's life.

By the way, the Library of Congress owns a notebook draft of the poem, in which lines 3–4 run thus:

One, two, three, four, on jail and square and people
They dingled down.

Wilbur points out that the deletion of the reference to the jail is a great improvement. "Suspense," he says, "requires that the reason for the man's intent listening should not be divulged until we come to the second stanza. Contrast requires too that the 'morning town,' as it is called in the first stanza, be simply presented as a crowded market place down to which the steeple clock almost gaily tosses its chiming quarters."

WILLIAM CARLOS WILLIAMS

The Dance (p. 721)

Williams's "The Dance" is in free verse, but the abundance of dactyls (as in "Breughel's great picture," "dancers go round," "squeal and the blare") gives it a sort of stamping effect appropriate to sturdy dancers wearing wooden shoes.

A "Voices and Visions" videocassette of William Carlos Williams is available from Longman Publishers.

ROBERT FRANCIS

The Pitcher (p. 722)

In presenting Robert Francis's "The Pitcher" to the class, ask if anyone knows the etymology of "eccentric" (cf. "eccentricity" in line 1). You may have to provide the answer yourself, but in any case you can explore with the students the ways in which a pitcher's art is "eccentricity."

Note that the first four stanzas do not rhyme, but they miss by only enough to "avoid the obvious" and to "vary the avoidance." "Aim" in line 1 comes as close as a word can to rhyming with "aim" in line 2, but the line drops off and misses by the merest fraction of a foot. And if "obvious/avoidance" and "comprehended/misunderstood" aren't strictly consonant, they are eccentrically so. No question about consonance or slant rhyme in "wild/willed." But perfect rhyme is reserved for the last couplet, which everyone (except the by-now-paralyzed batter) can see is a perfect strike. The rhyme scheme, the economical couplets, the tense but erratic repetition in sentence structure, the eccentric placement of caesuras (in 4 and 9), all of course contribute to the poem's wit in imitating the performance it describes.

We have found that students enjoy discussing the devices in the poem, one perception leading to another. But line 6 ("Throws to be . . . misunderstood") and line 10 ("understand too late") can cause trouble. Is the poet saying that poets are willfully obscure? Or that they like to challenge readers so that readers can have the pleasure of (after a little thought) enjoying complexity?

We have enjoyed Francis's collection, *Late Fire, Late Snow: New and Uncollected Poems* (1992).

GALWAY KINNELL

Blackberry Eating (p. 727)

Much of the fun of the poem is in the saying of it, the feeling of the sounds in the mouth, especially of the word *squinched*, in which the tongue presses against the palate and (given the context) crushes an imaginary blackberry in the mouth. But even in reading the poem silently one gets a sense of the pleasures of the sounds, for instance, in "The stalks very prickly," and perhaps— though we may be going too far here—in these words one almost *sees* (because of the verticality of the *t*, and the *l*'s, and the *k*'s) the prickly stalks.

Exactly what does Kinnell mean when he speaks of (lines 4–6) "the stalks, very prickly, a penalty / they earn for knowing the black art / of blackberry-making"? Does "they" refer to the blackberries, and is he playfully saying the blackberries are punished with prickles because they traffic in forbidden arts ("the black art / of blackberry-making")? Or does "they" refer to blackberry lovers, in which case he is playfully saying that those who gather the berries are punished for converting the berries into tasty objects? In any case, we think most readers will agree that the poem offers an almost sensuous delight.

For students, the best point of departure is Kinnell's *Selected Poems* (1982). Kinnell has also written a book of criticism, *The Poetics of the Physical World* (1969), and a collection of interviews, *Walking Down the Stairs* (1978), ed. Donald Hall. For critical discussion, see Lee Zimmerman, *Intricate and Simple Things: The Poetry of Galway Kinnell* (1987).

WILLIAM CARLOS WILLIAMS

The Artist (p. 728)

This appearance of this poem on the page, like the appearance of Ferlignhetti's "Constantly Risking Absurdity," clearly tells the reader that (in Robert Frost's words) a poem is "a performance in words." Experienced readers know this, even when looking at a poem that seems ordinary in appearance—let's say a sonnet, or a pair of quatrains—but most students need some practice in reading before they understand that the structure of a work (and the structure may be invisible to the inexperienced reader) is part of its meaning.

Of course all poems other than prose poems make one aspect of their structure clear: The poet keeps returning to the left-hand margin even though space remains at the right, whereas prose returns to the left only because space at the right has run out. In "The Artist" the line proceeds in short increments, and keeps coming back to its beginning, much as a dance consists of repeated movements. (Williams tells us that this artist is a dancer, in "stood on his toes / heels together," "arms . . . curled above his head," "whirled," "entrechat," and "the figure.")

What makes the poem especially engaging is the fact that the artist is an unprepossessing man, a guy with funny hair, a guy wearing "a soiled undershirt," a guy whose own wife apparently does not know of his talent. Further, there is the nice contrast between the writer's mother, an invalid seated in a chair, and the dancer's wife, who, hearing the mother's "Bravo," "came from the kitchen." Williams nicely catches the wife's voice, and nicely ends the poem.

> What goes on here? she said
> But the show was over.

LAWENCE FERLINGHETTI

Constantly Risking Absurdity (p. 729)

Ferlinghetti has insisted that poetry be read aloud, and as a consequence, he writes poetry that is easily intelligible to auditors. (Not surprisingly, the one allusion in Ferlinghetti's poem ("a little charliechaplin man") is not to mythology or literature but to the liveliest and most popular art, film.) Easy intelligibility, however, means that the poet is "constantly risking absurdity." Of course the point is not to be absurd; absurdity is a risk one runs in trying to "perceive / taut truth" as one approaches "Beauty" and hopes to catch her.

The shape of the poem on the page more or less imitates the progress and the pauses of a performer on a tightrope, and perhaps it also imitates his balancing pole extending far out on each side. The poem is obviously related to many of William Carlos Williams's poems, especially to "The Artist." And it is worthwhile to remind students of Frost's comment that a poem is a "performance in words" (a point that we make—perhaps that we belabor—in our first chapter).

In addition to Ferlinghetti's typographical performance on paper, wordplay is part of the act: "above the heads /of his audience" (4–5), "climbs on rime" (7), "balancing on eye-beams" (9), "sleight-of-foot tricks" (14), "high theatrics" (15) "with gravity" (26).

A Note on Shakespeare's Sonnets

Shakespeare's 154 sonnets were published in 1609, although it is thought that most of them were composed in the middle 1590s, around the time *Romeo and Juliet* and *A Midsummer Night's Dream* were written. Francis Meres spoke of

Shakespeare's "sugared sonnets" in 1598, and two were published in an anthology in 1599. The order of the sonnets is probably not Shakespeare's, but there are two large divisions (with some inconsistent interruptions). Sonnets 1–126 seem to be addressed to, or concerned with, a handsome, aristocratic young man who is urged to marry and thus to propagate his beauty and become immortal. Sonnets 127–152 are chiefly concerned with a promiscuous dark woman who seduces a friend, at least for a while.

Wordsworth thought the poems were autobiographical ("With this key Shakespeare unlocked his heart"), to which Browning replied, "If so, the less Shakespeare he." Scholars have not convincingly identified the friend or the lady, and the whole thing may be as fictional as *Hamlet*. Certainly it *sounds* like autobiography, but this is only to say that Shakespeare is a writer who sounds convincing. The chief argument that the poems really may be autobiographical is that the insistence that the friend marry is so odd a theme. As C. S. Lewis says in *English Literature in the Sixteenth Century* (1954), what man (except a potential father-in-law) cares if another man gets married? One other point: Do the poems addressed to the beautiful friend suggest a homosexual interest? Certainly they suggest a *passionate* interest, but it doesn't seem to be erotic. Sonnet 20, a bawdy and witty poem, expressly denies any interest in the friend's body. It seems reasonable to say that what the speaker of the sonnets wants from the friend is not sex but love.

Suggested references: A facsimile of the 1609 edition of the sonnets is available in *Shakespeare's Poems: A Facsimile of the Earliest Editions* (1964). Facsimile repro ductions of each poem, along with modernized versions, are also available in the edition by Booth (mentioned in the next paragraph) and in the commentary by Vendler (listed below).

Several editions of the Sonnets are recommended to readers who wish to immerse themselves in academic details. For a massive summary of almost everything that was said up to the middle of the twentieth century, see Hyder Edward Rollins's New Variorum Edition of *The Sonnets* (2 vols., 1944). For intelligent, relatively brief annotations of each poem, see *Shakespeare's Sonnets*, ed. W. G. Ingram and Theodore Redpath (1964, rptd. 1978). Stephen Booth's edition of *Shakespeare's Sonnets* (1977) combines a facsimile of the 1609 text with a modernized text and offers a commentary that has the advantages and disadvantages of being infinitely ingenious; when it comes to finding meanings, Booth's imagination is unchecked. (This edition is not to be confused with Booth's earlier, much more temperate book on the Sonnets, listed below.) Readers who wish a more detailed commentary than Ingram and Redpath, and a more conservative commentary than Booth, may consult three scholarly editions: The New Penguin Shakespeare edition by John Kerrigan, *The Sonnets and A Lover's Complaint* (1986, with minor revisions in 1995); The New Cambridge Shakespeare edition by G. Blakemore Evans, *The Sonnets* (1996); and the Arden edition by Katharine Duncan-Jones, *The Sonnets* (1997). For a detailed commentary on the formal qualities of each sonnet—but it is not an edition, i.e., it is not concerned with matters of dating, identification of Mr. W. H., etc.—see the book by Helen Vendler listed below. Additional titles of interest follow.

Booth, Stephen. *An Essay on Shakespeare's Sonnets*, 1969.

Colie, Rosalie. *Shakespeare's Living Art*, 1974.

Dubrow, Heather. *Captive Victors: Shakespeare's Narrative Poems and Sonnets*, 1987.

Grazia, Margreta de. "The Scandal of Shakespeare's Sonnets." *Shakespeare Survey* 47 (1994): 35–49.

Gurr, Andrew. "You and Thou in Shakespeare's Sonnets." *Essays in Criticism* 32 (1982): 9–25.

Kernan, Alvin. *Shakespeare, the King's Playwright: Theater in the Stuart Court*, 1995.

Landry, Hilton. *Interpretations in Shakespeare's Sonnets*, 1963.

Leishman, J. B. *Themes and Variations in Shakespeare's Sonnets*, 1961.

Melchiori, Giorgio. *Shakespeare's Dramatic Meditations*, 1976.

Muir, Kenneth. *Shakespeare's Sonnets*, 1979.

Nicoll, Allardyce, ed. *Shakespeare Survey 15*, 1962.

Smith, Bruce R. *Homosexual Desire in Shakespeare's England: A Cultural Poetics*, 1991.

Vendler, Helen. *The Art of Shakespeare's Sonnets*, 1997.

Wright, George T. *Shakespeare's Metrical Art*, 1988.

WILLIAM SHAKESPEARE

Sonnet 73 ("That time of year thou mayst in me behold") (p. 733)

Sonnet 73 is chiefly a meditation on growing old, though the couplet relates this topic to the theme of love that is the subject of many of Shakespeare's sonnets. All three quatrains, in varying degrees, glance at increasing coldness and darkness, and each successive quatrain is concerned with a briefer period. In the first, the human life is compared to a year; in the second, to a day; in the third, to a few hours. In the first quatrain, there is a further comparison; the boughs of the autumnal trees are compared (in "Bare ruined choirs") to the churches that had fallen into decay after England broke with Rome. ("Sweet birds" refers primarily to the feathered creatures that recently sang in the boughs, but it also glances at choristers in the choirs.) Note, too, that it is reasonable to perceive, faintly, a resemblance between the shaking boughs and a trembling old person. The first quatrain, then, is rich in suggestions of ruined beauty and destroyed spirituality.

The second quatrain, by speaking of night as "Death's second self," explicitly introduces death into the poem. The third quatrain personifies the fire, speaking of its "youth" (i.e., the earlier minutes or hours of the blaze) and its "deathbed," and in its reference to ashes it introduces a common idea of the decayed body. (The idea, of course, is that the last embers lie on the ashes, which were the "youth" or earlier hours of the fire, and these ashes now help to extinguish the embers.) The year will renew itself, and the day will renew itself, but the firewood is utterly destroyed. In the final line the speaker is reduced to "that," not even "me."

WILLIAM SHAKESPEARE

Sonnet 146 ("Poor soul, the center of my sinful earth") (p. 734)

Shakespeare's Sonnet 146 is well discussed in Edward Hubler, *The Sense of Shakespeare's Sonnets* (1952), and more learnedly and elaborately discussed by Michael West in *Shakespeare Quarterly* 25 (Winter 1974): 109–22. Also useful is *A Casework on Shakespeare's Sonnets* (1964), ed. Gerald Willen and Victor B. Reed. See also an article by Charles A. Huttar, "The Christian Basis of Shakespeare's Sonnet 146," *Shakespeare Quarterly* 19 (Autumn 1968): 355–65, which rejects a reading that the poem ironically argues that spiritual health is achieved by bodily subjugation. The rejected reading holds that the advice that the soul exploit the body must be ironic, since if it were not ironic, the soul would be guilty of simony, the sin of buying (or attempting to buy) salvation. According to this ironic reading, the poet really is pleading for the life of the body against a rigorous asceticism which glorifies the spirit at the expense of the body. But Huttar argues (by citing Biblical sources and Christian commentaries) that the poem argues in behalf of the traditional Christian doctrine that the soul should be the master of the body; the body (which must in any case die) should not be allowed to cause the soul to "pine." The poem, Huttar says, is close to Jesus's words in Matthew 6.20: "Lay up for yourself treasures in heaven, where neither moth nor rust cloth corrupt, and where thieves do not break through and steal."

ADDITIONAL TOPICS FOR CRITICAL THINKING AND WRITING

1. In line 2, "My sinful earth" is doubtless a printer's error, an unintentional repetition of the last words of the first line. Among suggested emendations are "Thrall to," "Fooled by," "Rebuke these," "Leagued with," "Feeding." Which do you prefer? Why?
2. How would you characterize the tone of the first two lines? Where in the poem does the thought take its chief turn? What do you think is the tone of the couplet?
3. What does "array" (line 2) mean?
4. Explain the paradox in lines 13–14.
5. In a poem on the relation between body and soul, do you find battle imagery surprising? Commercial imagery (lines 5–12)? What other imagery is in the poem? Do you think the sonnet is a dull sermon?

JOHN MILTON

When I Consider How My Light Is Spent (p. 736)

Argument about the date Milton became blind need not concern us (Miltonists wonder how literally to take "Ere half my days"), but it should be noticed that one critic argues that the sonnet is not about blindness. The common title "On His Blindness" has no authority; it was first used by a printer in 1752. Lysander Kemp held (*Hopkins Review*, 6 [1952]: 80–83) that the sonnet deals with the loss not of vision but of poetic inspiration, but Kemp's view has not been widely accepted. The most sensible view is that the octave assumes that God requires ceaseless labor, and the sestet enlarges the concept of service to include those who though inactive are eagerly prepared for action.

Additional notes: In line 2, "this dark world and wide" suggests not only the dark world of the blind man but is also a religious stock expression for the sinful world; in line 7, "day-labor" suggests not only labor for daily wages but also labor that requires daylight, i.e., the power of vision; in line 14, "wait" perhaps means not only "stay in expectation" but also "attend as a servant, to receive orders."

For further reading, students might begin with the introduction, texts, and annotations in *Milton's Sonnets*, ed. E. A. J. Honigmann (1966). Anna K. Nardo, *Milton's Sonnets and the Ideal Community* (1979) is another good resource. But the liveliest (and most controversial) commentary on Milton's sonnets and how they should be interpreted is to be found in Stanley Fish, *Is There a Text in This Class?: The Authority of Interpretive Communities* (1980). See also Edward Jones, *Milton's Sonnets: An Annotated Bibliography, 1900–1992* (Medieval and Renaissance Texts and Studies, vol. 122, 1994).

JOHN CROWE RANSOM

Piazza Piece (p. 737)

"Piazza Piece" is a sonnet, and sonnets often treat the theme of love, but few if any others treat the old theme of "Death and the Maiden." It should be read aloud, and when it is read aloud, the apparently odd placement of "listen to an old man not at all" seems perfectly right, catching the old-fashioned tone of the suitor.

Not all students will know that "piazza" (Italian for square) in parts of the United States denotes a porch, verandah, or balcony; nor will they know that in the earliest days of automobiling the roads were not paved or covered with asphalt, so riders—in open cars, of course—wore dustcoats, coats that were ankle-length. Ransom, a Southerner who was born in 1880, catches the politeness and nostalgia that characterized (and still characterize) much of the South when a respectable woman was still "a lady," and a man was "a gentleman," and "Sir" was in common use.

Students can be directed to two collections, Ransom's *Selected Poems* (1945) and *Selected Poems* (1963). But they need to know that the first excludes many poems that Ransom had published previously, and the second, while more capacious, includes revised (and many have argued, *inferior*) versions of his earlier work. See Thomas Daniel Young, *Gentleman in a Dustcoat: A Biography of John Crowe Ransom* (1976), and, on the poetry, Robert Buffington, *The Equilibrist: A Study of John Crowe Ransom's Poems, 1916–1963* (1976).

X. J. KENNEDY

Nothing in Heaven Functions as It Ought (p. 738)

The poem is a Petrarchan sonnet, with the traditional contrast between the octave and the sestet. Kennedy's contrast of heaven and hell is not surprising, then, but in the contrasting rhymes and versification he plays an unexpected game. The off-rhymes and the hypermetric lines of the octave imitate the statement of the octave (things are askew), and the mechanical perfection of the sestet imitates the sestet's statement ("Hell hath no freewheeling part").

Kennedy has let us see an earlier version of the poem. You may want to invite students to compare the following version with the one in their text.

Nothing in Heaven Functions as It Ought (an early version)

Nothing in Heaven functions as it ought:
Peter snaps off a key stuck in the lock,
And his creaky gates keep crowing like a cock
(No hush of oily gold as Milton thought).
Gangs of the martyred innocents keep whoofing
The nimbus off the Venerable Bede
Like that of an old dandelion in seed.
The beatific choir take fits of coughing.

But Hell, sweet Hell, holds no unsteady part,
Nothing to rust nor rip nor lose its place.
Ask anyone: How did you come to be here?—
And he will slot a quarter into his face
And there will be a click and wheels will whir
And out will pop a neat brief of his case.

Kennedy is a very witty, inventive poet who enjoys exploring many forms and genres, though always with keen attention paid to meter and rhyme. *Cross Ties* (1985) is a selection drawn from a number of volumes of his verse.

ADDITIONAL TOPICS FOR CRITICAL THINKING AND WRITING

1. Roughly speaking, how does Kennedy characterize Heaven? Does his characterization strike you as disrespectful? Why, or why not?
2. "Nothing in Heaven" is a sonnet. How does the form of the poem help to convey the meaning?

BILLY COLLINS

Sonnet (p. 739)

This poem will cause students no difficulty, and we think they will greatly enjoy it. Collins does introduce talk about the difficulties of writing a sonnet—he even dares to compare the poet's burden to Christ's via dolorosa—but the tone is easy-going from start to finish. In our view, the comparison of the fourteen stages in Christ's journey to the fourteen lines of the sonnet is a bit of self-mockery rather than blasphemy, though of course other readers may disagree with our easy assessment.

We especially like the ninth line, where the Petrarchan sonnet regularly takes a "turn"; Collins's language suggests that the "little ship" of line 3 has become a speeding car, and the rhetorical "turn" becomes physical: "But hang on here while we make the turn." In line 10 he assures us that "all will be resolved" (we are confident that indeed it will be, as it is in any successful sonnet), and by the end of the poem Laura invites Petrarch into bed. Presumably the "crazy medieval tights" are removed, along with the eccentric behavior, just as the "storm-tossed seas" of line 3 have been weathered, and we are in the comfortable ordinary world where people "at last [go] to bed."

The amazing thing about this sonnet—often overlooked by students— is that it does *not* employ rhyme. Surely Collins is playing a little joke on his readers.

Collins is very popular—sales of his books have broken all records for poetry—and many critics and poets have spoken highly about his work.

> Billy Collins writes lovely poems— lovely in a way almost nobody's since Roethke's are. Limpid, gently and consistently startling, more serious than they seem, they describe all the worlds that are and were and some others besides.
>
> —John Updike

> Billy Collins is an American original— a metaphysical poet with a funny bone and a sly, questioning intelligence. He is an ironist of the void, and his poems— witty, playful and beautifully formed— bump up against the deepest human mysteries.
>
> —Edward Hirsch

> Billy Collins's poems are graceful, ironic, smart, and full of feeling. Sometimes wrongfully described as a defense against feeling, irony is, in fact, a deeply mixed feeling. In poems as good as Collins's, it is a mirror in which we see ourselves not by reflecting in lazy categories, but perhaps as experience sees us, and certainly as we imagine ourselves.
>
> —William Matthews

Source for these quotations: http://www.contemporarypoetry.com/dialect/poetry/index.htm.

Some critics, and some of his fellow-poets, however, find his style and approach unchallenging. Consider, for example, this passage from an essay on Collins by the poet-critic Jeredith Merrin, "Art Over Easy," *The Southern Review* 38:1 (Winter 2002):

> The big draw here, for both writers and readers, is that Collins makes it all look more than easy; a breeze. Collins might be dubbed, in fact, Our Laureate of Easiness. . . . The problem, though, with an esthetic of easiness—though it might at first seem the right homespun riposte to Continentally influenced modernist difficulty—is that it condescends to readers and tries to pass off as unhighfalutin' honesty what are in fact down-

right untruths. This is a writer who takes you for a walk on the mild side. What you already know on earth, he assures you, is all you need to know.

Students, especially in an introductory course, often find poetry "hard," and we think it is a good idea to raise this issue with them and explore it. And it helps if you can key the discussion to a specific literary work, like this poem (which we admire) by Collins. Is the poem easy? Is it too easy? What makes one poem easier than another? Should poetry be "hard," and what exactly does this term mean? What are some examples of "hard" poems in other chapters of this book? Is the hardness a matter of the language, or of the thoughts and feelings that the poet describes, or both?

Here are two more quotations to keep in mind as the discussion proceeds. Gerard Manley Hopkins says that poetry is "speech framed . . . to be heard for its own sake and interest even and above its interest of meaning." For his part, T. S. Eliot suggests that "poetry communicates before it is understood."

EDWIN ARLINGTON ROBINSON

The House on the Hill (p. 740)

Robinson believed that human existence was full of tragedies, failures, and disappointments. As one contemporary critic observed: "Always defeat—always failure: surely the theme of human failure, with all its variations and nuances, has been treated so exhaustively by no other poet as by Robinson. One would not have believed there were so many ways to fail." His poems usually make a very direct impression, but he is subtle and sensitive, sharply aware of the complicatedness of emotions and relationships. As the poem "Richard Cory" (Chapter 14) reveals, Robinson is a master at presenting balked, suppressed, frustrated feeling and its maddening impact on the mind and punishment of the heart.

Yet Robinson had a tough-minded admiration for the lost and lonely and defeated characters he describes, for the measure of courage they display in their sexual, emotional, and spiritual struggles. He was not an innovator; he operated within poetry's common forms and conventions. Yet he was dedicated to his craft, and in his early poems, before he embarked on the long verse narratives that seem tedious today, he offered a distinctive voice and an anguished but unflinching vision. "No poet ever understood loneliness or separateness better than Robinson," the poet James Dickey has said, "or knew the self-consuming furnace that the brain can become in isolation, the suicidal hellishness of it, doomed as it is to feed on itself in answerless frustration, fated to this condition by the accident of birth, which carries with it the hunger for certainty and the intolerable load of personal recollection."

Dickey's words "feed on itself," "fated," and "personal recollection" suggest to us that the villanelle must have been an especially congenial form for Robinson. In a villanelle—certainly in this example—the reader feels that the writer is obsessed with some thought (here, the deserted house), some word or phrase (here, especially "away" and "nothing more to say"), and keeps returning to them.

There is little recent work on Robinson. The following older studies are helpful: Hermann Hagedorn, *Edwin Arlington Robinson, A Biography* (1938); Ellsworth

Barnard, *Edwin Arlington Robinson: A Critical Study* (1952); Edwin S. Fussell, *Edwin Arlington Robinson: The Literary Background of a Traditional Poet* (1954); Wallace Ludwig Anderson, *Edwin Arlington Robinson: A Critical Introduction* (1967); and Louis Coxe, *Edwin Arlington Robinson: The Life of Poetry* (1969).

DYLAN THOMAS

Do Not Go Gentle into That Good Night (p. 741)

One might at first think that a villanelle is an utterly inappropriate form in which to urge someone to "rage," but in Thomas's "Do Not Go Gentle into That Good Night," addressed to a man on his deathbed, it proves appropriate because of its ritualistic, incantatory quality. In discussing the poem one can wonder why the night is "good." Probably because death is natural and inevitable (in line 4 "dark is right"), but surely too there is a pun on "good night" as an equivalent to death. Further, "the last wave" (7) is probably both a final wave of water (suggesting the last flow of life) and a final gesture of the hand; "Grave men" (13) of course alludes both to serious men and to men near the grave.

Thomas's distinctions between "wise men," "good men," "wild men," and "grave men" have aroused various interpretations. W. Y. Tyndall, in *A Reader's Guide to Dylan Thomas* (1962), suggests that wise men are philosophers, good men are moralists (perhaps Puritans), and wild men are "men of action and lovers of living." (He suggests that the grave men are poets.) M. W. Murphy, in *Explicator* 27, No. 6 (February 1970), Item 55, suggests that the wise men who preach wisdom are contrasted with the good men who live a life of wisdom. Both rage against death because they have accomplished nothing, the words of the former and the deeds of the latter having gone unheeded. The wild men are hedonists—who at death discover they have not caught time— and, in contrast to those Dionysian figures, the grave men are ascetic Apollonians who have missed the joys of life but who now, near the grave, see what they have missed. In short, for all men life is incomplete and too brief, and no one should "go gentle into that good night."

We see the poem along these lines: Despite "good night," "at close of day," "the dying of the light"—terms that suggest death is to be welcomed—the speaker urges passionate resistance. The "wise men" (4–6) do not go gently, because they have come to realize that their wise words "had forked no lightning"—that is, had not given them, or anyone else, enough energetic illumination to accept death. The "Good men" of the third tercet, people who had presumably tried to do good deeds, see that their deeds are "frail." The "Wild men," the poets who "sang" of the vitality of nature, see that their celebrations were really elegies. The "Grave men" (there is, again, a pun here) are highly serious people who, nearing death and seeing the joy they have lost, also rage. The speaker, then, tells his father, who is "on the sad height" of old age, to "curse" and to "bless" him, to curse presumably because the speaker will go on living in the world that the old man is losing, and to bless him because the speaker has instructed the father on how to die properly. "Curse, bless," then leads to "fierce tears."

If you are lucky, a pedantic student may ask you why "gentle" rather than "gently" is used. One answer is that "gentle" is an adjective referring to the understood subject "you," not an adverb modifying "go." In this view, Thomas is describing a condition he hopes his father will not be in, rather than describing the father's method of going. This point is clear if for "gentle" one substitutes, say, "ignorant." On the other hand, one can argue that "gentle" is not necessarily an adjective. Some authorities point out that verbs of motion and sensation take adverbs that do not end in *ly*: cf. "Go slow," "Think fast," "Sleep sound," and "Feel good."

See *The Poems of Dylan Thomas* (rev. ed., 1974); *Collected Letters*, ed. Paul Ferris (1985); and *The Notebooks*, ed. Ralph N. Maud (1967). For criticism and bibliography: R. B. Kershner, *Dylan Thomas* (1976); and John Ackerman, *A Dylan Thomas Companion* (1991).

ELIZABETH BISHOP

One Art (p. 742)

For a poem about the art of mastering losses, Bishop chooses a difficult form, the villanelle, which she has obviously mastered. In an interview in *The Paris Review* 80 (Summer 1981), she said that she usually had difficulty writing villanelles but this one came easily. (Bishop, incidentally, published very few works in traditional forms, though she did publish two sestinas and at least one double sonnet.)

It is almost a convention of villanelles, rondeaux, and other intricate forms for the poet to announce that the form is *not* difficult, an idea suggested in Bishop's first line and echoed in lines 6, 12, and 18. It is "the art of losing" that proves harder to master than the art of writing villanelles. The poem moves to increasingly serious losses, from lost keys and lost time ("hour"), to lost "places, and names." In line 10 we return to the specific ("I lost my mother's watch"), and then, less specifically, to "three loved houses," "two cities," "two rivers," and "a continent."

The final stanza reveals that the speaker has lost a beloved person (made concrete and visible to us in "the joking voice, a gesture / I love"), and it is clear—from "I love" rather than "I loved"—that this loss has not been mastered, and the memory of the beloved has not been easily abandoned. The italicized "*Write* it! " of the last line is a command to the self, to put into writing (and thus make final) the acceptance of the loss, but in this command, and in the final word ("disaster"), we hear a strain, an effort to bully the self into belief, that is not heard in the earlier lines. That is, the last line—"though it may look like (*Write* it!) like disaster"—is quite different from line 9 ("None of these will bring disaster"), where indeed the tone is almost flippant.

By its very nature the villanelle, with its repeated rhymes, has an insistent, incantatory quality, but Bishop's villanelle tends to minimize this tone; it is rather more conversational than most villanelles. How does Bishop achieve her effect? If students have paid attention to our comments about the caesura, enjambment, and feminine rhymes they will be able, perhaps with a little prodding, to see how Bishop's use of these things helps to give her poem a relatively conversational (as opposed to incantatory) tone. Heavy pauses (sometimes indicating the end of a sentence) occur in the middle of a line, the thought runs over at the ends of some lines, and feminine rhymes tend to soften the endings. Further, colloquial expressions such as "And look!" (line 10) and parenthetic expressions (there are two in the final stanza) also give the poem a somewhat improvisatory quality not normally found in a villanelle.

ELIZABETH BISHOP

Sestina (p. 744)

Anyone who knows even a trifle about Bishop will assume that this poem about a grandmother and a child draws on Bishop's autobiography: Bishop's father died when she was eight months old, her mother experienced nervous breakdowns, and at the age of five the child was sent to live with her maternal grandmother in Nova Scotia. But surely the fact that the poem is in part or even in great part autobiographical is no reason for anyone other than a biographer of Bishop to read it. We include "Sestina" in our book because we think it is interesting in itself, not only as autobiography.

In fact, a strict autobiographical reading—a reading that speaks of Bishop and her grandmother—probably falsifies the poem. Not until we began speaking about the poem in class did we realize that the child's sex (or should we say gender?) is never specified in the poem. (We take the "She" in line 7 to refer, like all of the other female pronouns, to the grandmother.) We are not sure what to make of this degendering of the child, but our guess is that it is part of a tendency in the poem to set forth a somewhat archetypal, somewhat mysterious narrative. That is, the poem gives us a rainy autumn setting, an "old grandmother," and a child. All of this is made somewhat mysterious by talk of "the Little Marvel Stove" (line 4), an almanac (5, indeed, a "clever almanac" in line 18, clever because almanacs such as *The Old Farmer's Almanac* include predictions), "little moons" (33), and an "inscrutable house" (39). Take "the Little Marvel Stove": In the first stanza it is just a prop, something beside which the grandmother and the child sit, but in line 11 "The iron kettle sings on the stove," in line 15 drops of water from the tea kettle "dance like mad on the hot black stove," and in line 25 the stove speaks:

   It was to be, says the Marvel Stove.

The almanac—we have already mentioned that almanacs make predictions, especially about the weather—in this poem also speaks, first in line 26 and again in line 37:

   I know what I know, says the almanac. . . .
   Time to plant tears, says the almanac.

In line 6, you will recall, the grandmother is "laughing and talking to hide her tears." The poem never tells us why the grandmother weeps, but readers can assume that she weeps for the missing parents or parent of the child, which is to say that she weeps for her own missing (dead?) child.

A sestina by definition repeats in succeeding stanzas the six end-words of the first stanza (here the words are *house, grandmother, child, stove, almanac,* and *tears*) in a complicated order, and thus almost inevitably has something of the feel of an incantation, a magic spell. In Bishop's poem the hint of the unearthly is heightened, as we have said, by the characters (grandmother and child), the season (rainy autumn), the speaking stove, and the prophesying almanac. But there is more along these lines. Consider, for instance, the sense that everything has its foreordained moment (*"It's time for tea,"* 13, and *"Time to plant tears,"* 37), or consider the image of the almanac hovering like a bird in lines 19–21 (presumably the book has opened, so the left and right pages resemble a bird's outstretched wings). Also relevant are the teacup (22, which may evoke thoughts of fortune-telling via tea leaves), and the child's drawing of "a winding pathway" (28) and an "inscrutable house" (39). And then there are "the little moons [that] fall down like tears / from between the pages of the almanac" (33–34). We are pretty sure that these little moons are chads—small circles of paper generated by punching holes in the almanac so that it can be hung from a nail by a string that goes through the openings—but conceivably the moons are merely the depictions of the phases of the moon in the almanac and they fall into the drawing of the flower bed only in the child's imagination.

The child lives in this mysterious world where sad things are ordained: The first line of the envoi says, *"Time to plant tears,"* but as early as the last line of the first stanza we encountered the tears of the grandmother. Still, although living in a sad world where unhappiness is ordained, the child is also beginning to create his or her own world—we might say the child is beginning to invent a life or to live a life—by drawing a picture, a picture that the child "shows . . . proudly to the grandmother." The picture the child draws, however, is itself disturbing: It contains "a rigid house," "a man with buttons like tears," and "another inscrutable house." For this child—we can say for Elizabeth Bishop, if we wish—life will be filled with mystery and tears. Probably most creative artists feel that in large measure they are fulfilling their unsought destinies; their gifts, which may be as much a curse as a blessing, were not sought, merely apprehended. (See our discussion, in this manual, of Anne Sexton's "Her Kind," where we briefly talk about the *poète maudit*.) That is, the poet can hardly imagine not being a poet; the act of writing, despite the countless revisions of the work, may seem to be a bringing to birth of that which has been ordained.

A sestina of course in large degree contains its end in its beginning. Once the end-words of the first stanza have been established, the writer probably feels that *"It was to be"* (25). The poetic form itself, "a rigid house / and a winding pathway," is an emblem of the poet's life.

Our first question in the text asks the students to think about Bishop's title. We don't mention it in the text, but her original title for the poem was "Early Sorrow." Apparently Bishop came to feel that this title was too explicit or said too much and so she simply called the poem "Sestina," a title that in fact many writers of sestinas use, cf. Kipling's poem, in this chapter, "Sestina of the Tramp-Royal." As we have indicated in our discussion of Bishop's poem, we assume she wants the reader to be fully aware of the poetic form, and to take that form to be an emblem of her life, or perhaps of life as many people experience it.

GEORGE HERBERT

Easter-Wings (p. 746)

We print the poem as it was originally printed, with the lines vertical rather than horizontal, so that the resemblance to wings—those of a bird or an angel—is immediately evident. (In the 1633 edition, however, the first stanza was on the left-hand page, the second on the right-hand page.) Note, too, that the upper part of each wing is notably smaller than the lower part; most books center each line so that the two sloping sides of each triangle are of equal length, thereby damaging the resemblance to a bird's wing or to the depictions of an angel's wing.

Some classical poets had written poems in the shape of a wing, but the resemblance was to Cupid's wings. Herbert's wings, as we have mentioned, evoke those of an angel (in the Bible, angels are intermediaries between human beings and God), or the wings may even evoke God, who in the Hebrew Bible is conceived as winged, for instance, in Psalm 17.8: "Hide me under the shadow of thy wings." Speaking more generally, we can say that wings, the instruments of flight, are universally associated with the dematerialized body, i.e., with release from the bonds of earth, in a flight toward heaven. In Herbert's poem, the image is part of the meaning: In the first stanza, when he says that human beings foolishly became "Most poor," those words are in the shortest line, and as he expresses his hope to rise, the lines expand. Here the wings presumably suggest those of the lark, specified in line 8, a bird that is noted for its swift heavenward ascent at light of dawn. Similarly, in the second stanza when he says he became "Most thin," the line is the shortest, the thinnest, and then the poem again expands as he expresses his hope that, joining his wing with God's, his flight to heaven will be successful.

The structure of the poem—the plot, so to speak—moves from a rather ordinary statement in the first stanza concerning the fall of man and the poet's traditional comparison of the poet with a lark to his much more original thought, in the second and more personal stanza, that he himself might "combine" with God by joining God's wing ("if I imp my wing on thine"). This shift is evident in the movement from "O let me rise / As larks" in the first stanza to "Let me combine [with the savior]" in the second stanza.

Some students may have to be told the special relevance of Easter—the time of death and rebirth, the time when Jesus rose to heaven—and most students will need to be introduced to the concept of the Fortunate Fall, the idea (implied in line 10, "Then shall the fall further the flight in me") that when Adam and Eve disobeyed God by eating the forbidden fruit, they fell from grace and were expelled from paradise, but this fall was fortunate because it brought about Christ's sacrifice. Had Adam and Eve not fallen, there would have been no Christ to show his love by dying for them on the cross, and human beings would not have ultimately experienced a state more glorious than that of Eden. The human "sicknesses and shame" of line 12, which are God's punishment for the "sin" of Adam (13), are an "Affliction" (20), but they also move him to hope that he may "combine" (17) with the savior, whose affliction has made salvation possible.

LILLIAN MORRISON

The Sidewalk Racer (p. 747)

The poem belongs to a genre variously called "pattern poetry," "shaped verse," and *carmina figurata*. Examples are as old as fourth century B.C. Greece and as modern as today. We include a contemporary example in Chapter 1—James Merrill's poem in the shape of a Christmas tree—but in modern times the form is especially associated with Dylan Thomas and John Hollander. Perhaps the examples best known to students of English literature are George Herbert's "The Altar" and "Easter-Wings," which are anthologized in all surveys of English literature. Some students may be familiar with "The Tale of the Mouse" in *Alice and Wonderland*, where the text is arranged to look like a mouse's tail.

Morrison's "The Sidewalk Racer" is shaped like a skateboard, but the poem is not so much about the board as about the skater's sensations, about the experience of motion. Because the poem is very short, in class you may want to ask your students to move through the poem line by line. The entire first line in this poem about motion is, appropriately, a participle ("Skimming"), more specifically a verb of movement in an incomplete state. The second line introduces a metaphor, the "asphalt sea," but there is still no subject and no completion; we are, so to speak, kept in motion. The third line begins and ends with "I," but if the first part does in effect give us what looks like a sentence ("Skimming / an asphalt sea / I swerve"), the end of the line, with another "I," keeps us going, propels us into the next line, where indeed we find the verb, "sway."

But before we comment on the fourth line we should call attention to the internal rhyme in the third: "I swerve, I curve." Rhyme of course is a pattern of sounds, with variations, and here it is a sort of analog to the speaker's body, which itself traces a pattern, i.e., it bends this way and then that way according to laws of physics. (If the skater doesn't "rhyme" properly—doesn't match movement X with movement Y—he or she will take a tumble.) The fourth line ends with "whirring," which in the next line leads to "sound," and this word leads to the next rhyme in the poem ("ground"); appropriately, talk about a whirring sound leads to such a sound.

But the poem is more about the "I" than about sound effects. We have already encountered "I" three times in the third line, and now we encounter it again in the sixth ("I'm the sailor" and the seventh ("I'm the / driver") and again in the ninth ("I'm the one and only"). The sense of ecstatic unity set forth in "I'm the sailor / and the sail" continues in "I'm the / driver and the wheel." This sense of unity, this independence engendered by an activity that requires no companions, leads to an engaging sense of solipsism: "I'm the one and only," in particular the one and only "single engine / human auto / mobile," where the last word of the poem ("mobile") appropriately conveys motion.

In the book we several times quote Robert Frost's comment that a poem is "a performance in words." Frost's comment is applicable to all poems, but it seems to us especially applicable here, where the performance involves (a) shaping lines into a picture, and, more important, (b) communicating a sense of emotion, moving from the description of what is seen ("Skimming / an asphalt sea") to the description of what is felt, via rhyme, onomatopoeia, repetition—and indeed to conveying a touch of amusing egotism ("I'm the one and only").

WALT WHITMAN

When I Heard the Learn'd Astronomer (p. 748)

In our discussion of the poem, we emphasize the division of the one-sentence poem into two units of four lines each, but we concentrate our discussion on the length of the lines, and we say little about the thematic contrasts in the two parts; e.g., the speaker indoors versus the speaker out of doors, the speaker with other human beings versus alone in the presence of nature, the speaker amidst noise (the lecture, the applause) versus the speaker surrounded by silence, the speaker sitting and passive versus the speaker moving and active (though the activity seems almost effortless: "rising and gliding," "wander'd off," "Look'd up").

Notice too that we discuss the poem as an example of free verse—which it is—but we also mention that the final line of the poem is iambic pentameter. Moreover, though of course one does not want to read this line mechanically, stressing every second syllable, it is appropriate here (as rarely elsewhere in poetry) to stress the prepositions ("up" and "at") as well as the more obviously important words, "silence" and "stars."

A "Voices and Visions" videocassette of Walt Whitman is available from Longman Publishers.

CAROLYN FORCHÉ

The Colonel (p. 749)

"The Colonel" comes from a book of poems. You may want to talk about the rather undefined genre of the prose poem. A prose poem looks like prose but is marked by a strong rhythm (often gained by repetition of grammatical constructions) and sometimes by abundant imagery. (The idea is that the chief characteristics of poetry are rhythm and imagery, and so a short piece of prose with these features can be called a prose poem.) Having said this, we must add that we don't think there is much point in worrying about whether "The Colonel" is poetry or prose.

Much of "The Colonel" probably is literally true. During one of her stays in El Salvador, Forché may indeed have visited a colonel, and he may have said and done exactly what this colonel says and does. Until we are told that the ear "came alive" when dropped into the glass of water, there is nothing unbelievable in "The Colonel," partly, of course, because television has informed us that atrocities are committed daily.

Forché's first sentence ("What you have heard is true") suggests that the speaker is addressing someone who has just said, "I heard that you visited

Colonel ————. Did you really? What was it like?" We get details about what seems to be a comfortable bourgeois existence ("daily papers, pet dogs") and also some menacing details ("a pistol on the cushion beside him," "Broken bottles were embedded in the walls"), all told in the same flat, matter-of-fact voice. The sixth sentence uses a metaphor ("The moon swung bare on its black cord over the house"), but even journalists are allowed to use an occasional metaphor, and a reader probably does not think twice about Forché's metaphor here, except perhaps to notice that it uses the same structure ("The moon swung bare . . .") as the previous, factual sentences ("I was," "His wife carried," "His daughter filed," "There were"). Again, for the most part the language is flat; when the speaker next uses a metaphor (the ears are "like dried peach halves") she (or he) flatly apologizes for this flight of fancy: "There is no other way to say this." But the next-to-last sentence takes us into a metaphorical (or mysterious) world: "Some of the ears on the floor caught this scrap of his voice."

Much of the power of "The Colonel" comes from the contrast between the picture of the colonel's bourgeois private life (pets, television, lamb, wine, etc.) and his brutal public life, a contrast that Forché emphasizes by not commenting on it (i.e., by allowing the reader to make the comment). The piece is masterful in what it doesn't say. The colonel asks how the visitor "enjoyed the country," but we don't hear the response. We can, however, guess it by what follows: "There was some talk then of how difficult it had become to govern." Presumably the colonel becomes annoyed with the visitor's comments, though at first we aren't told this in so many words. Instead we are told what the colonel did (he got a sack of ears, dumped them on the table, shook one in the faces of his guests, dropped it in a glass of water). Then we hear him: "I am tired of fooling around. . . . As for the rights of anyone, tell your people they can go fuck themselves." Irked but (as we see it) enormously confident, he says of the severed ears, "Something for your poetry, no?" Students might be invited to comment on the tone the colonel uses here. Is he complacent, wry, naive, or what?

Students might also be invited to comment on the last two sentences of "The Colonel." Does the next-to-last sentence indicate (let's say symbolically) that the oppressed people of the country know what is going on, and will ultimately triumph? Does the last sentence ("Some of the ears on the floor were pressed to the ground") mean that (1) some of the ears were pressed, presumably by being stood on, and (2) the dead were listening (and presumably waiting to be avenged)?

Forché is the editor of *Against Forgetting: Twentieth Century Poetry of Witness* (1993), a powerful collection of poems on politics, war, torture, repression, death, exile.

19

Students Writing about Poems

LOUISE GLÜCK

Gretel in Darkness (p. 754)

In *New Voices in American Poetry*, ed. David Allan Evans (1973, 106), Glück comments on her poem:

> To Hansel the escape from the forest was a means to an end: a future. To Gretel the escape is an end in itself. No moment in the ordinary existence she made possible by killing the witch and rescuing her brother can touch for her the moment of the escape. That moment was her triumph: it provided Gretel with an opportunity to experience herself as powerful. The whole episode, the drama in the forest, remains for her charged and present. It is in that episode that she wishes to imbed herself. Unfortunately, she is alone in this desire. Their adventure grows increasingly remote to Hansel, presumably because the new life answers his needs. The Gretel of the poem perceives, and passionately wishes to alter, the discrepancy between her investment in the forest and Hansel's.

Students might continue their study of Glück by reading *The First Four Books of Poems* (1995), which brings together separate volumes of her work published from 1969 to 1985. Another important book is Glück's *Proofs and Theories* (1994), a collection of essays on the art of poetry that includes commentary on the autobiographical sources for a number of her poems. The best interpretations of Glück's verse can be found in Helen Vendler, *The Music of What Happens* (1988) and *Soul Says* (1995).

ADRIENNE RICH

Aunt Jennifer's Tigers (p. 761)

We think that Fuentes does a very good job of discussing Adrienne Rich's poem. True, she doesn't say *everything* possible about it (she might, for instance, have commented on the unusual word "denizens," or on the "chivalric certainty" of the tigers), but we think she makes important points, especially the connection between the screen as a work of art and the poem (another work of art). This point in fact is implicit from the outset, in Fuentes's title, where the balance (X and Y) implies an equivalence.

We happen to like, also, the slight personal touch ("What especially pleases me . . ."), which for the most part is combined with a relatively impersonal style. If you and your students are concerned with the question of how personal an essay should be, you may want to discuss this essay as one kind of example. Obviously essays can be more personal than this one, and less personal, but we think this essay strikes a good balance. Notice that in the final sentence, for instance, the language seems impersonal (there is no "I") but in fact strong opinions about the poem and about society are being conveyed.

20

Poets at Work

WALT WHITMAN

Enfans d'Adam, number 9 (p. 787)

Recent studies of Whitman's work have given detailed attention to Whitman as a gay poet. These studies include Michael Moon, *Disseminating Whitman: Revision and Corporeality in* Leaves of Grass (1991) and Byrne R. S. Fone, *Masculine Landscapes: Walt Whitman and the Homoerotic Text* (1992), as well as a number of essays included in *Breaking Bounds: Whitman and American Cultural Studies* edited by Betsy Erkkila and Jay Grossman (1996). But it is not entirely clear what the term "gay poet" means. Does it mean that Whitman was a gay man who wrote poetry, or that he was a gay man who wrote in a style and with a content that we a century and a half later identify as "gay"? If he is a gay poet in this second sense, is he one all of the time in all of his poems or, instead, in only a number of them, where gay themes and subjects are treated explicitly? And if he is a gay poet, how much or how little does this fact alter our response to his many poems about the love between men and women?

It is difficult, then, to know for certain what it means and implies when we describe Whitman as a gay poet. But it is an important sign of change for the better in Whitman studies, and in literary and cultural studies more generally, that the issue of Whitman's sexuality, and the homosexual and homoerotic dimensions of his poetry, are now part of the critical conversation. When we studied Whitman in college and graduate school many years ago, this topic did not arise at all. Whitman was read and valued as the great poet of American democracy, who celebrates the splendor of all persons and embraces them with equal warmth and grandeur. He is still *that* poet, but now we also recognize and can discuss in the classroom the ways in which his sexual views, feelings, and attitudes are part of his democratic inclusiveness.

"Once I Passed Through a Populous City," in its published version, describes the love between a man and a woman. It is passionate and very intense, and it is a daring poem in the type of relationship that it portrays. The man and the woman are not married; rather, they met "casually" in a city and enjoyed a deep and sexually charged connection with one another. The speaker now seems to have separated from the woman; "we *were* together," he says, and he has forgotten "all else" besides the powerful erotic bond that existed between them. But then, surprisingly, it appears they are still together after all: "Again we wander. . . . Again she holds me by the hand. . . ." But the point, we think, is not that the man and woman are together, but, rather, that the speaker's memory of her is so vivid, so immediate to him, that it is as if she is still present—so much so that the speaker vows to himself that he must not go away from her. Which presumably, however, he has done.

This poem fits very well in the *Enfans d'Adam* (Children of Adam) section of *Leaves of Grass* (1860 ed.), a series of poems that explore, brood upon, and rhapsodize about heterosexual love. It is therefore all the more striking to study the poem in its manuscript version, where we can see that Whitman first conceived of it as a poem about two men. In the manuscript he wrote "only a man" and "that youth" (crossed out) and "one rude and ignorant man," but then he chose for the published poem "that woman" and "she holds me."

Some critics have speculated that perhaps Whitman was fearful about making the relationship depicted in the published poem a homosexual one. On the other hand, in other poems that he did publish he is very open and explicit, often quite beautifully, about love, including physical love, between men. Indeed, some of the poems in the *Calamus* section of *Leaves of Grass*— poems that express the rapture and heartache of "manly love"—are among the most moving he ever wrote. It is possible that he switched the gender from man to woman for "Once I Passed Through a Populous City" not because of moral and literary timidity, but because he needed another heterosexual poem for the *Enfans d'Adam* section.

It is worth remembering that in Whitman's era, intense same-sex friendships were very common and very important in the culture, and the men and women involved in them typically expressed their feelings in language that strikes us as highly erotic—and as evidence that the men were gay and the women lesbian. But of course we are looking back on lives that led in a pre-Freudian era; according to the *Oxford English Dictionary*, the first usage of the word "homosexual" was not until 1892, which, coincidentally, was the year of Whitman's death. We like to think of ourselves as far more sexually tolerant than those who lived in earlier decades, and for the most part we are probably right. But it is also true that in the nineteenth-century, in Whitman's America, many men and women were comfortable with and proud of same-sex relationships; these seemed quite normal and natural to them.

Late in life, Whitman recalled that Ralph Waldo Emerson had told him that some of the poems in *Leaves of Grass* were too graphic sexually, too explicit in the erotic phrases and images they used. Emerson went on to urge Whitman to revise or delete these poems from the book. But Emerson, interestingly, was referring to the poems in *Enfans d'Adam* about love between men and women. He said nothing about the *Calamus* poems, which may have seemed to him fairly conventional, not unsettling or shocking at all. It was *Enfans d'Adam*, and similar poems elsewhere in *Leaves of Grass*, that upset many readers and led in 1882 to the banning in Boston of Whitman's book.

One approach to the manuscript and published poem of "Once I Passed Through a Populous City" is to consider the change from the love between two men to the love between a man and a woman, the change from a "gay" poem to a "straight" one. But as our comments here suggest, we think that this approach, while worthwhile as a starting point, is insufficient and perhaps even misleading. We are mistaken if we fail to consider Whitman as a gay poet and also mistaken if we think of him as *only* that. The Whitman scholar James E. Miller, Jr., in an essay included in *The Chief Glory of Every People: Essays on Classic American Writers*, ed. Matthew J. Bruccoli (1973), refers to this poet's "omnisexual vision," and there is much to be said for this capacious, open-minded, and open-hearted phrase as the best one for Whitman.

CATHY SONG

Out of Our Hands (p. 788)

In class when we talk about any work of literature we almost always find ourselves discussing the title. The issue can be raised at any point during the discussion, but since the title is what the reader sees first, a discussion of the title can easily be used at the outset, to get the class going. Why is the work called X and not Y?

The draft is untitled, and when we first read it we thought that the opening line, "Out of a hat," would make a fine title, with its associations of magicians who pull rabbits out of hats. In our view, the line foreshadows the element of magic, of wonder, that the poem is concerned with, the magic of words— their power to touch us, to influence our behavior—and the magic of friendship, again with the power to influence us. You may want to ask students if they can think of any quotations about the power of words. In our experience, someone almost always comes up with Edward Bulwer-Lytton's line (though they don't know the author), "The pen is mightier than the sword." (Somewhat pedantically we note here that this line affords a nice opportunity to talk about metonymy, "pen" standing for ideas expressed through words, and "sword" standing for military activity.) One student said she recalled something relevant from N. Scott Momaday's *The Way to Rainy Mountain* but of course she could only paraphrase it roughly. At the next meeting of the class she produced the quotation, which gave rise to a stimulating discussion: "A word has power in and of itself. It comes from nothing into sound and meaning; it gives origin to all things. By means of a word can a man deal with the world on equal terms. And the word is sacred."

We have not yet found a student who was familiar with Franz Kafka's "A book must be the axe for the frozen sea inside us," but you may want to introduce this quotation (from a letter Kafka wrote), especially since it nicely sees the work of literature as itself a weapon, and in this case a weapon used on oneself, i.e., a device that frees us from the clichés we normally live by. As for the magic of friendship, Song touches on this in the passage we quote in the biographical note, where she comments on her respect and affection for Wing Tek Lum, and on his influence on her.

A second association that "Out of a hat" initially set up in our minds was generated by the second line, "on a piece of paper." For a moment we thought we were witnessing a lottery of some sort. The idea is not pursued in the poem but it too is harmonious with the mysteries of chance encounters.

But Cathy Song chose *not* to call the poem "Out of a Hat"; rather she calls it "Out of Our Hands," and these words set up a different but related train of thought. When we say, "It's out of my hands," we are saying that other powers will shape the ending of whatever is in question. Perhaps the most potent use of related words is Jesus's "Father, into thy hands I commend my spirit" (Luke 23.46), but even the most trivial use of the phrase, "out of my hands," suggests that powers, perhaps incalculable, are at work. So this line, too, gets at the magic that Song is concerned with.

The idea of magic continues in the second and third stanzas of the revised poem, where the letters dismantle the air (in the draft, the letters themselves dismantle "in the air," but in the revised version they dismantle the air itself, i.e., they strip or take apart the sky, displacing the sky with the message), forming "the bird / seeds of a language" that the poet "needed to know." Song in her note, you will recall, says, "The images of birds and flight, children and language have everything to do with the way gifts are given and received— serendipitous and yet, there are no coincidences." The birds reappear in the starlings of line 22, and perhaps even in the down-to-earth final line, with its celebration of "the glorious color of chicken fat." Query: The name "Wing" (the poem is dedicated to Wing Tek Lum) is a fairly common Chinese name, but can we say that it too is part of the poem's bird imagery? Probably no one who speaks Chinese would think so, but readers who do not know Chinese may notice (or invent) a connection.

Line 31, "The poem a subversive act," may be especially provocative. We assume that Song has in mind something of the sort that we have already introduced with the quotation from Kafka, so here we give a fuller form of that quotation:

> We need the books that wound and stab us. . . . We need the books that affect us like a disaster, that grieve us deeply, like the death of someone we loved more than ourselves, like being banished into forests far from everyone, like a suicide. A book must be the axe for the frozen sea inside us.

This is strong stuff, and students may protest that they do not read books in order to be grieved. But with a little help they probably can at least give some consideration to the idea books are a part of education, and education involves seeing things that we hadn't seen before, or seeing things more clearly. At this point (if you are lucky) a student may mention Plato's "Myth of the Cave," with its wonderful image of people who, when they first leave the cave and enter the daylight are pained by the light and would eagerly return to the cave, where they saw only shadows, not reality. To put it bluntly, growing pains are a part of education. In the case of the speaker of Song's poem, the poetry of Wing Tek Lum helped her to celebrate Chinese identity.

Cathy Song's books of poetry include *Picture Bride* (1983); *Frameless Windows: Squares of Light* (1988); and *School Figures* (1995). For critical discussion, see Gayle K. Fujita-Sato, "'Third World' as Place and Paradigm in Cathy Song's *Picture Bride*," *MELUS* 15:1 (Spring 1988): 49–72; and Patricia Wallace, "Divided Loyalties: Literal and Literary in the Poetry of Lorna Dee Cervantes, Cathy Song, and Rita Dove," *MELUS* 18:3 (Fall 1993): 3–19.

WILLIAM BUTLER YEATS

Three Versions of *Leda and the Swan* (p. 789)

Before we briefly talk about the differences among the three versions, we want to say something about rape in mythology and in art and literature.

Probably twenty years ago most people would have taught this poem without fretting about the possibility that Yeats is insufficiently concerned about the victim of the rape. Indeed, amazing though it sounds, discussions of the story of Leda—we are not talking about Yeats's poem, but about the legend—commonly did *not* use the word "rape." A standard handbook of mythology on our shelves, Michael Grant and John Hazel's *Gods and Mortals in Classical Mythology* (1973)—a book that announces it is a "Merriam-Webster Reference Book"—tells the reader that "Zeus seduced Leda" (423). This book and virtually all others of the same sort, in speaking of Zeus's assaults on Leda, Io, Europa, and others (usually female, but don't forget Ganymede), use a variety of euphemisms: he "made love" to them, he "seduced" them, he "pursued" them, he "took" them. Occasionally the books will say that he "abducted" X or Y or Z, but only very rarely that he "raped" someone. (The same euphemisms are used of rapes committed by other gods: Hades "took" Persephone, and Apollo "pursued" Daphne.) Consider Richard J. Finneran's astounding note on "Leda and the Swan" in his valuable edition of *The Poems of W. B. Yeats* (1983): "In classical mythology, the god Zeus comes to the mortal Leda in the form of a swan" (652). Comparably sanitized (and preposterous) language is used by the editors of *The Norton Anthology*, 6th ed. (1993), in their footnote to the poem: "In Greek mythology Zeus visited Leda in the form of a swan" (2: 1884).

The authors of the handbooks were perhaps being cautious—they knew that their books would be in school libraries—but, like Finneran, they were also simply reflecting the thought of the period. Speaking a bit broadly we can say that from the Renaissance onward much of the violence of the ancient myths has been reduced. For instance, in Leonardo's *Leda and the Swan* (the original painting is lost, but a copy exists), Leda stands, caressing the swan's neck while she smiles and gazes at two eggs on the ground, from each of which has emerged a pair of twins. Admittedly a swan for a father is a bit odd, but on the whole the picture shows a happy family. In Michelangelo's lost painting (again, copies exist and Yeats in fact owned a photographic reproduction), a recumbent and apparently relaxed Leda is kissed by a swan. As Diane Wolfthal points out in *Images of Rape* (1999), even paintings that do show more violence, such as Titian's *Rape of Europa* and Giambologna's *Rape of the Sabine Women*, were likely to be discussed in terms of color and composition. The emphasis, Wolfthal rightly says, was on the genius of the male artist, not on the emotions of the depicted women.

It's hard to speak authoritatively concerning the ancient view of rape (for one thing, "the ancient view" covers several centuries and, for a second, such evidence as there is is not entirely coherent), but it does seem as though these rapes (including Zeus's rape of Ganymede) were presented from the god's point of view: A human being was done the great honor of being brought into the realm of the gods, of being united with a god. Whether one can present this idea convincingly in class is a question; it may be of a piece with the quaint idea that whites conferred a blessing on black Africans by enslaving them and thereby freeing them from idolatry.

There is a further difficulty. Students may say that Yeats is saying that women don't mind (and perhaps even enjoy) being raped. After all, in line 6 in all three versions he speaks of Leda's "loosening thighs." We can only suggest that Yeats is speaking about one particular mythological episode, not about rape in general or women in general. We do not want to minimize the violence of the poem. Yeats emphasizes the violence, as one can see by comparing the opening lines: In the first version we get "Now can the swooping Godhead have his will," which is fairly strong but is weak compared to the second version, "A rush, a sudden wheel, and hovering still / The bird descends." Even this opening, however, is mild compared with the shocking violence of the final version: "A sudden blow." And in the fifth line of each version, Yeats speaks of Leda's "terrified" fingers that seek to push the bird away from her.

How to help students to see that Yeats is not condoning rape and is not saying that Leda participated in her own violation? The attack is sudden—Leda is taken so unawares that she can scarcely resist. All three versions ask a question, "How can those terrified vague fingers push / The feathered glory from her loosening thighs?" But the question is rhetorical; the only possible answer is that her fingers cannot push the swan away, since the attack was unforeseen and the bird's grip is firm. Caught (in the final version) between the "beating" wings of the first line and the "beating" heart of the eighth line, i.e., locked within the octave, her "loosening thighs" yield to "the feathered glory" and to "that white rush." With the "shudder in the loins" Zeus and Leda generate Helen and the Trojan War and the death of Agamemnon.

Still, even though Leda is presented as a victim, and Zeus is not the rapist lurking in the park but a supernatural power, students may have difficulty seeing the poem as something more than a presentation of a rape. Here is an approach that we have been thinking about and that we may conceivably try out in the classroom the next time we teach the poem. (But by the time that you read this, we may have abandoned the idea.) St. Paul in Acts 9.3–8 speaks of his sudden vision of Jesus, and in 2 Corinthians 12.2 he says he was "caught up to the third heaven," i.e., taken into paradise. Paul's enforced visit to paradise is commonly spoken of as "The Rapture of Paul," *rapture* here being defined as "the transportation of a person, especially to heaven." The word, which can also mean "the state of being transported by a lofty emotion," comes from the same Latin word that gives us *rape*. The Latin word also gives us *rapt* (in a state of deep delight or absorption). Now, we are not saying that because the Latin *rapere* (to seize) is at the root of several English words, and some of these words have favorable meanings, all of them therefore must have favorable meanings. Rather, we are saying that the rape of Leda may somewhat resemble the rapture of Paul, where a mortal suddenly, violently, encountered divinity. So shattering was Paul's vision of Jesus that he became temporarily blind, and for three days he neither ate nor drank. Caravaggio's great painting, circa 1601, is relevant. Whereas earlier painters had usually shown Jesus descending through the clouds, surrounded by angels, Caravaggio shows us Paul on his back on the ground. The experience of encountering Jesus has knocked him off his horse and now, sprawled on his back, his legs spread and his arms helplessly outstretched, the divine light strikes his body. At this point we may recall Yeats's comment, printed in our headnote in the text: "Then I thought, 'Nothing is now possible but some movement, or birth from above, preceded by some violent annunciation.'" When God or a god makes use of a mortal, things are not easy for the mortal.

Yeats's use of "annunciation" reminds us that he associated the beginning of a new age with the combination of the divine and the bestial; in "The Magi," for instance, Yeats speaks of "The uncontrollable mystery on the bestial floor," and in "The Second Coming" he asks, "And what rough beast, its hour come round at last, / Slouches towards Bethlehem to be born?"

If you have read thus far, you have been patient, but we are still not ready to comment on the drafts. We want to mention that much has been published on pictorial sources for the poem. Neither Leonardo's nor Michelangelo's picture of Leda is especially close to the poem; indeed, the Leonardo, with its standing Leda who caresses the swan, is very far from the poem. These pictures, and several others, are reproduced in Giorgio Melchiori, *The Whole Mystery of Art* (1960). In the *Times Literary Supplement* for July 20, 1962, 532, Charles Madge published a bas relief of the rape, exhibited in the British Museum—a favorite haunt of Yeats's—and published an illustration of it with his article. (It is also published in the first volume of Elie Faure's *History of Art*, English translation 1920, which Yeats owned.) Madge points out that in ancient art there seems to have been two traditions, one showing Leda "recumbent and acquiescent" and the other showing her "standing and . . . being taken by force." The British Museum relief is of the second type. The swan is pressing his bill against the standing Leda's neck, forcing her face against his breast, and he has encircled her legs with his feet. Interestingly, whereas the first version of the poem specifies that the swan has "bowed her face upon his breast," as in the relief, by the final version this detail has been replaced by "He holds her helpless breast upon his breast." Madge points out that the relief is not consistent with the "stretched body" mentioned later in the poem, but he says, quite reasonably, "Perhaps the poet has carried the scene a stage farther in his imagination to a point where the girl has been forced backwards on to the ground."

We don't doubt that Yeats could have seen (and probably did see) the British Museum sculpture, but we think that another source is equally likely. Charles B. Gullans, in an article in *TLS*, November 9, 1962, 864, reproduces a bookplate showing Leda and the swan, a woodcut, that Yeats's friend T. Sturge Moore designed for A. G. B. Russell. It was first published in *Modern Woodcutters, No. 3: T. Sturge Moore* (1921). Moore had designed bookplates for Yeats and for Yeats's father, so it is easy to believe that Yeats was familiar with the bookplate his friend designed for another friend. In this image Leda's face is not exactly bowed upon the breast of the swan (as in line 4 of the first version), but the swan's neck encircles Leda's neck, and her "helpless thighs" (draft, 2) are certainly "pressed / By the webbed toes" (2–3). Last words about visual sources for the poem: Yeats probably was familiar with all of the images mentioned, and with others, but there is no reason to believe that any one image played an especially significant role.

Incidentally, for a rich range of uses of the story in literature and in art, see the entry on Leda in *The Oxford Guide to Classical Mythology*.

Now for some comments on the three versions. The opening quatrain gave Yeats the most trouble ("nothing so difficult as a beginning," Byron said, and all writers know), and dissatisfied him the most. The relatively slow opening of the first version ("Now can the swooping Godhead have his will") in the second version is greatly speeded up: "A rush, a sudden wheel, and hovering still / The bird descends"). Notice, too, that the explicit reference to the "Godhead" disappears, perhaps because Yeats came to think it was too inflated and in any case unnecessary. The "helpless thighs" of the second line become "frail thighs" in the second version, and simply "thighs" in the final version because, perhaps, Yeats came to feel that the contrast between "frail thighs" and "all-powerful bill" was too obvious. It is not until the final version that we get "the staggering girl" (line 2) and "helpless breast." That is, Yeats deletes the relatively sentimental word "frail," and so far as Leda goes, he tells us only that she is "staggering" and that the swan "holds her helpless breast upon his breast." "The webbed toes" of the third line in the first version remain in the second, but in the final version they are replaced by the much more evocative "dark webs" which suggest mystery ("dark") and entrapment ("web"). Part of the mystery is that "A shudder in the loins"—a very brief action—can engender a tragic history of humanly unimaginable but inevitable painful and yet glorious consequences ("The broken wall, the burning roof and tower / And Agamemnon dead"), and part of the mystery is in the poet's unanswered question ("Did she put on his knowledge with his power"). The two earlier questions in the poem were rhetorical: "How can those terrified vague fingers push / The feathered glory from her loosening thighs?" and "And how can body, laid in that white rush, / But feel the strange heart beating where it lies?" The question that ends the poem, however, is unanswerable. If pressed for an answer, we would say, first, "No, she did not acquire Zeus's knowledge. Why would the victim of a sexual assault learn anything about the future?" And yet the very fact that Yeats raises the question, so different from the earlier rhetorical questions, makes us modify this response and makes us entertain the possibility that somehow Leda did understand that this astounding union would have astounding consequences. We may say of this question what Sir Thomas Browne said of other mysteries: "What song the Sirens sang, or what name Achilles assumed when he hid himself among women, though puzzling questions, are not beyond all conjecture." Conjecture, yes; decisive answer, no.

In short, the second version extensively rewrites the first four lines of the poem but retains the rest except for some changes in punctuation and for a revision of line 13. In the draft, 13 is "Did nothing pass before her in the air?"; in the second version it becomes "Did she put on his knowledge with his power," and this revision is retained in the final version. Interestingly, the off-rhyme of "up" and "drop" in lines 12 and 15, indicating Zeus's post-coital weariness or indifference now that he has finished using Leda, was present even in the first version. Speaking of the last line, notice, too, that in all three versions "beak" is used, and "bill" is used in the third line of each version. Why the change (putting aside the matter of rhyme)? We take "beak" to be more menacing than "bill," and so our guess is that Yeats wanted to suggest, even after the culmination of the act that Alexander Pope called "the fierce embrace," the violent character of the god.

If the glimpse of Zeus's mental condition at the end of the poem was present even in the first version, so too was the *absence* of any inner presentation of Zeus in the octave. For the most part we get what seems to be an objective view of the episode, though in speaking of Leda's "terrified vague fingers" (line 5 in all versions) we do get into Leda's mind, and we also see things from her point of view in "that white rush" and perhaps even in "The feathered glory," though this last expression celebrates Zeus. Still, the impression on the whole is objective—first a report of a past event in the present tense, and then, at the very end, a distancing of the event by putting it into the past ("Did she" and "could let her drop") and by asking a mysterious question.

Camille Paglia, in *Break, Blow, Burn* (2005), offers a reading—sometimes unconventional—of the poem. We quote two passages.

> Neither Zeus nor Leda is named in the text itself, so that the scene becomes archetypal: the poem records a pivotal moment of contact between humanity and divinity. The exchange is painfully one-sided but revelatory: "mastered by the brute blood of the air," Leda sees God for what he is—a sadistic marauder, as tarnished as a fallen angel (3). Sated, the swan lets her "drop" from his "indifferent beak," a curt phrase that accentuates her cumbersome materiality. . . . Losing interest, God callously discards his toys. . . .
>
> Visually, the last stanza's jagged pattern resembles a thunderbolt, Zeus's emblem. Yeats has projected himself into Leda's story: he wrote elsewhere, "We who are poets and artists . . . live but for the moment when vision comes to our weariness like terrible lightning, in the humility of the brutes" (*Per Amica Silentia Lunae*). . . . (115–18)

A *final point*: Yeats, an endless reviser of his work, in the 1908 edition of his *Collected Works* urged his readers not to search for his unpublished material.

Accursed who brings to light of day
The writings I have thrown away!
But blessed be he that stirs them not
And lets the kind worm take the lot.

But he didn't reprint the lines after 1908, perhaps because he thought they were not worth printing, or perhaps because he had changed his mind.

See *W. B. Yeats: The Poems*, 2nd ed., ed. Richard J. Finneran (1997), vol. 1 of *The Collected Works of W. B. Yeats*; this volume includes detailed "explanatory notes" for each poem. Biographies include A. Norman Jeffares, *W. B. Yeats: A New Biography* (1988), and R. F. Foster, *W. B. Yeats: A Life, The Apprentice Mage 1865–1914* (1997). Two rewarding books for students: A. Norman Jeffares, *A New Commentary on the Poems of W. B. Yeats* (1984), and *Critical Essays on W. B. Yeats*, ed. Richard J. Finneran (1986). Still useful, too, are two books by Richard Ellmann, *Yeats: The Man and the Masks* (1948) and *The Identity of Yeats* (1954). Some students might be interested in examining the *Variorum Edition* of Yeats's poems, ed. P. Allt and R. K. Allspach (1957).

21

Variations on Themes:
Poems and Paintings

JANE FLANDERS

Van Gogh's Bed (p. 796)

Ms. Flanders has kindly furnished us with some remarks about her poem. She writes:

> The desire for simplicity [expressed in van Gogh's letters] would seem to be at the heart of the painting. Likewise the poem is "simple," even crude, especially the stubby first line of each stanza with its list of rudimentary adjectives. But what we are given, in both instances, is, of course, the illusion of simplicity. In the painting the room ought to seem restful. Actually it excites the eye with its bright colors, bold strokes, and odd angles. Even the bed itself looks as if it might levitate or drive off like some magical conveyance. A childlike playfulness invites the poet's reverie.
>
> By what wonderful process was it made? What did he dream about when he slept in it? The artist's absence (the empty bed) which may at first seem innocuous or self-evident (he's busy painting the picture, isn't he?) also reminds us that he would have his first mental crisis a few months later and his suicide at the age of thirty-seven was little more than a year away. Likewise, in the poem's final stanza, concrete details give way to something more elusive—light, fragrance, and not happiness itself, but the memory of happiness, with its hint of loss and melancholy.

We hope we are not being presumptuous if we add a few remarks of our own.

1. Using the title as the beginning—the reader more or less has to go back and repeat the title at the start of each stanza—is unusual, interesting, and witty.

2. The bed is orange, "like Cinderella's coach." The coach, of course, was a transformed pumpkin (hence orange), and transforming things is what artists do.

3. The coach-pumpkin-sun image continues into the second stanza, where van Gogh is conceived as being carried "bumpily to the ball." Possibly the idea is that the pumpkin-coach carries him also toward the sun, i.e., he is brought violently toward one of his chief subjects.

4. Although we get some violence in the second stanza ("slept alone, tossing," "bumpily"), in the third stanza we get a glimpse of the "friendly . . . peasant" world that he moved in. If there is violence here ("beat") it is for good domestic purposes ("beat the mattress till it rose like meringue").

5. The last stanza begins a bit desolately ("empty") but immediately is filled with nature ("morning light pours in"), nature transformed by human beings ("wine"), nature and humanity ("fragrance"), and humanity ("the memory of happiness").

ADRIENNE RICH

Mourning Picture (p. 799)

Edwin Romanzo Elmer's painting has something of the stiffness that one associates with Sunday painters, who until the 1970s were called primitive painters. These painters lacked formal training in art, and as a consequence they were likely to be unskilled in linear perspective and in other ways of suggesting gradual recession in space. They were, however, usually deeply concerned with their own sort of realism, with (for instance) depicting all four legs of a cow because, after all, most cows *do* have four legs—even though in fact in certain positions a leg or two might be invisible. Another characteristic of the work of Sunday painters is that the figures seem posed, as though a photographer using a slow film had arranged his subjects and then told them to be sure not to move.

In fact, Elmer, a native of rural Massachusetts, did receive some formal training in New York at the Academy of Design, but this undated painting probably antedates his stay in New York.

Rich's poem seems to us to have something of the painting's almost unnatural specificity. For instance, the first line is careful to tell us—in a rather flat, unemotional, and yet rather solemn tone—that the chair is mahogany and that the rocker is cane: "They have carried the mahogany chair and the cane rocker / out under the lilac bush. . . ." But if the speaker's voice is akin to the world of the painting, matter-of-fact and yet hyper-keen (unblinking one might say) and otherworldly, these qualities are especially appropriate, since the speaker is the dead girl. That is, the speaker sees things as, in a way, they are but in a way that is not quite natural. For instance, she speaks of "the map of every lilac leaf." When you think of it, leaves do resemble maps because of their veins, but the perception seems unnatural, a sort of perception through a magnifying glass. (By the way, another of Elmer's paintings shows a landscape as seen not simply through a window but through a magnifying glass perched on a vase on a table.)

We don't want to overemphasize the strangeness of the voice, however; the perception of the maplike leaf leads to a more usual perception, "the net of veins on my father's / grief-tranced hand." This chain continues in lines 25–26 with the image of silk thread, which in 27 becomes "a web in the dew." But what exactly do we make of 25, "the silk-spool will run bare"? These words constitute the end of a sentence about the grieving mother; we might have thought that the silk spool would remain unconsumed, that is, the mother might have put away her domestic work when the child died. But Rich tells us, on the contrary, that the "silk-spool will run bare," possibly suggesting the three fates, who spin, measure, and cut a thread, thereby ending a person's life.

After writing the preceding paragraph, with its conjecture about the silk-spool, we came across an article about Elmer, written by his niece, Maud Valona Elmer (*Massachusetts Review* 6 [1964–65]: 121–44). She mentions that as a boy Elmer worked in a spool-silk factory (presumably a factory that wound silk thread on spools, or perhaps a factory that prepared silk to be wound on spools). She also mentions that after the death of their daughter, Elmer and his wife left the house shown in the picture and went to live with the wife's mother, in Baptist Corner (cf. line 24). Since other information about Edwin Romanzo Elmer is virtually nonexistent, one can safely say that the article in *Massachusetts Review*—and of course the painting, which the niece sold to the Smith College Museum of Art—inspired Rich to write the poem.

The veins of the leaf become, in line 29, the "skeleton" of the leaf, thereby continuing the death imagery and continuing, too, the somewhat strange quality of the imagery. This strangeness is evident, too, in the "shadowless" house (31), shadowless because the time is noonday (31), when the sun is directly above us, but also "shadowless" because death and sadness have not yet come to the house. At the end of the poem the speaker (we think, but we are far from certain) says that if she recreated the world she—having experienced death—could not leave out death from what had seemed an idyllic world, a world of loving parents, placid sheep, and a doll to be cared for.

One other point: We learn from Maud Valona Elmer's article that the lamb in the picture indicates that the child is dead. In old New England cemeteries the tombstones of children are sometimes adorned with a lamb, suggesting that the deceased was "a Lamb of God."

Having said all this, we still remain unsure about the poem, but here are the main lines of our thought:

1. In "Mourning Picture," Effie describes Elmer's picture. In the first stanza she sees that "they" (probably the parents, possibly servants, but it doesn't matter) have carried out the chair and the rocker, that the parents "darkly sit there," the house "stands fast," the doll lies in her pram. She sees the mourning, but interestingly she does not see herself, with the lamb, the largest figures in the picture. Effie believes that she could remake (like the artist) every particle of that world ("I could remake . . . [I could] draw out"), but does not.

2. The second stanza describes Effie's present self, which we are inclined to think means in the hours after death, while she (the shade of the dead) still inhabits the house. What she experiences is that "the dream condenses." (Life here, as at the poem's end, is a dream.) It doesn't vanish yet. During this period, while the family mourns, she is "visible and invisible / remembering and remembered."

3. In the last stanza she foresees her parents' future. She imagines making the world "again" (line 28) but will not. Her death ("*this*") is part of her life. She remains "Effie"; "you" (meaning her parents, the painter, the reader?) are *her* dream.

CATHY SONG

Beauty and Sadness (p. 801)

The poem concerns the unhappy artist who creates enduring beauty. In some versions, the artist creates beauty *because* he or she is unhappy, as the oyster creates a pearl out of its discomfort, and this apparently is what Song is suggesting when she says that the "inconsolable" Utamaro—inconsolable presumably because the women were "indifferent" (line 41)—"graced these women with immortality" (49). We can go a little further and say that when she speaks of "the dwarfed and bespectacled painter" (52) Song implies the Freudian idea of the artist who, suffering from unsatisfied longings, engages in fantasy wish-fulfillment—in this case, making pictures of the beauties he cannot in reality win. Speaking more generally, we can say that Song's poem touches on the venerable theme of *ars longa, vita brevis*.

A few notes: The term *ukiyo* originally was a Buddhist term for "the world of suffering," i.e., the fleeting, transient world of incarnation, but in Japan in the late seventeenth century, by means of a pun, it became "the floating world," i.e., the world of transient pleasure. (The pronunciation is the same, but the initial character is different.) Pictures of the floating world—e.g., of women and of actors—are called *ukiyo-e*. In Song's poem notice "floating world" in line 26, and "fleeting loveliness" in line 13. In line 12, "transfer" probably alludes on the literal level to the thin paper on which the artist drew his design. This paper, placed on the block, provided the carver with a guide for cutting.

CARL PHILLIPS

Luncheon on the Grass (p. 802)

We'll begin with a few comments about the painting. According to a contemporary, Manet said, "I'm told that I must do a nude. All right. I will. Back in our studio days, I copied Georgione's women. . . . I'm going to do it over." (The picture that he copied in the Louvre, *The Concert*, is now attributed to Titian.) Manet, regarded as "a painter of modern life" (a term Baudelaire used for slightly earlier realists such as Daumier), chose to do a nude in a modern setting, not in a classical or renaissance setting. Further, it is impossible to give to Manet's naked woman the allegorical implications (ideal beauty, truth, nature, etc.) that customarily were attributed to the nudes of earlier painters. But what is one to make of a nude who cannot be regarded as a part of secular or sacred history (e.g., Bathsheba) or mythology (e.g., Venus) or allegory (e.g., Beauty, or Virtue, or whatever)? A nude of the older sort is acceptable to a bourgeois audience because of its "higher meaning"; on the other hand, a nude who is only a naked woman, a woman stripped in the presence of clothed males, is a problem for the viewer who claims he or she (but it is usually a he) is engaging in a lofty aesthetic experience, looking at art, not at pornography.

We don't want to spend much more space on the painting; pretty much all that needs to be known about it is admirably set forth in Robert L.

Herbert's *Impressionism* (1988). The three figures at the left are unquestionably derived from an engraving (where they appear as two nude sea gods, and a nude nymph) by Marcantonio Raimondi, based on a lost painting by Raphael of *The Judgment of Paris* (c. 1520). (The engraving, like the Georgione or Titian, is reproduced in Robert L. Herbert's book.) There is an important point here; artists (and we include poets in this word) like to take earlier works and reinterpret them, partly out of a sense of fun—Manet's painting is almost a parody of his sources—but partly also in order, in Ezra Pound's famous words, to "Make It New." Thus, Shakespeare reworked Plautus in several comedies, and he reworked (and thereby reinterpreted) several earlier English plays, including *King Lear* and a lost *Hamlet*. In our book, the most obvious example of a reworking is Joyce Carol Oates's "Where Are You Going?," a reinterpretation of the old story of the Demon Lover.

To return to Manet; yes, he will do a nude, but he will not disguise the erotic interest in it by claiming that it is a lofty allegory or even history. Rather, he will insist that the viewer recognize the sexual content of the scene. He will "Make It New." The result, of course, was a scandal.

Now for the poem. Phillips begins by recognizing that the picture caused a scandal ("Manet's scandalous / lunch partners"). As a poet, he need not cause a scandal, but his job is to "Make It New," partly by using language in fresh, interesting ways. For a start we can look at a passage in the second and third lines:

> . . . The two men, lost
> in cant and full dress. . . .

Here we get an example of zeugma, since the word *lost* governs two words but in different ways. In "Lost in cant" (incidentally, we might have expected the more flattering "lost in thought"), *lost* suggests some sort of mental failure; in "lost in full dress" *lost* is used differently, for the word now acquires the meaning of being overwhelmed by some sort of physical paraphernalia. Our explanation is clumsy, but the point is evident if you recall some of Alexander Pope's examples of zeugma:

> . . . *stain* her honor, or her new brocade,

and:

> . . . *lose* her heart, or necklace, at a ball.

But of course Phillips does not rely only on zeugma in his effort to make it new. By saying that these pastoral loungers are spreading their legs "subway-style," he makes the picture (1863) new, makes it something of *our* "modern life" rather than only something of Manet's. In fact, this is very much what Ezra Pound was getting at. He did not mean that the poet should turn away from the art of the past, but, rather that the poet should rediscover its vitality and present it in contemporary forms.

And so Phillips says, in his last lines,

> . . . My dear,
> this is not art; we're not anywhere close
> to Arcadia.

This is probably close to what Manet was doing, when he painted his nude in a modern style, i.e., when he painted a scene that (unlike a Renaissance painting) could not possibly be sanitized by being interpreted as an allegory or as an image of a lost pastoral world. Manet in effect said, "Look, *this* is what a nude is—a naked woman, not an allegorical representation of beauty, not a nymph, and if the scene suggests sex, well, why not?"

Phillips sees this in the painting. He imagines his nude as an earthy person, someone who asks, "where's / the *real* party?" Further, he puts himself and a companion into the scene, or, rather, he brings the scene to mind as he contemplates his present condition, nude, with a partner who has removed one boot in order to scratch an itch—and who knows what this will lead to? If Manet's picture is remote from the traditional nude, say, the Renaissance nude by Georgione (or Titian) that he copied, so Phillips's scene is remote from Manet. Manet's picture, in part because the landscape is painted flatly rather than illusionistically, still has something of the artificial world, the "shape of romance" that earlier paintings of nudes had. On the other hand, the details of Phillips's reality—a partner scratching an itchy foot in line 17, a "rusted green dumpster" in line 23, some unwanted chicken salad in line 31, a bottle of beer (not wine) in lines 32–33—take us utterly out of the timeless world of Arcadia. Arcadia endures only in art; in the speaker's world a lover forgets that the speaker dislikes chicken salad, and beer goes flat, and the speaker acts "fitfully." All is not well in this realm:

> . . . My dear,
> this is not art; we're not anywhere close
> to Arcadia.

But of course this *is* art, since it is all set forth in a poem. Phillips is taking the old motif of Arcadia, the old motif of pastoral poetry, and, true to Pound, is making it new.

A publicity release for Phillips's newest book says that Phillips is a gay African American, so we decided to add this information in our headnote in the text. In what sense, if any, is this a gay poem? It seemed to us even before we received the publicity release that the partner is male. Why did we have that impression? We aren't sure, but perhaps the reference to boots and athletic socks (16–17) gave us this idea, though women can wear boots and athletic socks. Perhaps we were influenced by the words, "We are two to Manet's main group / of three"; if the first big change is that Manet's female nude is replaced by a male nude, the second, it seems, is that Manet's two clothed males are reduced to one. Or maybe we felt as we did because there is no praise of any aspect of the woman's appearance, whereas heterosexual poems concerned with love usually include such praise.

ANNE SEXTON

The Starry Night (p. 805)

We think that one can reasonably call some of the language of this poem surrealistic—particularly the description of a "black-haired tree" that "slips / up like a drowned woman into the hot sky." (A tree presented as having hair, and a woman drowning *upward* seem to us to qualify; and so does the passage, in the second stanza, about the moon pushing children from its eye).

Surrealism is characterized by dreamlike, fantastic imagery, often presented in finicky detail and therefore (because the realism seems to be at odds with the subject matter) the more disconcerting. Surrealism is quite different from Expressionism. Expressionistic painting—and van Gogh is considered to be the father of Expressionism—does not seek to offer the surreal world of dreams and fantasies, nor does it seek to offer the world as perceived by traditional painters, who aimed at reproducing nature. Rather, Expressionist painting, as is evident in many of van Gogh's pictures, seeks to present the artist's emotions, or emotional response to the ostensible subject matter. (Sexton, as a "confessional poet," quite naturally found van Gogh's work of special interest.) Thus, as van Gogh's letters indicate, his picture of his bed (see the text and this handbook) was supposed to convey the artist's sense of rest. In *The Starry Night* van Gogh gives us not the dark sky with a thousand points of light that all of us can and do see, but a blazing heaven that expresses his ecstatic feelings about eternity. (Stars are a traditional symbol of eternity.) Also expressive of his feelings, no doubt, is the writhing cypress. In a letter to his brother, van Gogh says that he sees the sunflower and the cypress as both opposite and equivalent. Bright yellow sunflowers embody the life force, but they go to seed and die; dark cypresses are associated with death, but they energetically rise toward heaven. (See Vojtech Jirst-Wasiutynski on van Gogh's cypresses, in *Art Bulletin* 75 [1993]: 647–70, especially 657–60.) Also expressive is the little town, which is so slight when compared to the grandeur of nature.

But if Sexton's imagery is surrealistic, her poem is nevertheless tightly ordered. (There is no contradiction here. Surrealists such as Dali and Magritte often use conspicuously formal compositions.) The first two stanzas closely resemble each other, most obviously in the number of lines and of course in the identity of the last two lines of each of these stanzas, but in other ways too; for instance, the first line of each of these stanzas is conspicuously shorter than the second line. Doubtless Sexton counted on the reader perceiving the formal connection between the first two stanzas because much of the force of the poem depends on the fact that the last stanza is truncated—five lines instead of six, and only two syllables in the final line, instead of four. That is, "I want to die" (the ending of the first and second stanzas) is diminished to "no cry," a silent ending to an unheroic extinction of the flesh ("no flag," "no belly").

Having said that the poet imagines an unheroic extinction, we are uncomfortably aware that in the first two stanzas she seems to want to go off in a blaze of light ("Oh starry starry night! This is how / I want to die"). Still, our sense is that the third stanza makes a reader see the first two stanzas in a new light.

Two other points: (1) van Gogh's painting, as the quotation from his letter suggests, is a religious painting, or, rather, an expression of the artist's sense of the divinity of nature, whereas Sexton's poem seems to us to have nothing to do with religion. (2) The poem comes from *All My Pretty Ones* (1962), a book of poems much concerned with death. (The book takes its title from *Macbeth* 4.3.216, where Macduff is speaking of the children whom Macbeth slaughtered. Both of Sexton's parents had died within a few months of each other in 1959, and her father-in-law, of whom she was very fond, had died a few months later.)

For Sexton: *Anne Sexton: A Self-Portrait in Letters,* ed. Linda Gray Sexton (1977); *No Evil Star: Selected Essays, Interviews, and Prose* (1985); and *Selected Poems* (1988). Interviews and essays on Sexton are gathered in *Anne Sexton: The Artist and Her Critics,* ed. J. D. McClatchy (1978). See also: *Critical Essays on Anne Sexton,* ed. Linda Wagner-Martin; and Diane Wood Middlebrook, *Anne Sexton: A Biography* (1991).

A note on the assignment in the text: If you use this assignment, which asks students to discuss in what ways the poem does and does not describe the painting, you may want to follow this procedure: Divide the class into two groups. One group, after conferring for 15–20 minutes, would then report on the ways the poem does not reproduce the picture; the other on the ways it does.

W. H. AUDEN

Musée des Beaux Arts (p. 807)

Useful pieces on "Musée" are in *College English* 24 (April 1963): 529–31; *Modern Language Notes* 76 (April 1961): 331–36; *Textual Analysis,* ed. Mary Ann Caws (a relatively difficult essay by Michael Riffaterre); and *Art Journal* 32 (Winter 1972–1973): 157–62—the last useful primarily because it includes reproductions of Brueghel's work and it reprints other poems relating to his pictures. We reproduce Brueghel's picture of Icarus (in the Brussels Museum of Fine Arts, hence Auden's title); for a larger color reproduction see Timothy Foote, *The World of Brueghel* (1968). Auden glances at some of Brueghel's other paintings (the children skating in *The Numbering of Bethlehem* are indifferent to Joseph and Mary, who are almost lost in a crowd; the dogs and the horses in *The Massacre of the Innocents*), and his poem accurately catches Brueghel's sense of nature undisturbed by what rarely happens to the individual.

As Otto Benesch points out (*The Art of the Renaissance in Northern Europe,* 1945, 99), in *Icarus* Brueghel gives us a sense of cosmic landscape. Plowman, shepherd, and fisherman go about their business, unaware of Icarus, who is represented in the lower right-hand corner simply by his lower legs and feet, the rest of him being submerged in the sea. Daedalus is nowhere represented; the yellow sun sets in the west, and the sea, coasts, and islands are transfigured with a silvery light. It should be noted that in Ovid's account in *Metamorphoses* 8.183–235, the plowman, shepherd, and fisherman beheld Icarus and Daedalus with amazement, taking the two for gods. Given Brueghel's diminution of Icarus—legs and feet, unnoticed by the other figures in the picture— it is fair to say that Brueghel is offering a comment on the pride of scientists. James Snyder, who makes this point in *Northern Renaissance Art* (1985), 510, also calls attention to the shiny pate of a recumbent man, a dead man, at the left margin, halfway up and all but invisible even in the original painting. This image, Snyder says, "assuredly is meant to express the old Netherlandish saying, 'No plow stops over the death of any man,' or over Brueghel's Everyman, a clever footnote that reveals, after all, that peasant wisdom can be as profound as that of the ancients."

Students are first inclined to see Auden's poem as an indictment of indifference; our own view is that Auden gives the daily world its due, especially in such phrases as "doggy life" and "innocent behind"; that is, he helps us see that all of creation cannot and need not suffer along with heroes. Auden's poem evoked a pleasant reply by Randall Jarrell, "The Old and the New Masters," *Collected Poems* (1959), 332–33. It begins, "About suffering, about adoration, the old masters / Disagree. . . ."

X. J. KENNEDY

Nude Descending a Staircase (p. 809)

Duchamp's picture was exhibited at the famous Armory Show in 1913. This exhibition was chiefly devoted to contemporary American art—quite traditional stuff as we now look at it—but it also included material from the School of Paris. Predictably, the European material provoked indignation, ridicule, and passionate defense. Today the Armory show is regarded as marking the introduction of contemporary European art to America.

Part of Duchamp's joke in *Nude Descending a Staircase* is that the picture is so *un*sensual, so disappointing to anyone who has expectations of looking at a nude. This is entirely in keeping with Duchamp's interest in the movements of the human body as akin to the movements of a machine. He was influenced by the chronophotographs of Etienne-Jules Marey (1830–1904), who superimposed sequential photographs of a figure in motion. For examples of Marey's work, see Aaron Scharf, *Art and Photography* (1968), and Beaumont Newhall, *The History of Photography* (1964), or, in fact, almost any history of photography. In Duchamp's painting, the curved lines—some made out of dots—derive from Marey, who used such lines to indicate what he called lines of force. (Duchamp also knew the somewhat comparable photographs of figures in motion made by Eadweard Muybridge.) Photographs of bodies in movement were of considerable interest to scientists. For instance, Dr. Oliver Wendell Holmes used photographic studies of men walking in his work in designing artificial limbs for soldiers wounded in the Civil War. Photographs, he reported, are

> a new source. . . . We have selected a number of instantaneous stereoscopic views of the streets and public places of Paris and New York, each of them showing walking figures, among which some may be found in every stage of the complex act we are studying.
>
> Qtd. in Newhall, 117

Duchamp's interest in the mechanics of motion continued throughout his life; in his later years, he amused himself by devising complex machines that performed no useful function.

He painted *Nude* not in flesh colors but in the color of wood precisely because he did not want it to be seductive; the picture was to be a sort of scientific study of the machine-like aspects of the body.

> When we consider the motion of form through space in a given time, we enter the world of geometry and mathematics, just as we do when we build a machine for that purpose. Now if I show the ascent of an airplane,

I try to show what it does. I do not make a still-life picture of it. When the vision of the *Nude* flashed upon me, I knew that it would break forever the enslaving chains of Naturalism.

Qtd. in Ian Crofton, *A Dictionary of Art Quotations* (1988), 57

For a longer comment by Duchamp, see *Theories of Modern Art*, ed. Herschel Chipp (1968), 393–95.

What is especially interesting in Kennedy's poem is the engaging sensuous—even sensual—content, evident in such words as "flesh," "A gold of lemon," "She sifts in sunlight," "With nothing on," "We spy," "thigh on thigh," "lips," and "her parts." Surely Kennedy is having a little joke, putting the missing nude back into the picture. In its day, in the Armory show, the picture provoked not only wrath from conventional art critics but also genial humor from those simple souls who wanted a sexy picture of a woman. The most famous quip that came out of all this is that the picture shows not a nude but an explosion in a shingle factory. Where was the nude? *The American Art News* offered a $10 prize. Here is the winning solution:

You've tried to find her,
And you've looked in vain
Up the picture and down again,
You've tried to fashion her of broken bits,
And you've worked yourself into seventeen fits.
The reason you've failed to tell you I can,
It isn't a lady but only a man.

Qtd. in Milton W. Brown, *The Story of the Armory Show* (1963), 136

Our point: Kennedy is not simply describing the picture as (dare one say it?) the naked eye sees it. Rather, he is recreating it, turning it into (indeed) a picture of a nude descending a staircase. At the same time, he *does* catch Duchamp's mechanistic view ("the swinging air / That parts to let her parts go by," "Collects her motions into shape"), and he does effectively use metaphors to describe what we see ("One-woman waterfall," "she wears / Her slow descent like a long cape").

SHERMAN ALEXIE

At Navajo Monument Valley Tribal School (p. 811)

First, some words about Skeet McAuley's photograph, which we found in McAuley's *Sign Language* (1989), a book of photographs of the Navajo. Probably the most famous photographs of Indians are those by Edward Curtis, taken for his forty-volume work, *The North American Indian* (1907–30). These are beautiful images—we reproduce one on page 889 of the text—and the motivation behind them was noble: Convinced that the Indians were a vanishing breed—one of his images, *The Vanishing Race*, shows a file of mounted Indians riding off into the darkness—Curtis wanted to capture scenes of a way of life that he was convinced would soon be lost. In recent decades he has been much criticized for his refusal to photograph Indians wearing Western clothing or using modern tools, or within a landscape that included telephone lines.

No doubt he was not recording his material objectively, but, rather, was shaping it so that it conformed with his particular vision. One might almost say he photographed not what was in front of his eyes (Indians wearing jeans, standing on sidewalks) but what was behind his eyes (Indians dressed in traditional garb, feathered bonnets and all)—though of course this is what all photographers do. They have a purpose, and they take the pictures that suit their purpose. But even here, "take pictures" is the wrong term for what photographers do; as Minor White said, "I don't take pictures, I make them." Again, all photographers have a purpose—perhaps to collect evidence of a crime, or to show beauty, or to call attention to social injustice. A photographer equipped with a camera is not an Innocent Eye.

Skeet McAuley does not hesitate to take pictures of today's Indians in today's surroundings—for instance, washing windows or standing near automobiles. We will not presume to say what his purposes are—in a moment we will let him speak for himself—but we do want to mention that among his most famous pictures are shots of golf courses, shots, that is, of artificial nature, of man-made environments that inevitably challenge us to think about the ways in which we rearrange or recreate nature. The image that we reproduce inevitably causes a wry smile. Here we are, in the Southwest, in the desert, with a mesa (a time-worn rock formations of subdued color) in the background, and we are looking at a bright green lawn marked with a goal post and with a scoreboard, surrounded by a track for runners. Now, no one—least of all McAuley—is saying that the Indians of the community should not have a track field because such a field desecrates the landscape. But the picture does set us thinking. And it moved us to write to McAuley, who generously responded. Here (with his permission) is part of his reply:

> For me, the image represents a peaceful coexistence of several concepts. These range from reading it as history and the present (and possibly the future), beauty and the beast, myth and truth, "natural" nature and fabricated nature, peace and conflict, innocence and knowledge, real and surreal. It is not about either/or, but rather about both—the potential of possibilities. As well as being an important social gathering place, it is an oasis of solitude, beauty, spirituality and reverence. I have been back to the place several times since the image was made and it is constantly changing. I have found this to be a wonderful lesson in the relationships of time and the truth of the photograph. I believe all photographs lie. It is at best a form of shorthand—a visual language of reduction. Because of this, the experience of being there is much more profound than looking at the image for me. It is a place for the imagination, a place to rest, a place to contemplate, a place of magic. With patience, it is a place that can teach. Maybe that part of its character is translatable even through the photograph and its shortcomings.

Now for a few words about Alexie's poem. The most obvious thing about it is that the epigraph ("from the photograph by Skeet McAuley") and the first line and a half ("the football field rises / to meet the mesa") do not at all lead us to expect what we now get: Alexie populates McAuley's uninhabited image, "Indian boys / gallop across the grass." Soon "unbroken horses" (admittedly, this is a metaphor for the adults who watch the boys) enter the poem, and in a moment we are squarely in what we might think is the paleface's world

("Everyone is the quarterback"), but, after all, why shouldn't Indians play foot-ball; palefaces play lacrosse.

As we read the poem, in the fourth stanza an element of conflict comes to the fore ("winners and losers"), but it is rejected since in the next stanza we are told that

> This is the eternal football game,
> Indians versus Indians. All the Skins
> in the wooden bleachers fancydancing. . . .

This picture of an apparent conflict that is really a unity, a joyous celebration of identity, next is complicated and enriched by the entry of "the eighth-grade girls' track team," which encircles the field—the circle is a nearly universal symbol of unity and of eternity. The final stanza, where the girls are compared to "wild horses, wild horses, wild horses," picks up the image of the "unbro-ken horses" (6) that had been used to characterize the elders. The fact that the last line consists of a three-fold repetition suggests, we think, the continuity implied in the circle, and it implies the continuity of life.

JOHN UPDIKE

Before the Mirror (p. 813)

Updike's poem, we believe, is at least as much about himself as it is about the painting. And many critics today would say that *all* comments about works of art—even allegedly objective accounts—are about the speakers, not the works of art. Works of art say nothing, we often hear; critics are ventriloquists who put words (meanings) into the works that they purportedly describe. We can-not hold such a view—we are pretty sure that *our* comments about works of literature are rooted in the works themselves—but we are uneasily aware, as we read the words of some earlier critics, that *they* certainly made the authors over into their own image.

In an essay called "What MoMA Done Tole Me," written for the magazine *Art and Antiques* and republished in Updike's collection of essays entitled *Just Looking* (1989), Updike anticipated some of the ideas of "Before the Mirror." Of his visits to the museum in 1955–57, when he lived in New York, he wrote:

> For me the Museum of Modern Art [MoMA] was a temple where I might refresh my own sense of artistic purpose, though my medium had become words. What made this impudent array of color and form Art was the mys-tery; what made it Modern was obvious, and was the same force that made me modern: time. Indeed, some of the works that arrested me—Picasso's *Girl before a Mirror*, its ice-creamy colors and fat satisfied black outlines posed in those days at the turning of the main stairs; Rouault's *Christ Mocked by Soldiers*, with its outlines of a coarser sort . . . dated from 1932 and were thus just my age, which seems to me now very young. (8–9)

Here is the germ of the poem, the identity of the viewer with the work that is viewed. And so in 1996, when Updike again saw the picture in the great exhibition "Picasso and Portraiture" at MoMA, he returned to the topic, noting with satisfaction that the picture is holding up just fine:

> . . . The blacks,
> the stripy cyanide greens are still uncracked,
> I note with satisfaction; the cherry reds
> and lemon yellows full of childish juice.
> No sag, no wrinkle. Fresh as paint. Back then
> they knew just how, I reflect, to lay it on.

And yet. . . . One need not be a deconstructionist, committed to the idea that texts are inherently contradictory, to be a bit unnerved by these last lines. The final words, "to lay it on," suggest vigorous action ("lay on, Macduff") but they also undermine the suggestion by implying insincerity (as in, "to lay it on with a trowel"). Or go back to the penultimate line: "Fresh as paint." A chirpy idiom, and witty here, since the speaker is talking about literal paint, but, alas, a cliché; the words (and also others, especially "I note with satisfaction" in line 21) call to mind some oldster cheering himself up.

Updike—do we have to say "the speaker," when the speaker so clearly is the author?—is looking at the picture, and seeing himself. He is using the picture as, so to speak, a mirror, most appropriately since the picture itself shows a girl looking into the mirror. But mirrors as symbols have several meanings: The mirror can symbolize truth ("The mirror doesn't lie," "Mirror, mirror, on the wall, / Who is fairest of them all?"); or it can symbolize vanity (again the wicked stepmother's question, since she believes the mirror will tell her that she is the fairest); or (and Updike, who knows a lot about art, must know this) it can symbolize the passage of time and the coming of death, as in paintings of a young girl looking into a mirror and seeing an ancient crone or a skull. Picasso glances at this last interpretation in *Girl before a Mirror*, since the girl herself—she is at the left, with her face shown both in profile and frontally—surely is more youthful than the mirror-image (at the right), which seems to reveal a witch-like figure.

The girl's profile has a pale virginal look; the front view, with lipstick and rouge, suggests a more sexually aware woman; and the face in the mirror suggests advancing years. (The standard comment is that in the frontal view of the girl's face we see the energetic sun, in the mirror-image we see the darkening moon.) Further, the boundary lines of the elongated oval mirror can be seen as suggesting a coffin that contains the image.

If the poem ends with an explicitly cheerful note, this ending only barely conceals intimations of mortality. The painting shows "No sag, no wrinkle," but that is because it is a painting; the viewer, who tells us he is in his sixties, must be showing some sag, some wrinkle. In fact, early in the poem he tells us that he belongs to "a dwindling population." And in lines 9–10 he echoes the line that greets the new arrivals as they enter Hell: "Abandon Hope, ye who enter here." True, Updike's line ("Enter here / and abandon preconception") implies new life, bestowed by a new kind of art, a new way of seeing, but in conjunction with "dwindling population" the line nevertheless casts a shadow over the poem.

Still, he is of a piece with the picture, he goes back to a day when "they knew just how . . . to lay it on." Reading this poem about a man looking at a picture of a woman looking in a mirror—a man looking at a picture which, mirror-like, shows him what he takes to be his own image—we perceive a bit of vanity, we sense the approach of death, and perhaps we even think (though this is nowhere explicit in the poem) that Updike's own works are still "uncracked" and full of "juice." Lookers-into-mirrors will go, images in mirrors will go, viewers of pictures will go, but the pictures, the works of art, remain fresh.

What do we make of our third question in the text, which asks about the girl's gesture toward the mirror? Our guess is that just as the viewer mentally reaches out to the picture, so the girl reaches out to her own image, seeking to make contact with what she knows is an illusion. Perhaps, too, she is (so to speak) saying, "No, this image of decay can't be true," and she reaches out to prove that the image is an illusion. Or perhaps she is moved by sympathy: "There, there, I know how you must feel." Or maybe Picasso simply felt that it was not enough for the two halves of the picture to echo each other, and that they ought to be tied together.

GREG PAPE

American Flamingo (p. 815)

Greg Pape's poem is a response to "American Flamingo," one of the beautiful hand-colored plates in John James Audubon's *Birds of America*, published in four enormous volumes (each plate is about forty inches tall and thirty inches wide) between 1827 and 1838. Each bird is shown lifesize; hence, the flamingo (in order to fit on the page) had to be shown with its head down. Audubon ingeniously shows the bird in other poses in the flamingos in the distance.

The illegitimate son of a French merchant and slave trader and a Creole woman of Saint-Domingue (now Haiti) in the West Indies, and a failure in several business ventures, Audubon had a dream, to which he came to devote his life: He wanted to paint every species of bird in North America. With courage and persistence, Audubon traveled throughout the United States and Canada, seeking always to draw the birds in their natural habitat. The American scientific community failed to recognize the brilliance of his work—his depiction of birds in action, so to speak, as living creatures within a particular environment rather than as inert specimens—and thus in 1826 he left the United States for England. There he found support and collaborators, and his work soon went into production and moved forward, even as Audubon himself made return visits to the United States for further research and drawing and painting for the volumes.

Audubon was a passionate writer as well as an artist; with William MacGillivray, he wrote the *Ornithological Biography* (5 vols., 1831–39) to accompany *Birds of America*. Over the years he has been criticized for sacrificing scientific accuracy for dramatic effect, and there is some truth to this charge. But it is also the case that on occasion Audubon drew birds in strained, near-to-impossible poses because that was, for him, the best means for showing something new and noteworthy—for example, a feature of a bird's coloring that might be hard to glimpse. Remember, he studied the birds in their setting, not in a museum or laboratory.

The force and romantic glamour of Audubon's pioneering personality helps to clarify the quotation from the Southern poet-critic Robert Penn Warren (1905–89) that Pape gives toward the middle of his poem. It is taken from Warren's long poem *Audubon: A Vision*, published in 1969; Warren was born in Guthrie, Kentucky, the state where Audubon lived as a young man and tried to make a success of himself in business. Section I, titled "Was Not the Lost Dauphin," begins with this stanza in part A:

> Was not the lost dauphin, though handsome was only
> Base-born and not even able
> To make a decent living, was only
> Himself, Jean Jacques, and his passion—what
> Is man but his passion?

Referring to Audubon by his baptismal name "Jean Jacques," Warren sets aside the familiar but false story that Audubon was the Dauphin, the son of the dethroned Louis XVI and Marie Antoinette. Interestingly, in the next stanzas, Warren describes Audubon in quest of the Great White Heron, which in *Birds of America* comes just a few plates before the American Flamingo that Pape focuses on. Perhaps the vivid color of the flamingo seized Pape's attention. Or, more simply but importantly, perhaps for this poem of his own, Pape needed to select a different bird from the one that Warren chose: It would hardly do to write about the same one.

Curiously enough—and this point may bear on the solemn, evocative tone of the second half of the poem—the American flamingo is now an infrequent visitor to Florida, and so it would be relatively unusual today to find these birds in Hialeah, the city (and site of the famous race track) in the southeast part of the state to which Pape refers. The birds at the race track are in fact imported captives. According to the Audubon Society's *Encyclopedia of North American Birds* (1995 ed.), the American flamingo "wandered formerly in large numbers to Florida, but now rarely"; to see these brightly hued, long-legged, and long-necked birds in large numbers, one must travel to the West Indies and the Bahamas or to the northern coast of South America.

The *Encyclopedia* also notes that the American flamingo is shy, vigilant, hard to approach, and this may suggest why Pape shows such steady, absorbed interest in the flamingo's watchful eyes. Pape admires and highly values the work that Audubon has done; in line 23, he says that the movements of the flamingos in the background are "stunning"—a tribute to the painter's craftsmanship. And the deliberate pace of Pape's lines itself functions as a more general form of praise, with the passionate care of the poem serving to illuminate Audubon's own passion for detail.

For us, and for students, the challenge of the poem is describing what it all adds up to. Pape's images are striking, especially in the second half, as when he depicts "the satin figures of the jockeys / perched like bright beetles on the backs / of horses. . . ." Here he nicely makes good work of the verb "perched," which we associate for a moment with the posture of a bird only to find that in this instance Pape is attaching it to the beetles on the horses' backs. Still, though they respond to such details, our students have wondered about the broader "point" of the poem, and we find ourselves wondering about the same issue. It could be that this is a mistake on our part—the wrong kind of question to ask. The point of the poem may not be an easily statable theme but, rather, may lie precisely in the exercise of the poet's craft, which, again, is meant richly to complement the passionate ornithologist Audubon.

But we suspect that there is, after all, a thematic point that Pape seeks to draw in this poem, and it is one that explores the ambiguities of past and present. Many decades ago, Audubon performed his dogged, extraordinary work, and it has eternalized the American flamingo and the other birds upon whom he lavished such care. For Pape, the American flamingo still lives—he saw them. Yet we must be more exact; they live in his memory—he saw them once, in a time now past, and even then part of the reason they awed Pape and the spectators is because they came, it seemed, from "the old world." Seeing them was unforgettable, and Pape records this memory in his poem, as his companion-piece to the unforgettable drawing that Audubon has given us.

Note: Students may puzzle a bit over the first lines of the poem: Was this lover of birds a hunter? Audubon was; he hunted all his life and even admitted that when he was a young man he sometimes shot wild animals and birds for the sheer fun of it. Hence Pape may be kinder to him—saying that he shot the birds to study them—than the truth warrants.

The best place to begin the up-to-date study of Audubon's work is *Birds of America: The Watercolors for The Birds of America*, ed. Annette Blaugrund and Theodore E. Stebbins, Jr.; catalog entries by Carole Anne Slatkin; with essays by Stebbins and others (1993). For a good short discussion, see Robert Hughes, *American Visions* (1997); also useful is the entry in *The Dictionary of Art* (1996). Somewhat dated, but still useful, is Constance Rourke, *Audubon* (1936). Biographies have been written by Alice Ford (1964) and Alexander B. Adams (1966). For a good selection of Audubon's writings, see the *Audubon Reader*, ed. Scott Russell Sanders (1986).

22

Three Poets in Depth: Emily Dickinson, Robert Frost, and Langston Hughes

EMILY DICKINSON

There are two useful guides to Dickinson criticism, both of which are edited by Joseph Duchac: *The Poems of Emily Dickinson: An Annotated Guide to Commentary Published in English, 1890–1977* (1979), and *The Poems of Emily Dickinson: An Annotated Guide to Commentary Published in English, 1978–1989* (1993).

A "Voices and Visions" videocassette of Emily Dickinson is available from Longman.

EMILY DICKINSON

These are the days when Birds come back (p. 819)

The time is Indian summer, that is, a day that seems summery but is late, hence it is a sort of sophistry of mistake or fraud. (By the way, it is not true that birds, deceived by Indian summer, return.) Lines 10–11 introduce religious imagery ("ranks of seed their witness bear," and the pun on alter-altar, which suggests a communion scene), anticipating the more overt religious images in the next two stanzas.

Some readers take the poem to suggest that just as the season can be deceptive, communion too can be deceptive or illusory. Other readers see the poem moving the other way: from the illusory season, which evokes nostalgic thoughts, to the real or firm joys of Christian immortality. Charles Anderson, in *Emily Dickinson's Poetry* (1960), gives a substantive analysis. He suggests that the season's ambiguity provokes the question, "Does it symbolize death or immortality?" and he answers that Dickinson does not give an answer but gives us "warring images poised in ironic tension."

TOPICS FOR CRITICAL THINKING AND WRITING

1. What season or weather is being talked about? Why does Dickinson use the words "mistake" (line 6) and "fraud" and "cheat" (line 7)?
2. Explain the pun on "altered" in line 11.
3. Take the first three stanzas as a group and summarize them in a sentence or two. Do the same for the last three. Then, in a sentence or two, state the relationship between these two halves of the poem.
4. Why "a child" in line 15?

EMILY DICKINSON

Papa above! (p. 820)

At one extreme, we have encountered readers who find the poem a bitter protest masquerading as a prayer, a scathing attack on the anthropomorphic God of Judaism and Christianity; at the other extreme we have encountered readers who find nothing but piety in the poem, albeit piety in a very Dickinsonian idiom, a piety rooted in affection for God's creatures, even the mouse or rat. Our own view is somewhere in the middle; we hear genial—even affectionate—satire of anthropomorphism, and we also hear acceptance of the strange government of the world. Chiefly, we think, the poem expresses—again, in a characteristically Dickinsonian way—the "primal sense of awe" that Charles R. Anderson commented on.

"Papa above!" begins with a domesticated version of the beginning of the Lord's Prayer (Matthew 6.9–13, "Our Father who art in heaven"; Luke 11.2–4, "Father"). In "Regard a Mouse / O'erpowered by the Cat" we hear a solemn (and perhaps a wondering) voice, although we grant that one might hear some comedy in the let-down. That is, a reader who expects, after the invocation of the deity, something like "Regard the sufferings of mortals," or some such thing, is surprised to find that the speaker calls attention to a mouse. Or if the reader expects something that continues the idea of the Lord's Prayer, the shift from the expected "Give us this day our daily bread" to a picture of a mouse overpowered by the claws or jaws of a cat is indeed shocking, first because of the implied violence, and second because of the ironic contrasts between the meal Jesus spoke of and the meal Dickinson shows.

In the next two lines ("Reserve within thy kingdom / A 'Mansion' for the Rat!") we hear primarily a serious if not a solemn voice, though others hear mockery in the juxtaposition of "Mansion" and "Rat." In any case, there is surely a reference to the comforting words Jesus offered to his disciples (John 14.2) when he assured them of reunion in heaven: "In my Father's house are many mansions." But a heavenly mansion (dwelling place) for a rat? We are by no means convinced that Dickinson must have abhorred mice and rats, and that therefore "A 'Mansion' for the Rat" must be ironic. As we see it, the poem thus suggests that the mouse (or rat), destroyed at the moment, has its place in the enduring heavenly scheme. Again, some readers take this to be so evidently absurd or so disgusting that they believe Dickinson is satirizing the idea of a divinely governed universe; others find a tolerant pantheism.

The first two lines of the second stanza get us almost into a Walt Disney world of cute animals—here the mouse is "Snug" and it is able to "nibble all the day"—but in the final two lines the camera draws sharply back from the domestic scene and gives us a world of immense space and time, a world indifferent to ("unsuspecting" of) the mouse (and by implication indifferent to all of us). If there is any satire here, we think it is of persons who believe the "Cycles" are concerned with their existence, but we do not take these lines to be the fierce condemnation of the Judeo-Christian God that some readers take them to be.

The poem raises enough difficulties in itself, but you may want to ask students to compare it with Frost's "Design" (also in the text). Is Frost's "Design" a sort of restatement of Dickinson's "Papa above!"? Or is Frost's poem something of a reply?

EMILY DICKINSON

Wild Nights—Wild Nights! (p. 820)

A reader tends to think of Emily Dickinson as the speaker of "Wild Nights" and therefore is perhaps shocked by the last stanza, in which a woman apparently takes on the phallic role of a ship mooring in a harbor. But perhaps the poem is spoken by a man. (In one of her poems the speaker says, "I am a rural man," in another the speaker refers to "my brown cigar," and in "A narrow Fellow in the Grass"—included in our text—the speaker identifies himself as male in lines 11–12.)

Possibly we are superficial readers, but we don't attach to "Might I but moor—Tonight— / In Thee!" the strong sexual associations that several critics have commented on. Some but not all assume that the image suggests male penetration. Albert Gelpi, in *The Tenth Muse* (1975, 242–43) says that "the sexual roles are blurred." He adds, "Something more subtle than an inversion of sexual roles is at work here, and the point is not that Emily Dickinson was homosexual, as Rebecca Patterson and John Cody have argued," but he doesn't clarify the point. (Patterson's discussion is in *The Riddle of Emily Dickinson* [1951]; Cody's is in *After Great Pain* [1971].) Paula Bennett, in *My Life a Loaded Gun* (1986), drawing on a discussion by L. Faderman, seems to reject the idea of a male speaker. She says that "the imagery of the poem, with its emphasis on entering rather than being entered, is . . . far more appropriate for one woman's experience of another than for a woman's experience with a man" (61). Christine Miller too insists that the speaker is a woman. In *Feminist Critics Read Emily Dickinson*, ed. Suzanne Juhasz (1983), Miller says that the speaker is a woman but she adds that "The woman is the ship that seeks to 'moor—Tonight— / In Thee!'—an activity more representative of male than of female social behavior" (137). Our own simple view: A reader need not find an image of penetration in "moor"; rather, we think that in this poem the word suggests a longed-for security.

Is the poem sentimental? We don't think so, chiefly because it is brief, controlled, and (in "Tonight") it does not claim too much.

In *Explicator* 25 (January 1967), Item 44, James T. Connelly pointed out that in letter No. 332 (T. H. Johnson's edition, *Letters,* II, 463), Dickinson writes, "Dying is a wild Night and a new road." Looking at the poem in the light of this letter, Connelly concludes that "to die is to experience a wild night on a turbulent, surging sea. Only by plunging into this uncharted sea of Death can one at last reach the port of rest and calm. The poem, thus considered, is an apparent death wish: a personification and apostrophe to Death whose presence and company are paradoxically exhilarating luxury." We are unconvinced, partly because the poem speaks not of "a wild night" but of "Wild Nights," and we cannot see how the plural form lends itself to this reading.

TOPICS FOR CRITICAL THINKING AND WRITING

1. Probably "wild nights" refers chiefly to a storm outside of the lovers' room, but it can of course also describe their love. "Luxury" (from the Latin *luxuria*, which meant "excess" or "extravagance") in line 4 probably retains some of the meaning that it first had when it entered into English, "lust" or sensual enjoyment. What does the second stanza say about the nature of their love? How does the third stanza modify the idea?
2. What makes this lyric lyrical?
3. Do you think that the poem is sentimental? Explain.

EMILY DICKINSON

There's a certain Slant of light (p. 821)

The poem seems difficult to us, and any questions about it therefore lead to difficulties, but perhaps our fifth question, below, on the rhyme scheme, is fairly straightforward. Some students may recognize that metrically the poem is close to the "common meter" or "common measure" (abbreviated C. M. in hymnals) of a hymn. (C. M. can be defined thus: stanzas of four lines, the first and third in iambic tetrameter, the second and fourth in iambic trimeter, rhyming *abcb* or *abab*.) In fact no two stanzas in the poem are metrically identical (if we count the syllables of the first line of each stanza, we find seven, six or seven, six, and eight), but despite such variations, the meter and especially the rhyme scheme (*abab*) seem regular. The second and fourth lines of each stanza have five syllables, and these lines end with exact rhymes, though the first and third lines of each stanza rely less on rhyme than on consonance. The regularity of the rhyme scheme, especially in such short lines, is something of a tour de force, and (because it suggests a highly ordered world) it might seem more suited to a neat little poem with a comforting theme than to the poem Dickinson has given us. Further, since the meter and some of the rhymes might occur in a hymn ("Despair," "Air"; "breath," "Death"), there is an ironic contrast between the form (a hymn, that is, a poem celebrating God's goodness) and the content of the poem.

But what, in fact, is the content? And what is the "certain Slant of light" that, perceived on "Winter Afternoons," makes "Shadows—hold their breath"? No two readers seem to agree on the details, but perhaps we can offer a few inoffensive comments. Like Hopkins (cf. "God's Grandeur"), Dickinson sees a divinity behind phenomena, but her nature-suffused-with-divinity differed greatly from his. "There's a certain Slant of light" begins with "light," which might suggest life and eternal happiness (think of Newman's "Lead, kindly light"), but soon becomes darker, and ends with "the look of Death." The ending is not really a surprise, however, since the "certain Slant of light" is seen on "Winter Afternoons," that is, a season when the year may be said to be dying and when light is relatively scarce, and a time of day when light will soon disappear.

This "Slant of light," we are told, "oppresses, like the Heft / Of Cathedral Tunes." Surely "oppresses" comes as a surprise. Probably most of us think that cathedral tunes (even funeral music) exalt the spirit rather than oppress it, and so most of us might have written something like, "That elevates, like the Lift / Of Cathedral Tunes." But of course most of us couldn't have written even this, since we would not have had the imagination to think of light in aural terms ("Tunes") and in terms of weight ("Heft").

In any case, a certain appearance in nature induces in the poet a sensation that requires such words as "oppresses," "Hurt," "Despair," "affliction," "Shadows," and "Death." These words might appear in a traditional hymn, but, if so, the hymn would move toward the idea that God helps us to triumph over these adversities. Dickinson, however, apparently is saying that on these wintry afternoons the slant of light shining in the air gives us a "Heavenly Hurt," that is, it moves us to a painful consciousness of God and nature, and to a sense of isolation. In the final stanza presumably we are back to the "Winter Afternoons" of the first. Projecting herself into the surrounding world, the speaker personifies nature: "the Landscape listens"— but hears nothing further. (By the way, "listens" to or for what? A "Slant of light"? Again, as in the earlier comparison of light to "Cathedral Tunes," Dickinson uses synesthesia.) If during the moment when one perceives the light or "listens" there is no further insight, and certainly no amelioration of the "Heavenly Hurt," when "it goes" there is an intensification of despair, since one is left with "the look of Death." Is Dickinson evoking an image of the remote stare of a corpse? And is she suggesting that this stare corresponds to the paralyzed mental condition of those who have perceived the "Slant of light"?

Earlier in this brief discussion we contrasted Hopkins with Dickinson. But, as Charles R. Anderson points out in *Emily Dickinson's Poetry* (1960), there is a connection between the two. The perception in this poem resembles Margaret's perception in "Spring and Fall" (876), where the child senses "the blight man was born for."

TOPICS FOR CRITICAL THINKING AND WRITING
1. In the first stanza, what kind or kinds of music does "Cathedral Tunes" suggest? In what ways might they (and the light to which they are compared) be oppressive?
2. In the second stanza, the effect on us of the light is further described. Try to paraphrase Dickinson's lines or interpret them. Compare your paraphrase or interpretation with that of a classmate or someone else who has read the poem. Are your interpretations similar? If not, can you account for some of the differences?
3. In the third stanza, how would you interpret "None may teach it"? Is the idea "No one can instruct (or tame) the light to be different"? Or "No one can teach us what we learn from the light"? Or do you have a different reading of this line?
4. "Death" is the last word of the poem. Rereading the poem, how early (and in what words or images) is a "death" suggested or foreshadowed?

5. Describe the rhyme scheme. Then, a more difficult business, try to describe the effect of the rhyme scheme. Does it work with or against the theme, or meaning, of the poem?

6. What is the relationship in the poem between the light as one might experience it in New England on a winter afternoon and the experience of despair? To put it crudely, does the light itself cause despair, or does Dickinson see the light as an image or metaphor for human despair? And how is despair related to death?

7. Overall, how would you describe the tone of the poem? Anguished? Serene? Resigned?

EMILY DICKINSON

I got so I could hear his name— (p. 821)

This poem is not as well known as others, but we think it is one of Dickinson's best, and it is one that students find very powerful. They respond to it, and are especially eager to probe its complexities, because they feel the immediacy of its subject. It is something that has happened to them, or that they fear might happen. One of our students in an American literature class said, "This is exactly what it feels like to have your heart broken."

The poem does express *that*, but it is also about somehow trying to recover from the pain. What measures might be taken to overcome a devastating loss? Dickinson is stunningly effective, we believe, in noting the physical closeness that the persons in her poem shared, and the wrenching experience of their separation—"all our Sinew tore." The detail about the letters is very powerful as well, for it describes precisely the terrible way we return to memories, to signs of the beloved's presence, when what we want is to get beyond them.

This is, then, a poem about feeling and confronting pain and seeking a means of self-control. In the final three stanzas, the speaker turns to God— though notice the distancing effect of "I think, they call it 'God'." Perhaps this higher force, outside the wounded self, might be able to heal it. Students find the last stanza somewhat obscure, and we agree. But the main thrust is clear enough: The speaker is uncertain whether any power exists that might aid her, and, if there is, whether this power would ever care about the pain felt by just one person. A good question to ask is how much or how little closure takes place in the final line. Does the speaker reconstitute, at least partially, her shattered self, through the process of articulating and working through, cathartically, her pain? Or is the poem the record of a pain that persists, that the speaker cannot find a remedy for?

Dickinson has legions of admirers, but in our experience, many students have trouble with her intense, gnomic, highly condensed verse. This, again, is a poem to which students do feel connected, and it is valuable as a point of entry into the study of Dickinson's life and work. See Richard B. Sewall, *The Life of Emily Dickinson* (2 vols., 1974), and Cynthia Griffin Wolff, *Emily Dickinson* (1986).

Two charged, self-dramatizing comments by Dickinson on herself, both from undated letters to the critic, editor, and journalist Thomas Wentworth Higginson: "I had no portrait, now, but am small, like the Wren, and my

Hair is bold, like the chesnut Bur, and my eyes, like the Sherry in the Glass, that the guest leaves"; and "I had no monarch in my life, and cannot rule myself; and when I try to organize, my little force explodes and leaves me bare and charred."

EMILY DICKINSON

The Soul selects her own Society (p. 822)

Richard Sewall, in *Voices and Visions* (1987), ed. Helen Vendler, calls this poem Dickinson's "most famous 'choice' poem" (72), and indeed he leaves the choice of its subject to the reader; it may be read as concerned with the choice of a lover, or a friend, or a kind of spiritual life. Even without being certain of the subject of this poem, one can sense how the form contributes to meaning. The even-numbered lines are shorter than the odd-numbered lines that precede them, and each even-numbered line ends emphatically with a monosyllable, thus contrasting with the previous lines with their feminine endings. And in the final stanza the short lines are even shorter (a mere two syllables each); the tight-lipped speaker leaves no doubt about the determination of the soul which has made a choice and now rejects all other suppliants, however noble. But details remain uncertain, and critics have not been so tight-lipped.

W. C. Jumper, in *Explicator* 29 (September 1970), Item 5, suggests that the soul (feminine because Latin *anima* is feminine) has a "divine Majority" because Thoreau had said in *The Duty of Civil Disobedience* that "any man more right than his neighbors, constitutes a majority of one." Jumper points out that the second stanza makes ironic use of two folktales, "The Querulous Princess" and "The King and the Beggar Maid." In the first of these tales, the wooers arrive in chariots, but the winner of her hand is he who will bow his head to enter through a low gate; in the second tale, the king kneels before a beggar maid and wins her. In "The Soul selects" the soul rejects two such humble wooers, having already made her choice.

The word "Valves" in the penultimate lines has especially disconcerted critics. *Explicator* 25 (April 1967), Item 8, suggests that it is connected with "Door" in line 2 via two old meanings: (1) the leaves of a double or folding door and (2) the halves of the shell of a bivalve such as an oyster, which closes its valve when disturbed and thus remains "Like Stone." Sewall takes "Valves" to refer to a double door and says that "the line simply dramatizes further the action of line two" (73).

EMILY DICKINSON

This was a Poet—It is That (p. 822)

To say "This was a Poet" is perhaps to cause a reader to think that the speaker is contemplating the ashes or the grave of a poet, or perhaps a picture of a poet, but this idea is not developed. George E. Fortenberry in *Explicator* 35:3 (1977) reads the poem as a remark Dickinson is making "about a flower she has just plucked from beside her door, and as she smells it, thinks of it as a poet resurrected as a flower" (27). (We will return to Fortenberry's view in a moment.) In our experience, most readers take "This" to refer to a poem or a book of poems; the speaker has just read something, and now contemplates on the nature of the writer.

The first two stanzas form a single sentence, even though the second does not end with a period. At the end of the first line presumably we must supply the word "which," i.e., the poem that stands for the poet is that which distilled (extracted the essence of, stops from perishing) or "Arrested" (line 8, i.e., caught and holds for us to see) the amazing content of what seemed to be ordinary experience but what in fact is an experience that—we now see, via the poet's presentation—causes us to "wonder" (7), i.e., brings wonder into our lives. (Students might be invited to say what they think is the value of art. Our own view is pretty much what we take Dickinson to be saying here. One might also consider Archibald MacLeish's "Ars Poetica," which is in the text.)

The awe-struck wonder of the first two stanzas gives way, in the remainder of the poem, to a more agitated tone. (There are five dashes in the first two stanzas—two in the first stanza, and three in the second—but there are six dashes in the third stanza, and nine in the fourth stanza.) The idea of the third stanza seems to be this: We see our poverty when we see the poet's wealth as a revealer, a "Discloser." In the final stanza, "Portion" probably refers to the poet's wealth, and the idea is that the poet is so unaware of his or her wealth (priceless ability)—because so inherently richly endowed—that thievery would cause no loss to the poet; the poet stands outside of the world of the rest of us ("Exterior—to Time—")—immortal. In George E. Fortenberry's view, Dickinson "compares her own poverty of portion to that of the poet, who is so unconscious of his portion that the taking (robbing) of the flower 'could not harm.' The poet's fortune is exterior to time; thus he may be resurrected as a flower" (27).

For a very different (and, for us, difficult to follow) interpretation, see E. Miller Budick, *Emily Dickinson and the Life of Language* (1985).

EMILY DICKINSON

I heard a Fly buzz—when I died (p. 823)

Dickinson's poem juxtaposes some conventional religious images ("the last Onset," "the King," "What portion of me be / Assignable") with the buzz of a fly, rather than with, say, choirs of angels, and so, as Charles R. Anderson suggests in *Emily Dickinson's Poetry* (1960), "The King witnessed in his power is physical death, not God." Should one go further, and suggest that Death-as-fly equals putrefaction?

The last line of the poem ("I could not see to see") especially has attracted attention. Gerhard Friedrich (*Explicator* 13 [April 1955], Item 35) paraphrases it thus: "Waylaid by irrelevant, tangible, finite objects of little importance, I was no longer capable of that deeper perception which would clearly reveal to me the infinite spiritual reality." The fall into skepticism, Friedrich says, demonstrates the inadequacy of the earlier pseudostoicism. John Ciardi took issue with this interpretation and suggested (*Explicator* 14 [January 1956]:

Item 22) that the fly is "the last kiss of the world, the last buzz from life," reflecting "Emily's tremendous attachment to the physical world"; the final line, in his view, simply means, "And then there was no more of me, and nothing to see with."

The Todd-Higginson editions gave "round my form" for "in the Room" (2), "The eyes beside" for "The Eyes around" (5), "sure" for "firm" (6), "witnessed in his power" for "witnessed—in the Room" (8), and "What portion of me I / Could make assignable—and then" for "What portion of me be / Assignable—and then it was" (10–11). It is worth discussing with students the differences these changes make.

EMILY DICKINSON

This World is not Conclusion (p. 824)

First, a brief comment about Dickinson and religion. She clearly was not fond of the patriarchal deity of the Hebrew Bible. "Burglar! Banker—Father," she wrote of this deity, and in a note to Thomas Wentworth Higginson she says that the members of her family, except for herself, "address an Eclipse every morning—whom they call their Father." She seems to have been amused by preachers. She said, of one, that "the subject of perdition seemed to please him somehow." Still, in the words of Charles R. Anderson, in *Emily Dickinson's Poetry* (1960), no reader can doubt that she "faced creation with a primal sense of awe" (17). And, as Anderson and everyone else points out, the Bible was "one of her chief sources of imagery" (18).

Now for "This World is not Conclusion." The first two lines sound like the beginning of a hymn ("Conclusion" presumably means "ending," not "inference drawn"). The poem is not divided into stanzas by white spaces, but clearly it moves in units of four lines. The first four lines assert that although a world beyond our own is (like music) invisible, we strongly sense it. "Positive" in line 4 perhaps refers both to our conviction that it exists and also to its goodness.

Line 5 introduces a complication: "It beckons, and it baffles." Although the rest of the stanza (i.e., lines 6–8) seems to affirm the initial confident (positive) assertion, it also raises doubts in the reader, since it dismisses "Philosophy" and "Sagacity," and it characterizes life (or is it death?) as a "Riddle."

Lines 9–12 seem more positive. They remind us that although human experience "puzzles Scholars," martyrs have given their lives to affirm religious faith, to affirm (in the words of the first line) that "This World is not Conclusion."

Lines 13–16, however, present "Faith" in a somewhat less heroic light: "Faith slips—and laughs, and rallies—Blushes, if any see." Surely this is in a much lower key than "Men have borne / Contempt of Generations," a couple of lines earlier. The enduring power of faith is still affirmed (Faith "rallies"), but in "slips" and "Blushes, if any see" we seem to be presented with a rather adolescent world. Further, the last two lines of the stanza (15–16) similarly diminish Faith, showing it clutching after "a twig of Evidence," and inquiring of a "Vane" (a weathervane, a most unstable thing). Perhaps, too, "Vane" hints at emptiness, insubstantiality (Latin, *vanitas*).

The final four lines at first seem more affirmative. They begin with a strong assertion that calls up a picture of a vigorously gesticulating preacher, and they reintroduce imagery of music (now "Strong Hallelujahs roll"), but these lines at the same time are unconvincing, or, rather, almost comic. A reader may find in the preacher's abundant gestures a lack of genuine conviction. (One thinks of the marginal note in the politician's speech: "Argument weak; shout here.") The "Strong Hallelujahs" may strike a reader as less potent than the "Music" that was "positive" in lines 3–4. Are the gestures and the hallelujahs "Narcotics" that don't quite work, that is, that don't quite convince us of the pious forthright assertion that "This World is not Conclusion"? Yet the poem ends with the word "soul"; if "Much Gesture, from the Pulpit" reveals a preacher who is not wholly convincing, we nevertheless cannot therefore lapse into the belief that this world is conclusion. Something "nibbles at the soul."

TOPICS FOR CRITICAL THINKING AND WRITING

1. Given the context of the first two lines, what do you think "Conclusion" means in the first line?
2. Although white spaces here are not used to divide the poem into stanzas, the poem seems to be constructed in units of four lines each. Summarize each four-line unit in a sentence or two.
3. Compare your summaries with those of a classmate. If you substantially disagree, reread the poem to see if, on reflection, one or the other of you seems in closer touch with the poem. Or does the poem (or some part of it) allow for two very different interpretations?
4. In the first four lines the speaker seems (to use a word from line 4) quite "positive." Do some or all of the following stanzas seem less positive? If so, which—and what makes you say so?
5. How do you understand "Much Gesture, from the Pulpit" (line 17)? Would you agree with a reader who said that the line suggests a *lack* of deep conviction? Explain.

EMILY DICKINSON

I like to see it lap the Miles (p. 824)

Whoever first called a train an "iron horse" had the gift of the poet, but Dickinson goes much further in "I like to see it lap the Miles," catching the beast's energy and (in the last three lines) its docility. She is interested in the sound and sight of the train (these are playfully set forth with lots of alliteration, beginning with "like . . . lap . . . lick"), but she displays no interest in the train as a symbol of progress, no interest in people or goods getting anywhere. Indeed, her train ends up—for all its rushing and roaring—"At its own stable door."

Charles Dickens, in *American Notes* (1842), describes a train ride. You may want to ask your students to compare Dickens's account with Dickinson's.

On it whirls headlong, dives through the woods again, emerges in the light, clatters over frail arches, rumbles upon the heavy ground, shoots beneath a wooden bridge, which intercepts the light for a second like a wink, suddenly awakens all the slumbering echoes in the main street of a large town, and dashes on haphazard, pellmell, neck-or-nothing, down the middle of the road. There—with mechanics working at their trades, and people leaning from their doors and windows, and boys flying kites and playing marbles, and men smoking, and women talking, and children crawling, and pigs burrowing, and unaccustomed horses plunging and rearing, close to the very rails—there—on, on, on—tears the mad dragon of an engine with its train of cars; scattering in all directions a shower of burning sparks from its wood fire; screeching, hissing, yelling, panting; until at last the thirsty monster stops beneath a covered way to drink, the people cluster around, and you have time to breathe again.

EMILY DICKINSON

A narrow Fellow in the Grass (p. 825)

"Fellow" (and the pronouns "Him" and "His," rather than "it" and "its") and "rides" in the first stanza help to assimilate the snake to the human world, as does "comb" in the second stanza. In these two stanzas there is some emphasis on the unexpectedness of the snake. He is "sudden" but not menacing. And in the beginning of the third stanza he seems almost an eccentric neighbor: "He likes a Boggy Acre." In the fourth stanza the reference to a whiplash introduces a more threatening note; "Nature's People" in the next stanza seems to bring us back to the comfortable world of the first stanza, but with the last line of the poem ("Zero at the Bone") there is communicated a terror that indicates a response to the snake as supremely hostile. (The snake is, after all, a traditional image of our satanic enemy.) The contrast between "a transport / Of cordiality" (which carries a sense of warmth, that is, warm-heartedness, via *cor,* heart) and the coldness of "Zero at the Bone" could hardly be greater.

Karl Keller, in a provocative book about Emily Dickinson, *The Only Kangaroo among the Beauty* (1979), says (268) that the poem "manages to make Freud trite." Keller says that Dickinson's "tighter breathing / And Zero at the Bone" indicate that "she finds her genitals alarmed," and that "she is shocked and attracted by the male erection ('His notice sudden is')." Keller patently misreads the poem when he says, "Her own sexual desires are she says very strongly aroused: she feels 'a transport / Of cordiality.'" Not so; the poem says that for "Several of Nature's People" she feels that transport "but" for this fellow she feels "Zero at the Bone."

Dickinson complained when the third line was printed with a question mark at its end. Apparently "did you not" is less a question than a tagged-on conversational filler like "don't you know" and a question mark causes too long and too strong a pause. Yet another point about the punctuation: Lines 11–16 describing the boy (the speaker is a boy, not Emily Dickinson) stooping to pick up what he thinks is a whiplash but what is in fact a snake that disappears are unpunctuated (until the end of 16) and thus suggestive of the speed of the event.

TOPICS FOR CRITICAL THINKING AND WRITING

1. Many of Dickinson's poems are rather like riddles. In this poem who or what is the "narrow Fellow in the Grass"?
2. How would you describe the speaker of this poem? What relationship does the speaker seem to establish with the reader?
3. In lines 17–20 Dickinson refers to "Several of Nature's People." Who or what might these be in Amherst in the later nineteenth century? Check "transport" and "cordiality" in a dictionary to see which meanings you think are especially relevant.
4. Why does Dickinson speak of the snake as "him" rather than "it" and of the animal world as "Nature's creatures"?
5. If you have read Lawrence's "Snake," write an essay of 500 words indicating the *purposes* of Dickinson and Lawrence. Include a discussion of how effectively each poet fulfills these purposes.

EMILY DICKINSON

Further in Summer than the Birds (p. 825)

We take the opening words "Further in Summer" to mean that the crickets chirping in the grass are more advanced in their span of life (nearer to autumn and winter and death) than are birds. Moreover their song is heard later in summer and thus they remind us of the imminent end of the season. The song is pathetic partly because the creatures are so small but probably chiefly because it reminds us of the passing of time and losses and of our consequent increasing loneliness. The final stanza provides another look. The first two lines of this stanza may mean that no disturbance as yet diminishes the beauty (no grace has been remitted, there is no "Furrow on the Glow" of summer), but we are somewhat inclined to take them as meaning: "Do not give back (reject) grace; the moment is undisturbed"—that is, continue to experience the blessedness of the moment. If this reading is right, "Yet" in the next line does not quite mean "but"; rather it means (we think) "still," "even so."

Charles Anderson discusses the poem at some length in *Emily Dickinson's Poetry* (1960).

TOPICS FOR CRITICAL THINKING AND WRITING

1. Paraphrase the first line.
2. What is the "minor Nation," whose pathetic sounds (here said to be a celebration of the Mass) are heard in the grass?
3. In this context, what does "Grace" (line 6) mean?
4. Does "Enlarging Loneliness" (line 8) mean "making loneliness greater," or does it mean "setting loneliness free," that is, releasing us from loneliness?
5. Is Dickinson saying that nature teaches us that all of creation shares in God's grace? Or is she saying—especially in the last stanza—that we must give up our imagined idea that Christian grace is found in nature? Or is she perhaps saying something else?

EMILY DICKINSON

Tell all the Truth but tell it slant (p. 826)

A student once brought up, by way of comparison, Polonius's

> And thus do we of wisdom and of reach,
> With windlasses and with assays of bias,
> By indirections find directions out. (Hamlet 2.1.64–66)

The last line especially seems to have affinities with Dickinson's first line, but the thrust of the two passages is fundamentally different. Polonius, worried about the behavior of his son Laertes, is sending Reynaldo to find out if Laertes has been misbehaving. He tells Reynaldo to slander Laertes, to see if Reynaldo's hearers deny the charges. Polonius thus is advocating deceit, whereas Dickinson is saying that because truth is too bright for our "infirm Delight," if we want to communicate, we must use indirection.

For Dickinson, the truth *is* splendid—it does "dazzle"—but we can perceive this splendor only after we have become accustomed to it, and we arrive at this condition "gradually."

The word "slant" nicely plays against "Circuit," and on rereading it may be taken to anticipate the word "lightning," which is often represented by a diagonal line. In any case, one of the charms of the poem is the homely comparison in lines 5–6, where the need to tell the truth "slant" is compared to offering "explanation kind" to children who presumably have been frightened by lightning. Telling the truth "slant" or "in Circuit" is not an attempt to deceive, but to be "kind."

An extant draft of the poem shows that Dickinson contemplated two possible changes, *bold* for "bright" in line 3, and *moderately* for "gradually" in line 7.

EMILY DICKINSON

A Route of Evanescence (p. 826)

An old discussion, Grover Smith's in *Explicator* 8 (1949–50), Item 54, seems to us to remain the most interesting. Smith points out that the phrase "A Route of Evanescence" is "a metonymy equating the bird with its own path across the field of vision." Smith goes on:

> The visual effect is the converse of that obtained photographically by multiple rapid-exposures of a moving object on a single plate; here the poet describes not the simultaneous presence but the simultaneous vanishing of the bird at every point. . . .

Speaking of the "revolving Wheel"—the wheel-like optical illusion produced by the rapid up and down motion of the wings—Smith points out that Dickinson's reference to the iridescent color on the bird's head and back uses synesthesia ("A Resonance of Emerald"). He also says that Dickinson uses onomatopoeia in this line and the next line ("A Rush of Cochineal"), though not every reader will agree that onomatopoeia occurs in "A Resonance of Emerald."

Equally challenging is his assertion that in the final two lines beside the image of the bird "is implicit that of a speeding railway train, the mail and express, and also that of the more common kind of mail—a letter. . . . A train travels upon a 'route,' it is borne along by many a 'revolving wheel,' its sound is a 'resonance' and a 'rush,' and on it people 'ride.'" We confess that we don't see this image in the lines, and Smith himself is apparently a bit uneasy with the idea, since he himself points out that of course no train crosses the sea from Tunis, and no "easy Morning's Ride" will get us there.

Other points: The words "Emerald," "Cochineal" (associated chiefly with North Africa), and "Tunis" bring the precious and the remote into the familiar garden. (By the way, we have been told that when hummingbirds leave New England they go to Mexico, not to North Africa.)

One of Dickinson's copies of the poem, according to Millicent Todd Bingham's *Ancestor's Brocades* (1945, 37), included several alternatives for "revolving" in line 2: *delusive*, *dissembling*, *dissolving*, and *renewing*. (The present location of this manuscript is not known.)

TOPICS FOR CRITICAL THINKING AND WRITING

1. Dickinson in her letters refers to this poem as "A Humming Bird." What is she getting at in line 2?
2. Dickinson uses synesthesia (the description of a sensory impression in terms of another sense) in "A Resonance of Emerald." What is the point of describing a color ("Emerald") in terms of sound ("Resonance")?
3. In line 7, why is "Tunis" preferable to, say, "New York"?

EMILY DICKINSON

Those—dying, then (p. 826)

The faith of her ancestors is, Dickinson apparently feels, no longer possible, but it serves to enrich behavior. An *ignis fatuus* (a phosphorescent light— caused by gases emitted by rotting organic matter—that hovers over a swamp) presumably resembles, however weakly, the beautiful flames of heaven and the demonic flames of hell. It is only a will-o'-the-wisp, but at least it is *some*thing. The image of amputation is shocking, but it can be paralleled in the Bible, for example by "and if thy right eye offend thee, pluck it out, and cast it from thee. . . . and if thy right hand offend thee, cut it off, and cast it from thee" (Matthew 5.29–30).

TOPICS FOR CRITICAL THINKING AND WRITING

1. In a sentence or two, state the point of the poem.
2. Is the image in line 4 in poor taste? Explain.
3. What is an *ignis fatuus*? In what ways does it connect visually with traditional images of hell and heaven?

EMILY DICKINSON

Apparently with no surprise (p. 827)

As in most nature poems, nature is humanized—but with a difference. If a flower is Wordsworthian in being at "play," the frost is not. It is a "blonde Assassin"; blonde because it is white, and the fact that this color is usually associated with innocence makes the personification the more shocking. (See Frost's white spider in "Design," in our text.) Note, too, that "at its play" can go with the frost as well as with the flower, in which case the frost is only play-ing, but happens to play too vigorously with a destructive (but unlamented) result. And still more shocking, at least on first reading, is the fact that God (like the sun) approves. God stands behind the world, approving of the acci-dental destruction of beauty and joy. One could, by agile philosophizing, justify the necessary destruction of beauty and joy—but the "accidental" destruction? The sun, as usual, measured off the days, but mysteriously withheld its warmth and allowed the frost to do its work. The flower, the sun, God, all seem indifferent; only human beings are shocked.

"Apparently," of course, has two almost opposed meanings: (1) evidently, clearly; (2) seemingly (but not really), as in "The magician apparently vanished into thin air." So the lack of surprise, and the impassivity of the sun and the approval of God *may* be unreal; maybe this is just the way things look or seem, not the way things really are. After all, it is only apparent (seemingly), not real, that flowers are "happy" and that they "play."

TOPICS FOR CRITICAL THINKING AND WRITING
1. What is the implication of the action described in lines 1–3?
2. Why is the frost's power called "accidental"?
3. Why is the assassin called "blonde"? What does this word contribute to the poem?
4. Is the last line shocking? Explain.

EMILY DICKINSON

I felt a Funeral, in my Brain (p. 828);
I felt a Cleaving in my Mind— (p. 830); and
The Dust behind I strove to join (p. 830)

The problem with most criticism of Dickinson's poetry is that critics typi-cally approach it from the outside in. They focus first on facts (or reports and rumors and legends) about Dickinson, or on historical contexts, or on philo-sophical ideas and themes about identity and the self, and then proceed to interpret the poems accordingly. On one level this makes good sense; we want to learn as much as we can about the life and times, and about the abiding themes, of a writer, in order to extend and enrich our understand-ing of his or her work. But the risk of this procedure is that it forces

Dickinson's language to conform to ideas and themes that in fact she intends to resist, challenge, and explore. When we read the poems intensively, the striking thing about them is that it is difficult to make them fit into any one pattern or theme.

For the teacher, especially in an introductory course, it is hazardous, in our view, to set out biographical and historical contexts or a dominant idea or theme before turning to the poems themselves. The students find Dickinson a very hard poet to begin with. If you suggest to them that there is a big, controlling idea they must first know about, or biographical and historical facts they must be aware of as they get underway, they will feel frustrated. They will conclude that they cannot really appreciate the poems because they will never know enough about Dickinson, her era, and so on.

The better approach, we think, is to turn immediately to the poems. Sometimes we have said at the outset of the discussion, "All of you probably have heard something about Dickinson's reclusive life, family, and history—all of these are interesting. But let's experiment today. Let's see what we can make of the poems on our own, and discover together what kind of portrait of Dickinson as a poet emerges from them."

With "I felt a Funeral, in my Brain," move through it carefully, asking the students to hear and feel the language, registering its meanings as Dickinson moves from one line to the next.

You'll want the students, for example, to note that the poem begins with "I." This is the point of departure, the sign that *this* voice is speaking, and that she is addressing us—or that we are overhearing her. "I felt a Funeral" is an intriguing phrase, not what we expect. *See* a funeral: that is something we are familiar with, that we can understand. But how does one *feel* a funeral? Dickinson is organizing her language to make us ask the question and imagine what it's like to *feel*, not see or watch or attend, a Funeral.

The comma after "Funeral" makes us pause. Dickinson is giving us a moment to picture the funeral. But no sooner do the scenes form than the next phrase, "in my Brain," complicates them. It's not a funeral that we conceive of, but one that the speaker imagines in *her* brain. It is a funeral, one might say, that takes place internally. It is not out there, but inside, an event on the landscape of her mind.

"And Mourners": Who are they? At whose funeral are they mourning? "To and fro"—such a curious phrase, a phrase with a bit of a playful rhythm that we often find used about children as they gambol, "to and fro." It's a phrase that makes an uneasy combination with the funeral and the mourners, and it is that disconcerting feeling that Dickinson wants.

"Treading" is a harder, more severe word. Its general meaning is to walk on, over, or along. But it means, more precisely, to press beneath the feet, trample; to crush or injure, to subdue harshly or cruelly. Dickinson uses the word twice, for greater impact, so that there is no missing its point and power. The mourners press their way back and forth, relentlessly—maybe one should even say, punitively.

"That Sense was breaking through"—a complex line, which is (as Dickinson intends) difficult to pin down to a single meaning. Is the speaker saying that finally she began to make sense of what the funeral was about? Or is she saying that the mourners finally began to make *their* sense known to her? The line has an agonizing import—the sense breaking through, like a wound in the skin. But this feeling that the line gives us is combined with the more positive cast that we frequently assign to a phrase like this one: "I thought for a long time about the matter, and at last it made sense to me—the breakthrough that I was hoping for came."

These comments on the first stanza are meant to show how you can work inductively on the poem in the classroom. It is a demanding experience for the students, but we have found it to be very productive. This kind of close scrutiny enables the students to perceive the astonishing unusualness of Dickinson's writing; they can see, hear, and feel what makes this poet special. The challenge for you as a teacher is to acknowledge that Dickinson is difficult even as you convey to the students why she is intensely interesting.

When you focus on this poem, or on others by Dickinson, you can launch the analysis yourself. But turn after a line or two to the students. Get them involved; get them *inside* the poem.

We want to add, keep your eye on the clock. You need to work carefully, deliberately. But make sure that the class has a good rhythm. If the pace becomes too slow, the students will begin to feel bogged down, as if they were in the midst of an exercise rather than engaged with a rich and stimulating, if hard and disquieting, poem.

Recently we taught this poem in an introductory course, a seminar for first-year students that emphasized weekly essays and oral reports. For the first part of class, we worked as a group on the text of "I felt a Funeral, in my Brain" as it is printed in *The Complete Poems of Emily Dickinson,* ed. Thomas H. Johnson (1957). This is the text as we know it today, the one that all of the introductory and American literature anthologies use when they print it. We then distributed to the class a packet of materials, which we have included in our book for your students to work with:

1. The poem as it appears in Dickinson's own hand—the manuscript version.
2. The poem as it appeared in *Poems by Emily Dickinson*, third series, ed. Mabel Loomis Todd (1896)—the first published version of the poem.
3. Two more poems, from Johnson's edition: "I felt a Cleaving in my Mind" and "The Dust behind I strove to join."

We divided the class of sixteen students into four groups. One separated off to examine and talk together about the manuscript; another discussed Todd's edition; and the other two were assigned one of the short poems from Johnson's edition. The question we asked was, "What does the manuscript or poem tell you about the poem we have been studying today?" After about fifteen to twenty minutes of discussion among themselves, the students then reassembled and the groups reported on their discoveries.

The subsequent general discussion went well. One group commented, for example, on Dickinson's change in line 10 of the manuscript, where she crossed out "Brain" and substituted "Soul." They noted too that this kind of revision differs from the more puzzling one at the end, where Dickinson seems to have written two concluding lines and not made a choice between them. Was Johnson right, they wondered, in omitting the final line of the manuscript from the poem? What led him to decide that the manuscript should be changed into the version that he prints?

Similarly, another group wondered why Todd not only made minor changes throughout, but, more boldly still, cut the entire last stanza. How does the poem affect us without the final stanza? Why, furthermore, might the final stanza in the manuscript have impelled Todd to conclude that it did not belong, that the poem would be better without it?

In their own way, the other two Dickinson poems also helped to reveal and dramatize the distinctiveness of "I felt a Funeral, in my Brain." As the students pointed out, "I felt a Cleaving in my Mind" has a different force. "Cleaving" is one thing, "Funeral" is another. "Cleaving" comes from a verb that means to pierce or penetrate, or to split or cut with a sharp instrument. Not an event, not a funeral, but an action, a cutting, wounding, rending action. Nor is "Mind" the same as "Brain." As one student remarked, we might have expected the line of the second poem to read: "I felt a Cleaving in my Brain," because a person's brain is something tangible, something that can suffer a disease, something that a doctor can operate on or a scientist dissect. The mind: We know it is there and can talk about how it works, but can we *see* a person's mind in the way we can see and analyze the brain?

When our students finish their study of Dickinson, we hope they will be interested enough to want to read more about her and the biographical, historical, religious, literary, and philosophical contexts that bear upon her writing. We do not mean to confine the students to the poems alone, and no more than that. But if students are to get anywhere with Dickinson, they will need to feel they can make something of the poetry on their own. Our task as teachers is to make these hard poems accessible—literary works that students will believe they have the capacity to read, struggle with, profit from, and, yes, enjoy.

For our purposes, the two best resources for studying Dickinson and becoming intimate with her as a writer are *The Poems of Emily Dickinson*, 3 vols., ed. Thomas H. Johnson (1955); and *The Poems of Emily Dickinson: Variorum Edition*, 3 vols., ed. R. W. Franklin (1998). These scholarly works meticulously examine the manuscripts and variant readings for each and every poem.

ROBERT FROST

Although in the text we give some of Frost's own comments on his poetry, here we want to quote two additional short comments. The first, from Frost's preface to his collection entitled *Aforesaid* (1954), is about the best way to read a poem:

> A poem is best read in the light of all the other poems ever written. We read A the better to read B (we have to start somewhere; we may get very little out of A). We read B the better to read C, C the better to read D, D the better to go back and get something more out of A. Progress is not the aim, but circulation. The thing is to get among the poems where they hold each other apart in their places as the stars do.

The second passage we want to quote, from a letter to Louis Untermeyer, January 1, 1917, is a bit more cryptic. We read it to students when we begin studying Frost's work, and we reread it occasionally during the course of the study:

> You get more credit for thinking if you restate formulae or cite the cases that fall in easily under formulae, but all the fun is outside saying things

that suggest formulae that won't formulate—that almost but don't quite formulate. I should like to be so subtle at this game as to seem to the casual person altogether obvious. The casual person would assume that I meant nothing or else I came near enough meaning something he was familiar with to mean it for all practical purposes. Well well well.

A "Voices and Visions" videocassette of Robert Frost is available from Longman Publishers.

ROBERT FROST

The Pasture (p. 833)

"The Pasture" is a rare example of a poem that uses no figures of speech—no metaphors, no similes. Every word can be taken literally. But the entire poem is a sort of figure. By placing "The Pasture" at the opening of his *Collected Poems* Frost allows us to read it as a figure; the invitation to accompany the speaker on a trip to the pasture can be read as an invitation to accompany the poet on a trip to the poet's work—his poems.

Reuben Brower, in *The Poetry of Robert Frost* (1963), rightly observes that in this poem "there is not a word or an order of words we might not use in talking," and that

> by using the commonest of leave-takings and a familiar phrase of artless begging, Frost balances perfectly the claims of both song and speech. Through the concealing art of this and other lines he aptly doubles his meanings, extending an invitation to seeing and doing country things while inviting his companion and the reader to a kind of poetry and to love. (11)

In Daniel Smythe's *Robert Frost Speaks* (1964), Frost offers a comment on this poem:

> I have always had an interest in that word, "confusion." I don't think I really thought of it in this poem, but it could be thought of in connection with it. I wrote it a long time ago. I never had a greater pleasure than on coming on a neglected spring in a pasture in the woods. We clean out the leaves, then wait by to watch the uncloudiness displace the cloudiness. That is always a pleasure to me; it might be taken as a figure of speech. It is my place to see clarity come out of talk and confusion. You didn't need to know that was in the poem. But now you see that was the way it was used. (56–57)

ROBERT FROST

Mending Wall (p. 834)

Some critics applaud the neighbor in Frost's "Mending Wall," valuing his respect for barriers. For an extreme version, see Robert Hunting, "Who

Needs Mending?" *Western Humanities Review* 17 (Winter 1963): 88–89. The gist of this faction is that the neighbor wisely realizes—as the speaker does not—that individual identity depends on respect for boundaries. Such a view sees the poem as a Browningesque dramatic monologue like "My Last Duchess," in which the self-satisfied speaker unknowingly gives himself away.

Richard Poirier, in *Robert Frost* (1977), makes the interesting point that it is not the neighbor (who believes that "good fences make good neighbors") who initiates the ritual of mending the wall; rather, it is the speaker: "I let my neighbor know beyond the hill." Poirier suggests that "if fences do not 'make good neighbors,' the *making* of fences can," for it makes for talk—even though the neighbor is hopelessly taciturn. For a long, judicious discussion of the poem, see John C. Kemp, *Robert Frost: The Poet as Regionalist* (1979).

TOPICS FOR CRITICAL THINKING AND WRITING
1. Compare and contrast the speaker and the neighbor.
2. Notice that the speaker, not the neighbor, initiates the business of repairing the wall (12). Why do you think he does this?
3. Write an essay of 500 words telling of an experience in which you came to conclude that "good fences make good neighbors." Or tell of an experience that led you to conclude that fences (they can be figurative fences, of course) are detrimental.

ROBERT FROST

The Wood-Pile (p. 835)

The poem contrasts a human being who "can forget his handiwork" because he lives for "turning to fresh tasks" with nature, a "frozen swamp" that is "Too much alike to mark or name a place by"; the swamp is not even a "here," but only something that tells the speaker he is "far from home." Nature is nothing in itself—or rather, nothing meaningful to humans—until a human gives it meaning; in this poem, meaning is imposed on it by the person who built the woodpile. And even though the wood is not burning in the fireplace, it nevertheless has been made into something coherent, and it shows the mark of a human as it rots and "warm[s] the frozen swamp as best it could." Nature, then, needs a human's collaboration, and, conversely, a human needs nature's collaboration, for nature completes what a human has abandoned. On this last point, notice that "Clematis / Had wound strings round and round it like a bundle"—though the line also suggests that nature is reclaiming from humans what is hers. For an excellent discussion of the poem, see Richard Poirier, *Robert Frost* (1977).

TOPICS FOR CRITICAL THINKING AND WRITING
1. What is the contrast that Frost makes between human beings and nature?
2. What does he say about the relationship between human beings and nature?

ROBERT FROST

The Road Not Taken (p. 835)

The diverging roads are pretty similar; the speaker chose the one less worn, as "having perhaps the better claim," but three times we are told that the difference was negligible: "just as fair"; "Though as for that, the passing there / Had worn them really about the same"; "equally." It is important to notice that although a reason is given for the choice ("it was grassy and wanted wear"), we are led to doubt that there really was a clear basis for choosing. Certainly there is no moral basis. Moreover, we may feel that had the speaker chosen the other path, the ending of the poem would have been the same; that is, he would remember the alternative path and would fantasize that he might someday return to take it, and would at the same time know that he would not relearn. And so he would find that it too "has made all the difference." The sigh imagined in the last stanza is not to be taken as an expression of regret for a life wasted, but as a semicomic picture of the speaker envisioning himself as an old man, wondering how things would have turned out if he had made a different choice—which is not at all to imply a rejection of the choice he did make.

Students are likely to take the poem too seriously and to press it too hard for a moral, for example, that Frost says we should choose the "less traveled," the unconventional, path. We have tried to suggest that the first two lines of the last stanza are playful, a reading that is supported by a letter in which Frost spoke of the poem as "my rather private jest." (See *American Literature* 50 [November 1978]: 478–79.) As Lawrance Thompson says in his introduction to *Selected Letters of Robert Frost* (1964, xiv), Frost wrote the poem after returning to the United States from England. In England, his friend and fellow poet Edward Thomas liked to take Frost on woodland walks and then fretted that perhaps he should have chosen a different path, which would have revealed different flora. This bit of biography does not prove that the poem cannot refer to moral choice, but it may help students to ease up on the highly moral interpretations that many are prone to make.

TOPICS FOR CRITICAL THINKING AND WRITING

1. Frost called the poem "The Road Not Taken." Why didn't he call it "The Road Taken"? Which is the better title, and why?
2. Consider a choice that you made, perhaps almost unthinkingly, and offer your reflections on how your life might have been different if you had chosen otherwise. Are you now regretful, pleased, puzzled, indifferent, or what? (For instance, what seemed to be a big choice may, in retrospect, have been a decision of no consequence.)
3. Suppose that someone said to you that the poem is simply about walking in the woods and choosing one road rather than another. In an essay of 250 words, set forth your response. (You may, of course, agree with the view, in which case you will offer supporting evidence.)
4. In a paragraph discuss whether it would make any difference if instead of "yellow" in the first line the poet had written "bright green" (or "dark green").
5. Why do you think that Frost says he (or, more strictly, the speaker of the poem) will later be telling this story "with a sigh"? Set forth your response in a paragraph.

ROBERT FROST

The Telephone (p. 836)

A student of ours, Jane Takayanagi, wrote an entry in a journal that we think is worth reprinting. In our opinion she is right in seeing that a quarrel has precipitated the speaker's walk ("When I was just as far as I could walk / From here today"), but it is hard to convince someone who doesn't sense it. In any case, here is the entry from her journal:

> As the poem goes on, we learn that the man wants to be with the woman, but it starts by telling us that he walked as far away from her as he could. He doesn't say why, but I think from the way the woman speaks later in the poem, they had a fight and he walked out. Then, when he stopped to rest, he thought he heard her voice. He really means that he was thinking of her and he was hoping she was thinking of him. So he returns, and he tells her he heard her calling him, but he pretends he heard her call him through a flower on their window sill. He can't admit that *he* was thinking about her.
>
> This seems very realistic to me; when someone feels a bit ashamed, it's sometimes hard to admit that you were wrong, and you want the other person to tell you that things are OK anyhow. And judging from line 7, when he says "Don't say I didn't," it seems that she is going to interrupt him by denying it. She is still angry, or maybe she doesn't want to make up too quickly. But he wants to pretend that *she* called him back so when he says, "Do you remember what it was you said?" she won't admit that she *was* thinking of him, and she says, "First tell me what it was you thought you heard." She's testing him a little. So he goes on, with the business about flowers as telephones, and he says "someone" called him. He understands that she doesn't want to be pushed into forgiving him, so he backs off. Then she is willing to admit that she did think about him, but still she doesn't quite admit it. She is too proud to say openly that she wants him back but does say, "I *may* have thought as much." And then, since they both have preserved their dignity and also have admitted that they care about the other, he can say, "Well, so I came."

Two other (small) points: (1) Why in line 11 does Frost speak of having "driven a bee away"? We think that maybe in a tiny way it shows the speaker's willingness to exert himself and to face danger. It's a miniature ordeal, a test of his mettle. (2) In line 17 the speaker says, "I heard it as I bowed." Of course "bowed" rhymes with "aloud," but putting aside the need for a rhyme, surely the phrase is better than, say, "I heard it as I stood," since it conveys a gesture of humility.

ROBERT FROST

The Oven Bird (p. 836)

Whether or not one has ever heard an ovenbird, the idea that its song is exceptionally unmelodious is clearly suggested in lines 4, 6, and 10, where we get

"he says" rather than "he sings." In case a reader missed the point while reading the first ten lines, Frost makes it explicit in line 12: "he knows in singing
not to sing." Notice, too, other ways in which Frost deemphasizes the bird as
a singer: the ovenbird "*makes* the solid tree trunks sound again," "he *knows*,"
and "he *frames*" a question.

Although Frost says in the opening line that everyone has heard the ovenbird, he carefully educates the reader who has not heard it, explaining that it
is heard in the interval between "the early petal-fall / When pear and cherry
bloom went down in showers" and "that other fall we name the fall." It is midsummer when leaves are abundant, but they are "old," and "the highway dust
is over all." This time of stasis is no time for the usual sort of birdsong.

Ask your students how many of them have ever heard an ovenbird. (In
some parts of the country few, if any, students will have heard it. By the way,
the North American ovenbird is not a true ovenbird; i.e., it does not belong
to the family *Furnariidae*, which contains birds that build elaborate domed
nests of clay or who dig tunnels in the ground. The North American ovenbird is a wood warbler [*Parulidae*] which looks like a miniature thrush.) You
might ask your students, too, after some discussion of "The Oven Bird," if
they believe that in order to enjoy the poem one must have heard an ovenbird. It's our guess that Frost adequately conveys the bird's song, partly in
that stressed, unexpected "Loud" at the beginning of line 2 (it gains an even
greater weight by being followed by a comma), and partly in the repetition
of "mid" in this line ("mid-summer," "mid-wood") there is a suggestion of the
repetition in a bird's song. Notice, too, that this line almost defies scansion;
certainly it can't be called predominantly iambic. The poet, like the ovenbird,
"knows in singing not to sing." Line 9 ("And comes that other fall we name
the fall") sounds flat, and one isn't certain about how much stress to put on
"we," "name," and "fall."

ROBERT FROST

The Vanishing Red (p. 837)

This must be one of Frost's most terrifying poems, because, in our reading of
it, Frost implies that in the human heart there is a sort of maniacal hatred of
what now is called "the Other." He is not saying we all would kill those who
are different from us, but he is saying that if we were the Miller's contemporaries, we might not judge him as we now do:

> It's too long a story to go into now.
> You'd have to have been there and lived it.
> Then you wouldn't have looked on it as just a matter
> Of who began it between the two races.

That is, for the modern reader, it seems to be a matter of who first did what to
whom. Did the white people injure the Indians, so that any counterattacks by
Indians are more or less excusable, or did the Indians savagely (!) attack the
new immigrants? (We might remember that although we now speak of
"Native Americans," these people in fact were not native to the continent; they

migrated to this hemisphere, but a good deal earlier than the whites did. And while we are remembering things, we might also remember that until recently it was regularly said that when Indians killed whites it was a "massacre," but when whites killed Indians it was a "battle.")

Well, why isn't it a matter "Of who began it"? Or, to put the question a bit differently, why did the Miller kill the Red Man? In lines 14–18 Frost gives us as much of an answer as he will give:

> Some guttural exclamation of surprise
> The Red Man gave in poking about the mill
> Over the great big thumping shuffling mill-stone
> Disgusted the Miller physically as coming
> From one who had no right to be heard from.

"Some guttural exclamation of surprise." About what? About the Miller's prices? About the Miller's behavior? About the way the mill worked? Frost doesn't tell us—because it doesn't matter. What matters is that the Red Man expressed something and he was a person "who had no right to be heard from," in the Miller's opinion. The Red Man was, we might say, a non-person, and here he was, like a person, acting uppity. By the way, when the poem was originally published in *The Craftsman* (October 1916), what is now line 18 ("From one who had no right to be heard from") was not one line but two:

> From a person who the less he attracted
> Attention to himself you would have thought the better.

The early version is interesting, but it does not convey the intensity and the craziness of the revised version, where Frost does what he can to tell us of the Miller's reason for his act: The Indian had "no right" to open his mouth.

And so the Miller decides to show John the wheel pit. (By the way, the Indian is named, but not the Miller, almost as though the Miller is not meant to be a single person.) The Miller shows John "The water in desperate straits"— in a moment John himself will be in desperate straits—then closes the trap door, whose jangling ring serves as a sort of funeral knell. Obviously self-satisfied, the Miller "said something to a man with a meal-sack / That the man with the meal-sack didn't catch—then." Frost doesn't tell us what the Miller said, but we can go back to lines 6–8, where Frost does tell us what the Miller's face seemed to say. And we can easily imagine that the last line of the poem ("Oh, yes, he showed John the wheel pit all right") is what he may have said to the man with the meal-sack. Frost tells us that whatever it was he said, it was something that the man "didn't catch—then." The "then," preceded by a dash, implies that later the man *did* get the words. Presumably at some point the Red Man was missed, perhaps the man with the meal-sack said he had seen him at the mill— and then, suddenly, the significance of the words became clear.

But we are offering mere conjectures about the narrative, about what the Miller's motive was, about what he said, about what made the man with the meal-sack later "catch" the meaning of the words. What is *not* conjecture, however, is the irony of the title. "The Vanishing Red" sounds as though the Red Man did some sort of magic trick and made himself disappear into thin air. The term (or a variant such as "The Vanishing Indian" or "The Vanishing Race") was of course a euphemism; white society liked to believe that the

Indians simply faded away, not that they were killed, or that they died of diseases brought by whites. Why, according to the old mythology, did Indians "vanish"? They "vanished" because whether they were imagined as noble savages (persons living close to nature, filled with natural goodness) or imagined as diabolical figures (persons lacking the virtues of civilization), they lived in an unchanging world, a world that did not participate in progress (technology). When technology came to dominate the land—when their world was superseded—they simply vanished. Such was the comforting view held by many whites. Frost gives us quite another view of the vanishing act. (We will return to this issue in a moment.)

The poem is unusual among Frost's work not only in its subject matter but also in its form. We are not thinking so much of the fact that the lines do not rhyme—Frost wrote a fair amount of blank verse—but of the fact that the pentameter is only loosely iambic. One other point: In a conversation, Frost once mentioned that he never read this poem publicly. He put it in a class with "Out, Out" (the poem about the boy who loses his hand while operating a buzz-saw), something too terrifying to inflict on a captive audience.

A few more words about the title, and about the representation of American Indians. First, a word about the word "Indian." It is Eurocentric, of course, and in recent years it has been somewhat displaced by "Native American," but (as we say in this handbook at the beginning of this chapter) many American Indians still prefer to call themselves Indians; in fact, it is our impression that whites are more likely than Indians to use "Native American." Second, whatever term is used, it probably erodes important ethnic and individual differences. One hears generalizations about Native Americans (or Indians) that would be inconceivable in speaking of "Europeans." For instance, in *The West as America* (1991), ed. William H. Truettner—a book that accompanied a highly controversial exhibition of art—the authors are very careful to indicate their views that the Indians were far superior to the whites who maltreated them, but we get such sweeping, unsupported comments as this: "Individuality, material status, and vanity . . . [are] all notions less highly regarded in Indian culture [than in white culture]" (149). It might come as a surprise to, say, the Sioux, the Navaho, the Pawnee, and the Seneca, that they have much in common. Still, *The West as America* is an invaluable resource for images of Indians.

Another resource is Edward S. Curtis's massive collection of photographs, *The North American Indian*. The first picture in the first volume (1907—only nine years before Frost's poem) is called *The Vanishing Race*. It shows a line of Indians riding from the foreground into a dark background—vanishing. It is conveniently reproduced as #56 in Christopher M. Lyman, *The Vanishing Race and Other Illusions* (1982).

ROBERT FROST

The Aim Was Song (p. 838)

The poem offers a playful, witty fable, in effect telling how human beings improved upon nature by inventing art. Frost talks about only one art, "song," the art dearest to him, but (as we will see in a moment) the fable implies the other arts too.

Nature is the rough wind, blowing loudly. Art is (to use Alexander Pope's words in *An Essay on Criticism*) "nature methodized." In Frost's playful terms in this poem, nature has to be "converted" (line 11, literally *turned around, transformed*) and changed into something governed "by measure." Poetry of course uses *measure*, i.e., meter (from the Greek *metron*, "measure"), but so do the other arts, such as music (where the metronome has its place), architecture (where symmetry is common), and even prose fiction (where one can chart recurring motifs, paired or contrasting characters, foreshadowing, and so forth).

Having said this, we must admit that Frost is talking chiefly about poetry, and in fact about lyric poetry (*song*) where, one might almost say, the sound is more important than the sense. After all, we *do* value some lyrics that barely go beyond *hey nonny nonny*. There is a staying-power in nonsense rhymes, counting-out rhymes, and so forth, and while no one would say that these are the highest kind of poetry, they do serve as reminders that music (measure) is at the heart of poetry.

ROBERT FROST

The Need of Being Versed in Country Things (p. 838)

We begin this discussion with some questions that we usually ask in class, and we follow these questions with our own responses.

TOPICS FOR CRITICAL THINKING AND WRITING

1. By the end of the second stanza the reader understands that the farmhouse has been destroyed by a fire. Why do you suppose (putting aside the matter of rhyme) in line 2 Frost wrote "a sunset glow" instead of (say) "a burst of flame"? And what is the effect of the simile in line 4? That is, what do these comparisons contribute to the poem? (If you are unsure of the meaning of "pistil," check a dictionary.)

2. In the fifth stanza Frost uses personifications: "the lilac renewed its leaf," and the "pump flung up an awkward arm," and "the fence post carried a strand of wire." What other personifications do you find in the poem? What effect do these personifications have on you? And why do you suppose there are no personifications in the last two lines of the poem?

3. In a sentence or two or three, characterize the speaker. (You can probably characterize him or her by means of an adjective or two or three; use the rest of the allotment to provide evidence, such as brief quotations.)

4. Much of the poem describes a scene, but the speaker also interprets the scene. How would you summarize the interpretation? How might you paraphrase the title? Does the speaker convince you of the "need" to be "versed in country things"?

5. Do you think the poem is sentimental? Or, on the other hand, cynical? Explain.

6. Suppose you were to write a parody of "The Need of Being Versed in Country Things." What scene might you use, or what objects might you personify? (A parody is an amusing imitation of the style of another work, often with an inappropriate subject. Thus, one might parody a sports writer by imitating his or her style, but the subject would not be an athletic event but, say, students engaged in peer review.) Suggestion: Consider the possibility of using your neighborhood or your workplace as a subject.

Our thoughts about the above questions may be of some interest.

1. Why "a sunset glow" in line 2, instead of say, "a burst of flame"? Frost's metaphor introduces, early in the poem, the motif that things are not what they seem. (Later his point will be that the birds seem to weep, but are not weeping.) The same might be said for the simile of the chimney as a pistil, in line 4, with the additional implication that the house is absorbed into nature.
2. The personifications in the fifth stanza suggest that the human perceiver of nature insists on finding human qualities in nature—a tendency that will be debunked (though that's too strong a word) by the end of the poem, where the speaker without figurative language states the facts. Other personifications in the poem are "the will of the wind" (7) and the "murmur" (15) of the birds.
3., 4.   Although at the end of the poem the speaker claims to be telling it as it is—that is, insisting that nature is not lamenting the catastrophe—a reader probably feels that the speaker regrets that this is so. After all, much of the poem is devoted to evoking a highly sympathetic image of a busy farm that has been destroyed and turned almost into a part of nature itself. In our reading we hear some confidence in the assertion that the phoebes are not weeping, but this confidence is undercut by or at least suffused with deep regret. Put it this way: Observers should understand that nature does not weep for human losses, but (and this is not explicitly said but we think it is evident in the tone) this is a pity.
5. Our own feeling is that the poem is neither sentimental (maudlin, and influenced more by emotion than by reason) nor cynical (sneering). As we indicated in the preceding paragraph, we hear objectivity tinged with regret. Obviously other responses are possible.
6. This suggestion for writing calls for a parody. If you assign this topic and receive some work of special interest, we hope that (after getting the student's permission) you will send it to us, with the student's name and address. If we think we can use it in the next edition of the book, we will get in touch with the student.

ROBERT FROST

Stopping by Woods on a Snowy Evening (p. 839)

Note: In Chapter 19 we include three essays—some good, some weak—on this poem.

On "Stopping by Woods," see John Lynen, *The Pastoral Art of Robert Frost* (1960). We number ourselves among the readers who see in the poem a longing for death ("frozen lake," "darkest evening of the year," "The woods are lovely, dark and deep" seem to support this view), but that is not what the poem is exclusively about. If there is a momentary longing for death in the poem, there is also the reassertion of the will to face the tasks of living. As Frost put it, at the Bread Loaf Writers' Conference in 1960, "People are always trying to find a death wish in that poem. But there's a life wish there—he goes on, doesn't he?"

Frost reads the poem in *Robert Frost Reading His Own Poems* (Record No. 1, EL LCB, 1941), distributed by the National Council of Teachers of English.

TOPICS FOR CRITICAL THINKING AND WRITING

1. As the manuscript indicates, line 5 originally read: "The steaming horses think it queer." Line 7 read: "Between a forest and a lake." Which version do you prefer? Why?

2. The rhyming words in the first stanza can be indicated by *aaba*; the second stanza picks up the *b* rhyme: *bbcb*. Indicate the rhymes for the third stanza. For the fourth. Why is it appropriate that the rhyme scheme differs in the fourth stanza?

3. Hearing that the poem had been interpreted as a "death poem," Frost said, "I never intended that, but I did have the feeling it was loaded with ulteriority." What "ulteriority" is implicit? How is the time of day and year significant? How does the horse's attitude make a contrast with the speaker's?

ROBERT FROST

Acquainted with the Night (p. 840)

Some years ago a student of ours, Joseph Kang, wrote an explication of this poem. It seems excellent to us, and we reproduce it here with his permission.

> The words in Robert Frost's "Acquainted with the Night," except "luminary" in line 12, are all common ones, but if we look closely at these words we see some *unusual* implications. Take the title: "Acquainted with the Night." We are usually acquainted with a person or with a fact, not with the night. And so "night" must have some special suggestion that is not yet clear. And to be "acquainted" with someone or something usually implies familiarity (as in "I am acquainted with John Jones") but not thorough knowledge. "I have been one acquainted with the night," then, is an unusual and cautious statement.
>
> The first stanza is matter-of-fact. It consists of three sentences, each beginning "I have," and each sentence fills exactly one line. It almost sounds flat, but is not flat because as I have said, "acquainted with the night" is an unusual expression. Also, the repetition of words and grammatical structure makes for special emphasis. Furthermore, when "I have walked out" turns into "I have outwalked the furthest city light," we realize that we are being told about a special journey, not just a literal walk. We don't yet know what this journey was, but even if this walk beyond "the furthest city light" was a literal walk, Frost also means for us to take it as a walk beyond man-made illumination, civilization, order. It must have been meant as an experience with something dark in the way that grief, ignorance, loss of faith, or loneliness are dark.
>
> The second stanza resembles the previous stanza but it is more expansive. It continues the use of "I have," but now only in the first two of its three lines, and only the first line is a complete sentence. And it introduces people other than the speaker, first in "the saddest city lane" (line 4), and next in the watchman (line 5). The lane cannot literally be sad; "saddest" implies that sad people live in the lane, or that the speaker feels sad when he thinks of the people who live in the lane. The watchman perhaps is one of these, and the speaker avoids his glance, explaining only

that he is "unwilling to explain" (line 6). The speaker, then, not only is walking alone but also isolates himself from his fellows. That is, he feels isolated and therefore shuns contact.

The third stanza begins with "I have," as five of the previous six lines have begun, but it is even less closely patterned on the first stanza than the second was; that is, the poem becomes looser. In fact, the thought overflows the stanza; the first stanza of three lines was three sentences, and their tone was assertive, almost confident: "I have been one acquainted . . . I have walked out . . . and back" (there is a survivor's note of understated triumph in that "and back"), and I have "outwalked" again a note of triumph. But the quiet yet firm self-assertion then begins to dissolve. The second stanza was two sentences, and now the third stanza cannot contain even one complete sentence—the sentence flows into the next two stanzas, running almost to the end of the poem. To put it slightly differently, all but the last line of the octave (final eight lines) of this sonnet is a single sentence.

In the second stanza the speaker ignores human society, suggested by the watchman; in the third and fourth stanzas human society ignores the speaker, for the "cry" (line 8) is not directed to the speaker: It is "not to call me back or say good-bye" (line 10). In addition to this suggestion of mankind's indifference to the speaker, there is a suggestion that the speaker almost doesn't exist—even in his own perceptions: "I have stood still and stopped the sound of feet" (line 7). A paraphrase of the last six words might be, "and stopped producing the noise of footsteps." Thus, by standing still the speaker or became inaudible not only to the city-dwellers but also to himself.

The "interrupted cry" on line 8 is sorrowful, for it is a "cry" and not a "call" or "shout" or "laugh." And the cry is mysterious because we do not know its cause, its source, its message, or why it is "interrupted." The fourth stanza continues to deepen the sense of mystery by referring to a clock "at an unearthly height." Maybe this is a real clock, perhaps with an illuminated face, high on a church or town hall, but it seems more likely that this "luminary" clock is something beyond "the furthest city light"; probably it is a metaphor describing the full moon, which is literally "unearthly." Its unearthliness is emphasized by the unusual use of the unusual word "luminary," for "luminary" is usually a noun meaning "a source of illumination," but here it is used as an adjective. In any case, a real clock can be right or wrong, and it can tell us that the time is right or wrong for eating, sleeping, attending class, or whatever. But this "luminary clock," at an "unearthly height," offers no heavenly guidance and it cannot be either corrected or obeyed. The speaker can only look at the clock (whether a real clock or the moon) and increasingly sense that he has nothing to communicate with.

The last line of the poem, a complete sentence in itself, repeats the first line exactly, and it restores the tone of assurance. Now we have a sharper idea of what the speaker means when he says he has been "one acquainted with the night," but we still cannot say that the "night" equals or symbolizes this or that. "Loneliness," for example, is too simple a translation, because loneliness implies isolation from people, and in the poem we sense that the speaker's isolation may be not only from other people but also from himself (from a sense of any individual purpose) and also from a meaningless universe. Moreover, we must also say—and the poem is as much about this as it is about "the night"—that the speaker is not crushed by the experience. The poem is not a lament, and not a descent into self-pity. The speaker does not sadly say "I *am* one acquainted with the night"; rather, the experience is put at a distance by being set in the past: "I *have been* one acquainted with the night." And though the memory of the experience is still sharp, the speaker keeps his response under control. The closest he comes to telling us explicitly of his feelings is in the terse first and last lines. For the most part he shows us the situation rather than tells us his feelings, and thus he conveys a sense of control—a sense, we might say, of being able to deal with the experience, to survive it (since the last line repeats the first line we can say that he literally comes out where he went in), and even to get it down on paper.

ROBERT FROST

Desert Places (p. 840)

Presumably the abundant alliteration and repetition of words, especially in the first stanza but also in the third, help to suggest the thick snow falling fast, almost uniformly covering the land. The first three stanzas emphasize blankness, but of course a reader is as interested in the speaker's tone (elegiac and sonorous, but fused with some witty word-play); the fourth stanza emphasizes the speaker's response to heavenly emptiness (i.e., to the vast spaces and to lifelessness) by diminishing them with a reference to his inner "desert places." Reuben Brower, in *The Poetry of Robert Frost* (1963), points out that in the fourth stanza "the scary place is thrust off 'there' by the emerging man of wit, by the mind that won't give way to 'absent-spiritedness.' But the gesture is a bit flamboyant and opens up a worse form of terror by bringing fear where the poet most lives alone. The taunting threat . . . is now replaced by a finer and more discreet irony" in the final lines.

The expression "desert places" appears in Chapter XVIII of *The Scarlet Letter*: Hester Prynne, outlawed from society, found that "Her intellect and heart had their home, as it were, in desert places, where she roamed as freely as the wild Indian in his woods." For two articles that seek to make much of the relation to Hawthorne, see A. J. von Frank and E. Stone in *Frost: Centennial Essays*, ed. Committee on the Frost Centennial of the University of Southern Mississippi. The poem (though not the alleged relation to Hawthorne) is also discussed by Brooks and Warren, *Understanding Poetry*.

ROBERT FROST

Design (p. 841)

On Frost's "Design," see Randall Jarrell, *Poetry and the Age;* Richard Poirier, *Robert Frost* (1990); Reuben A. Brower, *The Poetry of Robert Frost* (1963); Richard Ohmann, *College English* 28 (February 1967): 359–67; and Reginald Cook, *Robert Frost: A Living Voice* (1974), especially 263–67. Brower is especially good on the shifting tones of voice, for example, from what he calls "the cheerfully observant walker on back country roads" who reports "I found a dimpled . . ."—but then comes the surprising "spider, fat and white"—to the "self-questioning and increasingly serious" sestet. Here, for Brower, "the first question ('What had the flower to do . . . ') sounds like ordinary annoyance at a fact that doesn't fit in." The next question brings in a new note, and irony in "kindred." For Brower, with the last question ironic puzzlement turns into vision: "What but design of darkness to appall?" And then Brower says that in the final line "The natural theologian pauses—he is only asking, not asserting—and takes a backward step."

The title echoes the "Argument from Design," the argument that the universe is designed (each creature fits perfectly into its environment: the whale is equipped for the sea; the camel for the desert), so there must be a designer, God. Notice that the word—"design"—has two meanings: (1) pattern and (2) intention, plan. Frost certainly means us to have both meanings in mind. There seems to be a pattern and also an intention behind it, but this intention is quite different from the intention discerned by those who in the eighteenth and nineteenth centuries argued for the existence of a benevolent God from the "Argument from Design."

"Design" was published in 1922; below is an early 1912 version of the poem, entitled "In White":

> A dented spider like a snow drop white
> On a white Heal-all, holding up a moth
> Like a white piece of lifeless satin cloth—
> Saw ever curious eye so strange a sight?—
> Portent in little, assorted death and blight
> Like the ingredients of a witches' broth?—
> The beady spider, the flower like a froth,
> And the moth carried like a paper kite.
> What had that flower to do with being white?
> The blue prunella every child's delight.
> What brought the kindred spider to that height?
> (Make we no thesis of the miller's plight.)
> What but design of darkness and of night?
> Design, design! Do I use the word aright?

The changes, obvious enough, are discussed by George Monteiro, in *Frost: Centennial Essays*, published by the Committee on the Frost Centennial of the University of Southern Mississippi, 35–38.

By the way, an ingenious student mentioned that the first stanza has eight lines, corresponding to the eight legs of a spider. And the second stanza has six, corresponding to the six legs of a moth. What to do? We tried to talk about the traditional structure of the sonnet, and about relevant and irrelevant conjectures, and about the broad overlapping area. About as good a criterion as any is, does the conjecture make the poem better?

TOPICS FOR CRITICAL THINKING AND WRITING

1. Do you find the spider, as described in line 1, cute or disgusting? Why?
2. What is the effect of "If" in the last line?
3. The word "design" can mean "pattern" (as in "a pretty design"), or it can mean "intention," especially an evil intention (as in "He had designs on her"). Does Frost use the word in one sense or in both? Explain.

ROBERT FROST

Come In (p. 841)

This poem has fairly close associations with "The Need of Being Versed in Country Things" (the speaker at the end indicates his awareness that nature is *not* to be interpreted in the way that a less knowledgeable person might interpret it) and also with "Stopping by Woods on a Snowy Evening" (the temptation to enter into the darkness—to yield to some sort of impulse of self-surrender—is rejected, in favor of the assertion of the self in business as usual). The thrush's song is understood not as a "call to come in," but as "almost" (line 15) such a call (cf. the realism of the speaker of "The Need of Being Versed"), and the speaker is "out for stars," and therefore will "not come in" (cf. the end of "Stopping by Woods," where the speaker asserts the need to go for miles before he sleeps).

Reuben Brower, in *The Poetry of Robert Frost* (1963), speaks of "the doubling of tones in the poem" (32). Among the examples that he gives are the title, which suggests a friendly welcome at the kitchen door, and also a more mysterious invitation, and (in line 2) the word "hark," which has an old-fashioned grandmotherly tone and also a poetic tone of religious wonder. Notice also the two sets of images, darkness (in most of the poem) and light ("But no, I was out for stars"). "Pillared dark," incidently, wonderfully connects the trees with columns, presumably those of a temple.

ROBERT FROST

The Silken Tent (p. 842)

The idea of comparing a woman to a silken tent in the summer breeze seems fresh enough to us (probably swaying silken tents have been compared to young women, but did anyone before Frost see it the other way around?), and given this idea, one would expect passages about gentle swaying. If one knew the piece were going to be an allegory worked out in some detail, one might expect the tent pole to be the soul. But who could have expected the brilliant connection between the cords and "ties of love and thought," and the brilliant suggestion that only rarely are we made aware—by "capriciousness"—of our "bondage"? The paradoxical idea that we are (so to speak) kept upright—are what we are—by things that would seem to pull us down is new to most students, who think that one "must be oneself." With a little discussion they come to see that what a person is depends largely on relationships. We are parents, or students, or teachers, or—something; our complex relationships give us our identity. Sometimes, in trying to make clear this idea that our relationships contribute to (rather than diminish) our identities, we mention the scene in Ibsen's *Peer Gynt* where, in an effort to get at his essential self, Peer peels an onion, each removed layer being a relationship that he has stripped himself of. He ends with nothing, of course.

In short, we think this poem embodies a profound idea, and we spend a fair amount of our class time talking about that idea. But we also try to look at the poem closely. Students might be invited to discuss what sort of woman "she" is. What, for instance, do "midday" and "summer" in line 2 contribute? Frost could, after all, have written "In morning when a sunny April breeze" but he probably wanted to suggest—we don't say a mature woman—someone who is no longer girlish, someone who is of sufficient age to have established responsibilities, and to have experienced, on occasion, a sense of slight bondage. Among the traits that we think can be reasonably inferred from the comparison are these: beauty, poise, delicacy (in lines 1–4), and sweetness and firmness of soul (5–7).

TOPICS FOR CRITICAL THINKING AND WRITING

1. The second line places the scene at "midday" in "summer." In addition to giving us the concreteness of a setting, do these words help to characterize the woman whom the speaker describes? If so, how?
2. The tent is supported by "guys" (not men, but the cords or "ties" of line 10) and by its "central cedar pole." What does Frost tell us about these ties? What does he tell us about the pole?
3. What do you make of lines 12–14?
4. In a sentence, a paragraph, or a poem, construct a simile that explains a relationship.

ROBERT FROST

The Most of It (p. 843)

The "he" of the poem is not the speaker, of course; we are totally dependent on the speaker for our impression of this person, and we don't get even a single phrase of reported speech. Judging from what the speaker tells us, the "he" is a rather unimaginative person, someone who (at least in the first half of the poem) finds nothing of significance outside of himself. The world around him offers "but the mocking echo" of his own voice. As Richard Poirier suggests, in his shrewd analysis in *Robert Frost* (1977), 165, this is someone who cannot "*make* the most of it," someone, we might say, who is not a poet. But the reader, as distinct from the "he," perceives the grandeur of the surroundings— and this grandeur is so presented that as we read it we more or less project ourselves into the mind of the spectator, who stands in this landscape "bathed in a mythological heroism" (Poirier, 165), and we feel we are experiencing his experience. What we and the spectator get is not what the spectator wanted at the start, but is (again in Poirier's words) "a vision of some fabulousness beyond domestication" (165).

LANGSTON HUGHES

Students should approach poems by Langston Hughes with at least two goals in mind. It is important, first, to read each one carefully in its own right, paying close attention to the special way that Hughes handles vocabulary and imagery. Second, it is important, and one of the pleasures of reading Hughes, to notice the connections between one poem and others, the verbal and thematic links that organize Hughes's poetic enterprise as a whole.

Readers of Walt Whitman—following Whitman's lead—often refer to the many separate poems in *Leaves of Grass* as components of a single poem, a single massive act of expression in which Whitman seeks to convey and honor the multiple meanings of America. A similar description, we think, could be offered of Hughes's collected poems, and in this context it is worth mentioning that Whitman was in fact Hughes's great model, the precursor in the American literary tradition whom Hughes wished to emulate. He wanted to achieve for his people what he believed Whitman had achieved for white America, and, as David Perkins has observed in *A History of Modern Poetry* (1976), Hughes's "oeuvre makes a remarkably broad, rich, forceful, appealing impression," like Whitman's.

Notice, then, how the poem "The Negro Speaks of Rivers," with its evocative testimony of the poet's desire to speak what he has known and deeply acquired in his soul, is connected to the lines in "The Weary Blues": "Sweet Blues! / Coming from a black man's soul. / O Blues!"; and then, in turn, hear how the mood of "The Weary Blues" gets turned toward a dispirited, yet still somewhat wry, self-disdain in "Too Blue." Ponder the painful image of "the dead fire's ashes" in "The South," in contrast to the "clean flame of joy" in "Ruby Brown." Consider also the themes of injustice and betrayal—specifically, the betrayal of the American dream and the promises of equal opportunity.

When a poet is studied in depth, students can be encouraged to see affinities among poems, linkages in ideas and illuminations, shared patterns, and variations performed on the same or related subjects, as when, for instance, Hughes traces the plight of African-American women in "Mother to Son" and "Ruby Brown." Students will observe, too, that a number of these poems are *about* poetry, about writing, about finding a subject, a voice: "The Negro Speaks of Rivers"; "Poet to Patron"; "Theme for English B"; "Poet to Bigot."

For a discussion of Hughes's relationship to other African-American writers of the period, see Arnold Rampersad, "The Poetry of the Harlem Renaissance," in *The Columbia History of American Poetry*, ed. Jay Parini (1993). For background, see *Voices from the Harlem Renaissance*, ed. Nathan Irvin Huggins (1976), and David Levering Lewis, *When Harlem Was in Vogue* (1981).

Biographies too often make a writer's work seem less interesting and urgent than it is, but Rampersad's *The Life of Langston Hughes* (2 vols., 1986, 1988) is an exception to the rule and is highly recommended.

LANGSTON HUGHES

The Negro Speaks of Rivers (p. 846)

W. E. B. Du Bois noted in 1940 that "the longing of Black men must have respect; the rich and the strange readings of nations they have seen may give the world new points of view and make their loving, living, and doing precious to all human hearts." It is a version of this longing, this desire for expression, that is at the center of "The Negro Speaks of Rivers." It is important that students realize Hughes was still in his teens when he wrote it and that the poem is a bold as well as beautiful one. This young man was claiming to speak as a Negro on behalf of generations of his people. There is a grandeur to the aspirations he voices, and maybe behind the poem is Mark Twain's formidable rendering of the Mississippi River in

Adventures of Huckleberry Finn and other writings. But "the Negro" whom Hughes describes knows of many rivers, in an arc of experience that spans the globe.

LANGSTON HUGHES

Mother to Son (p. 846)

The main movement of this poem is clear enough: a mother urges her son to keep moving forward, working hard, whatever the hard obstacles he faces. But what makes the poem affecting is the manner in which Hughes evokes the mother's voice. Notice, for instance, the starkness of "bare" in line 7, which dramatizes both a literal fact about the stair ("places with no carpet on the floor") and the desolating emptiness that the mother feels but still strives to overcome.

On one level, the poem is affirmative and uplifting, but the reiteration of the phrase "life for me ain't been no crystal stair" complicates the mood, perhaps darkening it. Here it can be interesting to ask students what the effect would have been if Hughes had ended the poem at line 19: "I'se still climbin'." That would have given the poem, as it concluded, the surge of an upward movement. But Hughes had a different emotional aim; he wanted the mother to return to the hardness of her life, to her slightly comic but still wounded sense of the richer, more comfortable life that she lacks. The poem ends with the mother's voicing of what she does not have, the burden that she carries. She keeps on striving and struggling, not giving up, and she counsels her son to do likewise. But she does not deny to herself or to him that there is resistance, a weight of pain and disappointment, that she will always know is there.

Note: Be sure to make vivid for students what "crystal" is. They benefit from being reminded of its glimmering qualities (how it reflects light), and of its use in fine glassware and ornaments.

LANGSTON HUGHES

The Weary Blues (p. 847)

This poem ("weary" may pun on "wary") has been identified as one of the first by an African American to make use of the blues form. This is a key piece of information to pass along, but it does not take us very far. The phrase "the blues" is familiar, and is widely used, yet it is hard to define. In fact, part of the point seems to be the mysterious depth and mystery of the blues: You know what it is and when you are feeling it, but cannot *say* in so many words what it is. You simply got the blues, or, if you are a musician, you are playing the blues.

As *The Oxford Companion to Popular Music* (1991) indicates, "the blues remains a hazily poetical concept that still cannot ultimately be expressed more accurately than in the words of an old slave woman, quoted in the mid-19th century, who described it as music that could only be created with 'a full heart and a troubled spirit.'"

On the other hand, the literature, both popular and scholarly, on the subject of the blues is vast. We have found it to be a good one for reports by students, particularly those with an interest in contemporary music, jazz, gospel, and rhythm and blues. Teachers might recommend Le Roi Jones, *Blues People* (1963); *The Blues Line: A Collection of Blues Lyrics*, ed. E. Sackheim (1973); Robert Palmer, *Deep Blues* (1981); and P. Oliver, M. Harrison, and W. Bolcom, *The New Grove Gospel, Blues, and Jazz* (1986). See also M. L. Hart, *The Blues: A Bibliographical Guide* (1988).

For more immediate purposes in the classroom when teaching Hughes, we have cited Ralph Ellison, "Richard Wright's Blues" (1964): "The blues is an impulse to keep the painful details and episodes of a brutal experience alive in one's aching consciousness, to finger its jagged grain, and to transcend it, not by the consolation of philosophy but by squeezing from it a near-tragic, near-comic lyricism. As a form, the blues is an autobiographical chronicle of personal catastrophe expressed lyrically."

The jazz trumpet player Wynton Marsalis, in an interview published in *American Heritage* (October 1995), speaks suggestively as well: "Blues gives the jazz musician an unsentimental view of the world. Blues is adult secular music, the first adult secular music America produced. It has an optimism that's not naive. You accept tragedy and move forward. . . . Blues is such a fundamental form that it's loaded with complex information. It has a sexual meaning, the ebb and the flow of sexual passion: disappointment, happiness, joy, and sorrow. It has a whole religious connotation too, that joy and lift."

When we teach Hughes's poem, we tend to read it aloud and then, either through a mini-lecture or student reports, to provide a cultural context for it. Next, we read the poem again, lingering over the rhymes, the alliteration ("moan with melody"), and the other expert, subtle handlings of sound. One of us, indeed, always sings the lines that Hughes identifies as coming from the song of the musician. It may not be the best singing that the lines could receive, but it does alert the class to the closeness of Hughes's poem to song, to the way in which this blues poem derives from (and is) blues music.

LANGSTON HUGHES

The South (p. 847)

Hughes builds this poem on sharp contrasts of description and feeling, beginning with the first two lines: "The lazy, laughing South / With blood on its mouth." The first line could have led to a different kind of poem—sentimental, dreamy, wistful; Hughes, we think, counts on this possibility only to strike against it in the next line, with its graphic image of savagery. This is an angry, punishing poem, possibly one that is self-punishing too, as Hughes brings forth cruel images that, one feels, are etched in his consciousness, that he cannot break free from.

As the poem moves toward its conclusion, Hughes declares he will seek liberation from the South, and in our classes we have discovered that sometimes students too quickly regard the poem as proposing a straight exchange or polarity: the South is bad, impossible for the black man or woman to love, while the North is the land of bright prospects. Here, it's helpful to show how a phrase like "kinder mistress" is balanced against the reference to "cold-faced" and the distancing "they say" (the speaker is relying on others' reports—maybe these are wrong) in the preceding lines. In addition, if there is hope, it *may* exist (which differs from saying that it *will* exist) only for the next generation, not for the speaker.

We like to take the opportunity that this poem offers to recommend C. Vann Woodward's classic study, *The Strange Career of Jim Crow* (3rd ed., 1974), and I. A. Newby, *The South: A History* (1978). Advanced students will also find useful a good collection of essays, *Myth and Southern History*, ed. Patrick Gerster and Nicholas Cords (2nd ed., 2 vols., 1989). This is also a moment in the semester when one can refer students to Jean Toomer's collection of poems, prose sketches, and stories, *Cane* (1923), and to Richard Wright's collection of stories, *Uncle Tom's Children* (1938; enl. ed., 1940), and his wrenching autobiography about growing up in the South, *Black Boy* (1945).

LANGSTON HUGHES

Ruby Brown (p. 848)

This poem works well alongside "Mother to Son" as another example of Hughes's commentary on the predicaments of African-American women. The poem itself does not record a judgment on Ruby Brown's decline into prostitution, though the details are certainly disturbing ("the sinister shuttered houses"), and the church members, it is noted, no longer mention her name. But the speaker basically tells her story; he does not criticize or condemn her. Possibly there is even a hint of an ambiguity in the phrase "good church folk." Yes, they are good, but maybe just a bit complacent as well, unsympathetic to Ruby's situation, unable to fathom why she found her life of low-pay, joyless labor so deadening.

LANGSTON HUGHES

Poet to Patron (p. 849)

A short poem, with a ringingly clear point expressed in its angered, impatient tone. But there are some verbal effects here that students should be helped to see and appreciate. "Throw out pieces of my heart" is a wonderfully apt phrase. It suggests what the speaker is giving up to the patron, but even more precisely, it sounds a note of self-disgust: The precious pieces of his heart are thrown away like something that has no or little value. The patron is exacting something from the speaker, and the speaker is exacting something from himself. How could he allow himself to do this?

The implication here prepares the way for the harsher line, "I must sell myself," in the next stanza. The "perfumed note" in the next-to-last line, we think, says something mocking and derisive about the patron who sends the note, yet, once more, it conveys self-contempt in the speaker who is obliged to receive it. Notice that the speaker does not conclude by renouncing the patron. He dislikes the patron's demands, and he states that working in a factory might be better. But the final lines imply that he is still connected to the patron; he hasn't broken away yet. After all, if he worked in a factory, he would not be writing poetry. If he gave up his patron, he would be sacrificing even more than he does now. In this respect, the patron is still in control, whatever the speaker's resistance to him.

LANGSTON HUGHES

Ballad of the Landlord (p. 849)

This is another of Hughes's political poems, and it is a very effective one. In it Hughes shows what happens to a person who stands up for his rights and demands justice. As soon as he does, he is branded a dangerous radical who is bent on toppling the government and turning America upside down. The final lines are clipped and fast-paced, as Hughes bears witness to how quickly America contains (and eliminates) its internal foes. Part of the point is that versions of this same incident have occurred countless times before.

We talk about ballads—popular and literary—in Chapter 14.

LANGSTON HUGHES

Too Blue (p. 850)

This poem can be taught effectively next to "The Weary Blues"; it has a sad, wry weariness that is evident, for example, in the speaker's amused but glum observation that it would probably take two bullets to crack through his "hard head" if he tried to shoot himself.

LANGSTON HUGHES

Harlem [1] (p. 850)

The poet-critic Claude McKay, in *Harlem: Negro Metropolis* (1940), observes: "Harlem was my first positive reaction to American life—it was like entering a paradise of my own people; the rhythm of Harlem still remains one of the most pleasurable sensations of my blood."

Hughes sometimes celebrates Harlem in the way that McKay does, but in this poem the vision is more severe and terrible: Harlem is painted as the place on the edge of hell where African Americans face mistreatment and from where they glimpse all that is denied to them. Harlem is *here,* and "the world" is over there, gazed at from a distance.

When we teach this poem, we return for a moment to "The South," so that the students can measure what is said about Harlem in "Harlem [1]" against the freedom that the speaker (or at least his children) hopes to locate in the North. Students enjoy hearing poems in dialogue with one another, glossing and even challenging one another. Try to communicate to students how the poems of a writer like Hughes establish a structure of relationships, which, in turn, are part of the larger structure of the history of poetry within which the writer works.

See the critic Arthur P. Davis, in an essay included in *Images of the Negro in American Literature*, ed. Seymour L. Cross and John Edward Hardy (1966): "One must bear in mind that with Langston Hughes, Harlem is both place and symbol. When he depicts the hopes, the aspirations, the frustrations, and the deep-seated discontent of the New York ghetto, he is expressing the feelings of Negroes in black ghettos throughout America."

LANGSTON HUGHES

Theme for English B (p. 851)

We have found this poem to be very provocative for getting students to think about what constitutes the *identity* of a poet. The question has always been an important one, but perhaps in today's highly multicultural society it has become especially vexed and contentious. "So will my page be colored that I write?" Hughes's speaker asks. Does a poem inevitably reflect the race, ethnicity, gender, and/or class of its author? Can members of a different group *really* read and understand such a poem, or is a poem a circuit of communication that passes only from the author to the members of the group whose identity he or she shares?

For Hughes, persons cannot be separated off into groups, however much they might wish they could be. "That's American," he says. If there is an essential America, it lies in the fact that in America no one is truly separate from anyone else. Everyone is "part" of one another and has much to learn. No one can claim to be beyond the need of knowing about what others have to teach them. We like at this point both to commend Hughes's faith and query students whether they can accept it for themselves.

LANGSTON HUGHES

Poet to Bigot (p. 852)

Like "Theme for English B" and "Poet to Patron," "Poet to Bigot" is a poem about writing, reading, and interpretation. Invite students to draw out the implications of the opposing images of "stone" and "flower" in the final two stanzas. But then, by way of review and summary, ask the class to describe the range of feeling, the range of voice, that Hughes exhibits in the poems included in this section of the book. "My moment is / A flower." Call attention to the precise, concrete immediacy of this line, with its rich but fragile delicacy, and then prompt students to discuss moments in other poems where Hughes's voice displays a different tone and timbre.

23

Poetry and Translation

Can Poetry Be Translated?

An important purpose of this part of the chapter is to let students who are at ease in a language other than English—perhaps *more* at ease in it than they are in English—draw on their experience, make valuable contributions to the class, and increase everyone's understanding of poetry.

As long-time English teachers, we inevitably have read a fair number of discussions of translation, e.g., concerning Pope's *Homer*, the Greek dramatists, Roman poets, Old English poems, *The Rubaiyat*, etc., to say nothing of arguments about the worth of Ezra Pound's translations of works in languages that he did not know. More recently we have encountered discussions of the problems of translating Native American poetry. Most specialists in Native-American poetry insist that because such poems are not merely spoken, but are chanted and danced, a translation of the mere text, without indications of intonations, pauses, music, and so on, is necessarily misleading. On this topic see Arnold Krupat, "Identity and Difference in the Criticism of Native American Literature," *Diacritics* 13 (Summer 1983): 2–13; Brian Swann and Arnold Krupat, *Recovering the Word* (1987); and Brian Swann, ed., *Coming to Light: Contemporary Translations of the Native Literatures of North America* (1995).

In discussing translations of poetry it is commonplace to say that they fall (very roughly) into three kinds: (1) literal, where the information or content is paramount, and literary values are largely or entirely ignored (such translations are often in prose); (2) verse translations that seek to reproduce the form of the original (e.g., tercets, or ottava rime) and that of course seek to stay as close to the content as the translator can, within the confines of the form; and (3) free translations, concerned less with the poem as information than with the poem as an aesthetic object. Translators of the last sort are likely to claim that they have aimed at catching the "spirit" of the original, which may mean that they have departed very far from the content. Persons who favor the third type point to the translations of Ezra Pound, which (from the scholarly point of view) are filled with gross errors, and in any case sometimes are from languages that Pound did not know. Pound's translations (his translation of the Old English "The Seafarer" is the usual example), these critics say, have the spirit of the original and are good poems in themselves, and therefore the translations are superior to versions that are more accurate in terms of whatever information the original conveyed.

But, again, we include this chapter not primarily in order to allow for discussions of the art or craft of translation but in order to allow non-native or bilingual speakers of English to draw on their experience, enlarge their own understanding of poetry, and contribute to the enlargement of the understanding of their classmates.

Students are keenly interested in learning about the differences in languages—for instance, the use of the familiar form in French and Spanish, or the use of honorifics and the distinction between "man's language" and "woman's language" in Japanese, or the fact that Chinese poetry uses patterns of tone rather than of stress.

Students interested in the art of translation might enjoy Edwin Honig, ed., *The Poet's Other Voice: Conversations on Literary Translation* (1985). There is also a detailed entry and bibliography in *The New Princeton Encyclopedia of Poetry and Poetics*, ed. Alex Preminger and T. V. F. Brogan (1993)—a massive work that students ought to know about.

24

A Collection of Poems

We begin this chapter with some traditional ballads. We have found that they teach well, partly because they are narrative, partly because they are musical, and partly because students can be invited to talk about other ballads that they know. If you are lucky, a student in your class will sing some ballads.

Albert B. Friedman, in *The Viking Book of Folk Ballads*, reissued as *The Penguin Book of Folk Ballads* (1977), gives a comic version of "The Three Ravens" and an American version of "Edward." An American version of "Edward" is recorded on an album, *Child Ballads Traditional in the United States*, 1, issued by the Library of Congress (AAFS L57). Some of these resources may be useful in class discussion.

ANONYMOUS

The Three Ravens (p. 873)

"The Three Ravens," like many other ballads, is filled with mystery: How did the knight die? Why does the doe bury him? Is the doe his lover? But against these uncertainties the poem gives us considerable detail. There are three ravens, the field is "green" (death and life coexist), hounds and hawks loyally guard the knight, and the doe cares for his corpse, protecting it from the birds who would make it their "breakfast." Having given us stanzas in which death and life and bodily self-satisfaction and loyalty are juxtaposed, the poem goes on (with the fallow doe) to show us only gentleness and self-sacrifice. The final stanza, with its reference to a "leman," pretty clearly indicates that the pregnant doe is the knight's beloved and, equally important, suggests that even though the knight is dead, his life was a sort of triumph since it earned such loyalty. The last stanza offers explicit moralizing, but the poem as a whole has *shown*, not preached.

TOPICS FOR CRITICAL THINKING AND WRITING

1. The hounds and the hawks are loyal followers of the knight, as is the doe. How do the references to the hounds and hawks in some degree prepare us for the doe? Do you think this preparation is necessary? Why, or why not?

2. Why does the poet include the ravens? Do they confuse a poem on loyalty, or do they provide an effective contrast? Do the ravens help to give a fuller, more realistic picture of life? Explain.

3. What is your response to the final two lines? Do they strike you as an intrusive comment? Explain.

ANONYMOUS

The Twa Corbies (p. 874)

"The Twa Corbies," unlike the "The Three Ravens," is a poem about *disloyalty*—of hound, hawk, and lady—but we should not overlook the cozy, though macabre, domesticity of the fourth stanza, in which the corbies plan to dine and to patch their nest.

TOPICS FOR CRITICAL THINKING AND WRITING

1. The story in the poem is implied (in the second and third stanzas) rather than made explicit. In your opinion, what is the story? Is it the worse for being implicit? Explain.

2. Hair is usually "gowden" in ballads. What does this conventional detail tell us about the knight's age? Suppose instead of "gowden" (15) the poem said "graying." Would your response be different? How? Why?

3. What do you think the fourth stanza (especially 15–16) contributes to the poem?

4. Animals can't speak. Do you therefore find the poem absurd? Explain.

ANONYMOUS

Edward (p. 875)

Bertrand Bronson, in *The Ballad as Song* (1969), suggests that "Edward" may not be a pure folk ballad. Perhaps the strongest evidence of a "literary" touch is the fact that the surprise ending in the last line—which forces us to reconstruct our understanding of the mother—is unusual for a ballad. In traditional ballads, Bronson points out, people ask questions in order to learn what they do not know (or, in the case of riddling ballads, in order to test someone), but in "Edward" the questions and answers serve a sophisticated technique of character revelation and of plot-telling. By the way, the motifs of questions and answers and last will and testament, found in "Edward," are also in "Lord Randal," which is fairly well known among undergraduates.

TOPICS FOR CRITICAL THINKING AND WRITING

1. The poem consists of two parts. How does the structure of the first part parallel that of the second?
2. What might have been the mother's motives? Do you think that the story would be improved if we knew the motives behind her "counseils"? Explain.
3. How can you explain Edward's statements about his wife and children?
4. Line 21 offers a surprise, but it is topped by the surprise in the final four lines. Can you reread the poem with pleasure once you know the surprises? Explain.

ANONYMOUS

John Henry (p. 877)

There is a wealth of information about the origin of "John Henry" in Guy B. Johnson, *John Henry* (1929), and in Louis W. Chappell, *John Henry* (1933). These books, and many other scholarly writings on John Henry, are summarized in Richard M. Dorson, "The Career of 'John Henry,'" *Western Folklore* 24 (1965):155–63, reprinted in *Mother Wit from the Laughing Barrel* (1972), Alan Dundes. Albert B. Friedman, *The Penguin Book of Folk Ballads* (1977), prints six versions, and the song has often been recorded, e.g., by Huddie Ledbetter, *Leadbelly's Last Sessions*, Vol. 1, Part Two (Folkways Records FA2941 C/D).

Although "John Henry" was composed by blacks, sung by blacks, sung to blacks, and is about a black hero, Eldridge Cleaver suggests in *Soul on Ice* (1963, 164) that it suits the purposes of white racism: The black is all body and no brain. There is something to Cleaver's view, though ballads are scarcely likely to celebrate intellectual activity; when one thinks about the matter, one notices that ballads celebrating a white folk hero normally give him a touch of cunning and make him a fighter against injustice (e.g., Jesse James "had a hand and a heart and a brain," and he "stole from the rich, and he gave to the poor"). "John Henry" celebrates only physical strength (and sometimes sexual strength, in the reference to his women). But the vast majority of ballads celebrating white heroes are rather unimpressive sentimental pieces; "John Henry," however limited its view, has an aesthetic excellence that endures. And after all, no one expects any work of art to tell the *whole* truth.

TOPICS FOR CRITICAL THINKING AND WRITING

1. How does the first stanza contribute to John Henry's grandeur?
2. Some versions contain an additional stanza at the end:

> They took John Henry to the buryin' ground,
> And they buried him in the sand;
> And every locomotive come roarin' round
> Says "There lies a steel-drivin' man,"
> Says "There lies a steel-drivin' man."

Do you find the ending as given in the present text unsatisfactory? Do you have any doubt about John Henry's death?

SHERMAN ALEXIE

On the Amtrak from Boston to New York City (p. 878)

This piece takes the Anglo reader deep into the heart of "the Other." On the surface, the speaker is an affable guy—in a conversation with a stranger he nods his head acquiescently, he does not embarrass the woman by telling her she is talking foolishly, and he even brings her an orange juice from the food car. But we feel his rage at her superficiality and at Don Henley's show of concern for Walden. We also intensely feel his impotence as he makes plans (lines 34–37), which of course he will not act on, for the next occurrence of the same situation. The last line makes it explicit that whites are his enemy, but the reader knows that the whites who meet him on the train will never know it.

The woman's idea that "history" has been made only by whites is presented here in such a way that it is obviously absurd. But it is an idea that almost all whites have held until very recently. For instance, Robert Frost in "The Gift Outright" speaks, without any irony, of the pre-white world as "unstoried, artless, unenhanced."

Alexie is a poet, novelist, short story writer (we include one of his stories in Chapter 9), and writer of screenplays. Our favorite among his books is *Reservation Blues* (1996), which *The Reader's Catalog* summarizes as "a mythic tale of an all-Indian rock band traveling from reservation bars to Seattle and on to Manhattan." According to one review, *Reservation Blues* "does for the American Indian what Richard Wright's *Native Son* did for the Black American in 1940." An issue of the journal *Studies in American Indian Literatures*, 9:4 (Winter 1997), is devoted to Alexie. See especially John Purdy, "Crossroads: A Conversation with Sherman Alexie," 1–18.

Lynn Cline presents an illuminating profile of Alexie's life and literary career in "About Sherman Alexie," *Ploughshares* 26:4 (Winter 2000/2001): 197–202. Also helpful is Stephen F. Evans, "'Open Containers': Sherman Alexie's Drunken Indians," *The American Indian Quarterly* 25:1 (Winter 2001): 46–72, which treats Alexie's techniques as a satirist and social critic, in particular his exploration of ethnic stereotypes. See also John Newton, "Sherman Alexie's Autoethnography," *Contemporary Literature* 42:2 (Summer 2001): 413–28, included in a special issue on the topic "American Poetry." "Sherman Alexie: The Official Site" can be found at http://www.fallsapart.com/.

MATTHEW ARNOLD

Dover Beach (p. 879)

"Dover Beach" begins with the literal—the scene that hits the eye and ear—and then moves in the second stanza to Sophocles's figurative tragic interpretation, in the third to Arnold's figurative religious interpretation, and finally—the image of the sea now being abandoned—to the simile of the world as a "darkling plain" whose only reality is the speaker and the person addressed. The end thus completes the idea of illusion versus reality that began in the first stanza, where the scene that was "calm" (1), "fair" (2), and "tranquil" (3) actually contained the discords implicit in "grating roar," "fling," and so on. In fact, even the "tonight" of the first line implies some conflict, for the word suggests that on other nights the sea is not calm.

For a thought-provoking reading of "Dover Beach," consult A. Dwight Culler, *Imaginative Reason: The Poetry of Matthew Arnold* (1966). Culler argues (perhaps too ingeniously) that although some critics complain about a lack of unity in the imagery (no sea in the last section, and no darkling plain in the first), "the naked shingles are the darkling plain, and that we have no sea in the last section is the very point of the poem. The sea has retreated from the world. . . ." To this point of Culler's we add that the "pebbles" flung about by the waves (10) are an anticipation of "ignorant armies" that are "swept with confused alarms of struggle and flight" (36).

Gerald Graff includes a chapter called "How to Save 'Dover Beach'" in his *Beyond the Culture Wars: How Teaching the Conflicts Can Revitalize American Education* (1992). As the title of the essay and the subtitle of the book indicate, Graff believes that works such as "Dover Beach" can best be taught by recognizing that many of today's readers find some of their assumptions unconvincing and even incomprehensible. Graff imagines an older male professor (OMP) who throws up his hands at his students' indifference to the poem, and a young female professor (YFP) who says she understands how the students feel. In fact Graff's YFP goes on not to express indifference but rather to offer a challenging reading of the poem, or at least of the last lines ("Ah, love. . . ."). She says that this passage adds up to this:

> In other words, protect and console me, my dear—as it's the function of your naturally more spiritual sex to do—from the "struggle and flight" of politics and history that we men have been assigned the regrettable duty of dealing with. It's a good example of how women have been defined by our culture as naturally private and domestic and therefore justly disqualified from sharing male power. (38)

She goes on to say that it is precisely for this reason that we *should* teach the poem—"as the example of phallocentric discourse that it is." OMP objects that such a label "misses the whole point of poetry," and that YFP and her colleagues treat poems "as if they were statements about gender politics" rather than expressions of "universal concerns." YFP replies that literature *is*—among other things—about "gender politics." She goes on:

> What you take to be the universal human experience in Arnold and Shakespeare, Professor OMP, is male experience presented as if it were universal. You don't notice the presence of politics in literature—or in sexual relations, for that matter—because for you patriarchy is simply the normal state of affairs and therefore as invisible as the air you breathe. My reading of "Dover Beach" seems to you to reflect a "special-interest" agenda, but to me your's does, too. You can afford to "transmute" the sexual politics of literature onto a universal plane, but that's a luxury I don't enjoy. (39)

Again, Graff's chief point is that we should face the controversies—should let them enter into our teaching—and not ignore them. "For disagreements about 'Dover Beach' are not peripheral to humanistic culture; they are central to what we mean by humanistic culture" (56). And:

"Controversies from which we have been trying to protect 'Dover Beach' can do a lot to save it" (63).

Students will be greatly aided by the detailed annotations in *The Poems of Matthew Arnold*, ed. Kenneth Allott (1965; 2nd ed., ed. Miriam Allott, 1979). *Matthew Arnold: Selections*, ed. Miriam Allott and Robert H. Super (1986), is also well annotated and includes a good selection of Arnold's prose. We also admire the selection of Arnold's poems edited and annotated by Timothy Peltason (1994).

Though now somewhat dated, the range of essays on Arnold's life included in *Matthew Arnold*, ed. Kenneth Allott (1975), is still useful for teachers and students alike. Excellent biographies have been written by Park Honan (1981), Nicholas Murray (1996), and Ian Hamilton (1999). For an insightful brief account: Stefan Collini, *Arnold* (1988). Three books from the 1960s remain valuable: A. Dwight Culler, *Imaginative Reason: The Poetry of Matthew Arnold* (1966; rpt. 1976); G. Robert Stange, *Matthew Arnold: The Poet as Humanist* (1967); and Alan Roper, *Arnold's Poetic Landscapes* (1969). In our view, the most stimulating recent book is David G. Riede, *Matthew Arnold and the Betrayal of Language* (1988).

Note: Later in the chapter the book includes Anthony Hecht's response, "The Dover Bitch."

TOPICS FOR CRITICAL THINKING AND WRITING

1. What are the stated and implied reasons behind Arnold's implication that only love offers comfort?
2. The sea, described in the first stanza, puts the speaker in mind of two metaphors, one in the second stanza and one in the third. Explain each of these metaphors in your own words. In commenting on the first, be sure to include a remark about "turbid" in line 17.
3. Is there a connection between the imagery of the sea in the first three stanzas and the imagery of darkness in the last stanza? If not, is this a fault?

W. H. AUDEN

The Unknown Citizen (p. 880)

In "The Unknown Citizen" the speaker's voice is obviously not the poet's. The speaker—appropriately *un*identified in a poem about a society without individuals—is apparently a bureaucrat. For such a person, a "saint" is not one who is committed to spiritual values but one who causes no trouble.

TOPICS FOR CRITICAL THINKING AND WRITING

1. What is Auden satirizing in "The Unknown Citizen"? (Students might be cautioned to spend some time thinking about whether Auden is satirizing the speaker, the citizen, conformism, totalitarianism, technology, or what.)
2. Write a prose eulogy of 250 words satirizing contemporary conformity, or, if you prefer, contemporary individualism.
3. Was he free? Was he happy? Explain.
4. In a paragraph or two, sketch the values of the speaker of the poem, and then sum them up in a sentence or two. Finally, in as much space as you feel you need, judge these values.

JIMMY SANTIAGO BACA

So Mexicans Are Taking Jobs from Americans (p. 881)

The title, the first line, and indeed the whole poem have the flavor of ordinary but forceful speech, and we think this closeness to pugnacious speech, on both sides of the fence, accounts for much of the work's power. That is, it is not enough for a poem to set forth admirable sentiments, let's say, sympathy for the disenfranchised. We want it to be *a poem*, not just the expression of ideas we approve of.

Here we find art in the contrast between the title, which evokes the ordinary world, and the first line and a half, which give us a preposterous world of mounted bandits, and then the third line, which gives us, even more preposterously, a bandit asking us to hand over not money but our job: "Ese gringo, gimmee your job."

To our ear, the most successful lines in the poem are of this sort—lines that show an ear for common speech and a sense of the absurd—and the least successful are the straight, earnest lines of the advocate, such as "I see the poor marching for a little work, / I see small white farmers selling out / to clean-suited farmers living in New York." But we realize that what we have been saying, which in some measure separates literature from political activity, may be unconvincing to others.

In fact, *are* Mexicans taking jobs from Americans? Well, first of all, many of these "Mexicans" are themselves Americans of Mexican origin. Second, although the subject is much disputed, some reputable authorities insist that much of the work that Chicanos do—as migrant laborers, domestic workers, gardeners, and so forth—is in fact so low-paying that Anglos and African Americans will not do it. That is, the jobs wouldn't exist except for the fact that "Mexicans" are willing to do them.

Of Baca's books, we especially value *Immigrants in Our Own Land and Selected Early Poems* (1990 ed.) and *Working in the Dark: Reflections of a Poet of the Barrio* (1992).

AMIRI BARAKA

A Poem for Black Hearts (p. 883)

Most students know something about Malcolm X, and many of them will have seen the film by the African-American director Spike Lee that appeared in 1992. Still, it is useful to remind students that Malcolm X broke bitterly with the Black Muslims in 1963–64, having become pained by the corruption he perceived in the Black Muslim leadership, especially in the case of Elijah Muhammad, whom Malcolm X had revered as his spiritual father. After an inspirational journey to Mecca, the holy city of Islam, where he saw equality among different races, Malcolm X stopped preaching that all whites were evil and began work on a movement of his own, the Organization of Afro-American Unity. He was assassinated—it is widely believed—by Black Muslims in New York City on February 21, 1965.

This poem is a good one to compare and contrast with Brooks's on King. Both poems were written two years after the death of the figures they commemorate—which suggests that both were the product of reflection on the death and its aftermath. But where Brooks is mostly understated, with firm but short lines and stanzas, Baraka is angry, honoring Malcolm X and issuing an appeal for vengeance.

Baraka's poem always generates intense debate and discussion. The reference to breaking the face of "some dumb white man," for example, can prove upsetting. But we have had students remark that this very phrase may evoke sympathy, too: He is just some dumb white man, who maybe did not at all deserve the fate he suffered. Which then leads to the question whether Baraka intended such a reading of the phrase, or, instead, whether some readers want to find it there to mute the impact of his harsh words. Some students have also noted an irony in Baraka's indictment of whites and determination to rally black men for revenge, since it was a group of African Americans who killed Malcolm X.

Ossie Davis: "Malcolm was refreshing excitement; he scared hell out of the rest of us, bred as we are to caution, to hypocrisy in the presence of white folks, to the smile that never fades" (1965).

Maya Angelou: "Malcolm was a path, a way into ourselves" (1981).

Students might be directed to *The Autobiography of Leroi Jones/Amiri Baraka* (1984) and to two scholarly works: Kimberly W. Benston, ed., *Iamamu Amiri Baraka* (1978), and William J. Harris, *The Poetry and Poetics of Amiri Baraka: The Jazz Aesthetic* (1985).

Biographies of Malcolm X are somewhat disappointing; the best is Peter Goldman, *The Death and Life of Malcolm X* (2nd ed., 1979). The most valuable approach to him is through his own words, in George Breitman, ed., *Malcolm X Speaks* (1965), and *The Autobiography of Malcolm X* (1965).

ELIZABETH BISHOP

The Fish (p. 884)

Bishop's poem gives a highly detailed picture of a "venerable" heroic fish that, with its "medals" and its "beard of wisdom," becomes a symbol of courageous endurance. From the colors of the fish, seen and imagined ("brown skin," "darker brown," "rosettes of lime," "tiny white sea-lice," "white flesh," "dramatic reds and blacks," "pink swim-bladder," "tinfoil"), and from the colors of the old fish-lines, the poem moves to the rainbow in the oil in the bilge (the lowest part of the hull). The rainbow—the sign of hope and of God's promise to Noah to spare humanity—grows in the imagination until it fills "the little rented boat," illuminating (we might say) the speaker, who, perceiving the heroic history of the captive, forbears to conquer and returns the fish to the water.

For a discussion of the poem, see Bonnie Costello, *Elizabeth Bishop: Questions of Mastery* (1991).

TOPICS FOR CRITICAL THINKING AND WRITING

1. Underline the similes and metaphors, and think about their implications. Of course they help to describe the fish, but do they also help to convey the speaker's attitude toward the fish?
2. Why does the speaker release the fish at the end of the poem?

WILLIAM BLAKE

Infant Joy (p. 886)

In addition to the infant there is a second speaker, an adult—presumably the mother, but nothing in the text rules out the possibility that the adult speaker is the father.

The infant speaks the first two lines, the adult (asking what to call the infant) speaks the third. The infant replies, "I happy am, / Joy is my name" and the adult is then moved to say, "Sweet joy befall thee." Is it too subtle to detect a difference between the infant, who knows only that it is happy, and the adult, who, in saying "Sweet joy befall thee" is introducing (to the edges of our mind, or, rather, to the depths of our mind) the possibility that—life being what it is—joy may *not* befall the infant? That is, even here, in the *Songs of Innocence*, we may detect an awareness of a fallen world, a world where in fact people do not always encounter "Sweet joy."

The second stanza apparently is spoken entirely by the adult, but the language of the first two lines ("Pretty joy! / Sweet joy but two days old") is close to the language of the infant—not to the language of a real infant, of course, but to the language of Blake's infant, who began the poem by saying "I have no name, I am but two days old." Still, there is a difference between the speakers. The mother sings (a lullaby?), partly out of her own joy, and partly, perhaps, to reassure the infant (at least that is more or less the function of lullabies in real life).

For introductory students, secondary sources on Blake can offer more harm than good. We favor turning students toward Blake's *Poetical Sketches* and *Songs of Innocence and of Experience*. For the ambitious, the next steps might include *The Poetry and Prose of William Blake*, David Erdman and Harold Bloom (rev. ed., 1982), and *Blake's Poetry and Designs*, ed. Mary Lynn Johnson and John E. Grant (1979).

WILLIAM BLAKE

Infant Sorrow (p. 886)

In "Infant Joy" we saw not only the child's view but also the parent's. Here we see only the child's view, which regards the adult embrace not as an act of love but as a threatening constraint. It's not a question of which view—"Infant Joy" or "Infant Sorrow"—is truer. Both are true. In "Infant Sorrow" Blake lets us see life from the point of view of the infant, a creature who is helpless, distrustful of the parents, presciently aware that it has entered a "dangerous world" and aware that its cries sound like those of a "fiend" to all who cannot understand its distress.

The first stanza emphasizes physical actions—of the mother in labor, of the sympathetic father, and of the babe itself ("piping loud"). There is action in the second stanza too, but there is also something more; there is thought, really strategy. Confined by the father at the beginning of the second stanza, the infant decides it is best to turn to the mother ("I thought best / To sulk upon my mother's breast"), but in any case the infant is still trapped.

TOPICS FOR CRITICAL THINKING AND WRITING

1. A two-day-old infant cannot know her or his name, much less utter it. How, then, can you explain—make sense of—the first five lines of "Infant Joy"? What aspect of real life is the poet presenting?

2. In line 9 the mother says, "Sweet joy I call thee." Why does the mother give this name to the child? Do you think that the final line of the poem adds a somewhat dark note, implying that joy may *not* befall the child? Explain your position.

3. In "Infant Sorrow," why is the infant sorrowful? What does he or she struggle against? (Can you grant that, from a baby's point of view, it may be horrible to be powerless and utterly at the mercy of adults?) Does "like a fiend" suggest that the infant is inherently wicked and therefore should be repressed? Or does the adult world repress energy and thus make the baby seem fiendlike?

4. Why does the mother groan? Why does the father weep? Is the world "dangerous" to the infant in other than an obviously physical sense? To what degree are his or her parents enemies? To what degree does the infant yield to them? In the last line, one might expect a newborn baby to nurse. What does this infant do?

5. Compare and contrast "Infant Joy" with "Infant Sorrow." For example, each poem consists of two stanzas, but are the patterns of the two poems similar? (A two-stanza pattern might, for instance, be a question and an answer, or a generalization and a specific example, or a mental action and then a physical action.) Examine each poem closely, and then, so to speak, stand back and see if you find a pattern in each. (By the way, notice how much more active "Infant Sorrow" is—with "pip*ing*," "struggl*ing*," and so forth—than is "Infant Joy.")

WILLIAM BLAKE

The Lamb (p. 886) and The Tyger (p. 887)

E. D. Hirsch, Jr., in *Innocence and Experience* (1964), Harold Bloom, in *The Visionary Company* (1961), and Hazard Adams, in *William Blake* (1963), discuss these poems. "The Tyger" has engendered much comment. Of special interest are Martin K. Nurmi, "Blake's Revisions of 'The Tyger,'" *PMLA* 71 (September 1956): 669–85; Harold Bloom, *Blake's Apocalypse* (1963); and two pieces by John Grant and Hazard Adams reprinted in *Discussions of William*

Blake, ed. John Grant (1961). See also, for a collection of essays and extracts from books, *William Blake: The Tyger*, ed. Winston Weathers.

In the course of arguing on behalf of reader-response criticism, Stanley Fish, in *Is There a Text in This Class?* (1980), has some fun calling attention to the diversity of opinions. He points out that in *Encounter* (June 1954), Kathleen Raine published an essay entitled "Who Made the Tyger?" She argued that because for Blake the tiger is "the beast that sustains its own life at the expense of its fellow-creatures," the answer to the big question ("Did he who made the lamb make thee?") is, in Raine's words, "beyond all possible doubt, No." Fish points out that Raine, as part of her argument, insists that Blake always uses the word "forest" with reference "to the natural, 'fallen' world." Fish then calls attention to E. D. Hirsch's reading, in *Innocence and Experience* (1964), in which Hirsch argues that "forest" suggests "tall straight forms, a world that for all its terror has the orderliness of the tiger's stripes or Blake's perfectly balanced verses." In short, for Hirsch "The Tyger" is "a poem that celebrates the holiness of tigerness." Hirsch also argues that Blake satirizes the single-mindedness of the Lamb.

We find all of this very baffling. We are not specialists in Blake, but it seems to us that both poems celebrate rather than satirize or in any way condemn their subjects. In "The Lamb" (such is our critical innocence), innocence is celebrated; in "The Tyger," energy is celebrated. In "The Lamb" the speaker is a child, or is an adult impersonating a child. He asks the lamb a question and then gives the answer according to traditional Christian thinking. (In the Gospel of John [1.29, 35] John the Baptist twice greets Jesus as the Lamb of God, presumably drawing on the idea of the lamb as a sacrificial offering. And behind this idea is the Suffering Servant of Isaiah 53, who is compared to "a lamb that is led to slaughter.") The speaker uses a simple vocabulary (words of one and two syllables), and he uses end-stopped lines (one thought to a line). Lamb, God, speaker, and child are all united at the end of the poem.

In "The Tyger" the animal is "burning bright" because of its fiery eyes (6) and presumably because of its orange stripes, also flame-like. (Since the tiger is imagined as being created in a smithy, the poem also includes other images of fire in such words as "forge" and "furnace.")

Blake's question in effect is this: Was the tiger created in hell ("distant deeps") or in heaven ("skies")—and by Satan or by God? Blake hammers these questions into our minds, but it seems to us that Blake clearly implies an answer. The creator is "immortal," daring, "dread," and—most important— creative. In traditional Christian thinking, then, the answer is that God created the tiger. Lines 17–18 ("When the stars threw down their spears / And watered heaven with their tears") have engendered much commentary. Possibly the lines allude to the war in heaven in Milton's *Paradise Lost*, and Blake's gist might be paraphrased thus: "When the rebel angels cast down their spears in defeat, did the triumphant God smile at his success, i.e., What were God's feelings when he had to be tiger-like to an aspect of his own creation?" This makes sense to us, but we admit that, strictly speaking, in *Paradise Lost* the rebellious angels never do "cast down their spears," i.e., never surrender.

One last comment. Harold Bloom probably understands Blake as well as anyone else alive. In *The Oxford Anthology of English Literature* he gives this footnote, which we can't quite bring ourselves to believe. You may want to think about it and to try it out on your students:

However the poem is interpreted, the reader should be wary of identifying the poem's chanter with Blake, who did not react with awe or fear to
any natural phenomenon whatsoever.

Blake probably had considerable satirical intention in this lyric, as a
juxtaposition of his verbal description of the Tyger with his illustration
seems to suggest. [The illustration shows an unimpressive beast.] The
poem's speaker, though a man of considerable imagination (quite possibly
a poet like William Cowper), is at work terrifying himself with a monster
of his own creation. Though Blake may mean us to regard the poem's
questions as unanswerable, he himself would have answered by saying that
the "immortal hand or eye" belonged only to Man, who makes both Tyger
and Lamb. In "the forests of the night," or mental darkness, Man makes
the Tyger, but in the open vision of day Man makes the Lamb.

TOPICS FOR CRITICAL THINKING AND WRITING

1. What do the lamb and the tiger symbolize?
2. In "The Tyger" Blake asks a great question, "Did he who made the lamb
   make thee?" What is the answer?

WILLIAM BLAKE

London (p. 887)

"London," from *Songs of Experience*, is a denunciation of the mind-forged man-
acles, that is, of man-made repressive situations, not a denunciation of cities
and a glorification of rural life. The church assists in exploitation by promises
of an eternal reward, the monarchy slaughters men for private gain, and marriage drives the unmarried (or the unsatisfactorily married) to harlots.
"Chartered" (line 2)—not merely mapped but also licensed—is perhaps
almost acceptable for streets, but that the river, an image of freedom, should
also be chartered is unnatural and intolerable. As the poem develops, it is evident that children are licensed (as chimney sweeps), soldiers are licensed (to
kill and to be killed), and harlots are licensed (bought and sold). E. D. Hirsch,
Jr., *Innocence and Experience* (1964), suggests that there is a further meaning:
The English were proud of their "chartered liberties," rights guaranteed by
Magna Carta, but "these chartered liberties are chartered slaveries." For "ban"
in line 7 Hirsch offers four references: a summons to arms (king), a formal
denunciation or curse (church), a proclamation of marriage, and a prohibition
(king, church, marriage).

A few additional points. The church is "blackening" because (1) it is covered with the soot of an industrial (mechanistic) society; (2) it is spiritually
corrupt; and (3) it corrupts people. The chimney-sweeper's cry appalls the
church because the cry is a reproach, and "appalls" hints at "pall" (suggestive
of the dead church) and at its literal meaning, "to make pale," that is, the
hypocritical church is a whited sepulcher. In line 14, "the youthful Harlot's
curse" may be a cry (thus linked with the infant's cry, the chimney sweeper's
cry, and the soldier's sigh), or it may be the disease that afflicts her and is
communicated to others. In *Poetry and Repression* (1976), Harold Bloom offers
the astounding suggestion that "the harlot's curse is not, as various inter-

preters have said, venereal disease, but is indeed what 'curse' came to mean in the vernacular after Blake and still means now: menstruation, the natural cycle in the human female. . . . [Blake knows that one] curse or ban or natural fact (menstruation) blasts or scatters another natural fact, the tearlessness of the newborn infant."

In an earlier version, "dirty" stood in lines 1 and 2 instead of "chartered," and "smites" instead of "blights" in line 16.

For an analysis of several readings of "London," see Susan R. Suleiman and Inge Crosman, *The Reader in the Text.* Also important is an essay by E. P. Thompson in *Interpreting Blake,* ed. Michael Phillips.

Thompson has also written a richly contextualized study of Blake: *Witness Against the Beast: William Blake and the Moral Law* (1993). We also enjoyed the vividly written biography of Blake by Peter Ackroyd (1996).

ROBERT BLY

Driving to Town Late to Mail a Letter (p. 888)

There are hundreds of poems about snow, snowfall, and snowstorms. Your students may be familiar with two famous examples: Robert Frost's "Stopping by Woods on a Snowy Evening" and Wallace Stevens's "The Snow Man"—both of which, we suspect, haunt the margins of Robert Bly's "Driving to Town Late to Mail a Letter."

Perhaps the key word here, however, is "waste." It derives from the Latin word *vastare*—to lay waste, ravage. Used as a transitive verb, "waste" means: to lay waste; to bring to ruin; to cause to shrink in physical bulk or strength; to cause to become consumed or weakened; to wear away or impair gradually: to diminish by constant loss; to spend or use needlessly, carelessly, or without valuable result; to consume or employ to no purpose.

"Waste . . . time": we invoke this phrase so often that it may not feel vivid to us. But it's exactly this vividness that Bly restores to the word, placing it as he does at the close of a poem whose imagery has a clean clarity and directness. Coming where it does, it has to mean a lot: There is a burden of meaning that falls on the word.

What does it mean to say that we are "wasting time"? How is this different from spending time well? Is wasting time always a bad thing, or does it have its profitable uses? Don't we enjoy some occasions of wasting time, of doing nothing?

Bly's speaker seeks to waste time in relation to a privacy he values. "Love" (line 4) is, of course, a term we highlight in many contexts (I love baseball, I love a good meal, I love to read, etc.), but it matters above all in our accounts of special relationships—the man or the woman I love, I love my family, and so on. To us at least, it is a little unsettling to hear a reference to the *love* of "privacy." Most of the time, we hear people talk about their *need* for privacy, rather than their love of it. What would life be like if what people loved was "privacy"?

That's an urge we do feel—the speaker acknowledges this reality. But the other side of privacy's appeal is its wastefulness. Who do you love the most, yourself or others? Is the best feature of your life its privacy? Not solitude, but privacy. It has its rewards, but it may not be the best place for a person to dwell. There is something aimless and random in its attractiveness. And that is why we pursue human contact—perhaps by means of a letter dropped through the mailbox door, a detail that from the vantage-point of Bly's final line retrospectively gains much power.

For further reading: Ingegerd Friberg, *Moving Inward: A Study of Robert Bly's Poetry* (1977); and *Of Solitude and Silence: Writings on Robert Bly*, ed. Richard Jones and Kate Daniels (1981). See also an interview with Bly in *The Paris Review* 154 (Spring 2000).

GWENDOLYN BROOKS

Martin Luther King Jr. (p. 888)

Four years before King's death the African-American journalist Lerone Bennett wrote: "His grace, like Gandhi's, grows out of a complicated relation not to oppression, but the ancient scourges of man to pain, to suffering, to death. Men who conquer the fear of these things in themselves acquire extraordinary power over themselves and over others." King was assassinated in Memphis, Tennessee, on April 4, 1968—a white man named James Earl Ray was later convicted for the murder. Immediately upon King's death, race riots erupted in Detroit, Washington, D.C., and more than a dozen other major cities. Nearly 100,000 persons, including national and world leaders, attended King's funeral on April 9.

Brooks's poem places special emphasis on King as a preacher of the word "Justice," and it ends with the speaker's pledge that this word will, despite King's death, continue to be spoken and will surely be achieved. Yet students disagree about the kind of Justice that Brooks envisions. Some connect it to the healing and anointing powers that the speaker attributes to him, whereas others see something destructive in the "burning" that King's word causes—a sign, perhaps, of the revolutionary dimension of his program. Interestingly, students have sometimes interpreted this poem as a call for, or prophecy of, revenge—that Justice will eventually be done, and America forced to pay for the crime of King's murder.

Students will probably know about the controversy that arose in the 1980s about making King the focus of a "national" holiday and will be aware of the resentments that many persons still harbor toward him for the social changes he pioneered. It is worth pointing out to students that in fact there is no such thing as a *national* holiday. The president and Congress can legally designate holidays for federal employees, and the states can follow the lead, but neither Congress nor the president can declare a national holiday. Aside from New Year's Day, Independence Day, Labor Day, Thanksgiving, and Christmas, all states do not celebrate holidays on the same day. Most states, for example, celebrate Veterans Day on the fourth Monday in October, but a few use the old November 11 date. In 1986, King's birthday, January 15, was declared a *federal* holiday, not a national one.

Instructors might mention to students the following books: D. H. Melhem, *Gwendolyn Brooks: Poetry and the Heroic Voice* (1987); and Harry Shaw, *Gwendolyn Brooks* (1980).

On King, see Taylor Branch, *Parting the Waters: America in the King Years, 1954–1963* (1988); and David J. Garrow, *Bearing the Cross: Martin Luther King, Jr., and the Southern Christian Leadership Conference* (1986).

TOPICS FOR CRITICAL THINKING AND WRITING

1. You probably would not ordinarily say that someone "went forth." What does this somewhat unusual diction contribute to the poem?
2. Lines 2–4 offer three metaphors, asserting that King was "a prose poem," "a tragic grace," and "warm music." What do you take each of these metaphors to be saying about King?
3. Explain the meaning of line 5. What is the relationship of this line to lines 6–7?
4. In line 10 Brooks speaks of King's "word," but she does not tell us what that word was ("Justice") until line 13. What is the effect of delaying this information?
5. Is Brooks overstating her claim about King's power?
6. What is the effect of repeating, "So it shall," in the last two lines of the poem? Let's think a bit further about this final stanza. It picks up a word, "spoken," from the preceding stanza. Suppose the final stanza omitted line 14 ("So it shall be spoken"), and the poem ended thus:

    The word was Justice. It was spoken.
    So it shall be done.

    What might be gained or lost?
7. Do you find this poem inspiring? Does it express for you the reason(s) you admire—assuming you do—Martin Luther King Jr.?

ANONYMOUS

Funeral March for Martin Luther King Jr. (photograph, p. 889)

On the day of Martin Luther King's funeral, the Ebenezer Baptist Church, in Atlanta, Georgia, overflowed, and some ten thousand mourners gathered outside of the church. The coffin was placed on a mule-drawn farm wagon, symbolizing the Poor People's March to Washington. King had planned the March, but interrupted his plans to go to Memphis, Tennessee, to assist striking sanitation workers. It was in Memphis that he was assassinated. The thousands of people who followed the coffin were paying homage to King and were also implying that his work was still to be done. King was buried in Atlanta's South View Cemetery, under a marble monument inscribed with the words of a slave spiritual that he had often quoted: "Free At Last, Free At Last! Thank God Almighty! I'm Free At Last!"

Nearly all students have seen film of King's mighty delivery of these words at the close of his "I Have a Dream" speech, given before the Lincoln Memorial on August 28, 1963, as the keynote address of the March on Washington. But they would benefit from knowing King's other writings and speeches, gathered in the collection *A Testament of Hope: The Essential Writings of Martin Luther King, Jr.*, ed. James M. Washington (1986).

GWENDOLYN BROOKS
The Bean Eaters (p. 889)

Descriptions of old people, and especially of poor old people, are likely to be sentimental, portraying them as (a) too sweet, and (b) too weak, in an attempt to create a warm glow in the reader, but we think that Brooks stops short of getting us into this swamp. Her old people are poor (therefore doubly weak, i.e., aged and financially insecure), and indeed they are "Mostly Good," but "mostly" of course says that they are not entirely good. We can imagine that they have their irritable moments, states of mind unthinkable in (say) Mother's Day verse.

Brooks says (twice) that they engage in "remembering." She doesn't tell us explicitly what they remember, but "twinklings" suggests remembered pleasures, and "twinges" suggests remembered pains. Presumably the pleasures outweigh the pains, because even though their food and their lodgings are humble ("beans," "their rented back room"), they are surrounded with objects of their earlier years—"beads and receipts and dolls and clothes, tobacco crumbs, vases and fringes." The final word sounds terribly old-fashioned to us—we see ancient lamp shades and tablecloths with fringes, and of course it also suggests the outer extremes, and relatively fragile substances, almost an objective correlative for the old people, who are (so to speak) on the fringe of existence. Notice, too, that the last sentence dwindles from poetry into prose, more or less. True, the final word does rhyme with "twinges," but the line itself goes on and on, whereas all the earlier lines are relatively short. Further, it uses *and* four times, giving it a somewhat sprawling tone, conveying a life that lacks sharp emphases.

To get back to our first point, sentimentality. We have had good discussions in class centered on this topic. We ask students to define the term and then to offer their opinions on whether sentimentality in literature is a good or a bad thing—and *why*.

Your students might be interested in comparing this poem to those discussed in Richard Flynn, "'The Kindergarten of New Consciousness': Gwendolyn Brooks and the Social Construction of Childhood," *African American Review* 3 (Fall 2000): 483–99, which focuses on her as a poet-advocate for children and African Americans. For a cogent study, see Henry Taylor, "Gwendolyn Brooks: An Essential Sanity," *The Kenyon Review*, new series, 13 (Fall 1991): 115–31. We also recommend Martha Satz, "Honest Reporting: An Interview with Gwendolyn Brooks," *Southwest Review* 74 (Winter 1989): 25–35.

Additional resources include George E. Kent, *A Life of Gwendolyn Brooks* (1990); *A Life Distilled: Gwendolyn Brooks, Her Poetry and Fiction*, ed. Maria K. Mootry and Gary Smith (1987); and *On Gwendolyn Brooks: Reliant Contemplation*, ed. Stephen Caldwell Wright (1996). The Academy of American Poets Web site includes an entry for Brooks, with biography, bibliography, and a list of online resources. Visit the search tool at http://www.poets.org/poets/.

ROBERT BROWNING
Porphyria's Lover (p. 890)

Compared with "'My Last Duchess," this poem has more story and less of the diction of a particular speaker, but students can fairly soon see that the interest in "Porphyria's Lover" is not only in what happened but also in the speaker's mind. His insane egotism led him to attempt to preserve forever Porphyria's love for him. He believes that although she struggles to offer her love, her weakness (lines 21–25) made her require his assistance. Interestingly, in 6–15 she seemed energetic and efficient; perhaps there is even something a bit too efficient in making the fire before speaking to her lover. Or are we to remember that we are seeing things through the eyes of a madman (Browning published this poem along with another, under the title of "Madhouse Cells")? The speaker's egotism is tempered with solicitude (41–42, 50–54), making him less monstrous but certainly mad. Inevitably discussion in class centers on the lover's motives (do we believe them?). Surely he is mad. He apparently kills Porphyria in order to possess her forever—a state of mind that may suggest Miss Emily in Faulkner's "A Rose for Emily."

Is it possible, however, that Porphyria too is unbalanced? At the risk of blaming the victim, can one argue that she must have known what sort of a man the lover was. She regularly visited him, and (according to his account) in this instance without greeting him she tidied up his cabin and then placed his arm around her waist—very odd behavior, one might think. A student of ours, arguing along these lines, called attention to the following passage:

> But passion sometimes would prevail,
>   Nor could tonight's gay feast restrain
> A sudden thought of one so pale
>   For love of her, and all in vain: . . .

In this student's view, Porphyria takes delight—gets sexual excitement?—out of visiting and dominating a man who is very nearly catatonic. Our own view stops well short of this psychoanalytic interpretation of Porphyria, but. . . .

As for Question 2 below, which asks the students to serve as the murderer's lawyer: Probably the best defense is a plea of insanity, which in some twenty-five states in the United States means that a defendant who did not know what he or she was doing or that the acts were morally wrong is not criminally liable. Evidence that the speaker is insane: (1) He sees nature as hostile (the wind is "sullen," vexing the lake and tearing down the trees "for spite"); (2) he thinks Porphyria "worships" him—though perhaps she does, we can't tell; (3) he thinks that Porphyria, now dead, has her "utmost will"; and (4) he has sat "all night long" with her head on his shoulder.

By the way, a plea of insanity is usually accepted to mean that the defendant not only was mentally ill but was so ill that he did not have the capacity to control his actions or (and this is rather different) to appreciate the wrongfulness of the action. Thus a killing may be carefully planned and executed exactly according to plan, but the defendant may be judged not guilty by virtue of insanity. John Hinckley, Jr., who shot President Reagan, was so judged, although the prosecution argued that Hinckley planned carefully and was aware that he would get attention by attacking the president. In reaction to the Hinckley decision, some states have recently changed the laws governing the use of the insanity plea. That is, some states that used to allow juries to acquit a defendant if the prosecutor failed to prove beyond a reasonable doubt that the defendant was sane at the time the crime was committed now shift the burden to the defense: The defense must prove that the defendant was insane. The change is a big one, for the traditional constitutional concept of a criminal trial was that the defendant need do nothing to prove his or her innocence; the burden of proof was on the prosecutor. Students wishing to do some research on the insanity plea might look at two books: William J. Winslade and Judith Wilson Ross, *The Insanity Plea* (1983), and Norval Morris, *Madness and the Criminal Law* (1982).

TOPICS FOR CRITICAL THINKING AND WRITING

1. Exactly why did the speaker murder Porphyria?
2. You are a lawyer assigned to defend the speaker against the charge of murder. In 500 to 750 words, write your defense.

GEORGE GORDON, LORD BYRON

She Walks in Beauty (p. 891)

The lyric appears, as we mention in the text, in Byron's *Hebrew Melodies*, a book that supposedly offered poems that in some way resembled the poetry of the Hebrew Bible. In fact this poem is thoroughly secular, as are about half of its companions. The other half evoke, in one way or the other, the Psalms or other Hebrew material (e.g. "Oh! Weep for those that wept by Babel's stream").

What we get here is a pretty typical romantic lyric poem. Whereas the earlier lyric usually contained some element of narrative—consider for example "Western Wind," where in a mere four lines there is the suggestion that a lover once was with his beloved but now is separated from her—the romantic lyric often (not always, of course) has no noticeable narrative. In this poem we learn only that the woman is beautiful and that her beauty is a sign of "A mind at peace with all below, / A heart whose love is innocent." We are not told that she has died, or that the speaker is otherwise separated from her, or soon will join her, any other such narrative element.

The first ten lines use images of dark and light ("starry skies," "dark and bright," "tender light," "raven") to assert her distinctive quality: "One shade the more, one ray the less, /Had half impaired the nameless grace." Presumably the reconciliation of these opposing images indicates her uniqueness. The final eight lines assert, in Neo-Platonic fashion, that this distinctive beauty is a sign of virtue ("goodness" "A mind at peace," "A heart whose love is innocent"). In short, although the poem does not have a narrative in the sense of "then, but now," it does have a pretty clear structure: The poem moves from the physical to the moral and the spiritual.

We have known this poem since our high-school days, and in idle moments (e.g., while walking the dog) we find ourselves silently reciting it, or at least reciting the first stanza. Why? The essential Neo-Platonic idea of the poem is commonplace, at least to anyone familiar with Renaissance lyric poetry. Our guess is that the poem has stayed in our minds chiefly because of certain sound effects, notably in the first stanza the assonance of "like," "night," "climes," and "skies," and the the alliteration of "cloudless climes and starry skies" and of "gaudy day denies."

LUCILLE CLIFTON

in the inner city (p. 892)

This poem—from a book called *Good Times*—catches a distinctive voice, meditative and colloquial, the colloquialisms never slipping into merely cute dialect or local color.

For biographical and critical contexts, see Andrea Benton Rushing, "Lucille Clifton: A Changing Voice for Changing Times," in *Coming to Light: American Women Poets in the Twentieth Century*, ed. Dianne Wood Middlebrook and Marilyn Yalom (1985), 214–22; and *Broken Silences: Interviews with Black and White Women Writers*, ed. Shirley M. Jordan (1993). Also helpful is Wallace R. Peppers's entry on Clifton in *The Dictionary of Literary Biography* 41 (1985), 55–60.

JUDITH ORTIZ COFER

My Father in the Navy: A Childhood Memory (p. 893)

Most students will quickly see the imagery of death ("stiff and immaculate / in the white cloth," "an apparition") and the Christian imagery ("halo," "when he rose," "kept vigil," "like an angel / heralding a new day"). The sailor-father comes back to the living world from "below," and thus would seem to resemble the risen Jesus. But, at least as we understand the poem, it is the living (the speaker and her siblings) who, so to speak, bring life to the "apparition," whereas in Christian thinking it is Jesus who animates human beings, that is, gives them the possibility of eternal heavenly life.

For class discussion, you might consider asking the students to read and comment on Cofer's "And Are You a Latina Writer?" in *Mascaras*, ed. Lucha Corpi (1997), 11–19. Two interviews with Cofer are also rewarding. The first is in *MELUS* 18:3 (Fall 1993): 83–97; the second is included in *Speaking of the Short Story: Interviews with Contemporary Writers*, ed. Farhat Iftekharuddin, Mary Rohrberger, and Maurice Lee (1997), 57–74.

JOHN DONNE

A Valediction: Forbidding Mourning (p. 893)

Instructors may be so familiar with this poem that they may not recognize the difficulties it presents to students. The title itself leads many students to think (quite plausibly) that it is about death, an idea reinforced by the first simile. But this simile is introduced to make the point that *just as* virtuous men can die quietly because they are confident of a happy future, *so* the two lovers can part quietly—that is, the speaker can go on a journey—because they are confident of each other.

The hysterics that accompany the separation of less confident lovers are ridiculed ("sigh-tempests," "tear-floods"); such agitation would be a "profanation" of the relationship of the speaker and his beloved and would betray them to the "laity."

Thus the speaker and the beloved are implicitly priests of spiritual love.

The poem goes on to contrast the harmful movement of the earth (an earthquake) with the harmless ("innocent") movement of heavenly bodies, thereby again associating the speaker and the beloved with heavenly matters. (The cosmology, of course, is the geocentric Ptolemaic system.) The fourth stanza continues the contrast: other lovers are "sublunary," changeable, and subject to the changing moon. Such earthbound lovers depend on the physical things that "elemented" their love ("eyes, lips, and hands"), but the love of the speaker and his partner is "refined" and does not depend on such stuff. Moreover, if their love is like something physical, it is "like gold to airy thinness beat."

The three last stanzas introduce the image of a draftsman's (not an explorer's) compass, and they also introduce the circle as a symbol of perfection.

See Theodore Redpath's edition of *The Songs and Sonnets of John Donne* (1983), and see especially Clay Hunt, *Donne's Poetry* (1954), and Patricia Spacks, *College English* 29 (1968): 594–95. Louis Martz, *The Wit of Love* (1969, 48), says of line 20: "'Care less,' but is it so? The very rigor and intricacy of the famous image of the compass at the end may be taken to suggest rather desperate dialectical effort to control by logic and reason a situation almost beyond control."

TOPICS FOR CRITICAL THINKING AND WRITING

1. The first stanza describes the death of "virtuous men." To what is their death compared in the second stanza?

2. Who is the speaker of this poem? To whom does he speak and what is the occasion? Explain the title.

3. What is the meaning of "laity" in line 8? What does it imply about the speaker and his beloved?

4. In the fourth stanza the speaker contrasts the love of "dull sublunary lovers" (i.e., ordinary mortals) with the love he and his beloved share. What is the difference?

5. In the figure of the carpenter's compass (lines 25–36) the speaker offers reasons—some stated clearly, some not so clearly—why he will end where he began. In 250 words explain these reasons.

6. In line 35 Donne speaks of his voyage as a "circle." Explain in a paragraph why the circle is traditionally a symbol of perfection.

7. Write a farewell note—or poem—to someone you love (or hate).

JOHN DONNE

The Flea (p. 894)

Not all students will immediately understand that the speaker is a would-be lover, importuning his mistress (i.e., his beloved). We say "his mistress" because we assume that the speaker is a male who is addressing a female—such is the convention of love poetry of the period—but today a student may argue that the speaker can be a female addressing a male, or a female addressing a female, or a male addressing a male. In fact, the relationship clearly is heterosexual, since Donne draws on the traditional idea that a mingling of blood can result in pregnancy.

In the first stanza the lover patiently but eagerly delivers his little argumentative demonstration, hoping to get his pupil to agree with each stage of the argument: "*Mark* but this flea, and *mark* in this. . . ." "*Thou know'st that,* this cannot be said / A sin. . . ." "*Yet. . . .*"

In the second stanza, we learn at the outset that the woman has made some motion that threatens the life of the flea:

Oh stay, three lives in one flea spare.

What has the woman done? Since fleas are killed by being pinched or pierced with a finger nail, readers imagine that the woman holds the flea between two fingers, or immobilizes it by putting a fingernail on it. Why "three lives"? The flea now contains not only its own blood but also the blood of the man and of the woman. In this second stanza note the religious language ("marriage temple," "cloistered," "sacrilege," and "sins").

In the third stanza the reader learns that in the space between the second and third stanzas the woman has killed the flea by shattering it with a fingernail:

Cruel and sudden, has thou since
Purpled thy nail in blood of innocence?

In short, although we do not hear the woman speak, through the speaker's report we see her in action. The hyperbole of "Purpled thy nail in blood of innocence" perhaps evokes thoughts of the Slaughter of the Innocents, i.e., continues the religious imagery.

The woman has replied to his argument not with words but with a decisive action, refuting his argument that to kill the flea is to engage in three sins (murder, self-murder, and sacrilege—sacrilege because the flea has been called their marriage temple). He then trumps her card by saying, in effect, "Yes, and you see, nothing bad has happened; similarly, nothing bad will happen if you yield to me." The last lines of the poem are unadorned, a strong contrast to the metaphors of the second stanza, where the flea is said to be a "marriage bed" and a "marriage temple" because it contains the blood of the man and the woman. Now, at the end, the woman's action having inadvertently proved the lover's case, the lover can employ simple, direct language:

'Tis true. Then learn how false fears be:
Just so much honor, when thou yield'st to me,
Will waste, as this flea's death took life from thee.

JOHN DONNE

Death Be Not Proud (p. 895)

This is one of Donne's *Holy Sonnets*, which is to say that it is related to "Batter my heart three-personed God," a poem printed in Chapter 17.

Students may not at first notice the surprising cheekiness of the beginning of the poem: Donne boldly addresses death (the figure of speech used is the apostrophe) and speaks to him in dismissive terms. In the opening four lines, however, Donne offers no evidence to support his initial assertion that Death should not be proud; evidence isn't really given until line 5, and even in lines 5–8 we get very little supporting evidence.

Not until the sestet do we get a battery of *reasons*: Death is the slave of "Fate, Chance, kings, and desperate men"; Death dwells with unsavory fellows ("Poison, War, and Sickness"); "poppy or charms can make us sleep as well." And then, picking up the word "sleep" from line 12, Donne goes on to contrast the "short sleep" of Death (13) with our eternal awakening. He thus ends triumphantly, "Death, thou shalt die," but in fact he has moved from reasoning to the assertion of faith. That is, the reasons he offers as evidence of death's unimportance really do not in any way support the assertion that we live eternally, and it is this last assertion (if it is true) that most emphatically diminishes death. A reader probably is entertained rather than convinced by the early arguments, e.g. that if from "rest and sleep" (mere pictures of death) we get pleasure we will therefore get even more pleasure from death (lines 5–6). The abundance of reasons allows the speaker to ask Death, "why swell'st thou then?" (i.e., why is Death swollen—puffed up—with the pride mentioned in the opening line?), and perhaps here we detect a depth of feeling that is not evident earlier, in the allegedly logical arguments.

The couplet seems to us to be especially effective, with the contrasts between *sleep* and *wake* and between *short* and *eternally* in line 13, and the final paradox, "Death, thou shalt die." In speaking about the couplet, instructors will probably want to call attention to the fact that line 13 is entirely monosyllabic except for the last word, "eternally," which is to say that the choppiness of the daily life of this world ("One short sleep past, we wake" is displaced by eternity. The poem in fact abounds with monosyllabic words and with strong stresses, especially evident in the final four words: "Death, thou shalt die."

RITA DOVE

Daystar (p. 896)

The poem comes from Dove's Pulitzer-prize book *Thomas and Beulah* (1986), which contains sequences of poems about African Americans who migrated from the South to the North.

In thinking about a poem, one can hardly go wrong in paying attention to the title. Here, why "Daystar"? "Daystar" can refer either to a planet—especially Venus—visible in the eastern sky before sunrise, or to the sun. Both meanings are probably relevant here. The speaker's brief period of escape from (at one extreme) the children's diapers and dolls and (at the other) Thomas's sexual demands are perhaps like the brief (and marvelous) appearance of a planet at a time when one scarcely expects to see a heavenly body; and this moment of escape—a moment of wonderful independence—is perhaps also like the sun, which stands in splendid isolation, self-illuminating. Sometimes, as she sits "behind the garage," she is closely connected to the visible world around her (the cricket, the maple leaf), but sometimes, with her eyes closed, she perceives only herself. (The mention, in the last line of the poem, of "the middle of the day" perhaps indicates that the chief meaning of "daystar" here is the sun, but we see no reason to rule out the suggestion of the other meaning.)

Dove's *Selected Poems* (1993) is a good place to start for further reading. We also value her collection of stories, *Fifth Sunday* (1985), and her novel, *Through the Ivory Gate* (1992). An interview with Dove appears in *Black American Literature Forum* 20 (Fall 1986). For critical discussion: Arnold Rampersad, "The Poems of Rita Dove," *Callaloo* 9:1 (Winter 1986): 52–60; and Robert McDowell, "The Assembling Vision of Rita Dove," *Callaloo* 9:1 (Winter 1986): 61–70. See also the section on Dove in Helen Vendler, *The Given and the Made: Strategies of Poetic Redefinition* (1995).

TOPICS FOR CRITICAL THINKING AND WRITING

1. How would you characterize the woman who is the subject of the poem?
2. What do you make of the title?

BOB DYLAN

The Times They Are A-Changin' (p. 896)

In *The Unraveling of America* (1984), the historian Allen J. Matusow notes that the song "The Times They Are A Changin'" quickly "became a generational anthem," adding that "it was no less appropriate for Dylan to sing at the 1963 March on Washington than for Martin Luther King to deliver a sermon there."

It is sometimes hard to convey to students why Dylan was such an important figure, and why his music was so radical and evocative, so much a part of the angry rebelliousness, sense of newness, and spirit of hopefulness of the 1960s. Some students will have seen Dylan's recent appearances on MTV, but these make him seem just another aging rock star from long ago.

On the other hand, students do find that "The Times They Are A-Changin'" fits perfectly with what they know (or have heard) about the 1960s. And most students seem able to look closely at details of the language— the criticism of senators and congressmen, the complaint about unsympathetic parents—and make connections between these and the antiwar movement, civil rights campaign, and student activism that were so central to the 1960s.

Yet it is a curious fact about the song that it came early in the decade—in 1963—and in this sense it did not so much reflect what was widespread as tell and prophesy of what was its opening phases. Making this point is a good way to help students understand how lyric and song can at least in part create the conditions that they describe, serving as a source of inspiration and empowerment.

Other important Dylan songs from this era include: "Blowin' in the Wind," which became especially important to those involved in civil rights struggles; and "A Hard Rain's A-Gonna Fall," which was inspired by the Cuban missile crisis of 1962. Curiously, this social protest album, *The Freewheelin' Bob Dylan* (1963), was followed by *Another Side of Bob Dylan*, where, as the music critic Jon Wiener has noted, Dylan "dismissed social issues and sang personal songs that expressed, among other feelings, considerable bitterness toward women."

Instructors might also ask students if "The Times They Are A-Changin'" speaks directly to them. Is it a great lyric of the 1960s, but only that? Or is it a lyric that in a timeless manner dramatizes the changes and transitions that each new generation faces? In this respect, the general nature of Dylan's language is worth remarking on. There is no reference in it to a specific historical figure or event; and except for the mention of senators and congressmen, there is nothing in "The Times They Are A-Changin'" that even ties it to the United States.

See Anthony Scaduto, *Bob Dylan* (1973), and Robert Shelton, *No Direction Home: The Life and Music of Bob Dylan* (1987).

T. S. ELIOT

The Love Song of J. Alfred Prufrock (p. 898)

Among the useful introductory books are Elizabeth Drew, *T. S. Eliot* (1949); Northrop Frye, *T. S. Eliot* (1968); and Grover Smith, *T. S. Eliot's Poetry and Plays* (1974). On "Prufrock," see also Rosenthal and Smith, *Exploring Poetry* (1955); Hugh Kenner, *The Invisible Poet: T. S. Eliot* (1965, 3–12); and Lyndall Gordon, *T. S. Eliot: An Imperfect Life* (1999). See also the biography by Peter Ackroyd (1984), and the interesting volume of Eliot's letters, vol. 1, 1898–1922, expertly edited by Valerie Eliot (1988).

It is well to alert students to the fact that "Prufrock" is not a Browningesque dramatic monologue with a speaker and a listener, but rather an internal monologue in which "I" (the timid self) addresses his own amorous self as "you." (Not every "you" in this poem, however, refers to Prufrock's amorous self. Sometimes "you" is equivalent to "one.") Possibly, too, the "you" is the reader, or even other people who, like Prufrock, are afraid of action.

Among the chief points usually made are these: The title proves to be ironic, for we scarcely get a love song: "J. Alfred Prufrock" is a name that, like the speaker, seems to be hiding something ("J.") and also seems to be somewhat old-maidish ("Prufrock" suggests "prude" and "frock"); the initial description (especially the "patient etherised") is really less a description of the evening than of Prufrock's state of mind; mock heroic devices abound (people at a cocktail party talking of Michelangelo, Prufrock gaining strength from his collar and stickpin); the sensuous imagery of women's arms leads to the men in shirt-sleeves and to Prufrock's wish to be a pair of ragged claws.

The poem was first published in *Poetry* magazine. When it later appeared in book form it differed only in punctuation (e.g., square brackets instead of parentheses) and two verbal changes—"soot" instead of "spot" in line 19, and *no doubt* instead of *withal* in line 114.

In graduate school, one of us had the privilege of studying Eliot's poem with an eminent critic of modern literature, who has written well about Eliot, Joyce, and Pound. A student in this class, somewhat impatiently, asked, "So what does the poem mean?" To which the instructor replied: "It doesn't mean anything."

That reply seems at first a bad one that is likely to add to students' confusions and perplexities when they encounter "The Love Song of J. Alfred Prufrock" for the first time. It doesn't mean *anything*? But what the instructor was getting at, and what he proceeded to describe, was the ample pleasure that the reader can take—and that Eliot took himself—in the mixed playful and serious rhymes ("In the room the women come and go / Talking of Michaelangelo"); in the clever imagery (e.g., yellow fog that's like a cat); and in the management of sounds ("I grow old . . . I grow old / I shall wear the bottoms of my trousers rolled") that echo the verbal patterns that such nineteenth-century poets as Longfellow and Tennyson mastered.

On one level, Eliot is engaged in an act of high literary seriousness, as the allusions to Dante, Shakespeare, and the Bible attest. But these features of the poem sometimes prove more appealing to critics and scholars than to beginning students, who do not always possess the background needed to appreciate and ponder them. You'll want to talk about the allusions and give students some help with them. But remember, too, that there are many kinds of verbal effects in the poem, many different moments in the organization of its language. You can read lines and stanzas aloud and linger over them with students. This is obvious enough, but it works especially well in Eliot's case and overcomes students' worry that this poem is "too hard" for them.

Sometimes students do indeed find "The Love Song of J. Alfred Prufrock" intimidating—which, with its epigraph in Italian, probably was one aspect of Eliot's intention. But only one: The poem is actually quite engaging to students, quite accessible, when it is read aloud, and when Eliot's phrases and lines are enjoyed in all their craftsmanship.

A "Voices and Visions" videocassette of T. S. Eliot is available from Longman Publishers.

TOPICS FOR CRITICAL THINKING AND WRITING

1. How does the speaker's name help to characterize him? What suggestions—of class, race, personality—do you find in the name? Does the poem's title strike you as ironic? If so, how or why?

2. What qualities of big-city life are suggested in the poem? How are these qualities linked to the speaker's mood? What other details of the setting—the weather, the time of day—express or reflect his mood? What images do you find especially striking?

3. The speaker's thoughts are represented in a stream-of-consciousness monologue, that is, in what appears to be an unedited flow of thought. Nevertheless, they reveal a story. What is the story?

RALPH WALDO EMERSON

Concord Hymn (p. 902)

The poem presents a reader with no difficulties, but because we happen to be deeply attached to it—the writer of these pages was required to memorize it in the eighth grade, and has treasured it ever since—we will talk at some length about "Concord Hymm" even if sometimes tangentially.

During Emerson's lifetime the poem was published under the title of "Ode"as well as "Concord Hymn." Both titles point to the loftiness or solemnity of the theme, though "Hymn"—perhaps from the Greek *hymen*, referring to a song of joy at a marriage—today is almost always reserved for a song in praise of God.

In any case, Emerson's subject is lofty, though he treats it in a simple, lucid manner. At the beginning of the poem we are in a humble setting—by a "rude bridge." As Emerson says in lines 7–8, in his own day the bridge was gone. In 1874, in preparation for the centennial, a bridge was built, but it did not resemble the original and it was later replaced. The present bridge is said (Allen French's *Historic Concord and the Lexington Fight*) to be a replica of the original, though "higher and stronger." In this humble setting stand ordinary men, "farmers." And of course most of the men really were farmers; only in Boston would there be a substantial non-agricultural population. In the final stanza, after their action has been recorded, the farmers are called "heroes." But even in the first stanza there is a faintly heroic (larger-than-lifesize) note: The Concord River is a "flood," and the farmers seem to be assisted by nature itself ("Their flag to April's breeze unfurled"). Still, on the whole the scene is unprepossessing, but at this pastoral site the farmers "fired the shot heard round the world." And they really did. By Emerson's day, the country had doubled in territory, and it had become a player in the international scene. Less than a decade after Emerson wrote the poem, Matthew Calbraith Perry commanded a naval squadron off Africa in support of a British blockade of the slave trade, and in 1853 (less than two decades after Emerson wrote the poem) Perry anchored four ships in a Japanese harbor.

The Concord monument ("votive stone" in line 10, "shaft" in line 16) is an obelisk. A study of obelisks can take a student into some very interesting byways in the history of ideas and of iconography, particularly into the Egyptian Revival in Europe and England in the late eighteenth century and in the United States in the early nineteenth. Briefly, the obelisk—a four-sided tapering stone pillar, topped by a pyramid—came to America via Europe, and to Europe via Egypt. The obelisk, whose top was sometimes gilded in order to catch the first rays of the sun, may have originated as a phallic symbol, but it is usually thought to represent the *axis mundi* ("world pillar," "axis of the world"), an imaginary pillar in the center of the flat earth, supporting the heavens. It is thus the symbol of stability and of a well-ordered universe. After Rome's victory over Egypt at the Battle of Actium (31 B.C.), Augustus imported an Egyptian obelisk to serve as the gnomon for a giant sundial, and later other Egyptian obelisks were imported. In 64 A.D. Nero crucified Christians (including, according to tradition, St. Peter) in the Circus of Nero, where there was an obelisk that Caligula had imported. This obelisk was allowed to stand when St. Peter's basilica was erected on the site of the Circus of Nero, because it had witnessed Peter's martyrdom, and because it was from the land where Moses had lived. The obelisk thus acquired additional suggestions of holiness.

What we have said thus far is preliminary to the Egyptian Revival, stimulated by Napoleon's Egyptian campaign (1798). Books illustrating Egyptian monuments and designs provided Europeans and Americans with a repertory of motifs that can still be seen in furniture and in architecture, for instance, in libraries and in cemetery gates. The Concord obelisk still stands ("Time and Nature," in accordance with Emerson's wish in lines 15–16, have indeed spared the monument), though tourists visiting Concord's North Bridge tend to focus on Daniel Chester French's statue, *The Minute Man of Concord*, on the other side of the bridge. In thinking of obelisks that are used as patriotic symbols in the United States, one should also recall the Washington Monument and the Bunker Hill Monument, although these are not true obelisks since they are not monoliths.

We've had good luck when we directed students to *Emerson in His Journals*, ed. Joel Porte (1982), a judicious culling of the sixteen-volume edition of the journals published by Harvard University Press. Though over half a century old, Ralph Rusk's *The Life of Ralph Waldo Emerson* (1949) remains excellent. Among recent books, one stands out: Robert D. Richardson, Jr., *Emerson: The Mind on Fire* (1995).

TOPICS FOR CRITICAL THINKING AND WRITING

1. Other poems commemorating battles are Francis Scott Key's "The Star-Spangled Banner," originally entitled "The Defense of Fort McHenry," and Melville's "The March into Virginia," both given in our text, along with Lanier's poem on the death of Stonewall Jackson, at the Battle of Chancellorsville. What other poems commemorating battles can you think of? Examine one poem, studying the particular aspects of the battle—for instance self-sacrifice, courage, pity—that the poem is chiefly concerned with, and compare it with the qualities celebrated in "Concord Hymn."

2. The memorial was (and still is) an obelisk—the "shaft" Emerson speaks of in line 16. Exactly what is an obelisk? And why do you suppose obelisks—rather, say, than boulders—are frequently used as memorials?

3. Line 11 is curious. Why does Emerson suggest that memory must "redeem" the deed of the Minutemen? (If you are in doubt about the exact meaning of "redeem," look it up in a good dictionary. You might also check the brief entry—a short paragraph—on *redemption* in *The Perennial Dictionary of World Religions*, or the long entry—almost six pages, double-columns—in *The Anchor Bible Dictionary*.) Think about what other words Emerson might have used instead of "redeem," and consider how a substitution would change the meaning of the line.

4. We hear about "sires" and "sons" (line 12) but nothing about mothers and daughters. And the "farmers" (line 3) who "fired the shot heard round the world" are men. Does the sexism of the poem disturb you? Explain.

MARTÍN ESPADA

Bully (p. 902)

The editors of *An Introduction to Literature* belong to a generation that was taught, in grade school and in high school, that Teddy Roosevelt was a hero. Some of his words entered the classroom, just as half a century later some of the words of John Kennedy—notably the Inaugural Address—entered the classroom. In school we heard such Rooseveltisms as "I wish to preach, not the doctrine of ignoble ease, but the doctrine of the strenuous life" (1899), "In life, as in a football game, the principle to follow is: Hit the line hard" (1901), and "There is no room in this country for hyphenated Americanism. . . . The one absolutely certain way of bringing this nation to ruin, of preventing all possibility of its continuing to be a nation at all, would be to permit it to become a tangle of squabbling nationalities" (1915). In the fifth question below, we quote yet another (in)famous remark, expressing the opinion that all immigrants should be required to learn English within five years. Persons who doubt that Roosevelt was regarded as one of America's greatest heroes need only call to mind Mount Rushmore National Memorial, in South Dakota, where an enormous bust of Roosevelt, along with busts of Washington, Jefferson, and Lincoln, is carved. Although the sculptures (visible for some sixty miles) were not finished until the 1950s, the monument was dedicated in 1927, and in effect it represents the values of the 1920s.

In our third question below, we ask about the word "bully," as an adjective and as a noun. Roosevelt used the adjective, meaning "excellent," in a famous comment, to the effect that the presidency is a "bully pulpit." But given Roosevelt's enthusiasm for military action, in particular for the Spanish-American War (a war whose name somehow omits the efforts of the Cuban patriots who fought for independence), it is hard not to think of the other and more common meaning of the word. Certainly in this poem entitled "Bully," where it is said of Roosevelt that "each fist [is] lonely for a sabre," the image that comes across is of someone who pushes other people around. A century ago Roosevelt stormed San Juan with his Rough Riders, but today Puerto Rican children invade Roosevelt High (line 11). The end of the poem, with its reference to Roosevelt's "Victorian mustache / and monocle," presents a hopelessly outdated and somewhat comic figure who contrasts with the vitality of the "Spanish-singing children."

TOPICS FOR CRITICAL THINKING AND WRITING

1. If you're not sure what Theodore Roosevelt was famous for, consult an encyclopedia. What *was* he famous for? In the first stanza, what words best express Espada's attitude toward him?

2. In the second stanza, what does Espada mean when he says "Puerto Rico has invaded Roosevelt"? What does he mean by an "*army* of Spanish-singing children"? Who are the *Taíno*?

3. What does "bully" mean as a noun? As an adjective?

4. Roosevelt was a great believer in what is called The Melting Pot Theory of America. What is this theory? Do you think there is a great deal to it, something to it, or nothing to it? Why?

5. Here is a quotation from one of Roosevelt's speeches:

> Every immigrant who comes here should be required within five years to learn English or leave the country.

What do you think of this idea? Why? Suppose that for some reason (perhaps political, perhaps economic) you decided to spend the rest of your life in, say, Argentina, or Germany, or Israel, or Nigeria. Do you think the government might reasonably require you to learn the language? Why?

ALLEN GINSBERG

A Supermarket in California (p. 903)

The poem evokes Walt Whitman by name and evokes his poetry in the long, unrhymed lines and in the catalogs of commonplace objects of American life. But Ginsberg's America is not Whitman's, for Ginsberg makes the point that Whitman too was lonely while he lived and finally encountered the loneliness of death. The allusion to the Spanish poet García Lorca is to his poem on Walt Whitman and also calls to mind yet another homosexual poet whose love was unreciprocated. As we see it, the "self-conscious" poet, his head aching (line 1), draws inspiration from Whitman, who lived in an earlier and more innocent age, an age when a man could unselfconsciously celebrate male beauty and comradeliness. But that age is "the lost America of love" (11), and in any case the Whitman who celebrates it and who is the poet's "courage-teacher" (13) was himself "lonely" (again 13) and, like all mortals, at last lost all. By the way, in the first sentence, Ginsberg seems to confuse Lethe (the river of forgetfulness) with Styx (the river across which Charon poled his ferry).

Students will enjoy Barry Miles, *Ginsberg: A Biography* (1989). Another good source is Carolyn Cassady, *Off the Road: My Years with Cassady, Kerouac, and Ginsberg* (1990). Somewhat dated, but still interesting, is *Allen Verbatim: Lectures on Poetry, Politics, Consciousness*, ed. Gordon Ball (1974). There are also a number of Internet sites devoted to Ginsberg, the best of which is Welcome to Allen Ginsberg: Shadow Changes into Bone, http://ginzy.com/; this site is especially useful for its links to interviews.

TOPICS FOR CRITICAL THINKING AND WRITING

1. Ginsberg calls his poem "A Supermarket in California." Need the market be in California, or can it be anywhere?
2. In the second line, Ginsberg explains why he went into the supermarket. Is the explanation clear, or puzzling, or some of each? Explain.
3. In the third section ("What peaches and what penumbras!"), what *is* a penumbra? Are the aisles full of them?
4. In line 8 ("Where are we going, Walt Whitman? The doors close in an hour. Which way does your beard point tonight?"), is Ginsberg hopeful or not about where he and Walt Whitman will stroll?
5. Read two or three Whitman poems (reprinted elsewhere in this book). In what ways does Ginsberg's poem resemble Whitman's poems? In what ways is "A Supermarket" pure Ginsberg?

NIKKI GIOVANNI

Master Charge Blues (p. 904)

For some comments on blues, see the note on Langston Hughes's "Evenin' Air Blues," in this handbook, p. 198. For a concise overview, see William J. Harris, "Sweet Soft Essence of Possibility: The Poetry of Nikki Giovanni," in *Black Women Writers, 1950–1980*, ed. Mari Evans (1984), 218–28. Good critical studies include Anna T. Robinson, *Nikki Giovanni: From Revolution to Revelation* (1979), and Virginia C. Fowler, *Nikki Giovanni* (1992). Some of your students might be interested in two books that dramatize the literary and social crises and debates of the 1960s and early 1970s: *A Dialogue*, by James Baldwin and Nikki Giovanni (1973), and *A Poetic Equation: Conversations between Nikki Giovanni and Margaret Walker* (1974).

LOUISE GLÜCK

The School Children (p. 905)

On the surface, the poem seems loaded with pictures of cute children on their way to school, bringing the traditional apples for the teachers: "with their little satchels," "apples, red and gold," "their overcoats of blue or yellow wool." Even "how orderly they are" (said of the nails on which the children hang their coats) can be taken as a benign comment on this happy scene.

But by the time we finish the second stanza we realize that this is not a Norman Rockwell scene. The children must cross to "the other shore" where they are confronted by people "who wait behind great desks." Further, these people are not presented warmly. Rather, they are presented (we never see them) as godlike figures who wait "to receive these offerings."

The third stanza is perhaps even more menacing, with that orderly row of nails, waiting to accept the pretty coats. The text speaks—horribly—of "the nails / on which the children hang. . . ." As we continue to read the sentence the meaning changes radically, of course, and we see that it is not the children but "their overcoats" that hang on the nails, but the thought lingers; the mind retains a vision of the children hanging from nails.

The last stanza reintroduces us to the teachers, who "shall instruct them in silence," a menacing expression that we take to mean (1) shall teach them silently (a terrifying way of teaching), and (2) shall teach them to be silent (a terrifying condition). The stanza does not end, however, with the teachers or with the children. Rather, it ends with the mothers, who "scour the orchards for a way out," i.e., who seek to equip their children with the "offerings" (line 7) that the gods require. That is, the mothers seek (by propitiating the gods) to protect their children from the severe socialization that awaits them, but it is already too late, because "the gray limbs of the fruit trees" (it is now autumn) bear "so little ammunition."

In the last stanza, why "The teachers *shall* instruct them," and "the mothers *shall* scour the orchards," rather than "will instruct" and "will scour"? Although older handbooks say that *shall* expresses simple futurity in the first person (and *will* expresses determination in the first person), it is our impression that *shall* has almost disappeared. Indeed, part of what made Douglas MacArthur's "I shall return" so memorable was that he used an unusual construction. To our ear, the use of *shall* in the last stanza of Glück's poem has a voice-of-doom quality; the teachers must act as they will, and the mothers must act as they will—and the children will be the victims.

TOPICS FOR CRITICAL THINKING AND WRITING

1. Which words in the poem present a cute picture-postcard view of small children going to school?
2. Which words undercut this happy scene?
3. In the last stanza we read that "the teachers shall instruct" and "the mothers shall scour." What, if anything, is changed if we substitute *will* for *shall*?

H. D.

Helen (p. 906)

Most students know something about Helen of Troy—her extraordinary beauty; her marriages to Menelaus and Paris; and the fact that the Trojan war, which Homer recounts in the *Iliad*, was waged over her. But whenever we teach this poem, we use it as an occasion to send students to the library to read about Helen in such reference works as *The Oxford Classical Dictionary*, ed. N. G. L. Hammond and H. H. Scullard (2nd ed., 1978) and *The Oxford Companion to Classical Literature*, ed. M. C. Howatson (2nd ed., 1989). Both have lengthy entries on Helen of Troy and flesh out well the bare bones of the students' knowledge. Most of us consult reference books, dictionaries, specialized encyclopedias often—it's hard to imagine doing research and teaching without them. But many students are unfamiliar with scholarly tools of this kind; they know about general multi-volume encyclopedias and handy desktop-size dictionaries, and that's about it. Reference works come as a revelation to many students whom we have taught, and we try to get them into the habit of making use of these books, not only for reading literature but, even more, for paper-writing assignments, so that students can comment in detail on allusions, references, names, and terms that a poem relies upon.

H. D.'s poem depends for its effect on the aura of Helen, known and expressed throughout the ages. And it is made all the more evocative through the clear, clean, precise choices of language that H. D. has made—"the still eyes in the white face," "the beauty of cool feet." The verbs are effectively placed—for example, the sharply focused "hates" in line 1, and the keenly rhymed combination of "reviles/smiles" in lines 6–7.

Note: As a way of indicating Helen's mythic status, we make sure to quote Marlowe's famous lines from *Doctor Faustus*: "Was this the face that launched a thousand ships / And burnt the topless towers of Ilium?" It doesn't hurt to mention other sources (e.g., Goethe's *Faust*), including a few that might be less well known, such as the line from Shakespeare's *All's Well That Ends Well*: "Was this fair face the cause, quoth she, / Why the Grecians sacked Troy?"

Students respond well to H. D.'s poetry and might be directed toward her longer work, *Helen in Egypt* (1961), and to her *Collected Poems, 1912–1944*, ed. Louis L. Martz (1983). Useful secondary sources include Barbara Guest, *Herself Defined: The Poet H. D. and Her World* (1984), Susan Stanford Friedman, *Penelope's Web: Gender, Modernity, H. D.'s Fiction* (1990), and *Signets: Reading H. D.*, ed. Susan Stanford Friedman and Rachel Blau DuPlessis (1990).

THOMAS HARDY

Ah, Are You Digging on My Grave (p. 906)

The narrative structure, as well as the motif of the "unquiet grave" (see the ballad of that title in Albert B. Friedman's *The Penguin Book of Folk Ballads* [1977]), derives from traditional ballads.

Also ballad-like is the use of the clichés or stock epithets (e.g., "My loved one," "My nearest, dearest kin"), but note that the chief cliché of thought (in the next-to-last stanza, with its stock idea of animal fidelity) is offered only so that it may be debunked in the final stanza.

It is worth discussing Samuel Hynes's contention (*The Pattern of Hardy's Poetry* [1961, 53]) that the poem—based on the idea that no affection survives death—is neither true (as Hardy's own poems to his dead wife demonstrate) nor effective (Hynes finds the poem's irony "gross and automatic," "clumsy and cynical").

JOY HARJO

Vision (p. 907)

The view that the earth is sacred is found in many societies, but it is apparently especially strong in the thought of Native Americans.

Some students—not necessarily only those who are Native Americans—may know something about Native American beliefs, and they may provide a way of entry to the poem. It may also happen that some students may know that according to Genesis 9.12–17, God established the rainbow as a token of a covenant with Noah and his descendants. If this concept comes up, you may want to contrast it with Harjo's poem and to compare Harjo's poem with Wordsworth's "My Heart Leaps Up":

> My heart leaps up when I behold
> A rainbow in the sky:
> So was it when my life began;
> So is it now I am a man;
> So be it when I shall grow old,
>   Or let me die!
> The Child is father to the Man;
> And I could wish my days to be
> Bound each to each by natural piety.

For Wordsworth, "piety" is "natural piety," something rooted in the human being's perception of (responsiveness to) nature, rather than something based on Scripture. We take it that Harjo's vision is close to Wordsworth's.

We are not saying, of course, that the visions are the same, but we do find a close resemblance in the emphasis on the perception of nature as animating the human. For Harjo, the rainbow animates the earth, giving "horses / of color" to humans, "horses that were within us all of this time / but we didn't see them. . . ."

Students will profit from a series of interviews Harjo has given, collected in *The Spiral of Memory: Interviews*, ed. Laura Coltelli (1990). For critical discussion of Harjo and other contemporary poets, see *Feminist Measures: Soundings in Poetry and Theory*, ed. Lynn Keller and Cristanne Miller (1994). We also recommend *Reinventing the Enemy's Language: Contemporary Native Women's Writing of North America*, ed. Joy Harjo and Gloria Bird (1997).

ROBERT HAYDEN

Those Winter Sundays (p. 908)

Students can learn something about writing by thinking about the length of the four sentences that constitute this poem. The first stanza consists of a fairly long sentence (four and a half lines) and a short one (half a line, completing the fifth line of the poem). The brevity of that second sentence reinforces the content— that no one thought about the father—and the brevity also, of course, adds emphasis by virtue of its contrast with the leisurely material that precedes it. Similarly, the fourth sentence, much shorter than the third, adds emphasis, an emphasis made the more emphatic by the repetition of "What did I know?"

Next a confession: We thought about glossing "offices" in the last line, for students will almost surely misinterpret the word, thinking that it refers to places where white-collar workers do their tasks. But we couldn't come up with a concise gloss that would convey the sense of ceremonious and loving performance of benefits. And it may be just as well to spend some class time on this important word, because the thing as well as the word may be unfamiliar to many students. After the word has been discussed, the poem may be read as a splendid illustration of an "office." Like the father in the poem, who drives out the cold and brings warmth (by means of love, of course, as well as coal) to an unknowing child, an "austere and lonely" writer performs an office, shaping experience for another person's use.

One may want to raise the question in class of whether the knowledge that the author was black affects the poem's meaning.

The most important books for the study of Hayden are *Collected Poems*, ed. Frederick Glaysher (1985), and *Collected Prose*, foreword by William Meredith, ed. Frederick Glaysher (1984). Students can begin with this cogent introduction: Fred M. Fetrow, *Robert Hayden* (1984). And, for more depth and detail, they can next consult John Hatcher, *From the Auroral Darkness: The Life and Poetry of Robert Hayden* (1984).

TOPICS FOR CRITICAL THINKING AND WRITING

1. In line 1, what does the word "too" tell us about the father? What does it suggest about the speaker (and the implied hearer) of the poem?
2. What do you take to be the speaker's present attitude toward his father? What circumstances, do you imagine, prompted his memory of "Those Winter Sundays"? What line or lines suggest those circumstances to you?
3. What is the meaning of "offices" in the last line? What does this word suggest that other words Hayden might have chosen do not?

ANTHONY HECHT

The Dover Bitch (p. 909)

Andrews Wanning, to whom the poem is dedicated, was a teacher of literature. Like the title, the subtitle ("A Criticism of Life") is derived from Matthew Arnold, who in "The Study of Poetry," *Essays in Criticism, Second Series*, speaks of poetry as "a criticism of life." Hecht's poem, which at first glance is a parody of Arnold, therefore is also a criticism of poetry (though Arnold's "Dover Beach"—in our text—survives it), and, as we will argue in a minute, also a criticism of life. Hecht's poem must be discussed in connection with Arnold's, but sooner or later the discussion probably ought to get to matters of tone in "The Dover Bitch."

Much of Hecht's poem purports to give the girl's point of view, though we should remember that the speaker is not the girl but a rather coarse fellow who knows her. This speaker sympathizes with her (to "be addressed / As a sort of mournful cosmic last resort / Is really tough on a girl"), but his sensibilities are not of the finest (he tells us that although she is "Running to fat," he gives her "a good time"). If he introduces a note of sexuality that is conspicuously absent from Arnold's poem and that affords some comedy, one's final impression may be that the poem shows us the bleak, meaningless, loveless world that Arnold feared. As Christopher Ricks puts it in *Victorian Studies* 6 (1968), Hecht's "brilliant and poignant poem is by no means flippant. . . . Having subjected Arnold to an unprecedented skepticism, [the poem suddenly reveals] the superiority of Arnold—and of all he epitomized—to that knowing speaker whose worldliness was at first refreshing. The poem, we realize, is in important ways a tribute to Arnold, though hardly a reverential one . . ." (539–40).

Hecht is also a stimulating critic; his books include *Obbligati: Essays in Criticism* (1986), *The Hidden Law: The Poetry of W. H. Auden* (1993), and *On the Laws of the Poetic Art* (1995).

TOPICS FOR CRITICAL THINKING AND WRITING

1. Do you think that the first six lines of Hecht's poem are too chatty and informal? What might be the poet's purpose in writing in this style?
2. Line 8 seems somewhat puzzling. Is "that bitter allusion to the sea" the kind of phrase that the speaker of the first few lines would use? Take note as well of the word "blandishments" in line 15, and the phrase "mournful cosmic last resort," line 18. Are the tone and diction of these lines consistent with that of the rest of the poem?
3. What, finally, is the point of Hecht's poem? Is he simply making fun of the stuffy, solemn author of "Dover Beach," or, beyond that, does he seek to present and explore a point of view of his own—for example, on the nature of male/female relationships?
4. Does "The Dover Bitch," to be effective, require that we know "Dover Beach"? If you came across Hecht's poem by itself and had never read Arnold's poem, what do you imagine your response to "The Dover Bitch" would be?

ROBERT HERRICK

Delight in Disorder (p. 910)

Our discussion is indebted to F. W. Bateson, *English Poetry and the English Language* (1934). Leo Spitzer in *Essays on English and American Literature* (1962) takes issue with Bateson and makes some interesting points, but we believe that on the whole Bateson in on the right track.

Almost every line of the poem except the last contains a word that, although describing clothing, suggests a bit of naughtiness or passion. The most obvious of these words are "disorder" (1), "wantonness" (2), "distraction" (4), "erring" (5), "Enthralls" (6), "neglectful" (7), "tempestuous" (10), "careless" (11), "wild" (12), "bewitch" (13), but in this context even "Kindles" (2), "thrown" (3), and "confusedly" (8) hint at sexuality, i.e., at the sexuality of the wearer. Spitzer disagrees. He says,

> Very civilized ladies may wear daring dresses that in some of their detail may make the impression of wantonness, neglectfulness, carelessness, etc. . . . I see, then, in the series of animated, or animized, pictures of pieces of clothing an anticipation of Walt Disney technique as they whirl around a figure of a woman who is not there. (14–35)

It is not at all clear to us why Spitzer is so eager to deny that clothes make the (wo)man, i.e., that the clothes reveal the wearer, or at least they send a message indicating the person the wearer wishes to be seen as.

Perhaps it is relevant to mention that this poem of fourteen lines (a sort of sonnet, but in couplets) is itself often a bit "neglectful" or "erring" in its rhymes. Although we can't be certain how these words were pronounced in the seventeenth century, probably there are off-rhymes in *thrown / distraction, there / stomacher*, and *tie / civility*, and perhaps elsewhere too, but at the end Herrick is careful to nail down the poem with an exact rhyme, *art / part*. Further, the metrical variations (e.g., line 2 begins with "Kindles," a trochee instead of an iamb, and line 10 contains dactyls) perhaps suggest, in a tiny, restrained way, this "sweet disorder" and "wild civility" (this last, a nice oxymoron). In any case, they prevent the poem from being "too precise in every part" (14).

The poem can be taught effectively in conjunction with Jonson's "Still to Be Neat," which immediately precedes it in the book.

GERARD MANLEY HOPKINS

God's Grandeur (p. 910)

The world (including the human world) has divinely created beauty in its charge (care), but "charged" in line 1 is also a scientific term (referring to electricity), leading to "flame out" in the next line; "foil" in line 2, Hopkins explained in a letter, refers to "foil in its sense of leaf or tinsel." Most of the first quatrain asserts the grandeur of God, whose divine energy may be manifested either suddenly ("flame out") or slowly ("ooze of oil / Crushed"). "Crushed," at the beginning of line 4, is part of this celebration (probably alluding to olives or seeds), but this word itself of course also suggests destruction, and the rest of the octave is about human corruption of the self and of nature. "Man's smudge" in line 7 probably alludes to original sin as well as to the destruction wreaked on the countryside by factories. The octave thus moves from an excited or urgent proclamation of God's grandeur to a melancholy reflection on our insensitivity to this grandeur. The sestet reintroduces a joyous affirmation of God's grandeur. Lines 13 and 14 allude to the traditional representation of the Holy Ghost as a dove, but Christ is here seen also as the dawning sun, giving warmth and light, and thus we go back to the reference to light in line 2; "bent world" probably evokes the curvature of the horizon, the world distorted by sin, and perhaps backbreaking labor.

Paul L. Mariani, in his excellent *Commentary on the Complete Poems of Gerard Manley Hopkins* (1970), suggests that the last lines are connected with the first quatrain: "If we can picture the dawning sun before it breaks over the horizon, we may recall how the rich light seems precisely to 'gather to a greatness' in density and brightness . . . until the orb of the sun itself seems to spring forth, and then the sun flames out in strong rays like wings from its center." W. H. Gardner, in *Gerard Manley Hopkins* (1948), vol. II, 230, suggests that the obvious meaning of the poem is that the world is a reservoir of divine power, love, and beauty, and that the deeper meaning is that life must be jarred before the presence of God can be felt. On "verbal resonance" and other sound effects in the poem, see Brooks and Warren, *Understanding Poetry*, 4th ed. (1976), 538–40. See also Terry Eagleton in *Essays in Criticism* 23 (1973): 68–75. Students might be invited to compare the poem with this entry (Dec. 8, 1881) from one of Hopkins's notebooks, reprinted in *The Sermons and Devotional Writings of Gerard Manley Hopkins*, ed. Christopher Devlin (1959), 95: "All things therefore are charged with love; are charged with God and if we know how to touch them give off sparks and take fire, yield drops and flow, ring and tell of him."

GERARD MANLEY HOPKINS

Pied Beauty (p. 911)

Ultimately this poem is rooted in the Argument from Design, the ancient idea that if one looks around one, the evidence of a benevolent creator is obvious. Thus, Newton in a comment added in 1713 to his *Principia* wrote:

> This most beautiful system of the sun, planets, and comets, could only proceed from the counsel and dominion of an intelligent and powerful Being. . . . He is eternal and infinite, omnipotent and omniscient; that is, his duration reaches from eternity to eternity; his presence from infinity to infinity; he governs all things, and knows all things that are or can be done.

This idea is found in Greek and Roman thought, and also in Judeo-Christian thought, notably in Psalm 19.1:

> The heavens declare the glory of God; and the firmament showeth his handwork.

Hopkins was much taken with this idea. For instance, in his *Journal* for May 1870 he wrote:

> I do not think I have ever seen anything more beautiful than a bluebell I have been looking at. I know the beauty of our Lord by it.

The poem argues similarly, moving from external nature—"skies of couple-colour as a brinded cow" and non-human creatures of the world (trout, chestnuts, finches' wings)—to the landscape with the marks of human beings ("Landscape . . . fold, fallow, and plough") and then more explicitly to human beings (the "trades," "gear," "tackle," and "trim" of line 6). In line 8, in "Whatever is fickle, freckled," we almost meet a changeable pied human being, though of course in Hopkins's context "fickle" and "freckled" can also equally apply to a leaf or a beast. In any case, we advance from the created variable world to the unvarying creator:

> He fathers-forth whose beauty is past change:
> > Praise him.

The clouds, the landscape, the fish in the stream, the cow in the meadow, and the bird on the wing all reveal God—but they cannot praise Him; only human beings can see this infinitely varied evidence of God and can joyfully celebrate His existence. And so Hopkins does not end his poem with a celebration of pied beauty, of "couple-colour," of "rose-moles all in stipple," of contrasts ("swift, slow; sweet, sour; adazzle, dim"). Rather, after the inventive "fathers-forth" he ends with a simply stated command to the reader (and to himself) to celebrate the unchanging creator who has created all this change: "Praise him."

Another way of putting it is to say that the poet moves from his solitary observation of pied beauty—again we emphasize the progress from the inanimate to the animate non-human and then to the human—to an implied society, in which the reader who has overheard the poet's joyous outburst is now invited to join the poet in praising the unchanging God.

A question. Can non believers enjoy such a poem? It has been our unambiguous experience that they can. We have found that Hopkins's enthusiasm is infectious, his artistry compelling. The poem does not persuade non-believers, of course, but it may give them a strong sense of what it feels like to be a believer. We know that many instructors hesitate to teach religious poetry, for fear of offending believers or non believers. Our own practice has been to teach the poem as an aesthetic object, not as a statement that is true or false, and we have never encountered any hostility in class. We have noticed with interest that many students who became keenly interested in Hopkins are students who do not share Hopkins's Roman Catholicism.

A. E. HOUSMAN

To an Athlete Dying Young (p. 911)

The poem presents no difficulties to readers, we think, except possibly the word "lintel" in line 23, the horizontal beam that spans an opening, in this instance the upper member of a door frame. Interesting, at least to pedants, is the fact that *lintel* ultimately comes from the Latin *limen*, "threshold"—this English word appears in the poem in line 7— and *limen* comes from *limes*, "limit." Death is largely a matter of crossing a threshold, of reaching a limit and going beyond it.

While we are fretting about *lintel* we should mention that Housman's manuscripts show that before he wrote "And hold to the low lintel up" he wrote

> And hold to the dark lintel up.

"Dark" is obvious enough for the realm of death, probably too obvious; surely "low" is far superior. The poem celebrates the athlete's latest triumph (he holds "the still-defended challenge-cup") but it also indicates that he carries it into a constricting realm. When we encounter the word "low" here, we almost feel our knees bend and our head lower—i.e., we *feel* the stooping involved.

While we are talking about the small but important change from "dark" to "low," we will mention another change: Housman first wrote "Wise lad" and then changed it to "Smart lad" in line 9. In our view, "Smart" is more colloquial, more suited to the speaker (a fellow townsman of the athlete), though we certainly do not want to insist heavily on a distinction between the speaker and the poet. That is, Housman clearly is not going to any great effort to create a country lad who is distinct from the professor-poet, in the way that (say) Browning's duke is distinct from Browning. We suppose that Housman himself, the Professor of Latin, might well have spoken of one of his students as a "smart lad," but, again, we think the word is more suited to the situation—townsman speaking about a local athlete—than is "wise."

The motif—early death as a sort of triumph—is not rare in literature, but we can't think of any other poem on this motif that students are likely to know. Still, you may want to quote a famous passage from Ben Jonson's "To the Immortal Memory and Friendship of That Noble Pair, Sir Lucius Cary and Sir H. Morison" (each was about twenty when he died):

> It is not growing like a tree
> In bulk, doth make man better be,
> Or standing long an oak, three hundred year,
> To fall a log at last, dry, bald, and sere:
> A lily of a day
> Is fairer far in May
> Although it fall and die that night;
> It was the plant and flower of light.
> In small proportions we just beauties see,
> And in short measures life may perfect be.

Here the note of triumph dominates unambiguously. We can contrast it with the last lines of Dryden's "To the Memory of Mr. Oldham" (Oldham, a poet, died at the age of thirty):

> Once more, hail and farewell; farewell thou young,
> But ah too short, Marcellus of our tongue;
> Thy brows with ivy, and with laurel bound,
> But Fate and gloomy Night encompass thee around.

The young man is compared to Marcellus (the nephew of Augustus), whose early death is memorialized in the *Aeneid*, and he is said to wear crowns of ivy (an evergreen, and therefore symbol of enduring strength) and of laurel (awarded to athletes, emperors, and poets)—but despite the young man's association with Marcellus and with strength and triumph, the poem ends by emphasizing his weakness, his subjugation by fate and darkness.

Housman's poem, we have already suggested, seems to us far more celebratory. Yes, there are ominous touches—"townsman of a stiller town," "shady night," "earth has stopped the ears," "low lintel"—but on the whole we think the emphasis is on victory. Certainly the final stanza does what it can (in contrast to Dryden's final lines) to emphasize the athlete's enduring triumph:

> And round that early laurelled head
> Will flock to gaze the strengthless dead
> And find unwithered on its curls
> The garland briefer than a girl's.

So far as subject matter goes, the obvious poem with which to compare— really, to contrast—"To an Athlete Dying Young" is Updike's "Ex-Basketball Player," where the emphasis is on a man who is a shell of his former self. Housman's fifth quatrain pretty much contrasts the dead youth with Updike's survivor:

> Now you will not swell the rout
> Of lads that wore their honors out,
> Runners whom renown outran
> And the name died before the man.

At the risk of moving away from the poem—the specific artifact—to a general idea, we want to quote a remark that Boswell attributes to Samuel Johnson: "It matters not how a man dies, but how he lives. The act of dying is not of importance, it lasts so short a time." As we say, the danger with introducing such a comment is that the discussion in class then shifts from the poem to a heated argument about—well, about other things, such as life. Still, although we firmly believe that in literature what is important is *how* things are said, i.e., the precise ways in which meanings are generated by exceptional uses of language, we do recognize that literature is connected with life, and we think it is sometimes appropriate to discuss the "idea" as well as the work itself. Discussion of "To an Athlete Dying Young" will, rightly and inevitably, go beyond Housman's words and will engage—how shall we put it?—a larger issue.

A. E. HOUSMAN

When I Was One-and-Twenty (p. 912)

The "wise man" seems to offer two pieces of wisdom, but they are closely related. One is, in effect, "Don't give your heart away," that is, don't fall in love; the second is, "If you do give your heart away, you will suffer." The speaker ignored the advice, and now, at twenty-two, has learned its truth. The last line of the poem, with its repetition, suggests that the speaker takes his youthful sorrow very seriously ("And oh 'tis true, 'tis true"), but surely the line strikes readers (and is intended to strike them) as a trifle maudlin. And since the poem jingles nicely and almost suggests a nursery rhyme, we can hardly take the grief too seriously. We listen with sympathetic amusement to this tale of disillusionment, but we are pretty confident that he will survive, and probably will live to love another day.

Norman Page has written a good biography (1983), and there is a valuable, if dated, selection of criticism in *A. E. Housman: A Collection of Critical*

Essays, ed. Christopher Ricks (1968). For students, we recommend B. J. Leggett, *The Poetic Art of A. E. Housman: Theory and Practice* (1978). But John Bayley, *Housman's Poems* (1992), is worth consulting as well.

A. E. HOUSEMAN

Loveliest of Trees (p. 912)

The motif of course is *carpe diem*, a motif the students will already have encountered if you have taught Herrick's "To the Virgins, to Make Much of Time" or Marvell's "To His Coy Mistress." We will talk about this motif in a moment, and also about a related concept, *Memento mori*, but first we want to talk a bit about the tone of the poem. Are we in the world of "Eat, drink, and be merry, for tomorrow we die"? (Incidentally, this quotation comes from the Hebrew Bible [Isaiah 22.13], and although it advises that one should seize the day, the larger context indicates that such a response is foolish.)

In our view, Housman's poem is chirpy, cheerful, and we think that some critics have gone overboard in emphasizing an undercurrent of death. To the best of our knowledge, this melancholy view originated with Winifred Lynskey in *Explicator* 4:8 (June 1946), Item 59, who began her short article thus: "The undertone of death in this poem should surprise no reader of Housman. Housman's preoccupation with death appears most vividly in the midst of youth, strength, beauty, and earthly ecstasy." Lynskey went on to say, "Even in the first stanza, 'Eastertide' has its own associations with death." We can stop right here, and mention that, yes, Easter is certainly associated with death but, much more important, it is also associated with the Resurrection, and with *eternal life*. Lynskey ends her article thus: "Here [i.e. in this poem] and elsewhere, in poem after poem, the melancholy Housman looks at 'things in bloom' and sees them hung with death, as the cherry is with snow."

Well, this seems all wrong to us. For one thing, the cherry is hung with white blossoms, here metaphorically seen as snow. Why is snow associated with death? (We are not in the world of Jack London's "To Build a Fire.") True, snow is associated with winter, and winter sometimes with death, but that's getting pretty far from the poem. This is a poem about the beauty of *spring*, and Housman insists upon the season, mentioning it twice, in line 7 and again in line 10. Nor is there any reason to talk about the "melancholy Housman" when discussing *this* poem. (We think that one of the wisest things ever said is Bishop Joseph Butler's comment: "Everything is what it is and not another thing.") Yes, other poems by Housman are melancholy—"With rue my heart is laden," or "Into my heart an air that kills / From yon far country blows"—but this poem seems to us to be very different: True, the twenty-year-old speaker introduces the idea of the end of life when he speaks of his "threescore years and ten," but he does bit of arithmetic and tells us that he will use this spring (and we infer he will use he remaining springs) effectively, enjoying their beauty. This is no moping speaker: He is up and at it; and he has even proven his case mathematically. "Since" in line 9 is pretty much like "therefore" in a syllogism. Further, and more important in a poem than logic, the speaker proves his case *wittily:* Readers enjoy hearing this clever young man who can do sums in rhyme, and who tells us of his delight in seeing cherry-trees in flower.

True, when one thinks about it, when one moves away from the actual words of the poem and begins to talk more generally about youth and spring and beauty, one can easily say that there is a melancholy undertone to any statement to the effect that one should live intensely for the moment because life is brief. But Housman's poem puts much less emphasis on the underlying sorrow than, say, Shakespeare does in "O Mistress Mine" (from *Twelfth Night*). We quote the second stanza of Shakespeare's song:

> What is love? 'tis not hereafter;
> Present mirth hath present laughter;
> What's to come is still unsure:
> In delay there lies no plenty,
> Then come kiss me, sweet and twenty,
> Youth's a stuff will not endure.

Here in six lines we get "not hereafter," "unsure," "no plenty," "not endure." Shakespeare ends by emphasizing the brief shelf-life of youth; Housman ends by emphasizing, by means of a metaphor, the beauty of the cherry blossoms. Yes, both poems can be said to share the theme of *carpe diem* but they are utterly different poems.

Now for a few additional words about *carpe diem*, and also about a darker doctrine, *memento mori* ("remember that you have to die"). The words *Carpe diem* (i.e. seize the day) appear in a poem by Horace (*Odes* 1.11) that urges the reader to live for the moment because life is brief: *Spatio breui spem longam reseces; dum loquimur, fugerit invida aetas: carpe diem, quam minimum credula postero*," i.e., "life is brief, cut back long-range plans. Even while we speak, envious time has run on; seize the day, put as little trust as possible in the future." Again, our point is this: Yes, beneath the injunction to live for the moment there is the idea that the future is uncertain—other than that we will die—but this thought need not obliterate the joy of the present. In short, we distinguish it from *memento mori*, which indeed is an injunction to remember that one is mortal and *therefore* to act with humility, with decency. A sort of Judeo-Christian equivalent is found in Ecclesiasticus 7:36: "In whatever you are doing remember the end that awaits you; then all your life you will never go wrong" (Revised English Bible). Clearly there is nothing of this strong moralizing in Housman's poem, but we think it is equally clear that Housman's use of *carpe diem* is as cheerful as possible, partly because Housman's poem is witty (the mathematics), and partly because Housman emphasizes the beauty of "woodland ride."

JAMES WELDON JOHNSON

To America (p. 913)

The poem consists entirely of questions, and this fact about its structure is a good place to begin discussion. Students are able to grasp readily enough that this African-American poet is speaking on behalf of his race to white Americans. But they might not see at first the meaningful choice of title. Johnson does not say "white America," but simply "America," implying the way in which the idea of America has been wedded to whiteness, and at the expense of the black

Americans who did so much to build the nation. In Johnson's view, white Americans tend automatically to define the nation as *their* nation, and not as one in which black persons should be incorporated as equals.

See Eugene Levy, *James Weldon Johnson: Black Leader, Black Voice* (1973).

BEN JONSON

On My First Son (p. 913)

A helpful interpretation of this poem is given by Sara J. van den Berg, in her book *The Action of Ben Jonson's Poetry* (1987). Van den Berg describes how in this "intensely personal, even self-absorbed epitaph for his son," Jonson "merges himself with his son in a poignant wish to deny the permanence of his loss" (103).

Here is a section of van den Berg's analysis:

> The poem is constructed around a series of puns: on the name of the boy (Benjamin: "son of my right hand"), on the contrast between a contractual bond between God and man and the familial bond between father and child, and on the implicit analogy of father and poet as makers. The poem can bare-ly contain his feelings: He blames himself for the boy's death ("My sin was too much hope of thee"); he wishes he could somehow free himself of grief: "O, could I lose all father now." But neither the line nor the grief can end. The consolations that he could bring to bear on his grief for his daughter [the reference here is to Jonson's "On My First Daughter," who died of the plague in November 1593; see below] here seem harshly thrown up against his wish to deny and escape the feelings that overwhelm him. He presents the conven-tional themes of consolation not as statements but as questions: "For why / Will man lament the state he should envy? / To have so soon 'scaped world's and flesh's rage, / And, if no other misery, yet age?" The questions go unanswered, as he finally moves beyond protest to a hollow recognition of his loss. (103)

We agree with van den Berg about line 2—that the poet blames himself for the boy's death. But we hear bitterness and anger in this line as well. Why should it be sinful to feel so hopeful about one's child? Jonson did feel this hope, and he was punished for it—a punishment he both did and did not deserve, a punishment that he accepts even as it strikes home to him and to us as unfair and extreme. One is tempted to quote King Lear's belief that what-ever his faults, ultimately he is "more sinned against than sinning."

Perhaps the point is that Jonson was too proud—that the hope he felt was not really for his son but for himself as a father, for what he could experience himself through the boy's life. And for this pride (that is, presumption), he was struck down: His son was taken from him. Such a harsh, relentless form of jus-tice! If you allow your feelings to stray outside a hard-to-define set of bounds, you pay for it—the person you love, dies.

The monetary terms in lines 3–4 intensify the bitter reality of Jonson's loss and deepen the tone of bitterness and resentment. It is right that a person pays back a loan on the day that it is due; but to Jonson, this is, again, both right and not right or fair ("just") at all. With cruel, self-wounding precision, Jonson places "pay" at the end of one line, and "exacted" at the beginning of the next line, in order to give the point its maximum impact. No escape from this contract is possible.

"O, could I lose all father now": As van den Berg indicates, Jonson "wishes" here that he could free himself of his sorrow. But this is a wish that takes the form of an exclamation, an outcry. It is a terrible moment—a father is so consumed with grief that he would rather give up the memory of fatherhood altogether. In this respect it is worth noting that the standard edition of Jonson's poetry, edited by C. H. Herford and Percy and Evelyn Simpson (1947), prints "loose" rather than "lose." We hesitate to press a matter that may simply be the result of the vagaries of early seventeenth-century spelling, but "loose" is, we think, just as effective or more so than "lose." "Lose" brings out the sense of losing sight of or contact with someone or something, with the implication in this context that one never wants to find it again. "Loose" suggests breaking free from a tie or bond, implying that Jonson still feels connected to his son and—because the connection to the beloved is so painful—wishes he did not. He feels part of the boy, and this fact drives him mad with grief.

We have found two sets of questions in particular work well in class discussion.

1. Ask the students to comment on the meaning of the poet's reference to himself in line 10—which is also a reference to the son, who shares his father's name. And—to develop this line of questioning further—ask the students, too, why Jonson identifies the son as his father's "best piece of poetry." Is this too formal, too literary? To refer back to van den Berg: Is such a phrase a sign of Jonson's self-absorption?
2. The final line: Ask the class what Jonson means by the distinction between "loves" and "like." Why would Jonson say that his vow from now on is never (a strong word) to "like too much" what he loves? Does such a distinction make sense? Is the issue too much liking, or, instead, excessive love?

When we examine this line in class, students usually comment nicely on it and offer good speculative points about its key words. But there is often a fair amount of disagreement among the students. This, we think, helps to make an important point about the poem. On one level, it reaches a resolution—the poet has learned something (though it is a painful lesson indeed), and he says he will feel differently in the future. But on another level, there is no real resolution here—the poem is in truth open-ended, for it is in fact very hard, if not impossible, to make clear and firm the distinction between loving and liking that the poet expresses.

If Jonson's poem can be said to reach resolution at all, it does so with the most piercing kind of double-insight—first, that we must accept the death of a person whom we have loved and must move forward; and second, that we can never accept it, never stop thinking and feeling intensely about what this person meant to us.

Note: You might wish to bring to class a copy of "On My First Daughter":

Here lies to each her parents' ruth,
Mary, the daughter of their youth;
Yet, all heaven's gifts being heaven's due.
It makes the father less to rue.
At six months' end she parted hence

With safety of her innocence;
Whose soul heaven's Queen (whose name she bears),
In comfort of her mother's tears,
Hath placed amongst her virgin train;
Where, while that severed doth remain,
This grave partakes the fleshly birth;
Which cover lightly, gentle earth.

Astute surveys of Jonson's life and writings include Rosalind Miles, *Ben Jonson: His Life and Work* (1986), and David Riggs, *Ben Jonson: A Life* (1989).

BEN JONSON

Still to Be Neat (p. 914)

The contrast here is between the first stanza, in which the woman is "dressed / As you were going to a feast," i.e., is "powdered [and] perfumed," and the second stanza, which praises "simplicity" and "sweet neglect," specified as "Robes loosely flowing, hair as free." There is lots to talk about here. First of all, what is wrong with getting dressed up for a fancy affair, a "feast"? One might say that what is wrong in getting dressed up is that one loses one's identity. To take an extreme case, all men in tuxedos look pretty much alike (except for the jerks who wear maroon bow-ties). But, come to think of it, all students, wearing jeans and T-shirts, and toting backpacks, also look pretty much alike. Where is the "identity" or individualism that they are said to prize? When we dress for a role—and we all do dress for roles, every day, whether we are going to class or going to a job interview or going to a party—we are creating a self that helps to enlarge our identity. (Some sage has said, All clothing is drag.)

Put it this way: If we really believed that our appearance should be "natural," men and women would not cut their hair, and men would not shave. (The writer of this page has always found it strange that the Romantics, for all of their talk about "natural" behavior, and for all of their cult of the "primitive," were clean-shaven.) Come to think of it, we probably wouldn't bathe, either.

Let's return to the poem, to "Robes loosely flowing, hair as free." This praise of what would seem to be naturalness—presumably the robe is not highly tailored—is rhetorically effective, but ask those students who wear tight jeans if they plan to switch to baggy clothing. Baggy clothing too has its adherents; it makes a style statement, and those who wear baggy clothing would not be caught dead in form-fitting clothing.

Our point is not to disparage Jonson's poem, which is a poem that we treasure. Nor do we mean to suggest that there is nothing substantial to the praise of nature over art, but we do want to suggest that much that is commonly thought of as "natural" is artificial. Indeed, your students have probably bought manufactured products that are meant to give the buyer a "natural" look.

Our own view is that both art and nature have their place. The loosely flowing hair that we may seek for ourselves, or admire when we see others with it, may well be the product of art, but of an art that conceals itself. (Cf. the Latin saying, *ars est celare artem*, i.e., the real art is to hide art.) Or, come to think of it, the art may not at all be hidden. No one thinks that such a hairdo as cornrows is natural. The wearer presumably enjoys the—how shall we put it?—ceremonial treatment of the head, and viewers may rightly admire it.

On rereading what we have written, we are uneasy that we seem to be disparaging the poem. Not at all; we greatly admire the poem, a work that is of course a highly artificial (e.g., rhymed) praise of naturalness. Jonson has skillfully hidden his art. In fact, his seemingly spontaneous praise of naturalness—"Give me a look, give me a face, / That makes simplicity a grace"—is partly bookish; the subject had been treated by several classical authors whom Jonson had read carefully.

Note: The next poem in the text, by Robert Herrick (one of the "Sons of Ben"), continues the theme of the superiority of nature to art and it can effectively be taught in conjunction with Jonson's poem.

JOHN KEATS

To Autumn (p. 914)

The poem is discussed in books on Keats by Walter Jackson Bate, Douglas Bush, and Helen Vendler, and also in Reuben Brower, *The Fields of Light* (1951), and in Geoffrey Hartman, *The Fate of Reading, and Other Essays* (1975).

Some gleanings: One can see, in the three stanzas, the progress of autumn from the energetic first stanza (note "load," "bless," "bend," "fill," "swell," "set budding") with its "apples" and "mellow fruitfulness" before the harvest to the more languid second stanza with its "half-reaped furrow" and its cider press with "last oozings," and then the "stubble plains" in the third. We move from richness and fruition in the first stanza, to a sense of loss and also of drowsiness in the second, and finally to a full awareness of death in the third ("soft dying," "mourn," "wailful"), though death is seen in the context of fulfillment. Thus the images of death are in various ways modified. If the day is dying, it is "soft-dying," and if we get stubble rather than swaying grain, the stubble is "rosy."

One can also see the progress of a single day. The "maturing sun" of the first stanza may suggest noon, the resting figure of the second suggests mid-afternoon, and then "the last oozings hours by hours" suggest late afternoon; and of course the third stanza explicitly indicates the end of the day, by "soft-dying day" and "gathering swallows." There is also a movement from the cottage garden with its fruit trees and flowers in the first stanza, to the granary, cider press, and fields of a farm in the second, and then to the hills and skies (though including the "garden-croft") of the third.

X. J. KENNEDY

For Allen Ginsberg (p. 916)

This poem is a multi-leveled tribute. It is Kennedy's tribute to Ginsberg; Kennedy's tribute to William Blake, a poet whom Ginsberg esteemed and whose poem "The Tyger" Kennedy echoes; and Kennedy's tribute, one might suggest, to his own poetic prowess, as he seizes upon Blake's vivid words and adapts their rhythm into witty, exuberant praise of a poet whom Kennedy admired.

Blake's poem begins: "Tyger! Tyger! burning bright." Kennedy keeps the second part of the line but changes the first into "Ginsberg, Ginsberg," which, as one of our students noted, may lead readers to see Ginsberg in the image of the fearsome, fierce tiger: Blake's tiger has become Kennedy's Ginsberg. This is not what we would visualize as the appropriate animal for the peace-loving Ginsberg, but it is in tune with the fun-making spirit of the poem.

Kennedy clearly took a good deal of pleasure in composing this playful elegy. The pun in the phrase "*Queen* of Maytime" gets at the festive frolics in which the radical Ginsberg delighted, and also alludes to his homosexuality (as does the earlier word "Queer"). Kennedy took pleasure too, we are sure, in the double alliterative phrases "foe of fascist" and "bane of bomb" in line 9.

Kennedy changes the rhythm of the poem at line 13. There is a significant pause after "What a catch for Death," which may be Kennedy's way of dramatizing his (and our own) recognition that the vital, wild Ginsberg is dead—that the person whom Kennedy has been making so present and real has departed from us, and that all we retain are memories of Ginsberg's antics.

It intrigues us that Kennedy focuses almost exclusively on Ginsberg the merry-making prankster and social critic. He mentions the fact that Ginsberg was a foe to "proper poets," but he does not compliment Ginsberg *as* a poet. What have we lost with Ginsberg's death? "Glee and sweetness, freaky light." That's a fine and noble line of sentiment, but different from lamenting the departure from us of a great poet. It strikes us that "For Allen Ginsberg" pays tribute to Ginsberg the personality even as it may also imply Kennedy's assessment of Ginsberg the poet. At the least it raises the possibility that Ginsberg will endure because of who he was rather than because of the poetry he wrote.

YUSEF KOMUNYAKAA

Facing It (p. 916)

The title is both literal (he is facing the wall) and figurative (he is confronting the terrible memories of past experiences).

Soldiers in other wars, too, underwent traumatic experiences, and the experience of a combatant is almost bound to include episodes that seem unreal or surreal. But the fact that the Vietnam War had so little popular support—was not convincingly bolstered by the idea that it was being fought for a good cause—was particularly disconcerting and demoralizing. Much of Komunyakaa's poem catches a sense of unreality, and a sense of the loss of self. Thus, a black man looking at his reflection in the black wall finds his reflection literally disappearing; at the same time, if the wall has caused his reflection to disappear, it has nevertheless caught the man himself, drawn him back into the horrible experiences that the wall in effect memorializes. (Strictly speaking, the wall memorializes those who died, not the war itself. That is, the Memorial does not say that the war was either good or bad, only that certain people died in the war.)

From the title on, the speaker is "facing it"—facing the painful memories aroused by standing in front of the wall and confronting or reliving the war experiences. He sees a vision of the booby trap that killed a comrade, Andrew Johnson, and, as reflected in the wall, the loss of the arm of a veteran, who therefore is standing near the poet. At the end of the poem the violence is transformed by the return to the world outside of the wall. In the wall the poet sees a woman "trying to erase names," that is, apparently engaged in a futile action, though one hopes that the memories of the war can be diminished if not erased. But then he corrects himself and realizes that the wall is in fact mirroring an act of affection: "No, she's brushing a boy's hair."

Some of your students may have visited the wall. If so, you may want to ask them to report their experience.

For a good selection of Komunyakaa's verse, we recommend *Neon Vernacular: New and Selected Poems* (1993). Students might also enjoy *The Jazz Poetry Anthology*, ed. Sascha Feinstein and Yusef Komunyakaa (1991); and *The Second Set: The Jazz Poetry Anthology*, vol. 2, ed. Feinstein and Komunyakaa (1996). Komunyakaa has discussed his life and work in two interviews: Vicente F. Gotera, "'Lines of Tempered Steel': An Interview with Yusef Komunyakaa," *Callaloo: A Journal of African American and African Arts and Letters* 13:2 (Spring 1990): 215–29; and Muna Asali, "An Interview with Yusef Komunyakaa," *New England Review* 16:1 (Winter 1994): 141–47. For critical commentary on *Dien Cai Dau* (1988), Komunyakaa's poems about the Vietnam War, see Vicente F. Gotera, "'Depending on the Light': Yusef Komunyakaa's *Dien Cai Dau*," in *America Rediscovered: Critical Essays on Literature and Film of the Vietnam War*, ed. Owen W. Gilman, Jr., and Lorrie Smith (1990), 282–300; and Kevin Stein, "Vietnam and the 'Voice Within': Public and Private History in Yusef Komunyakaa's *Dien Cai Dau*," *Massachusetts Review* 36:4 (Winter 1995–1996): 541–61.

TOPICS FOR CRITICAL THINKING AND WRITING

1. The poem's title is "Facing It." What is the speaker facing? How would you describe his attitude?
2. Three people, whose names we don't know, briefly appear on the wall. How might we describe their actions? Try to paraphrase: "I'm a window. / He's lost his right arm / inside the stone."
3. At the poem's end, has the speaker "faced it"? What is your evidence?
4. If you have seen the Vietnam Veterans Memorial, describe it and your reaction to it in a paragraph or two. If you haven't seen it, try to describe it from "Facing It" and any written or photographic accounts you have seen.

MAYA LIN

Vietnam Veterans Memorial (photograph, p. 917)

The monument was commissioned by the Vietnam Veterans Memorial Fund, which held a design competition. Any U.S. citizen over the age of eighteen could enter a design. The criteria were as follows: The monument had to (1) be reflective and contemplative in character; (2) be harmonious with its surroundings; (3) include the names of the nearly 58,000 persons who died or who remain missing in action; (4) make no political or military statement about the war; (5) occupy no more than two acres of land. The competition was won by Maya Ying Lin, an undergraduate at Yale University. Her design consists of two 250-foot walls of polished black granite, meeting at a 136-degree angle. The walls are ten feet tall where they meet, but taper off into the sloping ground. The names of the dead are inscribed, chronologically in order of death. The names begin not at the left end of the monument, but at the intersection of the two walls, at the top of the right-hand wall. The names continue along the wall, and when space on the right-hand wall is exhausted (where the tip of the wall points to the Washington Monument) they continue at the western end of the left-hand wall (whose tip points to the Lincoln Memorial). Thus, the names of the first who died in the war (on the left-hand side of the right-hand wall) are adjacent to the names of the last to die (on the right-hand side of the left-hand wall).

When the winning design was announced—there were 1,421 entries—it met with much opposition. It did not convey heroism, it was not made of white marble (the traditional material of memorials), and it was not representational. Despite the controversy the memorial was built—though as a compromise, a flagpole and a realistic sculpture of three soldiers (two white, one black) were erected nearby. Today the monument is universally recognized as a masterpiece, though it is very difficult to explain why visitors find it so deeply moving. Something has to do with the site (pointing, as we have said, to the Washington Monument and the Lincoln Memorial), something has to do with the sequence in which the names are inscribed, but much has to do with the reflective black granite sinking into the sloping grass. The criteria, you will recall, included the monument be reflective—and it *is* reflective, in a literal way that the committee doubtless had not envisioned. Visitors looking for the names of friends and loved ones see themselves in the monument. It is not too much to say that the living and the dead meet here, set in an area rich in historical associations. Perhaps we can also say that although the Vietnam Veterans Memorial is indeed a memorial, it is not gloomy, chiefly because it is animated by images of the living, but also because of the site, a grassy slope in an area flanked by memorials to Washington and Lincoln.

One wonders, too, to what extent viewers are moved by the knowledge that the memorial was created by a young woman—an undergraduate!—of Asian ancestry. It is appropriate at this point to quote Maya Lin's own comment on her work. We find it interesting but far from definitive:

> I thought about what death is, what a loss is . . . a sharp pain that lessens with time, but can never quite heal over. A scar. The idea occurred to me there on the site. Take a knife and cut open the earth, and with time the grass would heal it. As if you cut open the rock and polished it.
>
> *American Institute of Architects Journal* 72 (May 1983): 151

Useful discussions of the memorial can be found in Jan C. Scruggs and Joel L. Swerdlow, *To Heal a Nation: The Vietnam Veterans Memorial* (1992), and in an article by Charles L. Griswold in *Critical Inquiry* 12 (1986): 688–719. (Griswold's article is reprinted in *Critical Issues in Public Art,* ed. Harriet F. Senie and Sally Webster, rev. ed., 1998.) Somehow, no discussion does much to account for the experience of visiting the memorial.

ARCHIBALD MACLEISH

Ars Poetica (p. 918)

See Donald Stauffer, *The Nature of Poetry* (1946, 121–25), and W. P. Standt in *College English* 19 (October 1957): 28–29. Standt points out that in the first and second sections there are similes, but in the third section we move from similarity to identity; i.e., metaphors replace similes. Moreover, identity is stressed in the quasi-mathematical formula at the beginning of the third section.

This poem easily gets the class into a discussion of the nature of art. And a discussion of MacLeish's poem inevitably gets into whether MacLeish practices his precepts; the abundant detail gives us a sense of felt reality ("be"), but doesn't MacLeish also "mean"? Certainly "A poem should not mean / But be" has meaning; and note, too, that MacLeish is not content to give us "An empty doorway and a maple leaf," for he prefaces this with an explanation, telling us that it stands "For all the history of grief."

It is useful to ask students to comment in detail on the figures. The figure of an empty doorway and an autumn leaf standing for grief is clear enough, but how is "A poem . . . motionless in time / As the moon climbs"? Perhaps the idea is that a poem, because it stirs the emotions, seems to move, yet it is itself unchanging.

MacLeish can be studied in detail in the following sources: *Letters of Archibald MacLeish, 1907 to 1982*, ed. R. H. Winnick (1983); *Archibald MacLeish: Reflections*, ed. Bernard A. Drabeck and Helen E. Ellis (1986); and Scott Donaldson, *Archibald MacLeish: An American Life* (1992).

CLAUDE MCKAY

America (p. 919)

McKay's focus is highly personal—how he responds to America, its ideals and values. This poem is very effective in showing students the complex response that many minority poets have expressed toward the nation. America makes McKay angry—it feeds him "bread of bitterness." (Note that McKay characterizes America as female at first, though later he uses the image of "a king in state.") Yet America also invigorates McKay, supplying him with the strength that he needs to combat America at its worst. For McKay, America is both enemy and ally, cruel foe and potent supporter and friend.

Lines 11–14 are somewhat puzzling. Does the image of "priceless treasures sinking in the sand" intimate that America's monumental glory will persist decades into the future (like the Egyptian pyramids), or that America, however mighty now, will one day be no more than a historical memory, fading into oblivion, covered up by the sands of time?

HERMAN MELVILLE

Misgivings (p. 919)

First, we want to say that we think Melville is an interesting poet—no, make it more than "interesting," let's say "talented" and "moving." So far as we can tell his poems are neglected. Our evidence? In earlier editions of *An Introduction to Literature* we have included "Shiloh," "The March into Virginia," and "Dupont's Round Fight," but our colleagues tell us that they do not teach these poems. Nevertheless we have retained one of the poems, "Dupont's Round Fight" (the accompanying map itself ought to draw interest), and we have introduced two others: "Misgivings" and "The Tuft of Kelp." We keep trying, and we hope some day to hear that instructors are teaching Melville's poems with pleasure and with success.

"Misgivings" (1860) begins with a description of an autumn storm; no one will be surprised to learn that the storm is symbolic of the Civil War that broke out a year later. Melville explicitly tells his reader that the storm causes him to think about his "country's ills:"

> When ocean-clouds over inland hills
>   Sweep storming in late autumn brown,
> And horror the sodden valley fills
>   And the spire falls crashing in the town,
> I muse upon my country's ills—
> The tempest bursting from the waste of Time
> On the world's fairest hope linked with man's foulest crime.

Exactly what is "man's foulest crime"? Stanton Garner, in *The Civil War World of Herman Melville* (1993) says,

> To many modern readers it has seemed that "man's foulest crime" must have been slavery, but to a conservative such as Herman the disintegration of the union was the more foul, and he linked that disintegration to the worst crime of all fratricide . . . Yet the poem allows the reader to choose whatever crime best suits his preconceptions. (61)

Are we being too literal if we take "the spire falls crashing in the town" to suggest that traditional spiritual beliefs are collapsing or have collapsed? And are we mistaken in thinking that although Melville disapproved of slavery, he sees the storm not as a product of a particular Southern practice but as a product of human imperfection that infects the nation ("I muse upon my country's ills"), indeed of dark forces in human nature that have at last burst out and that for a while will be unstoppable? "Nature's dark side is heeded now" suggests, to our ears, something close to the doctrine of original sin, a force that threatens to overwhelm the noble but relatively frail constructions of human beings. Melville's sonnet ends thus:

> The hemlock shakes in the rafter, the oak in the driving keel.

On the simplest level—a level not to be neglected—Melville is speaking about houses and ships, i.e., about society on land and sea, but we think it may not be not fanciful to see in this line faint allusions to the hemlock rafters of the house that is the Union and to the oak keel of the ship of state. The ship of state is a traditional figure, but the house as an image of the Union must have been in everyone's mind in 1860 because Lincoln had given the famous "house divided" speech only two years earlier, where he said,

> "A house divided against itself cannot stand." [Lincoln is quoting Mark 3.25] I believe this government cannot endure permanently half slave and half free. I do not expect the Union to be dissolved—I do not expect the

house to fall—but I do expect it will cease to be divided. It will become all one thing or all the other.
—"Speech at the Republican State Convention," June 16, 1858

HERMAN MELVILLE

The Tuft of Kelp (p. 919)

This short poem will cause no difficulty—provided that students know that kelp is a greenish brown seaweed. Still, there are things in it that are worth discussing.

To begin with, why "lonely sea"? After all, the sea is not lonely; it doesn't have feelings. For a moment let us digress from Melville, and talk about the sea. Contemplation of the sea, especially if no ship is visible, normally evokes a great sense of otherness, greater than, for instance, contemplation of a landscape, which perhaps stimulates thoughts of fertile fields that nourish human beings, or of lofty trees that provide welcome shade. One of the great poetic statements of this view of the ocean is at the beginning of Matthew Arnold's "To Marguerite—continued":

> Yes! in the sea of life enisled,
> With echoing straits between us thrown,
> Dotting the shoreless watery wild,
> We mortal millions live *alone*.

Now back to Melville's "lonely sea." The device of attributing human emotions to inanimate nature is called (somewhat awkwardly) the "pathetic fallacy," i.e., the fallacy of attributing feelings and human abilities to such things. (John Ruskin invented the term in 1856.) Also involved, of course, is the ancient device called personification, in which any non-human thing (animate or inanimate) is given human attributes, for instance feelings (as in the pathetic fallacy) or merely appearances (e.g., the *brow* of the mountain in Melville's "Misgivings," line 10—though even in this example Melville in fact uses the pathetic fallacy because he speaks of "the moody brow"). The sea presumably is "lonely" because, so far as the poem goes, it is uninhabited; its sole denizen was the tuft of kelp, which has now been "cast up."

Further, is the sea—even Melville's sea—"lonely," or, rather, is it the tuft of kelp that is lonely? Yes, we may think of the sea as "lonely" in that nothing is said of ships merrily sailing on it or bathers splashing in it, but probably we also more or less transfer the idea of loneliness to the tuft of kelp, cast up by the sea and, for the purposes of the poem, the only thing that exists other than the sea. In short, we take "lonely" to be an example of the figure of speech called *transferred epithet*. (Examples: In Gray's *Elegy* we are told that "drowsy tinklings lull the distant folds." The tinkling bells cannot literally be "drowsy"; the word is transferred to the bells from the sheep that wear them.)

Melville apostrophizes (another figure of speech!) the kelp, asking it:

> If purer for that , O Weed,
> Bitterer, too, are ye?

He doesn't give an answer, and even in our quest for figures of speech we refrain from saying that the question is a rhetorical question. It is simply asked, but we think a reader probably conjectures that Melville's answer is "Yes, the kelp is more bitter for having been battered by the sea and then cast up. If we press a little harder, we can say that Melville is raising a question that is often raised when we talk about anyone who has undergone great suffering. We try to salvage something out of the suffering, and so we may speak of some sort of improvement, of some sort of purification. Certainly when we talk about a tragic hero, for instance King Lear, we are likely to say that he "learns by suffering," that he achieves an *anagnorisis*, and so on. In Melville's term, we may say the tragic hero is "purer." Thus, in classrooms it is commonly said that Hamlet ultimately puts aside his bitter jesting, his harsh treatment of Ophelia, even his self-hatred, and ultimately achieves some sort of inner peace. Again, the idea is that somehow the suffering was necessary for the person to achieve purification. We happen to think that this idea that suffering is necessary for some sort of tragic purgation is much overrated, even in discussing tragedies, and much more so in discussing episodes in real life. A hurricane hits a town, and we hear on the TV news that the survivors are "stronger," have been "brought together," etc. Maybe. Does suffering often embitter rather than purge the sufferer? A topic for discussion.

PAT MORA

Illegal Alien (p. 920) and Legal Alien (p. 920)

The speaker of the first poem is a legal alien or a citizen, but of course the point at the end of the poem is that she—not the illegal alien whom she addresses—is "the alien" because she cannot offer the appropriate response to her comrade. The implication is that she has become too assimilated, capable of offering only "cooling words" when what is needed are "soothing hands."

The companion poem begins with assertions of competence ("Bi-lingual. Bi-cultural"), and indeed the opening stanza—a single sentence after the one-word fragment "Bi-lingual"—is elegant and forceful with its repetitions ("able to slip," "able to sit," "able to order," "perhaps exotic, / perhaps inferior") and its alliteration ("definitely different"). But even in the first stanza there is a strong suggestion of dislocation in *"Me'stan volviendo loca"* (i.e., they are driving me crazy), and the second stanza makes it clear that the speaker who in the first stanza seemed so comfortable in both worlds in fact in both worlds experiences "discomfort" (line 20), "being pre-judged/ Bi-laterally").

CAROL MUSKE

Chivalry (p. 921)

We begin by asking students about the meanings of the word "chivalry." Students usually know that the term refers to the medieval system, principles, and customs of knighthood—bravery, honor, loyalty. They are not always aware that it also connotes gallantry toward women.

The central claim that Muske makes, in stanza 3, then becomes the focus of our discussion. The speaker says that she has seen few acts that are like this one—an act of "true chivalry." But the act itself is one that may make many American readers, accustomed to different burial practices, uneasy and uncomfortable. Not all of our students, but a fair number of them, have found this poem disturbing. How could a man who loved his wife burn her body?

Yet this is the point of the poem, or, rather, the burden of meaning that Muske has taken on, as she declares and seeks to convince us that this is a noble, loving act. She uses the word "reverence," which connotes profound love, awe, deep respect. Muske wants to claim about this scene what we might at first find hard to accept—that it is a beautiful gesture that shows the "bereavement" (the desolate loneliness) that the old man feels.

Muske sets this moment against the broader span of the "familiar carnage of love." We ask students why they think Muske ended the poem with this line. Does it fittingly conclude Muske's reflections on the scene, or, instead, does it somewhat jar against the solemn mood she has created? Is there anger in this final line? Bitterness? "Carnage" is a strong word—massive slaughter, as in war, a massacre; corpses, especially of those killed in battle. Such "carnage" is "familiar," Muske observes: We have witnessed it all too often.

But we push this point further. What kinds of experiences is Muske alluding to through this phrase? Do members of the class agree with this claim, which is after all a grand and shocking one? Should Muske have done more to establish for us what "the familiar carnage of love" (at least it still *is* love) entails and how it stands in contrast to the kind of chivalric gesture she had depicted here?

In *An Octave Above Thunder: New and Selected Poems* (1977), Muske presents twenty years of work in verse. For interested students, this book pairs nicely with another that she has written in prose, a collection of essays titled *Women and Poetry: Truth, Autobiography, and the Shape of the Self* (1977).

TOPICS FOR CRITICAL THINKING AND WRITING

1. Do you find the poem shocking? Even more to the point: Do you find it shocking that the speaker refers to this scene as an example of chivalry?
2. What is the meaning of the final line? Why the word "carnage"? How does this word in particular fit (or, in your view, not fit) in the structure of the poem as a whole?

SHARON OLDS

Rites of Passage (p. 922)

One of our students wrote a good paper about this poem, calling it a "poem about perspective." We liked the way he noted the difference in size between the speaker and her son and the other "short men" attending the party, and his movement from this observation to verbal details that illuminate the speaker's point of view. This student said that the speaker in fact takes two points of view—two perspectives—on the boys, seeing them as children and as small adults (i.e., the persons they will grow up to be). We think it's helpful to ask students to consider how the speaker perceives the boys, how they view themselves ("they eye each other"), and—a broader issue—how Olds means for readers to understand the lesson of the poem. What exactly is its tone? What is our own perspective on its descriptions supposed to be?

Here one can focus on Olds's title. What is a "rite of passage" and in what respect is this birthday party an example of one? Turn next to specific moments in the poem's language, as when the speaker quotes the boys' warnings: "I could beat you up" and "We could easily kill a two-year-old." Students, we have found, react very differently to these phrases. Some judge them to be comic—it's funny and familiar to hear little boys making large threats—whereas others maintain that Olds wants us to hear these words as ominous, as a sign of the hard masculine world that these "short men" will inhabit (and promote) when they get older.

The discussion of "Rites of Passage" is always lively and becomes more so as it proceeds. A student in one of our classes wondered if this is a political poem. Is Olds using this scene to assail patriarchy, a system in which boys "naturally" assume manly poses and, while still small, are already looking and sounding like "bankers" and "Generals"? It is intriguing, too, to invite students to imagine other perspectives on this same subject. Would the boy's father (note that no mention is made of him) interpret the scene differently from the mother? Is there a similar kind of typical scene at a girl's birthday party against which this one could be compared?

Responses to these questions can be keyed to the poem's final phrase: "celebrating my son's life." The word "celebrate" can be connected to the word "rites"—it has a sacred and solemn meaning, as in celebrating a marriage or a mass. More commonly, "celebrate" suggests showing joy at an event; being part of a festive, happy occasion; rejoicing in an opportunity for honoring someone (i.e., celebrating a person's achievements). Does Olds want her readers to hear her final line as ironic, or, as students have sometimes told us, does she instead mean it more straightforwardly, as if she were saying, "I've made my amused, satiric points but it's really a happy day after all, and I do love my son"? Don't neglect the word "my," however. It's one of those small words that students tend to pass by, but it's an important one. It indicates the speaker's connection to the child (he is *her* child), renewed at the end of the poem. Yet while the speaker takes responsibility for him in one sense, this is balanced against the detachment, the separation, evident in the speaker's perception that her small boy is a man in miniature, not her child as much as an adult in the making. The words in this last line are finely placed, reaching a complicated, disquieting balance.

Olds's recent books of poetry include *The Wellspring: Poems* (1996) and *Blood, Tin, Straw* (1999).

LINDA PASTAN

Love Poem (p. 923)

"Love Poem" is not a love poem as such but, rather, a poem about the speaker's intention to write a love poem. "I want" is a nice beginning; it could suggest at first "I want *you*," but instead it introduces the desire to "write," a desire that in line 2 reveals itself more precisely as the desire to compose a love poem. "Headlong" means without deliberation; rashly, recklessly, heedlessly;

without delay or pause. The resonances of the word complicate the poem's first movement: "I want to write you" has a deliberate sound, whereas "headlong" evokes something or someone out of control, carried by its own momentum, not directed by human will or agency.

This tension is evident also in the juxtaposition of the headlong creek and the couple who "stand" on the bank—firmly in place. Yet the next line says "dangerous," so the standing is perhaps firm but in this location is perilous.

We wonder about the word "dangerous." Does it make the speaker's point too overtly? Might the effect in fact be more compelling if the action of the creek were described as "headlong" without the signaling of "dangerous"? We have a similar question about "every." We see its purpose: It conveys the absoluteness and finality of the creek's operation. But does it over-accent the meaning?

Notice that there is no punctuation in Pastan's poem—there's just the array of short lines, with their brisk pace. The lack of punctuation makes the reference to "every scruple" more surprising and more strategic. The reader is following the action of the creek and then suddenly encounters the abstract word "scruple," with the "every" taking the reader back to the two preceding uses of "every" in a more precise context. But this interpretation isn't quite accurate. "Scruple" does indeed mean an ethical consideration; a moral principle that inhibits action. But its root meaning is a small, sharp stone; a "scruple" is also a small unit of measure. For us, the particularity of the scene of the rushing creek activates the root meaning of "scruple," giving the word a richer sense.

We are drawn to Pastan's "swollen" as well. "Swollen" means to increase in volume; to grow larger or bulkier; to expand by internal pressure or growth; to fill out, dilate; to rise above or extend beyond a level, surface, or border. It also implies: to become filled with pride and arrogance; to become puffed up; to behave or speak in a self-important manner. There may be a sexual undertone in "swollen" too.

If this is indeed a love poem, or a poem about the yearning to write such a poem, it is an unnerving one. When the speaker and her beloved "grab" one another, there is desperation in their act—they hold on to one another for dear life against the forces that simultaneously allure and threaten them; even they endanger one another. One is reminded of the way in which desperate drowning persons can cause the death of their rescuers.

This effect is crucially the result of Pastan's choice of "grab," which means: to take or take hold of by a sudden motion or grasp; to seize, clutch, capture, restrain, arrest; to get or appropriate to oneself unscrupulously." "Grab" is rough and sudden, and intimates a person or a thing violated, which may reach back to the image of the "headlong" creek.

"Love Poem" does not present a tender scene. The scene instead is one of fascination, fear, and threat. Love means an exposure to risk, and to destruction and death. Even as we say this, however, we note with intense curiosity the image of the soaked shoes, which isn't glamorous or dangerous. Having soaked shoes is just embarrassing and uncomfortable. Shoes do get wet, but then they dry out. It is not a big deal. The image is perplexing in its placement, but we confess we like it, for it is in keeping with the unexpected play of meanings and feelings that "Love Poem" offers throughout.

The best point of departure for studying Pastan is her *Carnival Evening: New and Selected Poems, 1968–1998* (1998). For secondary sources: *Dictionary of*

Literary Biography, Volume 5: American Poets Since World War II, first series, ed. Donald J. Greiner (1980), 158–163. See also: "'Whatever Is at Hand': A Conversation with Linda Pastan," in *The Post-Confessionals: Conversations with American Poets of the Eighties*, ed. Earl Ingersoll, Judith Kitchen, and Stan Sanvel Rubin (1989).

MARGE PIERCY

To be of use (p. 923)

One of the best features of "To be of use" is how it employs in line 1 a common phrase and claim that, as the poem unfolds, Piercy makes vivid, deepens, and complicates.

"The people I love the best": that's simple enough, the first part of a definition. "The people I love the best" *are those who*. . . . And the first stanza by itself might make for a good poem. Piercy thus would be saying, boosted by the energy and verve of her well-placed verb "jump," that she loves above all people who know what they want to do and who decisively, emphatically, do it. The image of the seals is complimentary and affectionate—and comical too, evoking something splashily funny about the dedicated workers whom Piercy in this stanza celebrates.

We hear in these lines an allusion to a famous phrase in Conrad's novel *Lord Jim* (1900), where the character Stein says:

> A man that is born falls into a dream like a man who falls into the sea. If he tries to climb out into the air as inexperienced people endeavour to do, he drowns—nicht wahr [won't he]? . . . No! I tell you! The way is to the destructive element submit yourself, and with the exertions of your hands and feet in the water make the deep, deep sea keep you up. So if you ask me—how to be?

The pleasure and interest of the poem overall lie in Piercy's expansion and exploration of the opening line, carried on in a sequence of stanzas, and in an array of images. When we teach "To be of use," we encourage students to describe the impact, and the implications, of the imagery in the first stanza, and then we move to the second, asking, "How do the images of the ox, the water buffalo, pulling the cart change or modify the sense of the people whom Piercy loves?" Same question about the third stanza, with its imagery and its relationship to what has been expressed before. Then, as the poem moves into the final stanza: How do the preceding stanzas prepare the reader for the conclusions that the speaker reaches about the nature of "the work of the world"?

When we teach this poem, we move through the text slowly: we want the students to register and be conscious of the specific meanings and implications of Piercy's words. Often, that's more than half the battle in helping students to enjoy poetry.

"Botched," for instance, in line 19, derives from a Middle English word for "mend." But "botch" in fact means the opposite—to mend not at all, or to mend badly: "to ruin through clumsiness; to make or perform clumsily; bungle; to repair or mend clumsily." When the work is "botched," it "smears the hands." "Smear: to spread or daub with a sticky, greasy, or dirty substance; to apply by spreading or daubing: *smeared suntan lotion on my face and arms*; to stain by or as if by spreading or daubing with a sticky, greasy, or dirty substance; to stain or attempt to destroy the reputation of; vilify: *political enemies who smeared his name*; slang: to defeat utterly; smash." Press the students, then, to see and feel that "smearing," and then to hear and absorb the different range of association in "crumbles to dust," which perhaps alludes to Genesis 3.19: "For dust thou art, and unto dust shalt thou return."

For further reading, we suggest *Circles on the Water: Selected Poems of Marge Piercy* (1982). Students might also enjoy *Early Ripening: American Women Poets Now* (1988), which Piercy edited, and her memoir, *Sleeping with Cats* (2002).

For a helpful listing of primary and secondary sources, and other materials (e.g., interviews with Piercy), visit the Marge Piercy Home Page: http://www.margepiercy.com/.

In an interview, Piercy has identified key "influences" on her work; we are fond of quoting the passage in the classroom because it dramatizes for students that good writers see wide-ranging reading as the background from which their own vocation and craft emerge:

> In the beginning there were the romantics, Byron and Shelley and Keats, and also Whitman and Dickinson. That was the beginning, at fifteen. My earliest passions. Then came Eliot. Then came Blake and Yeats and Joyce, Joyce and Yeats and Blake, intense and burning passions. I discovered Muriel Rukeyser very early, when I was a senior in high school, and I loved her always. Always. Then came William Carlos Williams and Neruda and Vallejo. But all this is a gross simplification, because I was always reading so much. I left out Pope. I left out Wordsworth. They were both terribly important. As were Edith Sitwell and Edward Arlington Robinson. I loved Elizabethan lyrics and Wyatt. Just as I put in a lot of time reading fairy tales, tales of all sorts, the basic stories, I put in a lot of time with ballads. Child's ballads and the variations [Francis James Child's *English and Scottish Popular Ballads*]. Ginsberg liberated my imagination at a critical time, 1959. My reading style was heavily influenced by Black poets in the late sixties—not that I imitated what they did, which would have been silly and meretricious, but that they inspired me to figure out how to put my poems across: Sonia Sanchez, June Jordan, Don L. Lee.

SYLVIA PLATH

Daddy (p. 924)

C. B. Cox and A. R. Jones point out, in *Critical Quarterly* 6 (Summer 1964): 107–22, that literature has always been interested in perverse states of mind (Greek and Roman interest in the irrational; Elizabethan interest in melancholy, jealousy, madness, etc., and Browning's dramatic monologues). The "fine frenzy" of the poet himself (in the words of Shakespeare's Theseus), once associated with inspiration and even divinity, in the twentieth century links the poet with the psychotic personality. And apparently a sensitive (poetic) mind can make only a deranged response in a deranged world. Plath's "Daddy" begins with simple repetitions that evoke the world of the nursery rhyme (and yet also of the witches in *Macbeth*, who say, "I'll do, I'll do, and I'll do"). The opening line also connects with the suggestion of the marriage service ("And I said I do") in line 67. The speaker sees herself as tormented yet also as desiring the pain inflicted by her father/love ("Every woman adores a Fascist"). She recognizes that by accepting the need for love she exposes herself to violence. The speaker's identification of herself with Jews and the evocation of "Dachau, Auschwitz, Belsen" suggest some identity between the heroine's tortured mind and the age's. Death, Cox and Jones go on to say, is the only release from a world that denies love and life. The "Daddy" of the poem is father, Germany, fatherland, and life itself, which surrounds the speaker and which the speaker rejects.

In *Commentary* (July 1974 and October 1974), there is an exchange of letters on the appropriateness of Plath's use of Nazi imagery in a poem about her father. Roger Hoffman, in the July issue, argues that the imagery is valid because in a child's mind an authoritarian father is fearsome. Irving Howe, in October (9–12), replies that this argument is inadequate ground "for invoking the father as a Nazi." The speaker of the poem is not a child, Howe says, but "the grown-up writer, Sylvia Plath." He goes on: The "unwarranted fusion of child's response and grown-ups' references makes for either melodrama or self-pity." Howe also rejects Carole Stone's argument (July) that the images are acceptable because "one individual's psyche [can] approximate the suffering of a people." Howe replies that the victims of the concentration camps didn't merely "suffer"; they were methodically destroyed. He questions the appropriateness of using images of the camps to evoke personal traumas. There is, he says, a lack of "congruence" between the object and the image, "a failure in judgement." Some useful criticism can also be found in *The Art of Sylvia Plath* (1970), ed. Charles Newman.

Camille Paglia, in *Break, Blow, Burn* (2005), 167–76, offers a provocative commentary on the poem. We quote a few passages from it.

> "Daddy" is a rollicking nursery rhyme recast as a horror movie. Its arguable premise, simplistically read, is that women are kept in a state of perpetual childhood by domineering fathers and husbands. . . .
>
> Taking in far more than the festering female condition, "Daddy" is a tragicomedy of the isolated modern self. The public structures of creed and nation have failed, and emotion has become blindingly all-consuming in the seething crucible of the nuclear family. . . .
>
> To what degree is it justified for Plath, with her comfortable middle-class upbringing and privileged education, to appropriate the unspeakable annals of "Dachau, Auschwitz, Belsen"? . . .
>
> Plath's facile association of her father with Hitler is equally problematic. . . .
>
> The looming menace produces a dubious generalization: "Every woman adores a Fascist" (48). Is Plath saying that nature, for procreative reasons, implants in women a hormonal attraction to dominating men? Is the sex drive inherently demeaning? Or does Plath believe that women are socially conditioned for subservience? She seems to conflate emotional manipulation with physical violence ("the boot in the face"). . . .
>
> "The black telephone's off at the root, / The voices just can't worm through": this stunning metaphor, regressively fusing the modern with the archaic, portrays miscommunication and a dying family tree as a tech-

nology on the blink (69–70). We normally say a phone is "off the hook," not "off at the root"; the wire, slithering into the ground like a snaky vine, has been cut. . . .

Ironically, the last line of "Daddy," where the poet is at her boldest, is swamped by her father. In her dispute for mental territory with him, "I" appears thirty times in the poem (in English and German). But her exit line proclaiming victory grants him even more space: he appears there three times to her one. He has survived even with a stake in his heart. She has built his funeral monument: her best poem belongs to him. Father and daughter are locked together in psychic struggle for eternity.

Plenty here for students (and teachers) to think about, but the entire essay should be consulted if time is available.

A "Voices and Visions" videocassette of Sylvia Plath is available from Longman Publishers.

TOPICS FOR CRITICAL THINKING AND WRITING

1. Many readers find in this poem something that reminds them of nursery rhymes. If you are among these readers, specify the resemblance(s).
2. Some critics have called parts of the poem "surrealistic." Check a college dictionary, and then argue in a paragraph or two why the word is or is not appropriate.
3. Is this a poem whose experience a reader can share? Explain.
4. The speaker expresses her hatred for her father by identifying him with the Nazis, herself with the Jews. Is it irresponsible for a poet to compare her sense of torment with that of Jews who were gassed in Dachau, Auschwitz, and Belsen?

EZRA POUND

In a Station of the Metro (p. 927)

While these two lines have not generated quite as much commentary as the "two-handed engine" in "Lycidas," they have generated a good deal—beginning with Ezra Pound. In *T.P.'s Weekly* (June 6, 1913) Pound talked about the poem and then elaborated his comment, as follows, in *Fortnightly Review* (September 1, 1914):

> Three years ago in Paris I got out of a "metro" train at La Concorde, and saw suddenly a beautiful face, and then another and another, and then a beautiful child's face, and then another beautiful woman, and I tried all that day to find words for what this had meant to me, and I could not find any words that seemed to me worthy, or as lovely as that sudden emotion. And that evening, as I went home along the Rue Raynouard, I was still trying, and I found, suddenly, the expression. I do not mean that I found words, but there came an equation . . . not in speech, but in little splotches of color. . . .
>
> The "one image poem" is a form of super-position, that is to say, it is one idea set on top of another. I found it useful in getting out of the

impasse in which I had been left by my metro emotion. I wrote a thirty-line poem, and destroyed it because it was what we called work "of second intensity." Six months later I made the following hokku-like sentence ["In a Station of the Metro"]. I dare say it is meaningless unless one has drifted into a certain vein of thought. In a poem of this sort one is trying to record the precise instant when a thing outward and objective transforms itself, or darts into a thing inward and subjective.

What is left for commentators to say about the poem? A great deal, since Pound says nothing about any of the specific words in the poem. Thomas Hanzo in *Explicator*, February 1953, made the following points.

1. "In the first line the word 'apparition' suggests the supernatural or the immaterial and a sudden and unexpected appearance."
2. "Since only faces are mentioned," we have a sense of "bodiless" substances. "The faces are likened to 'petals on a wet, black bough.' We know therefore that they are the faces in the windows of a train which has drawn up at the station, for the likeness can only be between the faces framed in the windows of the long, dark train and petals which have fallen on a bough after a rain."
3. "The important point of similarity is that the train has made one of its momentary stops, just as the bough is only momentarily black because it is wet from the rain which has just broken the petals from their stem."
4. What interests Pound is *not* that beauty can be found in a subway (a point made by Brooks and Warren), "but that the vision of beauty has occurred in the one instant before it vanishes, when it has been released from the accidents and particularly of its material embodiment."

John Espey, writing in the June 1953 issue of *Explicator*, took issue with some of Hanzo's points. Espey argued that Pound's comment (unlike Hanzo's) keeps the faces "precisely where the poem places them, 'in the crowd,'" rather than in the windows of subway cars drawn up for a moment at the station. Further, Espey points out, the Parisian subway cars were not dark either inside or out, since they were illuminated and they had colorful exteriors.

What to do? Hanzo's comment that the detached petals can be taken to refer to faces in the windows strikes us as reasonable and perceptive, especially since "apparition" allows for a sort of disembodiment corresponding to faces viewed without bodies, but against this is Pound's own statement that the faces were in the crowd—presumably the crowd he saw on the platform as he got out of the car. Well, we all know that we don't have to take the author's word (Wimsatt and Beardsley taught us this truth in "The Intentional Fallacy"); still, one wants to think as carefully about an author's comments as one does about a critic's.

Let's start over. We can probably all agree that although the most memorable (because the most visual?) thing in the poem is the image of "Petals on a wet, black bough," the word "apparition" is extremely important, since it (paradoxically) makes somewhat ghostly or unreal the vivid image of the faces as petals. Yoshiyuki Iwamoto, in *Explicator*, February 1961, presses this point. He begins by arguing that the second line adds up to something like this: Life is violent (the rainstorm), and such violence is essential to the continuity of life. But, he says, the word "apparition" calls all of this into doubt, and thus the poem as a whole is linked to Buddhist thought about the unreality of the tumultuous life that we think is real. There is surely plenty here that can provoke lively debate in class.

Other points:

1. "The transition from the Metro station to the wet boughs somewhere outside liberates us from 'space limits,' and the transition from the present faces to the remembered petals breaks down 'time limits.'" (Hugh Witemeyer, *The Poetry of Ezra Pound* [1969, 34].)
2. Perhaps we can more humbly reword Witemeyer's point along these lines. The second line perceives beauty in the subway (underground, enclosed) and also takes us out of the subway, above ground and in the open air, and in connection with "apparition" suggests the mystery of existence. (If we seem to be making a fuss about "apparition," consider how different the poem would be if the word were "appearance.")
3. Can one go further and say that this poem, often thought of as simply a vivid image, not only suggests (a) the fragility or transience of life and (b) the mystery of life, but it also suggests (c) the pathos of urban, mechanized life?

A "Voices and Visions" videocassette of Ezra Pound is available from Longman Publishers.

WYATT PRUNTY

Learning the Bicycle (p. 927)

When we teach this poem, we usually begin with a leading question: "Is this poem too sentimental?" In a sense, this is a bad question. It is too big to begin with, and it risks pushing the discussion too much in one direction. We plead guilty. But we nonetheless find that this question works well. Nearly always, after we ask it, there's a pause, and awkwardness is in the air. The students have trouble making a connection between the question and their experience of the poem, and that's because the careful language of the poem is shaping the scene and resisting the danger of a lapse into sentimentality. Prunty knows that the scene easily could become sentimental: The challenge for him is to keep *that* from happening.

Once the general discussion has run for a while (it can prove a bit labored, but don't worry, that's good in this instance), we proceed through the text, line by line. There are a number of nice images (e.g., "gyros") and word choices (e.g., "hard," "quit," "predictable," "tilt") you can touch on. And, as one of our topics indicates, you can also invite the students to comment on larger issues of structure. Frequently we "stop" the poem after the first stanza: How would the poem end if it stopped here? And then we turn to the second stanza: What is the purpose of this stanza? Why is it necessary—or not—to the poem's meaning? And why are there two stanzas for the poem rather than a single one of sixteen lines?

As our discussion of "Learning the Bicycle" winds down, we risk another perhaps bad question: "Well, what's the point of this poem?" The problem here is that we will make a literary work too formulaic, less a form of art than a demonstration. But what we are working toward is encouraging the students to see the poet as a teacher, who through his craft is making us see something special and revelatory in a common situation.

And that is why we then ask the students to recall their own experience of learning to ride a bicycle—when this took place, how they felt about it at the time, how they feel about it now. Students speak vividly and thoughtfully about this moment in their lives, and they realize, as they share their experiences, that Prunty's poem has helped them to perceive something about their lives that they might otherwise have missed. He has made them more sensitive.

DUDLEY RANDALL

The Melting Pot (p. 928)

It is often said that America is a land of immigrants—that all of us are or are descended from immigrants. But the fact remains that African "immigrants" were the only ones brought to North America forcibly, against their will, as slaves. The history of African Americans is inextricably tied to, yet separate from, the history of other races and ethnicities. And it is a bitter version of this point that Randall satirically presents through the voice of his character Sam in this poem.

Students might be asked to respond to the effectiveness of Sam's declaration, "But I'll be just what I am," which concludes the poem. One of our students noted in class that these words are a powerful affirmation of identity, but, she wondered, is it possible for any group to stand apart from the other groups it lives among? In its ironic, barbed, clever way, Randall's poem is suggestive commentary on African-American histories.

Note: The phrase "melting pot" comes from a play about Jewish immigrant life, *The Melting Pot*, by the Jewish author and philanthropist Israel Zangwill (1864–1926). The play opened in New York in 1908 and was a great success.

Jesse Jackson (1969): "I hear that melting-pot stuff a lot, and all I can say is we haven't melted."

Jimmy Carter (1976): "We become not a melting pot but a beautiful mosaic. Different people, different beliefs, different yearnings, different hopes, different dreams."

Helpful studies include John Bodnar, *The Transplanted: A History of Immigrants in Urban America* (1985); Nathan Glazer, ed., *Clamor at the Gates: The New American Immigration* (1985); Maldwyn Allen Jones, *American Immigration* (1960); and David M. Reimers, ed., *Still the Golden Door: The Third World Comes to America* (1985). Students might also be referred to the *Harvard Encyclopedia of American Ethnic Groups*, ed. Stephen Thernstrom (1980), and to John Higham's important book on immigration and nativism, *Strangers in the Land: Patterns of American Nativism, 1860–1925* (1963).

ADRIENNE RICH

For the Felling of an Elm in the Harvard Yard (p. 928)

Adrienne Rich's "For the Felling of an Elm in the Harvard Yard" is an early poem, probably not the equal of the best of her later work, but we think that most people—students and instructors—will agree that it is impressive. It begins by giving us the reason why the tree is to be felled: The roots are not getting adequate nourishment. The second stanza seems to accept the explanation ("So the great spire is overthrown"), though surely the reader is meant to wonder if indeed the "sharp saws" should hurtle through "The rings that three slow centuries wore."

The third stanza brings history to life by evoking two worthies, William James and Alfred North Whitehead, who were witnesses to the tree. And against these vanished philosophers Rich juxtaposes "young men" who watch the glinting axes. In the final stanza the trunk is dragged away—gone, with James and Whitehead—and Rich tells us that some viewers (the "young men"?) "turn the symbol to their own," i.e., see the episode symbolically in accordance with their predispositions. What do these viewers see? They "admire the clean dispatch / With which the aged elm came down." What we especially like in the poem is that Rich gives both sides their due; the tree and the philosophers have their grandeur—but the new age, with its "glinting axes," is not seen merely as destructive. The tree apparently *did* need to come down, and it has been taken down with "clean dispatch." True, the assault on the tree has its unlovely side (the saws go "hurtling through," and the hewn trunk is unceremoniously "dragged away"), but it is our impression that Rich is being fair to both sides, or, to put it another way, makes us interested in both sides.

We especially value Rich's *The Fact of a Doorframe: Poems Selected and New, 1950–1984* (1984), and *On Lies, Secrets, and Silence: Selected Prose, 1966–1978* (1979). For critical commentary, consult *Adrienne Rich's Poetry: Texts of the Poems, the Poet on Her Work, Reviews and Criticism*, ed. Barbara and Albert Gelpi (1975); and *Reading Adrienne Rich: Reviews and Revisions, 1951–81*, ed. Jane Roberta Cooper (1984).

ADRIENNE RICH

Living in Sin (p. 929)

If some of the woman's perceptions seem to indicate hyperesthesia (she hears "each separate stair . . . writhe"), for the most part her perceptions are fairly ordinary: "last night's cheese," bugs among the saucers, and so on. The man, however, does not perceive even these, and for the moment—since we see him through her eyes—he seems utterly oafish. Notice the description of the apartment, imagined as an attractive still-life ("A plate of pears, / a piano with a Persian shawl, a cat / stalking the picturesque amusing mouse,") in contrast to the apartment with "dust upon the furniture of love," scraps of food, a piano that is "out of tune," and a lover (temporarily absent) who needs a shave. Later she is back in love—more concerned with the man than with the things around them—but this is not a love poem, and the real interest is in the woman's diminished (more reasonable) view of love, even though she is now back in love. The "sin" of the title is not a matter of cohabiting without the blessing of the church; rather, the "sin" is that she has seen through the myth of romantic happiness in difficult circumstances. If the stairs no longer "writhe," she is nevertheless conscious of them and of the "relentless day." Presumably never again will she think the studio will "keep itself"; now she knows that love is not the whole of life.

ANNE SEXTON

Her Kind (p. 930)

We learn from Diane Middlebrook's *Anne Sexton* (1991) that the first draft of the poem was entitled "Night Voice on a Broomstick," and a later version was entitled "Witch." Sexton's final title is less explicit, but in the first line the speaker identifies herself: "I have gone out, a possessed witch," so students should not have much trouble seeing at least the boldest outline of the speaker. Sexton regularly began her public readings with this poem, letting the audience know what they were in for, or at least letting them know what sort of persona she wished to present to them.

A witch is a female in league with the devil and other evil spirits, endowed with magic powers (the male equivalent is a "warlock") and estranged from decent society. No doubt Sexton's deep mental problems made her feel alienated from much of society, and no doubt, too, she recognized that her gift as a poet also separated her from ordinary people. In this respect she takes a place in the Romantic tradition of the poet as one who voyages through "strange seas of thought, alone" (Wordsworth's phrase, though Wordsworth was speaking not of poets but of Isaac Newton). That the poetic gift, the gift of imagination, can become a curse that estranges the bearer is evident in the term *le poète maudit*. Such an idea may be new to your students, but if they have already read Coleridge's "Kubla Khan" they have encountered the powerful but alienated creator-poet at the end of the poem:

> . . . with music loud and long,
> I would build that dome in air,
> That sunny dome, those caves of ice!
> And all who heard should see them there.
> And all should cry, Beware! Beware!
> His flashing eyes, his floating hair!
> Weave a circle round him thrice,
> And close your eyes with holy dread,
> For he on honey-dew hath fed,
> And drunk the milk of Paradise.

Sexton's persona, in the first stanza "a possessed witch" whose mental deviation is given a physical equivalent in her twelve fingers (line 5), has engaged in "dreaming evil," but the second stanza modifies this persona: The witch in the second stanza is a sort of nourishing housewife who fills the skillets, fixes suppers. In this aspect, she is a benevolent witch, or at least in one mood she sees herself as such. But the final stanza returns to the witch as the person at odds with society: Here she is riding in a cart, on her way to be burned at the stake ("your flames still bite my thigh"). There also is a reference, in line 19, to the instrument of torture known as the rack: The victim's body was stretched out on a sort of table, with his or her arms and legs extended and tied. A wheel at each end was rotated, winding up the rope and thereby causing the limbs to be pulled out of their sockets. Sexton sees herself as being tortured to death because of her difference from society, but she is unrepentant:

> A woman like that is not ashamed to die.
> I have been her kind.

The question, we suppose, is whether this sort of self-dramatization is brave and refreshingly honest and makes readers confront their own selves and their views of outsiders, or whether it is melodramatic and self-indulgent.

WILLIAM SHAKESPEARE

Sonnet 29 ("When, in disgrace with Fortune and men's eyes") (p. 930)

For general information about Shakespeare's sonnets, see p. 254 of this handbook.

The rhyme scheme of Sonnet 29 is that of the usual Shakespearean sonnet, but the thought is organized more or less into an octave and a sestet, the transition being emphasized by the trochee at the beginning of line 9. The sense of energy is also communicated by the trochee that begins line 10 and yet another that introduces line 11, this last being especially important because by consonance and alliteration it communicates its own energy to the new image of joy ("Like to the lark"). As in most of Shakespeare's sonnets, the couplet is more or less a summary of what has preceded, but not in the same order. Line 13 summarizes the third quatrain; line 14 looks back to (but now rejects) the earlier quatrains.

The first line surely glances at Shakespeare's unimpressive social position, and line 8 presumably refers to his work. Possibly the idea is that he most enjoyed his work before it became the source of his present discomfort. Edward Hubler, in *The Sense of Shakespeare's Sonnets* (1952), notes that "the release from depression is expressed through the image of the lark, a remembrance of earlier days when the cares of his London career were unknown."

To this it can be added that although the poem employs numerous figures of speech from the start (e.g., personification with "Fortune," synecdoche with "eyes" in line 1, metonymy with "heaven" in line 3), line 11, with the image of the lark, introduces the poem's first readily evident figure of speech, and it is also the most emphatic run-on line in the poem. Moreover, though heaven was "deaf" in line 3, in line 12 it presumably hears the lark singing "hymns at heaven's gate." "Sullen" in line 12 perhaps deserves some special comment too: (1) The earth is still somber in color, though the sky is bright, and (2) applied to human beings, it suggests the moody people who inhabit earth.

TOPIC FOR CRITICAL THINKING AND WRITING

Disregarding for the moment the last two lines (or couplet), where does the sharpest turn or shift occur? In a sentence, summarize the speaker's state of mind before this turn and, in another sentence, the state of mind after it.

WILLIAM SHAKESPEARE

Sonnet 116 ("Let me not to the marriage of true minds") (p. 931)

Although the poem is almost certainly addressed to a man, because it is a celebration of the permanence of love it can apply equally well to a woman or, in fact, to a parent or child.

The first words, "Let me not," are almost a vow, and "admit impediments" in the second line faintly hints at the marriage service in the Book of Common Prayer, which says, "If any of you know just cause or impediment. . . ." In line 2 "admit" can mean both "acknowledge, grant the existence of" and "allow to enter."

The first quatrain is a negative definition of love ("love is not . . ."), but the second quatrain is an affirmative definition ("O, no, it is . . ."). The third begins as another negative definition, recognizing that "rosy lips and cheeks" will indeed decay, but denying that they are the essence of love; this quatrain then ends affirmatively, making a contrast to transience: "bears it out even to the edge of doom." Then, having clinched his case, the speaker adopts a genial and personal tone in the couplet, where for the first time he introduces the word "I."

Speaking of couplets, we can't resist quoting Robert Frost on the topic. Once, in conversation with Frost, the boxer Gene Tunney said something about the price of a poem. Frost replied: "One thousand dollars a line. Four thousand for a quatrain, but for a sonnet, $12,000. The last two lines of a sonnet don't mean anything anyway." Students might be invited to test the sonnets against this playful remark.

TOPICS FOR CRITICAL THINKING AND WRITING

1. Paraphrase (that is, put into your own words) "Let me not to the marriage of true minds / Admit impediments." Is there more than one appropriate meaning of "Admit"?
2. Notice that the poem celebrates "the marriage of true minds," not bodies. In a sentence or two, using only your own words, summarize Shakespeare's idea of the nature of such love, both what it is and what it is not.
3. Paraphrase lines 13–14. What is the speaker's tone here? Would you say that the tone is different from the tone in the rest of the poem?
4. Write a paragraph or a poem defining either love or hate. Or see if you can find such a definition in a popular song. Bring the lyrics to class.

ALFRED, LORD TENNYSON

Ulysses (p. 932)

Robert Langbaum, in *The Poetry of Experience* (1957), and Christopher Ricks, in *Tennyson* (2nd ed., 1989), offer some good remarks; Paul Baum, in *Tennyson Sixty Years After* (1948), assaults the poem. Henry Kozicki, in *Tennyson and Clio* (1979), a book on Tennyson's philosophy of history, argues that "Ulysses" reveals Tennyson's optimism about historical progress and his despair about the role of a hero. For a review of much that should not have been written, see L. K. Hughes in *Victorian Poetry* 17 (Autumn 1979): 192–203. By the way, it is worth mentioning to students that Homer's hero wanted to get home, Sophocles's (in *Philoctetes*) is a shifty politician (as is Shakespeare's), and Dante's Ulysses (*Inferno* XXVI) is an inspiring but deceitful talker whose ardent search is for *forbidden* things.

The first five lines emphasize, mostly with monosyllables, the dull world Ulysses is leaving. With line 6 ("I cannot rest from travel") we see a rather romantic hero, questing for experience, and indeed "experience" is mentioned in line 19, but it must be added that something is done in the poem to give "experience" a social context: Ulysses has fought for Troy (17), he wishes to be of "use" (23), and he wishes to do "some work of noble note" (52). Lines 22–23 apparently say the same thing four times over, but readers are not likely to wish that Tennyson had deleted the superbly appropriate metaphor of the rusting sword. "Gray spirit" (30) and "sinking star" (31) help (along with the heavy pauses and monosyllables in 55–56) to define the poem as a piece about dying, though students on first reading are likely to see only the affirmations. Even the strong affirmations in 57 ff. are undercut by "sunset" (60), "western" (61), etc. But the last line, with its regular accents on the meaningful words, affords a strong ending; perhaps the line is so strong and regular that it is a bit too easy. In line 45 Ulysses directly addresses the mariners, yet we hardly sense an audience as we do in Browning's dramatic monologues. If he is addressing the mariners, who are aboard, where is he when he refers to "this still hearth" (2) and when he says, "This is my son" (33)? (Some critics claim that lines 1–32 are a soliloquy: Ulysses supposedly would not speak publicly of Ithaca as stagnant and savage, or of his wife as "aged." Lines 33–43 are his farewell to the Ithacans, and the remainder is an address to his mariners.)

Probably the reader ought to see the poem not as a muddled attempt at a Browningesque dramatic monologue but as a somewhat different type of poem—a poem in which the poet uses a fairly transparent mask in order to express his state of mind and to persuade his readers to share that state of mind. The poem thus is closer to, say, "Prufrock" than it is to "My Last Duchess."

TOPICS FOR CRITICAL THINKING AND WRITING

1. Comment on Ulysses's voice.
2. Is Ulysses a hero or a suicidal egotist?
3. Compare Ulysses as he sees himself with Ulysses as we see him.

KITTY TSUI

A Chinese Banquet (p. 933)

We don't think students will have difficulty with this poem, or, rather, we don't think there are any lines or images in the poem that students will find difficult to understand except the reference to the dragon, in line 50—more about that in a moment—though some students may find it difficult to talk about the subject matter, a lesbian relationship.

The title suggests fun, "A Chinese Banquet," but the dedication, *"for the one who was not invited,"* immediately undermines any such suggestion. The language of the opening stanza (and of the entire poem) is conversational, the language one uses in speaking with friends and family, but the report immediately sets the speaker apart:

> it was not a very formal affair but
> all the women over twelve
> wore long gowns and a corsage,
> except for me.

Ask your students why she was not wearing a corsage. They will explain that presumably all the other women had been given corsages by their husbands or boyfriends. Ask them, too, why the second stanza begins with the same words as the first stanza, "it was not a very formal affair." Here there may be less unanimity. Our own reading is that the repetition suggests that the speaker is hurt and is going over and over the event in her mind, returning so to speak to the scene of the crime, wishing it could have been different. As the poem proceeds, she recalls the typical talk, buying a house, traveling, but she is "dreaming" of her partner, who has not been invited. Instead of the banquet being a pleasant social occasion for the speaker, it is a trial, with her mother speaking sarcastically, nagging her. The banquet is "very much a family affair" but so far as the mother is concerned, the daughter has no partner and indeed the partner has not been invited. Isolated from the family by her sexual orientation, she cannot (or at least she thinks she cannot) join in the conversation even about food and cars, or tell her family that her "back is healing," i.e., she thinks she cannot talk about what matters to her, her health and her partner.

A few words about line 50, "i dream of dragons and water." In Western thinking, the dragon is a symbol of Satan and of evil in general, but in East Asia the dragon is beneficent, the male principle assocated with rain (hence it is associated with the air, and in the poem with "the wide open sky"), bringer of nourishment and good harvest. The complement of the dragon is the tiger, the female principle. We don't want to press the poem for autobigrahical significance, but if the speaker is the author, Kitty Tsui, and if she conceives of herself (somewhat playfully) as a tiger—Kitty?—then it is not surprising that she dreams of "dragons and water," i.e., of her partner, her complement.

One other point: Why does the speaker not use any capital letters? We don't know. If she did not use a capital for the first person singular pronoun but used capitals at the beginnings of sentences, we probably would suggest that the lack of capitalization in the pronoun suggested her sense of littleness, apartness, unconventionality. But the lack of capitalization at the beginning of sentences suggests there must be a different reason. Perhaps—and this would be a perfectly good reason—it is just to set the work apart from prose, i.e., to indicate that this utterance is distinctive.

ADDITIONAL TOPIC FOR CRITICAL THINKING AND WRITING

Is the poem rooted in specific ethnic behavior, or might this family equally have been, say, of Russian Jewish background, or Italian Catholics, or WASPs?

JOHN UPDIKE

Ex-Basketball Player (p. 935)

Although the first lines of the poem set forth a matter-of-fact description of how to get to a place ("Berth's garage") we take it that the language evokes the glory days of the former basketball star. Notice "runs past," "Bends," "and stops, cut off," "a chance to go." The first stanza consists of two sentences, but the effect is of a periodic sentence, the meaning suspended until the end, sort of like a play in the game, which doesn't (so to speak) achieve its meaning until the play is over.

The second stanza continues to evoke the game ("stands tall," "Five on a side"), though to a lesser degree. Incidentally, gas pumps of the sort Updike describes probably no longer exist, and certainly "Esso" has disappeared (it is now Exxon).

Pathos is evoked, at least faintly, even in the first stanza ("Flick Webb . . . helps Berth out"), more so in the third and fourth stanzas, especially in the fourth, with the pitiful comic business of dribbling an inner tube, but most strongly in the final stanza, where the silence is deafening: "Flick seldom says a word to Mae, just nods," and the "applauding tiers" that once faced the high school athlete now are merely the racks with candy in the luncheonette. Somehow the final line, devoted entirely to a Homeric catalog naming the cheap candies, strikes us as especially sad.

Our mention of "epic catalog" reminds us that the poem is in blank verse, and although the diction certainly does not evoke John Milton, the piece might almost be called "Paradise Lost."

John Updike has been widely admired for his fiction and literary criticism, but he is also an accomplished poet in, for example, *Midpoint, and Other Poems* (1969) and *Facing Nature: Poems* (1985).

Your advanced students may enjoy *Hugging the Shore: Essays and Criticism* (1983) and *More Matter: Essays and Criticism* (1999), which are extraordinary in the array of topics that Updike examines in alert and thoughtful ways.

We also recommend *The Best American Short Stories of the Century* (1999), which Updike selected.

A stimulating critical study is William H. Pritchard, *Updike: America's Man of Letters* (2000), a cogent, accessible reader's guide to Updike's career as a writer, which began in 1954 with the publication of a short story in *The New Yorker*.

DEREK WALCOTT

A Far Cry from Africa (p. 936)

Many students—partly because they think that puns are always comic and that literature is always serious—will not see the double meaning in the title: (1) the poem is a lament from Africa, violated by colonialism and also by Africans themselves, and (2) the poet—a West Indian who lives part of the year in the West Indies and part in the United States—is a very considerable distance away from Africa.

Walcott, a black, sees not only the wickedness of British colonial rule but also the wickedness that Africans visit upon other Africans. Further, Walcott's tongue is English; he utters his cry (to use a word from the title of the poem) in English, not in an African language. In short, the two meanings of the title embody the themes of the poem—the pain that Africa is experiencing (inflicted not only by colonialists but also by Africans), and the dilemma of the English-speaking poet, who is black but who lives thousands of miles from Africa and who feels a loyalty to (and a love for) "the English tongue."

The place to begin is with Walcott's *Collected Poems, 1948–1984* (1986), but your more advanced students might enjoy exploring his epic poem, *Omeros*

(1990). See also *The Art of Derek Walcott*, ed. Stewart Brown (1991); Rei Terada, *Derek Walcott's Poetry: American Mimicry* (1992); and *Critical Perspectives on Derek Walcott*, ed. Robert D. Hamner (1993).

ANONYMOUS

Eighteenth-Century Slave Ship (engraving, p. 937)

You may want to talk about the illustration of a slave ship that we print.

As we indicate in our discussion of Wheatley's poem, we do not subscribe to the argument, current today, that Wheatley's poem is consciously ironic, that Wheatley *can't* mean what she says, etc. Wheatley, we assume, as a pious Christian thought that her condition of servitude was a small price to pay for salvation, especially since she was much fussed over. But we should remember the other aspects of slavery, beginning with the voyage from Africa to the United States.

It is estimated that 10 million Africans survived the transatlantic journey (the "middle passage") to slavery. Most were sent to Brazil and the West Indies; only 4 to 6 percent of the total were delivered to the American colonies. But 66 percent of the slaves in the New World were in the American South by 1860, the result of a high birthrate and relatively stable (if precarious) family relationships.

Students might be reminded, too, that in the 1760s and 1770s— Wheatley was brought to Boston in 1761—slavery was legal in every one of the thirteen colonies. In 1763 there were, for example, 5,200 black slaves in Massachusetts, employed as seamen, farmhands, lumberjacks, craftsmen, and domestic servants.

For a powerful first-person account of the horrors of the slave trade, students could be referred to *The Interesting Narrative of the Life of Olaudah Equiano, or Gustavus Vassa, the African, Written by Himself* (1789; rpt. Bedford Books, 1995). Other useful sources include Jay Coughtry, *The Notorious Triangle: Rhode Island and the African Slave Trade* (1981); ed. Steven Mintz, *African-American Voices: The Life Cycle of Slavery* (1993); and David Northrup, *The Atlantic Slave Trade* (1994); and Marcus Rediker, *The Slave Ship: A Human History* (2007).

PHILLIS WHEATLEY

On Being Brought from Africa to America (p. 938)

As the headnote informs students, Wheatley was educated by a pious white family and was kept from the company of other blacks. It does not seem at all surprising to us, then, that the values she sets forth in this poem are those of her owner-educators, rather than (to put the point strongly) those of today's African Americans. Among the basic views of the time were these two: (1) slavery conferred a benefit on the slaves, since it rescued them from pagan ignorance and brought them, through faith in Jesus, from bondage to Satan to everlasting life, and (2) the color of Africans suggested a special affinity with Satan, the Prince of Darkness. Thus, to Jeremiah's question in 13.23, "Can the

Ethiopian change his skin?"—in a context where Jeremiah is accusing the people of Judah of irredeemable sin—one can juxtapose a reply from Matthew 19.26 and Mark 10.27: "With God all things are possible."

Not everyone believed that the color of the African was a sign of special guilt and that slavery was justified because it conferred the possibility of salvation, but these beliefs were widespread, and it is easy to see why. They offered whites a comforting justification for a wicked practice that they wished to continue.

We do not find it at all unsurprising that Wheatley, a black, should echo the thoughts of her white owners. What are these commonplace white thoughts? In the first line she says that "mercy" (rather than, say, a desire for material profit from her labor) brought her from her "pagan land"; in the second line she says that before she learned about God her soul was "benighted," hence her capture in Africa and her transportation to America was a boon. We do not find it hard to believe that she is utterly sincere in this belief, and we are puzzled by modern commentators who find it impossible to believe that in the eighteenth century a favored slave, brought up in a pious household, might genuinely believe that his or her physical and *spiritual* conditions were infinitely superior to those of pagan blacks in Africa. Wheatley expressed the idea elsewhere, in a poem addressed to Harvard students, "To the University of Cambridge in New England." She says,

'Twas not long since I left my native shore
The land of errors and Egyptian gloom:
Father of mercy, 'twas thy gracious hand
Brought me in safety from those dark abodes.

This sort of thing was good eighteenth-century Christian thinking; given the conditions of her upbringing, it is almost inconceivable that Wheatley could have held another view.

But we should return to the poem in the text. The imagery of darkness continues in "sable race," which some say "is a diabolic dye." The poem ends with the thought that although Negroes (Wheatley's word) are "black as Cain," they "may be refined, and join th' angelic train." This is all evident enough, but some readers have been determined to find in the poem a message contrary to the surface statement, where imagery of darkness is associated with evil. That is, readers want to say that Wheatley is surreptitiously a protest poet. Thus, James A. Levernier, writing in *Explicator* 40:1 (Fall 1981), says that "Wheatley used her considerable linguistic talent to embed in the poem, at a very sophisticated level, a far different message than that which the poem superficially conveys" (25).

What message does he find? "By subtly inverting the connotations traditionally associated with light and dark imagery, she suggests that Christians do not always practice what they preach" (25). He finds puns on *die* and *Cain*, i.e., he says that the words call to mind indigo *dye* and sugar *cane*, produced in the Indies by slave labor.

Aware that both dye and cane were obtained through the sufferings of blacks who not only constituted a commodity in the triangular trade, but who also labored in sugar refineries (yet another word which Wheatley puns on in the poem) and dye and cane plantations in the Indies, true Christians boycotted these products . . . The point of these puns [is] that Christians should practice what they preach. (26)

Certainly we can all agree that Wheatley directly addresses whites ("Christians") in the next-to-last line and reminds them that blacks no less than whites may "join th' angelic train," but whether by means of puns Wheatley stresses the monstrous behavior of whites is, well, something that is debatable.

See *The Collected Works of Phillis Wheatley*, ed. John Shields (1988), a volume in the Schomburg Library of Nineteenth Century Black Women Writers series, published by Oxford University Press. This volume is excellent in many ways, but the main selection of Wheatley's verse is a photo-offset of the 1773 edition—the archaic spellings of which may prove nettling to students.

WALT WHITMAN

Reconciliation (p. 938)

In "Reconciliation" Whitman celebrates not simply the end of the war—though that in itself was a cause of celebration—but a loving union, or reunion, daringly symbolized by a kiss bestowed upon the dead enemy. The poem begins by announcing (1) that the very word *reconciliation* has an affinity with heaven ("beautiful as the sky"), and (2) that the fact of reconciliation will "in time" obliterate the terrible carnage of the clash of cultures. Whitman goes on to call Death and Night sisters; that is, he constructs a mythology—at least we are not aware of any system of mythology in which they are sisters. (In Greek mythology, Night is the mother of Death.) Whitman's two allegorical figures "incessantly softly wash again, and ever again, this soil'd world." Once he has given us this image, it seems obvious enough, but, again, it is new to us. Far from being portrayed as a cleansing force, Death customarily is portrayed as destructive (think of the classical image of the inverted torch, or the late medieval and Renaissance image of a skeleton carrying a scythe), or at best as offering an anodyne, a release from an unbearably painful world. Night, in traditional mythology, is not quite so grim, and is even beneficent to the extent that she brings her son, Sleep, but she is nevertheless destructive since, like Day, she leads to decay and death. In contrast, Whitman imagines Death and Night as washing (purifying) "this soil'd world"; in this specific context of this poem, which speaks of a corpse in a coffin, the allegorical figures surely are meant to be associated with persons washing (symbolically purifying) a corpse.

The purification effected by Death and Night is a purification of the speaker and of his enemy; now that the "carnage" has been washed away, the former enemies are (in the word of the title) reconciled, and the new relationship is symbolized (daringly) by a kiss. But we should notice that, almost as daring as the gesture of the kiss, Whitman daringly ends this poem with the dead man still dead; the last word in the poem is *coffin.* Unlike (say) Lanier's Stonewall Jackson, Whitman's dead soldier does not become enshrined in the heavens, nor does he, through noble words, live eternally in the minds of survivors. The closest a reader gets to heaven is in the first line, where (as we have seen) the word *reconciliation* is said to be "beautiful as the sky." Still, at least in our reading of the poem, the gesture of the kiss is so daring, so original, that it overcomes the horror of the carnage and the continuing death of the former enemy.

TOPICS FOR CRITICAL THINKING AND WRITING

1. "Reconcile" means to "restore to friendship, compatibility, or harmony." What is happening in the scene of reconciliation that Whitman describes?
2. Does this poem make you uncomfortable? How would Whitman reply to someone who had such a response?
3. Whitman wrote this poem in the same year that the Civil War ended, a war in which, in the words of one scholar, "at least 618,000 Americans died, 360,000 on the Union side and 258,000 on the Confederate." Wasn't Whitman mistaken to imagine that "reconciliation" could take place so soon?
4. Do you think we should always become "reconciled" with our enemies? Can you imagine a situation when this would be impossible?
5. In the second line of the poem, Whitman seems to be claiming that the passage of time will cause the horrors of war to become "lost," to disappear from memory. Does he really believe this? Do you believe it? if you do not, how does this affect your response to the poem?

WALT WHITMAN

A Sight in Camp (p. 938)

In his essay "Love and Walt Whitman," the novelist and literary critic J. M. Coetzee calls attention to a letter that Whitman wrote during the Civil War:

> In August of 1863 Private Erastus Haskell of the 141st New York Volunteers died of typhoid fever in Armory Square Hospital, Washington, D.C. Shortly thereafter his parents received a long letter from a stranger. "I was very anxious [Erastus] should be saved," the stranger wrote,
>
> & so were they all—he was well used by the attendants.... Many nights I sat in the hospital by his bedside...—he always liked to have me sit there, but never cared to talk—I shall never forget those nights, it was a curious & solemn scene, the sick & wounded lying around in their cots...& this dear young man close at hand...—I do not know his past life, but what I do know, & what I saw of him, he was a noble boy—I felt he was one I should get very much attached to....
>
> I write you this letter, because I would do something at least in his memory—his fate was a hard one, to die so—He is one of the thousands of our unknown young American men in the ranks about whom there is no record or fame, no fuss about their dying so unknown, but I find in them the real precious & royal ones.... Poor dear son, though you were not my son, I felt to love you as a son, what short time I saw you sick & dying there.
>
> The letter was signed "Walt Whitman," with a Brooklyn address.
> —*The New York Review of Books*, September 22, 2005

During the Civil War, Whitman worked among the wounded from both the North and the South, and, in his poetry and prose, he describes many scenes like this one. It was an extraordinary act of generosity and compassion, as Harold Bloom has eloquently stated:

I cannot think of a Western writer of anything like Whitman's achievement who ever gave himself or herself up so directly to meeting the agonized needs of the most desperate. There are a handful of American poets comparable to Whitman in stature: Emily Dickinson certainly, Wallace Stevens and Robert Frost perhaps, and perhaps even one or two others. Our image of them, or of our greatest novelists, or even of Whitman's master, Emerson, can move us sometimes, but not as the image of the wound-dresser Whitman must move us. Like the Lincoln whom he celebrated and lamented, Whitman is American legend, a figure who has a kind of religious aura even for secular intellectuals. If Emerson founded the American literary religion, Whitman alone permanently holds the place most emblematic of the life of the spirit in America.
—"The Real Me," *The New York Review of Books*, April 26, 1984

In "A Sight in Camp," as always in his work, Whitman shows a beautiful feeling for nuance and detail. We tend to think of him as a grand, boisterous, inspirational chanter of American democratic freedom and equality, and it is true that he loves large, sweeping effects. Nevertheless, he is, surprisingly, a quiet, subtle, restrained kind of poet too: he excels in this mode. Here, the speaker says he has risen early; the single word "sleepless" makes an important point about his state of mind and soul. He walks slowly, both because he has not slept himself and because he does not wish to disturb the other figures on the scene whom he later will tell us about, and who are still sleeping. The "cool fresh air" is a wonderful touch: we can feel it ourselves. The word "tent" is then used a second time, but it is in reference to a *hospital* tent, which clarifies and evokes the setting for the speaker's walk.

As you examine the poem with your students, no doubt you will make your way carefully from the first figure to the second to the third. What is distinctive about each of them? How are they related to one another? The phrases "dear comrade" and "sweet boy," for example, are connected to one another, yet are not identical: the words carry different connotations within the same range of feeling.

The focus on "the face of the Christ" in the final stanza is astounding. On one level, it symbolizes the profound sacrifices made by the soldiers in the war: they have given their lives for the cause they believe in. But when we discuss this stanza with students, we dare to ask them: Might Whitman be saying that Christ, literally, is present here among the wounded, dying, and dead—that this "young man" is not "like" Christ, but, instead, "is" Christ? You and I might want immediately to reply, "That is not the case, that is not possible." However, perhaps for Whitman it is.

Note: See also the Manual entry for Chris Adrian, "Every Night for a Thousand Years: A Story of the Civil War."

WALT WHITMAN

The Dalliance of the Eagles (p. 939)

Please notice that we reproduce Whitman's manuscript as our frontispiece. We have found that students are interested to see that real writers revise.

Not all of your students will know that "Dalliance" means play, sportiveness; especially, amorous play (as flirting or caressing).

During the nineteenth century, and into the twentieth, Walt Whitman was a controversial figure because of his frank, graphic, and often celebratory depiction of sexuality. Even this poem, "The Dalliance of Eagles," came in for critical scrutiny, as David S. Reynolds explains in *Walt Whitman* (2005):

> To his frustration, [Whitman's] candid treatment of sex enraged the moral censors of his era. Those who espoused the prudish view of sex did not approve of his sexual images, no matter how much he tried to couch them in religious or physiological language. When a British edition of *Leaves of Grass* appeared in 1868, the editors carefully pruned away sexual references, producing an expurgated edition. Publication of the 1881 edition was suspended by the Boston district attorney on the grounds that it violated public statutes concerning obscene literature. (The phrase "banned in Boston" came from this episode.)
>
> It tells us a lot about sexual mores of the time that these priggish censors complained of even the mildest references to heterosexual sex while finding nothing objectionable in Whitman's numerous images of same-sex love. Amazingly, the 1881 censors targeted even the tame "Dalliance of the Eagles" (about the mating of birds) while leaving untouched all but one of the homoerotic "Calamus" poems. (117–18)

"The Dalliance of Eagles" was first published in the 1881 edition (the seventh) of *Leaves of Grass*. According to Gay Wilson Allen, in *The Walt Whitman Handbook* (1946), the naturalist, essayist, and conservationist John Burroughs (1837–1921) said that "The Dalliance of the Eagles" was written from an account that he gave Whitman (p. 212). As James E. Miller has noted in *Walt Whitman* (1962) "The Dalliance of Eagles" contains "in its symbolic drama the entire complex view" of Whitman's conception of sexual life and experience— "the delirious abandon to the sexual merge, but with the persistence of personal identity and individuality" (110).

This short poem includes striking images and phrases. Note, for example, that the first detail that the speaker recalls about his walk is not what he saw, but, rather, what he heard—"a sudden muffled sound." It was this sound that caused him to look upward, where he witnessed the eagles at their amorous play. Note, too, the speaker's emphasis on the height of the soaring eagles— "high in space together"; this gives us a literal fact about the scene but also conveys the eagles' grandeur. Observe, too, how Whitman places the scene "high" in the air even as he vividly calls attention to the "clinching" and "interlocking" of the claws, which brings up into close contact with the eagles' bodies.

This, we have found, is perhaps the best way to help students to appreciate Whitman's poetry, working with them through the stunning details and powerful intricacies of this writer's organizations of language. As John Updike has remarked, Whitman's poetry "is a luminous wind that bears upon it small distinct seeds that stick like burr."

WILLIAM CARLOS WILLIAMS

Spring and All (p. 939)

This, the first poem in a book (1922) of the same title, is preceded by eleven pages of prose, the gist of which is the defense of a "new" American experimental writing. This introduction concludes with the words "THE WORLD IS NEW," and then the poem bursts upon us. It begins with the reference to the hospital (stock responses—which Williams dedicated his life to opposing—conjure up ideas of sickness and death, reinforced in "cold" and "dried," but it turns out that the poem moves on to the recovery of health, which after all is what hospitals are for); it moves on to a vivid and concrete description of bushes and trees that appear "Lifeless," then to a spring that "quickens," and finally back to the bushes and trees that "begin to awaken." What is "contagious" turns out to be not sickness, death, winter (all stock responses), but spring, and probably this contagious quality of spring is what the "All" of the title implies.

Characteristically, Williams seems "unpoetic." Although in lines 2–3 "the surge of . . . clouds" is metaphoric (clouds as waves), and in line 7 "standing water" is a metaphor (though only a dead metaphor), one can say that in the first part of the poem figurative language is conspicuously absent. Not until line 15 ("dazed spring approaches") does figurative language emerge; the following stanza (16–19) continues the image of nature as human ("They enter the new world naked"), making it clear that the hospital is as much a place of birth as of death, and essentially a place where life is preserved, but the poem also continues to record sharp literal perceptions ("the stiff curl of wildcarrot leaf"), enhancing the last, metaphoric words: "rooted, they / grip down and begin to awaken." The slight increase in the number of verbs (they are sparse in the beginning) helps to suggest the life that is pushing through the deadness. Whether literal or metaphoric, the lines seek (to borrow words which Williams used of his *Kora in Hell*) "to refine, to clarify, to intensify that eternal moment in which we alone live." See also, for a long discussion, Bram Dijkstra, *Cubism, Stieglitz, and the Earlier Poetry of William Carlos Williams* (1990).

A "Voices and Visions" videocassette of William Carlos Williams is available from Longman Publishers.

WILLIAM WORDSWORTH

The World Is Too Much with Us (p. 940)

We have enjoyed good success with this poem in the classroom, probably because many students—eager but quick to feel burdened and boxed in—connect readily with the world-weariness and disappointment of the opening lines. They know right away, or claim to know, what the speaker is talking about.

The important next step, however, is to press the students to describe carefully what this speaker means in *this* poem. What does he mean by his opening claim? How do the following lines flesh out and clarify his belief that "the world is too much with us"? And why does the speaker say "us," rather than "me"?

This is, we have found, a poem that highlights for students the importance of specific words and phrases—the choices that the poet makes in saying exactly *this*. Line 4 is a nice case in point. "We have given our hearts away" is a fairly familiar phrase, almost a cliché. But the context of the poem makes the phrase come alive, giving it a sharp pain. The next part of the line, "a sordid boon," shows the speaker's response to what he and we have done in giving our hearts away. If you direct students to look up the etymology of "sordid," they will learn that it derives from a Latin word that means "dirt"; "sordid" suggests something morally ignoble, base, or vile; something meanly selfish or mercenary, filthy, squalid. Similarly, by directing students to a dictionary they will learn that "boon" comes from Old Norse and Middle English roots that mean "prayer"; the word itself means a blessing or benefit; something that is asked; a favor sought. Ask the students what these words mean, and how the words function together and in relation to the earlier part of the line. And ask them to describe the tone of voice that these words reveal and dramatize in the speaker.

Some students find the second half of the poem unclear and confusing. What is the point, they wonder, of the invocation of Paganism? Why would the speaker rather be a Pagan? Here, it pays to be patient, giving close attention in particular to line 10. The speaker claims to want to be something that he knows is outdated—a "creed outworn." He is, it seems, expressing the wish for a perspective on life that he can never possess. What is it that believers in classical mythology enjoyed that he and we can long for, but not attain, now?

As we sum up, we like to ask students some pointedly challenging questions about the poem. For example: "So is the speaker saying that the situation is hopeless?" "Is the speaker describing an emotional affliction for which in the modern era there is no cure?" "Is there too much self-pity here?"

There are so many books on Wordsworth—it is painfully easy for a student to get lost among the biographies, reference books, editions, critical studies. We tend to direct introductory students away from the highly theoretical work of the past two decades—feminist, new historicist, and the like. Most of it builds upon, and takes issue with, the wide range of previous interpretations; if a student is unfamiliar with *that*, he or she is only going to become confused in the face of the sometimes illuminating, but often frustratingly opaque, new body of commentaries. We find ourselves often returning to David Ferry, *The Limits of Mortality: An Essay on Wordsworth's Major Poems* (1959; rpt. 1978), and—still the classic work in the field—Geoffrey H. Hartman, *Wordsworth's Poetry, 1787–1814* (1964; rev. ed., 1971). To sample the range of recent work, a student could be sent to *The Age of William Wordsworth: Critical Essays on the Romantic Tradition*, ed. Kenneth R. Johnston and Gene W. Ruoff (1987).

WILLIAM WORDSWORTH

I Wandered Lonely as a Cloud (p. 941)

On April 15, 1802, Wordsworth and his sister, Dorothy, took a walk, during which they saw some daffodils near a lake. Dorothy recorded the experience in her journal, and this entry affords us something close to the raw material out of which Wordsworth's poem was made. The entry is not, of course, Wordsworth's own experience; Dorothy's experience was not William's, and Dorothy's words cannot exactly reproduce even her own experience. (It should be noted, incidentally, that Dorothy's description is not entirely "factual"; her daffodils rest their heads, glance, dance, etc.) Still, the entry gives us something of the phenomena that stirred an emotion in Wordsworth, and for Wordsworth, poetry was made out of "emotion recollected in tranquility." Below is the entry from Dorothy's journal. (We sometimes photocopy the entry and ask the students to discuss the poem in light of the entry.)

It was a threatening, misty morning, but mild. We set off after dinner, from Eusemere. Mrs. Clarkson went a short way with us, but turned back. The wind was furious, and we thought we must have returned. We first rested in the large boathouse, then under a furze bush opposite Mr. Clarkson's. Saw the plough going in the field. The wind seized our breath. The lake was rough. . . . When we were in the woods beyond Gowbarrow Park we saw a few daffodils close to the water-side. We fancied that the lake had floated the seeds ashore, and that the little colony had so sprung up. But as we went along there were more and yet more; and at last, under the boughs of the trees, we saw that there was a long belt of them along the shore, about the breadth of a country turnpike road. I never saw daffodils so beautiful. They grew among the mossy stones above and about them; some rested their heads upon these stones as on a pillow for weariness; and the rest tossed and reeled and danced, and seemed as if they verily laughed with the wind that blew upon them over the lake; they looked so gay, ever glancing, ever changing. This wind blew directly over the lake to them. There was here and there a little knot and a few stragglers a few yards higher up; but they were so few as not to disturb the simplicity, unity, and life of that one busy highway. We rested again and again. The bays were stormy, and we heard the waves at different distances, and in the middle of the water, like the sea. Rain came on—we were wet when we reached Luff's, but we called in.

Two years after the walk, William presumably recollected and contemplated the emotion, and wrote "I Wandered Lonely as a Cloud," leaving out the threatening weather, the plough, the boathouse, the miscellaneous flowers and even the first group of daffodils, and the people (including Dorothy). Notice, too, that the sense of effort which Dorothy records ("we thought we must have returned," "we first rested," etc.) is not in the poem. The speaker "wandered," and he lies on his couch in "vacant or in pensive mood"; if he acts, it is with spontaneous joy, but chiefly it is the daffodils that act ("Fluttering and dancing in the breeze," "Tossing their heads in sprightly dance," etc.).

On Dorothy Wordsworth's *Journals* and William Wordsworth's "I Wandered Lonely as a Cloud," see Carl Woodring, *Wordsworth* (1968); Edward Rosenheim, *What Happens in Literature* (1960); David Perkins, *Wordsworth* (1964); and especially Frederick Pottle's essay in *Yale Review* 40 (Autumn 1950): 27–42, reprinted in *Wordsworth*, ed. Gilbert T. Dunklin (1951).

TOPIC FOR CRITICAL THINKING AND WRITING

Wordsworth first published the poem in 1807, but the version printed here (which is the one everyone knows) is that of 1815. The differences between the first and second versions are these: In the first version lines 7–12 are lacking; line 4 has "dancing" instead of "golden"; line 5 has "Along" instead of "Beside"; line 6 has "Ten thousand" instead of "Fluttering and"; line 16 has "laughing" instead of "jocund." Evaluate the revisions. In particular, what does the added stanza contribute?

WILLIAM WORDSWORTH

The Solitary Reaper (p. 941)

"The Solitary Reaper" is discussed in Carl Woodring, *Wordsworth* (1968); John Danby, *The Simple Wordsworth* (1960), 122–27; and G. Ingli James, *Essays in Criticism* (January 1965): 65–76. What follows is derived from these sources.

The situation in "The Solitary Reaper" is notably Wordsworthian: A single humble figure is in a landscape that is both dreary and richly mysterious. The poem opens with an exclamation of wonder and a hint of biblical or at least archaic language ("Behold her"); in line 4, with the consecutive stresses on "Stop here," we get one of the poem's very few metrical variations.

In the second stanza the vision widens to include an oasis in Arabia and the Hebrides off western Scotland; her voice is like a nightingale's telling the desert travelers that they approach life and a refreshing coolness, and like the cuckoo's heralding the warm spring in the cold north. In line 15 the trochee in "Breaking" perhaps helps to communicate a suggestion of strength or vitality.

In the third stanza the poet says he cannot understand the words of her song—possibly because she sang in Gaelic, possibly because she is distant. In any case, her song resembles the nightingale's and the cuckoo's in that it is a song and a sign of life, but it differs from theirs in that it is melancholy, and here Wordsworth again extends the vision now to the distant past and the present and the high and the low.

Note, too, that the melancholy is presented in a work of art, and it should be noted that although the song is melancholy there is no evidence that the *girl* is melancholy. Presumably—if the singer is like people in the real world—there is indeed a sort of joy to be gained from singing a melancholy song. We included the poem in this section partly in order to let students discuss this point.

The feminine rhymes ("ending" and "bending," in lines 26 and 28) perhaps suggest the continuity of the song, which, so far as the speaker was concerned, did *not* end. The redundancy in "motionless and still" (line 29) perhaps serves to communicate the poet's entranced state, though perhaps it is merely a redundancy.

JAMES WRIGHT

Lying in a Hammock at William Duffy's Farm in Pine Island, Minnesota (p. 942)

It seems to us that the title is somewhat paradoxical, in its implication of utter relaxation and apartness—lying *in* a hammock, *at* someone's farm, *in* an island—and (on the other hand) the almost pedantic or fussy specification of the locale. And we find the rest of the poem paradoxical too.

The speaker's eye ranges. He takes in the view above (a natural starting place for someone lying in a hammock), then looks "Down the ravine," then "to my right," and then, at the end, up again ("I lean back"), when he observes the chicken hawk. In a sense he ends where he began, but meanwhile he has explored (or at least surveyed) a good deal. He has, from his sleep-like condition in the hammock, begun by seeing a bronze-colored butterfly "Asleep," then has heard the distant cowbells, and has seen "The droppings of last year's horses" (so we get some extension into time as well as into space), and then glances again at the skies. This exploration—all from the hammock—is marked by keen yet imaginative observations.

Let's go back a moment, to the first perception, the "bronze butterfly / Asleep." The poet is describing the color, but the effect is paradoxical, giving the reader a fragile insect made of an enduring material. From perceptions of colors ("bronze," "black," "green") we go to aural perceptions ("the cowbells follow one another") and then back to visual perceptions (the horse droppings, now "golden stones"). In all of this beauty there is a keen sense of isolation—the cows and horses are not present, and even the chicken hawk is looking for home. Now, "as the evening darkens," the speaker has an epiphany, uttered in the final line.

The final line probably comes to the reader as a shock, and perhaps the reader is uncertain about how to take it. Is the speaker kidding? Or is he saying, in dead seriousness, all creatures except me seem to have their place in a marvelously beautiful, peaceful nature, whereas I am not even in my own home? Our own impression is that, whatever he says, *we* feel that he has not wasted his life, since he has so interestingly recorded his perceptions.

For further study of Wright, see *Collected Prose*, ed. Anne Wright (1983); and *Above the River: The Complete Poems*, with an introduction by Donald Hall (1990). The best critical discussions can be found in *The Pure Clear Word: Essays on the Poetry of James Wright*, ed. Dave Smith (1982). Also recommended: Kevin Stein, *James Wright: The Poetry of a Grown Man* (1989); and Andrew Elkins, *The Poetry of James Wright* (1991).

TOPICS FOR CRITICAL THINKING AND WRITING

1. How important is it that the poet is "lying in a hammock"? That he is at some place other than his own home?

2. Do you take the last line as a severe self-criticism, or as a joking remark, or as something in between, or what?

3. Imagine yourself lying in a hammock—perhaps you can recall an actual moment in a hammock—or lying in bed, your eye taking in the surroundings. Write a description ending with some sort of judgment or concluding comment, as Wright does. You may want to parody Wright's poem, but you need not. (Keep in mind the fact that the best parodies are written by people who regard the original with affection.)

WILLIAM BUTLER YEATS

Sailing to Byzantium (p. 943)

It is worth showing students a few images from Byzantium, especially mosaics since Yeats speaks of "the gold mosaic of a wall" (line 18). In these mosaics, showing holy figures, the background does not depict a landscape, or even a heaven with clouds; rather, the background is uniformly gold, in order to symbolize the uniform, unchanging nature of God. And the gold itself of course symbolizes preciousness. The standard college histories of the survey of art, such as H. W. Janson's *History of Art*, Marilyn Stokstad's *Art History*, or Hugh Honour and John Fleming's *The Visual Arts*, include a few appropriate reproductions. We suggest that the day before you teach the poem you ask your students if any of them are taking a survey course in art, and if some are, ask them to bring the text to class. This way you can have several books circulating among students, as opposed to a single copy that you might yourself bring. But you may also want to bring a copy of *The Glory of Byzantium*, the catalog of a great exhibition that was held at the Metropolitan Museum of Art. Most of the objects illustrated in this catalog of course are not mosaics, but even smaller works such as ivories and the covers of Bibles will convey a good idea of Byzantine art.

Byzantium, originally a Greek trading station, was rebuilt by Constantine, who in 330 renamed it Constantinople and dedicated it to the Christian God. The most important city of the Roman empire in the East, Constantinople became the cultural center of the Christianized Roman world. But in the early Renaissance, Byzantine art—because of its lack of interest in naturalism—fell into disrepute: Byzantine figures, swathed in heavy drapery, reveal almost nothing of the body (except for representations of Christ on the cross), and their postures are usually static. An important medium, mosaic—lightweight squares of colored glass set into cement—hardly lends itself to naturalism.

In short, Byzantine figures seem (to the unsympathetic eye) lifeless, unable to move or to feel. But for the aging Yeats (he wrote the poem when he was sixty-one), seeking an alternative for a failing body, Byzantine art, with its other-worldly images, provided intimations of immortality. He had seen Byzantine mosaics in Ravenna in 1907, but not until his visit to Palermo in 1924 did Byzantine culture come to have great meaning for him.

The poem: Students will not have much difficulty in drawing up lists of contrasts between (to put it bluntly), youth and age, transience and permanence, the body and the mind, the flesh and the soul. Examples:

"birds in the trees"	a bird of "hammered gold" on "a golden bough"
"fish, flesh, or fowl"	"sages standing in God's holy fire"
"those dying generations"	"once out of nature"
"whatever is begotten, born, and dies"	"monuments of unaging intellect"
"that sensual music"	"singing-masters of my soul"
"dying animal"	"artifice of eternity"
"the young in one another's arms"	"an aged man"
"That is no country"	"Byzantium"

That is, Yeats establishes a contrast between, on the one hand, Ireland (with its "salmon falls," line 4), which stands for the natural world, the cycle of birth and death, and, on the other hand, Byzantium, which stands for permanence.

The first stanza is largely devoted to presenting a memorable image of the natural world, the world of youth and of fertility. This world will be disparaged, but Yeats also lets us see its appeal, as in "The young in one another's arms, birds in the trees," "The salmon falls, the mackerel-crowded seas." But even as he shows us the attractive sensuous world, he reminds us of its transience: "birds in the trees / —Those dying generations at their song. . . ." And the stanza ends with a sharp put-down:

Caught in that sensual music all neglect
Monuments of unaging intellect.

The second stanza, devoted to the intellectual and spiritual life, contrasts
the physical world—now concisely symbolized as "an aged man," who is a
mere "tattered coat upon a stick" (a scarecrow)—with the "monuments" that
were introduced at the end of the first stanza. We are now told that the aged
man, or, more precisely, his "soul," must "sing" (a contrast with the song of the
dying birds of the first stanza), and that the soul learns to sing by "studying /
Monuments of its own magnificence." And, the speaker tells us, this is why he
has come to "the holy city of Byzantium." The poet was, so to speak, trying to
prepare himself for his final examination. In *A New Commentary on the Poems of
W. B. Yeats* (1984), Norman A. Jeffares quotes a statement Yeats composed in
1931 for a broadcast of his poems:

> Now I am trying to write about the state of my soul, for it is right for
> an old man to make his soul, and some of my thoughts upon that sub-
> ject I have put into a poem called "Sailing to Byzantium." When
> Irishmen were illuminating the Book of Kells [in the eighth century]
> and making the jewelled croziers in the National Museum, Byzantium
> was the centre of European civilisation and the source of its spiritual
> philosophy, so I symbolise the search for the spiritual life by a journey
> to that city. (213)

The third stanza introduces art and associates it with the wisdom that the
soul acquires. Notice, however, that the mosaic is introduced merely as a comparison: The sages are "standing in God's holy fire / As in the gold mosaic of
a wall."

The fourth stanza combines the permanence of art (the golden bird on a
golden bough) with the transient stuff of "nature" (25), which is in fact the
subject of most art. And whereas the first stanza showed "Fish, flesh, or fowl"
caught up in the richness of the present, this final stanza takes us into a fuller
world, a world of what is "past, or passing, or to come." Are we wrong in
thinking that this poem, about human weakness, human blindness, also celebrates human achievements—and that one of these achievements is the
poem itself?

Bibliographic note: The literature on this poem is enormous. A classic piece
is Elder Olson's essay in *University Review*, 8 (Spring 1942): 209–19, reprinted
in *The Permanence of Yeats*, ed. James Hall and Martin Steinman (1961). Less
readable, but highly impressive, are Curtis Bradford's study of Yeats's interest
in Byzantium and of the manuscripts, in *PMLA* 75 (1960): 110–25, reprinted in *Yeats*, ed. John Unterecker, and Jon Stallworthy's discussion of the manuscripts in *Between the Lines* (1963). For a hostile discussion of the poem see
Yvor Winters, *Forms of Discovery* (1967).

For further background and context, students might type into a search engine
"The Glory of Byzantium." This will bring up a link to a catalog published by
the Metropolitan Museum of Art, with many images available on the site.

ADDITIONAL TOPICS FOR CRITICAL THINKING AND WRITING

1. What place is "That" (the first word of the poem)? What does it come to
   stand for? By the end of the poem, what does Byzantium stand for?

2. We are, all of us, in this transient world, this world of flux, this world of birth and death. Would you say that Yeats despises it? Or does he reveal its attractions even while he seeks to turn his back on it?

3. Have you ever visited any place—perhaps the place where you or your parents or grandparents were born, or perhaps a house of worship, or perhaps a college campus—which you have come to see symbolically, standing for a way of life or for some aspect of life? If so, describe the place and the significance that you give it.

IV

Drama

25

How to Read a Play

Among useful basic studies are S. Barnet et al., eds., *Types of Drama*, 8th ed. (2001), an anthology with introductions and critical essays; Cleanth Brooks and Robert Heilman, eds., *Understanding Drama* (1948), an anthology with a good deal of critical commentary; J. L. Styan, *The Elements of Drama* (1960); and Eric Bentley, *The Life of the Drama* (1964). The reference works we find ourselves consulting first are Martin Banham's *The Cambridge Guide to Theatre*, New Edition (1995), and Patrice Pavis's *Dictionary of the Theatre: Terms, Concepts, and Analysis*, trans. Christine Schantz (1998). Students should also be referred to Marcia L. Ferguson, *A Short Guide to Writing about Theatre* (2008).

SUSAN GLASPELL

Trifles (p. 953)

Some students may know Glaspell's other version of this work, a short story entitled "A Jury of Her Peers." Some good class discussion can focus on the interchangeability of the titles. "Trifles" could have been called "A Jury of Her Peers," and vice versa. A peer is an equal, and the suggestion of the story's title is that Mrs. Wright is judged by a jury of her equals—Mrs. Hale and Mrs. Peters. A male jury would not constitute her equals because—at least in the context of the story and the play—males simply don't have the experiences of women and therefore can't judge them fairly.

Murder is the stuff of TV dramas, and this play concerns a murder, but it's worth asking students how the play differs from a whodunit. Discussion will soon establish that we learn, early in "Trifles," who performed the murder, and we even know, fairly early, *why* Minnie killed her husband. (The women know what is what because they correctly interpret "trifles," but the men are baffled, since they are looking for obvious signs of anger.) Once we

427

know who performed the murder, the interest shifts to the question of whether the women will cover up for Minnie.

The distinction between what the men and the women look for is paralleled in the distinction between the morality of the men and the women. The men stand for law and order, for dominance (they condescend to the women, and the murdered Wright can almost be taken as a symbol of male dominance), whereas the women stand for mutual support or nurturing. Students might be invited to discuss *why* the women protect Minnie. Is it because women are nurturing? Or because they feel guilt for their earlier neglect of Minnie? Or because, being women, they know what her sufferings must have been like and feel that she acted justly? All of the above?

The symbols will cause very little difficulty. (1) The "gloomy" kitchen suggests Minnie's life with her husband; (2) the bird suggests Minnie (she sang "like a bird," was lively, then became caged and was broken in spirit).

The title is a sort of symbol too, an ironic one, for the men think (in Mr. Hale's words) that "Women are used to worrying over trifles." The men in the play never come to know better, but the reader-viewer comes to understand that the trifles are significant and that the seemingly trivial women have outwitted the self-important men. The irony of the title is established by the ironic action of the play.

Does the play have a *theme?* In our experience, the first theme that students may propose is that "it's a man's world." There is something to this view, but (1) a woman kills her husband, and (2) other women help her to escape from the (male) legal establishment. Do we want to reverse the first suggestion, then, and say that (in this play) it is really a woman's world, that women run things? No, given the abuse that all of the women in the play take. Still, perhaps it is fair to suggest that one of the things the play implies is that overbearing male behavior gets what it deserves—at least sometimes. Of course, when put this way, the theme is ancient; it is at the root of the idea of *hubris*, which is said to govern much Greek tragedy. Glaspell gives it a very special twist by emphasizing the women's role in restoring justice to society.

On Glaspell, see Jean Gould, *Modern American Playwrights* (1966); Arthur E. Waterman, *Susan Glaspell* (1966); and C. W. E. Bigsby, "Introduction," *Plays by Susan Glaspell* (1987). Also useful is *Modern American Drama: The Female Canon,* ed. Jane Schlueter (1990).

TENNESSEE WILLIAMS

The Glass Menagerie (p. 963)

The books on Williams that have appeared so far are disappointing. The best general survey is Henry Popkin's article in *Tulane Drama Review* 4 (Spring 1960): 45–64; also useful is Gordon Rogoff, in *Tulane Drama Review* 10 (Summer 1966): 78–92. For a comparison between the play and earlier versions, see Lester A. Beaurline, *Modern Drama* 8 (1965): 142–49. For a discussion of Christian references and motifs (e.g., Amanda's candelabrum, which was damaged when lightning struck the church), see Roger B. Stein, in *Western Humanities Review* 18 (Spring 1964): 141–53, reprinted in *Tennessee Williams*

(1977), ed. Stephen S. Stanton. Stein suggests that the play shows us a world in which Christianity has been replaced by materialism.

Perhaps the two points that students find most difficult to understand are that Amanda is both tragic *and* comic (see the comments below, on the first suggested topic for writing), and that Tom's quest for reality has about it something of adolescent romanticism. Tom comes under the influence of his father (who ran away from his responsibilities), and he depends heavily on Hollywood movies. This brings up another point: It is obvious that Amanda, Laura, and Tom cherish illusions, but students sometimes do not see that Williams suggests that all members of society depended in some measure on the illusions afforded by movies, magazine fiction, liquor, dance halls, sex, and other things that "flooded the world with brief, deceptive rainbows," while the real world of Berchtesgaden, moving toward World War II, was for a while scarcely seen. If Amanda, Laura, and Tom are outsiders living partly on illusions, so is everyone else, including Jim, whose identification with the myth of science may strike most viewers as hopelessly out of touch with reality.

The Glass Menagerie has twice been filmed, most recently in 1987, directed by Paul Newman. Newman followed Williams's sequence of scenes, and he kept almost all the dialogue, yet the film strikes us as unsuccessful. Why? Probably this "memory play" needs to be somewhat distanced, framed by a proscenium. Further, the film's abundant close-ups seem wrong; they make the play too energetic, too aggressive. Such are our impressions; instructors who rent the film (Cineplex Odeon) can ask students to set forth their own impressions—in writing.

Though the critical writing on Williams is less than stellar, we can recommend Lyle Leverich, *Tom: The Unknown Tennessee Williams* (1995), the first of a two-volume biography.

ADDITIONAL TOPICS FOR CRITICAL THINKING AND WRITING

1. Discuss comedy in *The Glass Menagerie*. (Students should be cautioned that comedy need not be "relief." It can help to modify the tragic aspects, or rather, to define a special kind of tragedy. A few moments spent on the Porter scene in *Macbeth*—with which almost all students are familiar—will probably help to make clear the fact that comedy may be integral.)

2. Compare the function of Tom with the function of the Chorus in *Antigone*. (Williams calls his play a "memory play." What we see is supposed to be the narrator's memory—not the dramatist's representation—of what happened. Strictly speaking, the narrator is necessarily unreliable in the scene between Laura and Jim, for he was not present, but as Williams explains in the "Production Notes," what counts is not what happened but what the narrator remembers as having happened or, more exactly, the narrator's response to happenings.)

3. Explore cinematic techniques used in *The Glass Menagerie*. (Among these are fade-ins and fade-outs; projected titles, reminiscent of titles in silent films; the final "interior pantomime" of Laura and Amanda, enacted while Tom addresses the audience, resembles by its silence a scene from silent films, or a scene in a talking film in which the sound track gives a narrator's voice instead of dramatic dialogue. By the way, it should be noted that Williams, when young, like Tom, often attended movies, and that

this play was adapted from Williams's rejected screenplay, *The Gentleman Caller*, itself derived from one of Williams's short stories.) This topic and the next are ways of getting at the importance of unrealistic settings and techniques in this "memory play."

4. Compare the play with the earlier Williams short story, "Portrait of a Girl in Glass," in *One Arm and Other Stories*.

26

Tragedy

SOPHOCLES

Oedipus the King (p. 1019)

Though interpretations are innumerable, most fall into the following categories.

1. The gods are just; Oedipus is at fault. The gods are innocent because fore-knowledge is not foreordaining. (Jesus predicted that Peter would thrice deny him, but this prediction does not mean that Jesus destined Peter to deny him.) The prophecy told what Oedipus would do, but Oedipus did it because of what he was, not because the gods ordained him to do it. As we watch the play, we see a man acting freely—pursuing a course that leads to the revelation of who he is. (See especially Bernard Knox, *Oedipus at Thebes* [1971, 33–41].) Though Oedipus is often praised for relentlessly pursuing a truth that ultimately destroys him, the fact is that—until very late in the play—he believes he is searching for someone other than himself, and moreover, in this search he too easily assumes that other people are subversive. Oedipus is rash and even cruel in his dealings with Teiresias, Creon, and the shepherd. His rashness is his *hamartia*, and the gods punish him for it. Given the prophecy that was given to Oedipus, a man less rash would have made it his business never to have killed anyone, and never to have married. (But he thought Polybos and Merope were his parents, and he knew that the old man [Laios] was not Polybos and that the queen in Thebes [Iocaste] was not Merope.)
2. The gods are at fault; Oedipus is innocent. When Oedipus asked the oracle who his parents were, the god answered in such a way as to cause Oedipus to leave a place of safety and to go to a tragic destination.

Oedipus is a puppet of the gods; his *hamartia* is not rashness (a moral fault) but simply a mistake: He *un*intentionally killed his father and married his mother. The oracle was not conditional (it did not say, "If you do such and such, then such and such will happen"). The play is a tragedy of destiny; notice that at the end of the play no one justifies the gods, that is, no one exonerates them from forcing evil on Oedipus.

3. Oedipus is on the whole admirable (he pities his suffering kingdom; he has a keen desire to know the truth), but he is not perfect. The matter of his *intention* is irrelevant because the deeds of patricide and incest (irrespective of motive) contain pollution. The gods are mysterious, and though they sometimes shape men's lives terribly, they are not evil because they cannot be judged by human standards of justice or morality.

4. Sophocles is not concerned with justice; the play is an exciting story about a man finding out something about the greatness of humanity and about human limitations.

Walter Kaufmann, *Tragedy and Philosophy* (1968), has a long discussion of *Oedipus the King*, in the course of which he finds five themes.

1. The play is about man's radical insecurity (epitomized in Oedipus's fall); Oedipus was the first of men, but he fell.

2. The play is about human blindness. Oedipus did not know who he was (i.e., he was ignorant of his parentage); moreover, he was blind to the honesty of Creon and Teiresias.

3. The play is about the curse of honesty. Oedipus's relentless desire to know the truth brings him to suffering. (If one wants to hunt for a tragic "flaw," one can see this trait as a flaw or vice, but a more reasonable way of looking at it is to see it as a virtue. Would we regard a less solicitous ruler as more virtuous?)

4. The play is about a tragic situation. If Oedipus abandons his quest, he fails his people; if he pursues his quest, he ruins himself.

5. The play is about justice or, more precisely, about *in*justice, that is, undeserved suffering. (Here we come back to Kaufmann's third point: The reward of Oedipus's quest for truth is suffering. It is not even clear that he is being justly punished for killing Laios, for Oedipus belongs to the old heroic world, where killing an enemy is celebrated.) Another point about the play as a play about justice: Sophocles talks of *human* justice too. When Oedipus curses the unknown killer of Laios, he does not think that the killer may have acted in self-defense. And Oedipus's desire to punish Creon and Teiresias similarly shows how wide of the mark efforts at human justice may be.

The Norton critical edition of *Oedipus Tyrannus* (1970), ed. L. Berkowitz and T. F. Brunner, includes a translation, some relevant passages from Homer, Thucydides, and Euripides, and numerous religious, psychological, and critical studies, including Freud's, whose key suggestion, in *The Interpretation of Dreams* (1999), is that the play "moves a modern audience no less than it did the contemporary Greek one" because there is a "voice within us ready to recognize the compelling force of destiny [in the play]. . . . His destiny moves us only because it might have been ours—because the oracle laid the same curse upon us before our birth as upon him. It is the fate of all of us, perhaps, to direct our first sexual impulse towards our mother and our first hatred and our first murderous wish against our father."

An instructor who uses this quotation in class may wish to call attention to the male chauvinism: Freud's "all of us" really means "all males," although he did make various efforts to account for the Oedipus complex in women. It may also be relevant to mention that if the Oedipus of the play did have an Oedipus complex, he would have wanted to go to bed with Merope (the "mother" who brought him up) rather than Iocaste. Note, too, that when he kills Laios, Laios is to him a stranger, not his father. Indeed, his flight from Corinth is a sign that he does *not* wish to sleep with his mother or to kill his father. But perhaps such a view is too literal. Perhaps this is a convenient place to mention that Oedipus's solution of the riddle of the Sphinx (a human being is the creature who walks on four feet in the morning, two at noon, and three in the evening) is especially applicable to Oedipus himself (the weakest of infants, the strongest of men in his maturity, and desperately in need of a staff in his blind old age), but of course it applies to all the spectators as well.

In addition to the Norton edition, the following discussions are especially interesting: Stanley Edgar Hyman, *Poetry and Criticism* (1961); H. D. F. Kitto, *Greek Tragedy* (1939) and his *Poeisis* (1966); Richmond Lattimore, *The Poetry of Greek Tragedy* (1958); Cedric Whitman, *Sophocles* (1951); Bernard Knox, *Oedipus at Thebes* (1957); Charles Rowan Beye, *Ancient Greek Literature and Society* (1975), especially 306–12; Brian Vickers, *Toward Greek Tragedy* (1971), Vol. I; and R. P. Winnington-Ingram, *Sophocles* (1980). See also Simon Goldhill, *How to Stage Great Tragedy* (2007).

ADDITIONAL TOPIC FOR CRITICAL THINKING AND WRITING
By today's standards, is Oedipus in any sense guilty, and if so, of what?

SOPHOCLES

Antigone (p. 1062)

On *Antigone*, consult two books by H. D. F. Kitto, *Greek Tragedy* (1939), and especially *Form and Meaning in Drama* (1956). See also D. W. Lucas, *The Greek Tragic Poets* (1950); Cedric H. Whitman, *Sophocles* (1951); and R. P. Winnington-Ingram, *Sophocles* (1980). Hegel's view, most often known through Bradley's essay on Hegel in Bradley's *Oxford Lectures* (and reprinted in *Hegel on Tragedy* [1962], ed. Anne and Henry Paolucci), claims that both sides are right and that both are also wrong because they assert they are exclusively right. (For a long anti-Hegelian reading, see Brian Vickers, *Toward Greek Tragedy* [1971], which insists that Creon is brutal and Antigone is thoroughly admirable.) Bradley says, "In this catastrophe neither the right of the family nor that of the state is denied; what is denied is the absoluteness of the claim of each."

Most subsequent commentators take sides and either see Creon as a tragic hero (a headstrong girl forces him to act, and action proves ruinous, not only to her but to him), or see Antigone as a tragic heroine (a young woman does what she must and is destroyed for doing it). The critical conflict shows no sign of terminating. Mostly we get assertions, such as D. W. Lucas's "There is no doubt that in the eyes of Sophocles Creon is wrong and Antigone right," and Cedric

Whitman's "Antigone's famous stubbornness, . . . the fault for which she has been so roundly reproved, is really moral fortitude." One of the most perceptive remarks on *Antigone* is by William Arrowsmith, in *Tulane Drama Review* 3 (March 1959): 135, where he says that Antigone, "trying to uphold a principle beyond her own, or human, power to uphold, gradually empties that principle in action, and then, cut off from her humanity by her dreadful heroism, rediscovers herself and love in the loneliness of her death." He suggests, too, that the play insists on "not the opposition between Antigone and Creon, but [on] the family resemblance which joins them in a common doom."

John Ferguson, in *A Companion to Greek Tragedy* (1972), offers a fairly brief, commonsensical, scene-by-scene commentary on the play. Toward the end he argues that Hegel was utterly wrong in his view that both Creon and Antigone are right. Ferguson points out that Creon "behaves as a tyrant" and that Creon's law "is disastrous for the state." And Antigone is "wrong," Ferguson says, because although her "view of the situation is the true one," as a woman it was her duty to obey Creon. The play is about Antigone's *hubris*, and therefore it is properly titled.

We'd also recommend Charles Segal, *An Interpretation of Sophocles* (1981), which includes detailed studies of both *Antigone* and *Oedipus the King*.

ADDITIONAL TOPICS FOR CRITICAL THINKING AND WRITING
1. What stage business would you invent for Creon or Antigone at three points in the play?
2. In an essay of 500 words, compare and contrast Antigone and Ismene. In your discussion consider whether Ismene is overly cautious and whether Antigone is overly cold in her rejection of Ismene.
3. Characterize Haimon, considering not only his polite and even loving plea when he urged Creon to change his mind but also his later despair and suicide. In what way is he like his father and also (in other ways) like Antigone?

WILLIAM SHAKESPEARE
Hamlet, Prince of Denmark (p. 1108)

Probably the best short study of *Hamlet* is Maynard Mack's "The World of Hamlet," *Yale Review* 41 (1952): 502–23, reprinted in the Signet paperback edition of *Hamlet* (1998), in *Tragic Themes in Western Literature* (1955), ed. Cleanth Brooks, and elsewhere. Maurice Charney's *Style in Hamlet* (1969) is excellent, and so too is Harley Granville-Barker's book-length essay in *Prefaces to Shakespeare* (1984). For an essay that draws on the tenets of reader-response criticism, see Stephen Booth, "On the Value of *Hamlet*," in *Reinterpretations of Elizabethan Drama* (1969, 137–76). For a sampling of recent criticism, see *William Shakespeare's Hamlet*, ed. Harold Bloom (1986).

The nature of the Ghost has produced a good deal of commentary, most of it summarized in Eleanor Prosser's *Hamlet and Revenge* (1967). She says that for the Elizabethans a ghost can be only one of three things: the soul of a pagan (impossible in this play, for the context is Christian); a soul from Roman Catholic purgatory (impossible in this play, because it seeks revenge); or a devil (which is what Prosser says this Ghost is). Prosser argues that the Ghost is evil because it counsels revenge, it disappears at the invocation of heaven, and it disappears when the cock crows. But perhaps it can be replied that although the Ghost indeed acts suspiciously, its role is to build suspense and to contribute to the play's meaning, which involves uncertainty and the difficulty of sure action. Prosser sees Hamlet as a rebellious youth who deliberately mistreats Ophelia and descends deep into evil (e.g., he spares Claudius at his prayers only in order to damn him), but when he returns from England he is no longer the "barbaric young revenger . . . but a mature man of poise and serenity" (217). He is generous to the gravediggers and Laertes, "delightful" with Osric. In short, the young rebel has been chastened by experience and by the vision of death, and so he is saved. He "has fought his way out of Hell" (237). Prosser offers a useful corrective to the romantic idea of the delicate prince, as well as a great deal of information about the attitude toward ghosts, but one need not accept her conclusion that the Ghost is a devil; her evidence about ghosts is incontrovertible on its own grounds, but one may feel that, finally, the play simply doesn't square with Elizabethan popular thought about ghosts.

We comment on the Oedipus complex in our discussion of *Oedipus*. The view that *Hamlet* can be explained by reference to the Oedipus complex is most fully set forth in Ernest Jones, *Hamlet and Oedipus* (1949). Briefly, Jones's points are that Hamlet delays because of "some unconscious source of repugnance to his task." This repugnance is rooted in the fact that Claudius had done what Hamlet unconsciously desired to do (kill Hamlet Senior and sleep with Gertrude). Thus far Jones follows Freud. But Jones adds another reason: The desire to kill the father is *repressed* in infancy, and this repression continues to operate in maturity, which means that Hamlet can scarcely act on his desire to kill Claudius, for Claudius is now in effect his father.

Hamlet is a challenging, difficult play, of course, yet it is a play that in our experience works very well for students, more so than *King Lear* and *Coriolanus*, for example, which we admire greatly but which are less familiar as cultural monuments to students. Sometimes, as the moment for reading *Hamlet* approaches, we have asked members of the class to prepare a study sheet of important issues in it. Even students who haven't read *Hamlet* before are able to make reference to the Ghost, the Oedipus complex, delay, the play within the play, revenge, Hamlet's soliloquies. Working as a group, the class can assemble an impressive list of questions, problems, and themes, which they can then bring to (and test against) their actual experience of the play.

We always use one or more film versions of *Hamlet* as a resource for teaching, such as those that star Laurence Olivier (1948), Nicol Williamson (1969), Derek Jacobi (1979), and Mel Gibson (1990). It can be very helpful if you bring to class one or more of these films—all are available in VHS format—and discuss how an actor has delivered an important speech and how the dramatic context for it has been designed. This prompts the students to focus on *Hamlet* as a *play*, as a work meant for the theater, and enables them to become sensitive to the pace, rhythm, and tone of Shakespeare's dramatic verse. The *choices* that directors and actors make, as they construct an interpretation of the play, can come alive for students when two versions of a speech or scene are compared.

In a moment we will offer a scene-by-scene commentary on the play, but we want first to mention that another commentary of this sort—and a very good one—is available in Alfred Harbage's *A Reader's Guide to Shakespeare* (1963). For a commentary of more than 900 pages, emphasizing theatrical productions, consult Marvin Rosenberg, *The Masks of Hamlet* (1992). We make no claims for the originality of any of the following remarks. They are derived from decades of reading commentaries, seeing productions, teaching the play, and conversing with colleagues.

When we teach *Hamlet* in an introductory course, we usually allot five days to it, doing roughly an act per day. We spend part of at least two meetings having students perform a short scene, or part of a scene. Our practice is to use volunteers for the first of these scenes, but we then usually assign students for any other scenes that we may want to stage, simply because we have found that some students who hesitate to volunteer will nevertheless gladly participate if asked. We give each actor a photocopy of the pages of the scene, on which we have jotted some minimal bits of direction, and we assign another student to serve as the director. Sometimes we recommend that the director read the relevant pages in Rosenberg's book, so that he or she may try out some approaches. It is the responsibility of the students to meet twice for rehearsal. In order to make certain that they can indeed all meet, during the class meeting when we choose the performers, we set a time when they can meet to rehearse, e.g., Monday and Thursday, 4:00–6:00 P.M. The students are not expected to memorize the parts; while performing they read from the text, but they do engage in a certain amount of movement, e.g., sitting, embracing, gesticulating.

1.1 The play begins with soldiers and ends with a soldier's funeral. Although the idea that Hamlet is a romantic, melancholy figure who cannot make up his mind still has currency, we tend to emphasize Hamlet's energy, resourcefulness, courage, and even military skill. He is involved in a battle to the death, and we do not think it incongruous to conceive of Hamlet as a soldier. Fortinbras (literally "strong-in-arm"), you will recall, at the end of the play says that had Hamlet become king, he would in all likelihood have "proved most royal." (How Fortinbras could know this is, admittedly, unclear, but we assume that Shakespeare wanted his audience to take the comment seriously, and so we tend to interpret the play in a way that fits with this final evaluation.)

This opening scene is chiefly in blank verse, but most of the first twenty-five lines, chiefly short, often iambic, could pass as prose. These lines, though simple and direct, introduce the note of mystery. Further, as is apparent when one sees this scene on the stage, the element of unstabilizing doubt is strong: Francisco is the soldier on duty, so he ought to challenge the apparent interloper, but it is Bernardo (coming to relieve Francisco) who utters the first words, the challenging "Who's there?" Later in the scene we will learn that Bernardo and Marcellus have seen the Ghost on two previous nights, so it is not surprising that Bernardo is jumpy, and (hearing or seeing something) calls out "Who's there?" Francisco's response ("Nay, answer me. Stand and unfold") is not an answer to the question, and it thus further indicates to us the state of uncertainty and confusion. Our point: Hamlet is not the only character in the play who is puzzled by his encounters, and who is unsure of what is what and who is who.

In this commentary we will try to confine ourselves to the text, but here we want to mention that although we admire Kenneth Branagh's film (1996), we are not wild about its opening, with its shots of Elsinor in snow, an immense statue of Hamlet Senior, a rasping noise, and (here we quote from the printed version of the screenplay) "CRASH! A body, from right of frame, bundles [Francisco] forcibly to the ground. On the frozen ground they struggle, dangerous flashing blades in the gloom." All of this before the second line of dialogue is spoken. We think that if you simply read the first twenty lines aloud, or have students perform them, students will see that none of Branagh's embroidery is necessary.

Because the play was originally staged in daylight, Shakespeare has to inform his audience that the scene takes place at midnight, and this he does by having Bernardo say, "'Tis now struck twelve," a good dramatic hour. Francisco goes on to set the psychological scene: "'Tis bitter cold, / And I am sick at heart." The uncertainty is emphasized by additional questions ("Who is there?" "Who hath relieved you?" "What, is Horatio there?"), all within the first twenty lines. We in the audience are kept in the dark. Marcellus says, "What, has this thing appeared again tonight?" He goes on to speak of "this dreaded sight," and Horatio says, "Tush, tush, 'twill not appear," but the spectator or reader still does not know what "this . . . sight" or "this apparition" or this "it" is.

Bernardo begins to narrate the events of "last night," setting a cosmic stage ("When yond same star that's westward from the pole / Had made his course t'ilume that part of heaven / Where now it burns"), and in the very act of narration the Ghost appears, almost as though he has been waiting for his cue. How the Ghost entered in Shakespeare's theater we do not know. Perhaps he merely walked on, perhaps he rose through a trapdoor. Whose ghost is it? It is said to *look* like the king, but perhaps it is an imposter. Horatio asks, "What art thou . . . ?" (again, the element of uncertainty), and when "by heaven" he charges it to speak, it stalks away. Marcellus says the Ghost is "offended," but why? Because it is an evil spirit, disguised as the king, who cannot respond when charged "by heaven"? Or because it indeed is the king and is offended by Horatio's charge that it "usurps" the night and the "fair and warlike form" of the dead king of Denmark? The audience thus far has been put into suspense and then partly gratified: We at last see the "thing" or "apparition," but we still do not know whether it is the ghost of the king or a usurper, presumably an evil spirit in the form of the king. And all this within fifty lines.

Horatio informs us that "This bodes some strange eruption to our state," and (whether the Ghost is or is not the dead king) we are ready to believe him. Marcellus tells the men to "sit down," and presumably they do so, somewhat relaxing the tension— but only somewhat, since the narrative that Horatio proceeds to set forth, concerning King Hamlet and the Norwegians, is filled with anticipation of a future struggle. Bernardo conjectures that the Ghost is associated with the war with Norway; Horatio (evoking Julius Caesar) gives it a cosmic dimension. Probably we are so absorbed with the narrative that we are taken by surprise when the Ghost reappears.

Usually we linger a bit over Horatio's speech, in order to make sure that the students pick up the important political background that it provides about the former kings of Denmark and Norway, the men whose sons bear the same name as their fathers—Hamlet and Fortinbras. The elder Hamlet, "our last king," Horatio explains, fought a deadly duel with King Fortinbras of Norway. He states that old Fortinbras was incited by pride, and that Hamlet's father was obliged to accept the challenge.

It is not surprising that Horatio seeks to cast the king of his own country in a favorable light (though some scholars have wondered whether Horatio, who has come from Wittenberg University, is a Dane or not), but Shakespeare has crafted the line so that it is somewhat ambiguous. "Thereto pricked on by a most emulate pride" is meant by Horatio to refer to Fortinbras, but when we hear the line it seems for a moment also to refer to Hamlet. The annotation in our text states, "refers to old Fortinbras, not the Danish king," which bears witness to the ambiguity of the line: Our editor feels that there is something in the line he needs to straighten out. He is right, but part of the meaning is in our response to the line *before* it is straightened out.

Our editor glosses "emulate" as "ambitious," but in addition to this older meaning, we think that "emulate" also suggests "to strive to equal or excel, especially through imitation; to compete with successfully; to approach or attain equality with." Shakespeare is prompting us to consider how these two kings are both different and the same, both of them moved by pride and honor, both of them setting an example that their sons in their different ways—Hamlet with much more complexity and difficulty—will respond to powerfully.

Horatio says that Hamlet's success in the duel enabled him to gain Fortinbras's lands. But now, in violation of the pledge which the old kings made before the duel (the winner gets the other's lands), young Fortinbras is on the march for revenge. Horatio then reports that young Fortinbras has "sharked up a list of lawless resolutes," and is planning to regain what his father lost.

The shark is a predator of the sea—fierce, dangerous, deadly; here the word connotes something of the angry, indiscriminate way that the shark feeds on other fish—which looks forward to the imagery of food and eating in the next lines. The word can also refer to a ruthless, greedy, dishonest person (e.g., a loan shark)—which gives all the more charge to the word "lawless"—or to a person unusually skilled in a particular activity (e.g., a card shark). As a verb, "shark" means "to obtain by deceitful means; to practice or live by fraud and trickery." It's a wonderfully chosen word that reveals a central feature of both Fortinbras's character and the kind of men he has enlisted in his army of mercenaries, against whom Denmark is now hastily making preparations to defend itself.

"Lawless resolutes": such is Fortinbras's force as Horatio apprehensively describes it here. When we actually see the army in 4.4, it seems well-organized and disciplined, a fine fighting force, capably led by a "hot" (Horatio's word) but a decisive and efficient Fortinbras. His narrow intensity is impressive, and to an extent it dramatizes a limitation in young Hamlet, as he observes himself. But while Fortinbras is more focused, not deterred by brooding doubts, he is for that very reason less interesting than the self-examining Hamlet, who has so many more elements in his character.

Why in fact is the Ghost walking? To warn the Danes against a Norwegian threat? Or to warn against some other "feared events," perhaps of a cosmic nature? Later we will learn that it walks because its death is unavenged, but of course none of the figures on the stage knows that the king was murdered, so they have no reason to offer this explanation. The closest anyone comes to touching on this point is Horatio's suggestion that perhaps the Ghost appears because one of the living may do something to "ease" it, but this hypothesis appears along with several others, thereby emphasizing the uncertainty.

The cock crows, the Ghost mysteriously appears in various parts of the stage ("'Tis here" "'Tis here"), and then it vanishes. Just as no one knows how the Ghost appeared in the Elizabethan stage, no one knows how it vanished. Conceivably it exited through one door just as another identically costumed actor appeared briefly at a second door; or perhaps it disappeared through one trapdoor and rose through another. The ambiguous nature of the Ghost is sustained by the contrast between Marcellus's assertion that it is "majestical" and

Horatio's assertion that "it started, like a guilty thing / Upon a fearful summons," and that it cannot appear in the daylight. Marcellus goes on to suggest that it may be an evil spirit, something that cannot appear at Christmas time.

Is the Ghost "an honest ghost" or is it, as Eleanor Prosser learnedly argues in *Hamlet and Revenge* (1967), a demon impersonating Hamlet's father, with the aim of enticing Hamlet to damnation? Prosser assembles massive evidence that Elizabethans did not regard a son as obligated to avenge the death of a murdered father, and massive evidence to the effect that most Elizabethan revenge plays condemn revenge. Looking specifically at *Hamlet*, she argues that the Ghost is hellish (i.e., a demon, not the spirit of Hamlet's father) because it urges revenge, it leaves when heaven is invoked and again when the cock crows, and it darts about suspiciously. Nevertheless, against all of her evidence, the writers of these pages believe that the Ghost is what it claims to be, the spirit of Hamlet's dead father. We take the play *not* to be about what Prosser in effect suggests it is chiefly about (Hamlet's escape from the devil's plot to ensnare his soul), but, rather, to be about a man's heroic fulfillment, at the expense of his life and the lives of others, to bring a murderer to justice.

You may want to suggest to your students that they keep an eye out for passages concerned with Christianity. How Christian is the play? Probably the most explicitly Christian passages are Marcellus's speech here, the Ghost's later reference to purgatory, the scene in which Claudius prays, the burial of Ophelia, and Hamlet's comments on providence and on the Christian prohibition against suicide. On the other hand, all of these passages exist in a play in which revenge is never condemned. And it is scarcely an exaggeration to say that one of the moments when Christian doctrine is most in evidence is the passage when Hamlet decides not to kill the praying king (he believes that to kill the praying king would send Claudius to heaven rather than to hell), and it is precisely this bit of theological reasoning that has most deeply offended many viewers and readers.

Although 1.1 is filled with doubt, with surprise, and with dire talk, it ends lyrically, with the coming of dawn, described (not shown, of course, on the Elizabethan stage) by Horatio. We have moved from midnight to dawn, and from armed figures and an armed Ghost to a description of the dawn walking in homespun clothing, i.e., we have moved into a more comfortable world—but only for a brief while.

1.2 This scene is a bit long to do in class with student actors, but we have sometimes done the first part, up through Hamlet's first line ("A little more than kin, and less than kind"), or even up through the end of Hamlet's first soliloquy.

In contrast to the "dark" and sparsely populated opening scene, 1.2 begins with a fanfare of trumpets ("Flourish") and lots of colorfully dressed figures. Handsomely dressed members of the court crowd the stage, but Hamlet is set apart from these colorful figures, probably physically and certainly by black garments ("nighted color," "inky cloak"). This contrast is evident whether the costumes are Elizabethan (doublet and hose) or modern, or something in between, as in Branagh's film, which was set in the late nineteenth century, with the women in ball gowns and the men in colorful military attire—except for Hamlet, in black. One of the characteristics of any tragic hero is his isolation—his sensibilities set him apart—here made visible by Hamlet's costume and probably by his position on the stage. Branagh's published text tells us that

Hamlet stands at the other end of the hall, "a black silhouette." Even when the tragic hero has a confidant such as Horatio he is, finally, alone, as we will see. Claudius engagingly—or is it unctuously?—summarizes the recent history of Denmark. He assures his hearers that although the dead king still is very much remembered, the time has come to go about new business. He has married the queen, with the full knowledge and presumably the advice and consent of the court, and he thanks them for their help. He then turns to the present difficulty, young Fortinbras.

The speech, again, seems highly competent, even masterful, but perhaps its very polish, its abundant and perhaps too-adept use of antitheses, makes a hearer uneasy, makes a hearer sense that Claudius is trying to make the hasty marriage acceptable by tying it to the funeral. Consider the following passage:

> Therefore our sometime sister, now our Queen,
> Have we, as 'twere, with a defeated joy,
> With an auspicious and a dropping eye,
> With mirth in funeral, and with dirge in marriage,
> In equal scale weighing delight and dole,
> Taken to wife.

That image of one eye joyful and the other downcast (or perhaps dropping tears), as well as the mixture of "mirth in funeral" and "dirge in marriage" and "delight and dole," is enough (a) to reveal Claudius's skill as a shrewd politician and (b) to make us a bit queasy. The audience does not yet know that Claudius is a villainous hypocrite, but the lines certainly allow us to suspect hypocrisy.

A word about the marriage between Claudius and Gertrude. Hamlet will later call it incestuous, but if the Elizabethans regarded the marriage of a man to his sister-in-law as incestuous, why does Claudius go out of his way to speak of Gertrude as "our sometime sister, now our Queen"? Theoretically such a marriage was incestuous, but Elizabeth's father, Henry VIII, had married Catherine of Aragon, his sister-in-law, after the death of her husband, Henry's brother, Prince Arthur. Before making this marriage he had sought advice and was assured it was acceptable. Later, after he became infatuated with Anne Boleyn (and anxious for a male heir), he had moral doubts, and was assured that the marriage was not acceptable. In short, the Elizabethans were of two minds about whether such a marriage was incestuous; it seems that Claudius's view was acceptable, and so was Hamlet's.

The rest of this long speech by Claudius shows him efficiently going about his business as king, explaining to the court the state of affairs with Norway, and dispatching Cornelius and Voltemand to the king of Norway. We notice that whereas Hamlet Senior conquered Fortinbras Senior in battle, King Claudius—apparently not a heroic figure—prefers diplomacy; he instructs the messengers to tell old Norway to restrain young Fortinbras.

Claudius's next speech is one of our favorites for revealing Shakespeare's skill in suggesting character:

> And now Laertes, what's the news with you?
> You told us of some suit. What is't, Laertes?
> You cannot speak of reason to the Dane
> And lose your voice. What wouldst thou beg, Laertes,

That shall not be my offer, not thy asking?
The head is not more native to the heart,
The hand more instrumental to the mouth,
Than is the throne of Denmark to thy father.
What wouldst thou have, Laertes?

If we ask students to perform this scene, in the annotated pages that we give them we call attention to Claudius's repetition of "Laertes"—an obvious attempt (presumably successful) to ingratiate himself. A master of what Dale Carnegie later formalized as *How to Win Friends and Influence People*, Claudius names Laertes four times in nine lines, thus verbally caressing him. In our notes to student performers of the scene we suggest that perhaps Claudius put both hands on Laertes's shoulders at the beginning of the last of these lines. Or perhaps he puts an arm around Laertes's shoulders, or even around his waist.

Students will immediately see the effect of the repetition of "Laertes"; they are less likely, however, to notice another method Claudius uses in order to ingratiate himself with Laertes, his shift from the royal first person plural ("You told *us* of some suit") to the first person singular ("*my* offer"), and in addressing Laertes the shift from "you" to the more intimate "thou."

Laertes makes his brief speech (he came to witness Claudius's coronation; Horatio will explain that *he came* for the funeral of Hamlet's father), and Claudius—apparently deferring to Polonius in yet another ingratiating touch—grants Laertes's wish, such is the power of a king. Claudius then turns to Hamlet, again putting aside the royal form: "my cousin" and "my son" (not "our cousin" and "our son"). His response is a one-line speech with a bitter pun, probably uttered as an aside, and when Claudius speaks another line and is greeted with another bitter one-line answer, Gertrude intervenes, telling Hamlet not to "forever" mourn his father. Hamlet, still bitter, picks up Gertrude's word "seems," and insists that his feelings are genuine. This is one of the passages which have caused some interpreters to say that Hamlet is a nasty self-centered figure, always whining, morally quite inferior to King Claudius, who is doing his best to govern a kingdom that has recently lost its leader and that is threatened by Norway. (This interpretation never ceases to amaze us.) Claudius—a man who has murdered his brother— in the next speech has the chutzpah to tell Hamlet that his grief is "unmanly" and even "impious," that "It shows a will most incorrect to heaven." Claudius's moralizing lecture continues:

Fie, 'tis a fault to heaven,
A fault against the dead, a fault to nature,
To reason most absurd, whose common theme
Is death of fathers, and who still hath cried.
From the first corpse till he that died today,
"This must be so."

The speech takes one's breath away, especially when one recalls that "the first corpse" was that of Abel, killed by his brother, Cain—a parallel to the murder that Claudius has committed.

Having delivered this stern rebuke, Claudius again seeks to ingratiate himself with Hamlet, in effect announcing that Hamlet is his heir ("let the world take note / You are the most immediate to our throne"). At the same time he makes it clear that he wants to keep Hamlet under surveillance: "For your intent / In going back to school in Wittenberg, / It is most retrograde to our desire." The "our"—the royal plural—makes it clear that Claudius is issuing a command. Gertrude adds two lines, and Hamlet (in effect snubbing Claudius) says, "I shall in all my best obey you, madam." Claudius politely ignores the slight, seizes the favorable aspect of Hamlet's response, and puts the best gloss on it: "Why, 'tis a loving and a fair reply." Announcing that he is pleased by this response, he informs the court that when he drinks, the cannon will join the celebration, "Respeaking earthly thunder." Readers and viewers may remember this passage (and the later sounds of the cannon when the king drinks) at the end of the play, when Fortinbras orders the soldiers to fire cannon as a tribute to the dead Hamlet.

Hamlet's first soliloquy: Our text gives "sullied," in the famous passage ("O, that this too, too sullied flesh would melt"); the quartos read "sallied" (probably an alternative form of "sullied") but the Folio reads "solid." Students need not be bothered with a textual problem; "sallied" or "sullied" makes sense, but in our view "solid" goes better with "melt."

In this soliloquy Hamlet calls attention to the Judeo-Christian prohibition against suicide, and in the final scene of the play (5.2) he will make explicit reference to "Providence," but, interestingly, nowhere in the play does Shakespeare raise the issue of the relation of revenge to Christian morality. The point is important because one sometimes hears that Hamlet's delay is due to a conflict in his mind between the Ghost's command that Hamlet avenge his death and the Biblical injunction, "To me belongeth vengeance" (Deuteronomy 32.35; Hebrews 10.30). To repeat: The issue of the morality of revenge is never raised in the play.

The soliloquy clearly reveals Hamlet's sense of despair, despair engendered not only by the death of his father but by the hasty (as it seems to him) remarriage of his mother. Indeed, his mother's action seems to be the greater cause of pain. We pause here to mention that this tragedy is unusual in that the hero's tragic situation is *not* of his own making. For the most part, tragic heroes (e.g., Macbeth, Othello, Lear) take some action that brings about their suffering, but Hamlet has done nothing. He suffers, but not because of any action he has taken. And at this moment he gets, again without initiating the action, news of the Ghost, news that will somewhat lift his spirits. With Horatio, Marcellus, and Bernardo, Hamlet is among friends, though, as we will see, even Horatio cannot fully share his feelings. The scene ends (we are skipping a lot) with Hamlet significantly rejecting the formal farewell of the friends ("Our *duty* to your honor"), and substituting for it the much more intimate "Your *loves*, as mine to you." The very last lines of the scene, like the last lines of the first scene, end with a note of hope.

With so much to cover in each scene and act and in the play as a whole, we always feel hard-pressed to decide what to include in (and what, reluctantly, to exclude from) class discussion. But we do try to give special attention to one or more of Hamlet's soliloquies, both for their dramatic importance and for the immediate connection they have for the students, who are familiar with many of the famous lines. In this soliloquy, as we have noted, Hamlet is in despair, especially from the pain of his mother's remarriage. "That it should come to this!" Hamlet cries out:

But two months dead—nay, not so much, not two.

Hamlet corrects himself sharply in the middle of the line, with three negatives. He is wounded by the hard fact of how recently it was that his mother remarried and insists on getting the period of time right, perhaps because to do otherwise would almost amount to excusing his mother's deed. No, she could not claim it was as long as two months; it was less than that.

> So excellent a king, that was to this
> Hyperion to a satyr, so loving to my mother
> That he might not beteem the winds of heaven
> Visit her face too roughly. Heaven and earth,
> Must I remember?

"Excellent": This is Hamlet's word to describe his father's quality as king. His father, as king, was outstanding, superior, but more than that. In his *Dictionary* (1755), Samuel Johnson defines *excellent* as meaning "of great virtue; of great worth; of great dignity; eminent in any good quality." Virtue; dignity; worth; eminence. The word evokes a great deal about Hamlet's sense of his father's distinction, and the specialness of his reign.

Hamlet's father was Hyperion to the satyr that is Claudius. Hyperion, in Greek mythology, is one of the Titans, the father of Helios, god of the sun; Selene, goddess of the moon, and Eos, goddess of the dawn. The satyr, on the other hand, is one of the deities of the mountains and the woods, with horns, tail, and, sometimes, the legs of a goat. The satyrs are portrayed in Greek mythology as the companions of Dionysus; they drink, dance, play music, and pursue nymphs. And in these activities, the satyr, for Hamlet, makes a fitting figure for the dissolute and lecherous Claudius.

Hamlet is angry, grievously hurt, and his intense language shows how much he has suffered—and how punished he is each time he remembers and recapitulates to himself what his mother and uncle have done. Hamlet, at this point, is overwhelmed by the profligate sexuality his mother has displayed in remarrying so quickly; he does not yet know about his father's murder—this will not come until the Ghost's appearance in 1.5. What comes painfully to mind for Hamlet now are images of his father's graciousness and sensitivity; he loved his wife so much that he wished that the winds might not blow too harshly on her face. The delicacy of this image—though the reference to the "heavens" also conveys its grandeur—is in striking contrast to the next one:

> Why, she would hang on him
> As if increase of appetite had grown
> By what it fed on.

Hamlet represents his father as a man of power, of prominence, yet one who is lovingly attentive to his wife. She, however, crudely hangs on him, her sexual appetite increasing each time it is satisfied. The image Hamlet uses for her suggests a person somewhat desperate, out of control, who cannot keep in check her erotic desires. The implication is that she could not handle being without a husband—a husband who is depicted here as a victim, a man oppressed by his wife's sexual demands. Hamlet, too, may feel victimized by his mother's sexuality, which saturates his consciousness, and which in this speech hits home for him with sickening force. His mother might say in her own defense that she was deeply in love with her husband, but Hamlet's vision of this love is coarse, burdensome—she "hang[s] on him," consuming (as the image shifts) one meal after another.

The line concludes:

> And yet within a month.

The two months have been reduced to less than two and, now, to less than a single month. And the impact of these adjustments in time reinforces Hamlet's indignation. To Hamlet, it feels if anything less than a month; the new marriage seemed almost instantaneous. We realize we are stretching a point, but to us Hamlet suggests that his mother was unfaithful to her husband's memory, *and* unfaithful to this memory with such disturbing speed that she may have been unfaithful to him even when he was alive. How much longer could Hamlet's father have succeeded in satisfying her ever-growing sexual appetite? It was only a matter of time before she would betray him, if she had not already done so. The Ghost's characterization of Claudius as "adulterate" (1.5.43) suggests that Gertrude had been unfaithful while married to Hamlet Senior.

This soliloquy also offers a fine opportunity to work with videos of the play. Nearly always, we focus on the text first, reading the lines aloud, exploring the meanings and implications of words and images, getting a feel for the tone, the movement, the organization. Then we turn to one or two video clips to reflect on how much or how little the actor has come close to our own interpretation and sense of how Shakespeare is characterizing Hamlet—or maybe we should say, how Hamlet is characterizing himself—through this speech.

Laurence Olivier, in his film version, begins this soliloquy in voiceover; we hear Hamlet's words as we watch him move silently, thinking to himself and walking slowly in the shadowy hall that Claudius, Gertrude, and the others have just left. But we see and hear Olivier himself uttering the bitter words, "Nay, not so much, not two," as though this point is one he cannot keep held within. He does the same thing later, with "and yet within a month," emphasizing once more the unmistakable speed of his mother's remarriage. He cannot think of this in silence.

While Olivier's tone is haunted, soft, painfully internalized, Kenneth Branagh's in his film is fiercer, angrier, more aggressively agonized. Through his tone of voice he makes his contempt for Claudius very vivid in the "Hyperion to a satyr" contrast, and as he declares "Heaven and earth / Must I remember," he holds his hands against his head, wishing he could protect himself from the memories and images that cut into his consciousness.

This might be a good occasion for you to explain to students that there is a long, rich, complicated tradition of "playing Hamlet," and that indeed each new Hamlet is more or less obliged somehow to make *his* Hamlet different. When Branagh performed the part on the stage (and later on film) he was keenly aware of how the great Olivier had done the part. One way of understanding Branagh's performance in his film is in fact to perceive it as a response to Olivier's, every detail of which Branagh knows and which he is acting (or, rather, reacting) against.

This movement from the text to the film helps to remind students that *Hamlet* is a work to be read—enjoyed and explicated—and a work to be acted, brought to life anew in each production. Often, we have found that watching a film clip—say, of one of the soliloquies—will enable students to understand a word or line or image that they could not quite grasp while they were reading the text on their own. Sometimes, too, it works in the other direction; the students will conclude that an actor is misinterpreting a line, misrepresenting the tone of the speech as (according to the students) Shakespeare wants it to be heard and experienced.

1.3 This rather domestic scene with Laertes, Ophelia, and Polonius comes between Hamlet's plan to meet the Ghost and the meeting itself. It is sometimes said to relieve the tension, but it might also be said to increase the tension: We listen with some interest to these lightweight people—but perhaps we also have, at least at the edges of our minds, thoughts about how Hamlet and the Ghost will meet.

Laertes has inherited something of his father's windiness, and in his dispensing of worldly knowledge he also resembles his father. Ophelia, significantly, has little to say in the scene; her longest speech occupies six lines, but most of her speeches consist of one line or half a line, such as "Do you doubt that?" and "No more but so?" Some recent Ophelias, with heightened feminist consciousness, have delivered these lines forcefully, or playfully, rather than meekly. And during Laertes's long speech some Ophelias have glared, smiled contemptuously or condescendingly, or in other ways indicated their independence. After this sort of thing, it is not surprising to hear her say to her father, "I do not know, my lord, what I should think" and "I shall obey, my lord." On the other hand, she is certainly not without spirit. After enduring Laertes's thirty-four-line lecture, she amusingly urges him to follow his own advice.

"Enter Polonius," the text says, but how does he enter? Given his propensity to eavesdrop, in some productions he enters silently at the rear, unseen by Ophelia and Laertes, and he observes them for a while before he makes his presence known. What to make of Polonius's advice? It can be delivered mechanically or absent-mindedly, making Polonius seem a fool. But certainly much of the advice is sound, and at least half a dozen lines (probably more) have found their way into common speech with no ironic implications, e.g., "Neither a borrower nor a lender be," "The apparel oft proclaims the man," and "This above all, to thine own self be true." Putting aside this last bit for the moment, one can say that Polonius's advice consists of worldly wisdom, much of it venerable, with sources in Isocrates, Cato, and other ancients. Is it good advice? In William Blake's words (though we can't recall the source), "Good advice for Satan's kingdom." Consider "Give thy thoughts no tongue." We can all agree that there are times when it is right to hold one's tongue (not just shrewd and self-serving, but morally correct), but Polonius's words easily include advice to be hypocritical. "Neither a borrower nor a lender be," but surely there are times when we should be generous, willing to lend money even though it may not be returned. "Beware / Of entrance to a quarrel; but being in, / Bear't that th' opposed may beware of thee." Perhaps Laertes heeds this advice too well; once he enters into the quarrel, he will stop at nothing, not even at the use of a poisoned foil. The bit of advice that is perhaps most memorable is

> This above all, to thine own self be true,
> And it must follow, as the night the day,
> Thou canst not then be false to any man.

Exactly what "self" does Polonius have that he can be "true" to it? If he is essentially a somewhat fatuous dispenser of platitudes, and one who fawns on the king, is this the self he should be true to? As for Laertes, he talks about honor, and in 5.2 he is so concerned with his honor that he accepts Hamlet's apology only tentatively, explaining that before he fully accepts it he wishes to consult "some elder masters of known honor"—but while he is saying this very line he holds in his hand a weapon he knows has been tipped with poison. If anyone in the play strives to be true to himself, it is Hamlet. For what it's worth, when the writer of this paragraph discusses in class the idea of being true to oneself, he customarily mentions the scene in Ibsen's *Peer Gynt* when Peer, an individualist whose motto has been "Peer, to thyself be enough," finds that by living this sort of life he has lost himself. He strips off layer upon layer of an onion, each layer representing a human relationship that he has cast off, and of course he finds there is no core, no self, because, Ibsen suggests, the nature of the self is social. Another way of getting at this idea is to look at Frost's "The Silken Tent" (in our text), where Frost makes the point that the tent stands up because it is tied down by guy lines, "countless silken ties of love and thought / To everything on earth the compass round." A discussion of this sort does, admittedly, get pretty far from the play, from talk about Shakespeare's art, about Hamlet's problem, about revenge, about tragedy, but we think it is worth it. It's our guess that students will never again speak of "being true to themselves" without thinking hard about what they mean.

To get back to the play, and to 1.3, we like to tell students that although Shakespeare's genius is evident in the famous lines, some of which we have just quoted, it is evident too in Polonius's "Affection, pooh," his contemptuous (and contemptible?) but marvelously revealing response to Ophelia's comment that Hamlet "has made many tenders of his affection." Polonius, full of worldly wisdom, cannot imagine that Prince Hamlet may indeed love Ophelia and will not seek to seduce her. We mentioned that the tragic hero is isolated from others; certainly Hamlet's world is not Polonius's. And, not surprisingly, in his last speech in this scene, Polonius forbids Ophelia from maintaining any contact with Hamlet, which, of course, serves to isolate Hamlet still further, depriving him of a connection with a loving, decent woman.

1.4 The setting is the cold guard-platform on the battlements, but the flourish of trumpets and the firing of cannon ("two pieces go off") remind us that Claudius and his court are comfortably reveling. Hamlet's comments on this habit of firing cannon when the king drinks are worth discussing in class. First, we notice that although Hamlet is "native" and "to the manner born" (i.e., he is familiar with the custom from birth), he dislikes the custom; he is isolated, separated from his fellows. Second, commentators who see Hamlet as prone to delay because he thinks too much see in the long speech he makes just before the Ghost appears a tendency to philosophize, to generalize. The argument goes thus: Hamlet begins with a specific situation (cannon being fired when the king drinks), and from this he moves, first, to commenting that Danes drink too much and then that because they are known for their heavy drinking they have a bad reputation that overshadows their good qualities. From this he goes on to reflect about "some vicious mole of nature" or "the stamp of one defect" that destroys a person. He gives several possibilities: The mole (blemish) may be (1) "in their birth—wherein they are not guilty," or (2) it may be "some complexion" (i.e., a dominant trait of temperament), or (3) it may be "some habit."

When he goes on to say that it may be "nature's livery, or fortune's star," we may be justified in thinking that we are not quite clear about the categories, but in any case we do understand his point that whatever the virtues of the Danes, in the view of other people they "take corruption / From that particular fault."

The gist of the entire passage is clear enough, but the details are obscure, especially the end of the speech: "The dram of evil / Doth all the noble substance often dout, / To his own scandal." (The passage appears only in Q2, and what in our text appears as "evil" in Q2 is "eale," usually taken to be an error for "evil" but perhaps a word whose meaning we have lost. And where our text gives "often dout," Q2 gives "of a doubt.") In any case, some critics, as we have said, see in this episode a tendency for Hamlet to move from the particular to the general, or (to put it severely) to lose sight of the immediate issue. For them, this is Hamlet's tragic flaw. (We disagree.)

This speech about the "vicious mole of nature" is sometimes regarded as Shakespeare's discussion of Aristotle's concept of *hamartia*, a term that used to be translated as "tragic flaw" but now is more usually translated as "tragic error."

Despite the common image of Hamlet as melancholy, romantic, and indecisive, in the latter part of this scene he acts swiftly and bravely. He vigorously rejects the entirely reasonable warnings of Marcellus and Horatio, and he bravely approaches the Ghost. In fact, when he defies his comrades, he probably draws his sword when he says "I'll make a Ghost of him that lets me" ("lets" of course means "hinders," as in a let ball in tennis, not "allows"). A Hamlet who draws his sword here may then hold it in front of him, using the hilt as a cross that offers protection. Hamlet exits, following the Ghost; he will receive the information that will change his life and all of Denmark.

1.5 The Ghost says Hamlet is bound to "revenge" the father's death, and this issue has given rise to an immense amount of comment. We have already referred to Eleanor Prosser, who in her book argues that Hamlet does *not* have a duty to avenge his father. A good deal of comment along these lines argues that Shakespeare regularly recommends forgiveness, for instance, Cordelia forgives Lear. On the other hand, Macduff vows vengeance on Macbeth for killing his family, and no critics object.

The Ghost imposes restrictions: "Taint not thy mind, nor let thy soul contrive / Against thy mother aught. Leave her to heaven." Hamlet now has acquired devastating knowledge (his uncle has murdered his father, and his beloved mother not only has married promptly but married the murderer), and he has also acquired the duty to avenge his father. This is not all; he must, again, not contrive against his mother, and he must not taint his mind, i.e., he must not become so consumed with hatred that he himself becomes villainous. If readers or viewers ever thought that he should heed the platitudinous remarks of his uncle and his mother in 1.2, to the effect that his grief was excessive and that he should reconcile himself to his father's death, surely they now realize that, given the new information and the new charges laid upon him, his grief can only deepen.

In the ensuing soliloquy he is not mad but he is somewhat hysterical (consider his odd injunction to himself to record his observation that a villain can smile), as well he might be, given his experience. His mother is a "most pernicious woman," his uncle a "villain, villain, smiling damned villain." When Horatio and Marcellus return, Hamlet goes on to speak what Horatio accurately calls "wild and whirling words," but, again, one must consider the revelations that have been made to him.

When the Ghost speaks from below, telling the mortals to swear, it is unclear what they say or do. The stage direction ("They swear") is an editorial addition—there is no such authentic direction and there is no dialogue. Possibly they simply place their hands on the cross-like hilt of the sword, or they may kiss the sword.

Why does Hamlet caution his friends that he may put on an "antic disposition"? In the source, it was known who killed the king, and Hamlet was guarded lest he attack the killer. He therefore feigned idiocy in order to deceive the guards into thinking he was harmless. But in Shakespeare's play Claudius has no reason to think that Hamlet knows of the murder, and therefore Claudius has no reason to fear Hamlet. By feigning madness Hamlet can only attract attention to himself and cause Claudius to be suspicious. The commonest explanation for Hamlet's announcement that he may feign madness is that (given the burden placed upon him by the Ghost's revelations and commands) perhaps he knows that he will not always be able to control himself and he therefore is cautioning his fellows about his possible odd behavior. Later in the play he insists he is not mad (e.g., in 3.4, when he says to Gertrude, "I essentially am not in madness, / But mad in craft"), but in 5.2, when he apologizes to Laertes, he twice alludes to his madness and his "sore distraction."

The scene ends not with a couplet (a fairly common way of ending a scene) but with an unrhymed line following the couplet, which, so to speak, weakens what might otherwise be a strong ending. That is, the vigor of a pair of rhymed lines ("The time is out of joint. O cursèd spite / That ever I was born to set it right") is diminished by "Nay, come, let's go together." Possibly Horatio and Marcellus have stepped back, maybe even bowing, to allow their social superior to go out first, but Hamlet insists on their leaving with him, partly out of courtesy, partly out of a need for human closeness.

2.1 This scene, like the next (the act consists of only two scenes), is largely concerned with spying, in this instance a father spying (through his agent, Reynaldo) on his son. Hamlet's father was, from all that we are told about him, a heroic figure; the father whom we see in this scene is a very different sort of person. Reynaldo protests that the false charges Polonius suggests be spoken of Laertes would "dishonor" Laertes (28), but in fact they dishonor Polonius. Polonius in this scene is despicable, but he is also something of a comic figure, which is to say that the first part of the scene offers some comic relief.

Ophelia's report of Hamlet's visit to her closet (private chamber) has been variously interpreted. Our own view is—this seems perfectly obvious to us— that Hamlet, having been cut off by Ophelia, as Polonius had ordered ("I did repel his letters and denied / His access to me"), has now lost not only his father and (for all purposes) his mother, but also the woman whom he loves, and this final loss has very nearly driven him mad. Ophelia says he looked at her "As if he had been loosèd out of hell / To speak of horrors," and indeed he can speak of horrors, the report of the Ghost, who has been loosed out of purgatory. Polonius interprets Hamlet's behavior as a sign that Hamlet is "mad for thy love," which is almost right, but, more exactly, we take it that Hamlet is maddened not by love (Polonius's view) but by Ophelia's rejection of his love. His mother (by her marriage) shut the door on him, and the woman whom he loves has now shut him out of her life. Ophelia's report is of his anguished farewell to his beloved.

There are of course other interpretations. Bradley sees in Hamlet's visit a stratagem: Hamlet is putting on the antic disposition he mentioned earlier (he knows Ophelia will report his behavior to Polonius, who will report it to the king). Why? In order to disarm Claudius, i.e., in order to seem a harmless lunatic, mad for love. In our view, the description is too convincing, too moving, for us to take Hamlet's behavior as feigned. The most astounding interpretation we have encountered, however, is that of Harold Goddard, who in *Yale Review* (March 1946) argues that the episode reported by Ophelia never really took place. The whole thing, Goddard says, is Ophelia's hallucination; nothing in the play, he argues, confirms it, i.e., Hamlet never mentions the episode and no other character claims to have witnessed it. To the extent that there is no scrap of evidence in the play that specifically supports the view that the episode actually occurred, Goddard is right, but it seems to us so clear that Ophelia is speaking the truth that no confirmation is needed.

Polonius, we believe, is right in thinking that Hamlet's behavior shows "the very ecstasy [i.e., madness] of love," but wrong in not seeing that the "ecstasy" is caused by the anguish Hamlet experiences when rejected by Ophelia. A few more words about Polonius: The stage direction in Q2, "Old Polonius," easily lets us think of him as slightly doddering. Notice line 6, "Marry, well said, very well said. Look you, sir," with its repetition and its insistence on being heeded (note also "Mark you" in 44), and especially lines 53–54, when he loses his train of thought, lapses into prose, and then asks, "Where did I leave?"

2.2 This scene, the longest of the play, affords several passages that students can effectively perform in class. Consider the possibility of asking students to do the first thirty-nine lines, in which the king and queen talk with Rosencrantz and Guildenstern. This unit begins with Claudius preparing to make use of the two young men—the scene will end, many lines later, with Hamlet preparing to make use of the Players—and with a little coaching the student actor who plays Claudius can convey the cunning that lies beneath the apparent geniality. Although Claudius seems to be solicitous for Hamlet's sake, his real concern is his own well-being, and when in lines 14–17 he asks Rosencrantz and Guildenstern to "gather" and to "glean" information from Hamlet, he is in effect urging them to spy.

The queen immediately adds a bit of flattery ("Good gentlemen, he hath much talked of you"), and she ends her short speech with a thinly disguised offer of a bribe: "Your visitation shall receive such thanks / As fits a king's remembrance." Then comes this dialogue:

Rosencrantz. Both your Majesties
Might, by the sovereign power you have of us
Put your dread pleasures more into command
Than to entreaty.
Guildenstern. But we both obey,
And here give up ourselves in the full bent
To lay our service freely at your feet,
To be commanded.

King. Thanks, Rosencrantz and gentle Guildenstern.
Queen. Thanks, Guildenstern and gentle Rosencrantz.

The repetition of the word "both" (in the first line of Rosencrantz's speech and the first line of Guildenstern's) probably goes unnoticed, but no one can miss the almost comic repetition in the lines of the king and queen, where the names of the friends are reversed. The passage hints at the interchangeability of these two friends, two ciphers, we might say, which leads us to quote Goethe's shrewd remark in *Wilhelm Meister*:

> What these two persons are and do [Wilhelm says] it is impossible to represent by one. . . . These soft approaches, this smirking and bowing, this assenting, wheedling, flattering, this whisking agility, this wagging of the tail, this allness and emptiness, this legal knavery, this ineptitude and insipidity, . . . how can they be expressed by a single man? There ought to be at least a dozen of these people . . . for it is only in society that they are anything. They are society itself, and Shakespeare showed no little wisdom and discernment in bringing in a pair of them. Besides, I need them as a couple that may be contrasted with the simple, noble, excellent Horatio.

(When we coach students for the scene, we usually read this passage to them, and briefly discuss it.)

Another scene that acts well in class, and that helps students to see something of the ways in which Shakespeare characterizes his figures, is the episode in which Polonius diagnoses Hamlet and reads Hamlet's letter while the king and queen, barely able to contain themselves, listen to him. Polonius is so full of himself, so confident of his perceptiveness, that he probably doesn't realize he is lying when he tells Claudius and Gertrude that he had perceived Ophelia's love for Hamlet "Before [his] daughter told [him]."

Soon after Polonius proposes using Ophelia as bait ("I'll loose my daughter to him") so that Claudius can verify Polonius's diagnosis, a stage direction reads, *"Enter Hamlet reading a book."* Some directors, following a suggestion first made by John Dover Wilson, have Hamlet enter a dozen lines earlier, unseen; he hears the plot, retreats, and then enters more audibly. The idea behind this staging is to communicate to the audience that in the next scene, 3.1, when Hamlet speaks to Ophelia, he is really speaking for the benefit of the hidden Claudius and Polonius. You may want to raise the issue now and discuss it when you talk about 3.1.

Hamlet's conversations with Rosencrantz and Guildenstern, after Polonius leaves, also work well in the classroom. The passage begins with conventional phrases from Rosencrantz and Guildenstern ("My honored lord," "My most dear lord"), phrases that contrast with the earnestness or almost boyish enthusiasm of Hamlet's "My excellent, good friends! How dost thou, Guildenstern? Ah, Rosencrantz! Good lads, how do you both?" But Hamlet's remarks soon turn bitter. Of course in the first dozen or so lines he does not yet know that they are in effect spies, but presumably he senses (and we know) that they are not people with whom he can speak with ease, and very soon he sees through them, saying directly, "Were you not sent for?" They are no match for Hamlet, and a dozen or so lines later the two collapse and Guildenstern confesses, "My lord, we were sent for."

You may want to comment on Shakespeare's use of prose, or, rather, his uses of prose. We saw Polonius slip into prose when he lost his train of thought in 2.1.50; later in the play, when Ophelia becomes mad, she speaks in prose, a form that, in a play that is predominantly in blank verse, can indicate a loss of command of language. We have already seen prose used for Hamlet's letter, in 2.2, where Shakespeare wants to set off a form of discourse from the normal language of the play. (In blank verse plays, letters and proclamations normally are in prose.) In short, Shakespeare uses prose for a variety of purposes, and his prose is as shapely, as artful, as his poetry. Although prose is commonly regarded as the language of normal speech, we should remember that despite M. Jourdain's joke in *The Bourgeois Gentleman*, prose is *not* what most of us speak. Normally we utter repetitive, shapeless, and often ungrammatical torrents; prose is something very different—a sort of literary imitation of speech at its most coherent.

Shakespeare often uses prose for small talk, such as Hamlet's conversations with Rosencrantz and Guildenstern, but he uses it also for princely reflections on "What a piece of work is a man" in the present scene. Perhaps he uses prose here because in the very act of speaking about man's nobility he wishes to undercut the assertions—the "goodly frame" is for Hamlet a "sterile promontory," and the creature who is "like an angel" is for him the "quintessence of dust." In any case Shakespeare conducts his prose as carefully as his verse. One might, in fact, contrast this speech, with its deeply moving contrasts, with Polonius's rather dotty verse speech describing Hamlet, which also abounds in contrasts, but entertainingly pointless ones: "My liege and madam, to expostulate / What majesty should be, what duty is, / Why day is day, night night, And time is time, / Were nothing but to waste night, day, and time."

In the Player's speech, as in a letter or a proclamation in a play, Shakespeare uses a distinctive style—as he will again in the play-within-the-play—to separate it from its context. True, in the Player's speech he uses blank verse rather than, say, octosyllabic couplets, but it sounds different from the rest of the blank verse in *Hamlet*. Conveying this difference to students is not easy, however, because to inexperienced readers most of Shakespeare's verse sounds pretty strange, pretty extravagant. That's one reason why when we teach *Hamlet* we call attention to the apparent naturalness of the verse in the very first scene, for instance, in such a speech as "Horatio says 'tis but our fantasy, / And will not let belief take hold of him / Touching this dreaded sight twice seen of us," or even in the heightened language at the end of 1.1: "But look, the morn in russet mantle clad / Walks o'er the dew on yon high eastward hill." This language, they can see (with a little help), differs from the Player's bombastic speech: "The rugged Pyrrhus, like th' Hyrcanian beast," or "The rugged Pyrrhus, he whose sable arms, / Black as his purpose, did the night resemble / When he lay couchèd in th' ominous horse. . . . " Students may at first not quite hear the difference, but as you go on with the speech they probably will perceive its difference, its strangeness, at least in some lines.

But of course you won't talk only about the style of the speech, or even about the nice bit of imitation where "Did nothing" is emphasized (some would say "enacted") by the nothingness that makes up the rest of the line:

So as a painted tyrant Pyrrhus stood,
And like a neutral to his will and matter
Did nothing.

A question: Is the "hellish Pyrrhus" an image of Claudius, or is he an image of the avenging Hamlet? Or both? Certainly he resembles Hamlet in his quest for revenge and in (temporary) paralysis, and one can also argue that

Pyrrhus, "horribly tricked / With blood of fathers, mothers, daughters, sons," anticipates Hamlet, who is at least partly responsible for the deaths not only of Polonius, Rosencrantz, Guildenstern, and Claudius but also of Ophelia and Laertes (and perhaps we can add Gertrude). Our own view is that in the picture of Pyrrhus we see a bloodthirsty avenger who is an image of what Hamlet might be if he went cold-bloodedly or hot-bloodedly about his task; that is, ultimately the spectator (on reflection) contrasts Hamlet with Pyrrhus, to Hamlet's credit.

The scene ends with a long soliloquy in which Hamlet reproves himself, a soliloquy that provides some of the evidence for the view that Hamlet delays, that Hamlet is a man who cannot make up his mind, that Hamlet knows what he should do but invents excuses for not doing it. And yet, would one want him to go about his work as Pyrrhus does? Best not to be dogmatic here. Many intelligent readers and spectators have felt that Hamlet's plan to confirm the honesty of the Ghost ("the spirit that I have seen / May be a devil") is mere stalling; others have felt that it is entirely reasonable and, further, quite in character for a man who is thoughtful, unlike (for instance) the impetuous Laertes, who is easily manipulated by Claudius.

3.1 "To be, or not to be" is among the most famous lines in Shakespeare, and the soliloquy in which it occurs is probably the most extensively discussed passage in Shakespeare. In reading some of the scholarship, one inevitably recalls James Joyce's comment (well, OK, it's a comment that Joyce puts into the mouth of Buck Mulligan), "Shakespeare is the happy hunting ground of all minds that have lost their balance." Rather than seek to review the arguments about the precise meanings of certain words, and about the degree to which the speech is about human existence as opposed to being about Hamlet's particular problems, we refer you to Harold Jenkins's Arden edition (1982) of *Hamlet*, 484–90.

Spectators last saw Hamlet when he was energized by his plot to trap Claudius; now, in the soliloquy, he meditates. His problem is not merely to find a way to kill Claudius but to find some meaning in life, in a world of injustice and infidelity. Here again we call attention to the tragic hero as someone isolated from others, isolated by his heightened consciousness. True, Hamlet casts a wide net in his meditations; he has not (for instance) personally suffered "the law's delay." We can say, however, that his reflections are significantly rooted in his experience. If he has not in any very obvious way experienced "the insolence of office," he has nevertheless experienced Claudius's power to prevent him from returning to Wittenberg, and with Ophelia's rejection he has experienced "the pangs of disprized [i.e., unvalued] love."

Incidentally, "disprized" is the Folio reading; Q2 has "despiz'd." A small difference, but there are so many small differences that no two modern eclectic editions of *Hamlet* are the same. And while we are touching on small textual matters, we want to mention that when, after this soliloquy, Ophelia first addresses Hamlet and asks "How does our honor for this many a day?" he replies, in F (the text chiefly used in our book), "I humbly thank you; well, well, well." In Q2 there is only one "well," and many editors take F's repetition to be an unauthorized actor's addition—and indeed it may well be. No one doubts that this is the sort of thing that actors do, and F affords several examples. Still, and here is our point, the larger issue is this: Is the text of a play the play that the author drafts, or the play that the actors perform, with revisions made in the course of rehearsals and perhaps with the permission (or reluctant permission) of the dramatist? Since Shakespeare was a member of the company that performed his plays, we can be sure that he was aware of actors' interpolations. What he thought of them is something we cannot be sure of. Once a director has settled on a text, there is still the problem of how to deliver the lines. It's too simple to say, "Just speak the lines, don't 'interpret' them, don't 'give a reading' of them." One *must* interpret them, one *must* give a reading. In the present instance, does Hamlet speak "Well, well, well" bitterly? Absent-mindedly? Cautiously?

The verbal assault on Ophelia is shocking and distressing, especially since we have no doubt that Hamlet in the main is a noble figure. An occasional critic has argued that Hamlet thinks Gertrude is eavesdropping and that his words are really directed at her. We find this view unconvincing, but we do believe that the attack on women is prompted chiefly by Hamlet's thoughts of Gertrude, though the words fall on Ophelia's ears. In any case, surely the words are provoked by the unendurable distress he has experienced, caused by (a) the death of his father; (b) the murderer's apparent success (the unsuspected Claudius rules Denmark); (c) Gertrude's swift marriage to the murderer; and (d) Ophelia's rejection of Hamlet's love. We might also add (e) Hamlet's awareness that his friends Rosencrantz and Guildenstern are spying on him, but in the context of these other agonizing experiences, their treachery is almost beneath attention. And we might also add (f) Dover Wilson's theory that Hamlet has heard Polonius tell the king that he and the king should eavesdrop on Hamlet's conversation with Ophelia—but we do not believe this to be the case.

In any case, Hamlet's comments on the discrepancy between appearances and reality (e.g., "I have heard of your paintings, too, well enough. God hath given you one face, and you make yourselves another") have already been anticipated by several passages in the play. The most notable anticipation is Claudius's own reflection about cosmetics earlier in this scene, in the speech immediately preceding "To be, or not to be," when in an aside Claudius comments on Polonius's assertion that often with "pious action we do sugar o'er / the devil himself." Claudius's words are:

> O, 'tis too true!
> How smart a lash that speech doth give my conscience!
> The harlot's cheek, beautied with plastering art,
> Is not more ugly to the thing that helps it
> Than is my deed to my most painted word.

Claudius's words are very important because they seem to confirm that he is as guilty as the Ghost claimed. His words indicate that his conscience torments him; he recognizes that his pious actions conceal the work of a man who (in the word that Polonius used) is the devil himself. But it is not clear what Claudius is, or might be, guilty of: Is he referring here to the murder of his brother, or to the over-hasty marriage to Gertrude, or to both?

Whatever its exact source, Claudius's guilt cuts him like the lash of a whip—he feels its searing pain. "Smart" is a keenly chosen word, wonderfully fitting in this context. It means, first, "with a stinging sensation." But, second, it implies mental alertness, shrewdness, intelligence, as if to suggest that the lash itself knows the depth and degree of Claudius's guilty conscience. Claudius is looking inward, with self-contempt, and he sounds in his awareness of his inauthenticity a little like Hamlet in some of his brooding soliloquies.

In the next lines, Claudius compares himself to a "harlot." This word originally referred to a vagabond, beggar, rogue, rascal, villain, low fellow, knave, and (by the sixteenth to seventeenth centuries) a man of loose life, a fornicator; later, it came to refer to an unchaste woman, a prostitute, a strumpet, though it could apply to men as well. Claudius is suggesting that he is as false as a whore, who commits sexual sin while making herself look pretty—attractive on the outside, ugly within. To put the point more exactly: Claudius is saying that the harlot's cheek is to his deed as the harlot's makeup is to the fine-sounding (but false and falsifying) words he uses. Perhaps the cheek is pockmarked, scarred from smallpox, implying that this woman can only make her way in life by trying to cover up what she looks like and selling her body. The sexual reverberations of these lines may intimate that what is really on Claudius's mind is not the murder, but the remarriage, or, more likely still, the connection of the murder to the marriage. Possibly he wanted Gertrude as much as or more than he wanted the crown, and it was for this reason that he killed his brother.

In some productions, these lines are cut, perhaps because the director does not want Claudius to expose himself to the audience before the dumbshow and the Players' spoken play in 3.2. Apparently some directors conclude that if the lines are retained, 3.2 loses its suspense. On the other hand, one could argue that the suspense would still be there, just in a different form. The audience would come to 3.2 in possession of this revelation in 3.1 spoken by Claudius himself. The question, "How will the King react?" will be vivid and suspenseful in either case.

When Hamlet suddenly asks Ophelia, "Where's your father?" he may be manifesting his antic disposition (the question seems to come out of nowhere), or he may have seen the arras stir (in some productions, Polonius sticks his head out in order to see or to hear better, and Hamlet catches a glimpse of him), or he may see a foot protruding beneath the arras. In Branagh's film, responding to what Branagh's stage direction calls "a tiny noise," Ophelia "glances across the room. And then it dawns." Best, in our view, Hamlet may just suddenly—mysteriously, instinctively—sense that something is wrong, that he is being spied on.

The scene ends with Claudius correctly perceiving that Hamlet's condition is not due merely to love of Ophelia. In his next-to-last speech in the play, Claudius astutely speaks of Hamlet's "brains still [i.e., continually] beating" on a "something-settled [i.e., lodged] matter in his heart," and here he puts his finger on Hamlet's distinctive quality, a mind that cannot dismiss what he has experienced.

3.2 Hamlet's speech about acting and about the nature of drama may well tell us something about Shakespeare's own ideas, but we may also connect it with Hamlet's own character, particularly with his intense concern to get things right—again, that continually beating brain. The comment that drama holds the mirror up to nature, showing "virtue her own feature, scorn her own image," is ancient. Donatus attributed it to Cicero, and it was a Renaissance commonplace. In particular, the idea was especially relevant to satiric comedy: The theory basically holds that a spectator watches the play, sees how foolish certain behavior is (e.g., miserliness, or jealousy, or love-sickness), and, not wanting to be like the absurd person on the stage, reforms his or her own behavior. Whether anyone today believes this idea about the social function of comedy is perhaps questionable, but it is worth thinking about Bernard Shaw's formulation of it in the Preface to his *Complete Plays*:

> If I make you laugh at yourself, remember that my business as a classic writer of comedies is "to chasten morals with ridicule"; and if I sometimes make you feel like a fool, I have by the same action cured your folly, just as the dentist cures your toothache by pulling out your tooth. And I never do it without giving you plenty of laughing gas.

After the Players leave the stage, Horatio enters, the true friend, in contrast with Rosencrantz and Guildenstern, whom Hamlet now dismisses from the scene. Hamlet tells Horatio that he has selected him as his special friend because Horatio is a stoic. Horatio is:

> As one, in suffering all, that suffers nothing,
> A man that Fortune's buffets and rewards
> Hast ta'en with equal thanks. . . .

(There is a pun in "suffering": undergoing; experiencing pain.) Hamlet continues in this vein, praising the stoical man, the man who is "not a pipe for Fortune's finger," the man who "is not passion's slave." Such a man, he says, is Horatio, and therefore Hamlet has taken him to his bosom. We must believe that Hamlet's characterization of Horatio is apt, and we can see why Hamlet admires him, but it is also appropriate to point out that the very qualities that Hamlet praises in Horatio are qualities that make him *less* than Hamlet, *less* than a tragic hero. Hamlet's intense feeling or obsessiveness (remarked on by Claudius at the end of 3.1, when Claudius speaks of Hamlet's "brains still beating" on a "something-settled matter in his heart") is part of the essence of a tragic hero, whose response to experience is not stoical acceptance but rather is a passionate and an everlasting "no." The stoic is an unimpassioned bystander, not a heroic doer, not one who feels an obligation to set the time right.

The dumbshow has caused a good deal of odd comment. Why, critics ask, does Claudius tolerate the sight of the crime in the dumbshow, since he finds the sight intolerable when the Players follow it up in a spoken performance? Answers vary. The chief answers are: (1) Claudius doesn't see the dumbshow because he has been chatting with Gertrude; (2) the printed text mistakenly conflates two versions, i.e., in one version there was a dumbshow, to which the king responded, and in another version there was a spoken text, to which the king responded; (3) the king can put up with the dumbshow because he is not convinced that it proves Hamlet is aware of his crime, but when the crime is enacted a second time, he realizes that Hamlet indeed is sending him a message; and (4) the dumbshow is necessary for *us* (not for Claudius), because the spoken performance will be interrupted, i.e., Shakespeare considerately shows us the whole thing and then shows us what happens when Claudius responds in the middle of the spoken version. In our view, the last explanation is the most satisfactory. In fact, we see no problem.

The style of the play-within-the-play, especially its beginning, is notably old-fashioned (couplets in an elaborated style):

> Full thirty times hath Phoebus' cart gone round
> Neptune's salt wash and Tellus' orbèd ground,

And thirty dozen moons with borrowed sheen
About the world have times twelve thirties been. . . .

The reason for this distinctive style is of course to set it off from the "normal"
verse language of the play. Invite students to think of comparable examples in
film and television, where a flashback or a fantasy is presented. (Color may
yield to black and white, or normal speed to slow motion.)

In talking about the Player King's speeches we almost always call attention to two passages that are relevant to thematic concerns:

What to ourselves in passion we propose,
The passion ending, doth the purpose lose.
The violence of either grief or joy
Their own enactures with themselves destroy.

(Late in 4.7, Claudius will say something quite similar to Laertes: "That we
would do / We should do when we would, for this 'would' changes, / And hath
abatements and delays"). The second passage that we sometimes dwell on is
this:

Our wills and fates do so contrary run
That our devices still are overthrown;
Our thoughts are ours, their ends none of our own.

Examples of ironic happenings abound in the play, for instance, Claudius prepares poison for Hamlet, but Hamlet forces Claudius to drink it, and Laertes's
poisoned foil similarly is used against Laertes himself.

When the king rises, thereby interrupting the performance, he provides
proof that he is the murderer. But exactly *why* does he rise? Is it because (1) he
is shocked to learn that Hamlet knows that Claudius is the murderer, or
because (2) he is struck with guilt? This second interpretation gains some confirmation from several passages in the play. Earlier, Claudius has indicated that
indeed he has a conscience, when in an aside he says (3.1) of Polonius's speech
about hypocrisy, "How smart a lash that speech doth give my conscience."
Later, in the scene when he is praying (3.3), he does not spare himself: "O, my
offense is rank." It is not foolish to say that Claudius may be guilt-struck when
he sees the crime enacted in the play-within-the-play.

The delightful passage in which Hamlet plays upon Rosencrantz and
Guildenstern, while accusing them of trying to play upon him, can go over
very well in class. Again, we like to impress upon students that Shakespeare is
not all fancy language and high sentiments; he can write wonderful colloquial prose. A line such as "It is as easy as lying" (often said to be proverbial, but
we have never seen an earlier citation) is just as Shakespearean, and just as
good, as "To be or not to be." And it is noteworthy that after Hamlet has finished playing upon his former friends, he turns to Polonius and plays a bit on
him, with the business about the shape of the cloud.

In the final speech in 3.2, for instance, when he says, "Now could I drink
hot blood," Hamlet is rather like the poisoner Lucianus ("Thoughts black, hands
apt, drugs fit"), and in the next scene, when he contemplates killing the king
but holds off because he wants to be sure to send the king's soul to hell, he perhaps sounds like a Machiavellian villain such as Iago, but for the most part

Hamlet retains our sympathy, and even the speech about drinking hot blood modulates into this:

> Soft, now to my mother.
> O heart, lose not thy nature! Let not ever
> The soul of Nero enter this firm bosom.
> Let me be cruel, not unnatural;
> I will speak daggers to her, but use none.

Still, as becomes evident in a moment, his hope that in dealing with his mother he will not become "unnatural" (e.g., unfilial) does not prevent him from formulating an almost diabolic design against Claudius.

3.3 Claudius's first speech lets us know that he knows Hamlet is at war with him; Claudius is obviously getting Hamlet out of the way, but only later will we learn of Claudius's plot to have Hamlet killed. Guildenstern's first speech here is typical in is obsequiousness and its windiness ("Most holy and religious," "many many," "live and feed"). Rosencrantz's speech is no less obsequious, but it also sets forth the traditional view that the fall of a king is essentially different from the fall of a lesser person: "The cess of majesty / Dies not alone, but like a gulf doth draw / What's near it with it." Like Guildenstern in the preceding speech, Rosencrantz goes on to (in effect) repeat himself: "or it is. . . . " However true the speech is, it is (a) windy, and (b) unconsciously ironic, since these words consciously refer to Claudius but can be applied to Hamlet Senior, whose death in fact was brought about by Claudius. That is, this apparent praise of Claudius is utterly misplaced, since it was Claudius's act of murder that has brought suffering to Denmark.

In discussing the episode of the king at prayer, students may need some help in understanding the difference between remorse and repentance. Claudius himself is clear about the difference. He knows that he feels a gnawing distress or mental anguish for his action (remorse, from the Latin *re + mordere,* to bite), but he also knows that if he were repentant (from *re + pentir,* to be sorry) he would resolve to change. The obvious sign of a change would be that he would give up the fruits of his action (the crown and the queen), but he cannot bring himself to this second stage:

> But O, what form of prayer
> Can serve my turn? "Forgive me my foul murder"?
> That cannot be, since I am still possessed
> Of those effects for which I did the murder:
> My crown, mine own ambition, and my Queen
> May one be pardoned and retain th' offense?

He knows the answer. Still, he tries to pray. As it turns out, he knows that his prayer is not heartfelt; again, he is remorseful but not repentant—but Hamlet, observing Claudius at prayer but not knowing Claudius's state of mind, does not realize that Claudius is in effect unconfessed.

What are we to make of Hamlet as he contemplates killing the praying king? Almost all commentators agree that Hamlet's sentiments are dreadful. For those with an Aristotelian bent, Hamlet here commits *hybris*, trying to kill not only Claudius's body but also his soul. We may as well toss in the term *hamartia*; the word is commonly translated as "tragic flaw" or (better) "tragic error," but etymologically it is a matter of "missing the mark," and Hamlet indeed misses, not only in the sense of passing up an opportunity, but in the sense of misinterpreting what is happening, since the king in fact is not contrite. We hasten to add that we do not encourage the application of these Greek terms, at least not in this episode, but some students are familiar with them (or at least with "tragic flaw") and may bring them up. For most critics, Hamlet here is at his worst. For some critics, however, the words are so dreadful that he cannot really mean them. In this view, Hamlet is looking for an excuse not to kill Claudius, and so he falls upon this ingenious way of not acting. Such was Coleridge's view, and it survives in Bradley: "That this again is an unconscious excuse for delay is now pretty generally agreed."

Let's look at the situation a bit differently: How does an audience respond at this point? Our hunch is that most people (a) do not want Hamlet to kill Claudius while the king is praying and has his back to Hamlet, and (b) they do not want Hamlet to kill while he is in this somewhat demoniacal mood. Most of us probably feel immense relief when, a moment before he might strike, he interrupts his own action.

A few words about the staging: Claudius often kisses a cross before praying, and after his unsatisfactory prayer brushes the cross aside, or he may remove a crucifix that he has been wearing. Some Hamlets leave a token that the king (to his great distress) finds when he stops praying. Among the things that Hamlet has left in stage productions are a coxcomb that the antic Hamlet has worn, a gown that he has worn, or a weapon. In some productions Claudius puts down his own sword before kneeling to pray, Hamlet, unseen, removes the sword, and Claudius discovers the loss when he has finished praying.

3.4 This is the famous "closet" scene, almost always staged as a bedroom scene, but a closet is merely a private room (as opposed, for instance, to an audience chamber) and it therefore need not contain a bed. The Freudian reading (Hamlet, endowed with an Oedipus complex, desires to kill his father and sleep with his mother, and therefore he cannot bring himself to kill the man—Claudius—who in fact has done what Hamlet himself wanted to do) is widely popular and doubtless has contributed to the strongly sexual staging that the scene often gets today. But we do not need Freud or Ernest Jones to tell us that in this scene Hamlet is intensely concerned with his mother's sexuality, and as Rosenberg points out in *The Masks of Hamlet* (1992), pre-Freudian productions often made use of a bed in this scene.

When Hamlet compares the picture of his father with the picture of Claudius, in the twentieth century he has usually pulled from his bosom a miniature of his father, and from Gertrude's bosom a miniature of Claudius (lots of room for sexuality here), but sometimes the pictures are framed canvases hanging on a wall, and sometimes they are two coins that Hamlet pulls out of his pocket. Occasionally they are not a pair; the picture of Claudius may be a framed picture on a table, and the picture of Hamlet Senior may be a miniature that Hamlet wears on a chain around his neck.

We have not discussed the question of why Hamlet delays, or (as some critics put it) *whether* he delays. The implication in this last view is that although he reproaches himself for delay (in the present scene he speaks of himself as "tardy" [110] and the Ghost speaks of Hamlet's "almost blunted purpose" [115]), Hamlet in fact acts quite vigorously, i.e., he quite reasonably and systematically must first verify the Ghost. When he has established Claudius's guilt, he promptly stabs him, or thinks he does, only to find that he has killed Polonius rather than Claudius. In this view, although Hamlet reproaches himself for delay, and the Ghost also does, both of these figures are (understandably) impatient and they do not accurately represent the facts. Then there is the Freudian view, already mentioned, that Hamlet delays because he cannot kill the man who has done what he himself wishes to do. And there is a very old no-nonsense view, attributed to Thomas Hanmer: If Hamlet acted promptly the play would end too soon, so the playwright had to find excuses for delaying the killing. Our own experience, most recently confirmed when we saw Branagh's film, is that despite the occasional reference to delay, a spectator does not (so to speak) *feel* that Hamlet delays.

Two other points about the scene, or, perhaps, one point drawing on two passages. When we merely read the play, we hear Hamlet lecture his mother at some length but we may forget that this moralizing is delivered in the presence of a bloody corpse. When we *witness* the play, the corpse can be relatively inconspicuous, e.g., behind the bed, but usually it is very conspicuous, and presumably its presence strongly colors our response to Hamlet in this scene. It can be unnerving to hear Hamlet lecture, in the presence of a bloody body. The second passage that we have in mind is his final speech in the scene, where, thinking about Rosencrantz and Guildenstern ("adders fanged") he seems to take a bit too much relish in the thought of destroying them:

> For 'tis the sport to have the enginer
> Hoist with his own petard, and 't shall go hard
> But I will delve one yard below their mines
> And blow them at the moon. O, 'tis most sweet
> When in one line two crafts directly meet.

One doesn't want to press the point too hard, but isn't it reasonable to say that this is not the mood the viewer wants Hamlet to be in when he finally brings Claudius to justice?

This entire speech, in fact, presents Hamlet in a disturbing light. Not only does he show a zesty glee about the fate he will contrive for Rosencrantz and Guildenstern—he will "blow them at the moon"—but he also speaks demeaningly, coarsely, about Polonius, whose "guts" Hamlet hauls away. Perhaps Hamlet is correct to term Polonius a "foolish prating knave," but one need not conclude that Polonius therefore deserved to be killed. Hamlet acted hastily when he thrust the sword through the arras, and, one could say, he excuses himself for his dreadful error by putting the blame on his victim. Polonius, we should remember, is not only the overbusy counselor to the King, but is also the father of Ophelia, and she (and Laertes too) suffers grievous pain because of Hamlet's bloody deed.

In some productions we have seen, Hamlet speaks the lines of this speech hysterically. He is very worked up, frenzied, distracted. There's something to be said for this approach. It removes some of the coarseness from Hamlet's words about Polonius, and some of the formality of his goodbye to his mother ("good night," he says twice—sincerely? mockingly? sorrowfully?). From this point of view, Hamlet is not in full possession of his faculties as the tremendously charged scene with his mother concludes; and so we should not pin him too literally to the words that he uses. The words matter less than the complex feelings behind the words.

Hamlet's words have also been spoken in a soft, quiet, even contrite tone, the tone thereby taking some of the harshness out of the words. In more than one production we attended, the phrase "lug the guts" was omitted.

One more point, which you may wish to mention to the class: Lines 209–17 ("There's letters sealed . . ." to ". . . two crafts directly meet") are not in F and may pose a bit of a problem. They do not seem to jibe with what Hamlet later (5.2.4ff.) reports to Horatio, where he tells of discovering the murder-order in Rosencrantz and Guildenstern's papers. How, one wonders, has he found the "letters sealed," to which he refers?

The play is filled with intriguing puzzles of this kind. Some of them are hard (if not impossible) to resolve; others, it seems, can be resolved with interpretive effort and ingenuity. We try to find moments during class to bring up examples of the play's textual cruxes and perplexities—we mention a number of them in this commentary. It is important to explain to students what a Shakespeare play is—that an edition of the play that we read is the result of a demanding editorial process that involves the study of texts and manuscripts often filled with mysteries and contradictions. But we need to remind ourselves that *Hamlet* is a big challenge for students, and it may be risky to linger too much over this or that textual problem or issue. When we teach the play, we find that the students do best when they keep their attention on the main lines of character development and organizing themes.

4.1 It is impossible to know if Gertrude really believes Hamlet is "mad as the sea and wind" (line 7) or if she is covering for Hamlet. Similarly, her assertion that Hamlet "weeps for what is done" (27) cannot be verified. But what is especially interesting about this short, urgent scene is the growing separation between Claudius and his queen. In line 28 he says, "O Gertrude, come away!"; in line 38, "Come Gertrude"; in line 44, "O, come away!" Throughout this speech she remains silent, presumably moved by what Hamlet has told her during the closet scene. In stage productions, if Claudius seeks to put his arm around her waist or shoulder, she usually draws away from him. Note, too, that in his last line in the scene ("My soul is full of discord and dismay") he reveals that the battle with Hamlet (and with his own conscience?) is indeed unnerving him. And why shouldn't he be unnerved? If in the prayer scene Hamlet has left with Claudius a token, for instance, a coxcomb, Claudius may now be holding it nervously.

4.2 A reader may take this scene to be chiefly one in which Hamlet verbally displays his antic disposition, but in fact the scene is filled with physical action. There are the offstage shouts, then the bustling entrance of Rosencrantz and Guildenstern, who in effect have been pursuing Hamlet. Branagh's stage direction in the script for his film gives an idea of the physical business: "They circle each other in the large room. Wary of a quick move." In the film, as in many productions, courtiers and soldiers enter, and attempts are made to lay hands on Hamlet. In Branagh's film, "Hamlet grabs Rosencrantz around the neck, taking him hostage against the growing crowd," and ultimately "Hamlet throws Rosencrantz back to the crowd." Incidentally, the last sentence in the scene, Hamlet's "Hide fox, and all after" (doubtless a line from a game of hide-and-seek) appears only in F, and it is commonly regarded, probably rightly, as an actor's addition. So again we can raise the question: What is the text of a play by Shakespeare—the play that he wrote or the play that was produced?

4.3 In line 14 we learn that Hamlet now is "guarded," and when he appears on the stage his hands may be bound, or he may be surrounded by armed guards. In Daniel Day-Lewis's production he was confined in a straitjacket. The wit battle concerning the trip to England makes it clear that Hamlet and Claudius are at war. Here is how Branagh presents this passage in his filmscript. (We do not preserve Branagh's typography, punctuation, or spelling, only his words.)

> *Claudius*: . . . Therefore prepare thyself.
> The bark is ready, and the wind at help,
> Th' associates tend, and everything is bent
> For England.
> *Hamlet*: For England!
> *Claudius*: Ay, Hamlet.
> *Hamlet*: Good.
> (*Claudius will not give in to Mr. Smart-arse.*)
> *Claudius*: So it is, if thou knew'st our purposes.
> *Hamlet*: I see a cherub that sees them. But come, for England! Farewell, dear mother.
> *Claudius*: Thy loving father, Hamlet.
> *Hamlet* (*brightly*): My mother. Father and mother is man and wife, man and wife is one flesh, and so my mother. (*This last with real hatred.*)

This is warfare, and we are not surprised to hear, a few moments later, the king confess in a soliloquy that he has ordered "the present [i.e., instant] death of Hamlet." In our view (here we tip our hand) it is entirely appropriate at the end of the play for Fortinbras to order the soldiers to treat Hamlet as a soldier who died doing his duty: "Let four captains, / Bear Hamlet, like a soldier, to the stage. . . . "

4.4 This scene (along with Fortinbras's other scenes) is often deleted in productions, but it is an important scene, not only because it shows a contrast between Fortinbras in command and Hamlet in custody, but, of course, because of the great soliloquy in which Hamlet meditates on the distinction between man and beast, characterized by the human being's possession of (a) rationality and (b) a sense of honor. These two qualities may be in conflict; rationality may cause us to think carefully (we may find ourselves "thinking too precisely on th' event"), whereas our sense of honor may cause us to act impetuously, even rashly. Hamlet praises Fortinbras as a man of action, but notice how some of the diction in his speech quietly undermines the praise. Expressions such as "divine ambition puffed," "eggshell," "straw," "fantasy and trick of fame" make the hearer doubt the worth of the quarrel motivated by honor. True, the speech ends strongly: "O, from this time forth / My thoughts be bloody or be nothing worth!" yet even here, in "bloody," we may have mixed feelings about what Hamlet apparently is praising.

4.5 The scene begins with the queen, obviously agitated ("I will not speak with her"), seeking to put off an encounter with Ophelia, partly of course to avoid a stressful situation, but partly because the queen herself is almost distraught (in line 17 she speaks of her "sick soul"). Perhaps the Gentleman's speech describing the mad Ophelia is meant to prepare the viewers, lest they laugh when they next see her. What has driven Ophelia mad? Among the possible causes: (1) the death of her father, at the hands of the man she loved; (2) Hamlet's rejection of her; and (3) guilt at the thought that, on her father's order, she betrayed Hamlet.

In 1.4.90 Marcellus had said, "Something is rotten in the state of Denmark," and the truth of his remark is everywhere in evidence here—in Ophelia's madness, in Gertrude's soul-sickness, in Claudius's uneasiness in this scene ("Where is my Switzers? Let them guard the door" he calls out when he hears "a noise outside"). In fact, when Claudius speaks to Gertrude and enumerates the causes of Ophelia's madness, saying, "When sorrows come, they come not single spies, / But in battalions," we can rightly take his words to apply to his own distress, we might say his dis-ease. And notice, too, in this speech, how Claudius is becoming isolated from his wife. Twice he addresses her, once near the beginning of the speech and once near the end ("O Gertrude, Gertrude," "O my dear Gertrude") but he gets no response from her. (A bit later, however, Gertrude seizes Laertes in order to protect Claudius.)

We need comment only briefly on Laertes here. It is obvious that his angry words about the death of his father can be compared and contrasted with Hamlet's:

> How came he dead? I'll not be juggled with.
> To hell, allegiance! Vows to the profoundest devil!
> Conscience and grace, to the profoundest pit!
> I dare damnation. To this point I stand.
> That both the worlds I give to negligence,
> Let come what comes, only I'll be revenged
> Most thoroughly for my father.

Having seen Claudius work his charms upon Laertes in 1.2, we are not surprised to see that Claudius can easily disarm this angry young man, indeed partly by the same device of unctuously repeating Laertes's name:

>   What is thy cause, Laertes,
> That thy rebellion looks so giantlike?
> Let him go, Gertrude. Do not fear our person.
> There's such divinity doth hedge a king
> That treason can but peep to what it would,
> Acts little of his will. Tell me, Laertes,
> Why thou are thus incensed. Let him go, Gertrude.
> Speak, man.

Claudius calms Laertes, assures him that the crown is innocent, and that justice will be done. Claudius's last words in the scene are, "And where th' offense is, let the great ax fall." At the end of the play we will see that the ax falls on Claudius as well as on the others, innocent and guilty.

4.6 Hamlet's letter (in prose, as usual) reveals a confident tone, and it reports energetic action—in effect it refutes the idea that Hamlet is someone who cannot act decisively. Also noteworthy is the fact that Hamlet tells Horatio to give the letter (his word is "letters," but the plural form regularly has a singular sense) to the king, i.e., Hamlet does not contrive to make an unexpected appearance. As we will see in subsequent passages, his mood now differs from his earlier moods; he now is beyond contriving. Incidentally, in the next scene Claudius assures Laertes that Laertes can use an unbated foil without Hamlet noticing it because Hamlet is "Most generous, and free from all contriving."

4.7 The dialogue between Laertes and Claudius, or especially the portion beginning after Hamlet's letter and continuing up to the entrance of the queen, is a bit long, but students can perform it effectively in class. Laertes is not exactly dumb, but he is no match for the Machiavellian Claudius, and one almost feels sorry for him when Claudius says, "Can you devise me?" and Laertes replies, "I am lost in it, my lord." A moment later, when Claudius says, "Will you be ruled by me?" Laertes replies, "Ay, my lord, / So you will not o'errule me to a peace," and of course peace is the last thing that Claudius has in mind for Laertes. Claudius flatters Laertes ("You have been talked of since your travel much, / And that in Hamlet's hearing"), telling him that Lamord's report of Laertes "Did Hamlet so envenom with his envy / That he could nothing do but wish and beg / Your sudden coming o'er to play with you. / Now, out of this—" and Laertes, who has not quite followed what Claudius is getting at, rather simply asks, "What out of this, my lord?" Notice that Claudius does not directly answer the question, but instead keeps Laertes in suspense, and whets his appetite, by asking, "Laertes, was your father dear to you? One cannot help admiring Claudius, so skilled is he in manipulating the impetuous young man. Claudius continues, bringing up again the motif of action that may dissolve into nothing ("Time qualifies the spark"). Laertes assures Claudius that he would "cut [Hamlet's] throat in' the church," a sentiment seconded by the murderer Claudius, who piously observes that "No place, indeed, should murder sanctuarize." And then on to a passage we mentioned a moment ago, when Claudius rightly says that Hamlet, being "generous, and free from all contriving, / Will not peruse the foils." True, earlier Hamlet had been engaged in contriving, but when he returns from the sea journey he is changed for the better, willing to act at the right moment ("the readiness is all") but not plotting to establish the conditions of the moment.

If one wants to talk about *hamartia*, one can say that Hamlet is guilty of a "tragic error" (he does not peruse the foils), but certainly this error or mistake proceeds not from a flaw in character but from a virtue. In contrast to Hamlet's virtue is Laertes's dishonorable behavior; Claudius has suggested using an unbated foil, and Laertes not only consents to using it but adds that he will also poison the tip. Claudius then suggests that as a backup he will prepare a poisoned chalice. Surely it makes no sense to see Hamlet as flawed when one sees villainy such as this.

Laertes is (from the spectators' view) at a low point, but the report of Ophelia's death does get some sympathy for him. The audience's response, however, is probably complex. We sympathize, and perhaps are even touched by his grief, but we also know that the reason why he does *not* utter the "speech of fire" that blazes within him is that he is confident he will kill Hamlet in the duel.

5.1 The dialogue between the clowns is amusing even when it is acted by amateurs, and even when it is delivered to people not familiar with the footnotes. But why does Shakespeare include in this dialogue passages insisting on

Hamlet's age? Doubtless he wanted to convey the irony inherent in the fact that Hamlet was born on the very day that the gravedigger began his trade—it is almost as though the gravedigger has all this time been digging in anticipation of Hamlet's death—and Shakespeare also wanted to connect Hamlet's birth with the triumph of Hamlet's father over Fortinbras. Still, why did Shakespeare insist on Hamlet's age? Perhaps he wanted to emphasize Hamlet's maturity, lest the audience think too much about Hamlet as the moody student of 1.1.

We want to talk a bit about Hamlet's famous leap into the grave—a leap that maybe he does not make. Certainly Laertes leaps into the grave first. Laertes's dialogue clearly calls for his leap, and stage directions in Q1 and F confirm it. He says, "Hold off the earth awhile, / Till I have caught her once more in mine arms" and then, after leaping into the grave, he says, "Now pile your dust upon the quick and dead." Hamlet's leap is far less clearly established; in fact, it depends entirely on a stage direction a bit later in Q1, a so-called "Bad Quarto": "Hamlet leaps in after Laertes." This direction, not in Q2 or F, may well merely reflect a provincial production. It is attractive in some ways, since the leap into the grave can be taken as a sort of symbolic entrance into death, and the leap out as a sort of renewal of life. On the other hand, it serves to make Hamlet the aggressor, and many students of the play wish to see in the Hamlet who has returned from the sea journey a new, mature Hamlet, a Hamlet who proclaims his kingly identity with "This is I, / Hamlet the Dane." (Cf. Claudius's earlier use of "the Dane" to mean the king, when he says to Laertes, in 1.2, "You cannot speak of reason to the Dane, / and lose your voice."

Further, the dialogue pretty clearly indicates that Laertes is the aggressor. Hamlet says, "I prithee, take thy fingers from my throat," and "Hold off thy hand," perhaps indicating that Hamlet's mere announcement that he is "the Dane" has caused Laertes to climb out of the grave and to seize him. Such is the way the episode is staged in Branagh's film. Somewhat strangely, Laertes has no lines in this scene after he and Hamlet are separated, even though Hamlet directly addresses him, for instance with "Hear you, sir, / What is the reason that you use me thus?" (By the way, one may wonder how Hamlet can be unaware of why Laertes is enraged.) In some performances, Hamlet offers a hand or arm to Laertes, who angrily (and silently) rejects the offer. In other performances, Laertes is still being restrained by those who separated him a moment ago during the fight. You may want to invite students to talk about how they would stage the fight and the remainder of the scene.

5.2 We spend a lot of time discussing this scene in class, much of it on the question of whether Hamlet's change of mood after the sea journey is (to put the matter crudely) a Good Thing or a Bad Thing. Our own view is that he has brought himself into the proper frame of mind, proper in that it ultimately is satisfactory to the spectator. That is, he pretty much ceases to be the bloodthirsty avenger, the man scheming and at the same time upbraiding himself for not accomplishing his purposes. He becomes, in our view (speaking a bit broadly), the man who rightly understands that he has a task to fulfill and that he *will* fulfill it, but in a way not yet known to him. The Ghost had enjoined him, "Taint not thy mind" (1.5.86) but we have seen that Hamlet in his bloodthirsty moments, and especially in his desire to catch the king's soul, comes close to violating this command. Even the passage at the end of 3.4, when he contemplates with pleasure outwitting and destroying Rosencrantz and Guildenstern, has a disturbing edge to it:

> For 'tis the sport to have the enginer
> Hoist with his own petard, and 't shall go hard
> But I will delve one yard below their mines
> And blow them at the moon.

Now, however, in the final act his mood is different. In his second speech in 5.2 he tells Horatio that he acted rashly:

> Rashly
> And praised be rashness for it—let us know
> Our indiscretion sometimes serves us well
> When our deep plots do pall, and that should learn us
> There's a divinity that shapes our ends,
> Rough-hew them how we will. . . .

Telling Horatio about the letter ordering his death, he rightly says:

> Being thus benetted round with villains,
> Or I could make a prologue to my brains,
> They had begun the play

Thus, in a situation *not of his own making* (just as his initial situation—the death of his father and the remarriage of his mother—was not of his making), he responds more or less spontaneously, i.e., without the calculated villainy that characterizes a Machiavellian. His response, a forged letter that sends Rosencrantz and Guildenstern to death, has distressed some commentators, but we confess that our own uneasiness is *very* slight. In the traditional legend, Hamlet contrives a successful revenge, and obviously in Shakespeare's play there are traces of Hamlet as an intriguer. But in Shakespeare's play, interestingly, most of Hamlet's intriguing comes to nothing. The obvious exception is the execution of Rosencrantz and Guildenstern, but whatever uneasiness a spectator or reader might have about their end is diminished: (a) The deaths are reported, not seen; (b) we have little sympathy for the two victims; (c) Hamlet is acting under great pressure, with his own life at stake; (d) asked by Horatio how Hamlet "sealed" the letter, Hamlet replies, "Why, even in that was heaven ordinant," and we are inclined to believe him (more about this in a moment); and (e) no one in the play expresses grief over the deaths of Rosencrantz and Guildenstern. Horatio's dry comment probably expresses much the audience's sentiment: "So Guildenstern and Rosencrantz go to 't."

What about this business of heaven being "ordinant"? The play (unlike *Lear*) is set in a Christian world, with a ghost from purgatory, talk of "our Savior's birth," and so on. When we experience this play, do we strongly feel a divine providence? *Hamlet* is not a medieval biblical play with a heaven-sent avenging angel. On the whole, things seem to work out on a purely naturalistic level. And yet, the Ghost gives Hamlet information that is otherwise unknown; the traveling players appear from nowhere, so to speak, allowing Hamlet to confirm the Ghost's message; during the sea voyage Hamlet, unable to sleep, is mysteriously prompted to examine the commission from Claudius; he forges a different commission and providentially (he says) is able to seal it with the king's signet; a pirate ship comes out of nowhere, and Hamlet alone boards it; Laertes and Claudius, *not* Hamlet, prepare the unbated poisoned foil that will enable Hamlet to fulfill his revenge; this fulfillment is accomplished publicly, in circumstances arranged not by Hamlet but by Claudius. (Whether Hamlet holds the poisoned rapier by chance or not is something we will look at in a moment.) We do *not* want to say anything to the effect that the play shows God is always at work in the world in mysterious ways, but we do want to say that in some mysterious way things work out, and that Hamlet fulfills his revenge without becoming a villainous avenger.

We have not yet looked at several speeches in 5.2, after Osric's departure, in which Hamlet seems to some commentators to have achieved an inner peace (in contrast, for instance, to the end of the soliloquy in 4.4, when he says, "O, from this time forth / My thoughts be bloody or be nothing worth!"). To other commentators, however, these speeches indicate that he has lapsed into further inaction, inaction that he masks as resignation to heaven's will. The two most explicit passages are:

(1) I am constant to my purposes; they follow the King's pleasure. If his fitness speaks, mine is ready; now or whensover, provided I be so able as now.

(2) Not a white, we defy augury. There is special providence in the fall of a sparrow. If it be now, 'tis not to come, it will be now; if it be not now, yet it will come. The readiness is all.

In the second speech, the line about the "special providence in the fall of a sparrow" echoes Matthew 10.29: "Not a sparrow shall fall on the ground without your Father's knowledge." Writing about this passage, A. C. Bradley (in *Shakespearean Tragedy* [1904]) said that he did *not* find "any material change in [Hamlet's] general condition or the formation of any effective resolution to fulfill the appointed duty. On the contrary [the speech and some other speeches] seem to express that kind of religious resignation which, however beautiful in one aspect, really deserves the name of fatalism rather than of faith in Providence." H. B. Charlton, essentially a Bradleyite, in his own *Shakespearean Tragedy* (1949) says pretty much the same thing:

Worst of all, recognition of the will's impotence is accepted as . . . the calm attainment of a higher benignity, whereas it is nothing more than a fatalist's surrender of personal responsibility. That is the nadir of Hamlet's fall. (103)

We see the point, but we differ. We don't know how either of the two contrasting views (Hamlet as lapsing in fatalism vs. Hamlet as achieving a heightened state of awareness) can ever be proved to the satisfaction of those who begin by holding the other view, but it seems to us that Hamlet's move from blood-thirsty plotting to an awareness that he must make himself ready to act when the right moment comes represents progress. Further, his apology to Laertes indicates a healthier state of mind than he has sometimes earlier displayed. And what of his comment, shortly before the duel, that the culprit was not Hamlet but "Hamlet's madness"? We are uneasy here. Is he lying? If so, his behavior is reprehensible. We prefer to think he now understands that indeed some of his earlier behavior (his cruel rejection of Ophelia comes to our minds) was the result of an emotional stress that caused him to behave in ways that would be shameful for a rational person. Remember, too, that we in the audience know, but Hamlet does not know, that the man to whom he is apologizing is prepared to murder Hamlet. Surely the spectator's response during this speech when Hamlet shifts some of the blame for his actions to his madness is not condemnation of Hamlet for evading responsibility, but wonder about what Laertes's response will be. And what is Laertes's response? This man who is planning to use a poisoned foil insists in a fatuous and finicky way that he can accept Hamlet's apology only provisionally, and that before he can be certain that Hamlet's apology leaves Laertes's honor unbesmirched, he will consult "some elder masters of known honor." An audience that responds intelligently to Laertes's twisted sense of honor can hardly judge Hamlet adversely.

The duel between Hamlet and Laertes perhaps brings to mind thoughts of the conflict between Hamlet Senior and Fortinbras, an honorable battle, in the heroic manner, that contrasts strongly with the treachery that underlies the present encounter. Exactly what happens in this final duel is a bit uncertain. Does Hamlet, wounded by Laertes's unbated foil, suddenly realize that Laertes is out to kill him, and does he therefore wrest the weapon from Laertes's hand? Q1 (the "Bad Quarto") says, *They catch one anothers Rapiers, and both are wounded, Laertes falles downe, the Queene falles downe and dies.* The Folio says, *In scuffling they change Rapiers.* Q2, a good quarto, has no stage direction here. The problem, then, is this: Do they exchange rapiers because Hamlet knows that Laertes holds an unbated rapier? Or does the exchange result from chance, from a scuffle in which the weapons are accidentally exchanged? Is this fatal exchange one of "accidental judgments, casual slaughters" ("casual" from the Latin *casus*, "chance") that Horatio will mention when he tells Fortinbras what has just occurred?

Olivier in his film has Laertes thrust at Hamlet and draw blood. Hamlet, realizing that Laertes's foil is unbated, in the next round knocks the foil out of Laertes's hand, retrieves it for his own use, and gives Laertes the blunt-tipped foil. Branagh in his film has Laertes rush at Hamlet, nick Hamlet's shoulder, then run past him, stop, and face him. After a few seconds of slow circling, *"suddenly it's a free-for-all, and now Hamlet chases Laertes round the hall, in amongst the crowd. . . . A great leap from Hamlet trips Laertes up. His sword skids away. Hamlet rushes for it. He looks at the tip—enraged. He throws his own sword to Laertes and retains the poisoned one."*

Laertes confesses his treachery ("The foul practice / Hath turned itself on me"), blames the king, and says Claudius "is justly served," thus publicly vindicating Hamlet. "Exchange forgiveness with me, noble Hamlet," Laertes says, and we take seriously the word "noble." As we have earlier said at some length, Hamlet fulfills the Ghost's command, and—remarkably—he does so in a way that does not taint him with murder.

Horatio summarizes the "woe and wonder" (standard characteristics of heroic tragedy) that Denmark has witnessed:

> So shall you hear
> Of carnal, bloody, and unnatural acts,
> Of accidental judgments, casual slaughters,
> Of deaths put on by cunning and forced cause,
> And, in this upshot, purposes mistook
> Fall'n on th' inventors' heads.

"Purposes mistook" are evident: Laertes prepares a foil to poison Hamlet, but he himself dies by that foil; the king prepares a poisoned drink for Hamlet, but Gertrude drinks it, and ultimately Hamlet forces the king to drink it. The "carnal" and "unnatural acts" may include Gertrude's incest; the "casual slaughters" may include the murder of Polonius and the drowning of Ophelia. But we need not try to identify each of Horatio's words with a particular happening in the play. It is enough, we think, to see that Hamlet, thrust into a tragic situation that is *not* of his own making, has at last performed the arduous task that he was ordered to do. T. S. Eliot, in "Shakespeare and the Stoicism of Seneca," a bit snidely says that Hamlet, having made a mess, "dies fairly well pleased with himself." In our view, Eliot misunderstands the play, partly because he does not see that Hamlet has indeed been successful (though at a terrible cost), and partly because he does not realize that it is appropriate for the tragic figure to make a dying speech in which he sums up his essence. (Othello has been similarly criticized for, in Eliot's words, "cheering himself up.") Many of your students will know *Macbeth*, so you may want to remind them that we get a report of the final speech made by the traitor Cawdor, just before he was executed: "Very frankly he confessed his treasons, / Implored your Highness' pardon and set forth / A deep repentance: nothing in his life / Became him like the leaving it."

The play ends with Fortinbras ("strong arm," the man of action) awarding Hamlet a salute from the cannon ("*a peal of ordnance is shot off*"), a military tribute to a heroic figure, a tribute to a man who, though he apparently preferred the meditative life associated with the university, nevertheless fulfilled a tremendously demanding task. When we hear the sounds of the cannon at the end of the play, we may recall that earlier in the play the cannon was set off when the base king drank. Now at the end, it is evident that Denmark has been purged of a criminal king, by a man who "was most likely, had he been put on, / To have proved most royal."

27

Comedy

Among useful books on comedy are Louis Kronenberger, *The Thread of Laughter* (1952); L. J. Potts, *Comedy* (1948); Morton Gurewitch, *Comedy* (1975); and D. H. Munro, *Argument of Laughter* (1951), on theories of the comic. Two interesting anthologies of essays on comedy are *Comedy*, ed. Robert W. Corrigan (1965), and *Theories of Comedy*, ed. Paul Lauter (1964).

For bibliographic suggestions about *A Midsummer Night's Dream*, see the note at the end of this commentary on the play.

WILLIAM SHAKESPEARE

A Midsummer Night's Dream (p. 1223)

We have taught this play many times, have seen a number of productions, and have read a fair amount of criticism, so we can't resist discussing the play here at some length. No claim is made for the originality of any of the following comments; they draw on numerous published writings and productions, but we can no longer cite their source. We want to mention, however, that some of our best class hours have been when neither we nor the students talked about the play, but when the students acted out a scene or a portion of a scene. We usually choose a passage that will take about 10 or 15 minutes to perform, photocopy the pages, write some notes suggesting bits of business, and then put a student in charge as the director. The performers are told to study the parts individually, and then to meet at least twice to rehearse under the supervision of the director. (The students are not expected to memorize the part; they perform while reading from the text. On the day that you choose the students for the performance, it's best to set a time for rehearsals; if the times are not set at once, it will be hard to get a time when they can agree.) On the first occasion that we set up a performance, we ask for volunteers, and we usually get some people who have had some experience performing, but for later scenes we sometimes draft students, though we give students the opportunity to decline if they strongly feel that they don't want to perform. We have almost never had a student refuse; and, perhaps oddly, the draftees are just about as good as the volunteers.

We have had particularly good luck with performances of 1.2 (the mechanicals meet to get parts for *Pyramus and Thisbe*) and with 4.1.49 to the end of the scene (Titania awakens, the lovers are awakened, and Bottom awakens). In the following scene-by-scene discussion, when we get to these two scenes we will talk a little about some stage business that we suggest to the students.

The title: The reference is to the summer solstice (the longest day of the year), around June 23, but in fact the play is set in May. Still, the holiday of Midsummer Night is appropriate since this day was associated with magic (herbs gathered on this night could charm), with lovers' dreams, and with madness.

1.1 In class we go over this entire scene, line by line, or, rather, speech by speech. It's our impression that our students do not find the process dull. Truth to tell, they seem to enjoy it immensely. If asked questions about some of the ways in which the lines work, they usually come up with very perceptive answers.

The play begins (and ends) in what passes for the real world, that is, Athens, a city that supposedly stands for reason and law. Theseus (accent on the first syllable)—the highest ranking character—speaks first, in blank verse (the form that he and Hippolyta always use, except in the fifth act, where they sometimes speak in prose). (Shakespeare does a good deal to give different kinds of speech to the different kinds of characters. The young lovers in the wood will use rhyme, the fairies will use songs, and the mechanicals will use prose.)

In his first speech Theseus introduces the motif of marriage—and also of the moon—and though he is a mature rather than an impetuous lover, he conveys impatience at having to wait for the "nuptial hour." His comparison of himself—presumably a man of some years—to a "young man" is amusing and probably true to nature. (What older man in love thinks of himself as other than youthful? Probably also true to nature is the impatience and self-centeredness glanced at in the man's conception that the stepmother or widow is "withering out" what belongs to the young man.) We read this speech aloud, discuss it, and then ask a student to read it again, so that students can hear the tones—the affection in "fair Hippolyta," the enthusiasm in "four happy days," and the pained longing in "but, O, methinks." (Speaking of longing, notice the long vowels in "O," "methinks," "slow," "old," and "moon.") In short, this is the time when we begin to talk about the marvelous flexibility of Shakespeare's blank verse.

Hippolyta in her reply introduces the motif of dreaming, with its suggestion of unreality, reinforces the motif of the moon, and in the figure of the "silver bow" manages to suggest Diana and also to suggest her own Amazon nature. Her speech ends with a reference to "solemnities," a word which, combined with Theseus's reference (a line and a half later) to "merriments," pretty much gives us the tone of the play: Marriage is both a solemn and a merry affair.

In 15–18 we learn that Theseus and Hippolyta, now representatives of maturity, law, and order, were once combatants. Theseus's "I won thy love, doing thee injuries" introduces the motif of strange transformations. The chief of these are the transformations that the lovers undergo, that Titania's mind undergoes, and that Bottom undergoes, but there are other transformations; for instance, Hermia's defiance of her father turns his love to hate or at least to anger. Another word about the earlier histories of Theseus and Hippolyta: We hear, in 2.1.65, that Hippolyta has had some sort of affair with Oberon and that Theseus was once a seducer and a rapist. By the time we have finished with the play, we can reasonably feel that Shakespeare is saying something about youthful lawless passion turning into something more decorous. In any case, Theseus's war with Hippolyta has turned into love, and so too the quarreling young lovers will ultimately be reconciled.

Into this picture of loving harmony wrought out of strife, with its promise of solemn joy ("With pomp, with triumph, and with reveling"), comes Egeus (accent on the second syllable), "Full of vexation." He is almost inarticulate—comically so—with rage: "Thou, thou, Lysander, thou hast given her rhymes . . ." (28), and he too speaks of "love" (29), "moonlight" (30), and "fantasy" (32). As in much comedy descended from Greek New Comedy, he insists that a harsh law be enforced. The play ultimately will brush this law aside, and Athens will thus be transformed from a constricting place to a newly enlarged and newly happy society.

His words are harsh—"As she is mine, I may dispose of her"—but they are in accord with the law (44), and Theseus at this stage can only try to persuade Hermia to obey her father. Theseus is paternalistic but very different from the irascible and tyrannical Egeus. He speaks more gently than Egeus, and he ends by saying (one hears kindness in his tone) "Demetrius is a worthy gentleman." To Hermia's pert response ("So is Lysander") Theseus continues to try to speak in kindly fashion: "In himself he is; / But in this kind, wanting your father's voice, / The other must be held the worthier." Hermia persists ("I would my father looked but with my eyes"), and Theseus patiently tries again, picking up Hermia's words: "Rather your eyes must with his judgement look." Why is Hermia so bold? She herself does not know ("I know not by what power I am made bold"), but we do—the power of love.

Theseus at some length, and with some gentleness, sets forth the grim possibilities that await Hermia, and we feel that although he represents order and maturity, and although he is well-meaning and his speech is beautiful, the choice he now offers is monstrous. He himself is aware that it is harsh, and he urges her to "Take time to pause," and he manages to introduce a reference to his own forthcoming marriage.

Lysander makes the point that Demetrius "Made love to Nedar's daughter, Helena," and so it is appropriate that the play ends with Demetrius paired with Helena, and Lysander with Hermia. As Puck will say, "Jack shall have Jill." Theseus, that embodiment of reason and authority, confesses that he has heard of Demetrius's behavior and has been negligent in speaking to him, but notice that in line 115 he invites Egeus also to a conference, for some "private schooling." One can assume that Theseus will do what he can to persuade Egeus to relent—though we never get such a scene.

Left alone, Lysander and Hermia engage in a charming duet to the effect that "The course of true love never did run smooth"—a motif that we will see exemplified in the play. As these youthful lovers exchange their patterned lines

("O cross," "Or else," "O spite," "Or else") it is hard not to smile at them, not to think of them as charming puppets, but they are scarcely objects of severe satire. If we smile at them, we also sympathize with them, even as they talk prettily about tragic love stories. One of the things that is especially interesting here is that Shakespeare introduces tragic motifs into this comedy. Lines 140–49 would not be out of place in *Romeo and Juliet*. Our point: *MSND* is a comedy of love, but Shakespeare gives us a glimpse of the tragedy of love— and later, in the story of *Pyramus and Thisbe*, he will give us a glimpse of the comedy of the tragedy of love.

And so these two eager lovers, who in line 152 talk of exhibiting "patience," immediately decide to run away from "the sharp Athenian law" (162) to the "wood" (165), the realm which Northrop Frye has called "the green world," that enchanted place that occupies the middle of so many comedies—before the lovers troop back to the ordinary world. One notices that this wood is associated (1.1.167) with an "observance to a morn of May," that is, with May Day, a holiday of love. Hermia's longish speech (168–78), in which she vows true love, interestingly is filled with references to the fragility of love, notably Aeneas's betrayal of Dido.

One should notice, too, the pairs of rhyming lines in 171–78. Although for the most part the young lovers speak blank verse, we can say that couplets are one of their characteristic idioms. Notice that the couplets continue with Helena's entrance, and they go on to the end of the scene.

In Helena's long, final speech in this scene, it's worth pointing out that when she says, "Things base and vile, holding no quantity, / Love can transpose to form and dignity," Helena might almost be describing Titania's infatuation with Bottom. It's also worth pointing out that although in *A Midsummer Night's Dream* love's obsessiveness is comic, it can be tragic elsewhere. (Some students will know *Romeo and Juliet* or *Othello*.)

1.2 If the talk of tragic love in the first scene conceivably caused a viewer to think that perhaps the play would be a tragedy, this comic scene makes it clear that the play is a comedy. Although the play of *Pyramus and Thisbe* is a tragic tale demonstrating that "the course of true love never did run smooth," we can be assured that with these performers the play (and the larger play in which it is embedded) will afford laughter. Notice too, near the end of the scene, that Quince tells his fellows that they will meet "in the palace wood . . . by moonlight," thus assuring us that the story of these rustics will somehow be connected to that of the lovers.

This is one of the scenes (the other is 4.1) that we usually ask students to perform in class. It calls for six performers, and although the roles are all male, there is no reason not to use women. On the photocopies that we give the actors and the director, we suggest that at the beginning of the scene the performers huddle close together (they are insecure), until Bottom confidently and grandly says "Masters, spread yourselves." We also suggest that Bottom is a know-it-all, and that in his second speech ("First, good Peter Quince") his manner is somewhat that of a teacher lecturing to children. In "A very good piece of work" he sounds rather pompous. When he comes to discussing the part of the lover ("If I do it, let the audience look to their eyes") he is perhaps not so much pompous as childishly enthusiastic and self-satisfied. (Again, our practice is to scribble suggestions of this sort on the photocopies, in order to give inexperienced readers some help, but other instructors may want to leave everything up to the students.) Presumably he recites the grotesque verse ("The raging rocks") in what he considers a lofty vein, and then, pleased with his performance, he congratulates himself ("This was lofty!") but then briskly turns back to the business at hand: "Now name the rest of the players." Still, he can't quite forget his noble performance, so he immediately adds, "This is Ercles' vein, tyrant's vein."

Other points about this scene: Flute's "I have a beard coming" should probably be said in a whimpering tone, perhaps while he feels his face. Bottom's "Well, proceed," may be uttered in a hurt tone, though Bottom regains his enthusiasm when he expresses the desire to play the lion too. When Quince insists that Bottom play only Pyramus, he is flattering Bottom as he describes the role ("for Pyramus is a sweet-faced man," etc.), and Bottom accepts, but a bit unhappily ("Well, I will undertake it"). Near the very end of the scene, Bottom's "adieu" is perhaps said rather dramatically. Quince then adds a remark, but Bottom must have the last line: "Enough; hold or cut bow strings" (perhaps the "Enough" is accompanied by the gesture of raising his hand authoritatively). Bottom is an ass, but a likeable ass despite his bullying. One thing that makes him likeable is his utter confidence, whether among mortals or fairies.

2.1 "Puck" is not really the character's name; rather, he is "the Puck," that is, "the spook" or "the pixy" (the words probably are all related). Since he is reputed to be mischievous, he is propitiated by being called "Goodfellow," just as the Furies in Greek mythology are called the Eumenides ("the well-meaning ones"). In this play, Puck is turned into something like Cupid, that is, a blind force (he errs in applying the juice of the flower) that overrides reason. One should note, however, that although Theseus describes the power of the herb in 2.1.170–73, we have already seen this power at work in Hermia, who defied her father, and we have heard how it turned Demetrius from Helena to Hermia. The herb, then, is merely a sort of concrete embodiment of what we already know exists.

This scene set in the wood—traditionally a place of unreason—makes a contrast with the Athens of the first scene, though, truth to tell, despite Theseus's attempts to reason with Hermia, Athens did not seem very reasonable. In any case, the fairies' song marks the place as something very different from the blank verse world of Theseus or the prose world of the rustics.

The fuss about the changeling (20–31) is a bit of a puzzle. Why is Oberon so eager to get the boy? Perhaps the idea is that since the child is male, he belongs ultimately in the male world, and so when Titania yields the boy we see something comparable to the proper pairing of the lovers, to Jack having Jill. That is, order is restored, things are at last in their proper places. Perhaps one can go further, and say that Oberon's triumph over Titania is the proper (in the Elizabethan view) triumph of male will over female will, something comparable to Theseus's triumph over the Amazon Hippolyta. The trouble with this reading, however, is that surely readers and viewers side with Titania, who is loyal to her dead companion, and we probably see Oberon as a sort of spoiled child who petulantly wants the toy of another child.

Titania's accusations (65–73) that Oberon has courted Phillida and has some sort of attachment to Hippolyta give rise to Oberon's charge that Titania has favored Theseus. What is especially important here is the picture of Theseus as rapist and betrayer (78–80). The Theseus that we see in the play is a well-meaning, fair-minded, and self-restrained lover, but we are reminded that even this courtly figure has a badly tarnished history.

2.2 Again the fairies speak in a characteristic form (song). Titania is put to sleep with song, and she will be awakened by song—Bottom's raucous singing. (Later the young lovers will be put to sleep by fairy song and will be awakened by mortal music.) If you read passages aloud in class, don't neglect the opportunity to read 34–61, in which Hermia fends off Lysander. Lysander speaks romantically ("One turf shall serve as pillow for us both, / One heart, one bed, two bosoms, and one troth") but Hermia is not taken in: "Lie further off." One further point about this scene: Although in 2.1 Puck says he is mischievous (43–57), he is not being mischievous when he anoints the eyes of the wrong lover. Oberon has told him he will recognize the youth by his Athenian clothes, so the mistake is an honest one.

3.1 Bottom's faith that a prologue will diminish the power of the illusion that *Pyramus and Thisbe* will create allows instructors to talk about dramatic illusion, the power of art, realism versus convention, and soon we inevitably get into some of this, but we usually make a point of reading some of the scene's lines for laughs. And we always read Bottom's song, Titania's line when she awakens, and on through Bottom's "Reason and love keep little company together."

3.2 Puck's lines in 110–21 can hardly be neglected. It's worth discussing the most famous line, "Lord, what fools these mortals be." Is this Shakespeare's judgment on humanity? (No, it's the comment of one character in the play—but one feels that there certainly is *something* to it.) One can easily get into a discussion of engagement and detachment in drama, and of Horace Walpole's famous comment that life is a comedy to those who think, a tragedy to those who feel. That is, if one *feels* for the lovers (sympathizes with them), one suffers; if one *thinks* about them (i.e., if one is detached from them), they seem absurd. Also relevant is a remark (Hazlitt, if we recall) on Pope's *The Rape of the Lock*, to the effect that it is like looking through the wrong end of the telescope.

We enjoy the misunderstandings of the lovers; we can laugh at them because we scarcely *feel* their pain, and we scarcely feel their pain because Shakespeare takes care not to make their statements too powerful. The jingling couplets, for instance, help to make the lovers somewhat puppet-like.

As we mentioned a moment ago, Puck's error is innocent, not malicious. Oberon takes care to point out, when Puck talks of "damned spirits" and of those who "themselves exile from light," that "we are spirits of another sort," and he associates himself with "the Morning's love." Appropriately, then, Puck undoes his error by bringing the lovers together and by applying the juice yet again so that (in the last words of the scene) "Jack shall have Jill . . . and all shall be well."

4.1 We usually ask students to perform this scene. On the photocopies that we give the students (eleven roles, plus a horn player or trumpeter) we make suggestions along the following lines.

Bottom and Titania sleep (it's OK to sit) to one side; at the other side the four lovers sleep or sit. *Then* Puck enters from one side, Oberon from the other, and they stand by Titania and Bottom. Oberon's first line is spoken enthusiastically, the second is spoken in a more thoughtful, meditative tone. The five lines at the end of the speech are recited as a spell. Titania's waking words: The first line is spoken in a voice of awe, the second perhaps in a more puzzled way. When Oberon points to Bottom, Titania says, in a tone of revulsion, "O, how mine eyes do loathe his visage now!" "Now, when thou wak'st" is spoken to Bottom. In the next line, be sure (following the text) to take hands. No need to dance, but if the spirit moves you. . . . Titania and Bottom go off to one side, where the sleeping lovers are *not*.

Theseus's words should be spoken authoritatively but genially. (He is confident of his authority and need not be pompous.) Egeus is still the crabby old man. His first three lines here perhaps are spoken (as the fourth line indicates) in "wonder," but also in a somewhat fussy and explosive way. Certainly we hear his anger in his lines about "power" and about sleeping and dreaming, "Enough, enough, my lord; you have enough . . . They would . . . they would . . . you and me, / You . . . me." The same sputtering that we heard in the first scene of the play. Demetrius speaks with puzzlement, awe. When Bottom awakens, his "Heigh-ho" is rather like an ass's braying. And when he says "me thought I had," he puts his hand on top of his head, and feels to see if he has ass's ears. (Lots of opportunity for engaging in business here; with a good deal of trepidation he feels for the ears but of course doesn't find them, then checks once more, and then expresses great relief.) His last lines here are, of course, spoken with great self-satisfaction.

4.2 This scene brings an end to the complications of the play. The lovers are properly paired, and Bottom is restored to the theatrical company. Why, then, a fifth act? Because we in the audience know that there is to be a wedding, and because we want to see a performance of *Pyramus and Thisbe*. In short, what follows gives us not the pleasure of surprise but the pleasure of the fulfillment of expectation. Further, *Pyramus and Thisbe*—intended to be tragic—shows us how the lovers' story might have turned out but, fortunately, did not.

5.1 If one doesn't read every line of this scene aloud—and there probably isn't time to do so—one must at least read the first 26 lines, about "imagination" and its effects on "the lunatic, the lover, and the poet." As Northrop Frye somewhere says, what ability in literary criticism there is in Athens is possessed by Hippolyta (23–27). The passage is so rich that pages can be (and have been) written on it, but here we will point out only that the confident Theseus, who dismisses "antique fables," is himself an antique fable, that is, a character of legend. And if he is dismissive of "fairy toys," we have nevertheless seen fairies in this play, and we know that they attend upon his wedding. And we have seen that in dreams there is truth (e.g., Hermia's dream in 2.2 that Lysander laughed as her heart was being eaten away). Another word about Theseus: In 89–105 he sounds pretty complacent, and we probably should not try to whitewash him, but despite his self-satisfaction he makes some thoughtful points about taking a good intention for the deed.

The play-within-the-play: We have not been particularly lucky when we have had this scene performed in class. It looks easy, but it takes skillful actors to make it funny.

We can never refrain from reading Theseus's last speech, where he (presumably jocosely) acknowledges the existence of fairies ("'tis almost fairy time"), nor can we refrain from reading aloud the remainder of the play. In our general comment on 4.2 we mentioned that chiefly it fulfills our expectations—but now comes a surprise, for we probably did not expect to see the fairies again, although, come to think of it, we were told that they have come to Athens for the royal wedding. Further, their presence now reminds us that the mortal world—sometimes rational and sometimes irrational—is surrounded by a mysterious world that mortals can never comprehend. Puck speaks of the workaday world ("the heavy ploughman," "weary task," "a shroud," etc.), but these lines lead to an exorcism of evil spirits and to a benediction by Oberon and Titania. The "glimmering light" perhaps put Elizabethan viewers in mind of midsummer eve revels when torches were ignited at a "blessing fire" and were brought from the woods to the hearth to promote good luck and fertility. Finally, in Puck's last lines he suggests that the audience may regard this whole performance as a mere dream—but we have seen in this play that dreams (e.g., Bottom's) are real.

Bibliographic note: There are many valuable studies of the play, but among short introductions we especially recommend three: the chapter on the play in C. L. Barber, *Shakespeare's Festive Comedy* (1959); Frank Kermode's essay in *Stratford-upon-Avon Studies 3: The Early Shakespeare* (1961), ed. John Russell Brown and Bernard Harris, reprinted in the Signet Classic Edition of *A Midsummer Night's Dream*; and Alvin Kernan's discussion in *The Revels History of Drama in English*, Vol. 3, ed. J. Leeds Barroll et al. (1975). For a short readable book, see David P. Young, *Something of Great Constancy: The Art of "A Midsummer Night's Dream"* (1966). Also useful is a small book by Roger Warren, *A Midsummer Night's Dream: Text and Performance* (1983). Warren devotes his first 30-odd pages to a general study of the play, and the rest of the book (again about 30 pages) to an examination of several performances, from Peter Hall's 1959 production to Elijah Moshinsky's 1981 BBC Television production. If you have more time, you may want to read the essays collected by Harold Bloom in *William Shakespeare's A Midsummer Night's Dream* (1987) and study the Arden Edition of the play, ed. Harold F. Brooks (1979). This volume has a book-length introduction, detailed footnotes, and appendices on textual cruces and so forth. See also the texts and contexts included in the Bedford edition of the play, ed. Gail Kern Paster (1999).

A videocassette of Shakespeare's *A Midsummer Night's Dream* is available from Longman Publishers.

28

Two Plays about Marriage

HENRIK IBSEN

A Doll's House (p. 1281)

First, it should be mentioned that the title of the play does *not* mean that Nora is the only doll, for the toy house is not merely Nora's; Torvald, as well as Nora, inhabits this unreal world, for Torvald—so concerned with appearing proper in the eyes of the world—can hardly be said to have achieved a mature personality.

A Doll's House (1879) today seems more "relevant" than it has seemed in decades, and yet one can put too much emphasis on its importance as a critique of male chauvinism. Although the old view that Ibsen's best-known plays are "problem plays" about remediable social problems rather than about more universal matters is still occasionally heard, Ibsen himself spoke against it. In 1898, for example, he said, "I must disclaim the honor of having consciously worked for women's rights. I am not even quite sure what women's rights really are. To me it has been a question of human rights" (quoted in Michael Meyer, *Henrik Ibsen* [1967], 2:297). By now it seems pretty clear that *A Doll's House*, in Robert Martin Adams's words (in *Modern Drama* [1956], ed. A. Caputi), "represents a woman imbued with the idea of becoming a person, but it proposes nothing categorical about women becoming people; in fact, its real theme has nothing to do with the sexes. It is the irrepressible conflict of two different personalities which have founded themselves on two radically different estimates of reality." Or, as Eric Bentley puts it in *In Search of Theater* (350 in the Vintage edition, 1954), "Ibsen pushes his investigation toward a further and even deeper subject [than that of a woman's place in a man's world], the tyranny of one human being over another; in this respect the play would be just as valid were Torvald the wife and Nora the husband."

Michael Meyer's biography, *Ibsen* (1971), is good on the background (Ibsen knew a woman who forged a note to get money to aid her husband, who denounced and abandoned her when he learned of the deed), but surprisingly little has been written on the dramaturgy of the play. Notable exceptions are John Northam, "Ibsen's Dramatic Method," an essay by Northam printed in *Ibsen*, ed. Rolf Fjelde (in the Twentieth Century Views series), and Elizabeth Hardwick's chapter on the play in her *Seduction and Betrayal* (1974). Northam calls attention to the symbolic use of properties (e.g., the Christmas tree in Act I, a symbol of a secure, happy family, is in the center of the room, but in Act II, when Nora's world has begun to crumble, it is in a corner, bedraggled, and with burnt-out candles), costume (e.g., Nora's Italian costume is suggestive of pretense and is removed near the end of the play; the black shawl, symbolic of death, becomes—when worn at the end with ordinary clothes—an indication of her melancholy, lonely life), and gestures (e.g., blowing out the candles, suggesting defeat; the wild dance; the final slamming of the door).

For a collection of recent essays on the play, see *Approaches to Teaching Ibsen's "A Doll's House,"* ed. Yvonne Shafer (1985). Also of interest is Austin E. Quigley's discussion in *Modern Drama* 27 (1984): 584–605, reprinted with small changes in his *The Modern Stage and Other Worlds* (1985). Dorothea Krook, in *Elements of Tragedy* (1969), treats the play as a tragedy. She sets forth what she takes to be the four universal elements of the genre (the act of shame or horror, consequent intense suffering, then an increase in knowledge, and finally a reaffirmation of the value of life) and suggests that these appear in *A Doll's House*—the shameful condition being "the marriage relationship which creates Nora's doll's house's situation." Krook calls attention, too, to the "tragic irony" of Torvald's comments on Krogstad's immorality (he claims it poisons a household) and to Nora's terror, which, Krook says, "evokes the authentic Aristotelian pity."

One can even go a little further than Krook goes and make some connection between *A Doll's House* and *Oedipus the King*. Nora, during her years as a housewife, like Oedipus during his kingship, *thought* that she was happy but finds out that she really wasn't, and at the end of the play she goes out (self-banished), leaving her children, to face an uncertain but surely difficult future. Still, although the play can be discussed as a tragedy, and cannot be reduced to a "problem play," like many of Ibsen's other plays it stimulates a discussion of the questions, What ought to be done? and What happened next? Hermann J. Weigand, in *The Modern Ibsen* (1925), offered conjectures about Nora's future actions, saying,

> But personally I am convinced that after putting Torvald through a sufficiently protracted ordeal of suspense, Nora will yield to his entreaties and return home—on her own terms. She will not bear the separation from her children very long, and her love for Torvald, which is not as dead as she thinks, will reassert itself. For a time the tables will be reversed: a meek and chastened husband will eat out of the hand of his squirrel; and Nora, hoping to make up by a sudden spurt of zeal for twenty-eight years of lost time, will be trying desperately hard to grow up. I doubt, however, whether her volatile enthusiasm will even carry her beyond the stage of resolutions. The charm of novelty worn off, she will tire of the new game very rapidly and revert, imperceptibly, to her role of songbird and charmer, as affording an unlimited range to the exercise of her inborn talents of coquetry and playacting.

Students may be invited to offer their own conjectures on the unwritten fourth act.

Another topic for class discussion or for an essay, especially relevant to question 4 in the text: Elizabeth Hardwick suggests (*Seduction and Betrayal* [1974, 46]) that Ibsen failed to place enough emphasis on Nora's abandonment of the children. In putting "the leaving of her children on the same moral and emotional level as the leaving of her husband Ibsen has been too much a man in the end. He has taken the man's practice, if not his stated belief, that where self-realization is concerned children shall not be an impediment." But in a feminist reading of the play, Elaine Hoffman Baruch, in *Yale Review* 69 (Spring 1980), takes issue with Hardwick, arguing that "it is less a desire for freedom than a great sense of inferiority and the desire to find out more about the male world outside the home that drives Nora away from her children" (37).

Finally, one can discuss with students the comic aspects of the play—the ending (which, in a way, is happy, though Nora's future is left in doubt), and especially Torvald's fatuousness. The fatuousness perhaps reaches its comic height early in Act III, when, after lecturing Mrs. Linde on the importance of an impressive exit (he is telling her how, for effect, he made his "capricious little Capri girl" leave the room after her dance), he demonstrates the elegance of the motion of the hands while embroidering and the ugliness of the motions when knitting. Also comic are his ensuing fantasies, when he tells the exhausted Nora that he fantasizes that she is his "secret" love, though the comedy turns ugly when after she rejects his amorous advances ("I have desired you all evening"), he turns into a bully: "I'm your husband, aren't I?" The knock on the front door (Rank) reintroduces comedy, for it reduces the importunate husband to conventional affability ("Well! How good of you not to pass by the door"), but it also saves Nora from what might have been an ugly assault.

ADDITIONAL TOPICS FOR CRITICAL THINKING AND WRITING

1. To what extent is Nora a victim, and to what extent is she herself at fault for her way of life?
2. Is the play valuable only as an image of an aspect of life in the later nineteenth century, or is it still an image of an aspect of life?
3. In the earlier part of the play Nora tells Helmer, Mrs. Linde, and herself that she is happy. Is she? Explain. Why might she be happy? Why not? Can a case be made that Mrs. Linde, who must work to support herself, is happier than Nora?
4. Write a dialogue—approximately two double-spaced pages—setting forth a chance encounter when Torvald and Nora meet five years after the end of Ibsen's play.
5. Write a persuasive essay, arguing that Nora was right—or wrong—to leave her husband and children. In your essay recognize the strengths of the opposing view and try to respond to them.

CLARE BOOTHE LUCE

Slam the Door Softly (p. 1337)

In *The Quintessence of Ibsenism* Bernard Shaw argued that the mid-nineteenth-century play before Ibsen usually consisted of "an exposition in the first act, a situation in the second, and unravelling in the third." Ibsen, he said, changed all that with *A Doll's House*:

Now you have exposition, situation, and discussion; and the discussion is the test of the playwright. . . . Now the serious playwright recognizes in the discussion not only the main test of his highest powers, but also the real center of his play's interest.

"His or her," he should have said, in this analysis of the play with a thesis. Elsewhere Shaw replied to the criticism that his plays are all talk by admitting the truth of the charge: "My plays are all talk, just as Raphael's pictures are all paint, Michaelangelo's statues all marble, Beethoven's symphonies all noise." Shaw is having his fun, but he is also being serious in his assertion that drama can deal not only with action of the obvious sort but also with ideas worth arguing about. The writer of a play of ideas will, of course, make some use of settings, costumes, and gestures to communicate meaning, but the chief interest is in the examination of an idea, or, to use Shaw's word, the center of interest is the "discussion."

Clare Boothe Luce's play is in this tradition. To some degree every writer must see himself or herself as part of a tradition. When Sophocles wrote *Oedipus the King* he presumably said to himself, "The Oedipus story has often been told, by Homer and by the playwrights who are my contemporaries, but this is the way *I* see it." Furthermore, he must also have said to himself, "Our writers of tragedies do such-and-such; in this play I want to deepen, or enlarge, what tragic drama can do, and I want to deepen or enlarge our sense of the tragic." Similarly, when Shakespeare wrote *Hamlet* he was working in (and adding to) the tradition of the Elizabethan revenge play, a form already popular; indeed, at least one play on Hamlet had already appeared on the stage. And in his *King Lear* he is similarly indebted to an older play, the anonymous *King Leir*, which ends happily. Shakespeare must have thought, "No, no, no! The story ought to go thus. . . ."

Clare Boothe Luce's play is inspired by Ibsen's *A Doll's House* (the title alludes to the end of Ibsen's play). Presumably Luce did not feel that Ibsen got the story wrong, only that in 1970—ninety-one years after Ibsen wrote his play—the story could usefully be set forth a little differently. She follows the main line of Ibsen's plot but uses American characters and customs of the late twentieth century. She also employs her distinctive tone, which is unlike Ibsen's. Part of the fun of reading her play is to imagine Ibsen in the background while at the same time recognizing both what is new in the work and what is essentially Ibsenite. To take a single, simple example, at the end of the play Nora carefully explains that she is not slamming the door, just closing it carefully.

For biography, see Wilfrid Sheed, *Clare Boothe Luce* (1982), and Ralph G. Martin, *Henry and Clare: An Intimate Portrait of the Luces* (1991). Mark Fearnow, in *Clare Boothe Luce: A Research and Production Sourcebook* (1995), gives helpful information about Luce's plays and their productions.

29

Students Writing about Plays

A few words about Katz's essay on *Death of a Salesman*.

We think that Katz's preliminary notes are extremely edifying—especially her renumbering (i.e., reorganization) of the items under the heading "other women." The jottings nicely illustrate the point that outlines almost always need to be revised—and of course the draft written from what one thinks is the final outline will also need revision.

Katz's paper strikes us as thoroughly admirable, especially in its use of sources. She does not simply present an anthology of comments; rather, she steadily advances her own ideas, and she quotes in order to make points, not in order to pad.

Two points about her paper: (1) Although the title reveals only the topic (we usually suggest that students reveal their thesis in their title), the first paragraph clearly reveals the thesis, so readers have a good idea of where they will be going; (2) one colleague who saw this paper expressed uneasiness about some of the diction. For instance, he was disturbed by the aggressiveness of the following passage:

> It might be nice if Linda spent her time taking courses at an Adult Education Center and thinking high thoughts, but it's obvious that *some-one* in the Loman family (as in all families) has to keep track of the bills.

We understand our colleague's uneasiness, and we ourselves urge students to think twice before they adopt a wiseguy manner, but we think that on the whole the paper has an engaging human voice in it, and for that we are grateful. Whether you agree or disagree with our colleague's view, you may want to call the class's attention to this passage and to discuss matters of tone in student writing.

Reminder: Chapter 30 includes *Death of a Salesman*. Ruth Katz's essay might effectively be assigned in conjunction with the play.

30

A Collection of Plays

ARTHUR MILLER

Death of a Salesman (p. 1384)

(This discussion is an abbreviation of our introduction in *Types of Drama*.) The large question, of course, is whether Willy is a tragic or a pathetic figure. For the ancient Greeks, at least for Aristotle, *pathos* was the destructive or painful act common in tragedy; but in English, "pathos" refers to an element in art or life that evokes tenderness or sympathetic pity. Modern English critical usage distinguishes between tragic figures and pathetic figures by recognizing some element either of strength or of regeneration in the former that is not in the latter. Tragic protagonists perhaps act so that they bring their destruction upon themselves, or if their destruction comes from outside, they resist it, and in either case they come to at least a partial understanding of the causes of their suffering. The pathetic figure, however, is largely passive, an unknowing and unresisting innocent. In such a view Macbeth is tragic, Duncan pathetic; Lear is tragic, Cordelia pathetic; Othello is tragic, Desdemona pathetic; Hamlet is tragic (the situation is not of his making, but he does what he can to alter it), Ophelia pathetic. (Note, by the way, that of the four pathetic figures named, the first is old and the remaining three are women. Pathos is more likely to be evoked by persons assumed to be relatively defenseless than by the able-bodied.)

The guardians of critical terminology, then, have tended to insist that "tragedy" be reserved for a play showing action that leads to suffering which in turn leads to knowledge. They get very annoyed when a newspaper describes as a tragedy the death of a promising high school football player in an automobile accident, and they insist that such a death is pathetic, not tragic; it is unexpected, premature, and deeply regrettable, but it does not give us a sense of human greatness achieved through understanding the sufferings that a sufferer has at least in some degree chosen. Probably critics hoard the term "tragedy" because it is also a word of praise: To call a play a comedy or a problem play is not to imply anything about its merits, but to call a play a tragedy is tantamount to calling it an important or even a great play. In most of the best-known Greek tragedies, the protagonist either does some terrible deed or resists mightily. But Greek drama has its pathetic figures too, figures who do not so much act as suffer. Euripides's *The Trojan Women* is perhaps the greatest example of a play which does not allow its heroes to choose and to act but only to undergo, to be in agony. When we think of pathetic figures in Greek drama, however, we probably think chiefly of the choruses, groups of rather commonplace persons who do not perform a tragic deed but who suffer in sympathy with the tragic hero, who lament the hardness of the times, and who draw spectators into the range of the hero's suffering.

Arthur Miller has argued that because Oedipus has given his name to a complex that the common man may have, the common man is therefore "as apt a subject for tragedy." It is not Oedipus's complex, however, but his unique importance that is the issue in the play. Moreover, even if one argues that people of no public importance may suffer as much as people of public importance (and surely no one doubts this), one may be faced with the fact that the unimportant people by their ordinances are not particularly good material for drama, and we are here concerned with drama rather than with life. In *Death of a Salesman*, Willy Loman's wife says, rightly, "A small man can be just as exhausted as a great man." Yes, but is his exhaustion itself interesting and do his activities (and this includes the words he utters) before his exhaustion have interesting dramatic possibilities? Isn't there a colorlessness that may weaken the play, an impoverishment of what John Milton called "gorgeous tragedy"?

Miller accurately noted (*Theatre Arts*, October 1953) that American drama "has been a steady year by year documentation of the frustration of man," and it is evident that Miller has set out to restore a sense of importance, if not greatness, to the individual. In "Tragedy and the Common Man" (reprinted in our text), published in *The New York Times* in the same year that *Death of a Salesman* was produced and evidently in defense of the play, Miller argues on behalf of the common man as a tragic figure, and he insists that tragedy and pathos are very different: "Pathos truly is the mode of the pessimist. . . . The plays we revere, century after century are the tragedies. In them, and in them alone, lies the belief—optimistic, if you will—in the perfectibility of man." Elsewhere (*Harper's*, August 1958) he has said that pathos is an oversimplification and therefore is the "counterfeit of meaning." Curiously, however, many spectators and readers find that by Miller's own terms Willy Loman fails to be a tragic figure; he seems to them pathetic rather than tragic, a victim rather than a man who acts and who wins esteem. True, he is partly the victim of his own actions (although he could have chosen to be a carpenter, he chose to live by the bourgeois code that values a white collar), but he seems in larger part to be a victim of the system itself, a system of ruthless competition that has no place for the man who can no longer produce. (Here is an echo of the social-realist drama of the thirties.) Willy had believed in this system; and although his son Biff comes to the realization that Willy "had the wrong dreams," Willy himself seems not to achieve this insight. He knows that he is out of a job, that the system does not value him any longer, but he still seems not to question the values he had subscribed to. Even in the last minutes of the play, when he is planning his suicide in order to provide money for his family—really for Biff—he says such things as "Can you imagine his magnif-icence with twenty thousand dollars in his pocket?" and "When the mail comes he'll be ahead of Bernard again." In the preface to his *Collected Plays*, Miller comments on the "exultation" with which Willy faces the end, but it is questionable whether an audience shares it. Many people find that despite the gulf in rank, they can share King Lear's feelings more easily than Willy's.

Miller gathered his early plays, including *Death of a Salesman*, in *Collected Plays* (1957); this volume also contains his illuminating introduction. For crit-ical commentary, see *Death of a Salesman: Text and Criticism*, ed. Gerald Weales (1967), and also the collections of essays edited by Robert W. Corrigan (1969), Helen Wickham Koon (1983), and Harold Bloom (1986).

An excellent resource is *Understanding "Death of a Salesman": A Student Casebook to Issues, Source, and Historical Documents*, ed. Brenda Murphy and Susan C. W. Abbotson (1999). For a revealing account of the origins of Miller's play, see John Lahr, "Making Willy Loman," *The New Yorker*, January 25, 1999. For a cogent, highly positive review of the recent Broadway production that starred Brian Dennehy in the title role, see Ben Brantley, "Attention Must Be Paid, Again," *The New York Times*, February 11, 1999.

TOPICS FOR CRITICAL THINKING AND WRITING

1. Willy says Biff can't fail because "he's got spirit, personality . . . personal attractiveness. . . . Personality always wins the day." In an essay of 500 to 1,000 words, distinguish between "personality" and "character," and then describe each of these in Willy.
2. The critic Kenneth Tynan has written, in *Tynan Right and Left* (1967), "*Death of a Salesman* . . . is not a tragedy. Its catastrophe depends entirely on the fact that the company Willy Loman works for has no pension scheme for its employees. What ultimately destroys Willy is economic injustice, which is curable, as the ills that plague Oedipus are not." What do you think of Tynan's view?

LUIS VALDEZ

Los Vendidos (p. 000)

Students who have been told that stereotyping people is wicked and that char-acters (whether in fiction or in drama) should be well-motivated, believable, and so on may find it difficult to see anything of value in a work that uses one-dimen-sional stock characters. Perhaps one way to help them enjoy such a work is to talk briefly about stereotypes in films that they have enjoyed and admired. The roles performed by Chaplin, the Marx Brothers, Bogart—or even some roles in soap operas—may help them to see that stereotyped characters can be powerful.

Los Vendidos is comic in the sense of having some laughs in it, and also (at least to a degree) in the more literary sense of being a play with a happy end-ing. If one stands at a distance, so to speak, and looks at the overall plot, one sees the good guys outwitting the bad guys (Ms. Jimenez). In the talk about going to a party, there is even a hint of the traditional *komos* or revel.

It is of course entirely appropriate that the play includes amusing pas-sages. Valdez has said that he wanted to lift the morale of his audience (chiefly striking workers), and he wrote and staged comedies—in the sense of plays with happy endings—because he wanted to help change society. He did not want, obviously, to show the tragic nature of the human condition. He makes his aims clear in his short essay, "The Actos" (see Question 5 in the text). One might ask students to think especially about whether in this play he does anything to "show or hint at a solution" to the "social problem." In some *actos* the message is clear, for instance, "Join the union."

It's our view that *Los Vendidos* does not at all suffer by failing to give a "solution." (Of course it's implied that Anglos should not think of Mexican-Americans as stupid and lazy, should not expect them to be subservient, and should value them as people, but Valdez does not offer a solution for Anglo prejudice.) Much of the strength of the play seems to us to lie in the wit with which the stereotypes are presented, and also in the ingenuity of the plot, when the robots come alive and thus reverse the stereotype: The Mexican-Americans are shown to be shrewd and enterprising, and Honest Sancho is shown to be lifeless.

For further study, students might begin with Jaime Herrera, "Luis Miguel Valdez," in *Updating the Literary West*, ed. Max Westbrook and Dan Flores (1997), 379–85. See also Harry J. Elam, Jr., *Taking It to the Streets: The Social Protest Theater of Luis Valdez and Amiri Baraka* (1997).

ADDITIONAL TOPIC FOR CRITICAL THINKING AND WRITING

At the end of the play the Mexican-Americans are shown as shrewd and enterprising. Has Valdez fallen into the trap of suggesting that Mexican-American culture is not distinctive but is just about the same as the Anglo imperialistic (capitalistic) culture that he has satirized earlier in the play?

JANE MARTIN

Rodeo (p. 1467)

First a few comments not about the play but about rodeo (pronounced either *RO dee o* or *ro DAY o*, but the second pronunciation is more common amongst those who perform in the spectacle). *Rodeo* (from a Spanish word meaning "[cattle] ring," ultimately from *rodear* = to go around, to surround) apparently developed in the 1880s as a celebration of a successful round-up. Cowboys would demonstrate the skills of their trade, riding, lassoing, and wrestling animals to the ground. In any case, what was at first a home-grown event—in which the performers were also most of the spectators—soon became an entertainment for a larger public. The writer of this page, a New Yorker who knew horses only as creatures that were ridden by mounted policemen, recalls seeing rodeos in Madison Square Garden when he was a child in the 1930s. Obviously the audiences in the Garden were remote from the audiences that Big Eight speaks of:

> Used to be fer cowboys, the rodeo did. . . . Used to be people came to a rodeo had a horse of their own back home. Farm people, ranch people— lord, they *knew* what they were lookin' at. Knew a good ride from a bad ride, knew hard from easy.

What the viewer of Jane Martin's *Rodeo* comes to see is that Big Eight, though relatively uneducated, understands pretty clearly that what was once a good-natured, friendly demonstration of useful skills in front of an audience of (more or less) peers has become Show Biz, mere entertainment, run for the profit of capitalists and offered to an ignorant audience. Big Eight herself is not exactly a role model, with her earthy comments about the large breasts of Tits Nelson, or her dismissal of "some New York faggot," but in our view she comes across as thoroughly sympathetic, and indeed we believe that readers and spectators increasingly respect her as the play proceeds.

At first she is merely entertaining, a specimen of local color, but as she continues to talk we realize that what she says makes sense and is important. We realize, too, that she is indeed talking to *us*. You may want to help your students to see that her speech is not a soliloquy—not a character's revelation of inner thoughts addressed to no one (though of course a soliloquy gives information to the audience). Rather, in her monologue (from Greek, *monologos* = single speech) Big Eight is decidedly speaking to a listener. In this case the listener is the entire audience; all of us, as a collective body, are to be understood as a character whom Big Eight is addressing. And she is not just nattering or whining about losing her job, Rather, she is making valid points, first about the development of the rodeo, and second— a much larger point—about the commercialization of all sorts of activities, for instance, sport— and can we add education?

> Well you look out, honey! They want to make them a dollar out of what you love. Dress *you* up like Minnie Mouse. Sell your rodeo. Turn *yer* pleasure into Ice damn Capades. You hear what I'm sayin'? You're jus' merchandise to them, sweetie. You're jus' merchandise to them.

Having said this, we should also mention that there are those who believe that the rodeo, early and late, was and is a cruel entertainment, based largely on the pain of animals. PETA (People for the Ethical Treatment of Animals) and other organizations have charged that calf-roping, for instance, often results in serious injuries to the animals, and that bucking broncos buck because they are given an electric shock when the gate is opened and because the flank (or "bucking") strap is tightly cinched below the ribcage, causing pain. We have also heard that irritants are sometimes placed under the flank strap and also in the animal's anus to stimulate bucking. Rodeo officials deny these charges. Officials also point out that the human performers are more likely to sustain injury than the animal performers—an argument not convincing to persons who are aware that the human performers are volunteers but the animal performers are not.

If indeed part of the spectator's pleasure in a rodeo was or is sadistic, i.e., is not simply pleasure in seeing the accomplishments of the human performers but is partly rooted in witnessing the pain of animals, one might think twice before lamenting the decline of old-style rodeo. We are reminded of Thomas Macaulay's comment on the puritans' opposition to bear-baiting: "The Puritan hated bear-baiting, not because it gave pain to the bear, but because it gave pleasure to the spectators." One might well ask the class: Are there certain pleasures that indeed we should *not* be allowed to experience? Should we enjoy calf-roping? Cock fighting? Dog fighting? And do we want to restore public executions, where crowds can enjoy the spectacle of seeing someone hanged or shot or injected with a lethal dose?

Macaulay's comment will provoke some interesting responses, we think, but we recognize that it is not central to Jane Martin's play: The quotation will stimulate a discussion of rodeos, but not of Martin's *Rodeo*. Here is another quotation that we think can be useful in teaching the play iself. Ursula K. Le Guin somewhere says,

The story is not in the plot but in the telling. It is the telling that moves.

Le Guin is speaking about fiction, not about drama, but her comment gets us back to a point we made a moment ago: The play is a monologue, but the speech is not merely the revelation of a character's thought and it is not spoken in isolation. Rather, the monologue that constitutes *Rodeo* tells a story in an engaging way, and it is very much addressed to an audience: The entire audience in the theater is conceived as Big Eight's listener. The plot, so to speak, of *Rodeo* is in the telling, the shifts in tone. The speech begins with a pretty direct statement that indeed sums up Big Eight's point ("Shoot—Rodeo's just goin' to hell in a handbasket") but by the end of the monologue this statement has infinitely more resonance than at the beginning. Big Eight goes on to talk about the early days, when a rodeo was essentially for knowledgeable folk ("Used to be fer cowboys") and was a family affair ("Used to be a family thing"). Then we get the talk about the bankers and the New York faggots, about Mickey and Minnie Mouse, and so on, and near the end—though of course *all* of the monologue is addressed to the audience—the motif is broadened with the assertion that all of us are "jus' merchandise" in the eyes of folks who look only at the bottom line.

"The telling," to take Le Guin's term, is what holds us—allegedly Big Eight's telling but of course really Jane Martin's.

One tiny complaint: Are we being picky when we say that, on rereading in preparation for writing this note, we find ourselves disturbed by occasional inconsistencies in the rendering of the dialect? Thus, in the first paragraph we get "jest" (for "just"), but in the last paragraph we get "jus'" (again for "just"). In the second paragraph and elsewhere we get "fer" (i.e. "for") but elsewhere we get "for"; sometimes we get "ya" (i.e., "you") but elsewhere we get "you." If we were directing the play, we would tell the actor to be consistent.

A word about the last topic that we give in the text, in which we ask students to consider the effect of ending not with a blackout, as the playwright instructs, but with a fadeout. This question of course gets into the business of the "language" of drama: A play is not simply people talking, i.e., using "language" in the ordinary sense of the word. There is also body language (gesture), and the language of costume (Hamlet's "inky cloak" tells the viewers that he is in mourning), and—and this is what we are getting at here—the "language" of lighting, information conveyed to an audience by the kinds of illumination that are used. A blackout (the sudden extinguishing of all light on the stage) inevitably surprises the audience; it is a sudden blow, and in *Rodeo* it might be thought of as analogous to the shocking dismissal of Big Eight. On the other hand, a fadeout (the gradual lowering of the lights) usually conveys pathos, a sort of slow dying. Our own practice is to follow the playwright's instructions, simply because we believe that authors are entitled to have their plays staged the way they want them to be staged, but we nevertheless believe that in *Rodeo* the blackout is less effective, less meaningful, than a fadeout would be. We think that what a blackout gains in immediate effect it loses in meaning, the gradual extinction of a way of life. A topic for discussion.

AUGUST WILSON

Fences (p. 1471)

Some background (taken from our *Types of Drama*) on the history of blacks in the American theater may be of use. In the 1940s and 1950s black playwrights faced the difficult problem of deciding what audience they were writing for—an audience of blacks or of whites? The difficulty was compounded by the fact that although there were a number of black theater groups—for example, the American Negro Theatre (founded by blacks in 1940)—there was not a large enough black theater-going public to make such groups commercially successful. In fact, although the original ideal of the American Negro Theatre was "to portray Negro life . . . honestly," within a few years it was doing plays by white writers, such as Thornton Wilder's *Our Town* (not only by a white but about whites) and Philip Yordan's *Anna Lucasta* (by a white, and originally about a Polish working-class family, but transformed into a play about a black family). Further, the aim of such groups usually was in large measure to employ black actors and theater technicians; some of the most talented of these, including Harry Belafonte, Sidney Poitier, and Ruby Dee, then went on to enter the mainstream of white theater, on Broadway, or—a short step—in Hollywood. Meanwhile, such writers as James Baldwin and Lorraine Hansberry, though writing about black life, wrote plays that were directed at least as much at whites as at blacks. That is, their plays were in large measure attempts to force whites to look at what they had done to blacks.

In the mid-1960s, however, the most talented black dramatists, including LeRoi Jones (Imamu Amiri Baraka) and Ed Bullins, largely turned their backs on white audiences and in effect wrote plays aimed at showing blacks that *they*—not their white oppressors—must change, must cease to accept the myths that whites had created. Today, however, strongly revolutionary plays by and about blacks have difficulty getting a hearing. Instead, the newest black writers seem to be concerned less with raising the consciousness of blacks than with depicting black life and with letting both blacks and whites respond aesthetically rather than politically. Baraka has attributed the change to a desire by many blacks to become assimilated in today's society, and surely there is much to his view. One might also say, however, that black dramatists may for other reasons have come to assume that the business of drama is not to preach but to show, and that a profound, honest depiction—in a traditional, realistic dramatic form—of things as they are, or in Wilson's play, things as they were in the 1950s, will touch audiences whatever their color. "Part of the reason I wrote *Fences*," Wilson has said, "was to illuminate that generation, which shielded its children from all of the indignities they went through."

This is not to say, of course, that *Fences* is a play about people who just happen to be black. The Polish family of *Anna Lucasta* could easily be converted to a black family (though perhaps blacks may feel that there is something unconvincing about this family), but Troy Maxson's family cannot be white-washed. The play is very much about persons who are what they are because they are blacks living in an unjust society run by whites. We are not allowed to forget this. Troy is a baseball player who was too old to join a white team when the major leagues began to hire blacks. (The first black player to play in the major leagues was Jackie Robinson, whom the Brooklyn Dodgers hired in 1947. Robinson retired in 1956, a year before the time in which *Fences* is chiefly set.) For Troy's friend, Bono, "Troy just came along too early"; but Troy pungently replies, "There ought not never have been no time called too early." Blacks of Troy's day were expected to subscribe to American ideals—for instance, to serve in the army in time of war—but they were also expected to sit in the back of the bus and to accept the fact that they were barred from decent jobs. Wilson shows us the scars that such treatment left. Troy is no paragon. Although he has a deep sense of responsibility to his family, his behavior toward them is deeply flawed; he oppresses his son Cory, he is unfaithful to his wife, Rose, and he exploits his brother Gabriel.

Wilson, as we have seen, calls attention to racism in baseball, and he indicates that Troy turned to crime because he could not earn money. But Wilson does not allow *Fences* to become a prolonged protest against white oppression—though one can never quite forget that Troy insists on a high personal ideal in a world that has cheated him. The interest in the play is in Troy as a human being, or, rather, in all of the characters as human beings rather than as representatives of white victimization. As Troy sees it, by preventing Cory from engaging in athletics—the career that frustrated Troy—he is helping rather than oppressing Cory: "I don't want him to be like me. I want him to move as far from me as he can." But Wilson also makes it clear that Troy has other (very human) motives, of which Troy perhaps is unaware.

A note on the word black: The play is set in 1957 and (the last scene) 1965, before *black* and *African-American* were the words commonly applied to persons of African descent. The blacks in the play speak of "coloreds" and of "niggers." *Black* did not become the preferred word until the late 1960s. For instance, the question was still open in November 1967, when *Ebony* magazine asked its readers whether the *Negro* should be replaced by *black* or *Afro-American*. The results of polls at that time chiefly suggested that *Afro-American* was the preferred choice, but *black* nevertheless became the established term until about 1988, when *African-American* began to displace *black*.

Polls in November 1995 revealed, however, that a majority of blacks still prefer *black* to *African-American* or to *Afro-American*. But it is our impression that in the limited world of colleges and universities, a majority prefers *African-American*.

See Joan Fishman, "Developing His Song: August Wilson's *Fences*," in *August Wilson: A Casebook*, ed. Marilyn Elkins (1994), 161–81; and Harry J. Elam, Jr., "Of Angels and Transcendence: An Analysis of *Fences* by August Wilson and *Roosters* by Milcha Sanchez-Scott," in *Staging Difference: Cultural Pluralism in American Theatre and Drama*, ed. Marc Maufort (1995), 287–300. Also helpful is *May All Your Fences Have Gates: Essays on the Drama of August Wilson*, ed. Alan Nadel (1994).

A 30-minute videocassette of Bill Moyers's interview with August Wilson is available from Longman Publishers.

DAVID IVES

Sure Thing (p. 1523)

Students enjoy this play, and for a change of pace you might ask them to perform it. The chief problem, though, is that it allows only two students to perform. This has led us to consider the idea of using different students for each mini-play, i.e., for each unit of dialogue that precedes the sound of the bell. Such a production would inevitably change the meaning of the play, but we think there is much to be said for it (it involves more students, and it therefore allows for different voices, different tones).

One way of talking about the play is to introduce Aristotle's idea that a play has a beginning, a middle, and an end, i.e., a play begins with a situation that needs no preliminary explanation (here, a man and a woman in a cafe), moves into a middle (a complication that arises out of the beginning), and ends with an action that results from the encounter and that itself marks the completion of the encounter. That is, there is nothing more to be said. In Ives's play, only the last episode does *not* have an end; rather, it seems to be leading to a new beginning.

But consider the first episode as a sort of tiny play:

Bill. Excuse me. Is this chair taken?
Betty. Excuse me?
Bill. Is this taken?
Betty. Yes it is.
Bill. Oh. Sorry.
Betty. Sure thing. (*A bell rings softly.*)

A static situation (Betty seated at a table—that's the beginning) is disturbed by Bill's question (the beginning of the middle), and the middle turns into another static situation, i.e., after Bill apologizes and Betty accepts the apology, we have an end, a situation in which there is nothing more to be said. This formula is repeated over and over until the last episode, when there is an ending that is both an ending (the two seem to hit it off) and a new beginning (together they call for the check, and presumably will pay and leave, and start a new beginning).

We use the term "formula," which implies both the idea that propels the play and perhaps, too, its limitation. Students do enjoy *Sure Thing*: we want to allow them to keep this good feeling. But, still, when we discuss this work, we raise a question or two about both what it offers and what it does not. *Sure Thing* is a pleasing play. Is it a complex one? Does it deepen in its meanings each time we read it or see it performed? Or does our return to the play give us the same experience we had before?

Again, since it is important for students to feel they can enjoy literature, we would not press such questions too hard. But it's worthwhile to raise them, which one hopes will prompt students to reflect on the limits as well as the rewards of their experience of Ives's engaging work.

TERRENCE MCNALLY

Andre's Mother (p. 1532)

Andre's Mother says nothing, so it is difficult for us (or any reader or specta-tor) to offer evidence in support of any characterization that we might propose. Still, the fact that she says nothing says something. Her refusal to join in the conversation—her insistence on isolating herself from the three other charac-ters—tells us she is deeply hurt, but it does not tell us *what* she is hurt by. By her son's immorality (as she sees it)? By Cal, who may, in her view, have cor-rupted her son and then killed him (again, in her view)?

We learn that Andre had two reasons for not telling his mother that he had AIDS: he was "afraid of hurting [her] and [he was afraid] of [her] disap-proval." The mother's continued silence, even near the end of the play, causes Cal to say, "I'm beginning to feel your disapproval and it's making me ill," and a moment later he leaves the stage, without a comforting word from the moth-er. She presumably cannot accept her son's homosexuality—or if she can accept it, she probably blames it and his death on Cal, although Cal tells her that he himself "tested negative."

We know nothing of Andre's Mother other than that she probably lived in a rural society (Cal says that Andre was "a country boy"), but even this informa-tion is a bit soft: a New Yorker such as Cal might jokingly say that someone from, oh, maybe Kansas City, is a country boy. Probably it is enough for us to say that the mother is hostile toward homosexuality and quite understandably is grieved by the death of her son and that she in some degree blames the boy's partner.

What do we make of the ending, when the mother finally let go of the bal-loon? Cal gives a rather constricted interpretation of the balloons:

> They represent the soul. When you let go, it means you're letting his soul ascend to Heaven. That you're willing to let go. Breaking the last earthly ties.

Surely other people, even at this very graveside, might offer a different inter-pretation. One might reasonably say that one is not and should not be willing to "let go," i.e., one will treasure the memory and perhaps will daily or at least often engage in actions that are motivated by the enduring connection with the dead partner, but one lets the balloon sail into the air as a sort of emblem of the deceased's new kind of existence.

In any case, the final stage direction tells us several things about Andre's Mother:

> *Her lips tremble. She looks on the verge of breaking down. She is about to let go of the balloon when she pulls it down to her. She looks at it awhile before she gently kisses it. She lets go of the balloon. She follows it with her eyes as it rises and rises. The lights are beginning to fade. Andre's Mother's eyes are still on the balloon. The lights fade.*

It would be absurd for us to speak dogmatically about the thoughts of Andre's Mother. For one thing, she is a fictional character—she has no existence other than the words that her author puts into her mouth. But even if she were a historical figure, in which case we might more reasonably speak of her personality, we would have to be cautious lest we project our own views onto the subject.

Still, perhaps we can say something of use. First of all, we can assume that Cal's view of the symbolism may have had some effect on her. That is, her reluctance to let go of the balloon may suggest her reluctance to let go of her ideas about her son—that he *couldn't* have been gay, or if he was gay, that he was somehow seduced from his natural heterosexuality by Cal and that Cal is responsible for Andre's death. Perhaps when she lets go of the balloon she is letting go of some or all of these mistaken, destructive ideas.

McNally tells us in the stage direction that Andre's Mother "follows [the balloon] with her eyes" and that when the lights fade, at the very end, "Andre's Mother's eyes are still on the balloon." This does not sound to us as though she is "willing to let go," and indeed we—the writers of this page—don't think she should "let go" her love for and memory of her son. On the other hand, yes, she should "let go" whatever false ideas she had about him, and she should "let go" whatever anger she feels toward his lover.

She *does* let go—literally—of the balloon, so in a way she lets go of this symbol of her son, or, rather, this symbol of her son's soul. We take the white balloon to be a fairly obvious symbol of the soul. The sphere, a sort of three-dimensional circle, is a common emblem of endlessness and perfection. White is a common symbol of purity and of rebirth, even (we are told) in Black Africa, where young men after circumcision may cover their faces with white chalk, indicating that they are now "reborn" as responsible adults. In Japan the white lotus is associated with the Buddha's perfect knowledge. For all of these reasons, then, and because the helium-filled balloon rises into the heavens, the white balloon seems to us to be a pretty clear symbol of the soul released from the body.

One final point about the play, and then we will say something about McNally's video version of his play. As far as readers and an audience are concerned, the play ends with Andre's Mother releasing the balloon *after* Penny and Arthur and (a bit later) Cal have left. Nothing indicates that these others know her final action. Cal's last words to her are, as we said a moment ago, "I'm beginning to feel your disapproval and it's making me ill. . . . Goodbye, Andre's Mother." If at the very end the mother undergoes some change, however small, viewers must find it painful—can we say tragic?—that Cal does not know of the change. Although it is commonplace to say that in a tragedy the tragic hero experiences an *anagnorisis*, a recognition, a final illumination, in fact tragic heroes often do *not* know the whole truth, do *not* fundamentally change. For example, in *Oedipus the King*, the self-confident protagonist is, at the end of the play, still being bossy: in the next-to-last speech of the play (except for the final words of the Chorus), Oedipus tries to hold on to his children, and in the last speech (again, except for the Chorus) Creon quite reasonably tells Oedipus that he is no longer in a position to give orders. In *King Lear*, almost surely Lear dies with the mistaken belief that Cordelia is alive. Romeo unquestionably dies thinking Juliet is dead. Many other instances might be given. Our point simply is that tragedy usually deals with mistakes, with mistakes that contain an element of irony—Lear banishes the daughter who loves him most—and sometimes the mistakes, the ironies, persist even unto death. In *Andre's Mother* surely our sympathy is chiefly with Cal but probably it finally extends to Andre's

Mother, and perhaps we feel a twinge that Cal, a bit too self-satisfied at the end, does not see that she is not beyond redemption.

McNally's video, *Andre's Mother* (starring Richard Thomas and Sada Thompson), done for American Playhouse, runs 58 minutes, obviously far longer than the original play takes. The opening shot shows Andre's Mother, then her son, then we hear the narrator's voice, and then the mother says, "You took my son from me." We next get shots of a street, a vendor with white balloons, a released balloon, the interior of a church, the funeral service complete with white lilies and a singer rendering Mozart's *Shepherd King* ("I love him, I will be constant"), shots of people in pews, another shot of Andre's Mother in a pew, a scene at an airport in which Cal meets Andre's Mother and explains that Andre has just left for Hartford to try out for a role. Andre's Mother and Cal go to Cal's apartment and we learn that Cal is writing a book about a gay composer, Samuel Barber. On the wall of the apartment is a poster of Hamlet: remember, Andre is an actor, and in the printed version Cal pays tribute to Andre by reciting a line that Horatio addresses to the dead Hamlet, "Good night, sweet prince, and flights of angels sing thee to rest."

The mother—we are still talking about the television version—says "Maybe there's some things I'd just as soon not know," and then there is a cut back to the church which is the site of the funeral service. There is a scene in a museum with Andre's Mother and her own garrulous mother, then a scene in a restaurant with Cal, the two women, and an evidently gay waiter. In the cemetery, Cal denounces Andre's Mother but embraces her, and he lets his balloon slip away. Cut to a scene of a young mother with a small boy on the beach—this is presumably Andre and his mother in happier days—and then we go back to Andre's Mother in the cemetery, where we see her release the balloon. You get the idea; the play is "opened up," with lots of scenes that are not in the original. This is not a bad thing, and indeed we think the video is quite effective—but it is different from (much more explicit than) the original text.

For biography and context, see interviews in: *A Search for a Postmodern Theater: Interviews with Contemporary Playwrights*, ed. John L. DiGaetani (1991), 219–228; *The Playwright's Art: Conversations with Contemporary American Dramatists*, ed. Jackson R. Bryer (1995), 182–204; and *Speaking on Stage: Interviews with Contemporary American Playwrights*, ed. Philip C. Kolin and Colby H. Kullman (1996), 332–345.

31

Critical Approaches: The Nature of Criticism

For this part of the book, we can only offer the mixed nature of our own experience and invite you to make the decision that feels right to you.

When we teach an introductory course open to all students, we find we usually say little or nothing about critical approaches. We might comment on feminist theory, but we do so within the context of our discussion of a specific literary work. We do not treat the theory in much detail or depth, and about deconstruction and new historicism we are silent. These approaches are too complex for brief comment; the students cannot handle them well and end up feeling mystified or confused. Students are, we think, better off focusing on the literary works directly and examining the writers' uses of language in them.

But when we teach an introductory literature or literature and composition course designed for English majors, then we do make an effort to discuss critical approaches. Feminist theory and criticism: This is an approach that students can begin to grasp fairly quickly—they see its relation to the women's movement of the 1960s and 1970s—and can learn to apply themselves. The same holds true for reader-response criticism; students right away can talk about their responses to texts, and feel some affinity with the theories that Stanley Fish, Wolfgang Iser, Jonathan Culler, and others have proposed. Deconstruction and new historicism are harder; the first greatly depends on continental philosophy, and the second on a wide and dense range of knowledge about history, society, and culture. But we can make some headway if we are patient enough in our explanations and illustrate how deconstruction, for instance, "works" in the case of a Wordsworth lyric or how a new historicist analysis of the monarchy in Shakespeare's England reveals something new about kingship and the kingdom in *Hamlet*, *Macbeth*, or *King Lear*.

No sooner, however, than we make this distinction between general courses and courses for English majors than we must admit that some of our colleagues hold a different view. Some of them give a good deal of time in all of their literature courses to the subject of critical approaches. Indeed, one or two of our colleagues launch their courses with a discussion of critical approaches. When they use our book, they begin with this chapter, taking it as the point of departure for the rest of the course they are teaching. As one of these instructors said to us, "When the students read and write about a poem, they need to have something to look for, and that's what the critical approaches give them."

To us, this formulation is awkward and unpersuasive. Surely there must be "something" in a literary work that can affect us simply because the work is what it is and we are who we are. Must a reader study literary theory before he or she can be moved by a Shakespeare play, a Hawthorne story, or a Dickinson or Frost poem? But we know the point that our colleague is making. He is saying that, in his view at any rate, students need a critical vocabulary, and one that goes beyond such standard terms as plot, character, setting, theme, tone, and the like. Equip the students with the tools, and they will be able to extract meanings from texts. If we don't, so the argument goes, the students will not know what to look for, and they will have little to offer in class and in paper assignments.

In some English departments, this claim has become the principle according to which the curriculum is structured. The introductory courses are devoted to theory and criticism, and it is only after these courses are taken that students then move to author, period, and other kinds of literature courses. These teachers maintain that students require a set of terms and interpretive procedures in order to know how to speak and write about the literature they study. The theories, the approaches, it is argued, provide students with the power to read critically and productively.

Perhaps what comes into focus from these examples is a question that teachers and critics have been debating for some years now: How much theory, how much study of critical approaches, do the students in literature courses need? Obviously they need a certain amount of basic work on those familiar and inevitable terms such as character and setting. But after that has been done, how much more is necessary?

A good case can be made that a student planning on graduate school needs a lot more. For better or worse, much of the emphasis in graduate training is placed on theory and criticism; a student starting graduate school without some knowledge of deconstruction, feminist theory and criticism, and other approaches will have some serious catching up to do. For English majors in general: Here, we think the case can be made that they, too, will benefit from courses on critical approaches, but we think that these courses should come in the later stages of the students' undergraduate careers. Why not read many authors and many different kinds of literary works first, and then turn to the project of examining and comparing and contrasting the strengths and limits of critical approaches?

We risk making our point more strongly than we intend. There are many theorists whom we have learned from—Stanley Fish, in his reader-response criticism on Milton's poetry, immediately comes to mind. Others we have learned from and find well worth disagreeing with include Geoffrey H. Hartman and Harold Bloom. But for us what makes the best theorists valuable, stimulating, provocative, is that they are engaged, attentive readers. Even as they work with their theories, they strike us as being responsive to the specific works at hand. They do not mechanically "apply" this or that theory to a literary work from the outside, with no heed paid to whether the work calls for such a theory or not.

Richard Poirier, Helen Vendler, John Hollander, Frank Kermode—these critics, and others we could name, have an approach but not a theory. They are intensely curious about the ways in which a writer and a literary work can challenge and teach them, explore complex ideas and feelings, spark new insights, expand the borders of consciousness. What matters for them is the writer's relation to the verbal medium—what he or she is doing with words in the literary work—and the reader's engagement with the work that this author has performed. It is this quality of personal commitment and engagement, and the excitement of it, that we do not find often enough in the books of literary theory that we have read. And it is this quality that we believe is the one above all that should be made vivid and rich for students.

We have one or two suggestions to offer you and your colleagues on the vexed matter of critical approaches. We think it is important—though we concede it is not always easy—to make the discussion of and debate about this issue a "public" one for the students. If you are using this book in a multi-section course, you and one or two of your fellow-teachers might select a poem by Wordsworth, Blake, or some other poet and each describe how this or that approach illuminates the text. We have often done something like this ourselves, with the help of a colleague or two who visits a class one day, or else we have done a version of it through a panel discussion in the late afternoon that students are encouraged to attend.

There are other topics you could select for one or more panels or faculty presentations:

- The Critics Who Made Us—this would focus on a critic or critics (or a teacher) who played a central role in your own literary education.
- Literary Theory: For and Against—this would center on the question of what is gained, and what is or might be lost, when the study of literary theory and critical approaches takes center stage.
- Close Reading: What It Is and How It Is Done—this would explore the question of what it means to "read closely" and what the teacher/critics in your department mean by the term "close reading." What does it mean to be a "close reader" of literature? What makes one close reader better than, or at least different from, another?

We have found that students enjoy these events. It interests them to hear their teachers talking about their own literary experiences and educations. It also helps the students to see connections between the courses they take. Even seeing a difference between one course and another is making a useful connection. And it also clarifies and makes interesting a problem that students often face and wonder about, a problem that may seem quite natural and minor to us but that is very real to them: "My roommate and I are taking the same course, but we're enrolled in different sections. My instructor told our class that . . . But my roommate's instructor said something that sounds completely the opposite. . . . " We should be willing to explain as best we can how and why such situations occur, and explain, furthermore, what would be the consequences for literature and literary study if it turned out instead that instructors and critics were always in agreement.

A

Manuscript Form/Documentation

On the day that we assign the first paper, we remind the students about the importance of mechanics. Their importance is obvious enough to the instructor, but without such a reminder, some students will hand in papers without a title, without page numbers, and the like. Many of them will place quotation marks in the wrong place, or will not indent long quotations. We think an instructor would do well to highlight the issue in advance and direct the students to the section of our book where they can find the guidance that they need.

When we make our points to the class about title, page numbers, proper placement of quotation marks, and other details about manuscript form, we do it in a more general context. One way to proceed is simply to say to students, "It has to be this way: Do these things correctly on your paper, or else your grade will go down." Often this leads to the right results, but not always. It is better, we have found, to tell the students about the conventions of good writing, and the importance of such conventions in creating and maintaining a good relationship with the reader.

A student writing an analytical paper on a literary work enters into a kind of pact with his or her reader; the reader expects to find a well-chosen title, expects that the pages will be numbered, and expects that quotations will be presented correctly. It the reader fails to find these, then the writer has begun his or her job at a disadvantage. The reader may only have glanced at the paper, and already there are signs that it is not done well because it is not done right—not done in the correct form.

We tell students that each piece of work that they do is a "representation of themselves." From the moment that the reader picks up the paper and takes a first quick look at it, he or she is forming judgments not only about the paper, but about its writer. If a paper lacks a title and page numbers, or if it is printed out in a very light (and hence barely readable) type, then the reader will likely conclude: "This writer is not showing me much consideration: I can't say I am in the best of moods for reading this paper." Again, encourage the students to realize that they can easily avoid producing such a response. Not every paper may be brilliant, but every paper can be successful in its basic form.

But you can say more than that: We like to say that a paper that is good in its basic form is likely to be successful in other important ways. Writers who are careless or neglectful about page numbers, titles, and other such features of the form are likely to make other sorts of mistakes as well. Sometimes, students will wonder why it makes a difference whether their papers have titles and page numbers, and why it matters that their quotations should be presented correctly. Isn't it the content, their ideas, that count? the students ask. Yes, an instructor wants to read papers that show a strong thesis that is well developed and well supported with evidence from the text. But a good writer cannot be intermittently careful, paying attention to some aspects of good writing and not others. Writing well means writing well in every way, from beginning to end. We shouldn't assume that we can be careful about some things, and not so careful about others. It's hard for a paper to succeed with our reader if it is afflicted with easily avoidable mistakes.

Writing a Research Paper

At Wellesley College, where one of us teaches, each instructor in the Introductory course for the English major is required to assign a research paper. Not all instructors like this requirement. There is so much to cover in the Introductory course, and so much to be done with students on the writing of analytical essays: Who has the time to teach the students how to write a research paper too? But the requirement strikes us as a good one for several reasons, and we recommend that if you assign a research paper, you take a few moments to describe the reasons for your decision to the students.

You might start by noting that in an era where information abounds, and now in electronic as well as in print forms, it is essential for students to learn how best to locate and make use of it. This sort of knowledge can and should be acquired in mid- and upper-level courses, but students need to begin as early as the Introductory course. In our view, a student working on an English major must be able to write effective analytical papers *and* research papers. Both of these are important, and we must confess that it dismays us when a junior or senior in a seminar tells us that he or she "has never had to write a research paper before." Every student should possess the skills for examining and writing about a specific poem, story, or play, but should also be equipped to undertake research in secondary sources and—making good choices—integrate his or her discoveries in a more complex kind of paper.

This kind of skill—the ability to find, assess, and make use of information—is much in demand in today's economy. We feel no hesitation in stressing this point to students, and to parents when we meet them. The study of literature is a rich, wonderful experience in its own right, but along with it comes a set of skills that students will find valuable in just about any career they pursue.

With apologies to our colleagues in the Economics department, we might mention here a comment made to us by a student who had graduated with a double-major in Economics and English and who had returned to campus for a visit a couple of years later. She said that she had enjoyed and profited from her Economics courses, and was certain that this training aided in preparing her for the job she was offered and had accepted in a New York City investment bank.

But, she added, what made her very appealing at the outset to her employers, and what made her invaluable in subsequent months to her business colleagues, was her array of interpretive and writing skills. As she explained, "Lots of people have good ideas, but few of them know how to write well, organize material, research a project, and make good use of sources."

This student was a pleasure to teach because she loved literature. But while she was doing her literary work, and even more afterwards, she could see that her major in English was also giving her a training in writing and research that would prove beneficial for her career. Her career lends support to a view held by one of our senior colleagues, who says that if a student wants to become indispensable in the workplace, well, "Major in English!"

Another kind of case can also be made. All of us recall and treasure the excitement we have received from some special novel or poem or play we have read. But while this experience begins as something private and personal, we are drawn most of the time to share it with others. We want to tell our friends about this literary work, and are quick to urge them to read it too, so that they can experience the pleasure and insight we have received from it. Once they have done so, we are eager to hear about their responses. In this respect, reading leads to more reading, and to animated "talk" about what readers have read. It is a social and communal, as well as a private and personal, activity.

When a student does some research about Shakespeare or Hawthorne, for example, he or she is engaging in a version of this same activity—bringing his or her experience into the midst of others' reading experiences, and weighing and testing them against his or her own. Some of the students' findings in secondary sources will prove interesting and relevant; some of these will turn out to be perplexing or downright useless. That's fine: Remind the student that we are not obliged to agree with everything we encounter in the world of scholarship and criticism. Indeed, as teachers we are especially gratified when a student reports that this or that article or book chapter is "wrong," because it means that the student has a position that he or she believes can be defended.

Instructors differ on the point, but we tend to advise students to turn to secondary sources *after* they have reached a fairly clear notion of their own position. To be sure, they want to be open to other points of view, ready and willing to learn from these. But for a student in an Introductory course in particular, it can be confusing to head into secondary-source research before developing a feeling for his or her own response to and understanding of the literary work. We emphasize that a research paper must be launched in the same way that a basic analytical paper is, with lots of careful attention to the text itself. Encourage the students to read the text closely first, and next to get underway with the research. The student will then have something to be looking for while the research is being undertaken: "What can I locate that will aid me in presenting *my* thesis?"

Ultimately it is still the student's paper, even when it draws upon other views and voices. The thesis should be the student's own, but through research it is now offered and expressed in a broader context. It is still a presentation: "Here is my thesis." But it is also something of a conversation: "I have been listening to what others have said, have spoken *back* to them, and now here is what I think."

Index of
Authors and Titles